From Cotton Field to University

From Cotton Field to University
A History of Methodist University, 1956-2006

William H. Billings

Methodist University, 5400 Ramsey Street, Fayetteville, North Carolina 28311

From Cotton Field to University
A History of Methodist University, 1956-2006

© 2009 by Methodist University
All rights reserved. Published February 2009

No part of this book may be reproduced or transmitted in any form or by any means, electronic or mechanical, including photocopying, recording, or by any information storage and retrieval system without written permission from the publisher. For information, address
Methodist University, 5400 Ramsey Street, Fayetteville, NC 28311

Printed in the United States of America

ISBN-10: 0-615-22935-2
ISBN-13: 978-0-615-22935-5

This book was underwritten by Methodist University.

*It is dedicated to the saints who
labored in these fields,
and by daring to dream,
ennobled the human spirit.*

Contents

Preface ix

Introduction xiii

Chapter 1 A College Is Born, 1956-59. 1

Chapter 2 Methodist College Opens, 1960-64. 67

Chapter 3 The College Grows Steadily, 1965-69 139

Chapter 4 The Torch Is Passed, 1970-74 213

Chapter 5 Survival 101, 1975-79 271

Chapter 6 A New Leader, 1980-84. 321

Chapter 7 A 'Miracle' Unfolds, 1985-89 375

Chapter 8 New Programs Spur Growth, 1990-94 437

Chapter 9 Campus Grows On Many Fronts, 1995-2000 501

Chapter 10 College Becomes University, 2001-06 571

Epilogue 639

Appendices. 645

Index 737

Preface

In 2002, Methodist College President M. Elton Hendricks appointed me College historian and charged me with writing a history of the College's first fifty years. He said he wanted a College history book published sometime after the College's 50th anniversary celebration November 1, 2006.

I inherited this project from Dr. Sue Kimball, a retired English professor; she was the first choice of an advisory committee to write the first history of Methodist College. After a year of basic research and note-taking, however, Dr. Kimball decided to step aside. Dr. Kimball gave me her notes and later on, her opinions of my early chapters, which she proofread and edited. She is a remarkable lady, and I value her friendship.

Although I was trained to be a journalist and teacher, not a historian, I am honored that Dr. Hendricks thought I could do this. I want to personally thank him for this once-in-a-lifetime opportunity. In my fifteen years as director of public relations for the College, I wrote hundreds of news and feature stories, press releases, and promotional materials for the College and took thousands of photographs. So the president knew what to expect.

This is not my first experience with historical research. In 1980, while working for *The Courier-Times* in Roxboro, N.C., I was assigned the task of summarizing the 1930s for the *Courier's* Centennial Edition. There were two newspapers in Person County during the 1930s, so I spent many hours reading through old copies of *The Roxboro Courier* and *The Person County Times;* in those days *The Courier,* edited by John W. Noell, carried international, national, state, and local news. I also interviewed some old-timers who remembered The Great Depression, FDR, Shirley Temple, and the advent of Social Security.

Among the college histories Dr. Hendricks gave me to read were books from the University of Georgia, Randolph-Macon College, Wofford College, and Barton College, formerly Atlantic Christian College. It was clear to me that Dr. Hendricks wanted a detailed chronology of the history of Methodist College.

During the 2002-03 school year, I worked full-time on this project, visiting the North Carolina Collection at UNC, the Cumberland County Public Library, and the Duke Divinity School Library to read as much as I could about the founding of Methodist College. I also read through the transcripts of 45 oral history interviews collected by Lynn Clark from 2000-02. In 2003,

I was appointed half-time historian and half-time director of Monarch Press, the College print shop. The demands of the print shop job and the graphic changeovers associated with the name change to Methodist University in 2006-07, prevented me from spending half my time on the College history that school year and slowed my progress significantly.

I have done most of my work in a basement office in Davis Library, across the hall from where the College archives are housed. My primary sources have been minutes of the Board of Trustees, the oral history transcripts, copies of *The Bulletin of Methodist College* and *Methodist College Today*, and copies of old student publications: *sMALL TALK* (the student newspaper), *Carillon* (the yearbook) and *Tapestry* (the literary magazine). I have also interviewed a fair number of persons who were part of our history. I have spent many nights and weekends reading through old volumes, taking notes, writing and typing the various chapters.

From the outset, I have followed a straight chronology of College events, starting with 1955 and ending with 2006, weaving together the thoughts and actions of trustees, faculty, staff, students, church and community leaders. I have tried to include as many students as possible because I believe **they** are our *raison d'etre* (reason for being).

Chapters 1-8 are divided into five-year segments, Chapter 9-10 into six-year periods. Each chapter includes relevant photos and end notes. In the back of the book you will find a large number of appendices and an every-name index. Had time and space permitted, I would have done more personal interviews and used more anecdotes from College staff and alumni. If I left anyone out, please forgive me.

This has been a long and arduous journey but a very worthwhile learning experience. I am indebted to the following members of the College family for their help and words of encouragement: Elton Hendricks, R. Parker Wilson, Bill Lowdermilk, Bruce Pulliam, Charles McAdams, Gene Clayton, Lynn Clark, Arleen Fields, Katherine Watt, Earleene Bass, Jerry Keen, Kathy and Robert Christian, Alan and Elaine Porter, Frank Stout, Mike Harrison, Christina Alvarez, Maria Sikoryak-Robins and Carol Pope.

Credit must also be given to Charles McAdams, John Elkin, Bob Perkins, Bobby Ayers and Richard Small for their excellent photography. Finally, the late Norma Womack did a superb job of collecting our school's archives—catalogues, student newspapers, photographs, newsletters, minutes, *etc.*,—while serving as director of Davis Memorial Library. A complete set of archives on campus made historical research much easier.

From my own family, I must thank my wife, Cynthia Billings, for proofreading and my stepmother, Colleen Billings, for insisting that I "hang in there" and finish what I started. For the most part, this project has been a labor of love, and I thank God for helping me finish it.

In the local community, I am indebted to Juan Llanos of Worth Printing, Inc. for technical assistance and creating the every-name index, the staff in the history room of the Cumberland County Public Library for research assistance, and Charles Broadwell, publisher of *The Fayetteville Observer* for permission to reprint old photos. Thanks also to Jean Hutchinson '67, who proofread text and helped select photos for the book.

I earnestly hope that others who come after me, especially students, will delve further into our archives and write more stories about our illustrious past. I dedicate this book to all who have invested their time, talent, and money in Methodist University. Many of you made great personal sacrifices and worked extremely hard to make Methodist what it is today. Hundreds of you are mentioned in this book.

I have a special reverence for three of our founding fathers: Terry Sanford, Bishop Paul Neff Garber, and L. Stacy Weaver. With very little money and a small number of students, these men created a College out of a cotton field. They were eloquent and tenacious in promoting Christian education and the liberal arts experience. Moreover, they believed in academic excellence and personal integrity. I am sure I speak for many students who attended Methodist in that first decade when I say, "We got the message that there is more to life than making a living."

To each and every reader of this book, I hope you will see "that good people make all things possible" and that "good people" working at Methodist University have inspired students to go forth and "make a positive difference in the lives of others." As President Hendricks has said many times, our graduates are living proof that what happens here is important and worth doing. Yes, we are proud of our 10,000-plus graduates—45 classes. We are also thankful to God and our many friends and supporters for the "Methodist miracle" that is still unfolding on Ramsey Street in Fayetteville, North Carolina.

— WHB

Introduction

As I delved into the early history of Methodist University, I was shocked to read of the founders' struggles to obtain the funds and the students needed to start this school. While enrolled at Methodist from 1964-68, I was not aware of the difficulties leaders in the Fayetteville community and in The North Carolina Conference of The Methodist Church had encountered raising the funds to build this new institution. After six years of historical research, I would be remiss if I did not comment on this.

Although 30,000 Methodists in eastern North Carolina and 6,000 residents of Fayetteville and Cumberland County did contribute funds, mostly small amounts, to establish Methodist College, neither the community's goal of $2 million nor the Church's goal of $2 million was met during five years of fundraising. In 1957, the Fayetteville College Foundation was forced to borrow $1 million from First Citizens Bank, using College land as collateral, to finance construction of the first four buildings, underground utilities, streets, parking lots, and sidewalks. Between 1962 and 1968, federal loans were needed to build four residence halls and to help pay for an addition to the Student Union and the Reeves Auditorium/Fine Arts Building.

What kept the Fayetteville community and the church from reaching their College fund drive goals? There is no simple answer. But many Methodists in eastern North Carolina felt the church was unwise to try and build **two** new colleges—Methodist College and N.C. Wesleyan College—while keeping Louisburg College open as a junior college. The original recommendation of the Bishop's Long Range Planning Committee was to: 1) move Louisburg College to Rocky Mount and make it a four-year school, and 2) build **one** new four-year college elsewhere within The North Carolina Conference. After Louisburg residents mobilized and pleaded with church officials to keep their junior college open, a plan was approved to build new colleges in Rocky Mount and Fayetteville **and** to upgrade Louisburg. Many Methodists did not believe The North Carolina Conference could adequately support three colleges.

Although Fayetteville's top civic leaders worked hard to acquire Methodist, there were no large donors. The most valuable donations came in the form of land—from the Stouts, the Kinlaws, and the Taylors. In 1956, Fayetteville was primarily a retail center catering to the military. America experienced a major economic recession in 1957. The city already had Fayetteville State College, a predominately black school, and would soon have a technical institute.

Another problem, I think, was the view that the Methodists' new colleges would be racially integrated. There were many church leaders and state residents who did not want this to happen. I believe three people saved the day for Methodist. L. Stacy Weaver, the founding president, had a sterling reputation as an educator and Methodist lay leader. Bishop Paul Garber preached eloquently of the value **to the church** of church-related colleges serving a wave of "baby boomers." Terry Sanford, a dynamic Democrat, decided that Fayetteville needed a church-related college and furthermore, that every young person in North Carolina should have the opportunity to attend college.

Permit me to share some personal history to show what a difference "good people" made in the founding of Methodist College. My first cousin, Lois Stephenson, lived in Harnett County and was a member of Methodist's first freshman class. She encouraged me to apply to Methodist. In the fall of my senior year, Charles McAdams, Methodist's first director of public relations, came to College Night at Durham High School, showed slides of Methodist and talked about the new school. Mr. McAdams emphasized the small size of the school, the talent of Weaver and Sanford, the school's church-relatedness, and the opportunity to be part of something new. All his brag points resonated with me, and I was ready to apply right then and there. My family and I also knew that Stacy Weaver, former superintendent of the Durham City Schools, would stress academic excellence. I abandoned plans to go to Carolina, where I was already accepted.

Because of a family illness, I was unable to enroll at Methodist in the fall of 1963, but Sam Edwards promised to hold my scholarship and financial aid package for the fall of 1964. As governor of North Carolina, Terry Sanford had adopted and circulated the following slogan among the state's youth: "If you have the will and the skill, we will help you find a way to attend college." While I was a student at Durham High, Sanford spoke these very words to the student body.

In the summer of 1963, I wrote Governor Sanford a letter asking for help with college. Shortly thereafter, the governor's aide, Joel Fleishman, called me and said there were people in Durham who could help me. Before I knew it, I was sitting in front of George Watts Hill, CEO of Central Carolina Bank, and later Steed Rollins, publisher of *The Durham Morning Herald*, where I had worked as a copy boy in high school. Mr. Rollins gave me a job as a dispatch clerk in the Display Advertising Department of Herald-Sun Papers.

When I arrived at Methodist in the fall of 1964, I was ready to study! While I initially intended to transfer to Carolina to major in journalism, I fell in love with Methodist and could not leave. I got involved in student publications, student government, debating, and music (the MC Wind Ensemble). I lived in

Cumberland Hall and worked as a student assistant in the Admissions Office. I majored in English and went off to Richmond, Virginia to teach eighth graders.

Without Methodist University, I would not be where I am now, and you would not be reading this. In addition to being a student, I have been privileged to work at Methodist for the last 22 years (15 years as director of public relations) and to teach freshman English in the evening program. My jobs at Methodist have been challenging but always inspiring. What a privilege it was to work for "Uncle Bill" Lowdermilk, even when I had to work 50-70 hours a week to get the job done.

It should be noted that while Methodist struggled financially during its first 25 years, its students and faculty still achieved remarkable things, and the College developed an excellent reputation. Unfortunately, a 50 percent drop in enrollment from 1968-78 forced layoffs, a default on federal loans, and twice-yearly bank loans to meet operating expenses.

In the last 25 years, Methodist has enjoyed a remarkable renaissance under the leadership of Dr. M. Elton Hendricks, its third president. Dr. Hendricks has assembled a team of talented and hard-working faculty and administrators. Methodist has added academic programs, sports, and buildings; tripled its enrollment and endowment; raised tens of millions of dollars; achieved national prominence in golf management and intercollegiate athletics; and become a university. The school has still had to borrow money—more than $30 million—to finance new buildings and other campus improvements, and Methodist is still looking for a mega-million-dollar donor who might secure its future.

The survival of Methodist University is no longer an issue. The central question now before us is, "How good can this school become?" That was a question raised and answered 50 years ago, when our founders stated unequivocally their desire that Methodist become the best school of its type in North Carolina. This is a tall order, given the list of outstanding private colleges and universities that we have in North Carolina, many of them older and far richer than we.

It now behooves each and every person who loves Methodist University, especially its graduates, to: 1) plant seeds in the minds of philanthropists and potential students that Methodist needs and deserves their help to become the best small university in North Carolina, and 2) share the vision of Methodist's founders that those who best exemplify "truth and virtue" are those who put service above self.

The Fayetteville Observer

VOL. CXXXIX—NO. 195   TWENTY-FOUR PAGES   FAYETTEVILLE, N. C., TUESDAY, MAY 15, 1956   FINAL EDITION   PRICE: FIVE CENTS

COLLEGE TO BE LOCATED IN CITY

Reds Challenge West To Reduce Armed Forces

Russia Announces It Will Discharge Over Million Men

MOSCOW (AP) — Russia has told the world it will cut its armed forces by 1,200,000 men within the next year and challenged the Big Three Western Powers to follow the Soviet example...

U.S. TO STAY STRONG

Dulles Doubtful Soviets To Cut Military Power

WASHINGTON (AP) — Secretary of State Dulles said today Russia's proposed armed forces cut would not appreciably alter Soviet military power...

U. S. Couples Sought To Settle In Africa

HIGHLIGHTS TODAY'S NEWS

BULLETIN

Plane Crash

A small T-6 type Army or Air Force plane apparently crashed at the end of a Grannis Field runway this afternoon about 2:30 o'clock and instantly burst into flames...

Two AF Leaders Advise Caution

WASHINGTON (AP) — Two U. S. Air Force leaders testified today the announced cutback in Russian military forces will not...

Rhee's Only Opponent Hides On Election Day

House Group To Seek Boost In Parity Funds

14 Billion Dollars Advocated For Farm Price Supports

WASHINGTON (UP) — The House Banking Committee prepared today to push through legislation boosting the farm price support fund to a record 14 billion dollars...

BULLETINS

Driving Skill Of Girl Credited With Saving 30

NEW YORK (AP) — A 16-year-old girl, who guided a runaway school bus across a busy thoroughfare...

Eden Keeps Silent And Adds Fuel To Frogman Mystery

LONDON (UP) — Sir Anthony Eden's absolute refusal to explain the case of Lt. Comdr. Lionel Crabb turned the disappearance of the frogman today into one of the great unsolved mysteries of the cold war.

Long Takes Over As La. Governor For Third Time

BATON ROUGE, La. (AP) — Earl K. Long advocate of racial moderation and party loyalty, today became for a third time governor of Louisiana...

French Troops Kill 38 Guerrillas, Capture 30

Action Of N.C. Methodists Is Highly Praised

Louisburg To Retain Institution; Rocky Mount Gets College

By JIM PHARR

Fayetteville area citizens today were jubilant in praising the location of a four-year co-educational college here Monday by the North Carolina Methodist Conference in Goldsboro...

Brigadier General In Korean Command

Where It Is

	Sec. Page
Amusements	
Classified	
Comics	
Editorial	
Films and Focals	
Radio, TV	
Sports	
Women's News	

COUNTY AUTO TOLL
TO THIS DATE
1955 ....
1956 13
DEFENSIVE DRIVING IS SAFETY FIRST

The day after The North Carolina Conference of The United Methodist Church voted in special session in Goldsboro, N.C., to build a new college in Fayetteville, The Fayetteville Observer *reported the news on the front page, under a banner headline. Community leaders greeted the news with joy and pride and were quoted extensively by staff writer Jim Pharr. The photo showed J.E. Talley, Jr., a local attorney and member of the Fayetteville College Steering Committee; Col. Joel Wareing, XVIII Airborne Corps chaplain; and Terry Sanford, treasurer of the Fayetteville College Steering Committee.*

Chapter 1

A College Is Born
1956-59

"Education is a function the Church cannot surrender nor neglect if its purpose is to give mankind a Christian mind."

—Episcopal Address by the Council of Bishops,
General Conference of The Methodist Church,
April 25, 1956, Minneapolis, Minn.

The Frenchman Victor Hugo once wrote, "Greater than the tread of mighty armies is an idea whose time has come."[1] In 1956, Methodist College was an idea whose time had come. Simply stated, the interests of The Methodist Church and a southern city converged to bring a new college to eastern North Carolina.

Good salesmanship on the part of two men and inspired leadership on the part of a third would convert the idea of Methodist College into reality. The idealists were Bishop Paul Neff Garber of The North Carolina Conference of The Methodist Church and Terry Sanford, a Fayetteville attorney and master politician. The man recruited to build and lead the College was L. Stacy Weaver, a public school administrator and Methodist layman.

Civic leaders in Fayetteville, North Carolina saw Methodist College as a way to improve their city's image and to give area residents the opportunity to attain a high quality liberal arts education. Church leaders, on the other hand, wanted to provide Christian higher education to a new generation of "baby boomers" in eastern North Carolina and beyond.

For nearly five months, from October 1955 to March 1956, members of a Presbyterian College Steering Committee appointed by Fayetteville Mayor George Herndon tried to persuade a board of the Presbyterian Synod of North Carolina to put a new four-year college in their city. On the evening of March 6, 1956, however, the Presbyterians chose Laurinburg, N.C., as the site for their new college.

Fayetteville had offered the Presbyterians pledges of $1.3 million and three large sites as possible locations for the college. It wasn't enough. The loss of the new college was a painful blow to the city's civic pride and to Dr. R. L. Pittman, Steering Committee chairman, and Frank McBryde, vice-chairman. Both Pittman and McBryde were members of Fayetteville's First Presbyterian

CHAPTER 1

Church and prominent members of the community. A surgeon by training, Dr. Pittman built and operated Pittman Hospital in Fayetteville and later became involved in real estate development. McBryde was a local optician and immediate past president of the Fayetteville Chamber of Commerce.

Two Fayetteville residents, Charles G. Rose and Dr. R. L. Pittman, served on the Consolidated Presbyterian College Board of Trustees that selected Laurinburg. They said Laurinburg was chosen primarily because it offered $3,052,000 in cash and because of "bad press" about Fayetteville within the state. Rose told a local reporter that many of his fellow trustees felt parents would be reluctant to send their children to school in Fayetteville because of the city's reputation as a military town. [2] At that time, the 300 block of Hay Street in downtown Fayetteville was, in fact, a "red light" district, filled with bars and other types of entertainment catering to soldiers from Fort Bragg and airmen from Pope Air Force Base.

Fayetteville's best selling point in its campaign to secure a college proved to be a 577-acre site off U.S. 401 five miles north of downtown. Both the Presbyterians and the Methodists were impressed by it. In early 1956, Fayetteville architect Dan MacMillan inspected four potential sites for a college and concluded that the one north of the city was ideal. In a letter to J. Mel Thompson dated February 24, 1956, MacMillan said the Raleigh Road site was clearly the best parcel "[. . .] because there is an abundance of available land, exciting rolling terrain with fine trees and a magnificent view—broad panorama of hills and valleys, and the historical Cape Fear River, its eastern boundary; also because of its adaptability as a neighborhood—capable of providing pleasant surroundings for active work and play, and passive relaxation. [3]

Thompson had been a member of the Committee of 100 appointed by the Presbyterian College Steering Committee to subscribe or guarantee $1 million over a five-year period. He later served as treasurer of the Fayetteville College Foundation, forerunner of the Methodist College Foundation.

Fayetteville Turns to the Methodists

While most Presbyterians in Fayetteville mourned the loss of what would become St. Andrews Presbyterian College to Laurinburg, and some were angered by the church's decision, former state senator and Fayetteville attorney Terry Sanford, a member of the Presbyterian College Steering Committee, met with committee members March 9, 1956, and persuaded them to reorganize as the Fayetteville College Steering Committee for the purpose of seeking a new Methodist college. Sanford was a Methodist layman and a prominent Democrat with aspirations of becoming governor of North Carolina. Terry Sanford was widely known in North Carolina, having served as president of the North

Carolina Young Democrats in 1949 and as a state senator in 1952-54. He also managed Kerr Scott's campaign for the U.S. Senate in 1954.

Sanford took the lead role in selling Fayetteville to the Methodists. He knew that Bishop Paul N. Garber of The North Carolina Conference of The Methodist Church had formed a Long Range Planning Committee to explore the possibility of building a new four-year college in eastern North Carolina and moving Louisburg College to Rocky Mount to convert it from a junior college to a senior college.

With the approval of the reorganized Steering Committee, Sanford asked Garber to invite committee representatives to appear before his Cabinet March 13, 1956, at Trinity Methodist Church in Durham to present Fayetteville's bid for the new Methodist College. Garber revealed that four other cities—Wilmington, Rocky Mount, Lumberton and Kinston—were vying for the college.

At a planning meeting held March 12 at Fayetteville's Hay Street Methodist Church, the Steering Committee received a pledge of support from the Rev. O. L. Hathaway, Fayetteville District superintendent for the Methodist conference and a member of the Bishop's Cabinet. "We need a college here because it has a place and will bring good things," said Rev. Hathaway.[4] Committee members in attendance at the planning meeting were: Terry Sanford, Norman Suttles, the Rev. Graham S. Eubank, the Rev. Clyde S. Boggs, Gen. John R. Hodge (Ret.), Frank McBryde, Dr. Walker B. Healy, J. Mel Thompson, Wilson F. Yarborough Sr., Fayetteville Mayor George B. Herndon, J. W. Hensdale, Wilbur Clark, Bernard Stein, Coy Brewer, Joe Tally Jr., Tom McLean and Bruce McFadyen.

At the meeting of the Bishop's Cabinet in Durham March 13, Sanford served as spokesman for the committee, pledging up to $1,750,000 and 600 acres for the college, along with continuing support of $50,000 per year. Also speaking in support of Fayetteville's bid for the college were: Joe Tally Jr.; Dr. Walker B. Healy; Brig. Gen. Paul R. Weyrauch of Fort Bragg; Col. Theodore Kershaw of Pope Air Force Base; Gen. John R. Hodge; Dr. R. L. Pittman (committee chairman); and the Rev. Graham Eubank.

The Fayetteville delegation made the first presentation at the Durham meeting, followed by groups from Kinston, Lumberton, Rocky Mount, and Wilmington. A group from Louisburg asked that Louisburg College be left in that city and expanded into a four-year institution. However, Bishop Garber recommended that Louisburg College be moved to Rocky Mount to become a four-year college and that a new four-year college be established elsewhere in eastern North Carolina.

— CHAPTER 1 —

Church Leaders Visit Fayetteville

A Site Committee headed by the Rev. Dr. W. L. Clegg, Durham District superintendent, visited Fayetteville and Fort Bragg March 15, 1956. The group toured the proposed 577-acre site for the college and met with civilian and military leaders. Local leaders who spoke in support of the Fayetteville College Steering Committee's proposal to land the new college were: Terry Sanford; Joe Tally Jr., attorney; Dr. Walker B. Healy, pastor of First Presbyterian Church; Brig. Gen. Paul R. Weyrauch, deputy commander of Fort Bragg; Col. Theodore Kershaw, commander of Pope Air Force Base; Gen. John R. Hodge, U.S. Army Ret.; Dr. R. L. Pittman, Steering Committee chairman; and the Rev. Graham S. Eubank, pastor of Hay Street Methodist Church.

In preparation for the Site Committee visit, local developer Joe Stout used a bulldozer to create a road into the southern part of the proposed site for the college—the 120-acre tract on the west side of Ramsey Street that he and his wife had decided to donate. The Stouts lived on the opposite side of Ramsey Street from the tract.

Dr. Frank Stout, Joe Stout's son, recalled walking over the site with his father. "There were Civil War ramparts there," he said. "It's one of the highest points in Cumberland County. You could see the land on the other side of the Cape Fear River. My father said the members of the Site Committee were flabbergasted by the beauty of it." [5]

Addressing local leaders, Dr. Clegg estimated that a minimum of $5 million would be needed to construct a college for 600 students plus an endowment of $300 per student. He said the costs would have to be borne by The North Carolina Annual Conference of The Methodist Church and the community in which the college was located. Clegg's Site Committee subsequently visited Lumberton March 16, Wilmington March 17, Kinston March 19, Rocky Mount March 23, and Louisburg March 24.

A special meeting of the Bishop's Cabinet, the Conference's Long Range Planning Committee, and executives of the Board of Education and other conference boards was held March 27 at First Methodist Church in Wilson. The recommendation of Dr. Clegg's Site Committee —that a new four-year college be built in Fayetteville and that Louisburg College be moved to Rocky Mount and converted into a four-year college—was accepted. Clegg reported that Fayetteville's proposal was superior to those offered by other communities in terms of location, population concentration, desirability of site, and relationship to other schools. Meanwhile, Louisburg leaders restated their desire that Louisburg College be expanded and retained in their city.

Bishop Garber reported that the college plans would have to be approved by the General Conference of The Methodist Church's Board of Education and Commission on World Service and Finance, trustees of Louisburg College, and finally The North Carolina Conference. Garber announced that he would be calling a special session of The North Carolina Conference to act on the recommendations prior to the Conference's regular annual session in June. He instructed special committees to meet April 5 in Fayetteville and April 10 in Rocky Mount to draft specific agreements between the two communities, to be presented to his Cabinet and the Conference's Long Range Planning Committee April 11 in Rocky Mount.

Members of the Fayetteville College Steering Committee expressed confidence after the Wilson meeting that Fayetteville could obtain a new Methodist college. Letters were immediately sent to all persons who had made pledges in the Presbyterian college fund drive asking them to transfer their pledges to the proposed Methodist college and, if possible, increase their original offers of financial support. In the letter, the committee said it had assured the Methodists that Fayetteville could raise **$2 million** for the new college. The Steering Committee had increased the local commitment from $1.75 million to $2 million.

When interviewed in the fall of 2000, Mrs. C. Wallace "Pinky" Jackson of Fayetteville recalled that "maybe half" of the pledges made to the Presbyterian College were converted to Methodist College.[6] Mrs. Jackson served with Alton Murchison on the Publicity Board of the Presbyterian College Steering Committee and was also a charter member of the Fayetteville College Foundation.

The North Carolina Conference's College Site Committee, chaired by the Dr. W. L. Clegg, met April 5, 1956, at Haymount Methodist Church in Fayetteville and later visited the proposed site for the new college. Other committee members present were: Dr. E. B. Fisher of Durham, chairman of the Conference Board of Education; Dr. C. D. Barclift of Durham, chairman of the Conference Long Range Planning Committee; Dr. James E. Hillman of Raleigh, a member of the State Board of Education; and Dr. Walter C. Ball of Burlington. Also present were Wilson F. Yarborough Sr., chairman of the local College Site Committee, and Dr. R. L. Pittman, chairman of the Fayetteville College Steering Committee.

Dr. Hillman estimated annual operating cost for the new college at $150,000-$200,000, exclusive of student fees. Dr. J. D. Messick, president of East Carolina College in Greenville, said it would take at least $3.5 million to build the new college. Dr. R. L. Pittman told the visiting group that his examination of early pledges from citizens in the Fayetteville area showed that 60 percent of those who had promised support for the college had doubled their pledges. [7]

— CHAPTER 1 —

Ads Seek Local Pledges for New College

In late April, 1956, full-page ads appeared in *The Fayetteville Observer* exhorting local residents to pledge to the new college. The April 23 ad carried the following message in large, headline-size type: "In just 21 days [May 14 in Goldsboro] the North Carolina Methodist Conference will take final action on the new Methodist college for Cumberland County. $2 million in pledges must be in our hands by then. Do your part now! Pledge today." [8] This ad was paid for by two local businesses: Johnson Cotton Co. and Home Federal Savings & Loan Association.

The April 30 ad was headlined, "Light up the future for endless thousands of boys and girls with your pledges now." [9] This ad also announced a mass meeting for Wednesday, May 2 at Alexander Graham Junior High School; it was sponsored by First Citizens Bank & Trust Co., Branch Banking & Trust Co., Commercial & Industrial Bank, and Cross Creek Building & Loan Association.

Bishop Garber, Others Cite Need for New Methodist Colleges

The General Conference of The Methodist Church met in Minneapolis, Minnesota, April 25-May 7, 1956, and adopted a quadrennial emphasis on education as recommended by the Commission on Educational Emphasis of the Quadrennial Program. The Commission chairman was Bishop Paul Neff Garber, resident bishop of the Richmond Area, of which The North Carolina Conference was then a part, and the man who had already endorsed the establishment of a Methodist college in Fayetteville.

While championing Christian higher education, Garber drew heavily on his educational experience and expertise in the history of Methodism to bolster his case. A native of New Market, Virginia, Garber received his A.B. degree from Bridgewater College and the M.A. and Ph.D. degrees from the University of Pennsylvania. He did postgraduate work at Crozer Theological Seminary. From 1926-1944, he taught history and served as registrar and dean of Duke University's School of Religion, now known as Duke University Divinity School. Before he was elected bishop of the Richmond Area of The Methodist Church in 1951, he served seven years as bishop of the Geneva Area of The Methodist Church, made up of ten countries in Europe and North Africa. Those who served with him in The North Carolina Conference remember him as an eternal optimist and a man of boundless energy.

The actions of The Methodist Church at the 1956 General Conference reflected the growing recognition among Americans in the mid 1950s that a post World War II "baby boom" would require a massive expansion of America's public schools and colleges to handle the influx of additional millions of young people. In their episcopal address to the General Conference, the bishops of

1956–1959

The Methodist Church declared unequivocally that, "Education is a function the Church cannot surrender nor neglect if its purpose is to give mankind a Christian mind." [10]

Terry Sanford attended the 1956 General Conference in Minneapolis. As treasurer of the Fayetteville College Steering Committee, Sanford had played the leading role in the two-month campaign to persuade Bishop Garber and Methodist clergymen to award a new four-year college to Fayetteville. While The North Carolina Conference had not yet voted to build a new college in Fayetteville, Sanford was confident this would happen. On the evening of April 30, 1956, Sanford sent a telegram to Dr. R. L. Pittman, chairman of the Fayetteville College Steering Committee, reporting that the Church had just adopted a quadrennial program to expand its efforts in higher education.

In his telegram, Sanford sought to challenge the home forces and instill pride in those Fayetteville residents who had already devoted much time and money to the campaign for the new Methodist college. Sanford wrote:

> The new college at Fayetteville can become the national model for The Methodist Church in this new advance and can receive the support necessary to become a top-flight college if we in Fayetteville will do our part now. Vision, courage and sacrifice have been the beginning of every great school. I am proud to tell the church leaders out here that they can look to the people of Cumberland County, North Carolina, for vision, determination, sacrifice, and leadership in founding this new great college. I know we will reach our financial goal. I hope that every family in Cumberland County will pledge something and become numbered among the founders of an educational institution which will bring centuries of enrichment to North Carolina. [11]

It became evident at the 1956 General Conference of The Methodist Church that Bishop Paul Neff Garber had emerged as one of the Church's leading crusaders for education. The portion of the episcopal address devoted to education reflected Garber's desire that The Methodist Church restate its long-standing belief in "the primacy of education as a religious responsibility."

The episcopal address portrayed the Church's educational mission as urgent and compelling, stressing the following points:

—While the annual giving of the churches for current maintenance of the colleges has increased during the last quadrennium, the goal of one dollar per member is a minimum requirement if

— CHAPTER 1 —

Church-related Methodist colleges are to remain solvent and efficient. Furthermore, it is predicted that the number of young people going to college will double by 1970. To retain the Methodist student ratio (among America's college population) of one in ten, facilities for at least 250,000 additional students must be provided.
—In the beginnings of American Protestantism the importance of education guided by a Christian philosophy was wisely recognized. The first Protestant churches had two pastors, one to preach and one to teach.
—Eight of the nine colonial colleges still surviving were founded by the Church.
—Methodism has always recognized the primacy of education as a religious responsibility. The first two questions asked in the first Methodist Conference of 1744 were: "What shall we teach?" and "How shall we teach?" The time has come for the Church to restate its position. [12]

North Carolina Conference Votes to Build College in Fayetteville

The final decision to build a four-year Methodist college in Fayetteville came May 14, 1956, during a special session of The North Carolina Conference of The Methodist Church at St. Paul Methodist Church in Goldsboro, N.C. Bishop Garber convened the special session "to discuss and take action upon matters relating to higher education in eastern North Carolina, under the auspices of The Methodist Church." [13]

Garber opened the session by reading a paper "relative to the conditions existing in our colleges." The Rev. C. D. Barclift presented the recommendation of the Conference's Long Range Planning Committee: 1) that Louisburg College be moved to Rocky Mount and converted to a new four-year college, and 2) that a new Methodist college be established in Fayetteville. Speaking in support of the recommendation were E. B. Fisher, chairman of the Conference Board of Education, and Gurney P. Hood, chairman of the Commission on World Service and Finance.

The report projected that Methodist College at Fayetteville would accommodate 600 dormitory students and 200 day students and cost $4 million to build. It recommended that The North Carolina Conference of The Methodist Church: 1) raise $2,188,000 for Methodist College from the churches and other sources over a period of 15 years for capital outlay, and 2) provide $50,000 per year in continuing support or $130,000 per year for 600 dormitory students. [14]

Fayetteville's obligation was described in the report as follows: 1) to provide $2 million over a period of five years, plus the site (less the $188,000 owed on the site), plus an extension of utilities to the site, and 2) to provide $50,000 a year in continuing support from the opening of the college. [15]

The minutes of the special session do not indicate there was much, if any, discussion of the financial obligation the Conference would be assuming by adopting the report. But the report itself included a very detailed listing of the obligations of the Conference, as well as the cities of Fayetteville and Rocky Mount. Under the subheading "Plan for Raising These Funds" which appears on the final page of the report, it is recommended that the Conference: 1) borrow $2 million "from the federal government or a foundation at 2 3/4 percent to 3 1/8 percent interest to be retired by the Conference College Sustaining Fund within 30-40 years, at a total annual cost of about $100,000." 2) conduct a public campaign (from corporations and individuals) for $2.5 million in capital funds, and 3) employ a professional fund-raising agency to conduct the capital campaign. [16]

The special session included a report by Key W. Taylor, chairman of the Town and County Commission, on population trends in North Carolina. Dr. J. D. Messick, president of East Carolina College in Greenville, spoke on prospective college enrollment trends.

Methodist layman Terry Sanford presented Fayetteville's offer for the new college. Speaking in support of that offer were Chaplain Joel Wareing, representing Fort Bragg, and Joe Tally Jr., another Methodist layman representing the general Fayetteville area. The Fayetteville group described a proposed 600-acre site for the college bordering the Raleigh Road five and a half miles north of the Market House. The presentation lasted 23 minutes.

Ray Bandy, a Methodist layman from Rocky Mount, presented Rocky Mount's offer for the new college and was supported by D. S. Johnson and Leon Russell. The Rev. W. L. Clegg spoke of the need for a Methodist Academy within the bounds of The North Carolina Conference. The Rev. C. P. Morris presented the summary of costs for a senior, coeducational Methodist college.

Judge Hamilton Hobgood, a Methodist layman from Louisburg and a member of the Louisburg College Board of Trustees, appealed to the Conference to allow Louisburg College to remain in Louisburg as a junior college. The *North Carolina Christian Advocate* gave this account:

> Said Judge Hobgood, "We do not desire to protest Fayetteville, Rocky Mount or any other North Carolina town obtaining a Christian college, but we do protest the moving of Louisburg College." Citing the fact that there are six brick buildings at Louisburg, "placed there by the county or citizens of the county,"

— CHAPTER 1 —

Judge Hobgood went on, "In 1950 the Methodist Conference constructed the first building there. The site for the campus was originally given by the town of Louisburg." [17]

Hobgood's appeal was supported by Judge Marshall T. Spears of Durham, Mrs. B. B. Everette of Palmyra, Supt. Suey Chandler of Currituck County and Dr. James E. Hillman of Raleigh, chairman of the Louisburg College Board of Trustees.

D. E. Earnhardt enumerated reasons for moving Louisburg College to Rocky Mount, including the assertion that Louisburg "did not have a single fireproof building." Rev. Barclift moved the adoption of the report of the Long Range Planning Committee. Rev. C. P. Morris offered an amendment to the report, stating that the Conference would build senior coeducational colleges at Fayetteville and Rocky Mount, but maintain Louisburg College in Louisburg as a junior college.

Morris's amendment was adopted with a change offered by W. A. Cade declaring that the Conference would retain Louisburg College as a junior college and enlarge its capacity to 400 or 600 when the need warranted. A motion by E. C. Purcell to prohibit the borrowing of federal funds to build the colleges was defeated.

The Conference concluded its special session by adopting the report of the Long Range Planning Committee as amended, voting to build new four-year colleges in Fayetteville and Rocky Mount and to retain Louisburg College as a junior college. The final vote was taken at 4:05 p.m. by a show of hands. Of the 800 delegates present, only a handful voted against the report.

Bishop Garber thanked the delegates for "having faith enough and courage enough to do what we did today." [18]

Forty-five years later, Dr. L. Elbert Wethington, the man who was administrative assistant to Methodist College President L. Stacy Weaver from 1959-60 and the author of the first curriculum for Methodist College, said Bishop Garber "surprised everyone by accepting both offers [from Fayetteville and Rocky Mount] which seemed a bit wild at that time." [19]

Charles McAdams, the first director of public relations and development at Methodist College, expressed similar sentiments in a 2000 interview: "It would have been better to have built one college and then the Conference give all the support to one college [. . .] Bishop Garber at that time wanted to be sure both factions were satisfied, both Rocky Mount and Fayetteville." [20]

Fayetteville Celebrates

The Goldsboro decision was greeted with joy and pride by the Fayetteville College Steering Committee and the citizens of Fayetteville. The decision received front page coverage in the May 15, 1956, edition of *The Fayetteville Observer*. A news story by Jim Pharr was headlined "COLLEGE TO BE LOCATED IN CITY" and was accompanied by a photo of J. E. Tally Jr., local attorney; Col. Joel Wareing, XVIII Airborne Corps chaplain; and Terry Sanford, treasurer of the Fayetteville College Steering Committee.

The community leaders quoted by Pharr were clearly jubilant. Dr. R. L. Pittman, chairman of the Fayetteville College Steering Committee, said, "I feel that we have been greatly blessed by the action of the conference. It's now up to our people to give the college our entire support, and we will have one of the finest and largest colleges, of the highest standards, in the whole country. Our efforts were crowned with success through the combined efforts of everyone in the community." [21]

Joe Tally Jr., local attorney and Committee member, went further: "I consider this the beginning of the greatest cultural advance Fayetteville has ever known. Our people are to be congratulated on their cooperation, work and pledges that have made this day possible." [22]

Fayetteville Mayor George Herndon called the new Methodist college "the opportunity of a century for our city and county" and "one of the greatest things that ever has happened here." [23] He concluded his remarks by saying, "I would like to take this opportunity to thank the people of Fayetteville, Cumberland County, Fort Bragg and Pope Air Force Base for the shares they have bought in this four-year coeducational college and the youth of today and tomorrow." [24]

In a May 15, 1956, editorial, *The Fayetteville Observer* advanced an interesting thesis concerning the significance for Fayetteville of the Methodist Conference's decision to build a new college in Fayetteville. First, the paper congratulated local leaders for their "splendid and intelligent efforts" to gain the college. [25] Second, the paper acknowledged that the task of raising two million dollars in pledges and an annual supporting fund of fifty thousand dollars a year would not be an easy task. It also warned, "Now is not the time to take things for granted about the college or about Fayetteville's future growth." [26]

But the thesis of the editorial was this:

> It is also heartening that this community has been able to wage a successful educational program of its own against the fallacious belief that a community is somehow contaminated by the presence of men who wear the uniform associated with the armed defense of their country.
>
> In some respects, the effectiveness of this educational campaign appears to be just as important to us as the business of getting the community approved as the site for the new college. [27]

— CHAPTER 1 —

The editorial concluded by saying, "We have struck a blow for the growth of our city, for the future of our children and for the welfare of the military visitor in our midst. Let's strike another one." [28]

State News Media React

The News and Observer of Raleigh, N.C., provided front page coverage of the Church's special session in Goldsboro in its May 15, 1956, edition. Reporter Charles Clay covered the event.

The News and Observer followed up with an editorial May 16, 1956, entitled "Rejoicing and Dissatisfaction." The editorial began by saying there would have been no effort to move Louisburg College if it had received the support in the past to be the college that it ought to be. The editorial also decried the fact that 300 Louisburg students "are housed in non-fireproof dormitories." [29]

Commenting on the new educational program adopted by the Methodists at their special session, the editorial ended on a positive note:

> Such a program will not be easy of fulfillment. It will require greater sacrifices and increasing appropriations for the three colleges, new ones at Rocky Mount and Fayetteville and the old one at Louisburg [. . .] The united front achieved by the Methodists for a new educational adventure means a divine dissatisfaction with inadequate efforts to provide the kind of Christian education now proposed. The dissatisfaction should continue until all three colleges are providing the quality of education of which the church in this region can be proud. [30]

Ten days after the special session of The North Carolina Conference of The Methodist Church in Goldsboro, the *North Carolina Christian Advocate*, the official magazine of the Western North Carolina and The North Carolina Conferences of The Methodist Church, praised the Goldsboro action in an editorial entitled, "Three Steps Forward":

> Last week in Goldsboro The North Carolina Conference took three steps forward along the road to the realization of a dream. For many years the eastern section of the state has had to get along with only a junior college. Now it is to have two four-year colleges and will retain Louisburg Junior College under the mandate of the special session of the Conference. [31]

Acknowledging the opposition of Franklin County residents to the original proposal to discontinue Louisburg Junior College and the Keep Louisburg College Committee's success in winning an amendment to keep the college in Louisburg, the editorial writer observed, "One of the most encouraging features of the Conference session was the lack of acrimony in the discussions and the evident desire of all parties to do what was best for the cause of education." [32]

The editorial concluded, "The North Carolina Conference has set itself no easy task. It will take millions of dollars to establish and maintain the new schools and several hundred thousand to carry on Louisburg College. But the communities affected have pledged generous support and we believe that what is needed to be done can be done." [33]

Conference Approves College Charter, Trustee Nominations

The Board of Education of The North Carolina Conference of The Methodist Church met June 19 at Hay Street Methodist Church in Fayetteville and approved a proposed charter for the new Methodist college and a slate of nominees to a 24-member board of trustees for the new institution. The charter and the trustee nominations were approved at the 1956 annual session of The North Carolina Conference held June 25 in Greenville, N.C.

The proposed charter for Methodist College, Incorporated established a nonprofit corporation to operate a coeducational institution of collegiate grade "under the control and direction of The North Carolina Conference, Southeastern Jurisdiction, of The Methodist Church." [34]

The charter provided for a board of trustees of "not less than 24 and not more than 36 members," empowering the board to purchase and lease property, to borrow money, to construct and equip buildings, and to perform all acts necessary for the successful operation of the college.

The board was also given the authority to make rules and by-laws, to elect the faculty and president of the college and "such other employees as it may deem necessary." The charter established as officers of the corporation: a chairman of the board of trustees, a secretary and a treasurer, as well as an executive committee of "at least five and not more than nine members." [35]

Fayetteville College Foundation Formed

Recognizing the need to form a nonprofit foundation to secure funds for the new college, members of the Fayetteville College Steering Committee reorganized as the Fayetteville College Foundation June 22, 1956, to "aid, foster and promote the growth, progress and general welfare of the new Methodist College." [36] With Terry Sanford presiding, a group of 100 supporters met at Hay Street Methodist Church, approved a preliminary charter for the Foundation, and elected the following officers: Franklin Clark, president; Wilbur Clark, first vice president; D. P. Russ, second vice president; Norman Suttles, secretary; and Mel Thompson, treasurer.

Sixty trustees of the Foundation were elected at that meeting, including the five officers (See Appendix A) .

College Name Selected

Who selected the name Methodist College? Fayetteville merchant Ed Fleishman, a member of the Fayetteville College Steering Committee and a charter member of the Methodist College Board of Trustees, is generally given credit for that. However, J. Nelson Gibson, an original trustee from Scotland County, said Terry Sanford was the first to suggest "Methodist College." In a 2001 interview, Gibson said the name issue was resolved in the spring of 1956 when Terry Sanford, the Rev. Graham Eubank and he were walking across the site for the campus, consisting largely of cotton fields and trees.

As Gibson recalled it, Eubank asked, "What are we going to call the college?" Gibson said Sanford answered, "Let's name it The Methodist College." Gibson said he told Sanford, "You can't do that because it won't be The Methodist College. It might be the Methodist College in this town in North Carolina, but there are Methodist colleges all over the place." [37] Gibson said the three discussed the matter further and agreed to drop "the" and go with "Methodist College."

In June, when the proposed charter for the College was presented to the Conference Board of Education and shortly thereafter to the full Conference, the name "Methodist College" was used. Even then, however, the name was not final. In its report to the Conference, given June 26, 1956, in Greenville, N.C., the Board of Education recommended adoption of certificates of incorporation for the new colleges—Methodist College, Inc. and Rocky Mount College, Inc.—"subject to the approval of the University Senate and the Division of Educational Institutions and provided that the Boards of Trustees may determine the names of the colleges, subject to the approval of the Executive Committee of the Board of Education." [38] The board of trustees of the Rocky Mount college subsequently voted to name that institution North Carolina Wesleyan College.

Gibson said Terry Sanford later discussed the name issue with Ed Fleishman and asked Fleishman to support the name "Methodist College." When the College Board of Trustees held its second meeting September 27, 1956, after Joe Tally had read and explained the proposed charter and by-laws for Methodist College, Fleishman moved that the proposed charter and by-laws be approved "with the name to remain (until changed) Methodist College at Fayetteville." [39]

In Gibson's words: "So, the College, a Methodist Christian enterprise, was named by a Jew, and that was very nice, we thought [. . .] we were very grateful that he [Fleishman] was on the board anyway. He did a lot of good on it." [40]

Church Elects First Board of Trustees

During its annual session in Greenville June 25-28, 1956, The North Carolina Conference of the Methodist Church elected the 24 College trustees who were nominated and approved by the Conference Board of Education. One-fourth were from Cumberland County, one-fourth were ministers from the Conference, and three-fourths were Methodists.

Those elected were: Mr. J. M. Wilson of Fayetteville, Dr. Allen P. Brantley of Burlington, Mr. W. Ed Fleishman of Fayetteville, Dr. William Spence of Elizabeth City, Rev. O. L. Hathaway of Fayetteville, Mrs. Earl W. Brian of Raleigh, Mr. Wilson Yarborough Sr. of Fayetteville, Rev. W. A. Crow of Warrenton, General John R. Hodge of Fayetteville, Mr. J. Nelson Gibson of Gibson, Mr. L. Stacy Weaver of Durham, Mr. W. Robert Johnson of Goldsboro, Rev. Vergil E. Queen of Wilmington, Mr. Joe Tally Jr. of Fayetteville, Rev. Jack W. Page of Raleigh, Mr. Frank McBryde of Fayetteville, Mr. W. E. Horner of Sanford, Mr. Lenox G. Cooper of Wilmington, Dr. W. L. Clegg of Durham, Dr. R. L. Pittman of Fayetteville, Mrs. E. L. Hillman of Siler City, Mr. Terry Sanford of Fayetteville, Mr. Ernest L. Sanders of Tabor City, Rev. Graham S. Eubank of Fayetteville.

Trustees Secure Office Space, Begin Work

After The North Carolina Conference gave its approval, Methodist College and The Fayetteville College Foundation obtained temporary offices on the third floor of the Grace Pittman Building on Hay Street. Dr. R. L. Pittman provided a suite of offices *gratis*.

The Methodist College Board of Trustees held its first meeting July 3, 1956 at the Prince Charles Hotel in downtown Fayetteville. Prior to the meeting, board members visited the proposed site for the College, the 577-acre tract located off U.S. 401 North (Ramsey Street) five and one-half miles north of the Market House, Fayetteville's downtown landmark.

The Rev. W. Stanley Potter of Sanford, N.C., secretary of the Board of Education of The North Carolina Conference of The Methodist Church, convened the meeting. The Rev. Vergil Queen of Durham, N.C., gave the invocation, and Mr. W. E. Horner of Sanford, N.C., was named temporary secretary.

After Terry Sanford read a proposed draft of the articles of incorporation for Methodist College, the Reverend Graham Eubank presented a slate of

— CHAPTER 1 —

nominations for Board of Trustees officers and moved that the office of vice chairman be added. His motion carried.

The first officers of the Methodist College Board of Trustees were elected individually; there was one nomination for each of the five offices. Mr. J. M. Wilson nominated Terry Sanford for chairman. Reverend Eubank nominated Dr. W. L. Clegg for vice chairman. Mr. J. Nelson Gibson nominated Mr. W. E. Horner for secretary. Mr. Sanford nominated Mr. Frank McBryde for treasurer.

For the remainder of the first Board of Trustees meeting, Terry Sanford presided as chairman. He began by reporting that over 7,000 persons had pledged $1,800,000 to the campaign for the College. He then appointed Mr. Horner chairman of a Planning Committee which he charged with drafting detailed plans for financing, building, staffing and starting the College. Sanford also named Mr. Joe Tally Jr. chairman of a committee to draft the by-laws for Methodist College, Inc.

After the trustees' first meeting, Chairman Sanford sent out a series of memos. In Memo No. 1 dated July 18, 1956, Sanford appointed a committee to recommend a College president, naming the Rev. Vergil E. Queen chairman and Mrs. Earl W. Brian vice chairman. Other committee members were Frank McBryde, W. E. Horner and Joe Tally Jr., with Sanford serving as an ex-officio member.

In Memo No. 2 dated July 19, 1956, Sanford appointed the following trustees to serve on the Planning Committee with Chairman W. E. Horner: Dr. Allen P. Brantley, Dr. R. L. Pittman, Mr. J. Nelson Gibson, the Rev. Jack W. Page, Mrs. E. L. Hillman and Dr. W. L. Clegg, with Sanford again serving as an ex-officio member.

In Memo No. 3 dated July 26, 1956, Sanford appointed an Investment Committee consisting of Mr. Lenox Cooper, chairman, Mr. J. M. Wilson, and Gen. John R. Hodge.

Charter Members of the Methodist College Board of Trustees: L to R, seated Mrs. E.L. Hillman, Rev. Vergil Queen, W.E. Horner, Terry Sanford. Dr. W.L. Clegg, Frank McBryde, Mrs. Earl W. Brian; standing. Rev. O.L. Hathaway, Rev. Jack Page, Lenox G. Cooper, J. Nelson Gibson Jr., W. Robert Johnson, Rev. Graham Eubank, J.M. Wilson, Gen. John R. Hodge.

Planning Committee Consults Experts

The Planning Committee headed by Mr. W. E. Horner of Sanford, N.C., hit the ground running. Three committee members— Mr. Horner, Frank McBryde, and Norman Suttles— journeyed to Washington, D.C., July 16, 1956, to meet with Dr. Arthur Adams, president of the American Council on Education. They were referred to Dr. Adams by Dr. Frank Porter Graham, a Fayetteville native and former president of the University of North Carolina, who was then working for the United Nations.

During the meeting, Dr. Adams telephoned Mr. Jay Duvon of the U.S. Housing and Home Finance Agency and allowed Mr. Horner to talk with Duvon about the possibility of the College borrowing money from that agency under Title IV to erect dormitories and/or eating facilities. Mr. Duvon told Mr. Horner that the College would have to operate at least three years and submit detailed financial reports before any loan application could be processed and approved.

In the course of his discussions with the members of the Planning Committee, Dr. Adams offered four distinct recommendations for consideration by the Methodist College Board of Trustees.

His first recommendation was that the board of trustees seek out and employ a College president to develop and implement plans for the establishment of Methodist College. Adams suggested the trustees contact Dr. John O. Gross, secretary of the Division of Educational Institutions, Board of Education of The Methodist Church, in Nashville, Tenn., for suggestions on how to find a good president.

Dr. Adams' second recommendation was that the College employ a land-use specialist to develop a site plan for the land on which Methodist College would be built.

His third recommendation concerned money. He told the visiting delegation that "a million dollars cash on hand" would be needed for the College to start receiving students. He said the College would have to operate at least one year to get its curriculum and courses provisionally accredited by the Southern Association of Colleges and Schools.

During the meeting, Mr. McBryde and Mr. Suttles discussed with Dr. Adams "the possibility of the Fayetteville group, upon endorsement by people who believed in the future of the College, securing a loan in advance of the receipt of the money from the Fayetteville pledges and the conference and either 1) erecting the College *in toto*, or 2) erecting the part that the projected million dollars would pay for." [41]

Dr. Adams' fourth recommendation concerned the possibility of securing foundation funding for Methodist College. Dr. Adams said the Rockefeller, Ford, and Carnegie foundations "had never contributed capital expenditure

— CHAPTER 1 —

funds to any college; that their grants had been to existent four-year institutions for specific purposes such as increments to salaries." [42] Adams suggested that the trustees send someone to visit Dr. Robert M. Lester, executive director of The Southern Fellowships Fund in Chapel Hill, N.C., and solicit advice on what foundations they might approach for financial support.

As "conclusions" to its first report to the Methodist College Board of Trustees September 27, 1956, the Planning Committee listed all four of Dr. Adams' recommendations from the July 16 meeting. With regard to Point 3 concerning the need for a million dollars, the committee recommended that the Fayetteville College Foundation be asked, "to take this matter to their hearts, and see how soon they can come up with hard cash money to pay for the site and get it debt free, with the immediate goal being a million dollars so plans may be made forthwith towards opening for students." [43]

Dr. Robert Lester Sounds Warnings

Planning Committee Report No. 3 dated September 25, 1956, reported on a conference that committee members had with Dr. Robert M. Lester, executive director of the Southern Fellowships Fund in Chapel Hill, N.C. The report states that Dr. Lester was formerly associated with the Carnegie Foundation, was a Methodist, and was the son of a Methodist preacher.

Dr. Lester told the committee that Methodist College was "ten years away from foundation help," adding, "No foundation in many years has appropriated money to a beginning institution to draw plans or erect buildings, nor even in recent years to one already existent." [44]

The fund director said he was opposed to the Methodists building two new four-year colleges in North Carolina, one in Fayetteville and one in Rocky Mount. "The Methodists can't and aren't maintaining the colleges they already have in a manner worthy of the name of higher education," he said. "They don't need two more in this state. The Methodists should operate several junior colleges and one good four-year college, whose quality of instruction should be better than a public institution, and where the B.A. degree should be a better badge of education than a B.A. from Chapel Hill." [45]

In a second warning, Dr. Lester predicted the following: "Attrition in your pledges will be nearer 50 percent than 10 percent; experience proves it, unless there are several huge gifts which will raise the percentage for dropouts of smaller donors [. . .] don't sell any of your 700 acres to get ready cash; every college that has done this has lived to regret it [. . .] There will be students aplenty, in a few years, more than state institutions can handle." [46]

In the report, Mr. Bill Horner, Planning Committee chairman, quoted Dr. Lester as saying that because there was no need in North Carolina for more four-year colleges, "these colleges must adhere in their entrance requirements to what their catalogs said and not admit the unworthy or unqualified." [47]

Sanford Addresses Churches

In September 1956, Trustees Chairman Terry Sanford sent a progress report on Methodist College and a cover letter to the ministers of all Methodist churches in The North Carolina Conference.

Sanford's cover letter invites each minister to serve on a Conference Advisory Committee to the College and to select three other church members to serve with him. He said the Advisory Committee "will render a threefold service by advising with us, representing us, and meeting with us occasionally. They will serve as our 'honorary alumni' until we can build an alumni group." [48]

Included in Sanford's mailing was a self-addressed post card in which he offered to arrange for a member of the Board of Trustees to speak to the church's Men's Club (or any other organization or the full congregation) about Methodist College. The post card asked each minister to list a choice of several dates when a speaker might come.

One of the first churches to accept Sanford's offer was Edenton Street Methodist in Raleigh, N.C. Sanford spoke to the Men's Club there September 10, 1956. In his remarks, Sanford said, "It is highly important that the church does not relinquish its traditional role of leadership and influence in the field of higher education at this critical time [. . .] As an alumnus and a devoted friend of the University of North Carolina, I can afford to say that it would be a dreadful day if we allowed the state to assume and pre-empt the field of higher education." [49]

Sanford also declared that the "primary emphasis" at Methodist College would be placed on the faculty which he saw as the main and essential ingredient in the type of quality college the church sought to establish in Fayetteville. "The Board of Trustees knows that a college, fundamentally, is neither more nor less than its faculty," he said, noting that the board was already studying faculty salaries and soliciting special endowments for this purpose, "with the view of setting the highest possible scale to attract the very best in the profession." [50]

Sanford made a similar presentation to the Trinity Methodist Church Men's Club in Elizabethtown, N.C. in early January 1957.

Trustees Approve Charter Application, By-laws

At their second board meeting September 27, 1956, Methodist College trustees received a report from Franklin Clark that the Fayetteville College Foundation was continuing its efforts to secure pledges for establishing and supporting the College.

— CHAPTER 1 —

On a motion by Joe Tally, the trustees approved the proposed by-laws and charter application for Methodist College, Inc. Dr. Clegg nominated Mr. F. D. Byrd Jr., superintendent of the Cumberland County Schools, to succeed L. Stacy Weaver of Durham, N.C., as a trustee. Weaver had resigned from the board, citing his conflicting duties as a member of the (Methodist) conference World Service Commission.

Treasurer Frank McBryde's financial statement showed total receipts from pledges of $80,007.15, along with campaign and operating expenses of $31,258.19, leaving a bank balance of $48,258.96. McBryde said the first campaign receipts, up to $188,000, would be applied to the amount due on the purchase of the College site. Mr. Wilson Yarborough Sr. reported that deeds for all tracts needed for the College would be obtained soon.

Chairman Sanford reported that the following educators had agreed to serve on the Special Advisory Committee to the trustees' Planning Committee: Dr. Frank P. Graham, New York City; R. B. House, UNC; Dr. Harold Tribble, Wake Forest College; Dr. Charles E. Jordan, Duke University; Dr. Dennis H. Cooke, High Point College; Dr. J. D. Messick, East Carolina College; Dr. Harold W. Hutson, Greensboro College; Dr. J. L. Stokes, Pfeiffer College; Dr. Cecil Robbins, Louisburg College; Dr. W. W. Pierson, Woman's College, UNC; Dr. Cecil Spruill, UNC; Dr. Charles Phillips, Woman's College, UNC; Dr. A. K. King, UNC.

Rev. Queen, chairman of the Committee to Nominate a President, reported that over 100 letters had been written to Methodist colleges all over the United States seeking suggestions for a College president. He said his committee would review and classify all suggestions and report later.

Mr. Horner presented a letter from the Department of City and Regional Planning at UNC, proposing that a graduate student be given a stipend of $750 and expenses to prepare a site plan for the College based on a topographic survey. On a motion by Mr. Brantley, a special subcommittee of the trustees' Planning Committee was authorized to spend up to $1,200 for the site plan. The minutes of the next board meeting identified the UNC graduate student as William Davis.

College Receives Charter Nov. 1, 1956

Methodist College, Inc. became a legal entity November 1, 1956, when its 24-member Board of Trustees filed a Certificate of Incorporation with North Carolina Secretary of State Thad Eure in Raleigh, N.C.

Eure signed the charter in his office in the state Capitol with three College trustees present: Terry Sanford, board chairman; the Rev. Vergil Queen, trustee and president of The North Carolina Conference of The Methodist Church's Board of Education; and the Rev. W. L. Clegg, vice chairman of the board.

November 1, 1956: N.C. Secretary of State Thad Eure signs the charter creating Methodist College, Inc. at the State Capitol. Others present are, left to right, the Reverend Vergil E. Queen, Terry Sanford, and Dr. W. L. Clegg.

The Certificate listed 19 articles defining the objects, authority, and scope of the College, whose chief objects would be: [. . .] to establish, maintain and operate at Fayetteville, Cumberland County, North Carolina, a coeducational institution of collegiate grade to be known as Methodist College, under the control and direction of The North Carolina Conference, Southeastern Jurisdiction, subject to the provisions of the Discipline of The Methodist Church." [51]

Article IV states that Methodist College shall have no capital stock and through its Board of Trustees "shall be conducted and operated as a non-profit corporation, for the purpose of Christian higher education and to extend the influence of science, art, and Christian culture." [52] (See Appendix D, Certificate of Incorporation of Methodist College, Inc.)

"We're officially in business now," said Sanford, "and with the support of thousands of financial backers already on the dotted line and other thousands from throughout The North Carolina Conference [of The Methodist Church], we have the highest hopes of reaping rich educational dividends for this and future generations." [53]

Duke Official Briefs Trustees

At their third board meeting November 15, 1956, the Methodist College trustees voted to borrow "not in excess of $75,000 for six months to complete payment on College tracts." It was reported that "two tracts were given outright; three were bought at low market price and one at market value." [54]

— CHAPTER 1 —

Franklin Clark reported that the Fayetteville College Foundation had employed Lloyd Advertising Inc., at a cost of $100 weekly, to "administer and assist in the fund drive and to act as temporary executive assistant to officers of the Foundation and to the Board of Trustees until such time as the Board of Trustees takes action to set up a permanent organization and a paid assistant." [55]

Mr. Horner, chairman of the Planning Committee, submitted reports 4 (curriculum suggested by UNC officials), 5 (Wake Forest conference), 6 (conference with Dr. Cecil Robbins of Louisburg College) and 7 (Atlanta conference with Dr. Donald C. Agnew concerning accreditation).

On a motion by Mr. Horner, the trustees instructed Chairman Sanford to appoint a finance committee to audit and report all expenditures to date and recommend an overall financial plan and accounting system showing receipts and payments of the Fayetteville College Foundation.

Dr. Charles E. Jordan, vice president of Duke University and a member of the Special Advisory Committee to the trustees' Planning Committee, addressed the board at some length concerning how the trustees should proceed with the establishment of the College.

Dr. Jordan offered the following observations and recommendations:
— There is a need for colleges tomorrow, but of 55 accredited colleges in North Carolina, only six are filled to capacity. Unless there is an elevated ambition to make this a really good college, the trustees should cease and desist, as there is no need in this state for further four-year mediocre colleges.
— The day of junior colleges is drawing to a close, with the entrance of the state into the community college field.
— Early accreditation and a strong curriculum are necessary.
— Student fees should be set high enough to ensure operations in the black.
— The College president should be a Methodist with a background in education; must be a good businessman, a promoter and a good public relations man, personable to the public; should not teach.
— None of the College land should be sold; it will be a gold mine in the future. The College should be visible from the highway and have double the amount of parking space the most liberal estimates say is necessary.
— The College should develop a master plan anticipating future growth.
— Buildings should be constructed in this order: classroom

with administrative offices, library, dormitories for men and women, cafeteria, auditorium, and chapel.
— The board of trustees should have an executive committee and standing committees on buildings and grounds, finance, and academic matters.
— The president should be responsible to the trustees and the faculty to the president, the trustees being responsible to the [Church] conference or conferences participating in the support of the College.
— An area of the campus should be set aside for faculty housing, with half-acre lots being sold or leased to faculty members. [56]

Planning Report No. 7 quoted Dr. Donald C. Agnew of Atlanta, Ga., executive secretary, Commission on Colleges and Universities, Southern Association of Colleges and Schools, as voicing doubt that eastern North Carolina could assimilate, all at one time, the college program to build two four-year colleges as approved by the special session of the North Carolina Annual Conference of The Methodist Church. Dr. Agnew also expressed the opinion that, "Fayetteville has more potential support in the way of students and finances from the community than Rocky Mount [. . .]" [57]

A former president of Coker College in Hartsville, S.C., Dr. Agnew gave the trustees' Planning Committee twelve general recommendations concerning the establishment of Methodist College and a list of the twenty-one standards the College would have to meet to be accredited by the Southern Association of Colleges and Schools.

Agnew's general recommendations included the following, as summarized by Mr. Horner: "[. . .] 2) we need an architect with imagination and alive to the new techniques in building and who is dedicated first of all to saving money [. . .] 11) small colleges we should study and perhaps pattern ourselves after include: Guilford, Emory & Henry, Southwestern College [Memphis, Tenn.], Florida Southern, Kentucky Wesleyan, and Centenary College [Shreveport, La.]." [58]

Bill Horner's Reports & Letters

Early records of the Methodist College Board of Trustees indicate that Board Secretary W. E. "Bill" Horner of Sanford, N.C., worked tirelessly as chairman of the trustees' Planning Committee. A native of Durham, N.C. and a 1922 graduate of The University of North Carolina, Horner was the publisher of *The Sanford Daily Herald*. From July to November 1956, Horner's committee produced seven reports detailing how the new College should be structured and financed, based on advice gleaned from visits with

— CHAPTER 1 —

leading administrators in the field of higher education. In a memo to the trustees dated October 29, 1956, to which Terry Sanford attached copies of Planning Committee Reports 4-6, Sanford wrote, "Mr. Horner and his associates on the Planning Committee are to be congratulated upon the thoroughness of their approach to matters falling within their purview." [59]

The Planning Committee reports were thorough and detailed, containing facts and figures, as well as suggestions for fund-raising, curriculum, facilities, annual operating costs, staffing, land-use planning, public relations/student recruitment, and other important issues. Horner's previous experience as a state legislator (he served five terms in the N.C. House of Representatives) and his previous service as a trustee (at Louisburg College, UNC, and Fayetteville State College) might explain why he was so focused and how he knew who to consult about starting a college.

Horner was noted for being open and direct, and he was proud of that fact. In several letters to Terry Sanford, he was insistent that the new College be operated in a businesslike, fiscally responsible manner. In a letter dated November 23, 1956, Horner told Sanford that the Board of Trustees should immediately adopt "a stable financial plan establishing the responsibility and function of the Fayetteville group (Fayetteville College Foundation) and the trustees in the matter of collecting pledges, spending money and making commitments for spending money." [60]

Fort Bragg, through its commanding officer, Maj. Gen. Paul D. Adams (center) contributed $31,000 to Methodist College from the military post's Community Fund Jan. 23, 1957. The general, a strong booster of the college movement from the early stages, hands the check to Wilbur Clark (R), one of the drive leaders, as Charter Warren (L), president of the Fayetteville Chamber of Commerce looks on.

Horner said he was "greatly concerned about the necessity of borrowing $75,000 to purchase land with 20 percent of $1,750,000 in pledges ($350,000) due to be collected by December 31, 1956." [61] "We'll never get this College started if the folks don't pay the first year's pledges by the due date," he wrote[. . .] I hope the folks down there will understand my views: tighten up on spending, collect the pledges, get ready to build a college." [62]

Horner sent Frank McBryde, board treasurer, a copy of his November 23 letter to Sanford. McBryde responded in a letter dated December 5, 1956, telling Horner the Fayetteville College Foundation had already collected $100,000 of the $350,000 expected during the first year and saying that "pledgers have until June 1, 1957, not December 31, 1956, to meet their first-year payment on schedule." [63]

The Fayetteville optician continued, "This isn't a poor performance when you consider no pressure has been applied and there's been no physical activity on the grounds to suggest that construction is in any way imminent." [64]

Trustees Interview Architects

On the afternoon of February 21, 1957, the Board of Trustees convened at the Prince Charles Hotel and heard presentations from seven architectural firms interested in planning and designing the buildings for Methodist College. Presenters included: George Watts Carr of Durham, Dan MacMillan of Fayetteville, H. R. McLawhorn Jr. of Greensboro, Charles C. Hartmann of Winston-Salem, Gorrell R. Stinson of Winston-Salem, Basil G. Laslett of Fayetteville, and Arthur C. Jenkins Jr. of Fayetteville. Following the architects' presentations, Willliam K. Davis, a graduate student at UNC-Chapel Hill, presented the preliminary findings of a long-range land use study which the trustees had commissioned.

At the same meeting, Dr. R. Wright Spears, president of Columbia College, presented information and suggestions for creating and starting the College, under the headings of curriculum, land use, buildings, standing committees of the board of trustees, and the relationship of the board to the College president and to The North Carolina Conference of The Methodist Church.

Board Treasurer Frank McBryde gave a financial report which showed receipts of $152,748 and disbursements of $115,613, including $109,337 for land. Trustee and Methodist lay leader Nelson Gibson gave a brief report concerning lay meetings on higher education which were being held at various places throughout The North Carolina Conference of The Methodist Church.

— CHAPTER 1 —

Foundation Issues Report

In February 1957, the Fayetteville College Foundation distributed a six-page booklet entitled "A Report On Methodist College." The booklet contained a brief progress report by Trustees Chairman Terry Sanford; an aerial view of the College site; information about the College charter, financial pledges secured by the Fayetteville College Foundation and The North Carolina Conference of The Methodist Church; and a letter of appreciation from Paul N. Garber, the resident Methodist bishop.

A message on the inside front cover of the booklet proclaimed, "Upon the solid bedrock of faith in God and selfless dedication of human resources in glorious fulfillment of a noble concept, the spiritual spires are rising heavenward." [65] The back cover listed the members, officers and committees of the Methodist College Board of Trustees; and the officers of the Fayetteville College Foundation.

In his message, Terry Sanford described the acquisition of the 600-acre site on which the College would be located as the most important single development to date. He also announced that the Fayetteville College Foundation would present the land to the Methodist College Board of Trustees in a brief ceremony on the College site February 21, 1957. Sanford also reported that the Board was interviewing candidates for the position of College president.

Under the heading "Cooperative Action," the booklet restated the commitments made by the Church and the community in support of Methodist College:

1) The North Carolina Conference of The Methodist Church has committed $2,188,000 in capital funds for Methodist College over a 15-year period and $130,000 per year in continuing support.
2) The citizens of Fayetteville and Cumberland County have pledged $2 million in capital funds over a five-year period (ending June 30, 1961) and $50,000 per year in continuing support from the opening of the College. [66]

The brochure closed with a letter from Bishop Garber to Terry Sanford, in which Garber expressed his deep appreciation to Sanford and other citizens of Fayetteville and Cumberland County for their leadership in the founding of Methodist College. Repeating a statistic he had previously given, Garber wrote, "It is estimated that the college population in America will triple by 1970 and unless we have new colleges like Methodist College the educational door of opportunity will be closed to many young people." [67]

1956–1959

Foundation Presents Land for Campus

On the morning of February 21, 1957, the Board of Trustees and hundreds of supporters gathered at the College site for a ceremony in which the Fayetteville College Foundation symbolically transferred the 577-acre site to Bishop Paul Garber, resident bishop of The North Carolina Conference of The Methodist Church, and the College trustees in a brief ceremony. Shivering onlookers gathered in front of a flat-bed trailer on which a podium and sound system were installed. Music was provided by the Fayetteville High School Band.

Fayetteville Mayor George Herndon recognized Mr. and Mrs. John C. Kinlaw and Mr. & Mrs. Joe W. Stout as important benefactors who had given large portions of the College tract. The Kinlaws gave 47.5 acres and the Stouts 120 acres. The remainder of the land—eight tracts— was purchased from the Kinlaws and other land owners by the Fayetteville College Foundation. Large tracts were purchased from Dr. and Mrs. J. W. Baggett, Mr. and Mrs. G. S. Quillin, M. T. and Lillian Mae Taylor, Richard E. and Linda H. Taylor, and the trio of T. Taylor, Richard E. Taylor, and Thomas L. Dale. A combination of woodland and farmland descending to the Cape Fear River, the site was considered ideal because of its highly favorable soil and drainage conditions. The tract fronted U. S. 401 for a half-mile, widening out and extending eastward for more than a mile to the Cape Fear River.

Trustee Wilson F. Yarborough, Sr., chairman of the Site Committee of the Fayetteville College Foundation and a member of the trustees' Building Committee, described the land as "the finest site available in the state and the South for a college," [68] mentioning its scenic attractions and river frontage and averring its scenic attractions, including a lake and river frontage. The Foundation and College trustees had authorized Yarborough to negotiate with various property owners to obtain the land needed for the College. [The deed for the ten tracts comprising the campus were conveyed from Wilson F. Yarborough Sr. and wife Mary P. Yarborough to Methodist College June 10, 1959.]

Franklin Clark, local attorney and president of the Fayetteville College Foundation, presented to Bishop Garber the freshly cut top of a longleaf pine tree growing on the premises, following the English custom "delivery of seizins." After accepting the land for The North Carolina Conference of The Methodist Church and for the College trustees, Garber thanked the people of Fayetteville and the area for "not waiting for a crisis in higher education to come before taking proper steps to ensure Christian higher education for the youth of the area and state soon to be knocking at college doors." [69]

Bishop Garber ended his address by saying, "This is the happiest day of my official career." [70]

— CHAPTER 1 —

Franklin Clark, Fayetteville attorney and president of the Fayetteville College Foundation, presents a pine bough to Paul Garber, bishop of The N.C. Conference of the Methodist Church, in a symbolic conveyance of 577 acres of land to Methodist College Feb. 21, 1957.

Davis Completes Land Use Plan/Campus Design

During the summer of 1957, UNC graduate student William K. Davis completed his study entitled "A Long Range Program for Campus Development: Proposed Fayetteville Methodist College." The trustees had hired Davis the previous year to do a land use plan for the College. The resulting plan which Davis presented to the trustees was his thesis for a Master of Regional Planning degree.

Davis' plan was divided into five chapters. In "Chapter I: College Objectives," the author noted that of sixty-two four-year colleges affiliated with The Methodist Church, twenty-seven were deemed "high quality" by the American Association of Universities in a 1948 list of accredited schools. He said the trustees had made it clear that they wanted Methodist College to be one of high standards, one with first-rate professorial talent and library materials and a policy of selective admittance. "This high caliber of instruction is exemplified by such institutions as DePauw University, Randolph-Macon College and Davidson College," wrote Davis. [71]

In "Chapter Two: Present Conditions," the topography of the College site is described as typical of the "sandhills" section of the coastal plain, with the principal land forms being: 1) the highway tableland, 2) the central hilltop, 3) the southern hill, and 4) the northeast valley plain. (See Appendix E, Topographic Map, Methodist College Campus.) He noted that the entire tract, including two small streams, drained eastward into the Cape Fear River. Like the architect hired by the College, Davis suggested that most buildings be erected on the highway tableland fronting U.S. 401.

This chapter refers to college population projections for North Carolina that the "baby boom" of the late 1940s would cause college enrollments to nearly double by 1975. It also notes a projection that the population of Fayetteville and Cumberland County would increase 50 percent by 1975, from 60,000 to 90,000 in the city, and from 75,000 to 150,000 in the county. The plan is based on trustees' Planning Committee reports which recommended that the College open with 300 students, half of whom would be day or commuting students, and that the campus be developed to ultimately serve about 2,500 students.

"Chapter III: Space Needs" outlines space and building needs in three phases, based on enrollments of 300, 1,000 and 2,500. Using tables, Davis projected a Phase Two enrollment of 1,000 students would require 91,800 square feet of dormitory space, 13,200 square feet of dining space, 26,200 square feet of library space, and 38 classrooms totalling 30,500 square feet. He projected 15,000 square feet would be needed for administrative offices during Phase II.

In addition to the learning, residential, and administrative space, Davis' plan suggested: an auditorium/theater with seating for 800, an amphitheater, a park, and parking space amounting to 1.75 acres (Phase I), 5.5 acres (Phase II), and 14 acres (Phase III). Also recommended were: a bell tower, an outdoor swimming pool, tennis courts, gymnasium, baseball fields, and a football stadium/track with seating for 6,000.

In Chapter IV, Davis projected a circulation plan of three intersecting loop roads accessible from U.S. 401 at two points. He produced a map showing ideal locations for dormitories, academic buildings, a stadium, athletic facilities, both single family and apartment housing, fraternity courts and a small park. (See Appendix F, Plan for Ultimate Enrollment.) At the end of his study, he also included campus maps for Florida Southern College, Drake University, Concordia College, Jacksonville (Fla.) Junior College, and the University of Miami.

Recognizing that the site for the College was more than one mile outside the city limits of Fayetteville and therefore not subject to city planning and zoning regulations, Davis recommended that the City of Fayetteville request special legislation from the N.C. General Assembly to extend the city's planning, zoning and regulatory jurisdiction to include the Methodist College campus. In an appendix to his study, Davis included the proposed draft for a bill entitled "Legislation for Site Protection."

To facilitate continuous physical planning for the College, Davis suggested the College president appoint a Campus Planning Board from key members of the faculty and administration. He also suggested that the College retain a planning consultant on a part-time, long-term basis.

Although there is only passing reference in Board of Trustees' minutes to Davis' campus development plan, it is clear that the plan was forwarded to

— CHAPTER 1 —

Stevens and Wilkinson, the Atlanta-based architectural firm selected by the trustees in June 1957 to design the Methodist College campus. The Stevens and Wilkinson site plan incorporated many of Davis' ideas and placed many of the facilities in the same locations that Davis had envisioned.

Trustees Appoint Stacy Weaver President, Select Architect

At their fifth meeting, held June 22, 1957, the College trustees took two very important actions. The Rev. Vergil Queen, chairman of the Special Committee to Recommend a President for Methodist College, reported that the committee unanimously recommended Lucius Stacy Weaver, 52, superintendent of the Durham City Schools and a prominent Methodist layman, for president of Methodist College. On a motion by Queen, seconded by Ed Fleishman, Weaver was unanimously elected on a standing vote.

Arriving a few minutes later, Weaver expressed appreciation to the board for its vote of confidence and pledged his best efforts in an opportunity afforded few men in "building a college from the ground up." [72] He said Methodist College would adhere to two fundamentals from the outset: 1) academic integrity— "The College shall rigidly observe intellectual honesty in all it undertakes." and 2) the Christian concept of life — "The institution must faithfully apply the sanctions of religious and moral precepts of Christian teaching in the development of character." [73]

A native of Lenoir, N.C., Methodist's founding president received his A.B. degree from Duke University and his master's from Columbia University. He would later receive an honorary doctorate from High Point College in 1958 and an honorary doctorate from Duke University in 1971. He began his career as a professor of Latin and Greek at Rutherford College, later serving as its president and subsequently as president of Mount Park Junior College in Surry County. He was principal of a consolidated school in Jonesville, N.C., for seven years, superintendent of the Statesville City Schools for six years, and superintendent of the Durham City Schools for ten years.

Stacy Weaver came from a prominent family of educators. His father, Dr. Charles C. Weaver, was a Methodist minister and former president of Davenport College (a precursor to Brevard), as well as Emory and Henry College. Weaver's brother Jim Weaver, was commissioner of the Atlantic Coast Conference and former director of athletics at Wake Forest College. His brother, Philip Weaver, was assistant superintendent (and later superintendent) of the Greensboro City Schools. Another brother, C. C. Weaver, Jr. had been principal of the Methodist Orphanage in Raleigh. His sister, Janie Weaver, was a teacher (and later guidance counselor) at Reynolds High School in Winston-Salem.

A College press release announcing Weaver's selection as president indicated that Queen's committee interviewed nearly 100 candidates. Weaver's appointment was greeted with enthusiastic approval from community, church, and education leaders. Methodist Bishop Paul Garber said Weaver was an outstanding Methodist layman with a background of achievement in education and "would have the full endorsement of the N.C. Conference of The Methodist Church and of all friends of the new College." [74]

Dr. Hollis Edens, president of Duke University, complimented the College trustees on their selection, saying Weaver possessed "the stature and educational experience required for setting the new school off on a high plane." [75]

Rev. Queen's committee recommended a salary for the president of $12,000 per year plus travel allowance and funds for office support and administrative assistance to be determined in a budget submitted by the president. The committee also recommended that the trustees provide a suitable residence for Dr. Weaver and his family. On a motion by Dr. Pittman, the matter of the president's salary and residence was referred to the trustees' Executive Committee where it was approved.

Reporting as chairman of the trustees' Building Committee, Dr. Pittman said his committee recommended that the firm of Stevens and Wilkinson of Atlanta, Ga., be commissioned to prepare plans and supervise construction of the Methodist College campus. This recommendation was also forwarded to the Executive Committee.

During a brief meeting of the Executive Committee, Dr. Weaver's salary was set at $12,000 per year, and Trustees Chairman Terry Sanford appointed a committee consisting of J. Mel Thompson, treasurer of the Fayetteville College Foundation, and Ed Fleishman to look for a suitable home for the president. On a motion by Frank McBryde, the Executive Committee voted to employ Stevens and Wilkinson of Atlanta, Ga., as College architects.

Terry Sanford Asks Local Citizens To Catch Up On Pledges

In the August 29, 1957, edition of *The Fayetteville Observer*, Methodist College Trustees Chairman Terry Sanford was quoted as saying that slow payments on Methodist College pledges could postpone the opening of the College for one year. The trustees had originally wanted to open the College in September 1959.

"Everything is shaping up on schedule except the money," said Sanford. "I suspect many people have put off paying their pledges until the need was more urgent and the accomplishments more apparent [. . .] If by next March—two years after the first pledges were made—everybody has paid two installments, then we can proceed on schedule and start actual construction. If just a few

— CHAPTER 1 —

College President L. Stacy Weaver, seated at left, meets with members of the Fayetteville College Foundation at the Pittman Building in downtown Fayetteville.

fail to pay on time, we can be thrown off schedule and delayed in our opening by at least a year." [76]

The newspaper article said local office workers had just mailed nearly 7,000 statements to area residents who had made pledges to the College as part of Fayetteville's $2 million commitment. As examples of progress in the development of the College, the article mentioned the recent acquisition of the 577-acre campus site and the employment of L. Stacy Weaver as College president.

Sanford also appealed to area residents to increase their pledges and to new residents to make a pledge. "We need new pledges and increased pledges," he said. "I know we will receive them, along with full payment of present pledges, and that soon I will have only good news for you." [77]

Trustees Purchase Home, Auto for President

On September 5, 1957, the Executive Committee approved a subcommittee recommendation that the trustees purchase for the president's home a house under construction by the Broadwell brothers at 1717 Raeford Road, at a price not to exceed $28,000. The group also authorized the purchase of a 1957 Buick for the president's use and authorized President Weaver to hire a secretary.

Trustees Chairman Terry Sanford expressed appreciation to Dr. R. L. Pittman for providing rent-free a suite of three offices for the president and his staff in the Grace Pittman Building on Hay Street in downtown Fayetteville. Weaver began work as president of Methodist College September 1, 1957.

1956–1959

Methodists Approve $5 Million Capital Funds Campaign

The 56-member Commission on Christian Higher Education of The North Carolina Conference of The Methodist Church held a special meeting September 18, 1957, at St. Paul Methodist Church in Goldsboro, N.C. concerning the Conference's $5 million Capital Funds Campaign planned for January 1- April 15, 1958. The Commission then made a formal report and recommendation for Conference approval.

"We reaffirm our concern for the education of our youth through all the institutions which we have long been associated and declare our confidence that our two newest colleges will enable us to enlarge and enrich the scope of this ministry," said the Rev. Paul Carruth, executive director of the Commission." [78] Carruth announced that the Conference had retained Ward, Dresham and Reinhardt, Inc. of New York to conduct the campaign and praised the Western North Carolina Conference of the Methodist Church for its recent decision to launch a capital funds campaign of $3 million to aid Greensboro College and High Point College.

Representatives from Methodist College, N.C. Wesleyan College, Louisburg College, Duke Divinity School, and the Wesley Foundation made funding requests totalling $5.2 million. Methodist and Wesleyan each asked for $2.2 million. The Commission approved the following allocations from the Capital Funds Campaign in two waves. After payment of campaign expenses of $200,000, the first $2,225,000 would be allocated: $1 million to Methodist College, $1 million to N.C. Wesleyan College, and $225,000 to Louisburg College. The balance of income from the campaign would be allocated: $1 million to Methodist College, $1 million to N.C. Wesleyan College, $100,000 to the Divinity School of Duke University, $150,000 to the Wesley Foundation, and $50,000 each to Greensboro College and High Point College, which had previously been supported by the Conference.

Final approval of the Capital Funds Campaign came November 4, 1957, at a special session of The North Carolina Conference of the Methodist Church held at Hay Street Methodist Church in Fayetteville.

In a two-hour meeting, over 800 delegates approved by unanimous vote the allocations recommended by the Commission on Christian Higher Education, giving Methodist College a total of $2 million, N.C. Wesleyan College $2 million, Louisburg College $50,000, and Duke Divinity School $100,000.

Bishop Deflects Integration Issue

During the Conference's special session in Fayetteville, Bishop Paul N. Garber avoided a major controversy by ruling out of order a resolution offered by W. F. Perry of Warrenton, N.C. which would have affirmed a segregationist admissions policy at the two new colleges. Garber said the only business before this special session was the adoption of the fund-raising campaign and said, "In Methodist educational institutions, matters relating to faculty, curriculum, admission of students and similar items are in the control of the boards of trustees." [79]

Garber released a lengthy written statement on his ruling, saying Perry's resolution should be addressed directly to the boards of trustees of the Conference's colleges or presented at the Conference's annual session the following June for discussion and debate. At the delegates' request, Garber's ruling was printed in the minutes of the special session and in the *North Carolina Christian Advocate.*

After the business meeting ended, nearly 1,500 delegates and guests gathered at the Methodist College campus site north of the city for a picnic lunch prepared by 225 Methodist women from Fayetteville area churches.

Trustees Approve Site & Building Plans

The Building Committee of the Board of Trustees met December 28, 1957 and approved a preliminary site plan for the College as prepared by the architects, Stevens and Wilkinson. When the Methodist College Board of Trustees met January 30, 1958, the trustees approved the architects' site plan which had already been reviewed by the Building Committee. Messrs. Wilkins, Barnett and Shirley of the architectural firm of Stevens and Wilkinson were present and answered questions about the site plan for the College, as well as preliminary drawings and floor plans for eight buildings: Administration, Classroom, Library, Fine Arts, Chapel and Bell Tower, Cafeteria and Student Union, Science, Gymnasium.

In his first report to the Board of Trustees, President Weaver made two recommendations: 1) that Stevens & Wilkinson be authorized to proceed with drawings and specifications for the Classroom Building, and 2) that the Executive Committee be empowered to employ a landscape architect to work with the architects. Both recommendations were approved by the board. Weaver estimated that the College would be able to take bids on the Classroom Building in about three months

President Weaver suggested in his report that Methodist College should plan to open with approximately 1,000 students—400 commuting students and 600 boarding students. He also predicted that the cost of constructing the buildings needed for opening the College might exceed the $4 million previously estimated, half of which was to be raised by the Fayetteville community and half by The North Carolina Conference of The Methodist Church.

A building estimates handout attached to Weaver's report projected the cost of building the Classroom Building, Library, Science Building,

1956–1959

Cafeteria/Student Union, Administration Building, Bell Tower, Heating Plant & Utilities at $1,764,372 plus $79,396 for architects' fees and $176,437 for equipment, making a grand total of $2,030,205. (See Appendix H, Building Estimates.) He said the College would need capital funds of $150,000 to purchase library books. He said the cost of landscaping and paving had not been determined.

Weaver praised the decision by The North Carolina Conference of The Methodist Church to postpone the campaign for capital funds for the three colleges for eight calendar months, but added, "This delay in the acquisition of Church funds makes the work of the Fayetteville College Foundation of the greatest importance and urgency." [80]

Noting that federal construction loans to institutions of higher learning were currently available only to schools that had been in operation two years, Weaver said legislation pending in Congress might liberalize this rule, by reducing the requirement to one year of operation.

Weaver concluded his report by expressing his thanks for the many courtesies he had received from the trustees, the Fayetteville community, representatives of The Methodist Church, and the educational world. "Having put our hand to the plow, we shall not look back, but by our united effort

The Greatest Gift: Mr. and Mrs. Joe W. Stout, shown here with Terry Sanford, chairman of the Methodist College Board of Trustees, made the largest gift of land to the College, conveying 120 acres of rolling woodland "near the center of the southern portion of the college site" October 17, 1956. An official of Southern Builders, Inc., and a successful land developer, Stout said, "We are happy to have a part in boosting the college project along, and we hope this will lighten the problems facing the institutions's trustees."

shall move onward to the accomplishment of the vision which brought this undertaking into being," he said. [81]

In other actions at the January 30, 1958, trustees meeting:

— Franklin Clark, president of the Fayetteville College Foundation, reported that the Foundation had collected just over $300,000 in capital funds for Methodist College.

— Rev. Paul Carruth, executive director of the North Carolina Conference of The Methodist Church's Commission on Higher Education, said the church would seek gifts from selected donors between April and May, then appeal to local churches between August 27 and December 21. He said the total sum sought would amount to about $30 per Church member in the Conference and be payable over three years.

— Trustees directed the Finance Committee to investigate the possibility of borrowing money to finance College buildings.

Trustees Opt for Contemporary Architecture

The "contemporary design" for the campus developed by Stevens and Wilkinson of Atlanta was used as a major selling point for Methodist College during its first decade. The first College catalogs were filled with pictures of the Classroom Building, bell tower, Science Building, and Student Union along with sketches of buildings yet to come. In a 1960 press release prepared for a "Methodist College section" of *The Fayetteville Observer*, Director of Public Relations Charles K. McAdams quoted Board Chairman Terry Sanford as saying the choice of architecture was "particularly significant."

The Atlanta firm had won many awards for its designs and had extensive background in campus design and college structures, having designed many of the buildings at Georgia Tech and the University of Georgia. McAdams' press release states that Stevens and Wilkinson received an award from a national architectural magazine "for the creativity and unity of design for the Methodist College campus." [82]

The Methodist College design had three striking architectural features: 1) unique vaulted roof structures, 2) extensive use of masonry (honeycomb) sunscreens over the windows, and 3) use of open courts in the center of several buildings (most notably the Classroom Building and the Science Building). The College's now famous honeycomb sunscreens were made of pre-cast concrete blocks twelve inches in depth and placed approximately two feet in front of the windows.

The PR director quoted College President Stacy Weaver as saying, "We shall get a lot for our money with this type of architecture," after considering comparative costs of different types of architecture. [83]

Waxing eloquent, McAdams concluded his press release with this paragraph:

> The overall architectural scheme is a very striking one in which the buildings themselves seem to have life. As one comes into the atmosphere of the architecture on this campus, he is immediately challenged by the high degree of imagination and originality in the total campus development. The basic campus is a group of interlocking malls, each adapted to its particular elevation and site topography. [84]
> (See Appendix I, Architect's Site Plan for Methodist College.)

The original site model (see page 39) showed a stadium and track at the back of the campus where a golf driving range was built in 1988. The gymnasium was located on the hill west of the Boiler Plant and south of the Classroom Building, where Margaret and Walter Clark Hall now stands.

The Rev. Dr. F. Belton Joyner, a retired minister and former trustee of Methodist College, offered this observation about Methodist's architecture:

> The architecture of the campus has always appealed to me [. . .] there are some who say they prefer the traditional Georgian look at N.C. Wesleyan, but my heart always beats a little faster at the more modern look [. . .] I have never seen the Florida Southern [College] campus that Frank Lloyd Wright designed, but the Methodist College campus has always reminded me of pictures I have seen of that campus. [85]

Dr. R. L. Pittman, the trustee who chaired the trustees' Building Committee, had worked with Stevens and Wilkinson on several of his development projects. Fayetteville resident Hugh Burton, who worked for the Rose Group and later as the site manager for Stevens and Wilkinson on the Methodist College project, said in a 2002 interview, "Dr. Pittman developed a lot of shopping centers up in the Richmond area, and Stevens and Wilkinson was doing his design work for him. So that is how they got involved with Methodist College." [86]

Developers Announce Plans for College Lakes Subdivision

The economic impact of Methodist College became apparent February 17, 1958, when Paul Thompson and Tom McLean announced plans to build the College Lakes subdivision on 1,200 acres opposite Methodist College, on the west side of Ramsey Street.

— CHAPTER 1 —

Stevens and Wilkinson of Atlanta, Georgia, designed a central mall dominated by the bell tower, with the Administration Building and Student Union at opposite ends.

Thompson and McLean said they had purchased the site of the Golden Belt Peach Orchard, Inc. from R. H. Barbour for $750,000. The realty firm of Thompson-McLean, Inc., announced that residential lots in College Lakes would be a minimum of one-half acre each and that the subdivision would have a dual-lane entrance at Rosehill Road.

Trustees Make Construction Decisions

Several matters related to construction of the campus were decided at a meeting of the trustees' Executive Committee May 2, 1958. The firm of Godwin and Bell, landscape architects, was employed to landscape the campus for a fee of $5,600 plus a per diem for supervision. Sol Rose was employed to make a topographic map of the College site at a fee not to exceed $2,730.

President Weaver submitted a proposed operating budget for 1958-59 of $33,253; $29,125 to come from the North Carolina (Methodist) Conference and the remainder from the rental of property. The committee also authorized Weaver to have an official corporate seal designed for the College.

Official depositories for College funds were designated as follows: First Citizens Bank and Trust Co. for the capital account; the Foundation operating account at Commercial and Industrial Bank, and the College operating account at Branch Banking & Trust Co.

After reviewing engineer's estimates of the cost of building and operating an electrical distribution system for the College, the committee decided that the College should own its own electrical distribution system and that it should be an underground system.

The committee authorized President Weaver to instruct the architectural firm of Stevens and Wilkinson to prepare working drawings for the Science Building, Library, Administration Building, Power Plant, streets, sidewalks, and parking areas. It was also decided that contractors would be invited to bid on College buildings, but that no public announcement would be run.

Finally, President Weaver reported that the dormitories, cafeteria, and infirmary buildings would be eligible for federal loans after the school had been in operation for one year. Board Chairman Terry Sanford said he would appoint a committee to investigate the possibility of securing such a federal construction loan.

Horner Reiterates Concern

Just prior to the May 27, 1958 "annual meeting" of the Board of Trustees, trustee and Board Secretary W. E. Horner (also Chairman of the trustees' Planning Committee) sent a letter to President Weaver reiterating his

Stevens and Wilkinson presented this site plan for the Methodist College campus to the Methodist College Board of Trustees in December 1957.

previously-expressed concern about the slow collection of five-year pledges to the College by the Fayetteville College Foundation. He had sent a similar letter to Terry Sanford and fellow trustees in November 1956.

In a letter dated May 22, 1958, Horner reminded the trustees that the board needed one million dollars cash to get Methodist College started. He expressed his concern that less than half of the $800,000 in pledges due at that point had been collected. "In my travels from college to college, expert to expert, I heard too many statistics about the depletion and shrinking of original pledges not to be genuinely alarmed at the current situation," wrote Horner [. . .] I am grieved and worried because after all the work and planning we put into this College, the pledges have not been paid as agreed upon." [87]

Horner said the trustees should ask the people of Fayetteville and Cumberland County to come current with their pledges and immediately take steps to secure additional pledges. He concluded by saying, "As we prepare to ask Methodists to contribute to this College, I deem it the first duty of the people of the area where the College is to be located to get current with their obligations. Until they do this, I see less hopes of a successful denominational-wide campaign." [88]

Sanford Disbands Two Committees

At its May 27, 1958 meeting, the Board of Trustees authorized the Executive Committee to take bids for construction of the Classroom Building in June, approved the nomination of six trustees for new four-year terms, and re-elected board officers and appointees to the Executive Committee.

Board Chairman Terry Sanford announced that he had not appointed a new Planning Committee or Building Committee, that the duties originally assigned to the Planning Committee would be assumed by the President and that the responsibility of the Building Committee would be absorbed by the Executive Committee.

Sanford expressed his appreciation for the "invaluable contributions" made by Mr. Horner and his Planning Committee and Dr. Pittman and his Building Committee. He also asked the Finance Committee to investigate the possibility of securing temporary construction loans for self-liquidating projects, as referred to in the President's Report.

Mr. Franklin Clark, president of the Fayetteville College Foundation, reported that the Foundation had been incorporated with twelve directors and that this group would be conducting an intensive campaign with 250 workers the following week to bring all pledges to the Methodist College Campaign up to date. Board Treasurer Frank McBryde reported that the College had a current bank balance of $75,392.

President Weaver reported that he and Chairman Sanford and other representatives had visited Washington to explore the possibility of obtaining federal construction loans for self-liquidating projects, specifically, two dormitory units and the Student Union-Cafeteria. He said the group learned that the College could apply for federal construction loans after being in operation one year, provided such application contemplated the assumption by the federal government of a then-existing temporary construction loan. Weaver said the working drawings on these facilities would have to be ready by October 1 in order for the buildings to be ready for the College's projected September 1960 opening.

Trustees Award Contract for First Building

The Executive Committee of the Board of Trustees met August 7, 1958, received bids on the Classroom Building and awarded a contract to McDevitt & Street Company of Charlotte, N.C., the low bidder among eleven firms participating. The total cost was $441,100.

Trustees, VIPs Attend Groundbreaking

The Board of Trustees met at Hay Street Methodist Church the morning of August 26, 1958, after which they attended a luncheon at the Church followed by an afternoon ground breaking ceremony at the College site. Guest speakers at the luncheon included Dr. Hollis Edens, president of Duke University, and Dr. William Friday, president of the University of North Carolina.

During the business session, President Weaver told the trustees that planning for the construction of the College was virtually complete and that the rate of construction would depend on financial support from the Fayetteville community and the Methodist conference. He explained that the collection of all pledges as currently due would be needed to pay for the Classroom Building. He said final plans for the Library, Science Building, Administration Building, and Power Plant would be completed by the architects and ready for bids within two to three months.

The College ground breaking occurred on a Tuesday afternoon under a tent during a "hurricane rain," with Methodist Bishop Paul N. Garber wielding a gold-painted shovel. Invited guests included William Friday and Hollis Edens, as well as the commanding general of the U.S. Army's 82nd Airborne Division at Fort Bragg, Maj. Gen. Hamilton H. Howze; Sgt. Ben Weeks, representing the enlisted men at Fort Bragg; and Lt. Eugene P. Richter of Pope Air Force Base.

A total of 2.6 inches of rain fell in Fayetteville that day, courtesy of Hurricane Daisy which was churning in the Atlantic a few hundred miles southeast of Wilmington, N.C. The temperature was about 70 degrees.

— CHAPTER 1 —

The day after the ground breaking, August 27, 1958, *The Fayetteville Observer* carried news stories and photos of the Methodist College ground breaking on the front pages of Sections A and B.

Reporter Gibson Prather, who covered the event, estimated that fewer than 100 persons attended. Prather's story indicated that after Bishop Garber had broken the ground with his shovel, Fayetteville College Foundation President Franklin Clark, who presided at the ceremony, presented Garber with an inscribed box holding the first shovelful of dirt.

Bishop Garber praised the people of Fayetteville and Cumberland County for their support of the College and also "the faith that has made this occasion possible." [89] Garber then offered this observation: "This is the North Carolina Way of Life. It can be summed up in that saying, 'First at Bethel, farthest at Gettysburg, last at Appomattox.' We North Carolinians don't need to boast of our accomplishments in advance. We do them and then we can make statements such as this." [90]

Terry Sanford, chairman of the Methodist College Board of Trustees, sounded one note of warning: "We shall have done a worse thing than never embarking in faith upon this venture if we ever allow it to wear the label of mediocrity. In every plan we make, in every step we take, we must be certain that we are laying foundations on which academic freedom can flourish." [91]

The Fayetteville Observer story noted that North Carolina Governor Luther Hodges had sent a message from Asheville congratulating the College trustees and saying, "We need more colleges and we need more boys and girls to go to college." [92]

A sidebar story in the Fayetteville newspaper headlined "Bishop Garber Came Prepared," indicated that the biggest laugh of the day came after Terry Sanford introduced Dr. R. L. Pittman, chairman of the trustees' Building Committee. "I feel out of place here with all this brass," Pittman said. "Here's the president of the University of North Carolina and the president of Duke. Also, (turning to Sanford) there's my honorable political opponent."

Methodist Bishop Paul Garber turns the first spade of dirt at the ground breaking ceremony for Methodist College Aug. 26, 1958, as Franklin Clark (holding box) and Stacy Weaver (holding umbrella) look on.

That brought down the house, because Sanford is a sure bet to run for governor and Dr. Pittman to support him. ⁹³

The (Raleigh) *News & Observer* also covered the Methodist College ground breaking. Like Fayetteville's newspaper, *The News & Observer* opted to run a photo of President Weaver with Presidents Friday and Edens with its story. The lead paragraph quoted Bishop Garber as saying this was his first college ground breaking.

Raleigh reporter David Murray also covered the luncheon at Hay Street Methodist Church which preceded the ground breaking. Murray reported that Dr. Friday called for a constant awareness of the high purpose of education and said there must be a determination to provide the "distinguished faculty so essential on an active campus." While describing the responsibility for education as "heavy and compelling," Friday added, "it is also challenging, exciting, and highly rewarding." ⁹⁴

Three presidents at the ground breaking for Methodist College. L to R, Dr. Hollis Edens, Duke University; Dr. L. Stacy Weaver, president of Methodist College; Dr. William C. Friday, the University of North Carolina.

Murray reported that Dr. Edens listed four ideas Methodist College could follow:
1. The College must ground itself solidly in the fundamentals of education.
2. It must set for itself goals that are attainable. These must be clear and concise enough to be understood by all.
3. The organization must have a set of convictions of its role in society.
4. The College must be concerned for what happens to man. ⁹⁵

Murray's story also mentioned that a rally to initiate a $5 million campaign for the three colleges within The North Carolina Conference of The Methodist

— CHAPTER 1 —

Church—Louisburg, Methodist, and N. C. Wesleyan—would be held in Raleigh Oct. 13 and that 186,000 Methodists from churches within the Conference would be asked November 16-23 to support the campaign for the colleges.

The News & Observer story concluded with the following observation: "Near the soaked ground breaking a drive-in movie advertised 'Under Water Warrior.' And a radio announcer completed his spot news coverage of the Methodist event by saying, 'This has been… with direct coverage from the site of the **Baptist** College.'" [96]

Methodists Rally in Raleigh to Launch College Fund Drive

More than 4,000 Methodists from eastern North Carolina gathered at Memorial Auditorium in Raleigh October 13, 1958, to launch the North Carolina Conference's $5 million college fund drive. The day-long rally featured a long list of speakers, dominated by church and government leaders.

During the morning session, Bishop Paul Garber issued a call to arms, calling higher education "a good right arm of Methodism." [97] He said the very first Methodist college was started in Kingswood, England, by the Wesleys, seeking to unite knowledge and religious piety. He said the first gift ever made toward the founding of a Methodist college in America was made by two North Carolina laymen in 1780—Francis Asbury and John Dickens. The result was Cokesbury College.

Garber continued:

"If Brother Asbury and Brother Dickens and Brother Bustian, three Methodists, and Gabriel Long, a non-Methodist, had faith enough to launch a Methodist college in the midst of revolution, I know that 187,000 Methodists of eastern North Carolina plus the assistance of thousands of Methodist friends can in 1958 launch two new colleges and can give dynamic support to our existing institutions and our Wesley Foundation." [98]

Garber cited statistics projecting phenomenal growth in the college population nationally and in North Carolina. He said the percentage of college-age students attending college in America had increased from four percent in 1900 to 40 percent in 1958¬ for a tenfold increase. He said North Carolina's college population was projected to double from 46,152 in 1957 to at least 90,000 by 1975. He said Methodists must do their part to meet an approaching tidal wave of college students.

The bishop offered another reason why Methodists should build more colleges, arguing that the American way of life and the North Carolina way of life were being challenged as never before by "aggressive atheism and a determined materialism." [99] He said Methodists "know that our institutions of learning are the church's indispensable bulwark against the encroaching

44

tide of secularism and unbelief [. . .] The centuries prove that the Christian Church builds itself into the culture of a people through its institutions of learning." [100]

He described as "marvelous" the action of citizens of Fayetteville and Cumberland County, as well as Rocky Mount and Nash County and Edgecombe County in pledging more than $4 million ($2 million in each community) to establish Methodist College at Fayetteville and North Carolina Wesleyan College at Rocky Mount. [The campaign also included funds for Louisburg College and the Divinity School of Duke University.]

North Carolina Governor Luther H. Hodges, a member of a Methodist church in Leaksville, echoed Bishop Garber's sentiments in an afternoon appearance. "The enormous salutary effect the new Methodist colleges will have on eastern North Carolina cannot easily be evaluated," he said. [101] The governor called on eastern North Carolina Methodists to "join hands and move forward together toward the realization of this great dream." [102]

The abundant publicity given to the kickoff rally for the college fund campaign and to the districts and churches within the North Carolina Conference of The Methodist Church as they worked to meet fund-raising quotas was probably unprecedented. Eastern North Carolina newspapers were generous in their coverage of the college fund campaign, as evidenced by scores of newspaper clippings that found their way into the conference archives. Many newspapers listed the dollar quotas and amounts raised in the conference's twelve districts and churches within those districts.

Immediately following the kickoff, Bishop Garber and other members of his cabinet fanned out across the conference's 12 districts to exhort Methodists to give to the campaign. Over the next two years, the state's newspapers (and other media) were filled with glowing accounts concerning the construction and opening of Methodist and Wesleyan.

Leaders Urge Churches, Community to Support College

Fayetteville District Methodists held a rally October 23, 1958, at Hay Street United Methodist Church to launch The North Carolina Conference of the Methodist Church's $5 million, three-year college fund drive.

The Fayetteville Observer reported that Bishop Paul Garber enumerated the dollar quotas for individual Methodist churches in the Fayetteville District to be paid over a three-year period. A news story in *The Fayetteville Observer* reported the following: "The bishop declared, 'We had better keep on supporting our free institutions in America, or some 'ism' may take over . . . We are not just raising five million dollars, but we are making a place for our girls and boys to go for Christian education.' Bishop Garber voiced the need for more colleges in North Carolina to provide for future population growth and asserted, 'I believe our Methodist Church should unite evangelism and education.'" [97]

Integration Issue Resurfaces

The issue of whether Methodist and N.C. Wesleyan colleges would be racially integrated or segregated, an issue originally raised at a November 4, 1957, special session of The N.C. Conference of the Methodist Church in Fayetteville, resurfaced in October 1958.

State Rep. Byrd I. Satterfield, a Methodist layman from Timberlake in Person County, stated that the General Board of Education of the Methodist Church "has an announced policy of integration" which leaves the Methodist colleges in Fayetteville and Rocky Mount "wide open to integration." [98]

The Rev. Vergil Queen, chairman of the N.C. Conference Board of Education and a Methodist College trustee, termed Satterfield's statement "weird and irresponsible," saying there were no plans for integration at either of the new schools. Queen also described The Methodist Church's General Board of Education as an advisory board with no control over any Methodist college. [99]

Satterfield answered Queen by saying that Articles 3 and 14 of the Methodist College charter made it clear that the College was subject to the Discipline of the Methodist Church and the Division of Educational Institutions of The Methodist Church. Satterfield also noted that Rev. Queen was on the staff of Duke Divinity School which had gone on record as favoring integration. [100]

Trustees Discuss Utilities

At its November 8, 1958, meeting, the Board of Trustees granted an easement to Fayetteville's Public Works Commission to build a sewer pumping station and sewer line across the College property. The board also authorized Stevens and Wilkinson to prepare working drawings and specifications for the Student Union-Cafeteria. President Weaver reported that plans for the Science Building were complete, but that no funds were yet available to call for construction bids.

Fayetteville District Churches Pledge $502,481

In late November, 1958, the Rev. O. L. Hathaway, superintendent of the Fayetteville District of The N.C. Conference of the Methodist Church, reported that forty-five Methodist churches in the Fayetteville District, about half the total, had met or exceeded their college drive quotas, generating $502,481 toward a three-year goal of $702,000. [101]

Editorial Urges Local Residents To Catch Up on Pledges

The Fayetteville Observer ran an editorial November 22, 1958 urging local residents to "catch up" on their pledges. While conceding that "a substantial financial recession" had occurred since the Fayetteville community offered $2 million toward construction of a four-year Methodist college, the editorial noted the time had come for local residents to catch up on their pledges so the College could open in the fall of 1960. The editorial writer said:

> During that recession many of the pledgers undoubtedly have had somewhat reduced incomes and the business of fulfilling said pledges has been somewhat more difficult than anticipated. But now the recession is vanishing in the economic distance. Business is on the advance. The prices of securities have soared to record heights.
>
> So now is the time for all of us to put our shoulders to the wheels and catch up on our pledges and enable Methodist College to achieve its goal of opening its doors in the fall of 1960. [102]

Fayetteville College Foundation Struggles to Raise Funds

Minutes of the Fayetteville College Foundation for the years 1958 and 1959 are full of references to the problem of past due pledges to Methodist College and how to collect them.

At the group's May 21, 1958, meeting, a Mr. Henke from the fund-raising company of Ward, Dresham, and Reinhardt told foundation members they would have to personally contact College donors in order to collect on unpaid pledges. Foundation President Franklin Clark said the Executive Committee had decided to name ten division heads with five captains under each head and five workers under each captain to personally contact local residents who were behind on their pledges.

The June 2, 1958 Foundation meeting was described in Foundation minutes as the kickoff of a program to bring pledges up to date, or "to get in 40 percent of the total pledge that is due now." [103]

Mr. Bert Ishee spoke of changing times and the importance of preparing for a large influx of college students within the state of North Carolina. He described what was happening on Raleigh Road, the building of Methodist College, as "the best thing that has ever happened to Fayetteville." [104]

At the July 8, 1958 meeting, Clark reported that the Foundation needed "a man to work on the collection of pledges and to secure new pledges." [105] Norman Suttles moved that the Foundation recommend to the College board of trustees that such a man be hired. His motion carried unanimously.

— CHAPTER 1 —

When the Foundation Executive Committee met August 11, 1958, President Weaver reported that a special committee appointed by Terry Sanford and made up of two Foundation members and two College trustees had hired Robert B. Isner as executive secretary of the Foundation at an annual salary of $6,000 plus $25 per month for car expense. Mr. Isner was then introduced to those present.

At meetings held September 18 and October 15, 1958, the Executive Committee discussed new ways to collect past due pledges. Norman Suttles was named chairman of a special committee to secure radio publicity.

College's Local Supporters Hold Loyalty Rally

On Monday evening, November 24, 1958, the Fayetteville College Foundation kicked off "Methodist College Loyalty Week" with a dinner/rally at Fayetteville High School. Barbecued chicken was served.

The keynote speaker was the Rev. Dr. D. D. Holt of Nashville, Tennessee, director of Financial Promotion, Christian Higher Education of the Methodist Church. Other speakers included Franklin Clark, Terry Sanford, Dr. L. Stacy Weaver, the Rev. O. L. Hathaway, and Robert B. Isner, executive secretary of the Fayetteville College Foundation. Mr. M. J. Weeks was the master of ceremonies.

The printed program for the rally contained a greeting from College President Stacy Weaver on the inside front cover addressed to "Friends of Methodist College" and headlined, "Pay Up and Build." Referring to the dual pledges of $2 million for the College from the Fayetteville community and The N.C. Conference of the Methodist Church, Dr. Weaver closed as follows: "With these two great forces at work, who can but say, 'What next? Why, a great college for the youth of America!.'" [106]

The Fayetteville Observer reported that a crowd of 250-300 "drawn mostly from civic clubs in the city" attended the loyalty rally. Fayetteville College Foundation President Franklin Clark told the gathering that the Fayetteville community had raised only $435,000 of the $850,000 now due on its original $2 million pledge. "We must do something about it," said Clark. "The money is here; we can get it." [107]

Dr. Holt, the keynote speaker, told the group not to be discouraged, that they would meet their fund-raising goal. He reminded those present that America's college population would double from three million to six million by 1975. "We face a crisis in education," he said, "and you are doing something about it." [108]

Holt said 55 percent of American college students were then enrolled in state-supported institutions, while 45 percent were enrolled in church-related and private schools. He said it was important that a dual system of higher education be maintained in America. The keynote speaker also contended that: 1) private education is less expensive than tax-funded education, and 2) that "It's good business to support education; you need trained people." [109]

State Announces Plans to Four-Lane U.S. 401

In early December, 1958, the N.C. Dept. of Transportation announced plans to widen 2.7 miles of U.S. 401 (Ramsey Street) from the Atlantic Coast Railroad overpass to the N.C. 59 (Country Club Drive) intersection with Tokay Drive.

Division engineer L. E. Whitfield said the four-laning of 401 would later be extended northward to Methodist College and possibly beyond the College. [110]

Trustees Discuss Construction Loan

Lennox Cooper, chairman of the trustees' Finance Committee, met with President Weaver and Terry Sanford December 17, 1958, regarding temporary financing of College construction. It was agreed that Mr. Sanford would contact a banking institution and Mr. Cooper would contact a life insurance company to "explore the possibility of securing any financing necessary to begin construction of our next building." [111]

Foundation Falls Short of Fund Goal

In a financial statement dated December 15, 1958, the Fayetteville College Foundation reported that it had collected $465,564 on outstanding pledges to Methodist College totalling $1,694,602. The balance to be collected was $1,229,038.

At its January 13, 1959, annual meeting, the Fayetteville College Foundation approved a motion by Mr. M. J. Weeks to amend the Foundation by-laws and increase the membership of the board of directors from twelve to eighteen. A slate of new officers and new members of the Executive Committee was elected as presented by Mr. Mel Thompson, chairman of the Nominating Committee. The new officers were: Mr. Alton G. Murchison, president; Mr. C. H. vonRosenberg, 1st vice-president; Mrs. Floyd B. Souders, 2nd vice-president; Mr. Robert B. Isner, secretary; and Mr. Thomas A. Hood, treasurer.

Mr. Murchison expressed his thanks and appreciation to Mr. Franklin S. Clark for the "very capable leadership" he had rendered as the first president of the Fayetteville College Foundation.

College President Stacy Weaver gave a progress report on the construction of the Classroom Building and said work would begin on the Science Building in a matter of weeks, financed with monies received from The Methodist Church (North Carolina Conference) campaign. He said bids on the Science Building would be opened March 10, and final

— CHAPTER 1 —

plans on the Student Union Building and Heating Plant would be ready for bidding May 1.

At the February 12, 1959, meeting of the Foundation's Executive Committee, President Weaver said contracts for any buildings needed for a College opening in September 1960 would have to be let by May 1959. He also reported that The North Carolina Conference of The Methodist Church's Board of Education had granted the Methodist College Board of Trustees permission to borrow $500,000 needed to complete the first three buildings. Dr. Weaver then stressed the necessity and pressing need for finding a way to build and furnish the library.

Executive Committee minutes for the March 12, 1959, meeting indicate that Robert Isner had tendered his resignation as executive director of the Foundation. President Weaver reported that construction of the Science Building would soon begin and that *The State* magazine had mentioned Methodist College in a recent issue featuring Fayetteville and Cumberland County.

The issue of *The State* to which Weaver alluded was the March 7, 1959, issue. Bill Sharpe, the principal writer of the Fayetteville/Cumberland County articles and the co-publisher of the magazine, ran a Stevens and Wilkinson architectural drawing of the central mall of the campus and made two brief references to the College in related articles about the city. The cutline under the drawing describes the College as "the biggest thing to happen to Cumberland since the establishment of Fort Bragg." [112]

Hay Street and the Market House, circa 1959.

At its April 20, 1959, meeting, the Executive Committee welcomed Mr. Frank H. Jeter Jr. as its new executive secretary. Dr. Weaver praised the appointment of Mr. Jeter, saying, "This is the most optimistic move that we have made since I have been here." [113] After lunch, Foundation members visited the Methodist College campus to see how construction was progressing.

The Executive Committee was briefed May 28, 1959, on plans to start a new pledge drive, using Fayetteville Public Works Commission records to create a list for a mass mailing to local residents.

When the Committee met July 23, 1959, Charles K. McAdams, the newly appointed director of development and public relations for Methodist College, spoke of "the real challenge before the people of Fayetteville" and of his plans to bring a closer relationship between the Methodist Conference and the College backers in the Fayetteville area. Mr. Jeter outlined plans for a "new direction" in pledge and collection work involving a much larger number of community volunteers.

The Foundation Executive Committee next met August 27, 1959. Dr. Weaver reported that The North Carolina (Methodist) Conference had paid $300,000 to the College thus far in 1959, while the Fayetteville College Foundation had paid only $125,000. "We must collect at least another $125,000 during the remainder of this year," said Weaver. [114] The president said all construction contracts needed for opening the College had been let, with the exception of the streets.

When the Executive Committee met September 24, 1959, Mr. Von Rosenberg said a Foundation audit showed that about one-fourth of the local pledges to the College had been paid. Mr. Jeter said the Foundation would conduct a mass mailing in October to all persons who had pledged. Foundation President Murchison said, "All plans are good, but we are so far behind it will take a long time to catch up." [115]

At the Executive Committee's October 22, 1959, meeting, Dr. Weaver reported that the College's building program was "about on schedule" for the Fall 1960 opening but that community contributions were lagging $250,000 behind what was needed for construction. He said The North Carolina Conference had paid the entire $350,000 pledged for 1959 as its share toward college building. "Community payments thus far have totalled $623,761, compared with $1,226,998 due on Fayetteville's pledges," said Weaver. [116]

Meeting November 24, 1959, the Foundation board heard opposing recommendations from two fund-raising firms: first, from Ketchum, Inc., and then from Ward, Dresham, and Reinhardt. After lengthy discussion, the board voted to launch a new College campaign for $1.2 million in the spring of 1960 under the direction of Ketchum, Inc. Ketchum representative Ed

— CHAPTER 1 —

Dodds said he thought about one million dollars could be collected out of current pledges. Mr. E. E. Armstrong, a representative of the other firm, said the drive should be delayed until 1961 when the present five-year pledges to the College would come due.

The Nominating Committee of the Fayetteville College Foundation met December 17, 1959, and proposed the following slate of officers for 1960: Mr. Bert Ishee, president; Mr. M. J. Weeks, 1st vice-president; Mrs. S. L. Elfmon, 2nd vice-president; Mrs. Elizabeth Ellis, secretary; Mrs. Charles Kistler, treasurer. Proposed as new members of the Executive Committee were: Mrs. Dennis Williams, Miss Dorothy Hutaff, Mr. John W. Hensdale, and Mr. Richard M. Lilly.

Executive Committee Authorizes Loan

When the Executive Committee of the Board of Trustees met January 20, 1959, President Weaver presented a list of the minimum number of buildings needed for the College to open and a projection of expected revenue from the Fayetteville College Foundation and the Church until September 1, 1960. Weaver said the College would have to borrow $500,000 to build the needed buildings and that any loan secured by the property of the College would have to be approved by the Executive Committee of the Board of Education of The North Carolina Conference of the Methodist Church.

On a motion by Joe Tally Jr., the committee authorized President Weaver, Trustees Board Chairman Terry Sanford, and the chairman of the trustees' Finance Committee to apply for a loan not to exceed $500,000 and to seek the needed permission of the Executive Committee of the Board of Education of the Methodist Conference.

Trustee W. E. Horner requested that local publicity be given to the fact that obligations to the College assumed by the Fayetteville community were not being made on time and the "feeling on the part of many members of the (Methodist) Church that this situation was handicapping the building of the College." [117] Horner said local residents should be urged to meet their pledges more promptly. Mr. James Pharr, a reporter for *The Fayetteville Observer* who was present to cover the meeting, agreed to publicize the matter.

The trustees' Executive Committee met April 3, 1959, and approved recommendations of engineers and architects that the College Boiler Plant be designed to burn No. 6 fuel oil with an alternate burner for natural gas. The committee gave President Weaver authorization to borrow an additional $500,000 (over the $500,000 already authorized) to complete the facilities needed to open the College by September 1960.

The committee awarded a grading contract to Sikes Brothers, Inc. for a base bid of $69,673 and a contract for construction of the Science Building to Anderson Construction Co. of Dunn, N.C. for a base bid of $402,600.

The group also authorized President Weaver to fill the positions of dean, business manager/comptroller, and director of public relations and development at the approximate salary levels of $9,000, $6,000, and $7,500 respectively.

Also approved was a design for a Methodist College seal bearing the motto "Veritas et Virtus" (Truth and Virtue), a depiction of Methodist Bishop Francis Asbury astride his horse, reading his Bible, and the year 1956—the date the College was founded—in Roman numerals.

Trustees Authorize $1 Million Loan

The Methodist College Board of Trustees met in annual session May 5, 1959. Mr. Alton Murchison, president of the Fayetteville College Foundation, and Mr. Frank Jeter Jr., executive secretary of the Foundation, were introduced and spoke briefly. Murchison said the Foundation was now composed of eighteen directors and that about 30 percent of the pledges to Methodist College—$536,242—had been collected.

The Rev. Paul Carruth, executive director of The North Carolina Conference of The Methodist Church's Commission on Christian Higher Education, reported on the progress of the Conference's campaign to raise $5 million for its three colleges—Louisburg, Methodist, and N.C. Wesleyan.

Dr. W. L. Clegg, chairman of the trustees' Nominating Committee, recommended six trustees for a new four-year term, as well as a slate of board officers, members of the Executive Committee, and members of other committees of the board. Terry Sanford was re-elected chairman and Frank McBryde was re-elected treasurer. New officers were: Mrs. Earl W. Brian, vice-chairman, and Jack Page, secretary.

In other matters, the trustees authorized President Weaver to seek approval of The North Carolina (Methodist) Conference Board of Education to borrow $1 million at five percent interest from First Citizens Bank & Trust Co. secured by a deed of trust upon the real property of the College. At President Weaver's request, the Fayetteville College Foundation agreed to pay $70,000 annually to amortize the College's $1 million loan with First Citizens Bank, in addition to making a $50,000 annual contribution to the College operating fund.

The board also approved a budget of $71,400 for 1959-60, and the appointment of Charles K. McAdams, associate pastor of Edenton Street

— CHAPTER 1 —

Methodist Church in Raleigh, N.C., as the College's director of public relations and development.

The board also received bids for the Student Union-Cafeteria, with McDevitt & Street Co. of Charlotte, N.C. submitting the low bid of $416,630. The board authorized the president to sign a contract with that firm.

In his written report to the board, President Weaver said he had deleted the library from the construction schedule until funds could be secured. He said he had worked hard for several months making speeches and appearances to church groups in support of the $5 million campaign for Christian Higher Education undertaken by The North Carolina Conference of The Methodist Church. He said he was optimistic that the campaign goal would be reached.

The president suggested the establishment by the trustees of a Development Committee and enlisted the help of each trustee to contact people who could assist the College in future building, endowment, and scholarship needs. Weaver expressed his thanks to Frank Jeter Jr. for doubling the return of collections on Fayetteville pledges to Methodist College since his employment September 1, 1958, as executive secretary of the Fayetteville College Foundation.

Weaver closed his report by saying, "Another year's work convinces me that the task to which we have set our hand is larger and longer than many realized in the beginning. This only serves to make it more worth doing." [118]

An aerial view taken in 1959 shows construction of the Science Building (lower right), Student Union (upper left) and the Classroom Building (upper right). Ramsey Street / U.S. 401 (upper right) was still a two-lane highway.

Trustees Award Contracts

The trustees' Executive Committee met June 3, 1959, and approved two additional contracts with Sikes Brothers, Inc., the firm hired to do grading work for the College. Sikes was awarded a contract worth $23,890 for building sanitary sewers and a $24,642 contract for building a water distribution system.

Meeting July 21, 1959, the Executive Committee received bids and awarded contracts for the Boiler Plant, steam distribution system, and underground electrical distribution system. McDevitt & Street Co. was the low bidder on the boiler plant at $118,700. The contracts for mechanical work for the plant and steam distribution system went to J. J. Barnes Inc. and totalled $202,843. The contract for the electrical distribution system, worth $49,278, was awarded to Howell Construction Co.

The Development Committee of the Board of Trustees met October 1, 1959, and approved a basic plan of development for the College. Dr. Weaver reported that the Classroom Building was nearly finished, that work on the Science Building and the Student Union-Cafeteria was on schedule, and that work had begun on the Power Plant. He said the next building priority was the Library.

A construction worker inspects a honeycomb sunscreen at the Classroom Building.

Mr. Charles McAdams, director of public relations and development, was authorized to produce and distribute any brochures, bulletins or pamphlets he felt were needed.

The trustees' Finance Committee met October 7, 1959, and approved a schedule of tuition and fees presented by Dr. Elbert Wethington, administrative assistant to the president. The committee approved an annual tuition fee of $400 and a general fee of $100. The group also voted to grant one-half tuition to ministerial students, sons and daughters of Methodist ministers, or ministers of any faith from Cumberland County. Also approved was a plan to award five merit scholarships granting full tuition to capable, needy students.

— CHAPTER 1 —

A report and breakdown of building costs versus revenues showed that the College needed $1,139,874 to complete the first phase of the campus. Collections projected through October 1 were: $229,166 from Fayetteville, $320,837 from The North Carolina Conference of The Methodist Church, $44,280 from cash on hand, and $545,594 from a bank loan.

Committee minutes state there was some discussion as to whether the Fayetteville College Foundation should plan a new campaign to raise funds for the College. As it turned out, a new fund drive was launched in early 1960 when the foundation retained Ketchum, Inc., a professional fund-raising firm, to design literature and conduct a $1.2 million building campaign.

Curriculum Approved

Meeting Oct. 8, 1959, the trustees' Academic Affairs Committee approved a plan for the College curriculum as presented by Dr. Elbert Wethington. The plan included a curriculum divided into six academic divisions, fall and spring semesters, provisions for conferring Bachelor of Arts and Bachelor of Science degrees, and graduation requirements of 120 semester hours with a minimum overall grade of C. The core requirements for all students were: English—12 semester hours, Foreign Language—6-12 s.h., Bible—6 s.h., Philosophy—3 s.h., Education and Psychology—3 s.h., Math—6 s.h., Science—8 s.h., Western Civilization—6 s.h., Fine Arts—3 s.h.

It was also agreed that emphasis would be given to the following vocational or professional interests: pre-ministerial; pre-engineering; premedical, dental and lab technicians; teacher training, including home economics; and business administration.

For an opening enrollment of 200 students, it was projected that the College would need four instructors of English and foreign languages, two instructors of Bible, four or five instructors of science and math, one history instructor, and one librarian.

The trustees' Building and Grounds Committee met Oct. 21 and reviewed plans for campus sidewalks, roads and parking lots, a building at the Boiler Plant to house physical education dressing and shower rooms, and a campus lighting layout. After inspecting the new Classroom Building, the Committee voted to accept it on the condition that several items be corrected.

Trustees Approve Fees

At its November 3, 1959, meeting, the Board of Trustees approved the fee schedule recommended by the Academic Affairs Committee and authorized Dr. Weaver to obtain plans and bids for the items discussed at the October 21 board meeting. The president was also authorized to negotiate a contract with

Carolina Power & Light Co. for electrical service and with the city's Public Works Commission for water and sewer service and also to obtain proposals for insuring College buildings.

When the trustees met November 24, 1959, the Rev. Paul Carruth, executive director of The North Carolina Conference of The Methodist Church's Commission on Christian Higher Education, reported that the campaign for the Conference's three colleges—Louisburg, Methodist, and N.C. Wesleyan—had collected $1,060,000 as of November 1, 1959.

The trustees also received reports from Mr. Alton Murchison, president of the Fayetteville College Foundation; Mr. Lennox Cooper, chairman of the Development Committee; the Rev. Vergil Queen, chairman of the Academic Affairs Committee; and Dr. R. L. Pittman, chairman of the Building Committee.

President Weaver announced that Mr. F. H. Eason, superintendent of the Franklinton City Schools, had been hired as College comptroller starting January 1, 1960. The president recognized Dr. Elbert Wethington, his administrative assistant, and Mr. Charles McAdams, director of public relations and development, and expressed his appreciation to both of them for their services to date.

Following the trustees' meeting, the Executive Committee approved a change order for the Boiler Plant construction project—the addition of dressing and bath facilities for the College's physical education classes at a cost of $25,000.

Garber, Sanford, Weaver Persist

Events of 1956-59 quickly taught those responsible for founding Methodist College that raising the money to build the College was not going to be easy. Leaders in The Methodist Church and in Fayetteville may have been overly optimistic that they could raise over $4 million within five years to build Methodist College.

The fact is, both the community and the church—equal partners in the Methodist College venture— failed to meet their fund-raising goals. The Fayetteville College Steering Committee promised to raise $2 million over five years to build Methodist College. By the end of the 1960, the Fayetteville committee had raised only $800,000 from about 6,000 contributors. But the Committee and then the Fayetteville College Foundation did manage to acquire 577 acres of land for the College, to pay an executive director and a secretary, and to establish a ledger card bookkeeping system for tracking payments on the original pledges to Methodist College.

In late 1958, The North Carolina Conference launched a $5 million campaign for its colleges; the campaign collected just over $3.5 million from approximately 30,000 Methodists. Methodist College in Fayetteville and N.C.

— CHAPTER 1 —

Wesleyan College in Rocky Mount received about $1.5 million each from the conference—$500,000 less than they were originally promised—to build their respective facilities.

Why did Fayetteville and the church fail to raise the funds needed to built Methodist College? First, many Presbyterians in Fayetteville who had pledged money to build a new Presbyterian college were not interested in supporting a Methodist college. Second, America experienced an economic recession in 1957-58. Third, rumors persisted among Methodists in The North Carolina Conference and among Fayetteville residents that the new Methodist colleges, Methodist and N.C. Wesleyan, might be racially integrated, although church leaders and College officials (including Terry Sanford) denied this would be the case. In 1958, four years after the U.S. Supreme Court ruled in Brown vs. Board of Education that segregation of the nation's public schools was unconstitutional, many people in eastern North Carolina were opposed to integrated schools at any level and did not want their money spent for this purpose.

Leaders of the Fayetteville College Foundation found themselves on the defensive and became very frustrated over their inability to get local residents to make good on their pledges. When gifts to the College did not materialize as expected, Garber, Sanford, and Weaver were forced to borrow the money needed, about $1.2 million, to build College facilities.

To obtain these loans, Methodist College had to pledge campus land as security. In short, the Methodist College land was both the College's salvation and Fayetteville's "greatest gift" because it made everything else possible. It should also be noted that the Fayetteville College Foundation agreed to pay $70,000 needed annually to amortize the College's $1 million loan with First Citizens Bank, **in addition** to making a $50,000 annual contribution to the College operating fund.

Despite fund-raising shortfalls, Paul Garber, Terry Sanford and Stacy Weaver continued to seek money for Methodist College in speeches to Fayetteville civic groups and to church groups throughout eastern North Carolina. In 1958, Sanford and Garber traveled to Washington, D.C. and persuaded North Carolina's two U.S. Senators, Kerr Scott and Sam Ervin, as well as Sen. John Sparkman (D-Ala.) to sponsor legislation relaxing a federal requirement that a college must have graduated one class and attained full accreditation to receive a federal construction loan. As a result, both Methodist College and N.C. Wesleyan College were able to obtain federal loans to build much-needed dormitories after only one year of operation.

President Stacy Weaver would have preferred that Methodist College not open with a temporary library (two classrooms), no dormitories (apartments were erected as "temporary" dorms in 1962) and no gymnasium (a metal "temporary" gymnasium was built in 1962). But he accepted the fact that money was short and continued traveling and speaking to church and community groups about the College's critical need for funds.

In a memoir written in 1984, Dr. Weaver said he was constantly on-the-go in the early years speaking at churches and at public meetings promoting Christian higher education. When he realized that contributions from the community and the church were not sufficient to build or to operate the College, Weaver said he "became a beggar for the Lord. Some people received me joyfully, others courteously and some almost insultingly. I became accustomed to this and rather philosophical about it. I received substantial donations from corporations, foundations and similar enterprises." [119]

Dr. Weaver also wrote in his memoir: "One of my regrets has been that necessary fund-raising took me off the campus so much that I did not have the opportunity to become more personally and intimately acquainted, not only with faculty members, but with students [. . .] But I may add, if I had stayed on the campus, Methodist College would not be there today." [120]

For the years 1956-59, the historical record is clear. It was the persuasiveness and persistence of Methodist Bishop Paul Garber, Fayetteville attorney Terry Sanford, and Methodist College President Stacy Weaver that enabled Methodist College to open. Methodist's "founding fathers"—Garber, Sanford and Weaver—were determined, articulate, and religious individuals. Emboldened by faith in their cause, they were able to convince thousands of Fayetteville area residents and Methodists in The North Carolina Conference that Methodist College was needed and would provide a high quality Christian liberal arts education. (See Appendices B, C and G for biographies of Garber, Sanford, and Weaver.)

Credit must also go to The North Carolina Conference of The Methodist Church for voting in 1956 and 1957: first, to build two new four-year colleges instead of one; and second, to raise $5 million for Christian higher education. These were unprecedented commitments, but most pastors and church members believed Bishop Paul Garber when he said Christian higher education was vital to the future of The Methodist Church and to this region.

Thirty thousand Methodists in eastern North Carolina and 6,000 Cumberland County residents gave what they could to the cause, but most were not affluent and could not make large gifts. With the exception of Mr. and Mrs. Joe Stout, who gave 120 acres for the campus, Methodist College found no six-figure donors during the period 1956-59. One of the "brag points" used early on by the Fayetteville College Foundation was the fact that $1.5 million of the $2 million pledged toward construction of the College consisted of gifts of $1,000 or less.

— CHAPTER 1 —

Although many in The North Carolina Conference of the Methodist Church, both clergy and lay members, would later say that Bishop Garber "bit off more than he could chew" by persuading the Conference to build two new colleges, the proposals to go forward, made in special sessions in 1956 and 1957, were openly discussed and overwhelmingly approved by ministers and lay persons representing all churches in the Conference.

As chief architect of the Conference's new venture in Christian higher education, Paul Neff Garber was hailed by many Methodists as a hero for his educational leadership and entrepreneurship. Although Garber would later become known as "the education bishop" of The Methodist Church, the Rev. Dr. F. Belton Joyner remembers him as a pragmatic and selfless man:

> "When I was a pastor at Wilmington, Bishop Garber came to a series of dinners to raise money for the schools. Someone started going on rhapsodically about, 'Wouldn't it be wonderful if they changed the name at one of the schools and named it Garber College in your honor for all you have done?' The Bishop replied, 'The greatest honor for me would be to pay for these schools.'" [121]

END NOTES
Chapter One

1. Victor Hugo, *Histoire d'un Crime* (1852), quoted in *Bartlett's Familiar Quotations*, 14th ed. Boston: Little, Brown and Company, 1968, p. 598.
2. *The Fayetteville Observer*, March 7, 1956, file.
3. Dan MacMillan to J. Mel Thompson, a letter dated February 24, 1956, minutes of the Methodist College Board of Trustees (hereafter referred to as TM), Book 1.
4. *The Fayetteville Observer*, March 13, 1956, file.
5. Frank Stout to Bill Billings, interview, July 17, 2003, file.
6. Mrs. C. Wallace "Pinky" Jackson to Lynn Gruber, interview, September 5, 2000, file.
7. R. L. Pittman, *The Fayetteville Observer*, April 5, 1956, file.
8. *The Fayetteville Observer*, April 23, 1956, file.
9. *The Fayetteville Observer*, April 30, 1956, file.
10. *Journal of the 1956 General Conference of The Methodist Church*, p. 52.
11. Terry Sanford to Dr. R. L. Pittman of Fayetteville, a telegram sent from Minneapolis, Minn. April 30, 1956, file.
12. Episcopal Address, *Journal of the 1956 General Conference of The Methodist Church*, p. 207.
13. Paul Garber, *Journal of The North Carolina Conference of The Methodist Church, 1956-57*, "Minutes of Special Session, May 14, 1956," at St. Paul Methodist Church, Goldsboro, N.C., p. 52.
14. "Report of the Long Range Committee to the Special Session of the North Carolina Annual Conference, Southeastern Jurisdiction, The Methodist Church," Goldsboro, N.C., May 14, 1956, file.
15. Ibid.
16. Ibid.
17. Hamilton Hobgood, *North Carolina Christian Advocate*, May 24, 1956, p. 4, file.
18. Paul F. Garber, *The Fayetteville Observer*, May 15, 1956, p. A-1, file.
19. L. Elbert Wethington to Lynn Gruber, interview, August 20, 2001, file.
20. Charles K. McAdams to Lynn Gruber, interview, December 13, 2001, file.
21. R. L. Pittman, *The Fayetteville Observer*, May 15, 1956, file.
22. Joe Tally, *The Fayetteville Observer*, May 15, 1956, file.
23. George Herndon, *The Fayetteville Observer*, May 15, 1956, file.

— CHAPTER 1 —

24. Ibid.
25. Editorial, *The Fayetteville Observer*, May 15, 1956, file.
26. Ibid.
27. Ibid.
28. Ibid.
29. Editorial, *The News and Observer*, Raleigh, N.C., May 16, 1956, p. A-4, file.
30. Ibid.
31. Editorial, *North Carolina Christian Advocate*, May 24, 1956, p. 2, file.
32. Ibid.
33. Ibid.
34. *Journal of The North Carolina Conference of The Methodist Church, 1956-57*, p. 132.
35. Ibid., pp. 133-34.
36. *The Fayetteville Observer*, June 23, 1956, file.
37. J. Nelson Gibson Jr. to Lynn Gruber, interview, August 23, 2001, file.
38. *Journal of The North Carolina Conference of The Methodist Church, 1956-57*, p. 132.
39. Ed Fleishman, motion before the Methodist College Board of Trustees, September 27, 1956, TM. Book 1.
40. J. Nelson Gibson Jr. to Lynn Gruber, interview, August 23, 2001, file.
41. Arthur Adams to W. E. Horner, *et. al.*, July 16, 1956 meeting in Washington, D.C., "Planning Committee Report No. 1," TM, Book 1.
42. Ibid., p. 3.
43. Methodist College trustees' "Planning Committee Report No. 3," presented September 25, 1956, TM, Book 1.
44. Dr. Robert M. Lester, in a conference with the Methodist College trustees' Planning Committee, reported in "Planning Committee Report No. 3," September 25, 1956, TM, Book 1.
45. Ibid., p. 2.
46. Ibid.
47. Ibid., p. 3.
48. Terry Sanford to ministers in The North Carolina Conference of The Methodist Church, a form letter mailed September 1956, TM, Book 1.
49. Terry Sanford, speech to Men's Club of Edenton Street Methodist Church in Raleigh, N.C., September 10, 1956, a Methodist College press release, file.
50. Ibid.

51. Certificate of Incorporation of Methodist College, Inc., September 27, 1956, TM, Book 1.
52. Ibid.
53. Terry Sanford, a Methodist College press release, November 2, 1956, file.
54. Terry Sanford, remarks to the Methodist College Board of Trustees, November 15, 1956, TM, Book 1.
55. Franklin Clark Sr., remarks to the Methodist College Board of Trustees, November 15, 1956, TM, Book 1.
56. Charles E. Jordan, remarks to the Methodist College Board of Trustees, November 15, 1956, TM, Book 1.
57. Donald C. Agnew, Planning Committee Report No. 7, November 15, 1956, TM, Book 1.
58. Ibid.
59. Terry Sanford to Methodist College trustees, a memo dated October 19, 1956, TM, Book 1.
60. W. E. Horner to Terry Sanford and other Methodist College trustees, a letter dated November 23, 1956, TM, Book 1.
61. Ibid.
62. Ibid.
63. Frank McBryde to W. E. Horner, a letter dated December 5, 1956, TM, Book 1.
64. Ibid.
65. "A Report on Methodist College," a booklet published by the Fayetteville College Foundation February 1957, TM, Book 1.
66. Ibid.
67. Ibid.
68. Wilson F. Yarborough, Sr., remarks to Methodist College trustees, February 21, 1957, TM, Book 1.
69. Paul F. Garber, remarks to the Methodist College Board of Trustees, February 21, 1957, TM, Book 1.
70. Ibid.
71. William K. Davis, "A Long Range Program for Campus Development: Proposed Fayetteville Methodist College," Master's thesis, The University of North Carolina at Chapel Hill, June 1957.
72. L. Stacy Weaver, remarks to the Methodist College Board of Trustees, June 22, 1957, TM, Book 1.
73. Ibid.
74. Paul F. Garber, a Methodist College press release, June 23, 1957, file.

— CHAPTER 1 —

75. Hollis Edens, a Methodist College press release, June 23, 1957, file.
76. Terry Sanford, *The Fayetteville Observer*, August 29, 1957, file.
77. Ibid.
78. Paul Carruth, *North Carolina Christian Advocate*, October 10, 1957, p. 4, file.
79. Paul F. Garber, *The Fayetteville Observer*, November 5, 1957, p. 5A, file.
80. L. Stacy Weaver, "President's Report to Methodist College Board of Trustees," January 30, 1958, TM, Book 1.
81. Ibid.
82. Charles K. McAdams, a Methodist College press release prepared for *The Fayetteville Observer* "Progress Edition," 1960, file.
83. L. Stacy Weaver, a Methodist College press release prepared for *The Fayetteville Observer* "Progress Edition," 1960, file.
84. Charles K. McAdams, a Methodist College press release prepared for *The Fayetteville Observer* "Progress Edition," 1960, file.
85. F. Belton Joyner to Lynn Gruber, interview, December 12, 2001, file.
86. Hugh Burton to Lynn Gruber, interview, July 30, 2002, file.
87. W. E. Horner to College President Stacy Weaver and Methodist College trustees, a letter dated May 22, 1958, TM, Book 1.
88. Ibid.
89. Paul F. Garber, *The Fayetteville Observer*, August 27, 1956, p. A-1, file.
90. Ibid.
91. Terry Sanford, *The Fayetteville Observer*, August 27, 1956, p. A-1, file.
92. Luther F. Hodges, *The Fayetteville Observer*, August 27, 1956, p. A-1, file.
93. R. L. Pittman, *The Fayetteville Observer*, August 27, 1956, p. B-1, file.
94. William F. Friday, *The News and Observer*, Raleigh, N.C., August 27, 1958, file.
95. Hollis Edens, *The News and Observer*, Raleigh, N.C., August 27, 1958, file.
96. David Murray, reporter, *The News and Observer*, Raleigh, N.C., August 27, 1958, file.
97. Paul F. Garber, *The Fayetteville Observer*, October 24, 1958, file.
98. Byrd I. Satterfield, *Durham Morning Herald*, October 25, 1958, file.
99. Vergil Queen, *Durham Morning Herald*, October 25, 1958, file.
100. Ibid.
101. O. L. Hathaway, *The Fayetteville Observer*, November 22, 1958, file.
102. Editorial, *The Fayetteville Observer*, November 22, 1958, file.
103. Minutes of the May 21, 1958 meeting of the Fayetteville College

Foundation Executive Committee (hereafter referred to as FCF), file.
104. Bert Ishee, remarks at a Fayetteville College Foundation meeting, June 2, 1958, FCF, file.
105. Franklin Clark Sr., remarks at a Fayetteville College Foundation meeting, July 8, 1958, FCF, file.
106. L. Stacy Weaver, Methodist College Loyalty Fund Program, November 24, 1958, file.
107. Franklin Clark Sr., remarks at a Fayetteville rally, as reported in *The Fayetteville Observer*, November 25, 1958, file.
108. D. D. Holt, remarks at a Fayetteville rally, as reported in *The Fayetteville Observer*, November 25, 1958, file.
109. Ibid.
110. *The Fayetteville Observer*, December 2, 1958, file.
111. Lennox Cooper, remarks in a Finance Committee meeting with President Weaver and Terry Sanford, December 17, 1958, TM, Book 1.
112. Bill Sharpe, *The State*, Vol. XXVI, March 7, 1959, p. 11, file.
113. L. Stacy Weaver, remarks at a Fayetteville College Foundation meeting, April 20, 1959, FCF, file.
114. L. Stacy Weaver, remarks at a meeting of the Fayetteville College Foundation Executive Committee, August 27, 1959, FCF, file.
115. Alton G. Murchison, remarks at a meeting of the Fayetteville College Foundation, September 24, 1959, FCF, file.
116. L. Stacy Weaver, remarks at a meeting of the Fayetteville College Foundation Executive Committee, October 22, 1959, FCF, file.
117. W. E. Horner, remarks at a meeting of the Executive Committee of the Methodist College Board of Trustees, January 20, 1959, TM, Book 1.
118. L. Stacy Weaver, "President's Report to the Methodist College Board of Trustees," May 5, 1959, TM, Book 1.
119. Stacy Weaver, his memoirs, 1984, file.
120. Ibid.
121. F. Belton Joyner to Lynn Gruber, interview, December 12, 2001, file.

Early in 1964, Dr. L. Stacy Weaver, the founding president of Methodist College, stepped outside his office in the Classroom Building to pose for this photo. Shown in the background are the bell tower (nearing completion), the Student Union, and site preparation for the library. At this point in time, the campus consisted of 12 buildings: three apartment buildings, the boiler plant, a metal temporary gymnasium, the Classroom Building, Science Building, Student Union, Garber Hall, Cumberland Hall, Weaver Hall, and Sanford Hall.

—photo by Charles McAdams

Chapter 2

Methodist College Opens 1960-64

> "I believe once Methodist College begins operation, there will be no better institution of higher education in North Carolina. It would be a great thrill to me to be a member of its first graduating class."
>
> —Harold Teague, quoted in *The Fayetteville Observer* in January 1960 when he was a senior at Massey Hill High School in Fayetteville, N.C. A member of the first freshman class and the first graduating class of Methodist College, Teague was also the first M.C. alumnus to earn a Ph.D.

The first *Methodist College Bulletin* was published in January 1960, and consisted of the College catalogue for 1960-61, the opening year. Prepared by Dr. L. Elbert Wethington, assistant to the president, the catalogue was printed in a 6 X 9-inch format and totalled 38 pages.

The cover featured an architect's drawing of the central mall of the campus and the slogan, "Chartered To Provide Highest Quality Christian Education." The title page indicated that the *Methodist College Bulletin* would be published quarterly and that an application for Second Class (periodical) postage was pending with the Fayetteville Post Office.

The inside of the catalogue contained an academic calendar for 1960-61, lists of College administrators and members of the Board of Trustees, a statement of purpose, a brief history of the College, a description of the campus, admission and graduation requirements, academic regulations, costs, and an outline of the curriculum consisting of six areas of study and a list of course offerings. Tuition was $400 per year, and fees were $100.

The catalogue restated the purpose of Methodist College, as defined by the College charter: to advance the cause of Christian higher education and to extend the influence of science, art, and Christian culture. Accompanying the statement of purpose was the following "Four-Fold Aim of Methodist College":

— CHAPTER 2 —

1. To share with students an intimate acquaintance with our spiritual and cultural heritage;
2. To assist students in seeing life from the vantage point of the Christian revelation as the best clue to the meaning of human existence;
3. To lead students in understanding the world in which we live and man's stewardship of all God's material and spiritual resources;
4. To inspire students to give themselves in service to the glory of God and the highest well-being of mankind. [1]

On January 3, 1960, *The Fayetteville Observer* carried a news story about Methodist College's first bulletin/catalogue and preparations for a fall opening. Dr. L. Stacy Weaver, college president, said 300 catalogues had been mailed to prospective students. Dr. Weaver estimated the College would open September 19 with 150-200 freshman day students.

The article contained the following list of recently hired administrators and faculty members: Dr. Clarence E. Ficken, dean, coming to Methodist after 14 years as dean at Ohio Wesleyan University; Frank H. Eason, comptroller, former superintendent of the Franklinton (N.C.) City Schools; Samuel R. Edwards, director of admissions and registrar, former Fayetteville Senior High School principal; Alva W. Stewart, librarian; the Rev. Samuel J. Womack Jr., assistant professor of Bible and chaplain, a doctoral student at Duke University;

Charles McAdams greets prospective students in February 1960.

Dr. Charles Ott, professor of chemistry, coming to Methodist from Guilford College; and Dr. Myron L. Simpson, professor of biology, coming to Methodist from Gettysburg College in Pennsylvania. [2]

College Accepts First Students/Sanford Files for Governor

In February, 1960, Dr. Weaver and Dr. Elbert Wethington, acting admissions director, announced the acceptance of the first seven students, all residents of the Cape Fear region, for the first freshman class at Methodist College. *The Fayetteville Observer* ran an article about the students Sunday, February 26, 1960, accompanied by a photograph. The students profiled were: Emma Barbee, Frances Hall and Samuel Marsden Pope of Fayetteville, Margaret Ann Weston of Fort Bragg, Irving Barefoot of Clarkton, Patricia Jackson of Hope Mills and Joseph Kelly Ward of Hallsboro.

Methodist College Trustees Chairman Terry Sanford filed as a candidate for the Democratic nomination for governor of North Carolina Thursday, February 4, 1960 in Fayetteville. After announcing his candidacy, Sanford called for a "New Day" in North Carolina and said improving the state's public schools would be his top priority as governor.

Trustees Approve Federal Loan to Build Dorms

The Building Committee of the Methodist College Board of Trustees met in early February, 1960, with President Weaver and reviewed preliminary plans for men's and women's dormitories to house 150 students each. Members voted to recommend to the Executive Committee that the College apply for a loan from the Federal Housing and Home Agency to build two dorms and the president's home.

Meeting in late February, the trustees' Executive Committee accepted the recommendation of the Building Committee and authorized Dr. Weaver to apply for a $1.3 million loan from the U.S. Housing and Home Agency to construct two dorms and the president's home. The Committee also increased the Boiler Plant construction contract with McDevitt and Street Co. $18,967 for a bathhouse addition for use by physical education classes. Also approved was an increase of $11,000 in a plumbing contract with J. J. Barnes. The Committee also authorized the college president to contract with Carolina Power and Light Co. for electric service and to contract for selective cutting of timber on College property.

In a written report to the trustees May 24, 1960, President Weaver said the Classroom Building and Science Building were complete, that the Student Union and Boiler Plant were nearly complete, that all utilities were in, and that

— CHAPTER 2 —

construction of streets, sidewalks, and parking lots was under way by Crowell Construction Co. He also reported that he had hired almost all the faculty needed for the College to open.

Dr. Weaver expressed concern at this meeting about the College's opening enrollment. "Student enrollments and applications are not encouraging," he said. "We had hoped to have 150 students, and the budget was based on that."[3] Weaver asked the trustees to refer prospective students to the College.

The president announced that a temporary library would be established in the Classroom Building and that he had secured an anonymous gift of $12,500, half the amount needed to purchase the 6,000 library books needed to meet accreditation requirements.

A Capital Fund report attached to the President's Report indicated the College owed a balance of $229,504 on construction contracts, but had only $29,715 on hand for that purpose. The costs for paving and equipment for the new buildings was estimated at $175,000.

Also meeting May 24, the trustees' Executive Committee authorized the College president to ask First Citizens Bank for an additional $125,000, bringing to College's total loan amount to $1 million.

The full Methodist College Board of Trustees then re-elected as Board officers: Terry Sanford, chairman; Mrs. Earl W. Brian, vice-chairman; Rev. Jack Page, secretary; and Frank McBryde, treasurer. Nominated to new four-year terms on the Board of Trustees were: Dr. R. L. Pittman, Mrs. E. L. Hillman, Terry Sanford, Rev. Graham S. Eubank, Dr. W. L. Clegg and Nello Teer Sr.

On a motion by Wilson Yarborough Sr., the Board accepted the recommendation of Mrs. Earl W. Brian, a trustee, that green and gold be adopted as the official colors of Methodist College.

Foundation Launches New Fund Drive

The Executive Committee of the Fayetteville College Foundation voted February 25, 1960, to hire Ketchum, Inc., a fund-raising firm, to conduct a spring campaign to raise $1.2 million in new money for the Methodist College building program. A total of $16,000 was budgeted for the new campaign, including Ketchum's fee.

At the Committee's March 15, 1960, John W. Hensdale was named general chairman of the campaign and John M. Wilson associate-chairman. Two other problems were discussed at some length at the March 15 meeting:

> [. . .]1) the $50,000 sustaining money which the Fayetteville community is pledged to give the College starting in the fall of 1960,

and 2) the matter of racial integration of the student body, which has been the subject of some comment in the community.

In the former matter, it was agreed that plans would be formulated at some later date--and the sustaining fund not linked in any way with the building program. On the latter, it was the consensus that the policy of the College administration, board of trustees, and the foundation itself is to continue the present pattern of racial separation now employed in all private colleges in North Carolina. [4]

A Foundation report dated April 1, 1960, showed pledges to the College totalling $1,725,880, but collections on those pledges of only $720,488. The Foundation held an open house at the College April 24, 1960, for employees of all local firms originally involved in the pilot campaign for Methodist College.

When the Foundation's Executive Committee met June 16, 1960, Mr. Dune Macdonald and Mr. Don Brewer of Ketchum, Inc., reported that 654 persons had pledged $391,209 in the new fund drive. Foundation minutes

In the spring of 1960, literature developed for the Fayetteville College Foundation's Methodist College Building Campaign to raise $1.2 million included attractive brochures, pledge forms, and signs to be put in store windows. Local residents were asked to make pledges of at least "a buck a week for five years." John W. Hensdale served as general chairman of the campaign, and John M. Wilson was associate chairman.

— CHAPTER 2 —

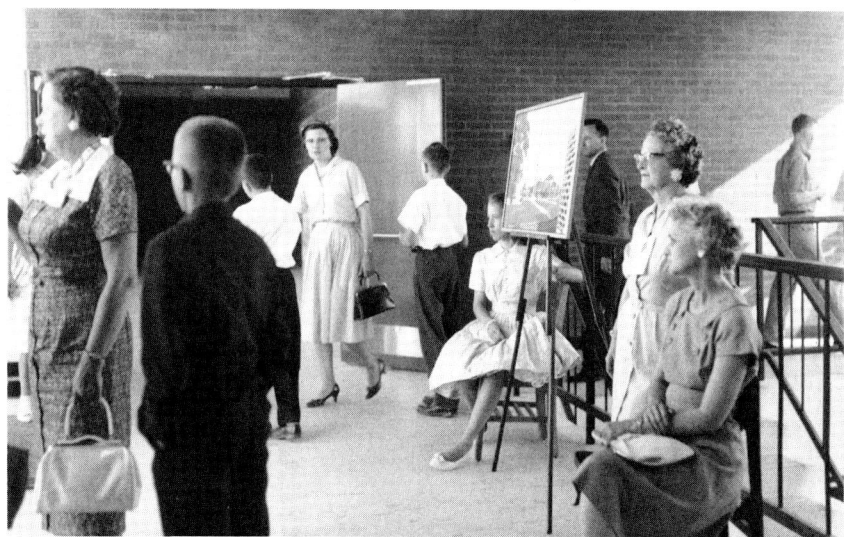
Visitors in the lobby of the Classroom Building during a Spring 1960 Open House.

state: "Mr. Macdonald and Mr. Brewer both expressed concern over the fact that more money had not been raised, but could not pinpoint the reason." [5]

Franklin Clark and John Hensdale thanked both of the Ketchum representatives for their work on the fund drive and said the Foundation would continue the drive "because we cannot fail in this great responsibility." [6]

College *Bulletin* Focuses on Fall Opening

The second issue of the *Bulletin of Methodist College* dated May 1960 was essentially a four-page newsletter focused on the fall opening of the College. The lead story on the front page consisted of questions frequently asked by prospective students and the answers thereto. The front also featured photos of the first seven students admitted as freshmen and photos of the Classroom Building, Science Building, and Student Union.

Also included in this *Bulletin* were short columns by President Weaver and Dean Ficken and comments from three accepted students—Irving Barefoot, Elaine Barbee, and Harold Teague—explaining why they chose Methodist College.

Profiles of the College's administrators and faculty members filled most of an inside page of the *Bulletin*. President Weaver's initial team consisted of persons with good academic backgrounds, experience in education, and strong religious ties. For his comptroller and for his director of admissions /registrar, Weaver selected public school administrators Frank H. Eason and Samuel R. Edwards, respectively.

Comptroller Frank Eason had been a schools superintendent, principal, teacher, and coach in small towns throughout eastern North Carolina. A native of Fuquay-Varina, Eason held the B.S. degree from Wake Forest College and the M.A. degree from East Carolina College. He was a certified lay speaker for The Methodist Church and had held major leadership positions in Methodist churches of which he was a member.

Registrar and Director of Admissions Sam Edwards was well-known in Fayetteville, having been principal of Fayetteville Senior High School since 1952. The Pennsylvania native held the B.S. degree from Mansfield State Teachers College and the M.A. degree from Duke University. He was also an active member of Fayetteville's Hay Street Methodist Church. Mr. Edwards also served as director of financial aid and as the College's first physical education instructor.

Methodist's first academic dean, Dr. Clarence Ficken, held impressive credentials. An Indiana native, he had served as dean and as acting president of both Ohio Wesleyan University and Macalaster College. He earned the A.B. degree at Baldwin-Wallace College, the M.A. degree from Northwestern University, and the Ph.D. degree from the University of Wisconsin. He was a member of Phi Beta Kappa and was an active lay leader in The Methodist Church. Dr. Ficken assumed the position of academic dean at Methodist April 1, 1960.

Alva W. Stewart, Methodist's first college librarian, was still in graduate school at U.N.C.-Chapel Hill when he was hired. A Georgia native, Stewart was an officer in the U.S. Air Force Reserve, held the A.B. degree from U.N.C. and the M.A. degree from Duke University, and would earn the M.S. degree in library science from U.N.C. during the summer of 1960. A Baptist, he had previously worked for the Charlotte/Mecklenburg County Public Library and as a journalist for newspapers in Asheboro and Greensboro, N.C. and in Rock Hill, S.C.

Samuel J. Womack Jr., assistant professor of Bible and college chaplain, was completing work on his Ph.D. at Duke University when he was hired. A native of Lakeland, Florida, Womack left a career in journalism to enter the ministry in the late 1950s. He had worked as a sports writer and managing editor of *The Lakeland Ledger* in his hometown and as a public affairs officer with the U.S. Army during the Korean conflict. He held the A.B. degree from Florida Southern College and the B.D. degree from Duke University and received his Ph.D. from Duke in September 1960. He was also a Methodist.

Dr. Charles Ott, professor of chemistry, came to Methodist after teaching chemistry for 16 years at Guilford College in Greensboro, N.C. Ott held the

— CHAPTER 2 —

B.S. degree from William Penn College and the Ph.D. from the University of Iowa and previously taught at William Penn College in Iowa and Central State College in Oklahoma. He had also worked as a research chemist for the Mid Continent Petroleum Company. He was a Quaker.

Dr. Myron L. Simpson, professor of biology, had previously taught at Gettysburg College, Washington College, and Westminster College. He held the A.B. degree from American University and the Doctor of Science degree from Johns Hopkins University. He had written extensively for scientific journals and was listed in "Who's Who in American Education" and "American Men of Science."

Dr. Willis Gates, professor of music, came to Methodist from Ohio University where he had been a visiting lecturer in the School of Music for one year; prior that he was professor of music and violin at Willamette University in Salem, Oregon, for ten years. Dr. Gates held a Bachelor of Music degree with honors from Peabody Conservatory in Baltimore, Maryland, and earned his M.A. and Ph.D. degrees from the University of North Carolina.

Dr. Marie C. Fox, instructor of history, held an A.B. degree from Duke, the M.A. from Northwestern University, and the Ph.D. from Cornell University. She had taught at Northwestern, Cornell, Smith College, the University of Massachusetts, the University of Arkansas, and San Jose State College.

The other members of the original faculty at Methodist College were: Mrs. Marie C. Ostborg, assistant in English; Grady K. Snyder, instructor of mathematics; Otis P. Lambert Jr., instructor of voice; and Mrs. Jean B. Ishee, instructor of piano and organ.

Sanford Wins Gubernatorial Nomination, Endorses Kennedy

Methodist College Trustees Chairman Terry Sanford's campaign for governor advanced two more steps in May and June, 1960 when he outpolled three opponents—John Larkins, Malcolm Seawell, and I. Beverly Lake— in the Democratic gubernatorial primary and defeated Wake Forest law professor I. Beverly Lake, a staunch segregationist, in a runoff primary to become the Democratic nominee for governor. He continued to campaign on a progressive platform and a pledge to improve the state's public schools and economic conditions.

In mid-July, 1960, Sanford caused quite a stir in North Carolina by endorsing Sen. John F. Kennedy (D-Mass.) for the Democratic presidential nomination at the Democratic National Convention in Los Angeles. Sanford hailed Kennedy as "another Franklin D. Roosevelt" in a speech seconding Kennedy's nomination. [7]

College Robbed

When College Comptroller Frank Eason reported to work Monday, September 19, 1960, he discovered that someone had broken into the Business Office in the Classroom Building and taken $2,500-$3,000 in cash from a small floor safe. A number of checks that were also in the safe were left behind.

The thief or thieves entered the preceding night or early that morning by breaking out a pane of glass at the north entrance. The office and safe were dusted for fingerprints by Fayetteville police. Eason said the loss was covered by insurance.

College Holds Opening Ceremony

Methodist College held a formal opening ceremony Monday, September 19, 1960, at 10:30 a.m. in the Student Union. Pre-opening events held the preceding week included faculty orientation Sept. 14 and freshman orientation/registration September 16-17. President and Mrs. Weaver hosted a tea for students and their parents Sunday afternoon, September 18 in the Student Union.

College President Stacy Weaver presided at the College's formal opening. Greetings were extended by Fayetteville Mayor George Herndon; Dr. W. H. Plemmons, president of the North Carolina College Conference; Bert Ishee, president of the Fayetteville College Foundation; and Terry Sanford, chairman of the Methodist College Board of Trustees.

Dr. Weaver compared the occasion to the birth of a child and offered congratulations to the parents of Methodist College—The North Carolina Conference of The Methodist Church and the Fayetteville College Foundation.

The College's formal opening ceremony was held in the Student Union September 19, 1960.

— CHAPTER 2 —

Mayor Herndon commended The Methodist Church, the people of the Fayetteville area, and "all others who have participated in making this dream come true." [8]

Dr. Plemmons said he was privileged to witness the opening of a new college and expressed the hope that Methodist College would "develop an educational program which will challenge existing patterns and point to new ones which will bestir the best that is within the rest of us." [9]

Speaking for the Fayetteville College Foundation, Bert Ishee assured all those associated with the College that "[. . .] you will have the continued support of this area in all of your endeavors, and in your growth and development." [10]

Trustees Chairman Terry Sanford challenged those present to make the name Methodist College synonymous with academic attainment and with excellence in the development of the mind. Sanford told the first group of students that they would be the ones to "give the final shape and character to this institution." [11]

Bishop Paul N. Garber, president of the Southeastern Jurisdictional Council of the Methodist Church and resident bishop of the Richmond Area (which included The North Carolina Conference), gave the opening address.

Garber spoke of college traditions and began his address by asking, "What traditions do we have at Methodist College?" [12]

The bishop then answered his question by noting that some traditions had already emerged during the development of Methodist College in the preceding four years:

> First [. . .] we believe in dreaming dreams and seeing visions—young people, don't let your dreams be upset or lost.
>
> Second, we believe in democracy [. . .] Who founded Methodist College? Not any one person or group, but some 6,000 people of the Fayetteville area and some 30,000 people of The North Carolina Conference of The Methodist Church and other friends, all of whom made financial contributions.
>
> Third, I hope that every boy and girl who comes to this college will always feel that a tradition of this College is that it is his or her personal duty to be a lady or gentleman.
>
> Fourth, we ought to continue the tradition here of being able to overcome hardships, handicaps, and difficulties.
>
> Fifth, here at Methodist College we believe in the spiritual forces of life [. . .] We cannot be just like another school. We

must have something special here, and that is Christian higher education with highest academic standards and freedom. [13]
Bishop Garber concluded his address by saying:

> We will look back to this day someday—some other generation will look back and say, we thank God that there were people in eastern North Carolina in 1956 to 1960 who believed in dreaming dreams; and seeing visions; who believed in the democratic way of life; who were not going to be discouraged when things went wrong; and who believed that religious principles should have a part in the building of this College. [14]

Special music at the opening ceremony included a violin solo by Dr. Willis Gates, professor of music, and a vocal solo by Otis Lambert Jr., voice instructor. Dr. Allen P. Brantley, executive director of the Commission on Christian Higher Education, N.C. Conference of The Methodist Church, gave the invocation. The Rev. J. W. Page, pastor of Fayetteville's Hay Street Methodist Church, gave the benediction. The ceremony was followed by a luncheon and a meeting of the Methodist College Board of Trustees.

Trustees Discuss Retirement Plan, Student Housing

When the Methodist College trustees met September 19, 1960, they approved an agreement with Teachers Insurance and Annuity Association of New York creating a retirement plan for Methodist College faculty and administrators. Under terms of a resolution presented by President Weaver, each contract employee of the College would contribute 5 percent of his or her monthly compensation to the retirement plan and the College would match that amount. On a motion by Dr. Allen Brantley, the trustees set a normal retirement age of 68, with provision for an extension to age 70 by vote of the trustees.

Noting that the College could not apply for a federal loan to build dormitories until it had been in operation one year, President Weaver recommended that small apartment buildings be built the next year to house students; he said these could be converted into faculty or married student housing after permanent dormitories were completed. The trustees' Executive and Building committees were instructed to pursue the matter.

In other matters, the trustees voted to hire a night watchman and to grant Carolina Telephone an easement for underground phone lines. They also decided not to meet on Founders Day November 1, 1960.

— CHAPTER 2 —

The first freshman class assembled in the Science Building Auditorium in September 1960.

College Opens With 128 Students

The first classes at Methodist College began Tuesday, September 20, 1960. The College opened with 128 day students, 101 from Fayetteville and Cumberland County, 25 from other parts of North Carolina, and two from other states. Full-time day students numbered 88. Another 41 students registered for evening classes. The original College faculty consisted of twelve persons.

The Rev. Millard C. Dunn Speaks at First Chapel Service

Methodist College held its first chapel service Wednesday September 21, 1960 at 11:30 a.m. in the Science Building Auditorium. (College chapel services were held from 11:30 to 11:50 a.m. Monday, Wednesday, and Friday of each week; attendance was required.)

The Rev. Millard C. Dunn, district superintendent of the Fayetteville District of The Methodist Church, was the guest preacher. He was invited by the Rev. Samuel J. Womack, assistant professor of Bible and college chaplain.

Dunn prefaced his message by saying, "This is one of the greatest moments of my life, and I have looked forward to the opening of this College as a little boy looks forward to Santa Claus." [15]

Dunn's thesis was simple: "The Church would like for you to discover some things, and four of these are:

1. You have a definite purpose in life—there will never be another you.
2. Never lose faith in mankind. People will at times hurt you—instead of holding a grudge, try to understand the other person.
3. The greatest power in the world is love. It may be difficult for you to see it at times because the wicked put on such a show.
4. Never judge eternity by the present moment. [16]

1960–1964

The Fayetteville Observer Features College in Special Section

In its September 24, 1960, edition, *The Fayetteville Observer* featured Methodist College in its 1960 Progress Edition. This 14-page section opened with brief messages from Methodist Bishop Paul N. Garber and College President Stacy Weaver opposite a full-page aerial photograph of the new campus.

Bishop Garber said Methodist College was founded for two reasons: 1) to serve a growing college-age population in North Carolina and the nation, and 2) to provide parents a place where their children could be educated under religious auspices and influences. [17]

Dr. Weaver's message expressed appreciation for "the great many minds, hands, and hearts" which had brought the College to its opening. He described the opening of the College as "a significant plateau but not the mountaintop," and said the College "must continue the building of facilities to take care of increasing numbers of young people and [. . .] begin undergirding of the operational phase of the College life. Endowments and scholarships in increasing number will be required." [18]

The *Observer's* "1960 Progress Edition" included articles about the history of Methodist College, its architecture and features of the new buildings, the first freshmen, the original faculty and administrative staff, and members of the Methodist College Board of Trustees. Almost all the articles were written by Charles McAdams, director of public relations at the College. Many photos were used throughout the section, shots of College facilities, registration day, members of the faculty and administration, and members of the Methodist College Board of Trustees.

Eleven businesses, one bank and three educational institutions bought congratulatory ads in the "Progress Edition." Full-page ads were purchased by Methodist College (thanking the people of Fayetteville for their support), Carolina Transformer Co., Inc., and First Citizens Bank. Campbell College in Buies Creek, N.C., and Edwards Military Institute in Salemburg, N.C., bought half-page ads. Other advertisers included: Armour's Variety Store, Walker Martin, Inc. (distributor of G.E. water coolers), Antex Exterminating Co., WIDU Radio, R. L. Pittman Investments, McCrory's Stores Corp., Dickinson Buick Co., Sol C. Rose (surveyor), and McDevitt & Street Co. (general contractor).

Trustees Approve Apartments, New Fund Drive

The Building and Executive committees of the Methodist College Board of Trustees met October 31, 1960, and authorized the college president to seek financing for two apartment buildings containing 16 rooms. Designed to serve as temporary dormitories, one was to house 32 males and the other 24 females plus a hall director.

President Weaver proposed and the trustees approved the following fees for 1961-62: tuition—$400, general fee—$100, board—$400, room—$180, making the total cost for a resident student $1,080.

The trustees' Executive Committee met December 21, 1960, to discuss the further development of the College. Winston McClellan, a fund-raising consultant from Durham, N.C., suggested the College conduct a special gift solicitation among selected prospects based on a preliminary survey. A week later, the trustees' Development Committee recommended that the College hire McClellan to do a preliminary survey for a fund drive to finance the further development of College facilities.

Fund-Raising Lags, Sanford Elected Governor

As 1960 came to a close, the Fayetteville College Foundation was faced with a marked decline in contributions compared to the previous calendar year. At the group's October 31, 1960, meeting, Executive Director Frank Jeter Jr. reported, "So far this year we've received only $128,406, which indicates we'll fall short of the $226,000 we collected in 1959."[19] Concern was also voiced that only $375 of the $50,000 in sustaining funds owed the College for its first year of operation had been raised.

Board members voted unanimously to seek a joint meeting of local College trustees and a delegation from the Foundation to discuss more effective ways of joint action. Foundation minutes state, "It was agreed that Terry Sanford, chairman of the Methodist College trustees, would be asked to arrange and attend this meeting, as soon after November 9 as possible."[20] (Sanford was elected governor of North Carolina November 8, winning 54.5 percent of the votes cast in a race against Republican Bob Gavin.)

In its annual financial report dated December 15, 1960, the Fayetteville College Foundation reported that it had raised $166,813 for the College in 1960 and that Fayetteville area residents had reached a cumulative total of $805,904 on their five-year pledge of $2 million to the College.

Meeting January 10, 1961, the Fayetteville College Foundation re-elected Bert Ishee as president. Other officers elected to serve with Ishee were: George Vossler, 1st vice president; Mrs. Dennis Williams, 2nd vice president; Mrs. Floyd B. Souders, secretary; and Newton Robertson Jr., treasurer.

Ishee described 1960 as a "less than successful year," and challenged his fellow board members to come up with some new activities to raise more money for the College in 1961.

Dean Clarence Ficken urged foundation members to "send students of quality to Methodist College" [21] and presented "pre-publication" copies of the second College catalogue.

College President Stacy Weaver discussed several pressing needs at the College, including student housing. Referring to fund-raising problems, Dr. Weaver acknowledged the possibility that, "We—the Methodists and Fayetteville—did not know what we were getting into [. . .]" but quickly added, "The tide is moving now; we shall have to move with it." [22]

Church Official Confronts College Foundation

Foundation minutes for 1961 indicate that "an urgent letter" from Dr. Allen Brantley, executive secretary of The North Carolina Conference of The Methodist Church's Commission on Higher Education, was read, a letter in which Brantley asked Foundation members to meet with him January 12 following a College board of trustees meeting, "so that he could tell the Fayetteville people what The Methodist Church is expecting of them." [23]

As requested, the Foundation board (12 members) met with Dr. Allen Brantley January 12, 1961. Brantley told the group that The North Carolina Conference of The Methodist Church had already transmitted $715,000 to Methodist College, adding, "People are looking to Fayetteville. What can we tell them?" [24] He asked if the $50,000 in annual sustaining money promised the College (once it began operation) had been raised. When told this had not been done, Brantley said Rocky Mount was supporting its college in both the building fund and the sustaining fund. The church official ended his remarks by asking that monthly reports on Fayetteville's fund-raising progress be sent to his office in Raleigh.

Approving a motion by E. N. Brower Sr., the Foundation board approved a budget (fund-raising goal) of $300,000 a year for Methodist College for the next four years ($250,000 to the building fund, $50,000 to the sustaining fund.) It was also agreed that the Foundation would launch a "big push" to collect College pledges Sunday, February 26 to coincide with a Methodist Church "emphasis" slated for all churches in The North Carolina Conference.

College Launches Concert-Lecture Series

The April, 1961 *Bulletin of Methodist College* featured photos of the first (fall semester) Dean's List (twelve students), Greensboro, N.C. Schools Supt. Philip J. Weaver (first lecturer in the Methodist College Concert-Lecture Series), and a group of physical education students bowling at Fayetteville's B & B Bowling Lanes.

— CHAPTER 2 —

Mr. Frank Eason inspects one of the pine seedlings planted at the front of the campus.

In his regular "Memo from the President's Desk" column, Dr. Weaver expressed pride in the College's Concert-Lecture Series and the fact that local civic clubs were beginning to hold meetings in the College cafeteria. The president noted that Philip Weaver gave an illustrated lecture on Russian education February 20, and the North Carolina String Quartet appeared in concert April 7, 1961.

In the ensuing years, the Methodist College Concert Lecture Series brought concert pianists, famous lecturers, opera singers, and scientists to the campus. Most were booked through a New York talent agency. One of the guest lecturers who left a lasting impression on Dr. Samuel Womack was a Dr. Andrews, a chemist. "He gave a lecture in which he said music was the ultimate stuff of creation: heat, light, and music. I was blown away because music is my great obsession. He said each cell of our body has its own musical note which we can't hear. He said there are eight basic elements, each represented by a musical note." [25]

Another article in the spring issue of the College *Bulletin* referred to three endowed scholarships recently established to honor the following: Charles Rankin of Fayetteville, Alex Bethune of Linden, N.C., and Arthur and Portia MacPhail Vann of Kenly, N.C. Also announced in this issue was the appointment of Dr. Charles Gilbert Rowe of Kerrville, Texas, as associate professor of foreign languages, effective in September. The author of *A French Review Grammar* textbook, Dr. Rowe earned the Ph.D. from the University of Illinois, the M.A. from Indiana University, the A.B. from Vanderbilt University and studied for one year at the University of Paris. He was scheduled to teach French and Spanish at Methodist.

A short article accompanied by a photo of Frank Eason, College comptroller, acknowledged a $150 gift from the Fayetteville Garden Club used to purchase 25 ten-foot willow oaks, four eight-foot ash trees, and four sycamore trees which were planted in areas surrounding the Classroom Building. Eason also reported that the College had planted: 275 hardwood and ornamental trees, 6,000 longleaf pines, 85 ginkgo trees, 44 flowering cherries, 14 river birches, 28 sycamores and 25 poplars.

Also announced in this issue was the construction of two small, air-conditioned dormitories in a wooded area south of the Classroom Building and the fact that each apartment building would house 28-30 students starting in September. One building was to house men, the other women. Construction was already under way when this article appeared.

Trustees Set Faculty Salaries, Re-elect Terry Sanford Chairman

Meeting January 12, 1961, the Methodist College Board of Trustees authorized the college president and board secretary to borrow $120,000 to build two small apartment buildings to house students. The board also voted to hire Winston McClellan to do a preliminary survey to prepare for a new capital fund drive for the College. It was agreed that McClellan would be paid $600 a week for six to eight weeks.

The trustees' Building and Executive committees met together January 17, 1961, to receive bids on two apartment buildings to be used as temporary dormitories. A construction contract for $97,942 was awarded to D. R. Allen & Son, contingent on Mr. Allen completing negotiations for a

Margaret Weston of Fort Bragg (seated) was crowned the College's first May Queen May 5, 1961.

— CHAPTER 2 —

construction loan to build the apartments. At its May 2, 1961, meeting, the Methodist College Board of Trustees heard a report from Winston McClellan, a fund-raising consultant, concerning prospects for securing funds to build the College library, chapel, and administration building.

Dr. Allen Brantley, director of The North Carolina Conference of The Methodist Church's Commission on Christian Higher Education, reported that $1,962,450 or 54 percent of the $3,571,189 pledged by church members to the Conference's college campaign had been collected, with $768,932 of that going to Methodist College.

Bert Ishee, president of the Fayetteville College Foundation, reported that $869,300 had been collected for the College in the Fayetteville area and that an honorary alumni group was being formed in Fayetteville and Cumberland County for the purpose of providing the $50,000 annual sustaining fund promised to the College.

Following a presentation by the Rev. Vergil Queen, chairman of the trustees' Academic Affairs Committee, the board approved a faculty rank, tenure and promotion policy with salary schedule. The schedule for faculty salaries ranged from $4,200 per year for an instructor to $6,900 per year for a full professor.

In other actions, the trustees: approved a $235,730 capital budget for 1961-62, authorized construction of a physical education facility (metal gymnasium) and athletic field east of the Boiler Plant, approved drawings for a gateway entrance to the College, and granted an easement for extension of a Public Works Commission sewer main to Ramsey Street.

Trustees re-elected Terry Sanford, the new governor of North Carolina, chairman of the board. Fayetteville attorney Joe Tally Jr. was elected vice-chairman, the Rev. Jack Page secretary, and Frank McBryde treasurer.

In a written report to the trustees, President Weaver noted the College had expended just under $2.7 million on buildings and equipment as of May 1, using $1,769,559 in cash plus $1 million in loan funds from First Citizens Bank. He said a $100,000 loan from State Capital Life Insurance Co. would pay for the two apartment buildings under construction.

Under the subheading "Students," Dr. Weaver said only 27 of the 41 students enrolled in the College's night school during the fall semester completed their courses and only fourteen enrolled for the second semester. "Unless a new direction can be found," he said, "it does not seem feasible to operate the night school." [26]

The president also expressed concern that student enrollment the first year was less than expected. "I am sorry to report that prospects for next year are not any more encouraging," said Weaver. "We understand a good many

Twelve students were named to the College's first Dean's List in early 1961.

reasons which have a bearing on this situation, but the total outlook is frankly puzzling to me." [27]

Faculty, Alumna Remember Spartan Surroundings

Sam Edwards, the man who held three administrative jobs (registrar, director of admissions, director of financial aid) and taught physical education, said of the latter experience:

"Teaching physical education at Methodist was quite an experience. We played softball, and the softball field was the parking lot for the Classroom Building. Somebody would hit the ball. You had to wait to see how many curbs it jumped over. We made all kinds of errors. But there was one girl who was very interested in dance, and she would put the girls through the exercises of dancers. They would come back the next day and could hardly walk." [28]

Jean Ishee, the first piano instructor, felt a little out of place in the Science Building. "I think I had five piano students my first year," she said. "We had an upright piano that we kept in the Science Auditorium. I remember the science faculty members saying they would scream if they had to hear that piano any

— CHAPTER 2 —

In 1960, Sam Edwards calls roll for his P.E. class.

longer. A few years later when the Music Department moved to one of the two small apartment buildings, we had this big old electronic organ which they hauled up to the second floor." ²⁹

Betty Neill Guy Parsons, a Fayetteville native who transferred to Methodist from Flora MacDonald College in the fall of 1961, has vivid memories of the campus, her classmates, and her professors:

> "The mud and sand spurs were terrible. We girls wore socks a lot. . . Many of our students were older and non-traditional and commuted to school. We often had lunch together at The Pizza Palace on Bragg Boulevard. . . One of the most colorful professors was Marjorie Ostborg who taught English. She once presented a poem by pirouetting into the room to a recording of *Swan Lake*. She said nature shows us its strength through trees, which we should go out and embrace. So we had this tree-hugging thing for quite a while. . . Grady Snyder turned me on to math. He made it fun and interesting. . . The thing I liked best about physical education was archery. I absolutely loved it. I guess it was because my dad had taught me to shoot rifles." ³

Bulletin Lists More Firsts

The June 1961 issue of the *Bulletin of Methodist College* announced another series of firsts for the College:

—Margaret Weston of Fort Bragg was crowned the first May Queen May 5.
—Dr. Howard P. Powell, pastor of Edenton Street Methodist Church in Raleigh, N.C., was the guest speaker for the first Religious Emphasis Week May 8-12.
—The first student music recital was held May 14 featuring

Students gathered in the Student Union in 1961.

Paul Ostborg, violist; Patricia Jackson, pianist; and Anne Bradford, soprano.

—The Methodist College newspaper staff organized, met with Gibson Prather, managing editor of *The Fayetteville Observer,* and announced plans to publish the first issue in the fall. Elaine Barbee was elected editor and Don Parsons was elected business manager.

The summer *Bulletin* also announced the appointment of Dr. James R. Heffern as associate professor of biology, effective in September. A former dentist, Dr. Heffern was then serving as professor of biology at Millikin University in Decatur, Illinois. He held a D.D.S. degree from the University of Kansas, a B.S. degree in biology, chemistry and health from Missouri State College, and had done graduate study in education at the University of Michigan.

Trustees Authorize Construction of More Apartments
At their July 19, 1961, meeting, College trustees authorized the president and board secretary to borrow $100,000 to build another apartment building for students. President Weaver announced a gift of $50,000 from R. J. Reynolds Tobacco Co. to the College's building fund.

— CHAPTER 2 —

The trustees' Executive Committee met September 28, 1961, and voted to recommend that the Methodist College Board of Trustees be increased to 36 members (from 24) by the addition of a maximum of 12 new members to be elected at large. The committee also authorized construction of 12 additional apartments for students at a cost of $150,000.

The full Board of Trustees met November 1, 1961, and approved the sale of ten shares of Burlington Industries stock and 380 shares of Reynolds Tobacco stock as needed for the Building Fund. The board also accepted D. R. Allen & Son's low bid of $139,791 for constructing 12 apartments "subject to completion of financing." [31]

In December 1961, the trustees' Executive Committee adopted a resolution in which the College applied to the U.S. Housing and Home Finance Agency to build two permanent residence halls, one for men and one for women.

Enrollment Doubles for 1961-62

The September 1961 *Bulletin of Methodist College* reported that the College began its second academic year by enrolling 314 students, 208 in the fall day program and 106 in the evening school. Included in that total were 28 transfer students. President Weaver said he was encouraged that Methodist's second freshman class was 76 percent larger than the first.

sMALL TALK Puts Gov. Sanford on Front Page

The lead story in the inaugural issue of *sMALL TALK*, the Methodist College student newspaper, was headlined "Governor Visits Campus" and reported on a speech given by North Carolina Governor and Methodist College Board of Trustees Chairman Terry Sanford during the College's second annual Founder's Day program November 1, 1961.

Barbee reported that Sanford directed his remarks to both the College "founders" who were present and the students. To the founders he said there were still a lot of foundations to be built. Addressing the students, he urged them to join the founders in creating the best college possible. Sanford said that because Methodist College was a new institution, "You are not chained by the habitual grooves of the past, and as you move out to establish a new program, you are free to plan and to think of the best." [32]

Another front page story profiled the Community Council, charged with coordinating extracurricular activities. The council was composed of five faculty members appointed by the president and five students elected by their peers.

1960–1964

Editor Elaine Barbee and Business Mgr. Don Parsons with the first newspaper in November 1961.

    A news brief on Page One announced that the faculty had voted to give the 11:30 a.m. Friday chapel period to the Community Council for class meetings and other student-led programs.

    A front page story on "chapel talks" quoted Dr. Sam Womack as saying the Monday chapel period would be reserved for the college president or faculty members to speak on the general topic, "This I Believe." He said the Wednesday chapel period would be reserved for guest speakers, and the Friday period for class meetings.

    The story went on to list Monday speakers who had filled in for President Weaver. These included: Dr. Charles Ott (chemistry), Mrs. Greta Duncum (psychology), Dr. James Heffern (biology), Dr. Charles Rowe (French) and Mrs. Marjorie Ostborg (music) who opted to lead the students in a "community sing."

    Some Wednesday "visiting speakers" included the Rev. Henry Johnson Jr., rector of Holy Trinity Episcopal Church; J. Bernard Stein, a local businessman, the Rev. Jack Page, pastor of Hay Street Methodist Church; and Mr. W. C. Fields, a local portrait painter.

    Another front page story recounted the experiences of sophomores Larry Warren and Amos McLamb, who were Methodist College delegates to the Seventh Quadrennial Methodist Student Movement Conference held August 28-31, 1961, at the University of Illinois. Warren and McLamb were part of a two-busload caravan of MSM members from North Carolina colleges who attended the conference.

— CHAPTER 2 —

Published in November, 1961, the first issue of *sMALL TALK* was a six-page issue. In the lead editorial entitled "What's in a Name?" Editor Elaine Barbee explained why the newspaper staff chose the name *sMALL TALK*:

> The campus of our college will have as one of its main characteristics a series of malls or shaded walks. It is on these that many important questions will be discussed by the students and faculty. By keeping attuned to these conversations, we of the newspaper staff hope that *sMALL TALK* will be a voice of students and faculty alike. It is our hope that big achievements from *sMALL TALK* will grow. [33]

Inside the first issue of *sMALL TALK* were a variety of stories about more College "firsts": the first performance by the Methodist College Chorus under the direction of Dr. Willis Gates, the first Sunday vesper service, a film series sponsored by the Student Christian Association, and "the first major sports event at Methodist College"—a volleyball contest between freshman and sophomore teams selected by Sam Edwards, physical education instructor (The freshmen won both games, defeating the sophomores 15-1 and 15-3).

One of three student-written columns in that first *sMALL TALK* was shared by correspondents from the Men's Dormitory and the Women's Dormitory housed in small apartment buildings on the southern edge of the campus. Each dorm had an adult counselor who lived on site—Mrs. Greta Duncum for the women and Mr. Alva Stewart for the men.

Barbara Rine of the Women's Dorm reported that one of the 24 residents there had left to get married, and that her dorm had acquired a "highly-prized doorbell" and a newly-furnished lounge.

Bob Reynolds of the Men's Dorm said the thin walls between apartments necessitated strict enforcement of quiet hours. He said the male residents there had only the bare essentials: "Through petition we have a water cooler, two pencil sharpeners, and a telephone line. We are still hoping for a petitioned 'Coke' machine." [34]

Bulletin Describes Arboretum Gift

The front page of the December 1961 *Bulletin of Methodist College* pictured the construction of a new apartment building/dormitory for 88 women with a cutline noting that the two small apartment buildings already in use would house men the following year.

Another story revealed that Fayetteville nurseryman W. G. Butler had given the College a collection of trees, shrubs, and other plants and had agreed to install, label, and maintain these in an arboretum on campus to aid in the instruction of botany students. Work on the arboretum was said to be underway in an area southwest of the physical education field where it would follow a stream bed and plateau between two ponds on the campus.

The winter *Bulletin* also announced the establishment of a Methodist College Advisors organization made up of over 400 representatives of local Methodist churches in The North Carolina Conference. Director of Public Relations Charles McAdams said local church pastors in eight districts (the Rocky Mount District was excluded in deference to N.C. Wesleyan College) had been asked to name one couple to be the contact between the College and the individual church. It was reported that 200 advisors had attended a fall orientation meeting held on a Sunday afternoon at the College.

Student Council Proposed

The lead story in the January 1962 issue of *sMALL TALK* carried a banner headline, "Student Council Proposed" and detailed the first step toward student government at Methodist College. That step was taken December 14, 1961, when the College faculty approved a set of three recommendations put forth by the Community Council. The first recommendation called for creation of a Student Council consisting of the four officers of the sophomore and freshman classes, the five student representatives then serving on the Community Council, and a faculty adviser appointed by the President. The Community Council's second request was that the new Student Council be charged with drafting a set of by-laws for a Student Government Association. The third recommendation was that extracurricular activities remain under the control of the Community Council until the faculty approved a set of by-laws for a Student Government Association.

sMALL TALK also reported on two Christmas-related events. A Bach cantata was presented on the evening of December 14, 1961, in the Student Union, featuring the Methodist College Chorus and the Hay Street United Methodist Church Choir, both under the direction of Dr. Willis Gates, professor of music at the College. The second annual Christmas dinner for students, faculty and staff was held the evening of December 15, 1961 in the College cafeteria. President Weaver delivered the Christmas message.

An inside story in the same issue reported that students had elected Ralph Hoggard president of the sophomore class and Shad Bosher president of the freshman class. Both Hoggard and Bosher were from Fayetteville.

In a sports column entitled "Sports Angles," Bob Reynolds, a student from Waynesboro, Va., lamented that Methodist College had yet to organize either

CHAPTER 2

intramural or intercollegiate athletic programs. Reynolds said Methodist's sister school, N.C. Wesleyan College in Rocky Mount, had already formed an intercollegiate baseball team and an intramural program. He ended his column by asking that any MC students interested in competing in intramurals or on a baseball team complete a clip-out coupon printed in the paper and bring it by the *sMALL TALK* office in Room C-106.

Foundation Elects Robertson President

The Fayetteville College Foundation elected Newton Robertson Jr. president January 9, 1962. Others elected to Foundation offices were: Richard L. Player Jr., vice president; Mrs. O. L. McFayden Jr., vice president; Mrs. Elizabeth Ellis, secretary; and Bert Ishee, treasurer. Robertson said he intended to "emphasize the things the College has already attained" [35] as he sought to raise funds in the community.

In February, the Foundation's Executive Committee launched a new policy of inviting two Methodist College students to their monthly luncheon meetings. Selected by Charles McAdams, director of public relations and development at the College, the following students were guests of the Foundation during the spring and spoke about their experiences at Methodist: Elaine Barbee, Bob Reynolds, Betty Bunce, the Rev. Kermit Weeks, and Walter Turner.

Trustees Accept Challenge Gift

Members of the trustees' Executive Committee voted February 16, 1962, to accept a challenge gift of $25,000 from the Richardson Foundation, Inc. to the College building fund. The gift was made on the condition that the College raise $225,000 for the building program by June 30, 1962. The College met the challenge.

At the same meeting, the trustees voted to build a temporary gymnasium (a metal Butler building) and to begin charging students a $25 per year Health and Activity Fee to cover health costs, nursing service, publications, public affairs, lectures, and entertainment.

sMALL TALK Describes ESP Experiment

The front page of the February 1962 *sMALL TALK* carried an interesting article about one student's interest in extrasensory perception (E.S.P.) and plans for an experiment involving MC students. Henry Walker, a sophomore, said he had visited with Dr. J. B. Rhine, noted psychologist and head of the Parapsychology Laboratory at Duke University, to obtain help in designing his experiment. (Dr. Rhine gave a public lecture at the College April 17, 1962.

Speaking on the subject "Parapsychology and Man's Search for Understanding," he emphasized the importance of understanding man as a spiritual being in a mechanical world.)

Mrs. Ingeborg Dent, the new Student Union hostess, was the subject of an inside feature story in the February *sMALL TALK*. A native of Duren, Germany and a graduate of the University of Cologne, she immigrated to the United States in 1954 and became a U.S. citizen in 1956. Her husband Bruce was a chief warrant officer in the U.S. Army. Mrs. Dent said she was planning to pursue an M.A. at the University of North Carolina so she could teach German at the college level.

The March 1962 issue of the student newspaper announced that the College was planning to build a temporary gymnasium and an athletic field and would employ a full-time physical education instructor in the fall to develop an intramural athletic program.

One entire page in the April 1962 *sMALL TALK* was devoted to student opinions on the question of whether Methodist College should adopt an honor system. Eight of the nine students offering opinions said they thought the College should adopt an honor system.

Dean Ficken, Jerry Wood, and Dr. Ott review a copy of an article by Wood and Ott in **The Science Teacher** *magazine.*

— CHAPTER 2 —

College Bulletin Lists More Firsts

The lead story in the March 1962 *Bulletin of Methodist College* reported that *The Science Teacher,* a national magazine, had accepted an illustrated article written jointly by Jerry Wood, a sophomore, and Dr. Charles Ott, chemistry professor. The article described a demonstration technique involving the protective action of a sacrificial magnesium anode as a rust preventative.

The *Bulletin* revealed that the University Senate of The Methodist Church had accredited Methodist College for meeting the requirements of the Church for the undergraduate training of ministers and that nine current students were planning to major in religion and enter the ministry.

The March newsletter included three photos of visitors to the campus: 22 German journalists and editors, the officers of the Fayetteville College Foundation with the *sMALL TALK* staff, and Congressman Alton Lennon of Wilmington, N.C., with Dr. Heffern in a science lab.

The June 1962 issue of the College *Bulletin* announced that the Board of Trustees had met a challenge by raising $225,000 for the building fund and would receive a $25,000 grant from the Richardson Foundation. Also announced in this issue was the creation of a $500 annual scholarship by the Belk-Hensdale Company of Fayetteville (to be awarded to one or more students from Cumberland County) and the appointment of Dr. Weaver to the Governor's Commission on Educational Television.

Dean Ficken Burned in Effigy

The first student demonstration at Methodist College occurred the evening of Thursday, April 19, 1962, and proved very controversial. Students submitted a petition to Dr. Clarence Ficken, academic dean, and the faculty April 18 requesting that Easter Monday be given as a College holiday. The next day, after Ficken and the faculty posted notices denying the request, a group of male resident students burned Ficken in effigy.

The incident was reported in *The Fayetteville Observer* Friday, April 20, 1962. The news story quoted a witness as saying the demonstration occurred around 9:30 p.m., about three hours after male and female students returned to their dormitory apartments from dinner to find a notice from Dean Ficken posted on their bulletin boards.

The notice said the petition for an Easter Monday holiday had been denied "by faculty action." Ficken said the College calendar was set a year in advance, that a spring recess had been observed March 29-April 4, and that any additional holiday would interfere with the final exam schedule.

A witness told *The Observer* that the initial demonstration began inside the men's dormitory but moved outside and soon attracted residents from the nearby women's dormitory. Bob Reynolds, one of the student demonstrators, recalled during a recent interview, that he and 11 other male residents burned the dummy in a vacant field across the street from their dormitory. He said he and the other demonstrators were suspended for two days and forbidden to leave campus. Reynolds said he personally apologized to Dr. Ficken later. He also said the petition was never formally presented to Ficken, just dropped off at his office.

A few weeks later, Dean Ficken announced during a College chapel program that he had requested and been granted retirement status, effective at the end of the current school year. Although many at the College felt the effigy burning prompted the dean to retire, Ficken said in his chapel announcement that he had submitted a retirement request to President Weaver in November, 1961.

Because Dr. Ficken was highly regarded by both staff and students, his decision to retire evoked tears and anger from many. The students responsible for burning Ficken in effigy were roundly condemned in two guest editorials that appeared in the May 1962 *sMALL TALK*.

Guest editorialist Kermit Norris said the demonstrators displayed "immaturity and inadequacy to meet the responsibilities of being adults." [36]

Connor Holland's editorial argued that the demonstration "pointed up the need for organized student government" [37] at Methodist to channel student spirit in the right direction. Holland said he did not believe the College faculty and administration wished to suppress student demonstrations but also felt the effigy burning was unjust to Dr. Ficken.

In a column entitled "Chapel Quotes," Virginia Kearn quoted Seldon Rapeleye as saying, "We now realize the harm done, and we are sincerely sorry for this regrettable incident." [38]

Dr. Samuel Womack, the College chaplain and assistant professor of Bible at the time of the incident, said in a 2000 interview that Dr. Ficken was "heartbroken" by the effigy burning. Dr. Womack said he met with the five male students responsible for the burning and tried to explain Dr. Ficken's position. He said to atone for their actions, the students cleared trees from a wooded area (where O'Hanlon Amphitheater is now) and built a small outdoor chapel in honor of Dr. Ficken.

sMALL TALK Recounts May Day Weekend, Lists New Faculty

The lead story in the May 1962 *sMALL TALK* described a successful May Day weekend and included photos of May Queen Dawn Hamby and members of her court: Pat Jackson, Tommie Parker, Barbara Rine, and Margaret Weston. Music for the May Dance was provided by the Sigmas of the University of North Carolina; the Student Union was decorated to illustrate the theme "At the Beach."

Other front page news in this issue was Dr. Ficken's retirement announcement and a story about new faculty members just hired for the 1962-63 school year. The new faculty included: Dr. Mary Emily Miller, dean of women and instructor of history; Joseph M. Daniel, assistant professor of physics and math; Earnest W. Schwarz, director of physical education; Bruce R. Pulliam, supervisor of the men's dormitory and assistant professor of history; Mrs. Pauline M. Longest, assistant professor of biology; Dr. Vearl G. McBryde, chairman of the area of Education and Psychology.

A separate news story on an inside page noted that Orren E. Dowd of Greenville, N.C. had been appointed dean of students at Methodist College effective in the fall of 1962. Mr. Dowd held B.A. and M.A. degrees from Duke University and had been principal of Greenville's J. H. Rose High School for 21 years.

This issue also included a photo tribute to Dr. Marie Fox, philosophy professor and advisor to the newspaper staff. Dr. Fox would announce in the late fall that her husband, an Army officer, was being reassigned and they would be leaving Fayetteville in December.

Trustees Award Residence Hall Contract, Re-elect Officers

At their May 1, 1962, meeting, the Methodist College Board of Trustees accepted the recommendation of the Building Committee and awarded a $1,137,800 construction contract for two three-story dormitories (Garber Hall and Cumberland Hall) to T. A. Loving & Company of Goldsboro, N.C. The men's dorm, Cumberland, was designed to house 160, while the women's dorm, Garber, had a capacity of 150. The dorms were financed for 40 years at a rate of 3 3/8 percent through the Community Facilities Administration, U.S. Housing and Home Finance Agency. Both residence halls were to be completed and ready for occupancy by September 1963.

At this same meeting, Dr. Allen Brantley informed his fellow trustees that the Commission on Christian Higher Education of The North Carolina Conference of The Methodist Church would propose to the Annual Conference in June that a new campaign for Christian education be held later in the year, seeking to raise $3 million in capital funds, $1 million of which would come to Methodist College.

1960–1964

The Board of Trustees nominated four persons to fill vacancies on the board: John M. Reeves of Pinehurst, N.C., the Rev. R. Grady Dawson of New Bern, N.C., John W. Hensdale of Fayetteville, and Lewis D. Isenhour of Sanford, N.C. All the nominees were elected at the 1962 session of The North Carolina Conference of The Methodist Church. The trustees re-elected Terry Sanford and three other board officers.

President Weaver's proposed budgets for 1962-63 were approved: $403,275 for operating and $219,624 for capital outlay and debt service. In his annual report to the board, Dr. Weaver said the College enrolled a total of 343 students in 1961-62, 246 in the regular day program and 97 in the evening school which was closed down at the end of the first semester. Dr. Weaver gave the following reason for discontinuing the evening school: "Since public institutions (e.g. Fayetteville Technical Institute) have been opened in the city within the past few months which essentially duplicate the work which was being done in our evening school, without any tuition charge to those who enroll, it does not now appear that there will be any demand for a continuation of these offerings." [39]

Mrs. Pauline Longest conducts a biology lab.

— CHAPTER 2 —

The president also expressed his appreciation to Gov. Terry Sanford and other members of the trustees' Executive Committee for their faithful and loyal service to the College during the preceding year.

Trustees Award Gymnasium Contract

The trustees' Executive Committee met July 10, 1962 and approved a contract with D. R. Allen & Sons, Inc. for the construction of a temporary metal gymnasium (Butler building) at a cost of $90,000. The College issued notes worth $55,000 to the Allen firm as partial payment for the building.

At the Oct. 10, 1962, meeting of the Board of Trustees, Dr. Weaver reported that Mrs. Walter R. Davis of Midland, Texas, had made a contribution of $100,000 to the College which would be used toward construction of a library. Mrs. Davis was the former Geraldine Tyson of the Gray's Creek community of Cumberland County.

The trustees held their final meeting of 1962 November 15, approving a loan agreement with the Community Facilities Administration of the federal Housing and Home Finance Agency and electing J. W. Hensdale of Fayetteville to replace the Rev. J. W. Page as board secretary. Rev. Page resigned as board treasurer but remained a trustee.

Members of a women's P.E. class plays volleyball on the courts behind the Boiler Plant.

1960–1964

College Enrolls 345, Intramurals Begin

Methodist College began its third academic year September 14, 1962, by enrolling 345 students; 307 were from North Carolina, 296 were from Methodist families in The North Carolina Conference, and 198 were freshmen.

The October 1962 *sMALL TALK* noted that Professor Loren Withers, piano instructor at Duke University, would give a recital October 23 at Methodist as part of the College's Concert-Lecture Series. This issue also offered profiles of Mrs. Greta Duncum, director of guidance, and Mrs. Esperanza Escudero, assistant professor of Spanish.

The October issue also announced the beginning of an intramural athletic program October 1, with five teams competing in eight-man touch football. The teams from the men's dorms were known as the "Yama Yama Men" (sophomores) and "Dorm No. 2" (freshmen). The three day student teams were known as "The Taggers," "The Untouchables," and "The Schmids." The November 1962 *sMALL TALK* reported that the Yama Yama Men were undefeated in touch football with eight wins going into the final round schedule.

Devised by the new physical education instructor Ernie Schwarz, the intramural program awarded points to various teams based on participation and order of participation in a sport. According to the schedule and point system printed in the November 1962 *sMALL TALK*, major team competition was to be offered in touch football, basketball and softball; minor team competition

Roommates Cynthia Walker and Sarah Jobe in their south campus apartment, ca. 1961.

— CHAPTER 2 —

in volleyball, bowling, soccer, track and field; individual competition in tennis, golf, table tennis, badminton, and horseshoes. A year-end banquet was slated for May 1963.

The lead story in the November 1962 *sMALL TALK* reported that a committee consisting of class officers for the three classes was still working on the draft of a proposed constitution and by-laws for a Student Government Association to be considered by the faculty. It was also reported that Dr. Bernard Boyd, chairman of the Religion Department at the University of North Carolina, would speak at Methodist Nov. 13 as part on the Concert-Lecture Series; his topic was "Towards a Higher Wisdom."

Other stories noted that the College would offer its first summer session of six-weeks duration in 1963 and that a student committee was meeting with representatives of ring companies to come up with a Methodist College ring design. Major Larry Fox, husband of Dr. Marie Fox, announced the establishment of the Marie C. Fox Philosophy Award to be given to a Methodist College student annually each spring. Dr. Marie Fox had served as professor of history and philosophy at the College since its opening in 1960. Dr. Fox had to leave the college in December 1962 to accompany her husband to Fort Leavenworth, Kansas, where Maj. Fox was to attend Command and General Staff College before being assigned to France, starting in May 1963.

A "Dorm Site" column by Billy Kelly and Cynthia Walker noted that "the girls" were having fun learning the "flop" and the "popeye," two of the newest dance crazes.

Gov. Sanford Delivers Major Address at Methodist

North Carolina Governor and Methodist College Trustees Chairman Terry Sanford delivered a major policy address on higher education at the College's third Founders Day program November 15, 1962. He was introduced by Dr. William C. Friday, president of the University of North Carolina. His address was entitled, "Education is the Only Path to Progress" and was covered by a large contingent of news reporters from across the state.

Governor Sanford began his address by asserting that, "North Carolina must say to the young people of the state, 'If you have the will and the skill, you can go to college.'" [40] He recalled that Governor Charles Brantley Aycock gave a speech in 1903 in which he said North Carolinians "must tighten their belts and put money into education for everybody. [41] Sanford said that while Aycock was governor, North Carolina built schoolhouses on the average of one a day, adding, "He left office unpopular and died almost repudiated; but the people supported education, and because they did, North Carolina began to move forward." [42]

Sanford's address focused on the recommendations offered in the Report of the Commission on Education Beyond the High School, under the general headings of Private Colleges, Community Colleges, Public Senior Colleges, and The University of North Carolina. Sanford appointed the commission in 1961, naming Irving E. Carlyle chairman.

On the subject of private colleges, Sanford said the state wanted private institutions of higher learning to flourish and increase their capacity and added, "I hope that all churches will increase the financial support they give their colleges." [43] He said he had been asked to create the mechanics whereby the private colleges could work together with the state, to give the benefit of their ideas for improving education to the Governor and the Board of Higher Education. "This we are doing," he said, "and we look forward to a fruitful partnership." [44]

On the subject of community colleges, Sanford cited two striking statistics. "By the end of this decade young people seeking admission to college in North Carolina will exceed the present capacity of public colleges plus the planned capacity of private colleges by more than 31,000." [45] He then decried the fact that North Carolina was sending a smaller percentage of its young people to college than four-fifths of the states. [46]

The governor said he endorsed the establishment of a community college system of public two-year post high school institutions offering college parallel studies, technical-vocational-terminal work, and adult education instruction tailored to area needs.

Referring to the state's nine public colleges (plus soon-to-be public-colleges at Asheville, Charlotte, and Wilmington), Sanford said these institutions needed additional funding from the General Assembly to upgrade their facilities. At this point, he offered the following opinion:

> There is sometimes an inclination to make every junior college a four-year college and every college a university, but this is vain and foolish. A good college is far better and is of far more influence that a sorry university. We cannot do without our four-year colleges and we cannot afford to have them second-rate. [47]

Speaking of the Consolidated University of North Carolina (at Chapel Hill, Raleigh, and Greensboro), Sanford said the Report recommended that state statutes be amended to: 1) define Consolidated University purposes,

— CHAPTER 2 —

Dr. Willis Gates conducts the chorus at the 1962 Founder's Day program in the Student Union.

and 2) authorize the Consolidated University Board of Trustees to establish additional campuses of the University where there is a clear need for graduate and professional programs.

Sanford said the Report of the Commission and the Southern Regional Education Board's "Goals Report" offered a sound path of progress for North Carolina to follow in higher education. He concluded his address by saying, "We have this plan; we have the resources, and now is the time to act together—to take the bold new steps which can give our state its time of highest achievement, its finest hour." [48]

As part of the Founders Day program, Dr. Harold Maxwell, president of the North State Exchange Clubs, presented a "Freedom Shrine" gift to the College from the Fayetteville Exchange Club consisting of 28 framed copies of historical documents, including America's Declaration of Independence, the U. S. Constitution, Lincoln's Gettysburg Address, and the United Nations charter. Terry Sanford accepted the gift for the College.

College Grounds Women

Women resident students at Methodist were grounded November 28, 1962, when the Committee on Student Affairs adopted a new closed study rule. The rule said women resident students would not be permitted to date or leave the campus after 7:30 p.m. Monday-Thursday starting December 3.

Dean of Students O. E. Dowd said the faculty members of the committee had analyzed mid-term grades and use of the library and concluded that too many women residents were neglecting their studies.

The new rule was the subject of a front page story in the December, 1962 *sMALL TALK,* as well as an editorial. Editor Kermit Norris opined that a blanket closed study rule was unfair to those women students who had proved themselves scholastically. He suggested the rule be modified to apply only to freshmen women and those on academic probation. He said upperclasswomen in good academic standing should be allowed at least two privilege nights during the week when they could leave the campus for dates or other reasons.

The Cuban Missile Crisis

The Cuban missile crisis in the fall of 1962 did not go unnoticed at Methodist College. The U.S. had obtained photographic evidence that the Russians were constructing intercontinental ballistic missile (ICBM) bases in Cuba. President John Kennedy demanded that Soviet Premier Nikita Kruschev immediately halt the construction, dismantle the bases, and cease shipments of missiles to Cuba. Kennedy also ordered U.S. ships to intercept and stop any Russian ships carrying missiles to Cuba.

Americans old enough to remember this crisis will recall that many of their countrymen were sufficiently frightened at the prospect of Russian missiles being launched from Cuba to start building fallout shelters in their backyards. One Methodist alumnus remembers an announcement made at his high school, "In the event of a national emergency you will be sent home." [49]

The November 1962 *sMALL TALK* interviewed several students, asking them, "If the Russians fail to dismantle their Cuban missile bases, what action should the United States take?"

Fran Abel responded, "In order to defend the Monroe doctrine we would have no alternative but to invade Cuba, although I believe this invasion would start World War III." [50]

Danny Nau answered, "For our way of life to exist our generation has the moral obligation to disarm Cuba; legally, we do not have the right." [51]

In "No Joking Matter," an editorial, the *sMALL TALK* editor said newspaper staff members were "astounded" that some students on campus were making jokes and wisecracks about the Cuban missile crisis. Upon further reflection, the writer said, the staff concluded that the whimsical response of some students was "a facade, a cover to hide the fears within." [52]

"Dorm Sites" columnist Tommy Manning wrote, "All the residents of the men's dorm keep looking in the mail boxes for those draft notices which should be coming any day now. We fellows may be 'bunking' with Uncle Sam before long. We might find him a worse roommate than the one we now have. We joke about it, but really we're all quite concerned." [53]

— CHAPTER 2 —

During its November 15, 1962 meeting, the Methodist College Board of Trustees adopted a motion by Ed Fleishman authorizing the Fayetteville and Cumberland County Council of Civil Defense to mark and stock designated qualified areas of the College buildings as fallout shelters.

College Foundation Votes to Move Offices

In June and July 1962, the Fayetteville College Foundation Executive Board adopted a budget for 1962-63 and voted to move the Foundation office from the Grace Pittman Building downtown to the College campus. Foundation President Newton Robertson Jr. reported that Founders' Certificates had been mailed to all local citizens who made and fulfilled their pledges in the initial five-year fund drive for Methodist College. E. S. Bosher suggested that a "Methodist College Day" be set aside in 1963 on which Foundation members would canvas prospective donors to the College.

At the August 16, 1962, Foundation meeting, members discussed a long list of recommendations for fund-raising from Col. Theodore Ellsworth, vice-president for development at New York University.

Foundation Executive Frank Jeter Jr. reported to the Executive Board October 18, 1962, that the Methodist conference's College Development

This is the way the campus looked from Ramsey Street in 1960.

Crusade for $3 million would be held November 28-December 21, with all proceeds collected at churches in the Fayetteville District going directly to Methodist College. As 1962 ended, the College Foundation reported it had raised $102,084 that year for Methodist College.

College Announces First Summer Session

Early in 1963, Methodist College announced it would offer its first summer session June 10-July 19. The announcement and schedule of 16 classes was carried in the January 1963 *sMALL TALK* and the February 1963 *Bulletin of Methodist College.*

The February 1963 College *Bulletin* also announced that Dr. Millard B. Burt would assume the duties of academic dean at Methodist College September 1, 1963. From the time of Dr. Ficken's retirement the previous summer until Dr. Burt's arrival, Mr. Sam Edwards served as acting dean.

Dr. Burt had served as academic dean at Atlantic Christian College for five years; prior to that he chaired the Dept. of Education and Psychology, and served as band director there. Methodist's second academic dean held an undergraduate degree from Atlantic Christian College and the M.A. and Ph.D. degrees from the University of North Carolina. He had also studied at the Sorbonne in Paris, France.

The February 1963 *Bulletin* reported that Dr. James Hillman of Raleigh, N.C., had accepted a part-time position as consultant on curriculum, with

Cumberland Hall is shown under construction in 1963.

— CHAPTER 2 —

particular emphasis on teacher education and general accreditation. Dr. Hillman previously worked for the North Carolina Department of Public Instruction.

The College *Bulletin* also announced four Weekend Visitations—one in February and three in March. Under this program, high school seniors and transfer students interested in attending Methodist College would be overnight guests of the College and would take scholarship examinations on a Saturday afternoon. Each visitation weekend lasted from noon Saturday to noon Sunday and included briefings by College officials, tours of the campus and meals.

Intercollegiate Athletics, Bids on Library, Chapel and Bell Tower Authorized

The Executive Committee of the Methodist College Board of Trustees met February 12, 1963, and voted to start a program of intercollegiate athletics in the fall "limited to basketball and minor sports." [54] The motion by Nelson Gibson to start intercollegiate competition stipulated that the basketball schedule be limited to 20 games, that no athletic scholarships be offered and that the faculty be asked to recommend academic qualifications for the student athletes representing the College.

Meeting February 23, 1963, the Executive Committee authorized President Weaver to sell stock in the Permian Corporation given to the College by Mrs. Walter Davis and to take construction bids for the library, chapel, and bell tower.

College Group Wows Lions in Hamlet

A story and photo in the January 1963 *sMALL TALK* reported that a "troupe" from Methodist College entertained members of the Hamlet, N.C. Lions Club January 4, 1963. Director of Public Relations Charles McAdams presented a slide show about the College and then introduced a group of five musicians from the College who led the Lions in a rousing sing-along.

The performers included "Jumpin' John" Roberts, Rita "Baez" Kemp, "Grave Dave" Herring, John "Stud" Hamilton, John "Knocky" Parker, and "Bags" Bud Beattie. The group opened with "Nothing Could be Finer Than to be in Carolina" and closed with "When the Saints Go Marching In." In addition, Kemp sang "Donna Donna," Roberts sang "Where Have All the Flowers Gone?" and Herring and Hamilton sang "Frogg." Dr. Parker (MC English professor) played "Honky Tonk Train" on the piano, accompanied by Bud Beattie on the wash-tub bass and Johnny Hamilton keeping rhythm on a chair.

In yet another indication that Methodist students were enterprising in those days, a short inside article pictured Lester Mason and Johnny Hall broadcasting on WTIP (Tower in the Pines, 650 KC) from their second floor apartment in the men's residence hall. Using a low power oscillator and a turntable, Mason played records and took song requests from his listeners; the signal did not reach beyond the residence hall area on south campus.

The back page of this *sMALL TALK* carried a photo of the Gates family: Dr. Willis Gates, professor of music, Mrs. Gates, and their four daughters with violins and violas in hand. The Gates family had given a concert on campus Jan. 11, 1964.

Inside the January 1963 *sMALL TALK,* Dr. Mary Emily Miller, dean of women and instructor of history, was profiled. While being interviewed, Dr. Miller gave some highlights of her tour of Europe the previous summer which took her to 23 countries in 82 days. Aside from traveling, she said she also enjoyed sailing, swimming, listening to music, and playing clarinet with the Fayetteville Symphony Orchestra.

Mr. Bruce Pulliam, assistant professor of history, dean of men, and hall director for Cumberland Hall, remembers Dr. Miller as a colorful character:

> Dr. Miller came to Methodist from Radciffe. During my first year she hosted teas at her campus apartment. She often wore sweat suits and smoked cigars. Once, when I was the residence hall director in Cumberland Hall, she came over to tell me something. I was entertaining Jim Gosier, a prospective student from New York, and his parents. The outside steps to my apartment were being repaired, so she had to knock on the window. I opened the window and she climbed in.
>
> The Gosiers were startled by her entrance. When she left, they asked, "Who was that?"
>
> "That was our dean of women," I answered. [55]

Betty Neill Guy Parsons also remembers Dr. Miller as a colorful character. "She wore flip-flops and a humongous aquamarine ring," she said. "Occasionally, she wore a fur coat, one we doubted was real." [56]

Student Killed in Auto Accident

The front page of the February 1963 *sMALL TALK* carried a news story about the death of Lela Croom, 20, a sophomore and copy editor of the newspaper, who died from injuries sustained in an auto accident January 26,

— CHAPTER 2 —

1963. The car in which Croom was a passenger had skidded off U.S. 401 between Raeford and Fayetteville and struck a tree. Her funeral was conducted by Dr. Samuel Womack at Jernigan-Warren Funeral Home January 28.

Another front page story reported on Dr. Weaver's announcement in chapel February 25 that Methodist College would compete in intercollegiate athletics the following year and that the new gymnasium (metal building) would be opened for use by physical education students February 26.

A Page 3 story indicated that a Freshman Valentine Dance organized by Tommy Yow had been a great success and that Janet McChesney was crowned Valentine Queen. Couples danced to Bill Vowell and his combo, playing "mood or easy listening" music. A few students complained that no "rock and roll" numbers were played.

Page 5 carried a feature on Dr. Charles Ott, chemistry professor, and a news article describing how 70 student volunteers had given blood specimens and filled out questionnaires in the Student Union February 7. Dr. George M. Johnson with the Raleigh office of the U.S. Public Health Service had come to campus seeking volunteers for a study of the Asian flu epidemic which began in Robeson County and spread to Cumberland County. Dr. Johnson returned to campus later to take follow-up blood specimens.

Students cast ballots in the first SGA election in April 1963.

1960–1964

Student Government Association Formed, Elected

The College reached another milestone in February and March 1963 when the Community Council, faculty, and students ratified a constitution for the Student Government Association. The April 1963 *sMALL TALK* contained a wealth of information about the April 19 S.G.A. election and the 40 students who were running for various offices.

The student body had met March 18 during the chapel hour in the Student Union to receive nominations for S.G.A. offices. Julian Jessup and Don Parsons were nominated for president, David Herring for vice president; Betty Neill Guy, Dawn Hamby, and Cynthia Walker for secretary; Connor Holland and Danny Nau for treasurer.

Immediately following the student body meeting, students met with their respective classes to nominate class officers and senators. Three senators were to be chosen from each class: two resident students and one non-resident (commuting) student.

The two candidates for S.G.A. president, Julian Jessup and Don Parsons, were profiled at length in *sMALL TALK*. Both were rising seniors.

Jessup was from Wallace, N.C., where he grew up on a farm. He graduated from Wallace-Rose Hill High School in 1959, attended Duke University in 1959-60, and served six months in the N.C. Army National Guard before entering Methodist College in the fall of 1961. A biology major, he received a local preacher's license from The Methodist Church in 1959. In his platform, Jessup advocated more student-sponsored chapel programs and the sale of yearly tickets to three S.G.A. dances

Don Parsons was a Fayetteville native and a 1960 graduate of Fayetteville Senior High School where he played varsity baseball and basketball. He entered Methodist in the fall of 1960 and took the fall 1962 semester off to tour Europe with a friend. During his campaign, Parsons said he wanted to foster a closer relationship between resident students and day students and between faculty members and students. He said he would also work for improved activities for students at the Student Union and the gymnasium.

Another Page 1 story in the April 1963 *sMALL TALK* concerned Methodist joining five other colleges to form the Dixie Intercollegiate Athletic Conference. The D.I.A.C. charter members were: Methodist College, North Carolina Wesleyan College, St. Andrews College, Charlotte College, College of Charleston, and Lynchburg College. The story noted that Methodist would field teams in 1963-64 in basketball, tennis and golf. Conference members approved plans to eventually sponsor competition in basketball, baseball, tennis, golf, soccer, track, cross country, and wrestling.

— CHAPTER 2 —

Trustees Acknowledge W. E. Horner Gift of $100,000

At their May 7, 1963, meeting, the Methodist College trustees expressed their thanks to Mr. and Mrs. W. E. Horner of Sanford, N.C. for establishing a $100,000 fund to build an Administration Building at the College. The trustees also thanked retiring board member Frank McBryde for his service as board treasurer.

In other business, the trustees approved operating budgets for 1963-64: $585,096 for operating expense and $144,795 for capital outlay. Included in the operating budget was $43,537 in interest on dormitory bonds. Speaking of future debt retirement on the two dormitories under construction, Dr. Weaver said, "The following year, 1964-65, we will have to contribute an additional $40,000 for amortization payments and to create a reserve fund." [57]

The trustees elected the following officers for 1962-63: Terry Sanford, chairman; W. Robert Johnson, vice chairman; J. W. Hensdale, secretary; and Wilson Yarborough Sr., treasurer. Trustees nominated to four-year terms ending July 1, 1967 were: V. E. Queen, Joe Tally Jr., Mrs. Walter Davis, J. W. Page, W. E. Horner, and Lenox G. Cooper.

The board approved President Weaver's recommendation that tuition be increased $50 per semester or $100 per year beginning in September 1964.

President Weaver presented the following low bids for construction of the library ($434,543), chapel ($101,281), and bell tower ($19,000) as submitted by D. R. Allen Co. of Fayetteville. The trustees accepted Dr. Weaver's recommendation to accept the bids on the library and bell tower and reject the bids on the chapel.

When the trustees' Executive Committee met July 18, 1963, the members voted to absorb the salaries and expenses of the Fayetteville College Foundation into the operating budget of the College and to make disbursements on behalf of the Foundation. It was agreed that the Foundation would transfer sufficient funds to the College operating budget to cover these costs.

In his annual report to the board, Dr. Weaver reported that Methodist enrolled 380 students during 1962-63 and that applications for 1963-64 were running 50 percent ahead of the same time a year ago. "Student patronage continues to be one of our problems," he said, "despite what you may read about the great flood of students which is overwhelming the colleges. It is not happening here. Perhaps this is to be expected in a new institution which is not known in a very wide area as yet, and which has not received formal accreditation." [58]

Dr. Weaver said the $90,000 costs for the new gymnasium (metal building) was paid for by a gift of $68,000 from R. J. Reynolds Tobacco Co.

and a $25,000 Foundation grant. He also expressed to the board his desire to hire a student recruiter to help Mr. McAdams and a full-time director of development for the College.

The president concluded his annual report for 1962-63 by extending special thanks to Board Chairman Terry Sanford and other members of the trustees' Executive Committee, to Director of Public Relations Charles McAdams (who attended 138 college day programs in North and South Carolina and Virginia), to Comptroller Frank Eason, and to Director of Admissions and Registrar Sam Edwards for their service to the College during the 1962-63 school year.

College Begins Third Year with Ten New Faculty Members

Methodist College began its third academic year, 1963-64, with 470 students, ten new faculty members, and two new residence halls—Garber Hall for women and Cumberland Hall for men. The College library was under construction.

In the fall of 1963, the student body consisted of 214 freshmen, 137 sophomores, 66 juniors, and 53 seniors. A total of 191 students were living on campus. Male students outnumbered female 275 to 195.

The new faculty members included: Addison R. Barker Jr., assistant professor of English—A.B. High Point College, M.A., University of North Carolina; George P. Chandler, instructor in philosophy—A.B. Elon College, B.D. Vanderbilt University, graduate study Emory University; Gene T. Clayton, instructor in physical education—A.B. Catawba College, M.Ed. University of North Carolina; Carlyle Cross, professor of English—A.B. Mercer University, M.A. Duke University, Ph.D., University of Georgia; Elizabeth F. Garthly, assistant professor art—B.F.A. University of Pennsylvania, M.S. Temple University, graduate study Pennsylvania State University; Helen Elizabeth Jones, assistant professor of English—A.B. Harvard University, M.A. University of Wyoming, graduate study University of Colorado; Alan M. Porter, instructor in voice—B.M. Mt. Union College, M.M. University of Illinois; Joyce Elaine Porter, instructor of French—B.A. Mt. Union College, M.A. Duke University; further study, University of Illinois; Allen P. Wadsworth Jr., instructor in sociology—A.B. Howard College, B.D. Southeastern Baptist Theological Seminary, M.Ed. University of North Carolina; Robert Parker Wilson, assistant professor of history—B.A. Wake Forest College, M.A. Peabody College, graduate study the University of North Carolina.

New staff members included the Rev. Bill Lowdermilk, assistant director of public relations, and John R. Parker, director of the Student Union. Lowdermilk came to Methodist after serving as pastor of Culbreth Memorial Methodist

— CHAPTER 2 —

Church in Fayetteville for five years. A native of Norman, N.C., he held degrees from Emory University and Duke University. Parker was a retired Army officer who had previously worked at Fort Bragg.

Marketing Methodist

The September 1963 *Bulletin of Methodist College* was designed as a recruitment brochure aimed at prospective students. Entitled "Your Invitation to A Stimulating Venture in Higher Education," this particular newsletter was filled with pictures of current students and campus buildings. In the early years of the College, the *Bulletin* was often used for marketing purposes. The College catalogue served as one of the *Bulletin's* quarterly issues, enabling the College to bulk mail large numbers of catalogues at Second Class (periodical) postage rates.

sMALL TALK Lists New Developments

The lead story on the front page of the October 1963 *sMALL TALK* concerned a pending accreditation visit to Methodist by the North Carolina College Conference Examination Board in October and a preliminary accreditation visit by the Southern Association of Colleges and Schools scheduled for spring 1964. Another story described the features of the new library which was under construction.

sMALL TALK Editor Lois Stephenson had plenty of milestones to report. There would be a new infirmary in the small apartment building formerly used as a women's residence hall, and the nurse was Mrs. Grady Snyder. Several walls had been knocked out to make new quarters for the Music Department

MC's first cheeleaders pose in the "tin can" gym in 1963.

In early 1963, a Jostens representative measured students for their class rings.

in the small apartment building that had served as a men's residence hall. The first yearbook staff, headed by Editor Reese Edwards, had chosen the name *Carillon*, referring to the bell system in the bell tower.

sMALL TALK's inside pages included two photos from spring 1963, one of May Queen Betty Neill Guy and another of Marlen Barnhardt and Jerry Wood receiving their class rings from a Josten's representative. A committee headed by John Ormond had worked with several companies on a class ring design the preceding year.

An article on the back page profiled Shad Bosher (Ernest Sheridan Bosher Jr.), a 21-year-old history major from Fayetteville who had spent the previous summer visiting London, Paris, Madrid, Rome, Athens, Berlin, Amsterdam, Jerusalem, and Algiers. In the course of being interviewed for this story, Bosher described some colorful characters he had met during his travels, persons who "made me aware of the many fears, drives, frustrations, beliefs and dreams that comprise human nature, regardless of the race or nationality involved." [59] He expressed a strong belief in individualism and the value of personal experience "in testing and placing a person's beliefs in proper sequence." [60]

In a "Letter to the Editor," Frank Jeter Jr., former executive director of the Fayetteville College Foundation, explained that although he had just purchased and intended to operate the *Spring Lake Times*, he would always remain close

— CHAPTER 2 —

In the fall of 1962 and 1963, Cumberland's Yama Yamas were the intramural football champs.

to Methodist College. "We have a great school here," he wrote, "destined for real service now and in the future. I'm proud that I have been allowed to be a part of it for the past four and a half years, and of course will always be one of the strongest supporters, in every way that I can, of this great cause." [61]

Trustees Approve New Loans

Members of the trustees' Executive Committee met October 30, 1963 and voted to apply for a new federal loan to build two more residence halls. The Committee also authorized President Weaver to borrow $100,000 to complete construction of the library and approved names for the new residence halls. Garber Hall, the new women's dorm, was named for Methodist Bishop Paul N. Garber, and Cumberland Hall, the men's dorm, was named in honor of those Cumberland County residents who had helped support and build Methodist College.

The full Board of Trustees met November 15, 1963 and approved a resolution of application to the federal Housing and Home Finance Agency, Community Facilities Administration, for a loan to build two more residence halls. The board also appointed four trustees—Joe Tally Jr., F. D. Byrd, W. E. Horner, and Grady Dawson—to a Presidential Inauguration Committee charged with planning the inauguration of Dr. L. Stacy Weaver as president of Methodist College April 9, 1964. The committee was also to have faculty and staff representation.

The following faculty and staff members were named later to serve with the trustees on the Inauguration Committee: Dr. Millard P. Burt, chairman; Alva W. Stewart, Frank Eason, Grady Snyder, Charles McAdams, Sam Edwards, Dr. Willis Gates, Dr. Charles Ott, and Dr. Samuel Womack.

MC Leaders Attack Speaker-Ban Law

Speaking at Methodist's fourth Founders Day program November 16, 1963, Fayetteville attorney and Methodist College trustee Joe Tally Jr. denounced the North Carolina General Assembly for enacting the "speaker ban law" prohibiting communists and those who had invoked the Fifth Amendment (refusing to answer questions based on the grounds of self-incrimination) from speaking at U.N.C. campuses and other state-supported institutions. The law was passed late in the 1963 session.

Tally said the law was a clear violation of the First Amendment to the U.S. Constitution, adding, "I do not know of any man who knows the process of education who could be for the act." [62] Saying he had enjoyed freedom of expression during a recent visit to the University of Moscow, Tally said the University of North Carolina should not be bound by a law prohibiting speeches by communists.

Tally said Methodist College "is conceived as welcoming all free and fair discussion so that we will have open minds on all things." [63] He then turned to the theme of his address, extolling the principles of "open heart and open mind."

"Man has not yet attained the true 'open mind'," he said. "There was no true conception of the individual being present until the time of Christ." [64] The speaker cited John Wesley, the founder of Methodism, for developing a "fresh" approach to religion in which each child of God is challenged to open his heart and mind to God's will.

Methodist's first bowling team performed well in 1963-64.

— CHAPTER 2 —

Tally concluded his address by defending freedom of speech and saying, "[. . .] the twins of God's creation, this open heart, this open mind, they dwell together in the temple of truth." [65]

In the November 1963 *sMALL TALK,* Methodist College senior Connor Holland took his own whack at North Carolina's "speaker ban law" with an allegory entitled "Question." In Holland's story, Citizen and his friend Minority embark on a journey to Freeland "to learn of the world and of truth." When the Scribes pass a law preventing subversives from speaking at the centers of education, Minority and Citizen object:

> [. . .] So those who were like ostriches and donkeys and isolationists in the Scribes expelled Minority and set upon Citizen angrily in their self-righteousness screaming 'Esse Quam Videri' (the N.C. motto—To be rather than to seem.) and tried and gagged him before he could protest. They tore his parchment from his hand and with it ran guiltily from the scene. [66]

Holland's story describes much rejoicing among the residents of the Darklands and Communeland upon learning of the new law enacted by the

The first men's basketball team took the floor in the fall of 1963.

Scribes. Meanwhile, Citizen was ostracized and received little support from his fellow Freelanders. But from behind his gag, Citizen "swore upon the altar of God eternal hostility against every form of tyranny over the mind of man." [67]

Holland's allegory was one of the earliest examples of political satire to appear in sMALL TALK.

In the ensuing years, the Student Government Association at Methodist, the State Student Legislature, and student leaders at most colleges and universities across the state lobbied the legislature to have the speaker ban law repealed. In February, 1968, in the case of Dickson vs. Sitterson, the U.S. District Court in Greensboro ruled the law unconstitutional.

The General Assembly finally repealed the law in 1995. An official in the North Carolina Legislative Library said state Sen. Aaron Plyler introduced the bill which finally repealed the act. [68]

MC Fields Basketball Team

The inauguration of intercollegiate basketball received front page coverage in the December 1963 sMALL TALK. The Methodist team lost its first five games, to Charlotte College, Campbell College, Guilford College, St. Andrews College, and Wilmington College. Methodist's first basketball victory came Jan. 7, 1964 at home against North Carolina Wesleyan College.

The starting five included: George Potts (captain), Carson Harmon, Herman Britt, Don Parsons, and David Altman Jr. The other squad members were: Bud Beattie, Larry Harris, Jerry Huckabee and Phil Levine Jr.

Seldon "Sparky" Rapelye was Methodist's lone entry in a Dixie Conference cross country meet Nov. 16, 1963, finishing 15th in a field of 31 runners.

The Monarch bowling team made its debut against North Carolina Wesleyan, winning three games and losing one. Reese Edwards was the team's leading scorer.

Campus Grieves Over JFK

The assassination of U.S. President John F. Kennedy November 22, 1963, in Dallas, Texas, stunned and deeply saddened members of the Methodist College family. On the morning of Kennedy's funeral, Monday, Nov. 25, 1963, Dr. Samuel Womack, college chaplain, had a television placed near the podium for the regularly scheduled chapel service in the Student Union. With volume muted, the TV was tuned to live coverage of the Kennedy funeral from Washington, D.C. Dr. Womack delivered a moving eulogy to Kennedy, as the audience watched images of the funeral cortege on the TV screen. It was a scene that many students and staff members would never forget.

— CHAPTER 2 —

In his eulogy, the college chaplain issued the following challenge to those present:

> Let us in these grim hours see ourselves for what we really are or may become. Let us not forget that those whom we are so ready to condemn for their terrible deeds are our brothers, nor that He whom we claim as Lord has told us that we are our brother's keepers. Let us not become ourselves victims of the very poison of hate which has so horrified us in the deeds of these past few days.
> Nor let us in these hours despair of man and his world. Despite the violence that has dominated our agonized attention, this is not a world gone mad; it is a world in which human dignity, human decency, the nobility of human character is being manifested all about us, as it was manifested so splendidly by the leader we mourn. [69] (See Appendix K for the complete text of Dr. Womack's eulogy.)

The editorial page of the December 1963 *sMALL TALK* featured a picture of Kennedy, a transcript of Dr. Womack's eulogy, and the following poem by David Herring, a Methodist College junior:

"a pocket full of why"

Someone standing brought a cheer
while no one squints an eye
Someone falling wrought a tear
"oh no" - - but no reply
many and more but mainly two
SUCH a lovely little town
but only she knew what to do
sit up to hold him when he fell down

see how red the innocent;
whisper "thou shalt not"
evil is no accident
now by was and who by what
a day can be a petty thing
so silent slipping by
but rear just once to take a life
then fade between the sky

so sing a song of sadness
a pocket full of why
a bullet sings so sad a song
to make a nation cry. [70]

Methodist celebrated Christmas in 1963 with a holiday dance December 6 featuring The Embers, a popular "beach music" band, and three other events: a Christmas chapel program December 18, a Christmas concert by the Methodist College Chorus December 19, and the president's annual Christmas luncheon for students, faculty and administration December 20.

Foundation Hires New Executive

The December 1963 *Bulletin of Methodist College* announced that Hank Perry had been hired as executive director of the Fayetteville College Foundation

Bill Wolfe and Betty Neil Guy gave a joint senior music recital February 9, 1964.

to replace Frank Jeter Jr. who resigned in September to take over publication of the *Spring Lake (N.C.) Times*.

A Fayetteville resident and a deacon at First Presbyterian Church, Perry had previously served as director of Camp Pineacres at Lakewood near Fayetteville, and as director of Christian education and administration at First Presbyterian Church.

First Students Named to Who's Who

The February 1964 *sMALL TALK* carried a short article about six seniors who had been tapped for inclusion in the 1964 volume of *Who's Who Among Students in American Universities and Colleges.* The honorees were: Betty Bunce, Reese Edwards, Robert Lapke, Louis Spilman Jr., Francis Stewart, and William Wolfe. Dr. Millard P. Burt, academic dean, announced the College's first Who's Who recipients in chapel January 7, 1964.

The first recital by senior music majors was the subject of a front page article and photo. William Wolfe and Betty Neill Guy gave a joint recital February 9, 1964. Guy sang songs by Schubert, Massenet, Haydn and Bohm. Wolfe performed works by Brahms, Scriabin, Mendelssohn, Debussy and Liszt. Wolfe performed Beethoven's "Fifth Piano Concerto" March 21 with the Fayetteville Symphony.

Coverage of Dr. Weaver's inauguration as College president dominated the front page and inside pages of the April 24, 1964 *sMALL TALK*. Dr. Weaver and his wife Elizabeth were profiled in separate feature stories on inside pages. Another front page story in this issue announced that David Altman, a junior from Olean, New York, had been elected S.G.A. president for 1964-65.

A short inside story recounted another milestone, Methodist College's first student dramatic production, March 5, 1964. Green and Gold Masque Keys, the drama club, had presented "America Speaks," written and directed by Miriam L. Usrey, instructor in English and speech. The production was done in a reader's theatre format, using a variety of readings about the American ideal.

Trustees Approve Hiring of Fund-raisers

In a March 9, 1964, meeting, the Executive Committee of the Methodist College Board of Trustees authorized President Weaver to hire Col. William Pope as assistant to the president for fund-raising, effective July 1, 1964.

Dr. Weaver told the Executive Committee there was an urgent need to raise funds to finish paying D. R. Allen Co. for construction of the library. The trustees authorized the president to hire Winston McClellan, a consultant from Durham, N.C., until June 1, 1964, to raise the necessary funds.

1960–1964

At the April 9, 1964, annual meeting, the Board of Trustees approved a list of 43 candidates for graduation on June 1 and President Weaver's proposed budgets for 1964-65: $844,632 for operating and $100,191 for capital outlay.

In his written annual report to the board, Dr. Weaver said Methodist had enrolled a total of 525 students in the fall and spring semesters of 1963-64 and 144 students in its first (1963) summer session. He said the new men's and women's residence halls achieved a 50 percent occupancy rate and that resident students made up 40 percent of the student body. He also reported that 44 percent of the full-time students were Methodist.

Dr. Weaver said the summer session included an outstanding reading development/laboratory experience enabling public school teachers to observe 92 school children (ages three-and-one-half to five) in demonstration classes taught by Dr. Vearl G. McBryde, professor of education. Dr. Weaver said 67 "bright" youngsters were enrolled in rapid reading classes and 25 others in remedial reading classes. He said all the youngsters made "startling" gains in reading proficiency.

In the area of finances, Dr. Weaver said Methodist's share of returns from the Methodist conference's campaign for the colleges had not been sufficient to meet payments for construction of the library. He said a $30,000 grant from the Mary Babcock Reynolds Foundation and $15,000 from the Kresge Foundation had made it possible to begin construction of the library. He said once the library was finished the College needed to begin retiring its $1 million debt to First Citizens Bank. He said the Fayetteville College Foundation was providing enough money to pay the interest on the $1 million.

Dr. Weaver ended his 1964 annual report with his usual rhetorical flair: "In fine, I should say that, barring our poverty, the state of the College is good; the heart of the College is strong; the vision of the College is eternal." [71]

College Offers Summer Scholarships to Teachers
The March 1964 *Bulletin of Methodist College* promoted the 1964 summer session slated for June 8-July 17. Twenty-nine courses, including private music lessons, were listed. For the first time, the College offered 25 full tuition scholarships for teachers employed in North Carolina public schools who needed certificate renewal credits.

Stacy Weaver Inaugurated College President
Dr. L. Stacy Weaver was formally inaugurated as president of Methodist College Friday morning, April 10, 1964 in an impressive ceremony in the Student Union. A large contingent of academicians processed from the Classroom Building to the Student Union.

— CHAPTER 2 —

The Fayetteville Symphony Orchestra, under the direction of Dr. Willis Gates, played "French Baroque Suite" as the prelude and the hymn "God of Our Fathers" as the academic procession entered the Union.

The audience included, in addition to College students, staff and supporters, 93 official delegates from other colleges, universities, church and professional associations. Dr. Weaver's mother, sister, three brothers, and two of his three sons were also present. Greetngs were brought by Julian Jessup, S.G.A. president; Charles Ott, professor of chemistry; Paul Garber, resident bishop, Richmond Area, The Methodist Church; and Ivy May Hixson, president, North Carolina College Conference. The Methodist College Chorus sang "O Give Thanks Unto the Lord" and a College song written by Virginia Kern, a member of the Class of 1964.

The guest speaker for the occasion was Dr. John R. Gross of Nashville, Tenn., general secretary, Division of Higher Education, Board of Education of The Methodist Church.

Speaking on the subject, "The Christian College Marches Backward Into the Future," Dr. Gross said modern higher education in America began with a "small spring of Christian idealism in New England" which led to a natural affinity between religion and the liberal arts. [72]

Terry Sanford assists Dr. L. Stacy Weaver, College president, prior to Dr. Weaver's inauguration.

Tracing the developments of the 19th century, Dr. Gross said Darwin's *Origin of the Species*, passage of the Morrill Act in 1862 (providing grants of land to states for the establishment of primarily agricultural colleges), and the influx of German trained professors in the graduate school shifted the focus of education from religion to science.

"In order for the church-related college to be a recognized part of American education," he said, "it must be a sound educational institution with an emphasis on the liberal arts and the Christian heritage. It must also be a place where students are not only educated to do something but to be something." [73]

President Weaver's inauguration received prominent coverage in the April 10 and 11 editions of *The Fayetteville Observer*. In his coverage of the main address by Dr. John Gross, the Methodist Church's top official in higher education, reporter Bill Wright emphasized a fear voiced by Dr. Gross and others involved in higher education "that the American college student is not now a crusader . . . and the belief that, "It is not good for the health of the nation to have its students standing on the sidelines and not identified with idealistic causes." [74]

Following Dr. Gross's address, Trustees Chairman and North Carolina Governor Terry Sanford gave the charge to the president and performed the installation. Bishop Paul Garber of The North Carolina Conference of The Methodist Church offered the prayer of dedication.

Dr. Weaver prefaced his inaugural address, "From Cotton Field to College," by saying he was being inaugurated seven years after he was hired because he chose to wait until the college had four classes on campus. His address focused primarily on the proper role of the "church-supported college" in America. He said the church college should train the future leaders of both the church and society.

He said the original Greek concept of liberal education for a leisure class had been broadened in the modern era to include the natural sciences, pre-professional training, and teacher education. Dr. Weaver said he favored a full year of professional training for teachers beyond the bachelor's degree, which could be attained in four calendar years at Methodist by the adoption of a three-semester academic calendar (fall, spring, summer).

Methodist's first president said the purpose of a Christian liberal arts education is "to release and harness the limitless power of the human spirit." [75] He also argued that, "Conscience, no less than competence, is the proper concern of the church college." [76]

President Weaver concluded his address by saying, "Development and strengthening of the spiritual nature of man once occupied a position of

— CHAPTER 2 —

pre-eminence among the purposes of higher education. Let it be restored." [77]
(See Appendix K for the complete text of Dr. Weaver's inaugural address.)

Trustees Honored, Residence Halls Dedicated

Following the inauguration of Dr. L. Stacy Weaver, an inaugural luncheon was held in the College dining hall for official representatives and guests. Those offering greetings to the president were: Wilbur Clark, mayor of Fayetteville; Richard L. Player Jr., president, Fayetteville College Foundation; A. C. Dawson, executive secretary, North Carolina Education Association; Charles F. Carroll, state superintendent of public instruction; William C. Archie, director, North Carolina Board of Higher Education; D. Trigg Jones, executive secretary, Southeastern Jurisdictional Council, The Methodist Church; C. P. Morris, executive secretary, Board of Education, North Carolina Conference of The Methodist Church. Joe Tally Jr., a Methodist College trustee, responded to the greetings.

President Weaver recognized the trustees of the College and presented each with a certificate of service.

May 1964: Reese Edwards presents the first **Carillon** *(yearbook) to Terry Sanford.*

After the luncheon, dedication and naming ceremonies were held at the two new residence halls: Garber Hall for women, and Cumberland Hall for men. Plaques were unveiled in the lobby of each residence hall, noting that Garber Hall was dedicated in honor of Methodist Bishop Paul Neff Garber and Cumberland Hall was dedicated to the residents of Cumberland County who had contributed to the founding of the College.

More Firsts Cited in *sMALL TALK*

The lead story in the May 1964 *sMALL TALK* described the May 16, 1964, presentation of Mozart's *Requiem Mass in D Minor* by the Methodist College Chorus and the Fayetteville Symphony Orchestra. Dr. Willis Gates conducted. Soloists were: Alan Porter, tenor; Sally Wyly, soprano; Katherine Stone, contralto; and Otis Lambert Jr., bass.

Also treated as front page news was a photo of *Carillon* Editor Reese Edwards presenting a copy of the first College yearbook to Trustees Chairman Terry Sanford. Another Page One story described "Shades of Shakespeare," a May 7, 1964, reader's theatre offering by Green and Gold Masque-Keys, the drama club. Actors Jim Davies, Nancy Best, Babette Persons and Dick Meissner performed scenes from *Hamlet, Othello, Richard III,* and *Henry IV.*

Inside news stories chronicled visits to the campus by Dr. Allard Lowenstein, a controversial civil rights activist and political science professor at N.C. State College, and Judge Richardson Preyer, candidate in the Democratic primary for governor of North Carolina.

Speakers for the College's first commencement were also announced in the May 24 *sMALL TALK*. Dr. Mark Depp, minister emeritus of Centenary Methodist Church in Winston-Salem, N.C., would deliver the baccalaureate sermon Sunday morning, May 31 at Hay Street Methodist Church in Fayetteville. Bishop Paul N. Garber would give the commencement address June 1.

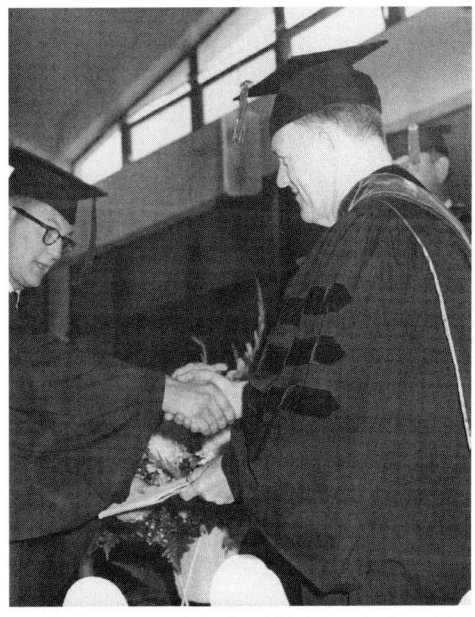

Guy Beattie received the first MC degree in June 1964

— CHAPTER 2 —

The editorial page featured insightful commentaries by Charles Stewart, defending the N.C. General Assembly for enacting a law (the famous speaker ban law) prohibiting Communists and invokers of the Fifth Amendment from speaking at state-supported colleges and universities, and Bob Harris, defending the college youth of his day.

Inside was a photo of the 1964 May Dance Court headed by Connie James, May Queen. Miss James was a sophomore from Fort Bragg. On the back page was a detailed diary account by Babette Persons of her weekend at the Azalea Festival in Wilmington, N.C., where she represented Methodist College. The sports page announced that Carson Harmon had been named Most Valuable Player in basketball and that Phil Levine had won the Outstanding Intramural Athlete Award.

College Graduates First Class

A week prior to Methodist's first commencement, Barbara Hauser of *The Fayetteville Observer* wrote a feature story in which she profiled the College's first graduating class. Her article was accompanied by a photo of the senior class officers: Ralph Hoggard, treasurer; Jerry Wood, president; Patsy Melvin, secretary; and Jimmy Johnson, vice president.

Methodist's first graduates, the Class of 1964, received their degrees Monday, June 1, 1964.

In her profile of the first graduates, Miss Hauser included the following facts:

— 34 would receive Bachelor of Arts degrees and nine Bachelor of Science degrees.
— 21 of the graduating seniors had enrolled as freshmen.
— 30 had completed teacher training.
— 21 were married.
— the class included two retired Army majors, many housewives, a grandmother, and a woman from White Oak, N.C., whose son was a junior at Methodist. [78]

Commencement activities for Methodist College's first graduating class began Sunday morning, May 31 with a baccalaureate service at Fayetteville's Hay Street Methodist Church. Dr. Mark Depp, minister emeritus of Centenary Methodist Church in Winston-Salem, N.C., delivered the baccalaureate sermon, entitled, "Living in Four Dimensions." At 4 p.m. that afternoon, President and Mrs. Weaver hosted a reception for the graduates and their families in the lobby of Garber Hall.

Methodist College awarded diplomas to its first 43 graduates June 1, 1964, in the Student Union. Dr. Millard P. Burt, academic dean, introduced the graduates and College President L. Stacy Weaver presented the degrees. Guy Beattie of Raleigh, N.C., received the first diploma, a Bachelor of Arts in Business Administration.

In his commencement address, Methodist Bishop Paul N. Garber cited Bishop Frances Asbury, the first Methodist bishop in America and the circuit rider portrayed in the College seal, as a figure of poverty, humility, sympathy and kindness who achieved an internal happiness through service to others. He urged the graduates to follow Asbury's example rather than seeking happiness through material things.

Four members of the Class of 1964 graduated with honors: *magna cum laude*, Ralph Finton Hoggard, Virginia Knox Kern; *cum laude*, Betty Graham Bunce, Louise Freeman Council. Ralph Hoggard received the first annual Lucius Stacy Weaver Award given to an outstanding member of the graduating class. Hoggard was selected by the faculty based on the following qualifications: exceptional scholarship, excellence of character, leadership abilities, devotion to Christian ideals, creative contributions to the total college program, and humanitarian service on and off campus.

— CHAPTER 2 —

Trustees Award Contracts

Meeting June 1, 1964, the Methodist College Board of Trustees awarded a construction contract for two additional residence halls (Weaver Hall, Sanford Hall) to D. R. Allen & Son of Fayetteville for $1,165,634. A separate contract for a new boiler for the Boiler Plant was awarded to J. J. Barnes, Inc., a local plumbing contractor, for $42,900. President Weaver announced that Mr. and Mrs. Wilson Yarborough Sr. had agreed to donate $20,000 for construction of the College bell tower.

The board also approved an amendment to Article XVII of the College charter to provide that in the event of dissolution of the corporation known as Methodist College, "all properties shall become the property of the North Carolina Annual Conference of The Methodist Church, Southeastern Jurisdiction of The Methodist Church." [79]

The trustees' Executive Committee met July 23, 1964 and approved a revised operating budget for 1964-65 of $830,430. The committee also elected Dr. Allen Brantley, a College trustee, to represent Methodist College on the board of trustees of The Methodist Foundation. President Weaver reported that construction of the College library was nearly complete.

Brantley Speaks at Founders Day, Trustees Meet

Methodist College observed its fifth Founders Day November 2, 1964. Dr. Allen P. Brantley of Burlington, N.C., one of the original College trustees, gave the keynote address.

Citing the importance of Christian higher education, Dr. Brantley said, "Living in an age of turmoil, tension and confusion, we must have an inward directiveness that guides us in our living. If not, life become merely a dead end [. . .] our job here is not only to make the world a better place for us to live but also a better place for the next generation." [80]

At the Board of Trustees later that day, President Weaver reported a fall enrollment of 619 students and two major gifts—$50,000 from Mrs. Gilbert Verney of Belle Haven, Greenwich, Conn. for library equipment and furniture and $50,000 from the Z. Smith Reynolds Foundation toward construction of the Administration Building.

President Weaver also reported that the College had received gifts totalling $150,000 toward the cost of building the Administration Building. Dr. Weaver also cited an urgent need to air-condition the Student Union Building before the 1965 summer session at an estimated cost of $40,000.

Finally, the Board approved the conferring of degrees to five students who had completed their graduation requirements during the summer term. As a result of that action, the Class of 1964 grew to 48 students.

1960–1964

Democrats Win *sMALL TALK* Poll

The front page of the November 1964 *sMALL TALK* featured a picture of Methodist's new library and carried the banner headline "Lyndon Johnson Wins Poll." The headline referred to a presidential preference poll in which 172 students participated. Lyndon Johnson, the Democratic candidate for president, was the choice of 86 students; 79 students voted for his Republican opponent Barry Goldwater. Students also preferred Dan K. Moore, the Democratic candidate for governor of North Carolina, giving him 99 votes to 65 for Robert Gavin.

Senior history major Walter Turner also made the front page. Turner had just been elected chairman of the North Carolina Federation of College Young Democrats.

An interview with Loraine Black, a junior from Baltimore, Md., was also featured on Page One. A native of Edinburgh, Scotland, Miss Black had just filed a petition to become a U.S. citizen.

sMALL TALK Editor Loche McLean ran a short editorial decrying conformity among college students, citing the current fad of wearing Bass weejun loafers along with Madras and tablecloth checkered shirts. McLean suggested that conformity in dress was a symptom of a larger problem. "Do people conform because they are afraid of being unpopular or afraid of being

Davis Memorial Library opened in the fall of 1964.

— CHAPTER 2 —

criticized?" he asked. "Or is it just easier to let someone else do your thinking? Think it over." [81]

College Wins Academic Recognitions

In October 1964, a visiting committee assembled by the Southern Association of Colleges and Schools visited Methodist College and recommended that the school be awarded early recognition and the status of candidate for membership.

In early November 1964, the North Carolina College Conference ruled that Methodist College had operated under senior college standards in 1963-64 and should be granted full accreditation effective in 1964-65. This action ensured that Methodist's first teacher education graduates (Class of 1964) would be fully certified by the North Carolina Department of Public Instruction and that other colleges in the state would accept course credits from Methodist.

These actions brought to three the number of academic recognitions won by Methodist College. The first recognition came in January 1962 when the University Senate of The Methodist Church ruled that the College had met the requirements of the church for the undergraduate training of ministers.

Juniors Win Book-Moving Contest

Accepting a challenge from S.G.A. President David Altman, Methodist College's four class presidents organized and directed a book-moving contest

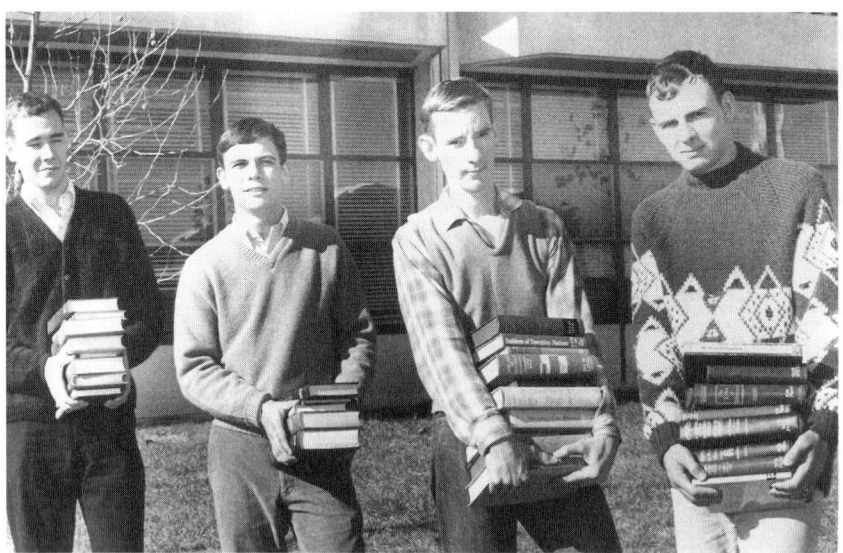

Students from the four classes moved books to the new library in November 1964. L to R, John Gardner, Bill Tarr, Larry Barnes, and Sparky Rapelye.

held Monday, November. 23, 1964. In a remarkable display of cooperation and school spirit, hundreds of students moved more than 20,000 books and an assortment of furniture and equipment from the temporary library in the Classroom Building to the new library on the bell tower mall. (Student volunteers did the moving during times they were not in class.) Long lines began forming outside the temporary library before 8 a.m. A scorekeeper's table was set up inside the door of the new library.

The junior class, led by Larry Barnes, won the contest and $40 by making 740 trips. The senior class, led by Sparky Rapelye, was a close second, followed by the sophomores (led by Bill Tarr) and the freshmen (led by John Gardner). More than 3,000 trips were made during the day, with many students running from building to building to increase the score for their class. Librarian Robert Mabson and five staff members were stationed in different areas of the new library to show students where to place each book or item of equipment. The necessary shelving had been previously installed on the main floor and the mezzanine of the new library. The move was completed without a hitch, and the library was open for student use the next day.

The Bulletin of Methodist College (March 1965) said the student book-moving project was the brainchild of Mr. Mabson, who had consulted with other librarians about the best way to move an entire collection. Mabson took the idea to Dean of Students O. E. Dowd; then Dowd and Mabson asked S.G.A. President David Altman to present the idea to the class presidents. It was agreed that the class making the most trips (in proportion to its size) would be named the winner, with a $40 prize going to the winning class and $20 going to the class that came in second.

Friends of Terry Sanford Raise $25,000 for Scholarship

Six thousand friends and supporters of North Carolina Governor Terry Sanford packed Dorton Arena in Raleigh, N.C., December 4, 1964, for a Sanford appreciation dinner. Sanford was slated to complete his term as governor in January, 1965.

The highlight of the evening came when Hargrove Bowles, Jr. presented Sanford with a check for $25,000 to establish the Terry Sanford Scholarship Fund at Methodist College. The money was contributed by Sanford friends and admirers from across the state.

The master of ceremonies for the evening was composer Richard Adler who had been a classmate of Sanford's at the University of North Carolina. A succession of speakers praised Sanford for his achievements as governor, saying his program to improve education in the state was a model for the nation. Those offering words of praise were U.S. Commissioner of Education Francis Keppel; Amory Houghton Jr., chairman of the board of Corning Glass Works, and Sidney Blackmer, actor and chairman of the advisory board of the North Carolina School of the Arts; and Hargrove "Skipper" Bowles Jr.

In a telegram to Governor Sanford, U.S. President Lyndon Johnson said Sanford's efforts in education and in the war on poverty "have set a standard for the whole nation, bringing recognition to your state and quality to the lives of your people."[82] Johnson told Sanford he was "confident that the monument to your term of office will not be built by the hands of men, but by the rewards of your efforts in the years to come." [83]

Local Resident Makes Plea for Funds

The December 1964 edition of *The Fayetteville Observer* carried a remarkably candid and detailed story by Barbara Hauser. Headlined "A Brick and a Promise Not Enough," the story concerned Fayetteville and Cumberland County's failure to raise the funds promised to Methodist College:

> [. . .] citizens of Fayetteville and Cumberland County are now $700,000 behind in their pledge for capital development and some $85,000 short in the total operating fund pledges for the past four years.
> Needless to say, when this amount has been planned in the budget of each year, it takes some astute juggling to cover necessary expenditures made from promises made which never materialized. [84]

The article noted that the Fayetteville College Foundation had recently come up with a Planned Effort Program (PEP) allowing local supporters to choose monthly, quarterly, semi-annual or annual notices of amounts due on their pledges to Methodist College.

Hauser concluded her article with the following appeal to local citizens: "Citizens of Fayetteville and Cumberland County purchased a college with borrowed money; time is past due to retire the debt and to aid with current operating expenses. A brick and a promise are not enough." [85]

President Briefs Trustees

As 1964 came to a close, College President Stacy Weaver reported to the Board of Trustees Dec. 16 that Methodist College had been accepted as a candidate for membership by the Southern Association of Colleges and Schools. Dr. Weaver reviewed the SACS accreditation standards the College would have to meet, noting that Methodist would be eligible for full accreditation in the fall of 1966 after graduating its third class.

The trustees took one major action at the December meeting, authorizing Weaver to borrow up to $100,000 from Branch Banking & Trust Co. to make the final payment due the contractor for work on the College library.

— CHAPTER 2 —

END NOTES
Chapter Two

1. *Bulletin of Methodist College* (first college catalogue), Vol. 1, No. 1, January 1960, file.
2. *The Fayetteville Observer*, January 3, 1960, file.
3. L. Stacy Weaver, "President's Report to the Methodist College Board of Trustees," May 24, 1960, TM, Book 1.
4. Minutes of the March 15, 1960 meeting of the Board of Directors of the Fayetteville College Foundation.
5. Dune Macdonald and Don Brewer to the Fayetteville College Foundation Executive Committee, June 16, 1960, FCF, file.
6. Franklin Clark and John Hensdale, meeting of the Fayetteville College Foundation Executive Committee, June 16, 1960, file.
7. Terry Sanford, in a speech seconding the nomination of John F. Kennedy as president, Democratic National Convention, Los Angeles, Cal., July 13, 1960, cited by John Drescher in his book, *Triumph of Good Will: How Terry Sanford Beat a Champion of Segregation and Reshaped the South*, Jackson, Miss: University Press of Mississippi, 2000, p. 230.
8. George Herndon, *Bulletin of Methodist College*, Vol. 1, No. 3, September 1960, file.
9. W. H. Plemmons, *Bulletin of Methodist College*, Vol. 1, No. 3, September 1960, file.
10. Bert Ishee, *Bulletin of Methodist College*, Vol. 1, No. 3, September 1960, file.
11. Terry Sanford, *Bulletin of Methodist College*, Vol. 1, No. 3, September 1960, file.
12. Paul N. Garber, *Bulletin of Methodist College*, Vol. 1, No. 3, September 1960, file.
13. Ibid.
14. Ibid.
15. Millard C. Dunn, *Bulletin of Methodist College*, Vol. 1, No. 3, September 1960, file.
16. Ibid.
17. Paul N. Garber, *The Fayetteville Observer* "1960 Progress Edition," September 24, 1960, file.
18. L. Stacy Weaver, *The Fayetteville Observer* "1960 Progress Edition," September 24, 1960, file.

19. Frank Jeter Jr. to the Fayetteville College Foundation board, October 31, 1960, FCF, file.
20. Minutes of the October 31, 1960 meeting of the Fayetteville College Foundation, FCF, file.
21. Clarence Ficken, remarks to the Fayetteville College Foundation board, January 10, 1961, FCF, file.
22. L. Stacy Weaver, remarks to the Fayetteville College Foundation board, January 10. 1961, FCF, file.
23. Allen P. Brantley, letter to the Fayetteville College Foundation, quoted in the minutes of the January 12, 1961 meeting of the Fayetteville College Foundation board, FCF, file.
24. Ibid.
25. Samuel J. Womack, interview with Lynn Gruber, June 28, 2000, file.
26. L. Stacy Weaver, "President's Report to the Methodist College Board of Trustees," May 1, 1961, TM, Book 1.
27. Ibid.
28. Sam Edwards, interview with Lynn Gruber, June 13, 2000, file.
29. Jean Ishee, interview with Lynn Gruber, July 5, 2000, file.
30. Betty Neill Guy Parsons, interview with Lynn Gruber, December 17, 2001, file.
31. Minutes of the November 1, 1961 meeting of the Methodist College Board of Trustees, TM, Book 1.
32. Terry Sanford, Founders Day speech November 1, 1961, quoted in *sMALL TALK*, November, 1961, Vol. 1, No. 1, file.
33. Elaine Barbee, editor, *sMALL TALK*, November 1961, file.
34. Bob Reynolds, columnist, *sMALL TALK*, November 1961, file.
35. Newton Robertson Jr. to the Fayetteville College Foundation board, January 9, 1960, FCF, file.
36. Kermit Norris, editorial in *sMALL TALK*, May 1962, file.
37. Connor Holland, editorial in *sMALL TALK*, May 1962, file.
38. Virginia Kearn, column in *sMALL TALK*, May 1962, file.
39. L. Stacy Weaver, "Annual Report to the Methodist College Board of Trustees," May 1, 1962, TM, Book 1.
40. Terry Sanford, Founders Day address at Methodist College, November 15, 1962, Addresses and Papers of Governor Terry Sanford, edited by Memory F. Mitchell, Raleigh: Council of State, 1966, p. 292.
41. Ibid., p. 293.
42. Ibid., p. 294.

— CHAPTER 2 —

43. Ibid., p. 295.
44. Ibid., p. 296.
45. Ibid.
46. Ibid.
47. Ibid., p. 298.
48. Ibid., pp. 300-01.
49. Bill Billings, oral history interview, file.
50. Fran Abel, *sMALL TALK*, November 1962, file.
51. Danny Nau, *sMALL TALK*, November 1962, file.
52. Kermit Norris, editorial in *sMALL TALK*, November 1962, file.
53. Tommy Manning, column in *sMALL TALK*, November 1962, file.
54. Minutes, February 12, 1963 meeting, Executive Committee, Methodist College Board of Trustees, TM, Book 1.
55. Bruce Pulliam, interview with Lynn Gruber, August 4, 2000, file.
56. Betty Neill Guy Parsons, interview with Lynn Gruber, December 17, 2001, file.
57. L. Stacy Weaver to the Methodist College Board of Trustees, May 7, 1963, TM, Book 1.
58. L. Stacy Weaver, "Annual Report to the Methodist College Board of Trustees," May 7, 1963,TM, Book 1.
59. Shad Bosher, quoted in a *sMALL TALK* feature article, October 1963, file.
60. Ibid.
61. Frank Jeter Jr., letter to the editor, *sMALL TALK*, October 1963, file.
62. Joe Tally, keynote address, Founders Day at Methodist College, November 6, 1963, as reported in a news story, *The Fayetteville Observer*, November 7, 1963.
63. Ibid.
64. Ibid.
65. Ibid.
66. Connor Holland, a parody, *sMALL TALK*, November 1963, file.
67. Ibid.
68. Brian Peck, librarian, North Carolina Legislative Library, telephone interview with Bill Billings, August 1, 2003, file.
69. Samuel J. Womack, chapel address given November 25, 1963, complete text printed in *sMALL TALK*, December 1963, file.
70. David Herring, poem, *sMALL TALK*, December 1963, file.
71. L. Stacy Weaver, "Annual Report to the Methodist College Board of Trustees," April 3, 1963, TM, Book 1.

72. John R. Gross, keynote address at the inauguration of L. Stacy Weaver as president of Methodist College April 10, 1964, *Bulletin of Methodist College*, June 1964, Vol. 5, No. 2, file.
73. Ibid.
74. John R. Gross, as quoted in a news article by Bill Wright, *The Fayetteville Observer*, April 10, 1964.
75. L. Stacy Weaver, inaugural address, *Bulletin of Methodist College*, June 1964, Vol. 5, No. 2, file.
76. Ibid.
77. Ibid.
78. Barbara Hauser, feature story, *The Fayetteville Observer*, May 24, 1964, file.
79. Minutes, June 1, 1964 meeting of the Methodist College Board of Trustees, TM, Book 1.
80. Allen P. Brantley, Founders Day address at Methodist College, November 2, 1964, *Bulletin of Methodist College*, December 1964, Vol. 5, No. 5, file.
81. Loch McLean, editorial, *sMALL TALK*, November 1964, file.
82. Lyndon B. Johnson, telegram sent to North Carolina Governor Terry Sanford December 4, 1964, published in *The Fayetteville Observer*, December 5, 1964, file.
83. Ibid.
84. Barbara Hauser, feature story, *The Fayetteville Observer*, December 6, 1964, file.
85. Ibid.

L to R, John M. Reeves of Pinehurst, N.C., Terry Sanford, and College President L. Stacy Weaver review architectural drawings for the future Reeves Auditorium and Fine Arts Building. Mr. Reeves gave $200,000 toward the construction of the building.
—*photo by Charles McAdams*

Chapter 3

The College Grows Steadily
1965-69

> "Moral and spiritual values should be inseparable from intellectual values. Adherence to Christian ideals and principles is seen as demanding an unwavering quest for academic excellence."
>
> —Statement of Purpose, contained in the President's Annual Report to the Methodist College Board of Trustees, May 3, 1966

The Executive Committee of the Methodist College Board of Trustees dealt with several financial matters January 14, 1965. First, the committee approved an application to the federal Housing and Home Finance Agency for an additional $35,000 in loan funds to cover construction cost overruns for two new residence halls (Sanford Hall for men, Weaver Hall for women).

Second, after College President L. Stacy Weaver reported that fee increases would be needed to meet the Southern Association of Colleges and Schools' new accreditation standard of financial support, the trustees authorized the president to increase student fees up to $200 for the 1965-66 academic year. Dr. Weaver said SACS would examine Methodist College for accreditation during the 1965-66 academic year. The president also proposed the enlargement of the Student Union Building and gave a financial report listing the current balances for both operating and capital funds.

When the trustees' Executive Committee met February 23, 1965, new salary schedules were approved for the president, faculty and administrative personnel, reflecting modest increases. The president's salary was set at $16,000 per annum; the academic dean's at $10,000. Faculty salaries ranged from $4,800 for an instructor to $8,200 for a full professor. The committee approved student fee increases for 1965-66 of $200 for resident students and $125 for day students.

At its April 2, 1965 meeting, the Executive Committee authorized the president to enter into a contract with Bass Air Conditioning of Fayetteville for the air conditioning of the Student Union/Cafeteria at a cost of $40,356. The group empowered Dr. Weaver to seek an appropriate means of financing the project.

— CHAPTER 3 —

Students Approve Revisions to S.G.A. Constitution

The February 1965 *sMALL TALK* reported that the student body had approved four revisions to the Student Government Association Constitution in a referendum February 8, 1965. The changes recognized the authority of the college president and dean of students to act in emergency matters involving suspension of students, gave the Judicial Council jurisdiction in cases when school was not in session, required a simple majority vote of the Judicial Council for conviction in a disciplinary action, and established a Student-Faculty Judicial Committee of nine members (four faculty appointed by the college president and the four S.G.A. officers, with the dean of students as an ex-officio member).

Enrollment Reaches 700

The March 1965 *Bulletin of Methodist College* reported that Methodist College had enrolled 619 students in the fall of 1964 and another 81 students in the spring 1965 semester.

President Speaks of Maturity

Reporting on College President Stacy Weaver's chapel address February 24, 1965, the March 1965 *sMALL TALK* noted that Dr. Weaver had used the theme, "Many are called, few are chosen." The president was quoted as saying the two things that constitute a call are: 1) need, and 2) the ability to meet the need.

Dr. Weaver said the goal of everyone called to be a college student should be maturity—social, intellectual, religious—in all aspects of living. "This maturity I cherish for you and for this college," he added. [1]

In his concluding prayer, Dr. Weaver asked that students realize "the urgency of what we do day to day. . . and take advantage of the opportunities" [2] available to them at Methodist College.

MC students elected Tommy Yow S.G.A. president April 14, 1965. A rising senior from Rockingham, NC, Yow defeated Rom Mason, an Army veteran and transfer student from Fayetteville. Yow promised to establish eight S.G.A. committees, form interclass and interclub councils, seek student representation on the Concert-Lecture Series Committee, and study the feasibility of establishing an honor system and an alumni association.

The May 1965 *sMALL TALK* announced the schedule of events and speakers for the spring commencement May 30-31. This edition also contained two photo pages showing highlights from the May Dance, the Green and Gold Masque Keys' production of *Everybody Loves Opal*, and the S.G.A. elections.

A profile of Dr. Millard P. Burt, the college's academic dean, occupied a full page in this *sMALL TALK,* along with the news that Burt had just

1965–1969

Candidates for SGA President Rom Mason and Tommy Yow cast their ballots in the April 1966 SGA election.

resigned. The student reporter noted that Dr. Burt had led an investigation of an unauthorized off-campus party in the fall of 1964 and recommended that five MC students be dismissed from school. The article praised the soon-to-be director of the Fort Bragg Division of N.C. State University for his skill in teaching the course, "History and Philsophy of Education."

A summary of MC athletics for 1964-65 reported that the golf team, coached by Ernest Schwarz, finished 6-7 and took second place in the Dixie Conference Tournament. The tennis team, coached by Gene Clayton, finished third in the conference; the cross country team finished second, the basketball team fourth, and the bowling team fifth.

Trustees Amend Charter

At the trustees' annual meeting May 4, 1965, the board voted to amend Article VI of the college charter to allow up to 36 members to serve on the Methodist College Board of Trustees. The revision provided that at least six members would be members of The North Carolina Conference of the Methodist Church; at least six would be residents of Cumberland County; and at least three-fourths would be members of The Methodist Church.

The following nominees to the board were approved: Mott P. Blair, J. M. Wilson, Allen P. Brantley, W. Ed Fleishman, William Spence, O. L. Hathaway,

CHAPTER 3

and Hargrove Bowles Jr. The following were nominated as board officers for 1965-66: Terry Sanford, chairman; W. Robert Johnson, vice chairman; J. W. Hensdale, secretary; Wilson Yarborough, treasurer.

James Auman, executive director of the Association of Methodist Colleges of The North Carolina Conference of the Methodist Church, reported that $240,000 had been collected for Methodist College in the current conference year, bringing church payments on the original $5 million capital fund goal for its colleges to $3.5 million.

The trustees approved a budget for 1965-66 of $1,266,753 for operating expense and $121,928 for capital expenditures. Also approved was a resolution authorizing the issuance of $1,325,000 in bonds and a trust indenture to finance the two dormitories under construction (Sanford Hall for men, and Weaver Hall for women).

The trustees met July 9, 1965 and accepted the only bid offered on the Methodist College Dormitory Bonds, a bid from the U.S. Community Facilities Administration with an annual interest rate of 3 5/8 percent over thirty years.

President Announces Reeves Gift of $200,000

In his annual report to the board (for 1964-65) May 4, 1965, President Weaver announced that Mr. John M. Reeves of Pinehurst, NC, had agreed to contribute $200,000 toward the construction of the college's auditorium and fine arts building. A college trustee, Methodist layman, and North Carolina native, Mr. Reeves was board chairman of Reeves Brothers, Inc., a New York-based textile firm. At the time of his gift, he was also serving as chairman of the North Carolina Ports Authority and as chairman of the board of trustees of American University in Washington, D.C.

In other portions of his annual report, President Weaver:
— expressed appreciation for the hard work of his administrative staff; William Pope, executive director of the Fayetteville College Foundation; and Mr. George Vossler, Foundation president.
— noted the appointment of Dr. Samuel J. Womack as academic dean, replacing Dr. Millard P. Burt who had been hired by NC State University as director of a new degree-granting division at Fort Bragg.
— expressed concern about the College's ability to find and retain high quality faculty due to "the salary we are able to offer." [3] He said the College had 41 instructors with faculty rank and that four administrative officers taught part-time. He reported that the College would need seven additional faculty for the following school year.

Following a custom established with the first graduating class, the Board of Trustees received a list of candidates for graduation May 31, 1965, and formally authorized the president to confer degrees upon the students listed, contingent on their completion of the current semester and all other requirements of the college. The list for the college's second spring commencement included 49 Bachelor of Arts candidates and 18 Bachelor of Science candidates.

First Alumni Banquet

Methodist College held its first alumni banquet Saturday evening May 29, 1965, in the college cafeteria, launching a very significant commencement weekend. Reese Edwards '64 presided, and Dr. Weaver was the keynote speaker. William Wolfe provided entertainment at the piano, and Seldon "Sparky" Rapelye '65 presented President Weaver with the keys to a trophy case, a gift from the Class of 1965.

Jerry Wood, president of the Class of 1964, announced the results of the balloting for the first officers of the Methodist College Alumni Association: Julian Jessup, president; Ralph Hoggard, vice president; and Betty Bunce,

First Alumni Association Officers: Julian Jessup, Dave Herring, and Betty Bunce.

secretary. Elected by the officers of the Class of 1964, the first alumni officers were installed by William P. Lowdermilk, Assistant Director of Public Relations. In a brief acceptance speech, Julian Jessup pledged to the college the full cooperation of the alumni association in the areas of public relations, student recruitment and financial support.

— CHAPTER 3 —

Also announced during the alumni banquet were the first members of Methodist College Scholars, a college honor society. Academic Dean Millard P. Burt announced that Virginia Kern and Ralph Hoggard of the Class of 1964 would be the first inductees, having demonstrated exemplary character and academic achievement. The academic standards were a grade point average of 3.75 at the end of the junior year and 3.60 at the end of the first semester of the senior year, or 3.50 at the end of the senior year.

Dean O.E. Dowd greets the Rapelye family; brothers Seldon, Peter and Gene all enrolled.

College Graduates Second Class, Dedicates Bell Tower/Carillon

Activities for Methodist College's second spring commencement continued Sunday, May 30, 1965, with the baccalaureate service and the president's reception for graduating seniors and their families. Bishop Paul Hardin Jr., resident bishop of the Columbia, South Carolina, Area of The Methodist Church, delivered the baccalaureate sermon entitled "A Mountain to Climb."

President Weaver conferred degrees upon 63 members of the Class of 1965 during commencement Monday, May 31, 1965. Dr. Paul F. Sharp, Chancellor of the University of North Carolina at Chapel Hill, delivered the commencement address. Barbara Allen Holmes, a music major from Fayetteville, received the second annual Stacy Weaver Award.

Immediately following the commencement, the Yarborough Bell Tower containing the Jones Memorial Carillon was dedicated on the central campus

Dedication of the Yarborough Bell Tower and Jones Memorial Carillon. Shown in the inset are Wilson F. Yarborough, Sr,. Dr. L. Stacy Weaver, and Mrs. Mary Franklin Jones McCoy.

mall. A 95-foot steel tower topped by a lighted cross, the bell tower was given by Mr. and Mrs. Wilson F. Yarborough, Sr. The electronic carillon in the top of the tower was given as a memorial to James Archibald and Mary McNair Jones of Laurinburg, N.C. by their children.

Following the commencement and the bell tower dedication, the Methodist College Board of Trustees met briefly and unanimously adopted a resolution governing academic freedom and faculty tenure.

On the subject of academic freedom, the policy stated:

> The Methodist College faculty member is expected to pursue the inherent truth of his discipline and to lead students to explore all avenues of the subject. Such academic freedom does not grant license

to use the classroom as a platform for non-related controversial prejudices, for the airing of grievances, or for the negation of the stated purposes of the institution. Academic freedom is not a valid defense for ineffectual teaching. . .Unprofessional criticism of colleagues and students, libelous or slanderous proclamations, or continual agitation that undermines the effectiveness of the institution shall be considered violations of the freedom of others and subject to appropriate action when substantiated. [4]

The section on tenure limited the tenure of a faculty member to the terms of the contract unless otherwise specified, but provided that a faculty member who had been appointed or reappointed on an annual basis for three years to five years would be granted continuous tenure without the necessity of annual reappointment. The policy also stated that tenure could be terminated only by formal action of the Board of Trustees for just cause. [5]

Enrollment Jumps 33 Percent to 818

The September 1965 *Bulletin of Methodist College* announced that the college began its sixth academic year with two new dormitories (Sanford and Weaver halls), 17 new faculty members, and 818 students. Enrollment increased 33 percent over the previous fall. In addition, 13 seniors received diplomas at the end of the summer term, bringing membership in the Class of 1965 to 76.

The freshman class, the Class of 1969, totalled 407, making it the largest in the history of the College. Of the total enrollment, 470 were resident students and 348 were commuting. The student body was comprised of 432 men and 366 women.

Two hundred ninety-nine full-time students were from Cumberland County, while 316 were from other North Carolina counties (56) and 180 were from other states (15). Wake County was second to Cumberland with 29 students. Virginia led the out-of-state enrollment with 84 students.

The *Bulletin* also announced seventeen new additions to the faculty and staff: Dr. Ofelia M. Balaez, associate professor of mathematics; Mrs. James D. Holmes, instructor in French and Spanish; Ingram C. Parmley, instructor in psychology; Mrs. Joy A. Jackson, instructor in English; Ray J. Kinder, instructor in history; Miss Stella Robbins, cataloguing librarian; Dr. John O. Tobler, associate professor of political science; John A. McAlexander, instructor in physics and mathematics; Fred C. Wansley, assistant librarian; Dr. Richard O. Hartman, associate professor of religion and philosophy; Dr. Fred G. Piercy, associate professor of Spanish; Miss Frances Douglas, assistant professor of physical education; Dr. Karl H. Berns, professor of education and psychology; Charles E. Matthews, instructor in English; Mrs. Edith C. Boushy, assistant professor of English; Bill R. Cain, instructor in sociology; and Dr. Bobby L. Crisp, assistant professor of biology. Six of these new faculty members were replacements, and eleven were additions. The faculty had thus grown to fifty members.

Elsewhere in the college's Fall 1965 newsletter, the Public Occasions Committee announced a 13-program Concert-Lecture Series for 1965-66. The lineup included: Dr. Y. Warner Kloepfer, Danforth lecturer on human genetics; Nathan Twining, pianist; The Fayetteville Symphony Orchestra; the Methodist College Chorus; Ursula Zollenkopf, contralto; Ottomar Borwitzky, cellist; Alan Porter, tenor; Dr. Jose Maria Chaves, Danforth lecturer on Latin American Affairs; Alirio Diaz, classic guitarist; and an oratorio by the Methodist College Chorus, Fayetteville Symphony Orchestra, and guest soloists.

The *Bulletin* also reported that sixteen Methodist College graduates from the first two classes had been accepted by graduate schools and seminaries and that Lois Blackburn '64 and Walter Turner '65 had been accepted by the Peace Corps.

Methodist Enrolls First Black Student

Methodist College enrolled its first black student, Mary Monroe, in the fall of 1965. A Fayetteville native whose father was in the Army, Monroe had received a scholarship from the Herbert Lehman Educational Fund which could be used at any college or university. Although her father wanted her to attend Fayetteville State University, she chose Methodist College because it was close to home and offered a degree in chemistry. She lived at home and commuted to classes. During her college years, she participated in several civil rights marches in Fayetteville.

In a 2001 interview with *The Fayetteville Observer,* Mary Monroe Atwater said being the first and only black at Methodist "wasn't as difficult as it could have been because I was used to living in a world like that. I made some friends there, and I had a great learning experience. The students and professors were nice and cordial to me." [6]

Atwater said she was elated when a second black student, James Speed, enrolled at MC in 1966. By the time she graduated, Methodist was home to six black students. After graduating *magna cum laude* in 1969, Atwater earned a master's degree in chemistry from UNC-Chapel Hill and a doctorate in science education from N.C. State University. She has taught at New Mexico State University, Fayetteville State University, and Atlanta University, now Clark Atlanta. She is now a professor of science education at the University of Georgia.

— CHAPTER 3 —

Mary Monroe was Methodist's first African American student.

In her 2001 interview, Atwater noted, "One thing I spend a lot of time trying to do is convince people about experiencing the richness that people can have when there is racial and ethnic diversity." [7]

College Receives Assets of Donaldson Academy

The lead story on the front page of the September 1965 *sMALL TALK* announced that Methodist College had received a major gift from the trustees of the Donaldson Academy and Manual Labor School in Fayetteville. Established in 1833, the school had not operated in many years; therefore, the trustees had voted to dissolve the school and distribute its assets to Methodist College and St. Andrews Presbyterian College in Laurinburg, NC. Methodist received real estate and securities worth $62,127. St. Andrews received cash assets of $56,644.

sMALL TALK Editor Larry Barnes announced that the student newspaper would become a bimonthly publication thanks to an increase in the student activity fee. Barnes also adopted as the newspaper's motto the following Thomas Jefferson quotation: "Where the press is free and every man able to read, all is safe." [8]

Freshmen Required to Wear Beanies

Another front page news story in the September 16, 1965 *sMALL TALK* announced the implementation by the Student Government Association's Executive Branch of a new Freshman Orientation Code designed to build camaraderie and school spirit. The code required that freshmen wear "Monarch caps" (beanies) the first month of school (these were optional for freshmen age 21 or older), refrain from wearing Bermuda shorts outside the dormitories, study and be tested on the S.G.A. Constitution, refrain from walking on the grass, attend every college function, and master the Alma Mater, fight song and college cheers. The month of freshman orientation would end with a freshman dance.

In an editorial entitled, "Beanies of Potential," Barnes welcomed the new freshmen, the Class of 1969, by observing that this class had been set apart by the new Freshman Orientation Code: "By the time of this publication, the 'Monarch caps' will have been removed. No green marks you now. However, your potential is the greatest ever to grace this campus. Now you must do the setting apart. You must make your mark in the academic life of this institution. Your must lead your class." [9]

Trustees Approve Minors

The college trustees' Committee on Academic Affairs met September 24, 1965, and approved the implementation of academic minors as a graduation requirement instead of the "related work" previously required. This was proposed by the faculty in the draft of its self-study report to the Southern Association of Colleges and Schools and was to be effective with the class entering in September, 1965. Minors were proposed for the following disciplines: English, History, Mathematics, Chemistry, Biology, Religion, French, Economics and Business, Music, Secondary Education, Spanish, Philosophy, Sociology, Psychology, Physics, and Political Science.

The committee also authorized the faculty and administration to advance any of six academic minors—Spanish, Philosophy, Sociology, Psychology, Physics, and Political Science—to major status as deemed appropriate, taking into account student needs and the availability of teaching personnel.

Trustees Approve Three Building Projects, Names for Buildings

The trustees' Executive Committee met September 28, 1965, and approved a resolution to borrow $435,000 from the U.S. Housing and Home Finance Agency, Community Facilities Administration to construct an addition to the Student Union/Cafeteria building. The board also gave the president authority to execute a temporary construction loan of $435,000 from a financial institution, once the federal loan was approved.

The Executive Committee voted to recommend to the full board that five buildings be named as follows: the proposed administration building: Horner Administration Building, in honor of Mr. W. E. Horner; the new men's dorm Sanford Hall, in honor of Mr. Terry Sanford; the new women's dorm Weaver

Hall, in honor of Dr. L. Stacy Weaver; the library Davis Memorial Library, in honor of Mrs. Geraldine Tyson Davis; and the proposed auditorium/fine arts building: Reeves Auditorium/Fine Arts Building, in honor of Mr. J. M. Reeves.

President Weaver reported to the trustees' Executive Committee October 26, 1965, that the proposed fine arts building/auditorium and the proposed administration building (estimated to cost $1,080,000) were eligible for federal assistance under the new Higher Education Act passed by Congress. He said the college could apply for a grant of $360,000 and a loan of $450,000 for the two buildings. The committee authorized the construction of the two buildings and application for a federal loan of $810,000.

The trustees' Development Committee met October 26, 1965, and discussed ways of raising the $275,000 in additional funds needed to construct the fine arts building/auditorium.

Professor Challenges Freshmen

In a brief essay which appeared in the October 4, 1965, *sMALL TALK*, Mr. Bruce Pulliam, assistant professor of social studies, challenged new freshmen to claim their cultural heritage through their studies at Methodist and to "fulfill the great expectations of those who know you best and love you most [. . .]" [10]

> If within the weeks and months ahead you can learn to govern yourself with respect to social conduct, moral standards and daily tasks; if you can come into full appreciation of freedom of thought and inquiry in the search for truth, both for yourself and for others; if you can fully appreciate academic standards and academic integrity, without evasion and without cheating; if you can come to understand and appreciate the essential unity of culture, science and religion, you will not only understand your school, but also you will be a part of it, and it will become a part of you. [11]

Hawks Prevail at Vietnam Day

October 29, 1965, was Vietnam Day at Methodist College, and the event was chronicled in the November 16, 1965, *sMALL TALK*. At a "voluntary" assembly organized by the Student Government Association, two Army officers from Fort Bragg addressed several hundred students. Lt. Col. Andrew Nisbet and Brig. Gen. Joe Stilwell of the John F. Kennedy Special Warfare Center at Fort Bragg said America was right to help South Vietnam prevent a communist takeover of southeast Asia. Nesbit and Stilwell also strongly defended America's role in the Vietnam War.

1965–1969

At the end of the program, S.G.A. President Tommy Yow and hundreds of other students signed a letter endorsing the U.S. stand in Vietnam. The letter was then mailed to U.S. military authorities in South Vietnam. Shortly thereafter, Yow received a letter from Gen. William C. Westmoreland, the Army's commanding general, in which he expressed his heartfelt thanks to the Methodist student body for its overwhelming display of support on Vietnam Day. He said he had forwarded the letter from Methodist students to the Command Information Officer for dissemination to the troops through the command newspaper. A copy of Westmoreland's letter was printed in the Letters to the Editor section of sMALL TALK December 1, 1965.

Cross Country, Volleyball Teams Win Conference Championships
November 1965 saw the Methodist College Monarchs win their first Dixie Conference championships, first in cross country and then in volleyball.

The cross country team, coached by Gene Clayton and captained by Jerry Huckabee, won the conference title over four other teams November 13, 1965, at St. Andrews Presbyterian College in Laurinburg, N.C. The Monarchs outpaced their closest competitor, St. Andrews, by 15 points; the final scores were M.C.-34, St. Andrews-49, Lynchburg-60, N.C. Wesleyan-102, and College of Charleston-116. Senior and team captain Jerry Huckabee finished the race in second place in 22 minutes and 5 seconds.

Coach Clayton said team members had set the goal of winning the conference title at their first practice and had worked hard to achieve it. "Very few people understand how much work and time and energy it takes to practice every day by running six to eight miles, then running four miles in a meet," said Clayton. "I would like to express my appreciation for their fine work and efforts this season." [12]

Six days later, the Monarch volleyball team, coached by Frances Douglas, defeated teams from N.C. Wesleyan, St. Andrews, and Lynchburg at Wesleyan in Rocky Mount. The Monarchs never trailed in the tournament and were only tied once. Team members were: Dave Cooper, Bob Ellis, Dale Marshall, Gary Miller, George Pearce, Peter Rapelye, D. K. Taylor Jr., and Ed Voorhees.

Honor Code Debated, Defeated
The November, 1965 issues of sMALL TALK carried news, letters, and editorials about a proposed Honor System for Methodist College. A committee appointed by S.G.A. President Tommy Yow presented a proposed Honor Code to the Methodist student body November 29 to be voted on December 13. S.G.A. assemblies were held December 1, 6, and 13 to explain the proposed Honor Code.

— CHAPTER 3 —

The 1965 Cross Country team won Methodist College's First Dixie Conference Championship.

At the November 29 student assembly, Bob Nardone spoke against the proposed system, saying it was an attempt to legislate or force self-government and that individual responsibility "like morality, cannot be legislated." [13]

At the same assembly, proponent Rom Mason argued the code would "shift the responsibility of policing student academic matters from the instructor to the students" and added, "Any student who would criticize another for valuing honor, for reporting dishonesty, is not worthy of the title 'friend'." [14]

In the November 16 *sMALL TALK*, News Editor Bill Billings argued that an honor system was not needed because Methodist College students were already required to sign the College's General Information Sheet, pledging adherence to the statement, "I promise to conduct myself everywhere in such a manner as to reflect credit upon myself, my family, and Methodist College." [15]

At the December 6 assembly, Henry Grant, a student opposed to the Honor Code, offered an amendment requiring a three-fourths majority for student ratification of the code. Only two of the 800 students assembled spoke against the amendment, and it carried. Ironically, an earlier poll taken during chapel showed that 50 percent of 471 respondents supported the idea of an academic honor system.

1965–1969

In a December 13, 1965, referendum, Methodist students defeated the proposed Honor System by a nine to one margin. In a letter to *sMALL TALK*, in which he predicted students would reject the code, Danny Nau expressed regret that the student body previously approved an amendment requiring a three-fourths majority for ratification, saying many students had failed to speak up for honor and the right to govern themselves. [16]

Rattling the Tin Can

The pounding of the metal walls of Methodist's "Butler Building" gymnasium became a hot topic when the 1965-66 basketball season began. *sMALL TALK* staffer Ken Murray reported in the December 13 issue that he had surveyed 268 students and found that 43 percent considered pounding the walls sportsmanlike and a show of school spirit, 37 percent felt it was unsportsmanlike, and 20 percent were undecided.

The pounding became a real issue December 1, 1965, during a basketball game between Methodist College and Campbell College. Mr. Jack Thomas, the college's superintendent of buildings and grounds, came forward and asked some students to stop kicking the walls. S.G.A. President Tommy Yow then exhorted the students to make more noise.

A guest editorial in the December 13, 1965, *sMALL TALK,* defended Mr. Thomas against student complaints that he was trying to stifle school spirit.

Basketball team members huddle in the "tin can" gym.

— CHAPTER 3 —

MC student Richard Alston said the gym walls were obviously dented and scarred, and contended [. . .] this type of abuse is not necessary for our teams to achieve victory." [17]

In a letter that appeared on the *sMALL TALK* Sports page, Tommy Yow said beating on the gym walls with hands and fists was initially done "to keep time with the cheerleaders and when our team had stolen a ball or scored a basket." [18] But Yow said the beating should now cease because of physical changes made to the gym since the preceding basketball season: "New goals have been erected with supporting wires attached to the walls; therefore, when students beat on the walls, they shake the goals." [19] He said another problem arose when the home bleachers were moved from one side of the gym to the other. "The hot water pipes are against the wall on the present home side, and the beating on the wall could cause them to either fail or burst," he continued. [20]

The S.G.A. president said students who maintained that beating on the gym walls was a sign of unsportsmanlike conduct were "only showing your ignorance. We were merely following a tradition." [21] He concluded his letter by saying the tradition should now cease for "purely practical reasons." [22]

Girls Pin Instructor

In 1965, a group of Methodist College cheerleaders enrolled in a sophomore physical education class hurled an unusual challenge at their instructor, Gene Clayton.

Gwen Pheagin Sykes Holtsclaw '68 remembers it well:

> He had a wrestling class prior to our P.E. class. Six of us cheerleaders walked in early and watched him finish up with the wrestling class. It looked liked fun, so when we got to our class we asked, "Coach, why can't we learn wrestling?"
>
> "Because you're girls," he answered.
>
> We said, "Like we couldn't pin somebody."
>
> He said, "All of you together couldn't pin me."
>
> That's when Merriam Palm—she was this tall, strong cheerleader—said, "Okay girls, on three—one, two, three."
>
> And we pinned Gene in two seconds. That convinced him, so he taught us wrestling moves. [23]

Foundation Raises $90,000 For Methodist

The Fayetteville College Foundation raised $90,190.71 for Methodist College during 1965, compared to $78,534.41 in 1964. George W. Vossler served as foundation president, and William P. Pope was the executive director.

1965–1969

The foundation held a kickoff breakfast for its 1965-66 PEP-Campaign November 5, 1965. Foundation minutes indicate that PEP stood for Progress-Education-Participation. At the breakfast, Mr. Vossler introduced Wilbur Smith as general campaign chairman and Mr. I. H. O'Hanlon as organizational chairman. Others who played an active role in the fund drive were Norwood Bryan Jr., Leon McBryde, Russell Crowell, Glenn Powell, and John Ormsby.

Trustees Deal With Money Matters

The Executive Committee of the Methodist College Board of Trustees took action on several money matters January 19, 1966. First, the committee approved a refinancing of the college's $1 million loan with First Citizens Bank and Trust Co. The committee approved an agreement with Northwestern Life Insurance Co. and the Pan American Life Insurance Co. to jointly lend the college $1 million for 30 years at an annual interest rate of 5 3/4 percent.

Second, the committee voted to increase a loan application to the U.S. Office of Education to assist in the construction of the administration building and the fine arts building from $1,080,000 to $1,276,480. President Weaver advised the group that a federal grant of $360,000 toward the cost of building an addition to the Student Union/Cafeteria had been approved, but that the college would need to increase the grant application to $425,493 to cover higher construction costs. Dr. Weaver estimated the college would need to contribute $319,000 toward the construction of the three projects.

The Executive Committee also voted to increase fees for 1967-68 by $100, $50 in board and $50 in tuition, making the total charges for one year $1,600 for a resident student and $800 for a commuting student.

The full Methodist College Board of Trustees met February 25, 1966 and approved a loan agreement with the U.S. Office of Education for funds to assist in the construction of a fine arts building and an administration building.

Meeting March 28, 1966, the trustees' Executive Committee voted to allow Carolina Power & Light Co. to purchase a 1.06 acre tract of land for a substation and to grant an easement for transmission lines from that substation.

President Weaver presented a request from the faculty Athletic Committee to add soccer, track, and wrestling as intercollegiate sports beginning in September, 1966. The committee approved the addition of the three sports pending inclusion of the costs of equipment and personnel in the college's 1966-67 budget.

sMALL TALK Covers Many Topics

As the spring 1966 semester approached, Methodist College said goodbye to Mrs. Miriam L. Usrey, instructor in English and speech, who resigned to

— CHAPTER 3 —

continue her graduate studies at the University of Indiana. The January 4, 1966 *sMALL TALK* carried a brief tribute and thank you to Mrs. Usrey, and the January 17 issue carried a resolution of appreciation from the English Department on the editorial page. A thank you from Mrs. Usrey appeared in the February 7, 1966 *sMALL TALK* under "Letters to the Editor," along with an original poem entitled "A Teacher's Prayer."

Mrs. Usrey was succeeded by Dr. George Dunlap, a Pennsylvania native and World War I veteran, who had just retired from Saint Paul's College in Virginia. Other newcomers that spring were Dr. Garland T. Knott, chaplain and professor of religion; Mr. Samuel Mason Sykes, instructor in physical education; and Dr. Jacob Shumelda, assistant librarian. Mr. Sykes assumed the teaching duties of Men's Basketball Coach Ernie Schwarz, who began a leave of absence to work on his doctorate at the University of North Carolina.

During Larry Barnes' tenure as editor of *sMALL TALK*, special interest columns became an important part of the student newspaper. They included: "Campus Concerns," an opinion poll by Kenneth Murray; "MC History" by Susan Sharp; "His Helping Hand," a devotional by Michael Hale; "What's In," a fashion column by Beverly Sprouse; and "The Monarch's Muse," a poetry column by Jean Hutchinson. Sprouse's column of January 4, 1966, listed as fashion fads among young women: the granny dress, mid-calf boots, and patriotic colors of red, white, and blue.

Students Active On Many Fronts

Methodist College observed its first homecoming weekend February 4-6, 1966, under the sponsorship of the Student Government Association and the Club Coordinating Council. Homecoming Chairman Bob Nardone, a junior from Durham, N.C., organized and coordinated the events, which began with a folk concert Friday evening by the men of Cumberland Hall.

Saturday events included the crowning of Cheryl Meacham as Homecoming Queen during halftime at the Methodist-Baptist College (of Charleston, S.C.) basketball game. A junior English major from Ellerbe, N.C., Meacham was chosen by the Monarch Club. Baptist College won the basketball game, 56-53. A homecoming banquet was held Saturday evening with brief remarks by President Weaver, Alumni President Julian Jessup, S.G.A. President Tommy Yow, and Director of Alumni Affairs Charles McAdams. The homecoming banquet was followed by a homecoming dance. The last event of the first homecoming weekend was an open house at Weaver Hall.

Cheryl Meacham

1965–1969

The Effigies, named for a famous incident in which MC's first academic dean was burned in effigy, perform at the first homecoming in February 1966.

Despite losing to Baptist College at Homecoming, the MC basketball team finished its third season with a 6-4 conference record and a third place finish in the Dixie Intercollegiate Athletic Conference Tournament. Coach Ernie Schwarz was named conference coach of the year and three MC players—Davis Bradley, Jim Darden, and Bill Honeycutt—were named to the all-tournament team.

The college's concert-lecture series for spring 1966 included: a tenor voice recital by Alan Porter, instructor of music; a lecture on Latin America by Dr. Jose Maria Chaves; a concert by Alirio Diaz, classical guitarist; and a concert by the Fayetteville Symphony Orchestra under the direction of Dr. Willis Gates, professor of music. The symphony concert also featured a piano solo by Roberta West, a senior music major at Methodist.

In March 1966, Brenda Heath, a freshman elementary education major, was crowned Miss Fayetteville.

Methodist's first annual Fine Arts Festival was held May 2-8, 1966, under the direction of R. Parker Wilson. The theme was "Fantasia 1966." Festival events included an art exhibit by students of Mrs. Elizabeth Garthley, a faculty talent night, presentation of two melodramas by the Green and Gold Masque-Keys, an intramural softball game between the male and female students, a concert sponsored by the Student Government Association, and the May Dance, followed by a Royal Feast.

— CHAPTER 3 —

The 1966 May Court: L to R, Susan Council, Charlotte Carmine, Pam Zollars (May Queen), Gwen Pheagin, Beverly Parks.

Steve Hopkins Elected S.G.A. President

In S.G.A. elections April 15, 1966, Steve Hopkins, a rising junior from Florence, S.C., defeated Charlotte Carmine, a rising junior from Richmond, Va., in a close contest for S.G.A. President. Other officers elected for 1966-67 were: Robert Nardone of Durham, vice president; Jean Hutchinson of Fayetteville, secretary; and Robert Landsberger of Greensboro, treasurer.

Trustees Set Fundraising Goal of $600,000

At the Methodist College Board of Trustees' annual meeting May 3, 1966, Dr. Mott P. Blair gave an extensive report from the Development Committee and moved that the board launch a fund drive for the $600,000 needed to build the Fine Arts Building/Auditorium without borrowing. Blair's motion carried, along with a second motion to form a Trustee Development Council, consisting of the Development Committee and the Finance Committee, to prepare a 10-year plan for the development of the college.

George Vossler, president of the Fayetteville College Foundation, informed the trustees that the foundation expected to meet its goal of raising $100,000 for the college in 1965-66. He said $50,000 would be contributed to the operating fund and $50,000 to make interest payments on the $1 million loan with First Citizens Bank & Trust Co.

In other actions, the trustees approved a list of degree candidates for the May 1966 commencement, made ten nominations for membership on the Board of Trustees, and re-elected the following as board officers for 1966-67: Terry Sanford, chairman; W. Robert Johnson, vice chairman; J. W. Hensdale, secretary; and Wilson Yarborough, treasurer.

President Weaver advised the board that the Visiting Committee from the Southern Association of Colleges and Schools, which had visited North Carolina Wesleyan College two weeks earlier, had informed college officials there that certain amendments would need to be made to the college charter before the college could qualify for SACS membership. Because the Wesleyan and Methodist charters were nearly identical, Dr. Weaver said the same changes would have to be made to the Methodist charter.

Article VI of the college charter was amended to read: "The business and affairs of this corporation shall be vested in, administered and managed by the Trustees of Methodist College, Incorporated." [24]

The second paragraph of Article VII, giving the Board of Trustees the right to remove any of its members, was amended by adding the words "for due cause" to the final sentence.

In his annual written report to the trustees, President Weaver noted that 866 students enrolled in 1965-66 and that 78 percent were from North Carolina and 48 percent were Methodist. He said the four residence halls were filled to one-half their capacity.

The president also reported that the Visiting Committee of the Southern Association of Colleges and Schools would visit the campus April 17-20, 1966; that majors in Spanish and Political Science would be added in 1966-67; that bids would be received June 1 for an addition to the Student Union/Cafeteria; and that architects' plans for the Administration Building and the Fine Arts Building would be ready for bids June 15.

The Methodist College Board of Trustees met November 2, 1966, following a Founders' Day program at which Terry Sanford gave the keynote address. At this meeting, the trustees:

—approved operating and capital fund budgets for 1966-67.
—voted to reject bids taken October 11, 1966, for construction of the administration building, fine arts building, chapel, and addition to the Student Union because they exceeded the funds available.
—voted to take new bids on all the building projects except the chapel.
—authorized the president to apply for additional construction funds for the three building projects from the U.S. Office of

— CHAPTER 3 —

Education and the Dept. of Housing and Urban Development.
—heard a request from Dr. Blair that each trustee give a list of prospective donors to Mr. William Pope, executive director of the Fayetteville College Foundation, and agree to give two days work to the College by the first of the new year.

Literary Magazine Makes Debut

The first issue of *Tapestry,* the Methodist College literary magazine, was published in May 1966 by Pastiche, the literary club. Ted Boushy was editor of the 31-page magazine. Jean Hutchinson '67 of Fayetteville, N.C. suggested the title for the magazine. Her reasons follow:

Most likely I was influenced by that beautiful poem, 'Weavings'! [written by Dr. Francis Merchant, one of Hutchinson's college English professors] I had also worked in the fabric department at Belk's and sewed outfits for use on mannequins in the store. . .and, of course, words woven together can make beautiful word pictures. More importantly, 'tapestry' as a word brings to mind something elegant and painstakingly created, with increasing value for posterity. [25]

Alumni Association Adopts Constitution, By-laws

The Methodist College Alumni Association held its annual meeting and banquet May 28, 1966. At the business meeting, the MCAA Board of Directors adopted a constitution and by-laws, defining an active member as anyone who had attended the college at least one academic year and was in good standing with the college.

Dr. Karl Berns, professor of education, was the guest speaker at the alumni banquet, to which members of the Class of 1966 had been invited as guests of the association. John W. Handy, president of the Class of 1966, presented a check to Dr. Weaver—a class gift to establish an endowed Class of 1966 Scholarship. Roger Williams '65 of Raleigh was installed as president of the alumni association for 1966-67, along with fellow officers David Herring '65, vice president; and Betty Bunce '64, secretary-treasurer.

College Graduates Third Class

Forty-nine seniors received degrees at Methodist College's third spring commencement May 30, 1966. Anne Butler, an English major from Marion, S.C., became the college's first *summa cum laude* graduate, and Roberta Dawn West, a music major from Mount Olive, N.C., received the Lucius Stacy Weaver Award, denoting her selection by the faculty as the senior who best exemplified academic excellence, spiritual development, leadership, and service.

Methodist Bishop John Owen Smith of Atlanta, Georgia, delivered the baccalaureate sermon entitled "The Higher Reach in Christ." Dr. Charles Carroll, state superintendent of public instruction, was the commencement speaker. In his address, Dr. Carroll expressed the hope that Methodist College would remain "a relatively small" liberal arts institution, maintaining a close relationship between faculty and students and among students themselves.

Faculty Grows to 57

Increased enrollment allowed the college to hire 22 additional faculty members for the 1966-67 school year.

Additions included: Dr. Walter Blackstock, English; Diane Cawman, physical education; Dr. William C. Cooper, chemistry; Dr. Yolana Cowley, Spanish; Dr. Anne Douglas, psychology and dean of women; Donald Green, art; Janelle Henwood, English; Rodney Hill, music and band; Mrs. Guler Johnson, physics and math; Dr. Anthony Kalina, history; Rowland Matteson, chemistry and math; Dr. Lorenzo Plyler, religion; Arthur Reinke, English and math; Dr. Vessalin Sarenac; Bruce Shelley, physical educaiton; Dr. King Wang, political science; J. Allan Wilson, economics and business; Mrs. Elizabeth Wilson, assistant librarian; C. H. Anderholdt, sociology; Eldon Woodcock, religion; Mrs. Betty Cline, sociology and diretor of guidance and placement.

Students "Sit Down" for German Shepherd

Chants of "We want Igor!" reverberated off the walls of Garber and Sanford halls on the evening of October 25, 1966, and in the early morning of October 26, 1966. The chants came from about 100 male resident students who staged a sit-down protest in the street between the two women's residence halls.

The students were protesting the capture and exile two weeks prior of Igor, a German shepherd dog that had lived on campus for about six months. When students learned the college administration had removed the dog, about 400 resident students signed a petition asking for Igor's return and submitted it to Mr. O. E. Dowd, the dean of students.

Dean Dowd referred the matter to the Student Life Committee, which set forth a list of conditions that would have to be met for Igor's return. The

— CHAPTER 3 —

committee said the dog would have to be kept in an off-campus kennel, would have to be leashed and muzzled, and would not be allowed in the gym.

S.G.A. President Steve Hopkins and *sMALL TALK* Editor Bill Billings met with Dowd to request that the dog be allowed on campus and without a muzzle. Dowd refused to lessen the conditions set forth by the Student Life Committee, and Hopkins appointed an S.G.A. committee to draw up a new proposal for keeping Igor on campus. On the evening of October 25, 1966, members of the committee reported to the four residence hall councils that Dean Dowd would not bend.

This news was not well-received in the two men's residence halls; a large group of residents voted to reject the conditions and then rushed *en masse* to the women's residence halls where they learned the women in one dorm were divided and those in the other were also opposed to the conditions. At approximately 11:45 p.m., 100 males sat down in the street between Garber and Weaver halls and began shouting, "We want Igor!" Scores of women in Garber and Weaver soon chimed in from their open windows.

At approximately 12:15 a.m. Oct. 26, Dean of Men Ingram Parmley and Dean of Students O. E. Dowd appeared and persuaded the male students to return to their residence hall lobbies to discuss the matter. In Sanford and Cumberland, the deans were peppered with questions: "Where is Igor? How do other colleges handle live animal mascots? Why is a muzzle necessary?" [26]

During the discussions, it was agreed each dorm would elect two representatives to a new committee to draw up a new proposal for the return and care of Igor. The committee adopted many of the ideas set forth by Kenneth Murray in an Oct. 17 *sMALL TALK* editorial: namely, that Igor be made the official college mascot and that a fund be set up to provide food and housing on campus. Jars were placed in the Student Union for donations to the Igor Fund.

Meanwhile, many MC students submitted letters to the editor and poems to *sMALL TALK* saying Igor deserved a reprieve. Some commuting students, however, wrote letters declaring the sit-down protest "unwarranted" and labeling the Igor issue "a trivial cause."

When S.G.A. President Steve Hopkins and *sMALL TALK* Editor Bill Billings presented a new proposal to College President Stacy Weaver for the care of Igor on campus, Dr. Weaver rejected it. Igor was not seen or heard from again.

Sophomore Dennis Bruce penned a fitting postscript to the Igor incident in his November 2, 1966 *sMALL TALK* column, "Behind the Power Plant." Bruce said the Igor demonstration had shown that "students have a voice. . .and will be heard ." [27] He said the Igor incident had validated the right and privilege of every American to peaceable assembly but had also shown the wisdom of considering both sides of a problem and acting maturely and responsibly.

When the Igor story was recounted in *Methodist College Today* twenty-five and thirty-five years later, a few of the former protestors wrote in to suggest the formation of an Igor Society and an Igor reunion.

Terry Sanford Proposes State Tuition Grant

Methodist College observed its 10th anniversary at a special Founders' Day program November 2, 1966, in the Student Union. Terry Sanford, chairman of the college's board of trustees, was the featured speaker.

In an address entitled, "Retrospect and Prospect," Sanford said church-related colleges had played a major role in the growth of America, but that private financial support would need to be doubled in the next five years to ensure that private colleges serve their purpose and flourish.

The former North Carolina governor offered three specific recommendations for increasing support of private colleges like Methodist:

1) That the North Carolina Methodist Conference double its allocation to its colleges. Even if the churches do not immediately follow suit, and even though we might fall short for several years, at least we will have set the goal which we must have to preserve the proper role and influence of the church.
2) That the contributions from Fayetteville residents (to Methodist College) be doubled.
3) That the state of North Carolina institute a scholarship program, providing a scholarship payment of at least $200 for every student (state resident) attending a private college in North Carolina. This would relieve the state of the higher costs required of it when the student attends a state institution, because the state must now put out about $400 for every college student in a public college. [28]

College President L. Stacy Weaver presided over the Founders' Day program, and trustees Dr. Allen P. Brantley and the Rev. O. L. Hathaway gave the invocation and the benediction, respectively. George Vossler, president of the Fayetteville College Foundation, and the Rev. James Auman, executive director of the Association of Methodist Colleges of the N. C. Conference of The Methodist Church, offered greetings.

Vossler ended his remarks by saying, "We resolve to focus our sights on the principles which have characterized our ten years of service: faith in God, citizenship responsibility, goodwill, and the affirmation of our faith in

— CHAPTER 3 —

The Methodist College Wind Ensemble debuted in 1966; Rodney Hill conducted.

Methodist College to become during the next decade, a Methodist university located on College Boulevard in historic Fayetteville, North Carolina." [29]

The College Chorus, the College Wind Ensemble, and a trio composed of Rodney Hill, flutist; Dr. Willis Gates, violinist; and Dr. John Tobler, pianist; provided special music.

At a luncheon meeting held after the Founders' Day program, college trustees voted to reject construction bids received in October for an administration building, fine arts building/auditorium, chapel, and addition to the Student Union, and to advertise for new bids to be opened November 22.

The Founders' Day issue of *sMALL TALK* included a biographical tribute to Dr. L. Stacy Weaver, president of Methodist College, written by Susan Sharp. Sharp's article included some lesser-known facts about Stacy Weaver:

—he started school at the age of five in Emory, Virginia, while his father was president of Emory and Henry College.

—at age 10 he entered Emory and Henry Academy, a college preparatory school.

—at age 14 he entered Emory and Henry College.

—at age 16 he worked a year as principal of a two-teacher school in Union County (while his father was pastor of a Methodist Church in Monroe).

—at age 17 Stacy taught a six weeks "cotton picking summer school," so named because this school allowed children to pick cotton during the fall harvest season.

—in 1922 Stacy transferred to Trinity College in Durham where he was a member of the Literary Society and an outfielder on the college baseball team. He majored in chemistry and minored in biology, but also took courses in Latin, Greek, and German. He graduated in 1924, the year Trinity College became Duke University.

—from 1924-32 he taught Latin and German at Rutherford College near Hickory, N.C., began a football team and became a coach of football, basketball, and baseball. He served as president of the college in 1932-33; the next year the college was consolidated with Brevard College in Brevard, N.C. [30]

Fayetteville Observer Commemorates College's 10th Anniversary

To mark the tenth anniversary of the chartering of Methodist College, *The Fayetteville Observer* published a 12-page special section recounting its early history and present status. A total of 62 local businesses bought congratulatory ads in the Methodist College section.

In Section C of the *Observer* Wednesday, November 16, 1966, the College announced (on the front page) an open house for the general public the next day, Thursday, November 17, 1966. Orren E. Dowd, dean of students, was in charge of the event. Members of the Student Government Association provided guided tours of the campus.

The commemorative section included a large College ad thanking the citizens of Fayetteville and Cumberland County for their support and noting that the College began the 1966-67 school year with 944 students—335 from Fayetteville and Cumberland County, 387 from 69 other counties in North Carolina, and 222 from 18 states and one foreign country.

Also included in this publication were interviews with Dr. L. Stacy Weaver, College president; Terry Sanford, trustees chairman; and George Vossler, Foundation chairman. Other articles concerned plans for three new buildings (auditorium, administration building, and addition to the Student Union), major benefactors, the faculty, the curriculum, the athletic program, cultural offerings, student organizations, the College's economic impact on the Fayetteville area, and financial aid. Photographs of MC student groups—athletes, the *sMALL TALK* staff, and cheerleaders—appeared throughout the section.

Soccer Team Begins Play

Methodist College launched a soccer team in the fall of 1966. The coach was Mason Sykes, who had been appointed to teach physical education in January of that year. He remembers his first season this way:

— CHAPTER 3 —

I had one fellow who had played soccer, Howard Arden, from Scarsdale, N.Y. I had one other fellow, Gary Miller, who had seen a soccer game. So I had to teach everyone the fundamentals first. Our first opponent was Lynchburg College, which had finished fourth in the nation the year before; they beat us 11-0. Then Campbell College beat us 7-0. We did not win a single game, but did manage to tie Pfeiffer on our field. They were playing for a berth in the District 26 NAIA playoffs. [31]

Mason Sykes

Ironically, the beginning of soccer also marked the beginning of the end for sand spurs, at least on the home field. Sykes told the team members if they didn't want to fall down on the prickly plants, they could dig them up. The players accepted the challenge and spend many hours removing sand spurs from the soccer field.

Because sand spurs grew in greatest profusion on the remote parts of the campus (the farm and fields between the dorms and the river), they were the source of a standing joke on campus. Students who came back to the dorms with large numbers of sand spurs on their clothing were invariably teased about finding "Splendor in the Sand Spurs."

SACS Grants Full Accreditation to Methodist College

November 30, 1966, brought good news from the Southern Association of Colleges and Schools when that body, meeting in Miami Beach, Florida, awarded full accreditation to Methodist College. The *Bulletin of Methodist College* for December 1966 devoted four and a half pages to this watershed event and to the decade of College history leading up to it.

Trustees Award Contracts for Three Buildings

The Executive Committee of the Methodist College Board of Trustees met November 22, 1966, and awarded contracts for three new structures—the administration building, fine arts building/auditorium, and an addition to the Student Union—to Player, Inc. of Fayetteville. The Player firm offered the low bid of $1,764,300 to build an administration building containing 12,000 square feet, a fine arts building/auditorium containing 30,000 square feet, and an addition to the Student Union totalling 15,000 square feet. The contract included a multi-effect fountain with reflecting pool given by the Fleishman brothers of Fayetteville in honor of their brother, W. Ed Fleishman, a charter member of the Methodist College Board of Trustees.

The trustees voted to apply to the federal government for increases in federal construction loans as follows: $21,750 for the Student Union addition and $253,653 for the fine arts building/auditorium and the administration building.

The December 1966 *Bulletin of Methodist College* announced that the family of Franklin S. Clark, the first president of the Fayetteville College Foundation, had established a $500 annual scholarship in Mr. Clark's memory. A local attorney, Mr. Clark had died in February 1966 at the age of 55. The scholarship was given by Mr. Clark's sisters, Mrs. Henry Anderson and Mrs. John C. Haskell, and by his sons and daughters William E. Clark, Margaret St. Clair Clark, Franklin S. Clark Jr., and Mary Pride Clark.

College Publishes Poetry Volume

In November 1966, Methodist College Press published *Leaves Before the Wind*, a collection of 98 poems written by Dr. Walter Blackstock, professor of English and chairman of the Area of Language and Literature. Subtitled "New and Selected Poems from Two Decades," the book was Blackstock's ninth volume of poetry. In October 1967, *Leaves Before the Wind* earned Blackstock his second Oscar Young Memorial Cup from the Poetry Council of North Carolina; in December of that year, the volume won the Roanoke-Chowan Award and Cup for poetry from the N.C. Literary and Historical Association.

Leaves Before the Wind was the first work published by Methodist College Press. Articles about the book appeared in the *Bulletin of Methodist College* and *sMALL TALK*, and college trustees were given copies. The English Department held a tea Thursday afternoon, October 27, 1966, in the Student Union to introduce Blackstock's work.

Blackstock had just come to Methodist from East Carolina College. In 1954-55, he studied with poet Archibald MacLeish at Harvard. In 1960, he edited the Selected Poems of James Larkin Pearson, poet laureate of North Carolina. In 1961, he received the Oscar F. Young Memorial Award from the Poetry Council, Inc., of North Carolina for his book of poems, Miracle of Flesh. A member of Phi Beta Kappa, the Modern Language Association, and the Poetry Society of America, Dr. Blackstock held a B.A. from the University of Georgia, an LL.B. from the Woodrow Wilson College of Law in Atlanta, an M.A. from Vanderbilt, and a Ph.D. in American literature from Yale. He was a native of Atlanta, Ga.

In the forward to *Leaves Before the Wind*, Norman Holmes Pearson of Yale University said of Blackstock:

CHAPTER 3

...what shapes his poems always, no matter what their immediate subject may be, is his hungering after height—his drive to see beyond the objects and situations which surround him and stimulate him. These become 'birds that brushed infinities of blue.' Over and over again he records this brushing of Infinity which the poet through the poem shares with his reader. [32]

Leaves Before the Wind
When there no longer is retreat from time,
And we must bow to circumstance like leaves
Before the wind—when there are no reprieves
For us—no morning bell nor evening chime
To stay our last goodbye—will some sublime
And fadeless word assuage the mind that grieves,
Remembering as gold-ripe summer sheaves
Recall the sun, or woods recall wild thyme?
Brave men might cry aloud for steel or stone
To stem their tears—but we were never brave;
We claimed no more than laughter as a shield—
No more than light-winged words that might have flown
With swallows long ago. So let us save
But smiles for then. . .a faith kept unconcealed.
—Walter Blackstock [33]

On the page facing his title poem, Blackstock used as a preface the following excerpt from Thomas Wolfe's novel *Look Homeward Angel*:

A stone, a leaf, an unfound door, and a stone, a leaf, a door, and all the forgotten faces. Naked and alone we came into exile. In her dark womb we did not know our mother's face, from the prison of her flesh have we come into the unspeakable and incommunicable prison of the earth.

Which of us has known his brother? Which of us has looked into his father's heart? Which of us has not remained forever prison-pent? Which of us is not forever a stranger and alone? [34]

Editor's Note: In 1969, Dr. Blackstock published his ninth volume of poems entitled, *Not As Leaves Are Shaken*. He left Methodist College in 1970.

English Prof Recalls His Time at MC

The Methodist College faculty of the 1960s included some older professors who had been lured out of retirement. One such person was Dr. George A. Dunlap, an English professor recruited in December 1965 to teach for the spring semester of 1966. Dr. Dunlap had retired in June 1965 from Saint Paul's College in Lawrenceville, Virginia (after 40 years of college teaching) and embarked on a two-month summer tour of Europe. Although hired initially for only one semester, Dr. Dunlap was persuaded to stay through the 1966-67 academic year.

Dr. Womack found Dr. Dunlap's name on the Retired Professors Registry kept by the American Association of University Professors. Dr. Dunlap was living in Haverford, Pennsylvania, when Dr. Womack phoned and asked him to take an interim teaching position at Methodist. The 70-year-old Pennsylvania native accepted an offer of $4,100 for the semester and agreed to report for duty January 17, 1966.

George A. Dunlop

Three years later, in the fall of 1970, Dr. Dunlap published a book about his college teaching experiences (Methodist was the 14th school at which he had taught) entitled, *Giving It the Good Old College Try*. The third chapter of his book, "Vignettes of Methodist College, 1966-67," includes a delightful description of college life "in the piney woods" and thumbnail sketches of administrators, faculty and students he encountered.

Dean Womack met Dr. Dunlap at the Fayetteville train station January 17, 1966, took him to lunch on the campus, and introduced him to Dr. John Tobler. That afternoon they toured the campus, and Dr. Womack escorted Dr. Dunlap to his second floor, two-bedroom apartment on the southern edge of the campus. The rent was $120 a month. The next day Dr. Dunlap learned he would be teaching one section of Freshman Composition 101, two sections of Freshman Composition 102, and one section of English Literature that spring.

Dr. Dunlap had a great wit and impressive credentials, holding an A.B. from Haverford College (Class of 1916) and A.M. and Ph.D. degrees from the University of Pennsylvania. A bachelor, he spent a lot of time in his apartment typing his memoirs. While living in the faculty/married student apartments, the English professor became close friends with Dr. Richard O. Hartman, head of the Area of Religion and Philosophy, who lived in a first floor apartment. The two of them enjoyed playing tennis and could often be found on the College courts. In his chapter about Methodist College, Dr. Dunlap recalled that Miss Stella Robbins (cataloging librarian) once invited Dr. Hartman and him to her apartment, where they listened to her Oriental records, sampled

— CHAPTER 3 —

her cookies, and partook of a new drink, "Quink", "manufactured expressly for loosening the tongue." [35]

In his book, Dr. Dunlap offered brief but laudatory descriptions of College President Stacy Weaver, Dean Sam Womack, Dr. Francis Merchant (English professor), Addison Barker (assistant professor of English and speech), Parker Wilson (the "live wire and stage-struck" history professor), Bruce Pulliam (history professor), Dr. Willis C. Gates (professor of music), Dr. Karl H. Berns (professor of education), Dr. Christopher Ryan (professor of economics and mathematics), and others.

In one anecdote, Dr. Dunlap recalled "Dr. Wang Day," May 10, 1967, when students honored a mild-mannered political science professor from Shanghai, China:

> Why the honor? The night before, Wang had single-handedly overpowered the Reverend W. W. Finlater [an avowed pacifist and pastor of Pullen Memorial Baptist Church in Raleigh] in a heated discussion of "Vietnam and Its Implications." Standing ovations had greeted Dr. Wang's stout defense of democracy. The kids vowed that for once his English was flawless. [Author's Recollection: At one point, Dr. Wang shook his finger at the reverend, saying, 'Communists are bad people!'] At first he regarded 'Dr. Wang Day' as propaganda, but before long he became convinced that he was all wrong: it was a sincere mark of admiration, even affection. [36]

Dr. Dunlap devoted considerable space to sketches of eleven students from his classes. Ted Boushy (son of an MC English professor) merited two pages, while most were profiled in a half page to one page. Don Culbreth and Terry Wicker were both tutored. Basketball standout Wayne Warren saved himself from failure by reading and interpreting some Dylan Thomas poems in English Literature. Paul A. McKee Jr., a freshman from Raleigh, came up with the most novel excuse for missing a one o'clock class. It seems the young wrestler had to lose ten pounds by two o'clock so he could weigh in at 137 pounds.

After leaving Methodist, Dr. Dunlap returned to Pennsylvania, where he wrote and published four more books: *A Collector of Colleges* (1973), *Not Every Day's a Banner Day* (1976), *Black, White, and Red: The Problem of Shawnee College* (1979), and *Summer with Timmy Harkins and Mark Ferris* (1979). He lived another two decades, well into his 90s, spending his last days in a skilled nursing facility in Paoli, Pennsylvania.

Speaking of kudos, former sociology and religion instructor Arnold Pope, who taught at the College from 1967-81, gave Samuel Womack high marks as academic dean. "Dr. Womack did a tremendous job as academic dean while I was there. How he was able to recruit the faculty he did with no more than he had to offer in the way of financial compensation was just amazing to me. He had high standards and yet could be a compassionate person. Somehow, I don't think a lot of people realize that." [37]

S.G.A. Drafts New Constitution

The Student Government Association dominated the front page of the December 19, 1966, *sMALL TALK* with two stories. The lead story, headlined "Senate To Consider New Constitution," reported that S.G.A. President Steve Hopkins and a special executive committee had presented the draft for a new S.G.A. constitution to the Fourth Senate. Senate President Bill Tarr then divided the draft into four parts and referred each part to a study committee. It was agreed the Senate would vote for or against the proposed constitution and then submit it to the student body for ratification.

Two of four S.G.A. Senate committees could not agree on a provision of the new S.G.A. constitution changing the structure of the Senate. Article VII of the new document provided for proportional representation (one representative for every 50 students) chosen from the residence halls and a "commuter council." It also provided for one representative from each class (freshman, sophomore, junior, senior), one of whom had to be a commuting student.

The existing Senate was composed of four senators elected from each class, one of whom had to be a commuting student. After considerable discussion, members of the Fourth Senate decided to present both proposals (proportional representation vs. equal representation) for restructuring the Senate to the student body in a subsequent issue of *sMALL TALK*, and then vote for one form or the other, based on student reaction. The Fourth Senate later asked S.G.A. President Steve Hopkins to submit both versions of the new constitution to the student body for ratification, one with Plan I (proportional representation) for Senate composition and one with Plan II (a continuation of four senators from each class, with an alternate). The proposed constitution, with both types of representation, was published in the March 20, 1967, *sMALL TALK*.

S.G.A. President Hopkins scheduled a referendum for May 31, directing that students vote for: A. the proposed constitution with Plan I; B. the proposed constitution with Plan II; or C. retention of the present constitution. He declined to endorse either plan for Senate makeup. By a two-thirds majority, the student body voted for the new constitution with Plan II (four senators and one alternate from each of the four classes). Of the 339 students who cast ballots, 202 voted for the new constitution with Plan II and 115 chose the new constitution with Plan I. Only 22 students favored retention of the old S.G.A.

— CHAPTER 3 —

Constitution. Student leaders were disappointed with the turnout, with less than 40 percent of the student body voting.

At its final meeting April 27, 1967, the Fourth Senate enacted a set of by-laws to accompany the new S.G.A. constitution.

Construction Begins On Three Buildings

The January 16, 1967, sMALL TALK reported that Player Construction Co. of Fayetteville had set up a mobile office and would shortly begin construction of three new buildings: the fine arts building/auditorium, an administration building, and an addition to the student union/cafeteria.

President Weaver and Hugh Burton, S&W site manager, review plans for Reeves Auditorium.

sMALL TALK also reported that:
—Homecoming Weekend, February 3-4, would include Friday concerts by the U.S. Army Field Band and The Tams, a basketball game against Campbell College (with crowning of the Homecoming Court at halftime), an alumni dinner, and a dance featuring the Catalinas.
—the Methodist College Chorus would embark on its first concert tour January 27, appearing in Gloucester, Virginia; Washington, D.C.; Waynesboro, Virginia; Leesburg, Virginia; and Goldsboro, N.C.

1965–1969

The February 1967 issues of sMALL TALK reported that:
—150 students had made the Dean's List for the fall semester.
—Pat Ball, a senior elementary education major from Raleigh, N.C., was crowned Homecoming Queen.
—Virginia Wesleyan College, Methodism's newest college, had opened its doors. The college was located between Virginia Beach and Norfolk.
—The 35-member Methodist College Wind Ensemble, under the direction of Rodney Hill, gave its first concert February 14, appearing with the Community Chorus.
—Full-time enrollment for the 1967 spring semester stood at 866, versus 920 for the fall 1966 semester.
—The men's basketball team, led by Johnson Murray and Jim Darden, finished third in the Dixie Conference Tournament in Rocky Mount. Lynchburg College defeated Greensboro College to win the tournament.
—Dennis Bruce, in his "Behind the Power Plant" column, chastised some MC students and the dean of women for being unduly harsh in their treatment of Bob Hearn, a transfer student who had been critical of the Student Government Association and student life policies and had become a close adviser to S.G.A. President Steve Hopkins.

Jim Darden hits a lay-up.

Students Choose Alma Mater

The MC student body selected a college song as their "alma mater" at a special assembly Monday, March 13, 1967, in the Student Union. An S.G.A. committee had been appointed the previous year to invite musical entries and stage a contest to find an acceptable song. During the 1966-67 school year, the S.G.A. committee became a joint student-faculty committee. Sammy Williams, president of the Methodist College Chorus, was the student chairman, and Dr. John O. Tobler, area chairman of Social Sciences and professor of political science, was the overall chair of the Alma Mater Selection Committee. Other members were Ray Ussery and Alan Porter.

— CHAPTER 3 —

L to R, Dr. John Tobler, Sammy Williams, Dr. L. Stacy Weaver, Ms. Lois Lambie

During the assembly, the Methodist College Chorus, under the direction of Alan Porter, performed four different songs received by the committee. One was based on a Brahms piece with words by Virginia Kearn, '64. The second was an original composition with words and music by Dean Clark. The third entry, written by Dr. John Tobler, was based on the melody of a Swiss anthem with words by Dr. Garland Knott. The fourth was an original work by Miss Lois Lambie, a music teacher at Seventy-First High School in Cumberland County.

At the alma mater assembly, copies of the words to the four songs and ballots were distributed to the 900 students in attendance. After the chorus performed each song, the students were invited to sing along. When the ballots were tallied, the student body had voted by an overwhelming margin for the song written by Miss Lambie.

Lois Lambie's alma mater was short and deliberately so, consisting of eight lines, while the other compositions proposed as alma maters were longer, with rather flowery lyrics. The full text of Miss Lambie's alma mater follows:

> Hail to thee our Alma Mater!
> Raise we now our hearts to thee,
> Singing forth our highest praises,
> Pledging our deep loyalty.
> Green shall grow thy fields of learning;
> Gold shall glow the torch of truth.
> Methodist College, God go with thee
> Now and thro' eternity.

In a 2001 interview, Miss Lambie recalled that Dr. John Tobler phoned her in November 1966, and invited her to submit an alma mater. Shortly thereafter, she had dinner with Mrs. Pauline Longest, a Methodist College botany instructor, and Mrs. Phoebe Emmons, a field worker with the North Carolina Education Association. "We got to comparing alma maters—high school ones, college ones—all of them horrible things," she recalled. "I knew the school colors were green and gold, and I wanted to use those in the song. I also knew an alma mater should be short, one verse, and that the tune should be very simple, less than an octave, if possible. There are six notes in the Methodist College one. One note is only used twice." [38]

"When I started to write the tune for Methodist College, I got to thinking about Methodists," she continued. "Duke (University) was Methodist. And I sort of inverted Duke's tune. It went da ta ta da ta ta da tum. Tum da ta ta da ta ta da, I just turned it upside down for the first little phrase." [39] The end result was an eight-beat phrase for the first line of the song.

Lois Lambie taught Latin and directed the chorus at Seventy-First High School for many years. She also directed the choir at McPherson Presbyterian Church. She held degrees from the College of Wooster, Ohio and the Eastman School of Music. Miss Lambie also wrote the alma maters for Seventy-First High School, Little Field (a grade school in Robeson County), Douglas Byrd High School, and West Harnett Middle School.

A week after the student body adopted Miss Lambie's song, Sammy Williams and Dr. Tobler and Miss Lambie presented a framed manuscript of the "Methodist College Alma Mater" to College President Stacy Weaver. Dr. Weaver presented Miss Lambie's composition to the Methodist College Board of Trustees May 2, 1967, and the trustees adopted it as the college's "official song."

Students Elect New Leaders

The fourth annual Student Government Association election saw Eddie Barber, a rising senior from Raleigh, and Bob Swink, a rising junior from Greensboro, wage a spirited and very close race for S.G.A. president. Barber defeated Swink by a narrow margin in the April 14, 1967, election.

Barber ran on a 15-plank "Can Do" platform, while Swink offered a 16-point program. A record 675 students—75 percent of the student body—voted. S.G.A. officers elected with Barber were: David Brown, vice president; Johnny Lipscomb, treasurer; and Joanna Cherry, secretary. Class senators and class officers were also elected; the class presidents were John Briggs, rising sophomore class; Richard Dean, rising junior class; and Milo McBryde, rising senior class.

sMALL TALK reported in its May 1967 editions that the Publications Committee had approved the election of Susan Sharp, a rising junior from Fairfax, Virginia, as *sMALL TALK* editor for 1967-68, and Dennis Bruce, a rising senior from Raleigh, as editor of *TAPESTRY* (the college literary magazine) for the next school year. Shortly thereafter, Bill Billings, a rising senior from Durham, was named editor of the *Carillon* (the yearbook).

— CHAPTER 3 —

The Royal Arts Festival held the first week in May, 1967, featured "An Evening in Rome," a talent show staged by *sMALL TALK*, a showing of the film *Becket*, starring Richard Burton and Peter O'Toole, and a Green and Gold Masque Keys production of the George Bernard Shaw play, *Androcles and the Lion*. The play was staged in the courtyard of the Classroom Building.

College Acquires Lafayette Papers

In April 1967, College President Stacy Weaver and Dr. Samuel Womack, academic dean, announced that the college had acquired a valuable collection of original letters and memorabilia relating to the Marquis de Lafayette, the French general who aided the United States during its War for Independence. Lafayette visited Fayetteville, N.C., the first city in America named for him, during a tour of the United States in the spring of 1825.

Mrs. Margaret McMahan, a Lafayette scholar, persuaded the college to purchase a collection of letters, monographs and realia from the Schindler Antique Shop of Charleston, S.C., for $3,800. To house the collection and to add new acquisitions, a group called "The Friends of Lafayette" raised additional money.

Trustees Elect New Chair

At its annual meeting May 1, 1967, the Methodist College Board of Trustees elected Dr. Mott P. Blair, a dentist and prominent Methodist layman from Siler City, N.C., board chairman to succeed Terry Sanford. Sanford had asked not to be reappointed chairman, but had agreed to remain a trustee. The trustees adopted a resolution of appreciation for Sanford's service, praising him for his tireless efforts to bring Methodist College to Fayetteville and to raise the funds needed to build the new college.

Trustees elected Henry B. Dixon, a retired Burlington Industries executive from Mebane, N.C., vice chairman of the board and tapped John W. Hensdale and Wilson F. Yarborough of Fayetteville to serve as secretary and treasurer, respectively.

In other actions, the board voted to accept the recommendations of its Executive Committee to name the new auditorium/fine arts building for John M. Reeves of Pinehurst and the library in honor of the late Geraldine Tyson Davis. A retired textile executive and a college trustee, Mr. Reeves gave $200,000 in 1965 toward the construction of the fine arts building. Mrs. Davis was a Cumberland County native and wife of Walter R. Davis of Midland, Texas. She gave $100,000 in 1962 to help build the library and served as a college trustee from July 1, 1963 until her death September 23, 1966.

In the area of fund raising, trustees received some good news and some bad news:

—Robert Milner, executive director of the Fayetteville College Foundation, said contributions to the college were running somewhat behind the previous fiscal year.
—the Rev. James Auman, director of the Association of Methodist Colleges of The North Carolina Conference, reported that his office was trying to complete payment of pledges on the Church's $5 million Capital Funds Campaign by the meeting of the Annual Conference in June, 1968, at which time Resident Bishop Paul Garber would be retiring.
—Dr. Blair, chairman of the trustees' Development Committee, reported that pledges of $26,087 had been received on the Second Decade Campaign, of which $10,172 had been paid.
—Trustee W. R. Horner of Sanford promised to contribute an additional $5,000 to the college if the rest of the Board of Trustees would match it with $45,000 by the end of the year. His challenge was accepted by his fellow trustees.

In his annual report to the Board of Trustees, College President L. Stacy Weaver noted that:
—the college enrolled 980 students in 1966-67, but opened with 45 empty beds in its residence halls.
—Methodist employed 57 persons with faculty rank.
—MC was currently offering majors in 12 fields and minors in five, and would add a major in sociology when it was able to obtain a teacher with a Ph.D.
—the college had a 1966-67 operating budget of $1,577,837 and an endowment valued at $553,545.
—student costs for 1967-68 would be $1,600 for a resident student and $800 for a day student.
—the college had refinanced its $1 million loan with First Citizens Bank and Trust Company and made the first two amortization payments.
—Methodist needed additional tennis courts, a paved parking lot behind the Student Union-Cafeteria, a soccer field, and facilities for track and field events.
—Dr. Karl Berns, former executive secretary of the National Education Association, had been appointed assistant to the president for development and would assume that post in January 1968. Dr. Berns would succeed Col. William Pope, who had resigned to become superintendent of Oak Ridge Military Institute.

— CHAPTER 3 —

—the Board of Trustees needed to amend the college charter to allow the board of its Executive Committee to sell property not contiguous to the college without the approval of the Board of Education of the North Carolina Conference of the Methodist Church.

—recommended that the board adopt the "Alma Mater" recently approved by the student body as the college's official song.

—presented a one-page draft of a new Statement of Purpose for the college.

At a called meeting May 29, 1967, the college trustees approved the new Statement of Purpose presented three weeks earlier by Dr. Weaver, as well as "Further Regulations in Regard to Tenure" (including the procedure for terminating tenured faculty), and the trustee committee appointments presented by Dr. Mott Blair, the new board chairman.

The trustees Executive Committee met June 21, 1967, and approved a contract for paving the parking lot behind the Student Union, a budget for 1967-68 ($1,683,089 for operating, $109,394 for capital expenditures) and fees for 1968-69 totalling $1,800 a year for a resident student and $900 for a commuting student.

Alumni Install New Officers

The Methodist College Alumni Association installed new officers for 1967-68 at its annual banquet and meeting Saturday evening May 27, 1967. The new officers were Jerry C. Wood '64, president; Ralph F. Hoggard '64, vice president; and Ella Rose (Hall) Smith '66, secretary-treasurer.

College Graduates Fourth Class

Sixty-eight seniors received degrees at Methodist College's fourth spring commencement Monday, May 19, 1967. An additional twelve seniors received degrees at the end of the summer session July 14.

Dr. Felix Robb, director of the Southern Association of Colleges and Schools, gave the commencement address. Speaking about power, Dr. Robb said education is the key to power. He also predicted, "The next hundred years can belong to the South if we successfully work out the human relations problem." [40]

Ima Jean Hutchinson, an English major from Fayetteville and a *magna cum laude* graduate, received the L. Stacy Weaver Award from Dr. Samuel J. Womack, academic dean. Given by vote of the faculty, the award is presented each spring to the senior who best exemplifies academic excellence, spiritual development, leadership, and service.

President and Mrs. Weaver receive Betty Lipscomb and brother Johnny at Betty's graduation.

In his baccalaureate sermon Sunday, May 28, 1967, Dr. Pierce Harris, pastor emeritus of First Methodist Church of Atlanta, challenged members of the Class of 1967 to choose wisely their level of living.

College Foundation Falls Short of Annual Goal

During 1966-67, the Fayetteville College Foundation fell $41,519 short of meeting its $120,000 annual commitment to Methodist College. The Foundation raised $70,258 from July 1, 1966-May 31, 1967 and gave $60,321 of that to the college.

Foundation President Jerome B. Clark Jr. explained the shortfall as follows at an April 20, 1967, board meeting: "Many are not aware of the college, its people and purposes." [41] To change this, Clark suggested the Foundation: 1) seek a deeper emotional involvement by everyone with the college, 2) recognize that since the college is not "established," it needs annual gifts, and 3) encourage greater campus visitation. [42]

The Fayetteville College Foundation Board of Directors received a fundraising proposal June 8, 1967, from Murchison and Bailey, Inc. of Fayetteville. For a fee of $13,5000, co-owner Alton Murchison said the firm would organize and direct a campaign to raise $150,000 locally in January 1968. At a July 13, 1967 meeting, the Foundation board voted to hire Murchison and Bailey to conduct the campaign.

— CHAPTER 3 —

Mr. Clark informed the Foundation board September 14, 1967, that the $150,000 raised in the campaign would be appropriated as follows: $30,000 to cover a 1966-67 deficit, $70,000 to amortize the $1 million loan (for initial construction of the college), and $50,000 to meet the foundation's annual commitment toward college operating funds.

Mrs. Raymond Thomason told the Foundation board October 12, 1967 that "Challenge for Excellence" would be the theme for the January 1968 campaign. Jerome Clark announced that Mr. I. B. Julian, vice president of First Citizens Bank and Trust Company, would chair the campaign.

Recruiting Students for Methodist

During the 1960s, recruitment of students was the responsibility of the Public Relations Office, more specifically, Charles McAdams, director of public relations, and Bill Lowdermilk, assistant director of public relations. It was their job to sell Methodist College to high school students along the East Coast and to youth who attended Methodist churches in The North Carolina Conference of the Methodist Church (eastern North Carolina).

Because both were Methodists (Mr. McAdams a prominent layman and Mr. Lowdermilk an ordained Methodist minister), they made a special effort to promote the college to Methodist churches. It was in 1959, while Mr. McAdams was on the staff of Edenton Street Methodist Church in Raleigh, that Methodist College President Stacy Weaver asked McAdams to join the college as director of public relations and development. One of Mr. McAdams's first actions after arriving at Methodist was to ask each church in The North Carolina Conference to appoint two representatives to visit Methodist College and to help recruit students. In addition, McAdams spent many Sundays at local churches in the Conference giving programs about the college.

The church connections of Charles McAdams and Bill Lowdermilk proved invaluable to Methodist College. McAdams and Lowdermilk often stayed in the homes of Methodist ministers and lay leaders when out on recruiting trips. During the mid 1960s, about half of the students enrolled at the college were Methodists.

From 1963-68, Bill Lowdermilk traveled widely, recruiting hundreds of students for Methodist College. "From September to December, I made the College Day programs of North Carolina," he recalled in a 2001 interview. "In January, I did the community colleges. In the latter part of February and the first part of March, I went to New Jersey. Then in April I went to Florida. In the summer, we used to get the Beta Club (high school honor society) lists from North Carolina, South Carolina, and Virginia; then we'd go through the lists trying to find students for majors Methodist was offering at that time." [43]

One of the high school guidance counselors who proved most helpful to Lowdermilk was Janie Weaver, Stacy Weaver's sister, who worked at Reynolds High School in Winston-Salem, N.C. In Lowdermilk's words, "When we went to College Day programs in those days, there would be 30 or 40 colleges there, recruiting in the gymnasium. At Reynolds, Methodist College was always at the center table in the front as you entered the gym. I remember another counselor at a high school in Salem, New Jersey, who always had five or six students lined up to talk to me." [44]

Lowdermilk lived on campus for most of his 32 years at Methodist and often used his culinary skills to recruit students for Bible study. After his Friday night Bible studies, he recalled, "I would feed them sinfully rich desserts. That was the way I showed students I cared about them and that they were important." [45] For Christmas 2001, Lowdermilk published a book for family and friends entitled *Uncle Bill's Recipes and Related Reflections*.

During an August 2001 interview, Lowdermilk offered high praise for the staff, students, trustees and friends of the college he knew during his 32 years at Methodist. Those specifically mentioned include: secretaries Cora Ann Turner and JoAnn Taylor, Larry Barnes '66 (an early president of the Methodist College Alumni Association), Ray Gooch '72 and Mike Safley '72 (who helped Lowdermilk prepare for Annual Conference meetings at the college), Dwight Cribb '80, Jerry Cribb '81, and trustee Ramon Yarborough.

Lowdermilk was especially fond of the "housemothers" who lived in the residence halls in the 1960s:

> Mrs. Nash was in Sanford Hall. She ran a country store. I mean she had cigarettes and matches, candy bars, whatever the students needed or wanted. . . There was Huldah Jones, a Baptist minister's widow, a more loving person you would never find in all your life. She always had extra linens, pillows, extra soap. . . Mildred Stanton in Cumberland loved going to car races and smoked her Camel cigarettes unfiltered. She was a good housemother who really cared about the students. These people were a good team and made a valuable contribution to the College. [46]

Former Dean of Men Arnold Pope also admired the housemothers:

> Pauline Jones in Cumberland Hall was just as homespun as she could be. One night a student was walking on the ledge outside his window and fell off. He was not seriously hurt, but Mrs. Jones said when they picked him up to put him in the ambulance, 'He looked

— CHAPTER 3 —

The large showers in the men's residence halls sometimes doubled as swimming pools.

like he was as stiff as a three-day old corpse.' We had this night watchman named 'Beanie.' Mrs. Jones' description of him was, 'He looked like somebody picked him before he got ripe.'

Mrs. Stanton sponsored a drag race and had some trophies in her apartment there in Garber Hall that her racer had won. She could keep order. She was probably not 80 pounds soaking wet, but I have seen her give some boys a rush out the door when they got out of line. [47]

College Begins Eighth Year With 1,069 Students

Methodist College began its eighth academic year September 14, 1967, with a record enrollment of 1,069 students, including 626 resident students. Enrollment increased 13 percent over the Fall 1966 figure of 944 students. Construction of the Administration Building, Fine Arts Building/Auditorium, and an addition to the Student Union continued on schedule.

The 60-member faculty included 15 new members: Dr. Ying Hsin, professor of economics and business administration; Dr. Clarence C. Hulley, professor of history; Mr. Fred Reardon, instructor in economics and business administration; Mr. Fred D. Wright, instructor in sociology; Dr. Paul Patterson, professor of biology; Mr. Tsung-Hsun Wu, assistant professor of physics and mathematics; Mr. William E. Woodall Jr., instructor in mathematics; Dr. Maria Salas-Calero, assistant professor of Spanish; Miss Ann Scott Thompson, instructor in French; Dr. Ivan Booker, professor of education; Bernon E. Byrd, assistant professor of English; Mrs. Edna Contardi, assistant professor of English; and Miss Nancy C. Massengill, instructor in English.

New additions to the administrative and teaching staff included Thomas Arnold Pope, dean of men and instructor in sociology, and Mr. Phillip C. Smith Jr., librarian.

Dr. Samuel J. Womack, academic dean, announced the creation of a new area of study, Area VII, formed by separating foreign languages from Area I, Languages and Literature. Dr. Charles Gilbert Rowe, professor of foreign languages, was named chairman of the new area.

The college opened its first language laboratory in the fall of 1967, using a downstairs classroom in the basement of the Classroom Building. The lab consisted of 24 carrels equipped with microphones and headphones for speaking and hearing practice. Twelve of the carrels contained tape decks for recording. The master console allowed the instructor or student lab attendant to play six different tapes simultaneously and to communicate with individual students, groups of students, or the entire class. It was estimated that 500 foreign language students would use the lab the first year.

In late September, Athletic Director Gene Clayton announced that Methodist's sports programs had been accepted for membership in the National Association of Intercollegiate Athletics (NAIA) District 26 (North and South Carolina and Virginia). The Dixie Intercollegiate Athletic Conference, of which Methodist was a member, joined the Carolina Intercollegiate Athletic Conference and nine at-large teams, including Campbell College and Wofford College, in NAIA's District 26.

Sherry Sellers Killed in South Carolina Wreck

Methodist College suffered a major tragedy September 23, 1967, when Sharon Ruth Sellers, a senior from Lockport, N.Y., was killed in a two-car collision in South Carolina. Driving alone, Sellers was on her way to Union, S.C., to hear her father preach at a revival.

The Student Government Association chose to remember the popular cheerleader by establishing the Sharon Ruth Sellers Memorial Scholarship. Donna Davis, Sellers' roommate, chaired a three-member S.G.A. Scholarship Committee with John Briggs and JoAnna Cherry.

Author Guy Owen Discusses *Flim Flam Man*

Dr. Guy Owen, former history professor at N.C. State University and writer-in-residence at Appalachian State University, was the featured speaker at a meeting of the Methodist College Literary Club October 5, 1967, in Davis Library. *sMALL TALK* reported that the poet and novelist gave an entertaining and fun-filled lecture about his novel, *The Ballad of the Flim-Flam Man*, and about writing in general. A Clarkton, N.C., native, Dr. Owen had attended a premiere of the film *The Flim-Flam Man*, which was based on his novel, October 4 in Elizabethtown, N.C. The film starred George C. Scott and featured the Cumberland County Courthouse in Fayetteville in one scene.

Dr. Owen told his audience he often used the names of real people in his stories and novels. He read a passage from *Flim-Flam* about a humorous encounter between Doodle Powell (a bootlegger) and Curley Treadaway at a liquor still. Asked what advice he would give to any aspiring author, Dr. Owen said, "There are two kinds of writers: the talking writers and the doing writers. The only way to be a writing writer is by doing and revising. There is no such thing as a 'writer.' There are only 'rewriters.' Try to emphasize being a creative writer. I would also say to read widely, not only to read but to scrutinize. . .read in depth." [48]

Freshmen Toss Beanies

In a student assembly October 9, 1967, freshmen ended their one-month orientation by taking a test compiled by the Student Government Association. Several frosh were also tried in a Kangaroo Court for violating the S.G.A. Orientation Code, which required among other things, that all freshmen wear beanies during the first month of school. Those found guilty of violating the code received sentences such as: singing under the bell tower at 5 p.m., sweeping the parking lots, counting all the pine trees on campus, and watering all the plants in the dorms.

At the end of the assembly, Bill Blalock, a junior, led the freshmen in the singing of the alma mater. Then, as reported by *sMALL TALK*, "Eddie Barber (S.G.A. president) gave the countdown and beanies flew into the air; orientation was finally over!" [49]

Homecoming '67 Features Little Anthony and the Imperials

Homecoming 1967 began with a bonfire Thursday evening November 2. The highlight of the four-day celebration was a concert by the rock and roll group Little Anthony and the Imperials (known for the hit "Tears on My Pillow," among others) November 3; the crowning of JoAnna Cherry of Charlotte as Homecoming Queen Saturday, November 4 (during halftime of a soccer game against Pfeiffer), an alumni banquet, and a dance that evening.

Dr. Graham Eubank Speaks at Eighth Founders' Day

Dr. Graham S. Eubank, Fayetteville District Superintendent of the Methodist Church and former pastor of Hay Street Methodist Church in

In the fall of 1967, freshman orientation ends as frosh toss their beanies into the air.

Fayetteville, was the keynote speaker at the college's eighth Founders' Day program Wednesday, November 1, 1967. One of the college's original trustees, Eubank said, "Of all the community enterprises sought and accomplished by the community of Fayetteville, none can excel the establishment of this college." [50]

Dr. Weaver used the occasion to announce a gift of $90,000 to establish scholarships in memory of Thelma Dingus Bryant, daughter of E. Bascom Dingus and Coral H. Dingus of Duplin and Pender counties.

In a November 14, 1967, editorial entitled "Where Were You?", *sMALL TALK* Editor Susan Sharp chastised the majority of the MC student body for "skipping" the Founders' Day program. She expressed embarrassment and outrage that only 100 of the 900 seats set up in the Student Union for staff and students were occupied.

Following the Founders' Day program, the college trustees dedicated Davis Memorial Library in memory of Geraldine Tyson Davis and held a brief luncheon meeting.

Outlaw Criticizes Chief Justice Earl Warren

Col. Wilbur Outlaw, North Carolina coordinator of the ultraconservative John Birch Society, told a group of 100 Methodist College students and faculty members November 1, 1967, that U.S. Chief Justice Earl Warren should be impeached "because of his pro-Communist leanings." [51] Outlaw accused the "Warren Court", as he called the Supreme Court, of attempting to rewrite the

CHAPTER 3

U.S. Constitution with recent rulings prohibiting compulsory prayer in public schools and placing new restrictions on the police in the handling of criminals.

Invited by MC's newly formed History and Political Science Club, Outlaw said the Birch Society was registered as a non-profit educational organization and was not political. The speaker said the society's motto was "Education is our total strategy; truth is our only weapon." [52] He listed the following as the group's primary goals: to fight communism, to seek less government, and to promote more citizen responsibility and a better world. Outlaw said the society had built up "a nationwide army with a fully paid staff" to fight communism and was spending more than $4 million annually to print and distribute literature.

Dr. Weaver Voices Thanks And Support For U.S. Troops

The December 12, 1967 *sMALL TALK* contained a timely news story about Methodist College President L. Stacy Weaver's Thanksgiving chapel address November 22, 1967. The story quoted Dr. Weaver as saying he was thankful for American troops fighting in Vietnam, that he didn't know the answer to the present situation there, but that he felt the time for protest was over because America was now fully involved in the conflict.

Dr. Weaver said if there were going to be protests against the Vietnam War, they should have been: "1) when John Foster Dulles put the United States into SEATO (the Southeast Asia Treaty Organization). If we wanted to be isolationists and cut ourselves off from the rest of the world, we should have said so then; 2) when President Eisenhower sent military advisers to Vietnam; and 3) when President Kennedy put arms into the hands of these men and told them if they were shot at to shoot back." [53]

"Now that we are sending drafted men into Vietnam to face bullets, I, for one, am not going to do anything to increase their difficulty," Weaver continued. "I will support them in every way that I can." [54]

President Weaver said he felt American affluence "was detracting from our gratitude" and added, "Thanksgiving was born and proclaimed in times of adversity." [55] Dr. Weaver also expressed his thankfulness for "the spiritual foundations of America; the freedoms which we enjoy, especially the freedom to govern ourselves; for the great men of the past and the present; for friends and for parents who at times were not afraid to say no." [56]

Students Confront Local, National Issues

In a February 1968 issue of *sMALL TALK*, S.G.A. President Eddie Barber announced that Methodist College would participate in CHOICE '68, a national college presidential primary being underwritten by Time Magazine.

He said 14 presidential candidates and three referenda issues would be on the ballot, and voting would take place April 24.

sMALL TALK found no shortage of news or student opinion in the spring of 1968. Ken Murray, a junior from Fayetteville, had assumed the editorship of the student newspaper at the beginning of second semester after Susan Sharp withdrew from college.

Academic Dean Samuel J. Womack appointed a special committee to study the college's class attendance policy after several faculty members complained about overcutting by Dean's List students (then granted unlimited cuts).

The MC wrestling team won the Dixie Conference wrestling championship February 10, 1967, by upsetting highly favored St. Andrews. The Monarch basketball team finished fourth in the Dixie Conference with an overall record of 10-13 and a conference mark of 8-7. The top finishers were St. Andrews, Lynchburg, and Greensboro.

The March 11, 1968, *sMALL TALK* contained two sharp jabs at some MC students. In a letter to the editor, Jesse Staton Jr. '70 criticized scores of his fellow students for rude behavior (talking, laughing, horseplay) during an assembly at which the Seventy-First High School Chorus performed under the direction of Miss Lois Lambie, composer of the Methodist College Alma Mater the previous year.

In the same issue, in a column entitled "Reflections at Fleishman's Pool," Gordon Herbert, a senior from Durham, roundly condemned what he called "pseudo or non-students at Methodist—those concerned mainly with "Glady's [the nearest source of beer], dating, intramurals, and gossip," those who were "fairly dull, intellectually artificial, and apathetic." [57] He ended his column by urging each of his fellow students to choose action and intellectual discipline over mediocrity and short-term gratification.

A front page story in the February 26, 1968, *sMALL TALK* reported that the number of MC students on academic probation had tripled from spring 1967 to fall 1968, growing from 57 to 149. Seventy-seven of those placed on probation at the end of the fall semester were freshmen.

In early March 1968, the S.G.A. Senate unanimously approved a resolution requesting that MC launch an intercollegiate baseball team at Methodist the following spring. It was noted that the Athletic Department supported this addition, and that Bruce Shelley, then serving as cross country, tennis and J.V. basketball coach, had agreed to coach the sport. The S.G.A. resolution was forwarded to the college Board of Trustees. In addition, *sMALL TALK* Sports Editor Richard Dean wrote an editorial in the March 25, 1968, issue supporting the idea and saying that N.C. Wesleyan College in Rocky Mount, N.C., was willing to reinstate baseball if Methodist fielded a team. He said MC would

— CHAPTER 3 —

Remember womanless weddings? Methodist's Circle K Club came up with the Miss Boiler Plant pageant in 1968; participants are shown taking a curtain call. Wayne Trousdale (in the print mumu) won this first one. Even College Controller Frank Eason once took to the runway!

construct a baseball diamond in the "cornfield" east of the men's residence halls.

Another news story from March 1968 concerned a joint meeting of the Student Academic Affairs Committee with the Faculty Academic Affairs Committee at which students voiced opposition to a tighter class attendance policy and raising the 3.0 GPA requirement for Dean's List to 3.25. On the other hand, the student committee urged discontinuance of the "lax policy" of allowing courses to be repeated with only the new grade being used to compute grade point averages. The committee suggested that the old grade be averaged with the new when a course was repeated.

The March 25, 1968 *sMALL TALK* also reported that the first phase of construction had begun on an amphitheater near a small pond on the south campus. Funds for this project were pledged by Mr. and Mrs. I. H. O'Hanlon of Fayetteville as a memorial to their son, Michael Terrence. The amphitheater was designed to seat 750 persons when completed.

The student newspaper also reported that Methodist College delegates to the March meeting of the State Student Legislature won passage in both houses of a bill to indemnify (pay the medical bills) of North Carolina residents who came to the aid of other citizens and were injured in the process. Based on a California law, the bill was forwarded to state legislators for their consideration.

The April 9, 1968, *sMALL TALK* carried a four-page "election section," giving the rules and dates for April 19 S.G.A. elections, along with the "platforms" of Bob Swink and Richard Dean, juniors seeking the post of S.G.A. president. The section also gave space to candidates for other S.G.A. and class officers to make their pitches.

That same issue of *sMALL TALK* also included a photo of Mary Alexander, a sophomore from Charlotte, N.C., who died in a local car accident April 2, 1968. A memorial service for Mary was held during the chapel hour the following week.

In its April 29 edition, the last of the 1967-68 school year, sMALL TALK reported that Bob Swink defeated Richard Dean by 57 votes and that 61 percent of the student body cast ballots. Others elected to S.G.A. offices were: Bill Blalock, vice president; David Hatchell, treasurer; and JoAnna Cherry, secretary.

The student newspaper also announced that Dr. Clarence Ficken, Methodist College's first academic dean, would address the Class of 1968 May 27 and that Methodist Bishop Paul Garber, presiding bishop for the Raleigh Area, would deliver the baccalaureate sermon May 26.

On three inside pages, sMALL TALK promoted the Royal Arts Festival/May Week activities, including an art exhibit by MC students, a sMALL TALK talent show ("To Broadway With Love"), a formal May Dance (theme: "Night Life in New York") featuring The Batchelors (a Virginia-based band), and three one-act plays by the Green and Gold Masque Keys (*Hello Out There* by William Saroyan, *Impromptu* by Tad Mosel, and *Ways and Means* by Noel Coward.) Trudi Jaber, a sophomore from Clarksville, Virginia, was crowned May Queen at the May Dance.

Students Wed in Chapel

Dr. Lorenzo Plyler officiated at the first wedding ceremony held at Methodist College March 9, 1968, in the small "classroom chapel" in the basement of the Classroom Building. The two students united in marriage were Robert Flynn, a sophomore from Roxboro, N.C., and Jeannine Faulkner, a freshman from Raleigh; they met while singing together in the Methodist College Chorus. After graduating from Methodist, Robert Flynn became a United Methodist minister in The North Carolina Conference.

In a December 17, 2002, e-mail to MC Alumni Director Tom Maze, Robert Flynn gave the following account of his courtship of and marriage to Jeannine:

> Jeannine and I met in the old Music Building when she tried out for the college chorus. Our chorus time was our dating time as well as our chorus travel time on the bus. We ate all meals together and even shared some study times. Our first date was a "group date" when we joined chorus friends on what we called a 'ghost search.' We dated only one other time. I proposed the last Thursday of February 1968.
>
> Dr. Lorenzo Plyler (area chair of religion and philosophy) officiated at our wedding, and Alan Porter (director of the MC Chorus) sang.
>
> President Weaver attended, and Charles McAdams (director of public relations) took photographs and

— CHAPTER 3 —

presented them to us as a gift.

After our wedding, we lived upstairs in the Infirmary, because Mr. Eason, the comptroller, said we had paid our dormitory space for the remainder of the school semester. [58]

Author's Note: The Reverend and Mrs. Robert Flynn are still happily married and the parents of four grown sons and a daughter. One of their sons, Jonathan Flynn, graduated from Methodist College in 1994.

Trustees Approve Names for Chapel, Classroom Building

At its annual meeting April 2, 1968, the Methodist College Board of Trustees approved the recommendation of its Executive Committee that the college chapel, the next building to be constructed, be named for John W. Hensdale, a Fayetteville trustee and a member of Haymount United Methodist Church. During the preceding five years, Mr. Hensdale had secured gifts totalling $54,995 from Belk-Hensdale Stores and the Belk Foundation. At his request, these funds were placed in a Chapel Fund.

Trustees also voted to named the Classroom Building the "Trustees Building" in honor of those who served on the original Board of Trustees and their successors in office. Finally, the board authorized President Weaver to execute a loan agreement with the U.S. Commissioner of Education for a loan under Title III of the Higher Education Facilities Act of 1963 to assist in the construction of the Administration Building and the Fine Arts Building.

In his annual report to the trustees, President Weaver said he was gratified that the college had enrolled a record 1,122 students in 1967-68 (both semesters) and had filled the residence halls. He also thanked Jerome Clark, president of the Fayetteville College Foundation, for 15 months of faithful and efficient leadership. (For the 1967-68 fiscal year, the Foundation raised

$108,571 locally for Methodist College; $96,312 for capital needs and $11,142 for operating expenses.)

The president said a federal loan for construction of the Fine Arts Building had been reduced by $52,000 because of funding cuts by Congress, which meant the college would now have to raise this amount. He noted that the college's 1968-69 budget would have to include $26,000 for amortizing the loan on the Student Union addition and $30,000 for retiring loans on the administration and fine arts buildings. He said the trustees' Executive Committee had authorized a student fee schedule for 1968-69 totalling $1,800 per year for a resident student and $900 per year for a commuting student.

Dr. Weaver said the college had assets of $8,070,273, liabilities of $4,062,303, and an endowment worth $406,754.

College Graduates Fifth Class

Methodist College awarded degrees to 112 students at its fifth commencement May 27, 1968. Both the May 26 baccalaureate service and the actual commencement ceremony took place in the newly-completed Reeves Auditorium/Fine Arts Building.

Donna Davis, a religion major from Raleigh, N.C., received the L. Stacy Weaver Award. Six members of the Class of 1968 graduated *magna cum laude*, and six graduated *cum laude*.

Dr. Clarence E. Ficken, Methodist's first academic dean (1960-62) delivered the commencement address, posing the question, "Where do we go from here?"

The June 1968 *Bulletin of Methodist College* reported that Dr. Ficken answered his question as follows: "The only place to go from here is to the cultivation of a creative response to the challenge of change. . .In order to make a creative response, man must be able to think and speak for himself. Also, man must be able to recognize his biases and prejudgments; he must develop a mental hospitality to new ideas." [59] Dr. Ficken challenged the graduates to discipline themselves for creative problem-solving in a tehnological world.

In his baccalaureate sermon, Bishop Paul N. Garber preached on "The Light of the World."

Methodist Conference Brings 1,050 To Campus

The 1968 session of The North Carolina Annual Conference of the United Methodist Church met on the Methodist College campus June 4-7, 1968, establishing what would become an annual tradition. Approximately 1,050 ministers and laymen attended the 1968 session of Annual Conference, and 540 of them were housed in the college's four residence halls.

— CHAPTER 3 —

Reeves Auditorium was completed in the spring of 1968, just in time for graduation.

Retiring Bishop Paul Garber, who had served the Raleigh Area for 17 years, presided over the conference. Guest speakers included Bishop Hazen G. Werner, Hong-Kong-Taiwan Area; Bishop Willis J. King, New Orleans, La.; and Bishop Walter C. Gum of the Richmond Area.

"We knocked ourselves out for them," said Bill Lowdermilk, then serving as director of public relations. "We made up 600 beds; we provided the pillows and the bed linens, towels, and everything. Ray Gooch and Mike Safley came down a week prior to Annual Conference. We went through the dorm rooms and noted everything that needed to be fixed. Then Maintenance made the repairs." [60]

For the next 18 years (in 1986 the Conference met at Duke University) and into the mid-1990s, Methodist College continued to host annual meetings of the Conference. Over the next 25 years, the college hosted scores of other Conference events, from annual meetings of the United Methodist Women to the Annual Conference Session (A.C.S.) of the United Methodist Youth Fellowship. These groups still meet annually at the college.

Bill Lowdermilk took great pride in the hospitality extended to his fellow Methodists during meetings at the College. The annual conference meetings in June were generally well-organized and very successful. At one meeting, however, half of a dossal curtain hanging from a metal pole fell while Bishop Cannon was leading a communion service in Reeves Auditorium. "Everyone just drew their breath as that lead pipe came down behind the bishop," said Lowdermilk. [61]

Uncle Bill's Flock

Rev. Lowdermilk helped Charles McAdams organize the Methodist College Alumni Association and worked closely with the group during four decades. The first alumni chapter meeting was held at the Flying Cloud Restaurant in Richmond, Va. He has vivid memories of one trip, when he and Larry Barnes, the alumni association president, were driving back from chapter meetings in Washington, D.C. and Richmond. "After we passed Richmond, it started snowing. It was 2 a.m. on a Sunday, and we both had to be back for Sunday school lessons. We were driving on I-95, and both of us were petrified . . . we kept sticking our heads out the windows so we wouldn't fall asleep." [61]

"Uncle Bill," is a nickname bestowed upon Lowdermilk by MC alumni, with whom he developed lifelong friendships. Many alumni remember the sermon Lowdermilk gave at a freshman orientation worship service; it was entitled "In Life You Are Always Starting Over." Other alumni remember Uncle Bill's Friday morning prayer breakfasts and the delicious desserts he served on those occasions. Lowdermilk presided at scores of alumni weddings; the first being that of Wayne Trousdale '68 at First United Methodist Church in Elizabeth City, N.C. He also baptized the children of College alumni and officiated at funerals of both alumni and alumni family members. Lowdermilk was the first person named an honorary alumnus by the Methodist College Alumni Association. [*Bill Lowdermilk's retirement program and memorial service would later be held in Reeves Auditorium, a place he knew and loved.*]

Foundation Changes Name

In July 1968, the Fayetteville College Foundation, Inc. amended its certificate of authority with the state of North Carolina and changed its name to Methodist College Foundation, Inc. The Foundation board had earlier amended its by-laws to expand the size of the board to 30 members, with "classes" of ten members elected on a staggered basis to serve three-year terms.

John C. Pate served as Foundation president for 1968-69; Pate was succeeded by I. H. O'Hanlon for 1969-70. The Methodist College Foundation raised $106,431 locally for the college in 1967-68 and $124,263 in 1968-69.

Fall 1968 Enrollment Declines

Methodist College began its ninth academic year, 1968-69, with an enrollment of 992 students, a faculty of 66 persons, three new building additions (Horner Administration, Reeves Auditorium/Fine Arts Building, north wing of Student Union), and four new administrators.

The Fall 1968 enrollment declined by 77 students from Fall 1967's 1,069, forcing President Weaver and the Board of Trustees to cut $126,105 from the operating budget previously adopted; yet the reduced budget of $1,928,103 still represented an increase of $245,014 over the 1967-68 operating budget.

Of the fifteen new faculty, ten replaced persons who had resigned, and five were additions. The new faculty included: Mr. Earl D. Martin, assistant professor of sociology; Mr. Jerry D. Lehman, instructor in education and psychology; Mr. Milton W. Loyer, instructor in mathematics; Mr. David N. Hutto Jr., instructor in art; Mr. James H. Price Jr., librarian/director of Material Center; Dr. James Howell, professor of English; Dr. Robert D. Bryant, assistant professor of sociology; Mrs. Ingeborg Dent, assistant professor of German and French; Mr. Edwin A. West, assistant professor of education and psychology; Mr. Roy F. McClelland, assistant professor of education and psychology; Mrs. Faye Lehman, cataloguing librarian; Mr. Robert S. Christian, instructor in English; Miss Frances C. Garrett, instructor in English; Dr. Sudhaker Gautam, associate professor economics and business; Miss Earlyne Saunders, director of guidance and placement.

In the administrative area, Mr. Bill Lowdermilk replaced Charles McAdams as director of public relations. Mr. McAdams left Methodist to become treasurer of the North Carolina Annual Conference of the United Methodist Church. Three other administrative changes were announced by President Weaver and Dean Womack. Mr. Charles McCullers, a Methodist layman from Dunn, N.C., assumed the new administrative post of Director of Institutional Advancement, charged with coordinating the work of the Director of Public Relations and the Director of Development.

Mr. Neil H. Thompson was named Director of Admissions, under the jurisdiction of Dean Womack. Thompson was to be assisted by Mr. Lowdermilk and Mr. Paul West, a transfer from the Comptroller's Office. (Mr. West later became the financial aid officer.) Mr. Sam Edwards, former admissions director, registrar, and director of financial aid, retained the title of Registrar.

Students Rate Faculty, Pick Nixon

The lead story in the first issue of *sMALL TALK* for 1968-69 concerned the release of the 1967-68 Student Academic Affairs Committee's evaluation of the Methodist College faculty. Committee Chair Donna Davis '68 released a report in which students had rated 55 professors and come up with a composite grade of 2.8 (C+) for the entire faculty.

Thirteen professors (25 percent) received "excellent" ratings, 25 received "good" ratings, 11 received "average" ratings, and six were rated "below average." The two curriculum areas rated highest by students for quality of teaching were Religion and Philosophy as well as Science and Mathematics, each receiving a 3.3 (B) rating. The faculty in the Social Science area received the lowest rating

Students of art instructor Donald Green inspect a wooden sculpture that Green built.

of 2.25 for what the committee termed an "extremely weak" economics and business department.

The committee offered two major recommendations: first, that the college raise the salaries of those faculty shown to be "dedicated, competent, and worthy," and second, that the academic dean and area chairmen make greater efforts to ascertain and upgrade the quality of classroom teaching.

At least one faculty member and several students wrote letters to *sMALL TALK*, questioning the methodology used in compiling the report and the committee's findings. The *sMALL TALK* story gave the following report of administrative feedback about the survey: "After reviewing the evaluation, both Dr. Weaver and Dr. Womack commented that it coincided with reports already in their possession." [63]

sMALL TALK Editor Ken Murray's lead editorial in the Sept. 17, 1968 issue caused a small uproar. Saying that speed bumps recently installed on campus were dangerously high and poorly placed, Murray said if the administration did not immediately remove at least half of the bumps and lower the other half by at least half, students would be justified in attacking the bumps with kerosene and a match. In the next issue, Larry Lugar said he agreed some of the bumps should be lowered, but noted that the real problem was "speed bums" who endangered pedestrians on campus. Lugar expressed outrage that Murray supported an act of vandalism (pouring kerosene on the asphalt speed bumps and setting them on fire) as a solution.

— CHAPTER 3 —

Howie Arden (R) eyes the ball in the fall 1968 homecoming game.

Results of the CHOICE 68 poll of Methodist College students conducted as part of a national poll in April revealed that 385 MC students (40 percent of those eligible) had participated. Results of the Methodist poll showed Richard Nixon was the top choice for president (with 39 percent of the vote). National poll results, however, gave Sen. Eugene McCarthy first place and Nixon third place.

The third issue of *sMALL TALK* announced that the spring 1968 issues of the student newspaper had been awarded a First Class rating by the Associated Collegiate Press.

Homecoming '68 Features Jay and the Americans

Homecoming Week 1968 (October 22-26) featured a Green and Gold Masque Keys production of *The Glass Menagerie* by Tennessee Williams, a Friday night concert by Jay and the Americans, a Saturday soccer game against St. Andrews Presbyterian College, and a Saturday dance featuring the Classics IV. MC lost the game to St. Andrews 3-0. Lyn Seacord, a junior from Scarsdale, N.Y., was crowned Homecoming Queen.

In November 1968, the S.G.A. Senate passed a bill written by Bruce Hiatt and Ronnie Russell setting up a committee made up of the presidents of each class and the chairman of Methodist's State Student Legislature delegation to select the college's delegates to the State Student Legislature. [The S.G.A. president formerly appointed delegates as a special committee.]

1965–1969

The Tower Rocks

One of the most famous Methodist College pranks involved the Yarborough Bell Tower. Early one morning during Homecoming Week of 1968, a group of men from Sanford Hall and Cumberland Hall patched into the wiring at the base of the tower, connected a portable cassette player, and proceeded to play rock and roll music through the speakers in the tower's electronic carillon. Around 1 a.m. on a weekday morning, the campus and neighboring community awoke to the raucous music of Doug Clark and the Hot Nuts blaring from the tower. The Reverend Arnold Pope, who was dean of men at the time and lived in a brick house on the southern front of the campus, heard the racket and set out on foot to investigate.

This is how Pope remembers the incident:

Arnold Pope

> I walked across the lawn and came up on the west side of the library . . . There had to be at least 200 people in a circle out there carrying on with this music playing. One of the boys saw me and screamed, 'God, it's Dean Pope!' It looked like a giant covey of quails flushed. I pulled the wire and player loose from the tower and started walking toward the men's dormitories. As I walked through the dorms, I was amazed at the number of boys who were sitting in their rooms studying. Many were having difficulty breathing, trying to catch their breaths. [64]

Many students who lived on campus during that period remember that Pope often marched around his yard in the late afternoon playing his bagpipes. He was also a competitive weight lifter and competed in the Scottish games at Grandfather Mountain (where he threw the stone and tossed the caber) for about 20 years.

In a 2000 interview, Pope recalled some other interesting experiences he had as dean of men and dean of students:

—One night the Sanford Hall housemother phoned me to say a group of boys was gathered in a circle behind the dorm howling at the moon. She wanted to know what she should do. I suggested she throw some meat out the window.

—Barney Vincellette, a student from New Jersey, liked things that glowed in the dark. One night Barney invited me to see

— CHAPTER 3 —

his room. I walked in and he closed the door and turned the lights off. Then all of a sudden I see stars up on the ceiling and recognizable constellations. He had painted the entire solar system on the walls and ceiling, with paint that glows in the dark. His motorcycle helmet was also painted with that and it glowed in the dark. He drove an old Chrysler with tail fins; it was painted green with gold trim. He had this toggle switch which he could flip, and the outside skin of the car became electrified. He also had a shortwave radio and broadcast radio programs from his dorm room. [Vincellete later earned his doctorate, made it into *The Guiness Book of World Records* (for creating the largest psychedelic light display on a house), went skydiving in the nude, and wrote a book entitled, *Bird of Paradise*.]

—One year during semester break, some students took a VolkswagonBeetle apart and reassembled it in a student's dorm room. When the student returned from break and entered his room, the car was actually idling.

—One night some students swiped a pig from a nearby farm and turned it loose in Garber Hall. Mildred Stanton [housemother from Cumberland Hall] came over, grabbed the pig by the hind legs, and threw it out the front door. I made the guys take the pig back to the farm.

— One spring some guys built a raft, intending to float down the Cape Fear River to the Azalea Festival [held each spring in Wilmington, NC]. They found some oil drums and two-by-tens. A boy from New Jersey donated his old Chevy car, and they welded paddle wheel spokes on the rear wheel rims. Before they could launch it, the thing was stolen. {Jim Darden '69 said he saw the craft spring a leak and sink in the middle of the river shortly after it was launched; he said the crew abandoned ship and swam to shore.]

— Once I followed this path down to the river and found one of our students playing Tarzan in a sycamore tree. He would grab hold of the vine with one hand and swing out over the river and come back to the tree and hit himself in the chest and make Tarzan noises. One time the vine twisted at the last minute, and all he could see was the sycamore tree right in his face. Luckily, he was not too badly hurt, and I was glad because I was so broken up laughing, I would not have been much help to him."[65]

Chapel Construction Begins

sMALL TALK began the second semester of 1968-69 with a new editor, Sonja Kendrick. The first issue of the spring semester noted that construction had begun on Hensdale Chapel at the east end of the Reeves Auditorium/Fine Arts Building.

The February 1969 *Bulletin of Methodist College* reported that Stevens & Wilkinson of Atlanta had designed a one story chapel with a vaulted roof and dormer and with red oak paneling inside. Player, Inc. of Fayetteville was the general contractor for the $71,650 project. Completion was projected for September 1, 1969. The simple design was a radical departure from the octagonal, diamond-shaped chapel with stained glass walls that was included in the architect's original plan for the campus and later depicted on class rings.

Faculty Raps 'Mickey Mouse' Assemblies

The February 11, 1969, *sMALL TALK* reported on the results of a questionnaire distributed by the student newspaper to MC faculty in January. The poll was designed to gauge opinion on four campus matters: the feasibility of having semester exams before Christmas, changes faculty would like to see in their departments, the faculty's relationship with the administration, and feelings about required convocations and assemblies.

The lead story on Page 1 proclaimed, "Faculty Urges Evaluation of Monday Assembly Programs" and included the following comment from Dr. Garland Knott, professor of religion: "The programs on Monday have been on an elementary level,. . .an insult to the students. The student body should be commended for its tolerance in being forced to attend 'Mickey Mouse' programs by the S.G.A. and other organizations."[66] The article went on to say that Dr. Knott's comment summed up the feelings of most faculty members questioned.

The February 25, 1969 *sMALL TALK* carried stories on both the front and back pages about the basketball team winning its first Dixie Conference championship. The Monarchs, coached by Gene Clayton, defeated the N.C. Wesleyan College Bishops February 13 in Rocky Mount by the score of 86-65. Senior Jim Darden scored 30 points in the title game. Darden and sophomore Roy Henderson were named to the all-conference first team. The Monarchs compiled an 11-3 conference record. Coach Gene Clayton was elected DIAC Basketball Coach of the Year.

In mid-March, Methodist's 10-member delegation to the 32nd annual session of the North Carolina State Student Legislature (held at Elon College) won passage in both houses of a bill entitled "Motivational Analysis Testing in Secondary Schools" and received "Honorable Mention" for its work. The delegation included: Ronnie Russell, chair; Bob Swink, Natalie Schwoyer,

— CHAPTER 3 —

Ronnie Bott, Barbara Schutz, Warren Southerland, Richard Swink, Georgena Clayton, Dale Leathers, and Tommy Smith.

The lead story in the April 1, 1969, sMALL TALK noted that the faculty academic affairs committee headed by Dr. Lorenzo Plyler had recommended new grade average requirements for students to remain in good standing with the college: a minimum 1.25 GPA at the end of the spring semester of the first academic year, 1.5 at the end of the second year, 1.75 at the end of the third year, and 2.00 at the end of the fourth academic year and thereafter. The policy stated that any full-time student who did not pass 16 semester hours of course work in a single academic year would be suspended.

College Registrar Sam Edwards reported that spring 1969 enrollment totalled 929, 63 students less than the 992 enrolled in the fall of 1968. He reported that 157 students had withdrawn since the beginning of the 1968-69 school year.

The student newspaper reported in its April 29, 1969 issue that a group of MC students had met with faculty members April 16 and proposed a SCORE (Student Committee Organized for Research & Evaluation) plan for evaluating the faculty patterned after a system used at UNC-Greensboro. The plan called for creation of a committee of seven students and seven faculty members, representing each of the seven academic areas of study at the college.

Dean Sam Womack was reported to be receptive to the idea. It was agreed a report of the ratings would be published for each academic area, but that ratings of individual faculty members would be withheld.

Under the SCORE system, students would evaluate professors by completing an 80-question booklet and answer sheet for each class. Evaluations would be turned in to the student member of the SCORE committee for the academic area to which the class belonged. The student and faculty SCORE representative of each area would then tally the responses given in each class and issue a report to the professor, the department head, the area chairman, and the academic dean.

The April 19, 1969, sMALL TALK also reported that the Sixth S.G.A. Senate had unanimously adopted a resolution from Howard Arden that, starting in the fall of 1969, the S.G.A. would support only one assembly program each week, that being Monday at 11:30 a.m. The resolution stated that special programs and class meetings could be held Wednesday at 11:30 a.m., that students should still be allowed three cuts (absences) each semester, and that the punishment for overcutting should be retained. It had become apparent to everyone that many students were not attending the two required assemblies (one secular and one religious) each week.

1965–1969

In its spring 1969 issues, *sMALL TALK* also reported that:
—Methodist students presented Samuel Beckett's controversial tragi-comedy, *Waiting for Godot,* April 29-20, 1969 in Reeves Auditorium. Bill Blalock played Estragon and Keith Hummer played Vladimir, two tramps waiting for the coming of Godot, but confronted instead by a master and his slave. Patrick Corn and John Williams played Pozzo (the Master) and Luck (the Slave) respectively. Raymond Conley, assistant professor of speech, directed the play.
—The MC tennis team finished third in the DIAC.
—The soccer team had a winless first season, with 11 losses and one tie.
—The cross country team finished second in the Dixie Conference.
—The wrestling team tied for second in the DIAC with teams from St. Andrews and Lynchburg.
—Pitcher Bob Costello fanned 16 batters as Methodist launched its first season of baseball against N.C. Wesleyan March 22, 1969. The Monarchs defeated the Bishops 2-1 in the first game of a doubleheader, but lost the second game 6-5. The initial win over Wesleyan was followed by 11 losses.
—The bowling team finished first in the conference and seventh among East Coast college teams playing in a post season tournament.

1969 Conference Champions: Monarch bowling team, shown with Coach Howard Baum (R).

— CHAPTER 3 —

—The golf team finished fifth in the conference.
—Howard Hudson of Garner, N.C., and Richard Swink of Greensboro, N.C., received the Outstanding Senior Athlete Awards.
—Religious clubs on campus, which had formerly been organized by denominations (*e.g.* Methodist Student Movement, Baptist Student Movement, Canterbury Club, Newman Club), decided to combine forces and form a new religious fellowship called Koinonia.
—Students elected the following S.G.A. officers for 1969-70 April 18, 1969: Jim Russell, president; Georgena Clayton, vice president; Diane Qualliotine, secretary; and Terry Self, treasurer. Camellia Sizemore was elected editor of the 1970 *CARILLON* (yearbook).
—Terry Self, a junior from Mebane, N.C., was crowned the 1969 May Queen.
—Caroline Norman of Fayetteville was named head cheerleader for 1969-70.

Bishop Cannon Addresses Class of 1969

Methodist College awarded degrees (157 Bachelor of Arts and 15 Bachelor of Science) to 172 students at its sixth annual commencement Monday, May 26, 1969.

The *Bulletin of Methodist College* reported that Bishop William R. Cannon, the new resident bishop of the Raleigh Area of The United Methodist Church, "gave counsel on 'how to live tomorrow'" [67] in his commencement address.

"We must live as best we can today," said Bishop Cannon. "Observe the law, heed the moral injunctions of holy scripture, and form a vital companionship with God." [68]

James Loschiavo, a math major from Fayetteville, received the L. Stacy Weaver Award. Five students—Loschiavo, Raymond H. Smith Jr., Mary Ann Monroe, Woodrow Wells, and Sandra E. Johnson—earned recognition as Methodist College Scholars, having earned a 3.6 GPA after the first semester of their senior year.

The Rev. Dr. Walker B. Healy, pastor of First Presbyterian Church of Roanoke, Va., delivered the baccalaureate sermon Sunday morning, May 25. President and Mrs. Weaver hosted a reception for graduating seniors and their families Sunday afternoon.

President Briefs Trustees on Declining Enrollment

At its annual meeting May 6, 1969, the Methodist College Board of Trustees approved an amendment to the college by-laws to allow the board to elect any active member who had served ten years and attained the age of 68 a "trustee emeritus."

On the recommendation of Norman Campbell, reporting for the trustees' Development Committee, the board adopted two goals: 1) to raise $80,000 for college operating expenses during the current fiscal year, and 2) to raise $80,000 for construction of a Field House and Maintenance Building.

Dr. James Auman reported for the Association of Methodist Colleges of The North Carolina Conference of the United Methodist Church that $40,000 in capital funds had been raised for the conference's three colleges (Louisburg, Methodist, N.C. Wesleyan) in 1969. Dr. Mott Blair, trustees chairman and United Methodist layman, said a group of United Methodist laymen was trying to obtain uncollected funds in the conference's capital drive for its colleges.

James Darden and Wayne Blake, president and vice president respectively of the Class of 1969, presented their class gift to the trustees—a framed portrait of College President L. Stacy Weaver to be hung in the board room of Horner Administration Building.

In his 10-page annual report to the trustees, President Weaver expressed concern that the college began 1968-69 with 45 empty beds in the residence halls and had 126 fewer applicants for 1969-70 than it had at the same point in 1968. He predicted another decline in total enrollment for 1969-70, "thus creating further budgetary problems." [69]

Dr. Weaver said someone had observed at a recent meeting of the N. C. Conference of The United Methodist Church's Commission on Christian Higher Education "that there are more Methodist students enrolled at East Carolina University alone than in all of the Methodist colleges in the state combined." [70] He said the reason was obvious—cheaper state tuition at E.C.U.—but also observed, "There are more young people preparing for full-time Christian service in The United Methodist Church and in other churches, enrolled at Methodist College alone, than there are young people undergoing such preparation in all of the public institutions combined, with their many thousands of students." [71]

The president asked each member of the Board of Trustees to direct college-age young people toward Methodist College.

Looking at college assets, Dr. Weaver reported that the college plant had a value of nine million dollars, a little more than half of which had been raised and paid. He said the college had received a little more than one and a half million dollars from The Methodist Church and hoped to receive the $450,000 still

— CHAPTER 3 —

remaining on this commitment. He said the original capital loan of one million dollars used for initial construction of Methodist College had been reduced to $958,597 and that the College had a balance outstanding on revenue bonds held by the federal government of $3,460,000. Finally, the president noted that the college endowment had a book value of $511,180.

Dr. Weaver said increased student fees for 1969-70—$2,000 for resident students and $1,000 for commuting students—might not be sufficient to support the college operating budget if enrollment continued to decline. He said he disagreed with some, including the president of the Ford Foundation, that the only way private colleges could survive in America was to obtain public funds. The president then added, ". . .it behooves us to be about the business of working out our own salvation. The ultimate answer to underwriting part of the cost of the operation of the college is endowment funds." [72]

At the end of his report, President Weaver said he did not intend to be "too somber" about the future of the college and wished to conclude by quoting John Ruskin, "who wrote some lines which aptly describe the undertaking in which we have been engaged for more than a decade." [73] Ruskin wrote:

> "Therefore when we build, let us think that we build forever. Let it not be for the present delight nor for the present use alone. Let it be such work as our descendants will thank us for, and let us think as we lay stone on stone that a time is to come when those stones shall be held sacred because our hands have touched them. And men will say as they look upon the labor and the wrought substance thereof, 'See, this our fathers did for us.'" [74]

At a special meeting held May 26, 1969, the college Board of Trustees unanimously passed a resolution opposing the proposed expansion of Fayetteville Technical Institute into a community college offering liberal arts courses for the freshman and sophomore years of college. The resolution said the proposed expansion by F.T.I. would adversely affect Methodist College and would represent a duplication of services already offered by Fayetteville State College and the N.C. State University Branch at Fort Bragg. The trustees' resolution was sent to each of Cumberland County's state legislators and to the chairman of the State Board of Education.

Trustees Adopt Budget, Fees

Meeting July 23, 1969, the trustees' Executive Committee approved a college budget for 1969-70: $1,900,863 for operating expense and $152,966

1965–1969

for capital expenditures. Tuition for 1970-71 was increased $50 per semester or $100 for the year.

At a meeting November 3, 1969, the trustees' Executive Committee discussed drawings for a proposed Maintenance Building (at a cost not to exceed $45,000) and gave the trustees' Building Committee authority to proceed with this project.

College Begins Tenth Year

Methodist College began its tenth academic year, 1969-70, with nine new faculty members and an enrollment of 903 students. Mrs. Pauline Longest, assistant professor of biology, was named chairman of Area IV: Science and Mathematics.

The new faculty members included: Mrs. Eleanor Howell, assistant professor of art; Dr. Deryl F. Johnson, associate professor of philosophy; Mr. Stacey H. Johnson, instructor in physics; Miss Marilyn Morgan, head librarian; Mrs. Georgia C. Mullen, assistant librarian; Mrs. Sondra M. Nobles, instructor in physical education; Mr. Howard W. Reisinger Jr., foreign language instructor; Mr. John Rider, music instructor; and Mrs. Elizabeth W. Wilson, reference librarian.

In September, William "Chip" Largent '69 became the first alumnus to be employed by the College. Hired as an admissions counselor by the Admissions

John Rider (L), Wind Ensemble director, and Alan Porter (R), choral director, collaborate.

— CHAPTER 3 —

Office, he recruited students for Methodist College in North and South Carolina, Virginia, and states in the Northeast.

Two new facilities—Hensdale Chapel and the Earth Science Laboratory—greeted students in the fall of 1969. During the fall semester, Sunday afternoon vesper services, two weddings, a baptism, and a Christmas candlelight service were held in the chapel. At a Founders' Day dedication November 3, John William Hensdale, the man for whom the chapel was named, commented that, though the building was small in size, he hoped it would serve a big purpose. [75]

The Earth Science Laboratory, financed with a matching federal HEW (Dept. of Health, Education, and Welfare) grant, was designed for Science 100, a two-semester course for non-science majors preparing for elementary education. The laboratory included a mineral and rock collection, geological maps and charts, a weather station, and a Polaroid MP-3 camera that could be used for making slides.

New Assembly Policy Takes Effect

A news story in the September 30, 1969, issue of *sMALL TALK* announced that a committee appointed by the college president (composed of students, faculty, and administration) to study assembly programs and the attendance requirement for students had drafted a new policy which had won the approval of the Administrative Committee.

Under the new plan, each student was required to attend 13 assemblies each semester versus the old requirement of two assemblies each week, which amounted to 36 assemblies per semester. The weekly assembly was held Wednesday at 11:30 a.m. Students were given slips of colored paper (each class had its own color) which they signed and dropped in boxes on leaving Reeves Auditorium. The Dean of Students Office was charged with recording student attendance and enforcing penalties against students who did not comply.

The October 14, 1969, *sMALL TALK* reported that the Monarch soccer team had defeated Guilford College 1-0, UNC-Wilmington 2-0, and Davidson College 3-2 before losing to Pembroke State College 5-2.

The newspaper staff revealed in its October 28, 1969 issue that College President Stacy Weaver had appointed students to seven faculty committees as well as the Student Life Committee, choosing from a list of students submitted by S.G.A. President Ronnie Russell. The same issue reported that only a few Methodist College students had participated in a Vietnam Moratorium October 15, 1969. This was a day when college students around the nation wore black arm bands to express their opposition to the Vietnam War.

Homecoming 1969 was held Oct. 27-Nov. 2, 1969, and featured a bonfire, a Green and Gold Masque Keys production of Maxwell Anderson's play, *The*

Wingless Victory, the Circle K Club's Miss Boiler Plant pageant, a homecoming dance featuring The Tempests, an alumni banquet, and a homecoming concert featuring The Drifters backed up by Maurice Williams and the Zodiacs.

The MC soccer team won its homecoming game against N.C. Wesleyan 5-0, led by Karl Woelfel who scored three goals. The Monarch soccer team finished its second season with a record of 7-3 and tied for first place in the Dixie Conference at the end of the regular season. This was a dramatic turnaround, for the Monarchs won no games in their first season. In addition, Coach Mason Sykes was named NAIA District 29 Coach of the Year, and two of his players, Karl Woelfel and Howard Arden, were named to the All-Conference and All-District teams.

In *sMALL TALK's* December 1969 issue, most of the dozen or so male students interviewed about the new federal draft lottery (in which birth dates were drawn and put in order for drafting priority) said the new system was fairer than the old method. On the editorial page, Editor Sonja Kendrick said farewell to her readers and welcomed her successor, Bill Flowers, a junior from Goldsboro, N.C. Flowers became editor in January 1970.

— CHAPTER 3 —

END NOTES
Chapter Three

1. Stacy Weaver, Chapel Address, February 24, 1965, *sMALL TALK*, March 1965, file.
2. Ibid.
3. Stacy Weaver, "Annual Report to the Methodist College Board of Trustees," May 4, 1965, TM, Book 1.
4. Minutes, May 31, 1965, meeting of the Methodist College Board of Trustees, TM, Book 1.
5. Ibid.
6. Mary Monroe Atwater, quoted in "Methodist College Grad Helped Open Doors," a feature article by Jeffery Womble, *The Fayetteville Observer*, February 11, 2001, file.
7. Ibid.
8. Thomas Jefferson, quoted by Larry Barnes, *sMALL TALK*, September 16, 1965, file.
9. Larry Barnes, *sMALL TALK*, September 15, 1965, file.
10. Bruce Pulliam, "The Heritage That Is Yours," *sMALL TALK*, October 4, 1965, file.
11. Ibid.
12. Gene Clayton, quoted in sports story, *sMALL TALK*, December 1, 1965, file.
13. Bob Nardone, quoted in news story, *sMALL TALK*, December 13, 1965, file.
14. Rom Mason, *sMALL TALK*, December 13, 1965, file.
15. Bill Billings, editorial, *sMALL TALK*, November 16, 1965, file.
16. Danny Nau, letter to the editor, *sMALL TALK*, December 13, 1965, file.
17. Richard Alston, editorial, *sMALL TALK*, December 13, 1965, file.
18. Tommy Yow, letter to the editor, *sMALL TALK*, December 13, 1965, file.
19. Ibid.
20. Ibid.
21. Ibid.
22. Ibid.
23. Gwen Pheagin Sykes Holtsclaw, interview with Lynn Gruber, October 26, 2000, file.
24. Methodist College Charter, Article VI, presented to the Methodist College Board of Trustees, May 3, 1966, TM, Book 1.

1965–1969

25. Jean Hutchinson, e-mail to Bill Billings, March 18, 2004.
26. News Story, *sMALL TALK*, November 2, 1966, file.
27. Dennis Bruce, column, *sMALL TALK*, November 2, 1966, file.
28. Terry Sanford, Founders Day Address, November 2, 1966, reported in *sMALL TALK*, November 21, 1966, file.
29. George Vossler, remarks at Founder's Day, November 2, 1966, minutes of Fayetteville College Foundation, November 1966, FCF, file.
30. Susan Sharp, feature story, *sMALL TALK*, November 2, 1966, file.
31. Mason Sykes, interview with Lynn Gruber, November 13, 2001, file.
32. Norman Holmes Pearson, forward to *Leaves Before the Wind* by Walter Blackstock, MC Press, 1966.
33. Walter Blackstock, *Leaves Before the Wind*, MC Press, November 1966.
34. Thomas Wolfe, *Look Homeward Angel*, quoted by Walter Blackstock in *Leaves Before the Wind*, MC Press, November 1966.
35. George A. Dunlap, *Giving it the Good Old College Try*, New York: Carlton Press, Inc., 1970.
36. Ibid.
37. Arnold Pope, interview with Lynn Gruber, August 9, 2000, file.
38. Lois Lambie, interview with Lynn Gruber, August 30, 2001, file.
39. Ibid.
40. Dr. Felix Robb, Commencement Address, May 19, 1967, *Bulletin of Methodist College*, May 1967.
41. Jerome B. Clark Jr, Meeting of the Fayetteville College Foundation Board, April 20, 1967, FCF, file.
42. Ibid.
43. Bill Lowdermilk, interview with Lynn Gruber, August 29, 2001, file.
44. Ibid.
45. Ibid.
46. Ibid.
47. Arnold Pope, interview with Lynn Gruber, August 9, 2000, file.
48. Guy Owen, quoted in *sMALL TALK*, October 18, 1967, file.
49. Eddie Barber, as quoted in a news story in *sMALL TALK*, October 11, 1967, file.
50. Dr. Graham Eubank, Founders' Day Speech, November 1, 1967, as reported in the *Bulletin of Methodist College*, November 1967, file.
51. Colonel Wilbur Outlaw, speech to Political Science Club, November 1, 1967, as reported in *sMALL TALK*, November 14, 1967, file.

— CHAPTER 3 —

52. Ibid.
53. Dr. L. Stacy Weaver, Chapel Address, November 22, 1967, as reported in *sMALL TALK*, December 12, 1967, file.
54. Ibid.
55. Ibid.
56. Ibid.
57. Gordon Herbert, columnist, *sMALL TALK*, March 11, 1968, file.
58. Robert Flynn, e-mail to Methodist College Alumni Director, Tom Mayes, on December 17, 2002, file.
59. Dr. Clarence E. Ficken, Commencement Address, as reported in *Bulletin of Methodist College*, June 1968, file.
60. Bill Lowdermilk, interview with Lynn Gruber, August 29, 2001, file.
61. Ibid.
62. Ibid.
63. News story, *sMALL TALK*, September 17, 1968, file.
64. Arnold Pope, interview with Lynn Gruber, August 9, 2000, file.
65. Ibid.
66. Dr. Garland Knott, as reported in *sMALL TALK*, February 11, 1969, file.
67. Bishop William R. Cannon, Commencement Address May 26, 1969, reported in *Bulletin of Methodist College*, May 1969, file.
68. Ibid.
69. Dr. L. Stacy Weaver, "President's Annual Report to the Methodist College Board of Trustees," May 6, 1969, TM, Book 2.
70. Ibid.
71. Ibid.
72. Ibid.
73. Ibid.
74. John Ruskin, quoted by L. Stacy Weaver, "President's Annual Report to the Methodist College Board of Trustees," May 6, 1969, TM, Book 2.
75. John William Hensdale, *Bulletin of Methodist College*, February 1970, file.

Dr. Richard W. Pearce

Chapter 4

The Torch Is Passed
1970-74

"I believe higher education is literally a mission field of the church . . . I have faith in the church-involved college."
—*Dr. Richard W. Pearce, in a Methodist College press release announcing his selection as the second president of Methodist College, April 3, 1973.*

Methodist College began its second decade of operation by initiating several academic innovations. These included: a two-year "pass-fail" option for upperclassmen taking elective courses; a course in Russian; two new "ecology" courses; and an art major.

Acting on a request from the Student Academic Affairs Committee, the faculty voted February 3, 1970, to allow a pass-fail option for a two-year trial period for juniors and seniors taking elective courses. The student committee requested the option as a means of encouraging more students to take electives outside of their major and minor fields.

For students choosing the Pass-fail option, the faculty opted to continue reporting letter grades to the Registrar, who would convert the grades to "Pass" (for grades of A, B, and C) or "Fail" (for grades of D or F). Students awarded a "Pass" grade in a course would earn the appropriate semester hours of credit, but no quality points would be awarded, and the course grade would not affect their grade point average. [The Methodist College Board of Trustees subsequently approved the new option after requesting that the grade of D be designated a passing grade or one what would not be reported under the pass-fail option.]

Foundation, Alumni Make News

sMALL TALK's lead news story February 10, 1970, reported that the Methodist College Foundation and the Methodist College Alumni Association had set fund-raising goals for 1970. The Foundation board launched its annual Community Loyalty Campaign January 13, 1970, with George B. Herndon and Glenn R. Jernigan serving as co-chairmen. The board set a goal of $120,000—$70,000 toward amortization of a $1 million construction loan and $50,000 toward the college's operating budget.

— CHAPTER 4 —

A sidebar story reported that the Finance Committee of the Methodist College Alumni Association would try to raise $5,000 from the college's 1,300 alumni before the May 1970 alumni banquet.

In its February 1970 *Bulletin*, the college announced that Harold J. Teague '64 had completed work on his Ph.D. in chemistry at N.C. State University, becoming the first Methodist College alumnus to earn a doctoral degree.

Chorus Tours Northern States

The February 10 *sMALL TALK* devoted an entire inside page to a photo feature showing highlights of the Methodist College Chorus's six-day concert tour of ten northern states during the break between first and second semesters. Traveling on a chartered Trailways bus, 35 chorus members, eight members of the Wind Ensemble, and Mr. Alan Porter, choral director, performed at Methodist churches in Roanoke and Alexandria, Virginia; McKeesport, Lafayette Hill and Philadelphia, Pennsylvania; Manchester, Connecticut; and Goldsboro, North Carolina.

Other news reported in the campus newspaper during the spring 1970 semester included:

—A February 8-11, 1970, visit by a seven-member committee of the Southern Association of Colleges and Schools. The committee was charged with reviewing Methodist College's adherence to eight standards required for reaffirmation of accreditation.

—The Monarch basketball team finished fourth in the 1970 Dixie Conference Basketball Tournament, defeating Greensboro College, but losing to UNC-Charlotte and St. Andrews Presbyterian College.

—The M.C. delegation to the 1970 session of the State Student Legislature achieved several milestones. The delegation's proposed population control bill for the state of North Carolina passed the House and Senate and was chosen Best Bill Presented by a Small College. After the bill was passed, the delegation sent a copy to the North Carolina General Assembly for its consideration. The second milestone was the election of three M.C. delegates—Natalie Schwoyer, Howard Arden, and Tommy Smith—as officers. Over 300 students from colleges and universities within North Carolina attended the 1970 S.S.L. session.

—The Kelly Springfield Tire Company, a division of Goodyear Tire and Rubber Company, opened a tire manufacturing plant a mile north of Methodist College.

1970–1974

—The M.C. tennis team entered the Dixie Conference tournament with a 4-1 record.
—Six seniors and one 1969 graduate were named Methodist College Scholars: Patricia Alston, Theresa Keller, Linda McPhail, Leven Nguyen, Diane Qualliotine, Leta Anne Smith, and Gloria Dailey '69.
—Methodist College placed five student athletes in the 1970 volume of *Outstanding College Athletes of America*: Roy Henderson, Bobby Hodges, Ronald Roberts, Howard Arden, and Karl Woelfel.
—Howard Arden and Roy Henderson were named Outstanding Senior Athletes at the 1970 Methodist College Sports Award Banquet. Arden was cited for outstanding play in the Dixie Conference Tennis Tournament (finishing No. 2 in singles and winning the doubles competition with partner Bently Hill). Henderson received Most Valuable Player awards in both basketball and baseball.
—Methodist College students observed "Earth Day" April 22, 1970, by planting a tree in front of Hensdale Chapel.
—President Weaver announced at the May 23, 1970 Alumni Banquet that Dean of Students O.E. Dowd would be retiring July 1 and moving to Greenville, N.C. Dowd had served as dean of students since 1962. The following newly elected officers of

The first and second levels of the campus mall circa 1970.

CHAPTER 4

the Methodist College Alumni Association were announced at the banquet: Tommy Yow '66, president; David B. Herring '65, vice president; and Gwen Pheagin Sykes '68, secretary.

Trustees Re-elect Mott Blair Chairman

At its annual meeting April 6, 1970, the Methodist College Board of Trustees re-elected as officers: Dr. Mott P. Blair, chairman; Henry B. Dixon, vice chairman; J. W. Hensdale, secretary; and Wilson F. Yarborough, Sr., treasurer. Trustees re-elected to four-year terms, in addition to Yarborough and Blair, were: F. D. Byrd Jr., J. W. Hensdale, William K. Quick, W. David Stedman, O. L. Hathaway, W. Robert Johnson, and T. Lynwood Smith. Trustees also elected Louis Spilman Jr., a member of the Methodist College Class of 1964, to a term ending July 1, 1971.

In an 11-page annual report to the trustees, College President L. Stacy Weaver noted that the college would soon complete its tenth year of operation, having graduated 810 young people. He expressed concern over declining residential enrollment, saying the college had 145 empty beds in the residence halls. He said the "overexpansion" of state institutions of higher learning "has placed the private and church-related colleges in North Carolina in a non-competitive position as far as students are concerned." [1]

Dr. Weaver then added: "It seems inevitable that Methodist College must recruit more students from other states where the cost of attending college, even in public institutions, more nearly approaches the costs which we are forced to assess against our students." [2]

The president said the college also needed to increase its faculty salary schedule, but could not afford to do as much as it should. Referring to the Methodist Church's original pledge of $2 million in capital funds for Methodist College and the fact that only $1.5 million of that amount had been received, Dr. Weaver said, "I am not optimistic that we will ever receive this money. By the contribution of $1.5 million, The North Carolina Conference of The Methodist Church has secured title to $9 million worth of property." [3]

Dr. Weaver also reported that a group representing private colleges in North Carolina had appeared before the state Commission on Higher Education and requested a state tuition grant to state residents attending private colleges, a grant based on the differential between tuition charged by public and private institutions in North Carolina. He asked the trustees to express their support for the state grant to their state legislators.

At this meeting, the college trustees also approved an amendment to Article IX, Section 2, Subsection G of the college charter making it clear that the college president is chairman of the faculty, but that the faculty elects its own secretary.

1970–1974

At a July 23, 1970, meeting, the Methodist College Board of Trustees approved an operating budget of $1,916,990 for 1970-71 and a capital budget of $131,519. The trustees also approved a $100 increase in tuition and the requirement of a $25 damage deposit from all resident students, effective with the 1971-72 school year. Trustees Chairman Mott Blair named his appointments to the following board committees: Executive and Finance, Nominating, Academic Affairs, Building and Grounds, Student Affairs, and Development.

John Brown Elected S.G.A. President

The May 12, 1970 *sMALL TALK* reported that John Brown, a rising senior from Piscataway, N.J., had been elected S.G.A. president for 1970-71, along with the following officers: Donald Leatherman, vice president; Kitty Cook, secretary; and Virginia Aydlett, treasurer. In a letter that appeared on Page 3, Brown said the two major goals of the S.G.A. the following year would be : 1) To stop the rise in vandalism, and 2) To give the Student Union Committee policy-making power.

Allen, Lewis Address Class of 1970

Durham, N.C., native George V. Allen, a retired U.S. ambassador and vice chairman of the Duke University Board of Trustees, delivered the commencement address to 156 seniors at Methodist College May 25, 1970. Speaking about international affairs, he said the role of policeman for the world had been thrust upon the United States and that he considered the prospect of an international federation in Europe "the brightest light on the international horizon." [4]

The Reverend Dr. John Lewis, pastor of First Baptist Church in Raleigh, N.C., and the father of Mrs. Jeannie Jessup, a member of the 1970 graduating class, gave the baccalaureate sermon entitled "Frontiers of Faith." He told the seniors they would be facing four frontiers—intellectual, social, political, and psychological—and challenged them to: go forth to love God "with all your mind in the intellectual frontier, your heart in the social frontier, your will in the political frontier, and your soul in the psychological frontier." [5]

Diane Qualliotine, a chemistry major from Fayetteville, received the L. Stacy Weaver Award, having been selected by the faculty as the senior who best exemplified academic excellence, spiritual development, leadership and service. Qualliotine graduated *summa cum laude* and was awarded a fellowship by the National Science Foundation to do graduate work in biochemistry at Wake Forest University's Bowman Gray School of Medicine.

— CHAPTER 4 —

Foundation Raises $114,428

Speaking at the kickoff luncheon for the Methodist College Foundation's Annual Community Loyalty Campaign January 13, 1970, College President L. Stacy Weaver reported that the college had graduated 616 students, of whom: 278 were teaching in the public schools, 170 held positions in business, 13 were ministers, and 60 were in graduate school.

In a June 1970 follow-up letter to an appeal sent out to local physicians in January as part of the Community Loyalty Campaign, Dr. Karl Berns, executive secretary to the Methodist College Foundation, noted that the college fiscal year could end June 30 with an operating deficit "as high as $75,000," and added, "Already, drastic retrenchments have been made in staff and facilities. It is impossible to cut further and provide top quality higher education. It is today that financial help is so urgently needed. Other local citizens have already contributed $110,000 in cash, restricted gifts, merchandise, stocks, scholarships and pledges. Let's show Fayetteville that physicians stand behind its college." [6]

When its fiscal year ended June 30, 1970, the Methodist College Foundation had raised a total of $114,428 from the greater Fayetteville community toward a goal of $120,000. At the Foundation board's August 11, 1970, meeting, local attorney Jerome B. Clark Jr. said, "Methodist College would receive much greater support if the people could receive the 'message.' There is a need for better communication." [7]

It was also announced at this meeting that Mrs. Hazel Horton, who had served as secretary to the Foundation since 1958, had resigned.

Meeting June 9, 1970, the Methodist College Foundation Board of Directors elected William O. Cordes, local plant manager of Black and Decker, president for 1970-71, along with the following: Norman Suttles, first vice president; Al Rummans, second vice president; Mrs. Elizabeth Ellis, secretary; and Mrs. James. B. Bundy, treasurer.

In November and December 1970, Foundation President Cordes reported that subcommittees had agreed on donor recognition levels—$50-$99, $100-$499, $500-$999, $1000 and up—for the 1971 Community Loyalty Campaign, as well as the design and content of a new campaign brochure.

College Begins 11th School Year

Methodist College began its eleventh academic year in the fall of 1970 with seven new faculty members and a total enrollment of 823 students. The freshman class numbered 233. Methodist also enrolled four foreign students: one from South Korea, one from Australia, and two from Thailand.

New administrators for 1970-71 included: Arnold Pope, dean of students; Jean Hutchinson '67, assistant director of public relations; Mrs. Margaret Love and Miss Sandra Matthews, admissions recruiters; and Thomas Manning, director of financial aid. New faculty department heads included: Dr. George Finch, English; Dr. Fred McDavid, Education and Psychology; and Dr. Frederick Arnold, Foreign Languages.

New to the academic area were: an art major, pass-fail options for upperclassmen taking electives, and two courses in environmental problems (ecology). The Science Department offered a one-semester course in environmental pollution, and the departments of Sociology, Political Science, Economics and History collaborated with the Religion Department to offer a one-semester sequel which studied environmental pollution from the standpoint of social, ethical, and religious considerations.

Freshmen Object To Beanies, Etc.

The September 29, 1970 *sMALL TALK* included the following in a column entitled "Dark Corners":

> The Fayetteville Brewers Association is finally making money again—the parking lot at Gladys' is full Monday-Thursday and deserted weekends. . . .
>
> This year's freshman class is "the best looking class yet," according to Dean Pope. Don't worry frosh. He's told that to every class for the past three years, and have you noticed the way the upperclassmen look? [8]

The October 13, 1970, *sMALL TALK* contained a complaint from a freshman about having to wear a beanie and meet other freshman initiation requirements during the first month of school. This was the fifth year of the "freshman orientation" code initiated by the Student Government Association. The writer observed that many freshmen, particularly commuting students, did not attend the required orientation sessions, especially the Kangeroo Court, a student assembly where freshmen who had failed to follow the initiation rules were tried and sentenced to lighthearted forms of punishment. The indignant freshman wrote: "Although Kangaroo Court was very enjoyable to many, some freshmen felt it was childish for a college campus and 'a public degradation of character' that served no useful purpose. They proposed that the upperclassmen devise an orientation initiation that would be more useful to the college than the wearing of beanies." [9]

The following filler appeared on the editorial page under the heading "Fun With Figures": "Googol" is a word coined by Dr. Edward Kasner,

CHAPTER 4

mathematician, to designate a number composed of the digit 1 followed by 100 zeros. It has been estimated that the number of raindrops falling on the city of Chicago in an entire century wouldn't add up to one "googol." [10]

A story on the sports page noted that Bentley Hill had become the first Monarch tennis player to be invited to play in the NAIA national championship. In the spring of 1970, Hill was undefeated in the Dixie Conference (18-0) and won the NAIA District 29 singles championship. Accompanied by his coach,

Student Assistant Chet Makowski works the Reeves Auditorium sound booth in 1973.

Mason Sykes, Hill had journeyed to Kansas City June 8-13, where he won three matches and advanced to the second round of the NAIA national tennis championship before losing to Ted Kople of Presbyterian College.

The October 13 and November 2 *sMALL TALK*s gave extensive coverage of Homecoming 1970, which took place October 23-24. The front page of the October issue featured large photos of the three bands slated to appear in the Homecoming (Saturday evening) concert: Liquid Smoke. Warm, and Lumbee. John Williams, chair of the S.G.A. Entertainment Committee, announced that Kallabash, Inc. would provide music for the Friday night dance. A photo of Vicki Barefoot being crowned Homecoming Queen appeared on the front page of the November 2 issue. Barefoot was crowned at halftime of the soccer game with St. Andrews Presbyterian College, a game which the Monarchs lost by the score of 4-0.

A news story in the November 24, 1970 *sMALL TALK* reported that Dr. Clarence Hulley, Professor of History, had signed copies of his new book, *Alaska: Past and Present,* during an autograph party at Davis Memorial Library.

1970–1974

The final *sMALL TALK* of 1970 dated December 15, reported that Bill Flowers had resigned as editor (due to student teaching obligations) and that Angie Vurnakes had replaced him. An inside story noted that the Community Chorus had joined forces with the Methodist College Chorus and the Fayetteville Symphony to present Parts I and II of Bach's "Christmas Oratorio" Saturday evening December 12, under the direction of Alan Porter.

College Bulletin Seeks Transfer Students, Salutes Alumni
During the first quarter of 1971, the Department of Public Relations at Methodist used its first three newsletters, officially known as the *Bulletin of Methodist College,* to appeal to prospective transfer and summer students and to highlight the activities of the Methodist College Alumni Association.

The February, 1971 *Bulletin* was a tri-fold entitled "Transfer Student Information." The inside text began with the question, "Interested in transferring to a small college with a modern campus and a friendly community atmosphere?" and listed grade requirements for entering transfer students, available majors, and a brief description of the college, including costs and admission procedures.

The May 1971 *Bulletin* carried the nameplate "Alumni News: a special alumni edition of the Methodist College newsletter." Alumni news items reported therein included the following:

—John Ormond '64 and Tommy Yow '66 were vying for president of the Methodist College Alumni Association. Yow had just completed one term as president. Candidates for other alumni offices, including seats on the board of directors, were also listed.
—In a meeting held April 17, 1971, the MCAA Board of Directors had approved a constitution for the Association's Cape Fear Chapter and created a new alumni award called the "Distinguished Alumnus Award."
—College officials had visited alumni chapters in Charlotte, Richmond, and Washington, D.C.
—Alumni had contributed $2,041 to the college in 1971.
—A page of class notes contained the latest news about 23 M.C. alumni.
—The seventh annual alumni dinner and installation of officers would be held Saturday evening, May 22 as part of graduation weekend.

One inside page of the special alumni edition was devoted to college news and reported that:
—Baseball Coach Bruce Shelley and his 1971 team of 19 players had completed construction of the new baseball field, including

— CHAPTER 4 —

two dugouts and a batting tunnel. Shelley said one Dixie Conference coach had paid him a back-door compliment by observing that the Monarchs had gone "from cow pasture to major league in one year." [11]

—Freshman P.E. instructor Sondra Nobles had added self-defense skills ("a combination of karate, judo and common sense") for women to her freshman course and published a basic self-defense guide.

—Methodist College would shift to the modified semester academic calendar starting in 1971-72, with the fall semester starting August 28 and ending before Christmas.

—David Patrick, a freshman from Chesapeake, Va., had finished sixth in the N.A.I.A. Wrestling Tournament held March 11-13, 1971, in Boone, N.C.

Students Help with Tornado Cleanup

An editorial in the March 2, 1971 *sMALL TALK* praised a group of Methodist College students for their efforts to help Ramsey Street residents and businessmen whose property was ravaged by a tornado February 23. The tornado struck near the V.A. Hospital, destroying several homes and businesses, uprooting trees, and knocking down power lines.

The same issue reported on a speech given Wednesday, February 25 in Reeves Auditorium by Terry Sanford, president of Duke University. In his speech, Sanford said state legislators were drafting a bill to provide tuition grants to North Carolina students attending private colleges in the state. The June 1971 *Bulletin of Methodist College* noted that a $4,000 gift from Mrs. Ruth Tyson of Mebane, N.C., given in honor of her late husband, Henry Page Tyson, had enabled the College to purchase 13 vinyl sofas and matching chairs, two carpets measuring 15 feet by 48 feet, and a pool table for the Student Union.

Faculty Cutback Sparks Outcry

In late February, 1971, the College community learned that two faculty members—Rowland Matteson in chemistry and Howard Reisinger in French—would not be rehired for 1971-72 because of declining enrollment. This lead to faculty petitions, a special assembly March 8, 1971, a special edition of *sMALL TALK* March 1971, the release of a typed statement by Dr. Samuel J. Womack, academic dean, and a flurry of letters to the editor.

At a campus wide assembly March 8, 1971, in Reeves Auditorium, S.G.A. President John Brown said the administration chose to cut faculty in the academic areas which had the fewest students enrolled in upper level courses. He then gave the floor to Dean Womack, who answered questions from students and faculty.

The front page of *sMALL TALK's* special edition of March 15 carried the banner headline, "Faculty Cutback Causes Concern." It contained two resolutions from faculty members in Area IV, Science and Math, and Area VII, Foreign Languages, supporting the two instructors, Rowland Matteson and Howard Reisinger, selected for non-renewal of their teaching contracts. It also included a chart showing student registration figures for all seven academic areas, interviews with Dr. Arnold, a Spanish instructor, and Mr. Philip Crutchfield, a biology instructor, sidebar articles on Mr. Matteson's lack of a Ph.D., and unsigned comments from science majors and French majors criticizing the non-renewals of Matteson and Reisinger.

The reverse side of the two-page special edition contained a sharply worded editorial which blamed "a lack of communication" by the administration on its decision not to renew the instructors' contracts for "rumors, misinterpretations, and the general lack of understanding between various groups [i.e. the administration, the faculty, and the students] here at Methodist." [12]

In the March 15 assembly, Dean Womack said *sMALL TALK's* special edition of that date was one-sided, contained erroneous and misleading information, and was a "faculty paper." *sMALL TALK* Editor Sarah Brady said the newspaper staff found there was more copy than the two-page issue could accommodate and that the printer had cut Dr. Womack's statement. She apologized to the dean for that fact and printed Dr. Womack's full statement in the next, March 30, edition.

Leatherman, Smith Vie for S.G.A. Presidency

The platforms of Donald Leatherman and Tommy Smith, two candidates for S.G.A. president for 1971-72, dominated the front page of the April 20, 1971, *sMALL TALK*. Leatherman offered three major goals or planks in his platform: 1) a new role for the S.G.A. as "organizer," not "leader," of students, 2) unification of the student body (commuting students and residential students), 3) more involvement of the S.G.A. in academic affairs (e.g. curriculum reform).

In the same issue, Natalie Schwoyer reported that the State Student Legislature had been renamed the North Carolina Student Legislature and that Tommy Smith had been elected president for 1972. The article went on to say that Methodist's S.S.L. delegation had won "Honorable Mention" for Best Bill from a Small School and for Best Delegation from a Small School.

The May 13, 1971, *sMALL TALK* was a "Year in Review" issue. The lead story on the front page profiled the May 1971 commencement speakers,

— CHAPTER 4 —

United Methodist Bishop Earl Hunt Jr., and Dr. Myron F. Wicke, secretary of the Division of Higher Education of The United Methodist Church. Another news story announced that students had elected the 1971-72 S.G.A. and class officers April 23, 1971. Those elected to S.G.A. offices included: Donald Leatherman, president; Chip Dicks, vice president; Kitty Cook, secretary; and Virginia Aydlette, treasurer. A significant arts-related event was the Methodist College's presentation of Gilbert and Sullivan's *Trial by Jury* May 10, 1971.

A 1970-71 sports review inside the paper reported that:
—the basketball finished second in the Dixie Conference regular season and tournament.
—the bowling team won the DIAC championship.
—the soccer team compiled a 2-8 record for the season.
—the baseball team finished 7-15.
—the cross country team compiled a 4-4 record.
—the golf team finished sixth in the Dixie Conference tournament.

A summary of S.G.A. legislation enacted by the Eighth Senate noted that the body:
—passed a resolution requesting that three non-voting students—the S.G.A. president, chair of the Student Academic Affairs Committee, and Senate president—be added to the Board of Trustees.
—created the office of Public Defender to assist any student who needed and requested it.
—passed a resolution written by Chip Dicks and Mike Safley to allow open dorms [*i.e.* visitation of men by women and *vice versa*]. The Faculty Committee on Student Affairs rejected the proposal.
—gave the S.G.A. president power to fill S.G.A. vacancies occurring between elections [September, February, April].

An article on an inside page presented results of a convocation survey taken several months earlier regarding the College advertising slogan, "Quality Education in a Christian Atmosphere." Students were asked to react to two statements: 1) "'Christian atmosphere' should be a major concern." and 2) "Quality of 'Christian atmosphere' by areas." The areas listed were: campus and social activities, student-faculty relations, dormitory life, academic matters, frequency and variety of worship opportunities, student-administration relations, student government, athletics, college-employee relations, planned religious activities.

For the first statement, students were asked to respond on a six-part scale from "strongly agree" to "strongly disagree." For the second statement, students were given four answer choices ranging from "excellent" to "poor."

Survey results indicated that a majority of the respondents (ranging from 55 to 76 percent) agreed with the statement that a "Christian atmosphere" should prevail in each of the listed areas of student life. In contrast, about half those surveyed rated the quality of "Christian atmosphere" as "fair" to "poor"

Members of Koinonia meet with Dr. Lorenzo Plyler in 1971.

in campus social activities, dormitory life, student-administration relations, and academic matters.

President Asks Trustees To Help With Student Recruitment

In a 13-page "annual report" given to the Methodist College Board of Trustees May 4, 1971, College President L. Stacy Weaver gave an extensive overview of the state of the College. With regard to the College's first seven graduating classes, 1964-1970, he said 353 of the 781 graduates were teaching in public schools and colleges, 206 were working in business, 87 were enrolled in graduate school, and 20 were pastoring churches or working in other Christian vocations.

Dr. Weaver expressed concern that College enrollment had declined by 75 students from 1969-70 to 1970-71, with most of the decline coming in residential students. He said freshman class size had fallen from 450 in 1965 to 233 in 1970. Dr. Weaver asked individual trustees to help with student recruitment and said he intended to asked the same of United Methodist ministers in The North Carolina Conference.

The president said he was gratified by the quality of students attending the College and the relatively high percentage of graduates entering graduate and professional schools. He also voiced pride that the College had recently [in December 1970] been reaffirmed for full accreditation by the Southern Association of Colleges and Schools.

In a lengthy discussion of College finances, Dr. Weaver observed, "It does not appear possible to increase student fees fast enough to compensate for the money lost due to the diminishing student enrollment. Therefore, we are faced with the necessity of increasing our outside contributions and reducing our cost of operation, wherever possible. About the only way we can make any reduction in our operating cost is to reduce the number of people employed." [13]

The president said the College plant was valued at $9.3 million and reported liabilities of $3,365,000 in capital debt for self-liquidating projects and $926,814 due on the original $1 million construction loan. He said the College held endowment properties worth $556,643.

Noting that 76 percent of the College's operating budget came from student fees, Dr. Weaver said The North Carolina Conference of the United Methodist Church was providing $171,021 toward operating costs and $7,267 in capital funds during the current fiscal year, while the Methodist College Foundation had provided $70,000 to amortize the $1 million loan and a small amount toward operating costs.

The president offered a candid assessment of the College's financial condition, saying the College might experience its first-ever deficit in the operating budget at the end of the 1970-71 fiscal year:

> The College began its operation with students eleven years ago without any money in the bank. We have operated these eleven years on the money we have taken in. . . . For the first eight of these eleven years, we built up a reasonable reserve fund. The past three years will have almost exhausted the favorable credit balance produced in the first eight years. Most private colleges have been conducting deficit operations for quite some time now." [14]

Dr. Weaver also noted that more than 3,000 persons would attend meetings at the College during the summer of 1971, indicating another area where the College was rendering a valuable service. Speaking of the United Methodist Church, Dr. Weaver said, "It is my belief that the church must continue to educate its leadership, if the church is to have that leadership. At the January meeting of the Methodist General Board of Education, it was reported that 80 percent of the graduate students in religion and 75 percent of the students now enrolled in theological and divinity schools who are now preparing for the pastoral ministry, did their undergraduate work in a church-related college." [15]

1970–1974

At the close of his annual report, President Weaver offered special thanks to Mr. W. E. Horner of Sanford, N.C., who was attending his last meeting as an active trustee. He said Horner was one of the original trustees, served as the first secretary of the board of trustees, chaired the original planning committee for the College, and had made generous gifts to the College.

S.G.A. President Asks Trustees To Open Meetings

At its May 4, 1971 meeting, the Methodist College Board of Trustees approved a list of degree candidates for the May commencement, re-elected the current board officers, and elected members of the Executive Committee.

John Brown, president of the Student Government Association, requested that the board appoint a special committee to study the possibility of students, faculty, and alumni participating in board meetings "with the privilege of the

SGA President John Brown works on student government matters in his campus office.

floor, but without vote." He suggested that certain officers of the participating organizations be automatically chosen to such representation." [16]

Board Chairman Mott Blair agreed to appoint an *ad hoc* committee as proposed by Brown, and also requested that the committee write down the basic operating procedures of the board.

Alumni Re-elect Yow; Three Faculty Members Retire

Results of the election of Methodist College Alumni Association officers for 1971-72 were announced at the alumni banquet May 22, 1971. Tommy Yow '66, then a United Methodist minister living in Fayetteville, was re-elected president. David Hatchell '69 of Washington, D.C., won the position of vice president, and Gwen P. Sykes '68 of Fayetteville was elected secretary. Larry Barnes '66 of Spivey's Corner, N.C., received the second annual Outstanding Alumnus Service Award.

College President L. Stacy Weaver announced the retirement of three faculty members at the alumni banquet: Dr. James R. Heffern, first professor of biology; Dr. William C. Cooper, chairman of Area IV, Science and Mathematics; and Edwin R. West, director of student teaching.

College Awards 150 Degrees

Methodist College awarded 150 degrees at the College's eighth annual commencement May 24, 1971. John Wayne Brown, a political science major from Piscataway, N.J., received the L. Stacy Weaver Award.

Dr. Myron F. Wicke, general secretary, Division of Higher Education, Board of Education of The United Methodist Church, delivered the commencement address. Wicke told the seniors, "Take thought of your personal gifts. Do not underestimate them. They are yours . . . use them for yourself and for other men and women. . . . Follow the messages that you have heard in life." [17]

Bishop Earl G. Hunt Jr., of Charlotte, N.C., resident bishop of the Western North Carolina Conference of the United Methodist Church, delivered the baccalaureate sermon. "Hunt said the concerns of young people today are essentially religious in nature and that youth now had the potential for bringing about the greatest spiritual reformation of all time." [18]

Duke Honors President Weaver

Methodist College President L. Stacy Weaver received an honorary Doctor of Laws degree from Duke University June 7, 1971. Duke President Terry Sanford, the first chairman of the Methodist College Board of Trustees, presented the degree to Weaver, Class of 1924 (A.B. in Chemistry).

Dr. Weaver's father, Dr. Charles C. Weaver, received an honorary Doctor of Laws degree from Duke in 1936. Stacy Weaver received his first honorary degree, a Doctor of Literature, from High Point College in 1958, and earned an M.A. at Columbia University in 1932.

Dr. Weaver was in distinguished company at Duke, which also awarded honorary doctorates to: U. Thant, Secretary General of the United Nations; Albert Coates, founder of the Institute of Government at Chapel Hill; Thomas G. Wicker, associate editor of *The New York Times;* Lewis M. Branscomb, director of the National Bureau of Standards; Mrs. Elizabeth Koontz, director of the Women's Bureau in the U. S. Department of Labor; and Bishop L. Scott Allen, United Methodist Church, Holston area of Tennessee and eastern Virginia.

Trustees Adopt Budget, Agree To Raise Funds

President Weaver told the Executive Committee of the Methodist College Board of Trustees July 21, 1971, that the College's capital and operating budgets closed the fiscal year "in the black with all bills paid, but that cash reserves declined by $89,012 which practically deleted the reserves in the operating budget." [19]

The president submitted an operating budget for 1971-72 of $1,855,717, a reduction from the 1970-71 budget of $1,916,9909. He said the trustees would need to raise $52,329, and the Methodist College Foundation would need to meet its goal in order to balance the operating budget. The proposed capital fund budget totalled $123,716, with the trustees agreeing to raise $28,002 of that amount.

Responding to a resolution presented earlier by the Student Government Association, the committee voted to increase the student entertainment fee from $5 to $15 for 1971-72 [giving $2.50 per student to each of the four classes in lieu of class dues] and thereafter to include the entertainment fee as part of the student activity fee. The committee then approved a $180 increase in tuition and a $5 increase in the athletic fee for 1972-73, bringing total costs to $700 per semester for a commuting student and $1,200 per semester for a resident student. The Executive Committee also approved the appointments to various board committees presented by Trustees Chairman Mott Blair.

An *ad hoc* committee of the Board of Trustees met October 13, 1971, and voted to recommend to the full board that the president of the student body and a faculty representative be allowed to attend trustee meetings with the privilege of the floor, but no vote. The committee also recommended that the full board of trustees adopt the following board operating procedures:

1) Agenda items for the annual [spring] meeting of the Board of Trustees must be presented to the college president at least 30 days in advance of the meeting.
2) Items to be presented at meetings other than the annual meeting must be presented ten days in advance.
3) The board will hear administrative appeals through its committees or upon request of the petitioner. [20]

College Begins 12th Year

Methodist College enrolled 764 students (727 full-time) for the fall 1971 semester, compared with 823 students in the fall of 1970. The freshman class numbered 198.

The first *sMALL TALK* of 1971-72, dated September 21, 1971, reported that four persons had joined the college faculty: Dr. Kathy S. Thompson,

— CHAPTER 4 —

This 1971 production of **Pygmalion** *starred Martha Eddy.*

assistant professor of psychology; Dr. Patrick D. Hollis, assistant professor of biology; Dr. William W. Horner, associate professor of chemistry; and Mr. William Harold Motes, instructor in economics and business administration.

The sports editor reported that Methodist had recruited some excellent athletes for cross country, soccer, and basketball. Soccer Coach Mason Sykes labeled his team "the best all-around squad as far as individual experience we've had. We are going to be a contender [for DIAC crown]." [21]

An inside feature article in the Oct. 5, 1971, *sMALL TALK* noted that Green and Gold Masque Keys (the drama club) would present George Bernard Shaw's *Pygmalion* Oct. 7-8, 1971, a musical with Phil Bauguess playing Professor Henry Higgins and Martha Eddy portraying Higgins's pupil, Eliza Doolittle. Parker Wilson directed the show, with assistance from Maurine Davidson.

Homecoming 1971 Stars Jimmy Webb

The front page of the October 5, 1971, *sMALL TALK* was used to promote Homecoming 1971, slated for the weekend of October 22-24. Large photos showcased singer/song writer Jimmy Webb ("Up, Up and Away," "MacArthur Park," *et. al.*) and a band from Montreal, Canada, called The Bells; these were the featured acts for the Saturday night Homecoming Concert. Another photo showed O.D. Grass, a band from Shallotte, N.C., which had been booked for the Friday evening Homecoming Dance. The final event of Homecoming 1971 was planned as an outdoor concert at the baseball field by Micropolis, a rock band from Atlanta, Ga.

Miss Peggy Bland, a junior from Pittsboro, N.C., was elected 1971 Homecoming Queen. The Monarch soccer team lost its homecoming game to the Marlins of Virginia Wesleyan College 2-1 in a driving rain Saturday afternoon, October 23, 1971. Rain also forced the Homecoming Committee to move what had been planned as an outdoor concert for Sunday afternoon indoors to Reeves Auditorium.

President Weaver Reflects

College President L. Stacy Weaver offered some candid observations when *sMALL TALK* Editor Sarah Brady interviewed him in October, 1971. Commenting on a three-year trend of declining enrollment at the College, Dr. Weaver said a declining birth rate and "the tremendous explosion of public education" [22] posed a dual threat to the college. He predicted it might take years to reverse the downward trend in enrollment. "We should not become discouraged by our problems; neither should we minimize them, " he said. [23]

The president urged students currently enrolled at Methodist to use their contacts with high school students to interest them in attending Methodist.

The president also reiterated his belief in a liberal arts education and the purposes for which Methodist College was founded.

Trustees Take On Fund-Raising Duties

The Development Committee of the Methodist College Board of Trustees met Nov. 1, 1971, on Founders' Day, with Chairman Norman J. Campbell presiding. Dr. Weaver reported that the College had a current enrollment of 760 students and expressed concern about the school's financial condition. He said the trustees needed to become more involved in fund-raising.

The president reported that the General Board of Education of The United Methodist Church was planning to launch a new program of public relations in 1972 to acquaint all citizens with the significant role of the private college in American life. He said the Church would also inaugurate a $400 million fund drive in 1973 to benefit 100 church-related colleges. He said Methodist College would contribute $900 to assist in launching the fund drive and that the Church's General Board of Education had retained a Baltimore public relations firm to plan the campaign.

Trustees Chairman Mott Blair presented a new proposal for fund-raising which was discussed at length. The Development Committee then voted to recommend to the full board that each member of the Development Committee assume responsibility for raising $6,000 for the College and that other trustees be asked to raise $3,000 by the end of the college's fiscal year, June 30, 1972.

At the same November meeting, the full Board of Trustees approved the recommendations of an *ad hoc* committee that the president of the student body and a faculty representative be allowed to attend trustee meetings, with privilege of the floor, "except at such time as the Board may find it desirable and necessary to go into executive session." [24] The board also adopted three *ad hoc* committee recommendations which specified the operating procedures of the board regarding agenda items and administrative appeals.

The board approved two recommendations of the Development Committee:

1) that Development Committee members agree to raise $6,000 each for the college during the current fiscal year and that other trustees raise $3,000 each during the same period.
2) that individual trustees assume responsibility for presenting the merits and needs of Methodist College to United Methodist churches in The North Carolina Conference, working in cooperation with ministers, other trustees, and interested laymen, students and alumni. [25]

The trustees referred to the Executive Committee for study a proposal from the Student Government Association, endorsed by the Faculty Committee on Student Affairs, that the new College baseball field be named Shelley Field, in recognition of Bruce Shelley, the baseball coach [and a licensed contractor] who, with the help of his players, had constructed the field.

O'Hanlon Amphitheater Dedicated

At Founders' Day services November 1, 1971, Dr. Sam J. Womack, academic dean, spoke about the College's academic mission and Gene Clayton, director of athletics, reported on the College's athletic program. The major highlight of the day was the dedication of the Michael Terrence O'Hanlon Amphitheater given by Mr. and Mrs. I. H. O'Hanlon of Fayetteville in memory of their son. Overlooking a pond on the southern end of the campus, the brick, multi-tiered facility was designed to accommodate 750 persons.

A long-time supporter of the College who served as president of the Methodist College Foundation in 1969-70, Mr. O'Hanlon told a group of trustees, family members, and church leaders gathered for the dedication,

> "The O'Hanlon name is associated with this amphitheater because our family loves nature. . . . We wanted to provide a

O'Hanlon Amphitheater, with seating for 750 persons, was completed in 1971.

beautiful, natural place where groups from the Church and the Fayetteville community could meet outside. The site where it is located is very lovely and appropriate. . . . I think culturally it will aid the community tremendously. . .and it will serve as a living memorial to our son Michael Terrence." [26]

sMALL TALK Cuts Back

The December 7, 1971, *sMALL TALK*, was one in which the editor and her staff threw down the gauntlet to the Methodist College student body. In a lengthy front page letter addressed to her fellow students and headlined "Does Anyone Care?," Editor Sarah Brady explained the purposes of the student newspaper, how it was financed (from student activity fees and ads), staff requirements, and proposed changes. She also answered critics of the paper, saying she had become "fed up with hearing sarcastic, destructive comments from students who cannot or will not be bothered with helping us." [27] Brady said the newspaper staff had spent long hours at night writing and typing to ensure that the paper came out every Tuesday.

She then announced, "Because of the apparent lack of interest on the part of the students and the pressing academic and private needs of the individual staff members, I have asked the staff to support my decision to change *sMALL TALK* from a bi-monthly paper to a monthly one, effective immediately." [28] Brady also asked students to take an interest and an active role in *sMALL*

CHAPTER 4

TALK by submitting articles, writing letters to the editor or rendering other assistance to the staff.

The back page of the December 7, 1971 *sMALL TALK* chronicled the fall achievements of Monarch athletic teams. The men's basketball team, led by freshman sharp shooter Elton Stanley, had defeated Pembroke State College in the Campbell College Tip Off Tournament before falling to Campbell in the championship game 77-65. The cross country team finished third in the conference behind Pembroke State and Lynchburg. The soccer team reached the semifinals of the DIAC tournament with a win over the N.C. Wesleyan Bishops, then lost to the undefeated Knights of St. Andrews Presbyterian College.

Spring 1972 Brings Innovations

Methodist College observed Faith and Life Week Feb. 14-18, 1972, with the Howard Hanger Trio, a vocal trio featuring religious music in a variety of styles, from classical to jazz. Led by the Reverend Howard Hanger, a United Methodist minister under special appointment to "the college campus," the trio performed five times during the week, offering everything from a Gregorian chant in 13-8 time to a Bach chorale to an abstract jazz-rock exercise. Many of the trio's concerts included light shows and multiple film projections.

A brief article in the February, 1972 *sMALL TALK* noted that the assembly attendance policy would be strictly enforced for the spring semester. All regularly enrolled students were required to attend an assembly each Wednesday at 11:30 a.m. in Reeves Auditorium. Students had to turn in attendance slips and were allowed five absences during the semester.

Methodist College began the spring 1972 semester with a new course in equestrian studies taught at the nearby Cedar Falls Equestrian Center and Riding Stables. Fifteen students signed up for the course which included two hours of instruction per week and one hour of free riding. Those completing the course were allowed to substitute it for the required sophomore level physical education courses, either P.E. 201 or P.E. 202.

The 1971-72 basketball team won its tenth game Jan. 22, 1972, by defeating the St. Andrews Knights 78-60. In a hard-fought battle at home, the Monarchs lost to Campbell College 100-69. The Camels, who had defeated Methodist earlier, shot 61 percent in the first half and 57 percent in the second and outrebounded the Monarchs 58-40.

The Monarch baseball team had an excellent fourth season, compiling a 10-4 record and winning a playoff spot in N.A.I.A. District 29.

In late February 1972, a break in an underground steam pipe, a ruptured water line, and a broken circulation pump in the Classroom Building forced the College to close for several days..

sMALL TALK's "Year in Review" issue published in May 1972 noted that the Ninth S.G.A. Senate and a committee chaired by Tommy Smith had revised the constitution and by-laws of the Student Government Association to create one document, "By-laws and General Provisions of the Student Government Association." The student body approved the documents during the April 14, 1972, general election by a vote of 323-23.

Major changes included the abolition of class officers and restructuring of the S.G.A. Senate. The new Senate consisted of: one representative from each of the four dormitories, three each from the four academic classes, and four representing the day students. Two new Senate committees were also created—the Appointments Committee and the Finance Committee.

In an unprecedented move, the S.G.A. Elections Committee invalidated student elections held April 11, 1972, citing numerous complaints of campaign rule violations by candidates and other students. In a new election held April 14, 1972, 400 students voted. John "Chip" Dicks was elected president, Winnie McBryde secretary, and Cindy Woltz treasurer. Two candidates for vice president were declared ineligible for academic reasons.

At the last meeting of the Ninth S.G.A. Senate, outgoing S.G.A. President Jim Ledford proposed and won ratification of the Joint Statement of the Rights and Freedoms of Students and the American Bar Association's Model Code for Student Rights and Responsibilities and Conduct.

Cultural highlights of Spring 1972 included a Methodist College performance of the opera *Down in the Valley,* a Green and Gold Masque Keys production of *Little Moon of Alban,* and the sixth annual Methodist College Juried Arts Exhibition held for students at Methodist and Fayetteville State University.

Methodist College students were encouraged to vote in North Carolina's first presidential preference primary Saturday, May 6, 1972. [Former Alabama Governor George Wallace defeated former North Carolina Governor Terry Sanford in that contest.]

A short news item reported that the College's Class of 1972 had presented a radio station to the College as its class gift. Based in the Student Union, the station was supposed to broadcast over campus wiring, enabling anyone with a plug-in radio to receive its signal.

President Briefs Trustees

At its annual meeting April 4, 1972, the Methodist College Board of Trustees received a sobering report from President Weaver about declining enrollment and College finances. Dr. Weaver noted that Methodist enrolled 822 students in 1971-72, 71 fewer than in 1970-71. He projected a further decline in enrollment for 1972-73. His annual report also included the following list of freshman enrollments for the past eight school years:

  1964=341
  1965=450
  1966=375
  1967=360
  1968=312
  1969=286
  1970=233
  1971=241 [29]

 Dr. Weaver endorsed a faculty resolution requesting that Dr. Charles Ott, the first professor of chemistry at the College, be given the status of Professor Emeritus. He said this matter and a proposal from a committee of the College chapter of the American Association of University Professors for a system of paid sabbatical leave for College faculty should be referred to the trustees' Committee on Academic Affairs. [Minutes of that committee indicate that members agreed to an emeritus classification for retired employees with at least ten years service, but rejected a proposal for paid sabbatical leaves due to the financial condition of the College. The committee noted that the College would continue its practice of assisting faculty members financially to complete doctoral programs.]

 In the area of finance, Dr. Weaver reported that 77 percent of the College's operating budget came from student fees and that The North Carolina Conference of The United Methodist Church had provided $171,021 for operating expense and $4,000 in capital funds. He said the $123,716 capital budget for 1971-72 had been raised, but that $48,503 needed to be raised to balance the operating budget. He said the 1971 session of the General Assembly of North Carolina made some modest appropriations to begin a pilot program of state assistance to private colleges. He said the College would receive a small appropriation in 1972-73 for each North Carolina resident enrolled, but said the total amount would not be sufficient to cover the newly mandated cost of providing unemployment insurance on all College employees amounting to three percent of their annual earnings.

 The president also reported that Methodist Colllege had joined in a six-year program by the National Association of Schools and Colleges of The United Methodist Church to 1) promote and advertise United Methodist schools to prospective students [a public relations firm in Baltimore, Md. was retained for this purpose], and 2) assist United Methodist institutions of higher learning in fund-raising. He said the General Board of Education of The United Methodist Church and member institutions would share in the cost. He said the cost to Methodist College would be the tuition charged one student in 1971-72.

The trustees Executive Committee met July 19, 1972, and declined to act on a request to name the baseball field for Baseball Coach Bruce Shelley, citing the board's policy that a major facility could only be named for someone who had furnished one-half the cost thereof. The committee also approved a College budget for 1972-73 of $1,904,320 for operating expense and $130,486 for capital expenditures.

College Holds Ninth Commencement

Methodist College awarded degrees to 141 students at its ninth spring commencement Monday, May 15, 1972. Dr. R. Wright Spears, president of Columbia College [Columbia, S.C.] was the commencement speaker.

Dr. Spears challenged members of the Class of 1972 to undertake a "mission imperative" —to become "actively involved in the spiritual awakening movement across the land . . ." and to respond affirmatively to their mission by ". . . contributing to world peace, helping others through human relationships and living a life of personal purity." [30]

In a baccalaureate sermon delivered Sunday, May 14, 1972, Dr. William O. Weldon, editor of *The Upper Room*, told the graduating seniors, "Without sacrifice you have not gotten the real meaning of the gift of life . . . Sometimes it takes the difficult to pull from us the response that shows that we are reaching for and striving for the highest of dreams." [31]

Larry Edward Lugar of Wilson, N.C., received the Lucius Stacy Weaver Award, signifying his selection by the faculty as the senior who best exemplified the education philosophy of President Weaver—academic excellence, spiritual development, leadership and service.

Foundation Passes $100,000 Mark

The Methodist College Foundation ended its 1971-72 year June 30, 1972, by raising a grand total of $111,849 for the College, an increase of $25,148 over 1970-71. Local radio executive Norman Suttles served as Foundation president for 1971-72.

College Accepts Carolina College Alumni Archives

In June 1972, the Public Relations Office published a special "Alumni News" tabloid edition of the *Bulletin of Methodist College*. The lead story noted that Methodist College had approved a new program that would enable exceptional high school graduates to earn 33 semester hours of college credit (one year) through the College Level Examination Program (CLEP).

— CHAPTER 4 —

Another Page One story reported that the Carolina College Alumni Association had accepted an invitation to affiliate with Methodist College. Carolina College in Maxton, N.C. was a Methodist college for women which operated from 1912-26. The agreement called for Carolina College Alumni Association archives and records to be transferred to Methodist College and to be housed in Davis Memorial Library.

An inside story noted that the Methodist College Alumni Association Board of Directors had awarded William P. Lowdermilk, Director of Public Relations, its Outstanding Alumni Service Award for service that goes beyond the call of duty. Mr. Lowdermilk thus became the first honorary alumnus to receive this award.

S.G.A. Calls Off Assembly Boycott

As Methodist College began the 1972-73 school year, the Student Government Association announced and then canceled a boycott of a September 20, 1972, assembly program to make the point that attendance at assembly programs should be a matter of individual choice and not an administrative requirement. S.G.A. President Chip Dicks explained in his "President's Corner" column in the October 1972 *sMALL TALK* that he canceled the boycott because the assembly speaker, The Reverend Gil Gillespie, was a member of a racial minority group, and he did not want the boycott to be misconstrued as racist.

In the October 1972 *sMALL TALK,* an Associated Collegiate Press article with a Washington, D.C. dateline reported that U.S. Secretary of Defense Melvin Laird had announced that draft inductions would end in December, six months ahead of President Richard Nixon's July 1, 1973, deadline. Laird estimated that 50,000 American men would be drafted for military service in 1972, down from a 1968 peak of 299,000.

On the political front, a short news item inside the October newspaper noted that a small group of Methodist College staff and students had attended a rally for Democratic presidential candidate George McGovern at the Gaslight on old Fort Bragg Road. The November 1972 *sMALL TALK* contained a strongly worded editorial by Editor Gene Dillman urging students to vote in the upcoming presidential election, the first time in American history that 18-year-olds would have the right to vote.

In his "President's Corner" column in the November 1972 *sMALL TALK,* S.G.A. President Chip Dicks reported that President Weaver and the College administration had agreed to an S.G.A. Senate resolution requesting that assembly programs be offered weekly during the spring 1973 semester and that students be *required* to attend any six of these programs. Dicks said if students adhered this plan, it would increase the likelihood that the S.G.A. could persuade the administration to make attendance at assembly programs totally optional in 1973-74.

Jim Croce Performs at Homecoming '72

A photo spread on the cover of the November 1972 *sMALL TALK* and a related article inside noted that Homecoming 1972, held Oct. 24-29, was a great success, as evidenced by the full participation of students in a wide variety of activities. The homecoming schedule included: a talent show, a field day with egg walks and sack races, the crowning of Gary Faircloth (Miss Vi Brator) as Miss Boiler Plant, a concert by pop singer Jim Croce, two parties at Cypress Lakes, a 4-0 soccer victory over UNC-G, an alumni/varsity basketball game, a spaghetti dinner for alumni (with entertainment provided by the MC Stage Band, directed by Mike Rogers), a dance featuring the band "Valley," and a Green and Gold Masque Keys production of the Greek comedy *Lysistrata* directed by Parker Wilson.

Jim Croce headlined at the 1972 homecoming.

The November *sMALL TALK* also carried a letter from college math instructor Frank Reid decrying the fact that Methodist College ranked last among 58 colleges and universities in North Carolina, South Carolina, and Virginia in average faculty salaries. Reid said few teachers at Methodist were receiving the maximum salaries for their rank and that not all teachers received a cost of living raise. He also acknowledged that declining enrollment meant the College could not afford to raise teacher pay.

Reid quoted Frank Eason, college comptroller, as saying that another reason the college could not pay teachers more was "because the citizens of Fayetteville and the surrounding area are not supporting the college with cash contributions to the extent that our founders thought they would." [31] Reid suggested that a committee of administrators, faculty, students and alumni be formed to study and seek solutions to the problems of declining enrollment and low teacher salaries.

— CHAPTER 4 —

President Weaver Announces Plans To Retire

College President L. Stacy Weaver announced during a Founders' Day program November 1, 1972, his intention to retire on or before June 30, 1973. He noted that he would soon reach the retirement age [67] set forth in the College bylaws, and that by year's end would have completed 50 years in education and 16 years as president of Methodist College.

Dr. Weaver's announcement led to a one-page special edition of *sMALL TALK*, which included a lengthy biography of Dr. Weaver and his full retirement statement, in which he promised to express "at a later and more appropriate time" his appreciation to the Board of Trustees, administrative officers, faculty, students, employees and friends "for their assistance in building Methodist College and bringing it to its present state of development." [33] Dr. Weaver's announcement was also reported in the November 1972 *Bulletin of Methodist College*.

At a trustees meeting following the Founders' Day program, Trustees Chairman Mott Blair appointed a presidential search committee to be chaired by J. Nelson Gibson. In addition to 11 trustees, Dr. Blair also appointed to the committee John "Chip" Dicks, S.G.A. president; Dr. Willis Gates, faculty representative; and Tommy S. Yow, alumni representative.

Dr. Weaver received a standing ovation from The Board of Directors of the Methodist College Foundation November 14, 1972, along with a resolution of appreciation. The resolution read in part:

> "Only a few can fully understand the awesome diversification of responsibilities in putting together in a short span of years, something so big, composed of so many parts, most of which are human parts None but a man with tremendous personal force, with prophetic vision, with every dimension of intelligence and with unlimited faith could have, as he has, made it appear easy. As part of the growing host who love Methodist College and cherish its ever-increasing worth to the people of our region, we, the Directors of Methodist College Foundation, wish to record our gratitude to Dr. L. Stacy Weaver for the spirit and quality of his tenure as President, and our gratitude to Almighty God that a man of his unique qualifications was in the right place at the right time." [34]

When the Presidential Search Committee met December 16, 1972, Dr. Weaver presented a job analysis for the post of College president. He proposed that the new president be an expert in every aspect of College life, be young, be able to raise money, and be involved in student life. He suggested the president did not have to be an educator. [35]

College Mourns the Passing of Karl Berns

The December 1972 *sMALL TALK* reported that Dr. Karl Berns, director of development at Methodist College, had suffered a stroke and died November 23, 1972, at the age of 74. Dr. Berns also served as Executive Secretary of the Methodist College Foundation and had previously chaired the Department of Education at the College. He was survived by his wife, Mrs. Bernice S. Berns.

A lengthy biography highlighted Dr. Berns' career as Assistant Executive Secretary for Field Operations of the National Education Association and a public school administrator. It was noted that Dr. Berns had directed a 1952 campaign which raised $10 million to build the National Education Association headquarters building in Washington, D.C. The Ohio native held both Ph.D. and law degrees and was considered an expert in school law.

S.G.A. President Reports on Presidential Search

Speaking at a campus assembly January 24, 1973, Chip Dicks, president of the Student Government Association and a member of the Presidential Search Committee, reported that the committee had agreed on six qualifications for the new College president:

1) 35-50 age range
2) ability to raise money
3) ability to obtain and retain students
4) ability to mingle with and understand students
5) ability to understand the "ropes" of the Methodist Conference
6) does not have to have a doctoral degree. [36]

Dicks said the committee had received more than 50 nominees and would soon begin preliminary interviews.

Trustees Discuss Declining Enrollment

Minutes of the The Methodist College Board of Trustees Executive Committee for February 21, 1973, indicate the committee discussed at length the College's financial problems brought on by declining enrollment. The committee directed President Weaver not to appoint a director of admissions or a dean of students "at this time" and further stipulated that the new president be consulted before these appointments were made. The minutes also noted that the present dean of students (Arnold Pope) had tenure as a faculty member and "would be offered a teaching position when employment contracts were sent out." [37]

In other actions, the Executive Committee:

—increased board $100 to $700 for 1973-74, bringing the total cost
 for a resident student to $2,500.

— CHAPTER 4 —

—approved a revised list of general course requirements (totalling 59 semester hours) and a new faculty salary schedule for 1973-74. The ranges for the various faculty ranks were:

Instructor	$ 7,500 - $ 9,000
Assistant Professor	$ 8,500 - $10,000
Associate Professor	$ 9,500 - $11,000
Professor	$10,500 - $12,000 [38]

Basketball, Bowling Teams Win DIAC Title

The front page of the March 1973 *sMALL TALK* carried a large photo of the 1973 basketball team over a sports clipping from *The Fayetteville Observer* headlined, "Flipping's 32-Point Show Keys Methodist To Title." Coached by Gene Clayton, the Monarchs won the Dixie Intercollegiate Athletic Conference Tournament February 24, 1973 in Greensboro, defeating Greensboro College 113-90. Methodist placed three players on the All-Tournament Team: Harry "Flip" Flipping, Craig Knight, and Elton Stanley. "Flip" was named Most Valuable Player of the tournament, scoring 32 points in three games.

The same issue carried a short announcement that the College would soon field an intercollegiate track team and that it would be coached by Paul L. "Buster" Sanderford Jr., a 1972 graduate of Methodist College. The article urged students interested in joining the track team to contact Coach Bruce Shelley.

Several events of March 1973 were designed to stretch the minds of the College community. Ethos, the sociology club, sponsored a March 14 showing of the film, *Future Shock* based on the best-selling book of the same name by British sociologist Alvin Toffler. A *sMALL TALK* news story promoting the film said it would shock viewers with computerized art, modular homes, the disposable body, robots, test tube babies, cloning and other futuristic concepts. The story then posed the following questions, "Do you dare face this opportunity to learn to perceive the future and understand how to control it? Do you want to control the future or do you prefer to live in a society gone mad? Honestly, do you realize the seriousness of the situation?" [39] The 42-minute film was directed by Alex Grasshoff and narrated by Orson Welles.

The drama club staged *The Night Thoreau Spent in Jail* March 15. Written by Jerome Lawrence and Robert E. Lee, the play featured Mike Casey in the role of Henry David Thoreau, Richard Baldwin as Ralph Waldo Emerson, and a supporting cast of ten players.

Fourteen members of the College's History and Political Science Club journeyed to Raleigh April 16, 1973, where they visited the State Archives

1970–1974

Methodist College's 1973 Basketball Team was No. 1 in the conference.

Building, attended an evening session of the North Carolina House of Representatives, and met with three members of Cumberland County's legislative delegation.

The Methodist College bowling team of 1972-73 won the Dixie Conference championship and represented Area 7 at the N.A.I.A. Championship held in Kansas City, Missouri, during May, 1973, finishing seventh in the nation. Coached by Howard Baum, owner of B and B Bowling Lanes in Fayetteville, the 10-member team averaged 5,576 pins [186 per member] during the N.A.I.A. qualifyng rounds. In the Dixie Conference roll-offs, Methodist placed five bowlers in the top 20 for all events: Elmer Hubbard, Steve Edwards, Bobby Ayers, Danny Fowler, and Mike Smith.

sMALL TALK'S year-end review issue for 1972-73 [published in May 1973] reported that students had elected Fayetteville native and Army veteran Bob Peele S.G.A. president for 1973-74, along with Gayle Evans, vice president; Yvette Rosa, secretary; and Mary Spilman, treasurer. The newspaper also announced that the *sMALL TALK* staff had chosen Carmen Evans, a rising junior from Lexington, N.C., editor for 1973-74.

— CHAPTER 4 —

Trustees Elect Richard W. Pearce President

The Methodist College Board of Trustees elected Richard W. Pearce president of Methodist College April 3, 1973, to succeed Dr. Weaver upon his retirement in June. Dr. Pearce, 49, was the vice president and dean at Florida Southern College in Lakeland, Florida. He held J.D., M.A. and B.A. degrees from Stetson University where he had taught business and chaired the Business Department. Prior to joining the faculty at Stetson, Pearce was in private law practice for ten years in Pierson, Florida.

Dr. Pearce was an active United Methodist lay leader, then serving as president of the Florida United Methodist Credit Union and as a trustee of the Florida Methodist Children's Home. He was quoted in a College press release as saying, "I believe higher education is literally a mission field of the church. . . I have faith in the church-involved college." [40] J. Nelson Gibson, chairman of the Methodist College Board of Trustees' Presidential Search Committee, said Pearce was chosen from 75 candidates as the individual who most nearly possessed all the qualifications they were seeking (see section entitled "S.G.A. President Reports on Presidential Search").

After his election by the trustees, Dr. Pearce was presented to the full board. He told the trustees he had studied Methodist College and found it "has a good reputation, a good faculty, and strong and active alumni." [41] In a later interview, he added, "I have a genuine and deep appreciation of the monumental task Stacy Weaver has done here." [42]

Richard Pearce was born in Glen Ellyn, Illinois, but his family moved to Hendersonville, North Carolina when he was a child, and he graduated from Hendersonville High School. After high school, he took machinist's training at Newport News Apprentice School, Newport News Shipbuilding and Dry Dock Co., for one year and joined the U.S. Navy Reserve, attending radio and radar school in the Washington, D.C. area. After completing his Navy service, Pearce attended the University of North Carolina for two years before enrolling at Stetson University.

A College press release noted that Dr. Pearce and his wife, the former Neva Mae Brock of Hendersonville, had two children, Richard Jr. and Karen Gail, who were students at Florida Southern College.

Minutes of the Methodist College Board of Trustees Executive Committee for April 3, 1973 indicate that the trustees voted to provide the new president: $25,000 per annum (to cover both salary and entertainment), payment of utilities for the president's home, a travel allowance of $2,000, an automobile for use on official business, moving expenses for both the incoming and outgoing presidents (using college personnel and rented trucks), and optional membership in the Teachers Insurance and Annuity Association.

Dr. Pearce had some serious concerns about conditions at Methodist when he accepted the job of president. In a 2001 interview, he recalled that when he was interviewed for the job, no one on the Presidential Search Committee could or would answer his questions about College finances and debt. He said on his first visit to the campus, he observed steam coming out of all the manholes, which indicated there were holes in the steam lines. He said he also noticed that many buildings were dirty inside. He said one of his first actions as president was to order the mahogany wall panels in the Student Union cleaned with Fantastic and Liquid Gold. [43]

Dr. Richard W. Pearce

Dr. Weaver Gives Final Report to Trustees

In other actions April 3, 1973, the Methodist College Board of Trustees approved an amendment to College by-laws granting emeritus classification to certain retired College employees under conditions previously discussed. Dr. Weaver was then unanimously elected President Emeritus of the College, effective upon his retirement.

In his final annual report to the trustees, President Weaver paid tribute to his late friend and colleague Dr. Karl Berns, describing him as "a man of great stature who left his mark upon everything he attempted to do." [44]

He also thanked the trustees for their assistance, service, and never-failing encouragement, and paid tribute to four persons who had worked with him from the beginning: Frank Eason, comptroller; S. R. Edwards, registrar; Dr. S. J. Womack, academic dean; and Dr. Willis Gates, chairman of the Fine Arts Division. Dr. Weaver extended best wishes to his successor, Dr. Pearce, and offered to assist him in any way possible.

Friends Pay Tribute to Dr. Weaver at Retirement Dinner

Approximately 300 persons gathered at the College May 12, 1973, to honor Dr. L. Stacy Weaver for his 50 years of service to education. The featured speaker was Dr. Terry Sanford, president of Duke University.

Special commendations were presented to Dr. Weaver by Fayetteville Mayor Jackson Lee, Cumberland County Board of Commissioners Chairman E. J. Edge, and Glenn Jernigan, member of the North Carolina House of Representatives. M.C. Alumn Association President Cynthia Walker presented Dr. Weaver with the association's first Distinguished Alumnus Award.

— CHAPTER 4 —

Charles K. McAdams, treasurer of The North Carolina Conference of The United Methodist Church, [and former director of public relations at MC] paid tribute to Dr. Weaver for his many years of service to The United Methodist Church, including several national committees.

Bishop Robert M. Blackburn of The North Carolina Conference of The United Methodist Church delivered the invocation, and special music was provided by Dr. Willis Gates, Grace Gates, Terry Terry, and Timothy Brown.

Dr. Mott Blair, chairman of the Methodist College Board of Trustees, presented a cash gift to Dr. Weaver on behalf of the president's friends.

Weaver Addresses Tenth Graduating Class

Dr. L. Stacy Weaver, college president, and Bishop Robert Blackburn of the Raleigh Area of The United Methodist Church, gave the baccalaureate and commencement addresses, respectively, at Methodist College's tenth spring commencement exercises May 13-14, 1973.

In a speech entitled "This I Believe," Dr. Weaver discussed his beliefs in: 1) the divinity of human personality, 2) the improvability of human personality, and 3) Christian education as the best means yet devised for the development of human personality.

The retiring president said the purpose of a church-supported college is "to assist the church in informing, directing, shaping and transforming the culture we call civilization." [45] He repeated the two goals to which he had dedicated Methodist College sixteen years earlier: academic excellence and the Christian concept of life.

Academic Dean Samuel J. Womack presented the Lucius Stacy Weaver Award to Kenneth Lee Williams. Trustees Chairman Mott Blair introduced President-elect Richard W. Pearce, who observed that "commencement means just that; it is a beginning." [46]

Twenty-two of the 147 members of the spring class graduated with honors, and nine were elected Methodist College Scholars for outstanding scholastic achievements.

Trustees Approve Budget

Dr. L. Stacy Weaver, outgoing College president, met with the College trustees' Executive Committee June 6, 1973, and presented proposed budgets for 1973-74: $1,696,936 [excluding the cafeteria budget] for the operating fund and $120,043 for capital expenditures.

The committee also appointed Oliver C. Culbreth comptroller, replacing Frank Eason, who was granted retirement due to illness.

Dr. Richard Pearce, the new president, met with the trustees' Executive Committee July 12, 1973, and recommended that the cost of board at Methodist be raised $30 per semester. He said the College cafeteria operated at a deficit the previous year and suggested the College might need to contract with A.R.A. Services to operate the cafeteria.

In other matters, the Executive Committee:

—approved five local banks and three local savings and loan associations as designated depositories for Methodist College funds.

—authorized trustee Wilson Yarborough, Sr., to sell the president's home at 1717 Raeford Road for no less than $62,000 and to place the proceeds in a capital fund for construction of a president's home on the College campus.

New President Addresses Foundation Board

Dr. and Mrs. Richard Pearce were guests of honor at the Methodist College Foundation Board of Directors meeting July 10, 1973. The Reverend William Lowdermilk, the College's director of public relations, introduced Dr. Pearce, who then shared some of his goals for the College.

The new president identified a three-year decline in enrollment, particularly residential enrollment, as the major weakness facing the College. He said the College would emphasize student aid, a quality educational program, and the College's religious affiliation in an effort to attract more students.

Dr. Pearce said he wanted the College to develop more educational and cultural opportunities for the general public, to show Fayetteville residents a return on their investment. As examples of new cultural offerings, he mentioned "quartets, a Dixieland band, and drama groups." [47]

The president said it was important to remember that Methodist College is an institution of The United Methodist Church and therefore obligated to provide students with a wholesome learning environment. He said he was preparing a "statement of commitment" so that the College's various constituencies would know that "Methodist College stands for certain things." [48] [See Appendix V.]

College Begins 14th Year

Methodist College began its 14th academic year August 23, 1973 with an enrollment of 617 students.

New faculty included: James Barger, psychology instructor; Dr. Margaret D. Folsom, assistant professor of biology; Joe Gallagher, head basketball coach; Robert C. Perkins, associate professor of history; Robert Wayne Preslar, assistant

— CHAPTER 4 —

professor of English; Eugene M. Rasmussen, assistant professor of sociology; Eugene Smith, assistant professor of mathematics.

New to the administrative staff were: Ivan L. Foster Jr., assistant comptroller; Dorothy T. Sparrow, news bureau director; and Louis Spilman Jr., part-time director of the Methodist College Foundation.

Changing Times

The October 1973 issue of *sMALL TALK* reflected a broad range of student concerns. One news story noted the passing of "Dr. Bernard Budd," a lizard which had resided in the Science Building. Another story reported that four MC faculty members had "thrashed" four upstart freshmen who had challenged them to tennis matches. The faculty won four out of six singles matches and two out of three doubles matches. Ray Kinder, Sid Gautam, Gene Clayton, and Mason Sykes won their matches, while Parker Wilson and James Barger lost.

In an editorial entitled, "What's Happening to Our Country?" *sMALL TALK* Editor Carmen Evans voiced her concern about America: "Our leaders seem to be working for their own betterment. We have become a nation where the ends justify the means. Many Americans have lost faith in our major institutions." [49] Citing the Watergate scandal and the resignation of Vice President Spiro Agnew for influence peddling while governor of Maryland, the editorial said political corruption was the country's most urgent problem, followed closely by runaway inflation brought on by the energy crisis. Evans concluded her editorial by saying America needed cohesion and by urging her fellow students to get involved in politics at the local, state, and national levels and to work together for the common good of the country.

Evans reported in a second editorial that in the preceding spring she had gotten the S.G.A. Senate to pass a resolution asking the Academic Affairs Committee to initiate a journalism class at the College and that the committee had agreed to offer "Journalism 303, News Writing and Editing" during the fall semester. She said the three-semester hour course would offer two lectures and three laboratory hours per week and would be taught on Tuesday and Thursday by Dr. Womack and Louis Spilman [both of whom had worked as newspaper journalists].

In response to President Pearce's announcement that he would maintain an open-door policy and welcome suggestions from students for improving Methodist College, one *sMALL TALK* staff member wrote an article suggesting that club presidents be asked to submit suggestions and participate in brainstorming sessions to be held at mid-term and the end of each semester. The writer of the article also offered the following specific suggestions: organize a Debating Society; encourage MC students to recruit by offering a $100 tuition credit for each student recruited; expand the scope of the Student Employment Office; initiate an anti-drug abuse program and require students to attend an orientation by experts in the field at the beginning of each semester; bring military parachute teams, bands and lecturers to the campus; create a fall [mid-semester] holiday; eliminate the class attendance policy.

The November 1973 *sMALL TALK* reported that Alan Porter, assistant professor of voice, had visited Florida Southern College for two days in October to explore the feasibility of organizing a hand bell choir at Methodist College. College President Richard Pearce sent Mr. Porter to Florida Southern because the college had an outstanding hand bell choir and gave academic credit for hand bell ringing.

The 1974 *Carillon,* the college yearbook, described Homecoming 1973, held November 1-3, as very successful. Highlights included the Miss Boiler Plant Pageant on Thursday evening, a Friday evening dance at the Ramada Inn featuring the band "Autumn," a Saturday soccer game in which Methodist defeated N.C. Wesleyan, the crowning of Linda Allvord [a senior from Bridgeport, N.J.] as Homecoming Queen, and two concerts featuring Wet Willy and Hugh and Cry.

President Pearce Outlines Goals

At his first meeting with the full Board of Trustees November 3, 1973, Dr. Pearce, the new president, received unanimous approval of the educational goals for the college that he had previously mailed to the trustees. The complete text of his statement of educational goals appeared in the November 1973 *Bulletin of Methodist College.*

Early on in his statement, Dr. Pearce said Methodist College could not be all things to all people and should market itself as a residential, undergraduate, church-involved liberal arts college designed primarily for 17-22 year-olds and offering "choice within limits" in both its academic and student life programs.

Dr. Pearce said the academic program should be characterized by: 1) flexibility and 2) choice for students to design their own academic programs, within the limits of a broad liberal arts education. In the area of student life, Dr. Pearce said students should be encouraged to govern themselves within limits and in accordance with the following minimal standards:

1. Use and possession of alcohol by Methodist College students is strictly forbidden. [See Appendix FF.]
2. Improper or illegal use of drugs or prescriptions is strictly forbidden.
3. There will be no open dorms.
4. There will be closing hours on girls' dorms.

— CHAPTER 4 —

Flower Power: Cumberland Hall residents change tires on a VW bus.

    5. All College activities will be chaperoned.
    6. Conduct befitting a lady or gentleman in today's world is expected of each student. [50]

Dr. Pearce also presented a "statement of commitment" for Methodist College.

The trustees approved a physical education major and referred a request from the Student Government Association that the baseball field be named in honor of Baseball Coach Bruce Shelley to the trustees' Executive Committee.

The president reported that the Yarborough Bell Tower and the exterior of Hensdale Chapel had been repainted and that metal work around the campus would be repainted soon. He said a summer commencement ceremony had been held and that a similar ceremony would be held in December.

Dr. Pearce said the College would receive $200 in state tuition grant money for each full-time North Carolina resident enrolled as of October 1, 1973, or an estimated total of $91,200. The president noted that the College had borrowed $200,000 for summer operating funds and repaid the loan from tuition and fees received when students enrolled in August. He asked the trustees to help him secure donations to avoid an operating deficit during the coming year.

The Executive Committee of the Board of Trustees met December 1, 1973, and approved a proposal to amend the College calendar by shortening the spring 1974 semester from 17 weeks to 15 1/2 weeks in order to reduce energy costs. President Pearce said the College was planning to take down 33

300-watt street lights, close down for extended Christmas holidays, and cut heating thermostats back to 68 degrees to save energy.

After hearing reports from Athletic Director Gene Clayton and Comptroller O. C. Culbreth, the committee voted to name the baseball field for Baseball Coach Bruce Shelley, concluding that Shelley had provided over one-half the cost of construction of the field in terms of equipment, labor, and supplies.

New Dean of Students Gene Clayton reported to the committee that a 36-member Student Union Board had been created to improve social activities on campus. Referring to requests that fraternities and sororities be allowed at Methodist College, Dr. Pearce said the College should allow Greek letter societies "so long as the societies abide fully with College rules and regulations and the College controls the Greek system." [51] He said there was nothing in the College charter or by-laws that prohibited the existence of Greek societies on campus. [In the spring 1974 semester, Methodist established its first sorority chapter, Alpha Xi Delta, and its first fraternity chapter, Pi Kappa Phi.]

New President Starts New Traditions

President Pearce wasted no time starting some new traditions at the College. These included the first December graduation, held December 21, 1973, in Hensdale Chapel. Lt. General Richard J. Seitz, XVIII Airborne Corps and Ft. Bragg commander, gave the commencement address, and 48 students received their degrees.

Dr. Pearce also established the first President's List during the fall 1973 semester, saying, "students who maintain a perfect 4.0 [A] average deserve special recognition." [52]

Leaders Discuss Energy Crisis

Approximately 85 persons gathered in the Science Auditorium January 22, 1974, for a follow-up seminar on the "energy crisis" sponsored by the College's Economics and Business Club. [As the result of an Arab oil embargo, gasoline prices in the U.S. soared in early 1974, leading to shortages and long lines of motorists waiting for fuel.]

A guest panel of speakers included: Fayetteville Mayor Jack Lee; Jack Clark, executive director of the Fayetteville Chamber of Commerce; Dr. Sid Gautam, professor of business administration and club advisor; and Denny Shaffer, president of the local unit of the Sierra Club.

Dr. Gautam called for Americans to adopted common sense energy conservation measures and for Congress to enact an Energy Conserving Act. Mayor Lee said the city had lowered thermostats and would purchase smaller, more fuel-efficient cars. Mr. Clark said Americans had been spoiled by low

— CHAPTER 4 —

energy costs and presented copies of a chamber brochure entitled, "Save America." Mr. Shaffer said oil and coal were non-renewable resources. He call for more recycling of "throw-away" products; more fuel-efficient cars and industrial equipment; more mass transit; and increased use of solar and wind energy.

At an all-day economy, energy, and ecology seminar held on campus in early April, 1974, five guest speakers shared their views on the energy crisis: Gen. John Tolson, secretary, N.C. Department of Military and Veterans' Affairs; Congressman Charlie Rose; Shearon Harris, president of Carolina Power & Light Co.; Fayetteville architect Dan MacMillan; James R. Westlake, senior staff advisor with the U.S. Environmental Protection Agency.

Citing tremendous waste of fuel and energy in America, Tolson said, "The only recourse to the problem is immediate conservation." [53]

Rose said, "We've got to move forward and make use of our nuclear generation facilities." [54]

Harris said CP&L would meet the needs of its customers, but conceded some conservation measures were needed, noting, "If we continue to use our fuel resources at the present level, we will have depleted oil by 1990, gas by 1995 and coal by 2050." [55]

MacMillan said architects must incorporate energy conservation features into their building designs.

Westlake said soaring demand for energy should not overrule environmental concerns, saying, "It's necessary to reduce resource demands and improve the quality of life. We should adapt to different travel and living standards as well as move back to inner-city living." [56] Methodist College President Richard Pearce said the College had responded to the energy crisis by reducing its use of electricity by one-third and its use of heating oil by one-fourth.

During an afternoon session, MC students Ed Kubisty and John Roberts gave presentations on thermopollution, and instrumentation and monitoring of air pollution, respectively. Dr. Sid Gautam, associate professor of economics, served as seminar moderator.

1974 sMALL TALK Reports Many Firsts

At the beginning of the spring 1974 semester, *sMALL TALK* reported that President and Mrs. Pearce had decided to host a formal dinner Saturday, May 4 for graduating seniors, to be followed by a dance for seniors and alumni, sponsored by the Methodist College Alumni Association. The president also announced that future baccalaureate and commencement services would be held on the same day, with the baccalaureate in the morning and the commencement in the afternoon.

A news story on an inside page reported that majors in French and Spanish had been temporarily discontinued due to a reduction of staff and courses.

1970–1974

Green and Gold Masque Keys presented *The Miracle Worker*, William Gibson's drama about Helen Keller and her teacher, Annie Sullivan, February 28 and March 1, 1974 in Reeves Auditorium. Sue Bailey played Annie Sullivan and Brenda Gail Roberts played Helen Keller. The play was directed by Parker Wilson, assistant professor of history.

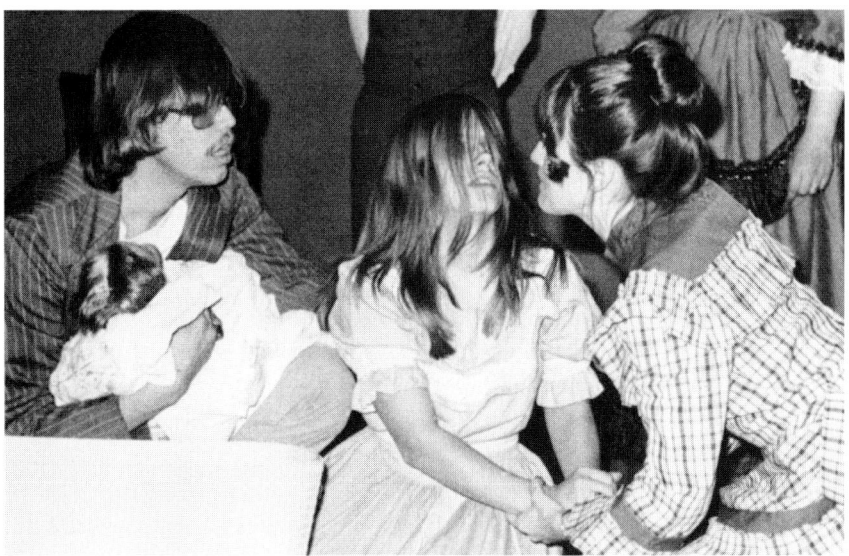

The Miracle Worker *(1974) starred Sue Bailey and Brenda Gail Roberts.*

The first annual Spring Art Festival, a juried exhibit, was held the last week of March, 1974. Five $20 cash prizes and five honorable mentions were awarded. The choral music program achieved a significant first in 1973-74, with the formation of a vocal ensemble from members of the Methodist College Chorus. The ensemble consisted of nine singers plus a pianist.

Methodist's bowling and basketball teams continued their winning ways during the 1974 spring semester. The basketball team, coached by Joe Gallagher and led by top scorers Greg Jones and Elton Stanley, won the Dixie Conference Tournament and advanced to N.A.I.A. District 29 play at Wilson, N.C., where the team lost to Virginia State 57-53. Coach Gallagher was named Dixie Conference Coach of the Year. The bowling team finished first in the conference at the end of the season, then lost in the conference tournament March 2 to St. Andrews.

Methodist students elected a new slate of S.G.A. officers for 1974-75 April 19, 1974: Fred Paddock, president; Tommy Dent, vice president; Brenda Hester, secretary; Danny Hood, treasurer; and Ken Reavis, chief justice. The

— CHAPTER 4 —

sMALL TALK staff elected Susan Githens, a rising junior from Hampton, Va., editor for 1974-75.

The May 1974 Year End Review issue of *sMALL TALK* contained a front page feature about Robert Pemberton and Larry Broach, two seniors who had just completed a "climatic environment" project in one of the Science Building courtyards. They installed a wide range of plants and created small pools for fish and turtles. Created for "Special Topics 450," the project was designed to replicate the three types of climatic conditions extant on the Methodist College campus: hydrophyte (wet), mezophyte ("happy medium"), and zerophyte (dry).

Pemberton and Broach said they had spent a lot of time in the woods on campus and bordering the river, observing plants and animals. Although they spent a year on the project, both said it was incomplete and would need to be finished by future students.

Streaking Fad Comes to Methodist

In March 1974, the streaking fad—running naked—reached its peak on American college campuses. Not to be outdone, a group of Methodist College baseball players decided that a streak would bring some much-needed publicity to the college.

Shortly before 1 a.m., Tuesday, March 5, 1974, between 20 and 30 male resident students at Methodist College took their clothes off and streaked from Sanford Hall up to the current site of the College president's home and back to their respective dorms.

News of a planned "midnight streak" began circulating on campus Monday. A number of male residents, most of them members of the baseball team, decided they wanted to set a record for the largest number of streakers at a small college. Dean of Women Inge Dent sent word that if a streak did occur, male students would not be allowed to enter the parking lots at Garber and Weaver halls and that women residents thereof would stay in their rooms.

Someone apparently notified *The Fayetteville Observer* of the planned streak, for the paper dispatched photographer Dick Blount to cover the event. Blount's photograph of three streakers, two with their heads covered, appeared on the front page of the *Observer's* local section Tuesday, March 6, along with a short cutline. The cutline ended, "Dr. Richard Pearce, Methodist College president, had no comment on the matter this morning." [57]

In a 1989 interview for *Methodist College Today,* former Dean of Women Inge Dent recalled that she prepared for the streak by parking her white VW Beetle in a clearing just west of Weaver Hall, in what is now the driveway to the president's home.

1970–1974

Paintings from the 1974 Spring Art Festival, a juried exhibit.

I turned my lights out and waited," she said. I had Maxi, my little daschund, with me. Sometime after midnight, these guys came running up the street wearing nothing but paper bags or ski masks and baseball socks and sneakers. The girls began cheering from the dorm windows.

When some of the guys began veering into the dorm parking lots, I turned on my lights and drove down the street to the dorms. Then I let Maxi out and told him to 'Go get 'em.' Maxi liked to grab pant legs, but at the sight of all those bare legs, he turned around and ran back to his seat in the car. For weeks, Dr. Pearce and the College staff joked that the streakers looked so bad, they turned off the dean's dog. [58]

Thirty-one years later, Bobby Cobb, one of the streakers, remembered the incident this way:

Methodist was a poor and struggling college. We were trying to bring some national exposure to our school. Some guys from

— CHAPTER 4 —

the baseball team came to see me at my apartment—I was already married at the time—and asked if I would streak with them. I asked my wife and she said 'Go ahead.' We started from Sanford Hall, but when we got to where the street runs between Weaver and Garber halls, all these car lights came on and we saw a sheriff's car. At that point, we ran into the woods and back to Sanford Hall. I did not realize a newspaper photographer was there and took our picture. A day or two later, my criminology class was observing a court case downtown. Suddenly, someone handed me a copy of the Fayetteville paper [*The Fayetteville Times*] and there I was, with several other streakers, on the front page!" [59]

The Fayetteville Observer reported on a national epidemic of streaking the first week of March, 1974, starting with 514 streakers at the University of South Carolina Monday night. At the University of Georgia the same night, police used tear gas to disperse 2,500 angry students following the arrest of a streaker. Two nights after the small group at Methodist streaked, about 85 students—75 men and 10 women—streaked at St. Andrews Presbyterian College in Laurinburg. An Associated Press story in *The Observer* reported that approximately 595 students at UNC-Chapel Hill streaked the evening of March 7, while a student band stood in front of a dormitory and played "The Stripper."

Local reaction to the Methodist College streaking incident was generally negative, prompting a flurry of letters to the editor of *The Fayetteville Observer* and *The Fayetteville Times*. In one letter, James Lancaster, a local resident, wrote: "The wages of sin is death. Some of the students at Methodist College did some streaking. It's an abomination in God's eyes. This event shows the imminence of Christ's return." [60]

sMALL TALK Editor Carmen Evans editorialized on the matter in the April 1974 issue, saying, "I am happy to say that streaking brought about more unity among the dorm students than has existed all year. Therefore, I say it served a purpose. I regret it was not a more constructive activity." [61]

Governor, Newspaper Salute S.G.A. Leaders

In late March of 1974, North Carolina Governor Jim Holshouser lauded a group of Methodist College students for proposing the United Student Appeal, a national charity for college students. After accepting a $400 check (funds donated by MC students) on behalf of the American Cancer Society, the governor said, "I'm sure the success of your drive will be carried to other college campuses across the nation." [62]

The United Student Appeal was the brainchild of S.G.A. President Mike Casey and Vice President Fred Paddock, who introduced the idea in a resolution passed at the March 1974 session of the North Carolina Student Legislature. The resolution called on other colleges to follow Methodist's lead and to ask every student to donate 25 cents to a national charity of their choice each school year.

An editorial in *The Durham Sun* commended the students at Methodist College for "taking steps to launch a new fad in which students throughout the state and nation will make donations to charity groups." [63]

Greeks Arrive, Signaling New Emphasis on Social Life

Social opportunities at Methodist advanced considerably in 1974, thanks in part, to the efforts of the Student Union Board and new Dean of Students Gene Clayton. The Board scheduled a "Give a Damn Week" for February 4-9, climaxed by a February 7 dance featuring Maurice Williams and the Zodiacs. A Spring Festival was set for April 8-13, followed by a Valentine's Dance. The Board also announced that ten feature films would be shown in the Student Union during the spring semester. Both Clayton and President Pearce indicated they were receptive to the idea of fraternities and sororities on campus.

The Delta Mu Chapter of Pi Kappa Phi, a national fraternity, held a chartering banquet on campus April 20, followed by a formal initiation ceremony at St. James Lutheran Church. Alvin Leslie of Fayetteville, president of the new colony, accepted the charter for the MC chapter. The *1974 Carillon* pictured 26 charter members of Pi Kappa Phi. One of the first projects of the Pi Kapps was a Miss Methodist College pageant held in late March, 1974, at which Cheryl Ann Matthews of Wade was crowned Miss Methodist.

A second fraternity, Lambda Chi Alpha, was chartered in early May, 1974. John Young of Raleigh was elected president of the service fraternity, whose "house" was established on the second floor left section of Sanford Hall. The colony began with 20 members.

Alpha Xi Delta, the College's first sorority, was installed as the Zeta Mu Chapter the weekend of April 26-28, 1974. Mrs. Elaine Porter, assistant professor of French, established the chapter, which initially consisted of 16 members.

Trustees Promote Lowdermilk, Hold Two-Day Meeting

Acting on the recommendation of College President Richard Pearce, the Executive Committee of the Methodist College Board of Trustees voted March 6, 1974, to create the position of assistant to the president and appointed William P. Lowdermilk, director of public relations, to that post.

The Executive Committee also authorized Wilson F. Yarborough, Sr., to sell the College president's home on Raeford Road with the stipulation that

— CHAPTER 4 —

the sale net not less than $50,000 for the College. In addition, the Committee voted to increase student charges for 1974-75 as follows: Board, $40; Tuition, $100; Fees, $10; for a total increase of $150.

The full Board of Trustees held a two-day meeting on campus Monday-Tuesday, April 1-2, 1974, "to give the board an opportunity to meet with the students, stay on campus overnight, evaluate the condition of the campus facilities, and study the curriculum and finances, in addition to examining the development and admissions programs." [64]

President Pearce reported to the trustees that:
— new majors would be added in fall 1974 in art education, physical education, and social work.
— the number of academic areas would be reduced from seven to five, under the titles Fine Arts, Humanities, Social Science, Natural Science, and Education.
— the faculty would be reduced by two and a half members in fall 1974, and student enrollment was projected to remain constant at 617 students.
— leakage from cracked underground steam pipes on campus was a serious problem.
— "The College's relations with the church [United Methodist] are good, but the results are poor. . . . It appears that our student presentations are our best recruiting and public relations devices." [65]

Garber girls give a 1970 Mustang a little TLC.

—100 dogwood trees were planted on campus in February.
—some long-range needs of the College are for: increased maintenance funds, a gymnasium, a small theater, endowed chairs [faculty], and endowments for the library and the concert-lecture series.

The trustees ended Day One of their meeting by dividing into four three-man committees: Development, Student Affairs, and Academic Affairs.

When the full board reconvened on Tuesday, April 2, 1974, trustees from each of the board's standing committee gave reports and recommendations. In the area of Academic Affairs, Mr. Leonard Doucette, a student, spoke of the need for a student evaluation of the faculty. On the recommendation of Dean Womack, the board approved creation of a Charlotte Lessem Memorial Scholarship to offer two full-tuition scholarships to persons age 65 and over.

Reporting for the Building and Ground Committee, the Reverend Wallace Kirby said the College needed $310,000 for immediate improvements: to fix breaks in steam lines, to solve a humidity problem in Reeves Auditorium, and to repair the men's dorms.

Speaking for the Student Life Committee, Dr. Mott Blair and W. Robert Johnson reported on their night's stay in Cumberland Hall. The board minutes report: "They spoke of the frank exchange of opinions they had had with the students who stopped by their room. Some of the students felt so much policing by deans showed a lack of confidence in them." [66]

Reporting for the Development Committee, Louis Spilman suggested formation of a trustees' Wills and Legacy Committee to actively solicit deferred gifts to the college, that a North Carolina practicing attorney be appointed to the board, and that national foundations be cultivated to help the College on a continuing basis. No action was taken on the suggestions.

Dr. Pearce followed Spilman by urging each trustee to: 1) find two or three persons annually could make sizeable contributions to the College, and 2) recruit students for the College. "If each trustee recruited three additional students," said Dr. Pearce, "our enrollment would increase by 16 percent." [67]

Shelley Field Dedicated at Spring Festival

Shelley Baseball Field was dedicated Saturday afternoon, April 20, 1974, just prior to a baseball game between Methodist and Virginia Wesleyan. The event was part of a four-day Spring Festival Weekend, which featured a Thursday evening semi-formal concert-dance in the Student Union to music by The Prophets, a Friday evening concert by Singletree, a Saturday picnic at the baseball field sandwiched between triple header baseball games with Virginia Wesleyan and the crowning of Dusty Woodbury as Spring Festival Queen.

The festival concluded with a semi-formal dance Saturday night in the Student Union; Pi Kappa Phi fraternity sponsored the dance, and The Sunstorms, a Fayetteville rock band, provided the music.

Speaking at the dedication of the baseball field, Baseball Coach Bruce Shelley said the field was the result of "lots of hard work and determination and dedication on the part of MY boys [the baseball players]. There were days when the players would have rather relaxed than paint bleachers. I gave them an ultimatum . . . paint the bleachers or run 10 miles. Of course, they painted the bleachers. This is really THEIR field." [68]

S.G.A. President Bob Peele presented a plaque to Coach Shelley and College President Richard Pearce praised Shelley for the work he had done for the College and the baseball team.

Mrs. Janet Mullen, wife of former baseball player Phil Mullen, then a semi-professional baseball player, read a letter to Coach Shelley from her husband, which read in part, "Coach Shelley taught me and the other players how to live." [70] Doug Nichol and Barry Willard, co-captains of the baseball team, unveiled a large sign that read, "Shelley Field, Dedicated April 20, 1974."

Sam Edwards Retires

More than 100 friends of Samuel R. Edwards gathered for dinner April 25, 1974, to honor Methodist College's first registrar, director of admissions and physical education instructor who had announced plans to retire July 1. Dr. Samuel J. Womack, academic dean, served as emcee for the event and was joined by other "patriarchs" who helped open the College: Edwards' son Reese [member of the Class of 1964], Dr. Willis Gates, professor of music; former controller Frank Eason; former chemistry professor Dr. Charles Ott; Louis Spilman Jr. [trustee and member of the Class of '64]; and Dr. James Heffern, former biology professor.

C. Reid Ross, former superintendent of the Fayetteville City Schools, said Edwards embodied quality education as a teacher, coach and high school principal while operating "with a firm, but just hand." President Pearce called Sam "Mr. Accuracy." S.G.A. President Bob Peele, co-worker Gayle Godwin, and Fred Kervin, a student enrolled in the Army's Bootstrap program, also praised Edwards, who received two plaques and a check in appreciation for his service to the College and its students.

Trustees Approve Nursing Program

At a May 12, 1974, meeting, the Board of Trustees adopted the following budget for 1974-75: $1,977,751 for operating expenses and $188,500 for capital expenditures, with all the capital expense money projected to come from contributions to the College.

In response to a report from Dean Womack, the trustees approved a proposal to implement a baccalaureate degree nursing program, admitting associate degree nurses as juniors.

At the August 10, 1974, meeting of the Executive Committee of the Board of Trustees, President Pearce reported that:

—Dudley Maxwell had agreed to draw plans and specifications for construction of the president's home for a fee of one percent of the construction cost.

—the College had received a $150,000 line of credit from Branch Banking and Trust Co.

—the College had to borrow a total of $200,000 the previous summer, in December, and again in May and June, 1974, to cover operating fund deficits; the loans were repaid upon receipt of student fees at the beginning of each semester.

—he [Dr. Pearce] had contracted for the interconnection of air conditioning systems for the two men's dorms, the Student Union, and two women's dorms, and was exploring the cost of installing tinted window film on the inside of the large exterior windows of Horner Administration Building, the Student Union, and Reeves Auditorium.

College Graduates 11th Class

Methodist's 11th commencement exercises were held on a rainy Sunday, May 12, 1974, in Reeves Auditorium. The College awarded bachelor's degrees to 107 seniors.

Dr. Lorenzo Plyler, associate professor of religion, delivered a baccalaureate sermon entitled "On the Christian Identity Crisis." Dr. Arnold K. King of Chapel Hill, special assistant to the president of the Consolidated University of North Carolina, gave the commencement address.

Dr. King told members of the Class of 1974 they were graduating at the end of the most turbulent decade in our nation's history, a decade marked by assassinations, the Vietnam War, a drug culture, a sexual revolution, an energy crisis, and the Watergate scandal.

"We're heading for an international disaster if the tide is not turned soon," said King. "We need to re-establish our faith . . . in God, in the system of justice, in the integrity of social process, and we must also learn to think for ourselves." [70]

Mrs. Nancy Coleen Shaw Doucette, a *magna cum laude* history and religion major from Fayetteville, received the Lucius Stacy Weaver Award from Dr. Samuel J. Womack, academic dean.

— CHAPTER 4 —

College Begins 15th Year With 622 Students

Methodist College began 1974-75, its 15th academic year, with 622 students (160 freshmen) and new majors in social work, physical education, and special subject teacher in art.

The College welcomed Gordon Dixon '66 as registrar, Alan Stowers as News Bureau Director, Susan Garrick Motes '71 as director of alumni affairs, and Bob Turner as student union director. Fayetteville residents Russell Crowell and Melvin M. Murry Jr. joined the Department of Business Administration and Economics as part-time instructors.

The Sept. 25, 1974, *sMALL TALK* reported that Dean Womack had established a student advisory subcommittee to work with the faculty's academic affairs committee on curriculum concerns. Laura Sullivan, a student representing the Fine Arts Department, was named chairperson of the subcommittee. Student representatives were also named from other departments: Mathematics, Religion, Social Studies, English, Foreign Languages, and Education.

10th Homecoming Features Denny Brooks, New Century Platters

Methodist College began its 10th Homecoming Weekend Thursday evening, October 3, 1974, with the Miss Boiler Plant Pageant, followed by a bonfire and pep rally. A Friday evening concert by ballad singer Denny Brooks was cancelled when a bomb threat grounded Brooks' plane in Los Angeles; Garber Hall saved the night with a bonfire and free food for students. At the Saturday lunch/picnic on the campus mall, the College handbell choir, chorus, and stage band performed. The picnic was followed by a soccer game with Lynchburg College (the Monarchs lost 2-0) and a Johnson Murray Memorial Basketball Game with two teams of varsity alumni, one coached by Gene Clayton and one coached by Ernie Schwarz. During halftime at the soccer game, Dusty Woodbury was crowned homecoming queen. Sanford Hall won the dorm decorating contest. The weekend ended Saturday night with a concert-dance featuring the New Century Platters.

sMALL TALK reported that 25 coeds from Garber Hall created a little extra excitement one evening during homecoming week. Around 9 p.m., the girls launched a water balloon assault on the men's dorms, hurling several dozen balloons at the windows of Sanford and Cumberland halls. An hour and a half later, 25 girls from Weaver Hall hit the men's dorms again, this time with over 200 water balloons. The men counterattacked and the battle moved outside. Finally, the men and women retreated to their respective dorms and by 11:15 p.m. all was quiet, "much to the relief of the house mothers." [71]

A critical review of a campus production of *The Mouse That Roared* which ran in the November 26 *sMALL TALK* caused a backlash from some students.

In their review, Kathy Ewing and Jim Nash labeled the performance "dull and mediocre" and the cast "amateur." [72] The December issue of the campus newspaper contained two letters to the editor, one from Tim Lloyd (a cast member) labeling the review "slanderous" and another from Winkie Lee defending the cast and the overall performance. [73]

The December 1974 *sMALL TALK* contained an announcement on the editorial page that Editor Sue Githens was resigning. Githens said she chose to resign after one semester because she was tired of the student apathy and criticism of the staff and newspaper, tired of doing one-third of the paper by herself, and tired of harassment from the administration. [74]

President Issues Challenge to Trustees

The trustees Executive Committee met November 3, 1974, and approved plans for the president's home. President Pearce reported that when the College exhausted its sinking fund for debt retirement, it could apply to the federal government for a waiver of interest upon provision that the *principal* on its loans be paid. He then recommended that the College increase its tuition for 1975-76 by $100, room by $50, board by $50, bringing the total cost for a resident student to $2,850.

Dr. Pearce said the faculty had been unable to select a faculty representative to the Board of Trustees and after three tie votes, had presented two candidates and asked that both be allowed to attend board meetings. After some discussion, the trustees voted to allow one faculty representative at each of its two meetings for 1975-76, giving the faculty the option to choose which of the two delegates they wished to attend each meeting.

The College president listed several urgent needs for the College: a new van ($6,000), repair and expansion of the tennis courts from four to six ($30,000), a new vinyl floor for the gymnasium ($25,000), equipment and uniforms for the Athletic Department ($5,000).

In the area of fund-raising, the president challenged the trustees to raise $50,000 from personal contact and to consider selling some of the 400 acres of campus land the College was not using or leasing a portion of land on U.S. 401 for commercial use or leasing farmland for commercial use. He said the resulting revenues would enable the College to cut its bonded indebtedness. Dr. Pearce said he was aware of the trustees' objection to selling any College land and "was in sympathy with them in not wanting to sell land unless it was absolutely necessary." [75]

When the full Board of Trustees met November 9, 1974, Dr. Pearce reported that the president's home on Raeford Road had been sold for $50,000. The board then voted to approve construction plans for the new president's home to be built on campus just west of Weaver Hall. The board also voted to borrow up to $50,000 from a local savings and loan association to build the home, and to seek donors to underwrite monthly payments on the home loan.

Dr. Pearce said the College had reduced its operating debt from $200,000 in September 1973 to $184,000 in September 1974.

Dean Womack reported that the College had a fall enrollment of 622, including 108 military connected students, that 22 students had received course credit by CLEP exam, that physical education and art education majors had been added, and that an interdisciplinary course entitled "Man's Future" would be offered in the spring semester.

Bill Lowdermilk, assistant to the president, reported that 2,500 persons had attended summer conferences, generating $34,000 in revenue.

The trustees approved a recommendation from Mrs. Earl Brian, chair of the Honorary Degree Committee, that the College wait a year to begin awarding honorary degrees. The board also approved a list of December degree candidates and referred to the Executive Committee a request from the Methodist College Alumni Association that the MCAA president be allowed to attend board meetings with privilege of the floor but without vote.

Dr. Pearce discussed briefly with the board rumors that Methodist College might be sold to the University of North Carolina system and work of The North Carolina Conference of the United Methodist Church's Joint Committee to Study the Future of United Methodist Higher Education. The discussion ended with the trustees approving by unanimous vote a resolution declaring their opposition to any sale of the College.

Dr. Charles Speegle Chairs Fund Drive, Heads Foundation

Directors of the Methodist College Foundation turned to a local veterinarian for leadership during the 1973-74 fiscal year. In December 1973, J. Scott McFadyen Jr., foundation president, and Louis Spilman Jr., executive secretary, announced that Dr. Charles Speegle, owner of Highland Animal Hospital, had agreed to chair the 1974 Community Loyalty Campaign.

At a campaign kickoff breakfast held in the College's Private Dining Room February 12, 1974, Dr. Speegle read a "Methodist College Day" proclamation from Fayetteville Major Jackson Lee. Approximately 80 campaign workers attended the breakfast. College President Richard Pearce delivered the campaign kickoff address.

In a preliminary report to the Foundation board March 12, 1974, Dr. Speegle reported that unrestricted cash and pledges totalling $71,640 had been received by the end of February, saying pledges were $8,000 ahead of the previous year and equal to the Foundation's best year to date.

Speaking at the June 11, 1974, meeting of the Foundation's Board of Directors, College President Richard Pearce reported that enrollment in the College's three summer terms, operated without residence halls and cafeteria services, would exceed 600. He also listed four goals for the College for 1974-75:

1. To establish the identity of the College.
2. To cement the College's relationship with the Church.
3. To make the College program more student-oriented.
4. To operate more economically. [76]

For the fiscal year ending June 30, 1974, the Foundation reported receipts and unpaid pledges totalling $89,448.96. In June, the Foundation issued two checks to Methodist College, one for $69,600 to the College's capital account, and one for $750 to the College's operating account.

At their annual meeting August 13, 1974, directors of the Methodist College Foundation elected Dr. Charles Speegle president for 1974-75. Dr. Pearce reported that new majors in physical education and sociology had been added at the College and that applications for the fall were running 10 percent ahead of the previous year.

At the September and October 1974 meetings of the Methodist College Foundation Board of Directors, College President Richard Pearce spoke at length about the potential tax advantages of charitable gift annuities, deferred charitable gift annuities, and gifts of appreciated property for persons using these methods of giving to Methodist College. His talks included many specific examples illustrating in dollar amounts the benefits that would accrue to donors making these types of gifts.

— CHAPTER 4 —

END NOTES
Chapter Four

1. Stacy Weaver, "Annual Report to the Methodist College Board of Trustees," April 6, 1970, TM, Book 2.
2. Ibid.
3. Ibid.
4. George V. Allen, Commencement Address May 25, 1970, *Bulletin of Methodist College*, June 1970, Vol. 11, No. 4, file.
5. The Reverend Dr. John Lewis, Baccalaureate Sermon May 24, 1970, *Bulletin of Methodist College*, June 1970, Vol. 11, No. 4, file.
6. Dr. Karl Berns, June 1970 letter to Fayetteville area physicians, Methodist College Foundation board minutes, June 1970, MCF, file.
7. Jerome B. Clark Jr., at a meeting of the Methodist College Foundation Board of Directors, August 11, 1970, MCF, file.
8. "Dark Corners," column in *sMALL TALK*, September 29, 1970, file.
9. News story, *sMALL TALK*, October 13, 1970, file.
10. Feature filler, *sMALL TALK*, October 13, 1970, file.
11. Alumni News Edition, *Bulletin of Methodist College*, May 1971, file.
12. Editorial, Special Edition, *sMALL TALK*, March 15, 1971, file.
13. Stacy Weaver, "Annual Report to the Methodist College Board of Trustees," May 4, 1971, TM, Book 2.
14. Ibid.
15. Ibid.
16. John Brown, S.G.A. president, remarks to Methodist College Board of Trustees May 7,1971, TM, Book 2.
17. Dr. Myron F. Wicke, Commencement Address May 24, 1971, *Bulletin of Methodist College*, June 1971, file.
18. The Reverend Dr. Earl G. Hunt Jr., Baccalaureate Sermon May 23, 1971, *Bulletin of Methodist College*, June 1971, file.
19. Stacy Weaver, report to Executive Committee, Methodist College Board of Trustees, July 21, 1971, TM, Book 2.
20. Ad hoc committee, Methodist College Board of Trustees, October 13, 1971, TM, Book 2.
21. Mason Sykes, sport story, *sMALL TALK*, September 21, 1971, file.
22. Stacy Weaver, interview story in *sMALL TALK*, October 1971, file.
23. Ibid.
24. Methodist College Board of Trustees, November 1, 1971, TM, Book 2.

1970–1974

25. Ibid.
26. I. H. O'Hanlon, remarks at dedication of O'Hanlon Amphitheater November 1, 1971, *Bulletin of Methodist College*, November 1971, file.
27. Sarah Brady, editorial in *sMALL TALK*, December 7. 1971, file.
28. Ibid.
29. Stacy Weaver, "Annual Report to the Methodist College Board of Trustees," April 4, 1972, TM, Book 2, file.
30. Dr. Wright Spears, Commencement Address May 15, 1972, *Bulletin of Methodist College*, June 1972, file.
31. Dr. William O. Weldon, Baccalaureate Sermon May 14, 1972, *Bulletin of Methodist College*, June 1972, file.
32. Frank Eason, quoted in a letter to the editor of *sMALL TALK*, November 1972, file.
33. Stacy Weaver, special edition of *sMALL TALK*, November 1972, file.
34. Resolution, Board of Directors, Methodist College Foundation, November14, 1972, MCF, file.
35. Stacy Weaver, remarks to Presidential Search Committee, December16, 1972, TM, Book 2, file.
36. Chip Dicks, S.G.A. president, speech at a campus assembly January 24, 1973, as reported in *sMALL TALK*, January 1973, file.
37. Executive Committee, Methodist College Board of Trustees, February 21, 1973, TM, Book 2, file.
38. Ibid.
39. News story, *sMALL TALK*, March 1973, file.
40. Richard W. Pearce, Methodist College press release April 3, 1973, TM, Book 2, file.
41. Richard W. Pearce, remarks to Methodist College Board of Trustees, April 3, 1973, TM, Book 2, file.
42. Ibid.
43. Richard W. Pearce, interview with Lynn Gruber, June 14, 2001, file.
44. Stacy Weaver, "Annual Report to the Methodist College Board of Trustees," April 3, 1973, TM, Book 2, file.
45. Stacy Weaver, Commencement Address May 14, 1973, *Bulletin of Methodist College*, May 1973, file.
46. Richard W. Pearce, speaking at commencement May 14, 1973, *Bulletin of Methodist College*, May 1973, file.
47. Richard W. Pearce, speaking to Board of Directors, Methodist College Foundation, July 10, 1973, MCF, file.
48. Ibid.

49. Carmen Evans, editorial in *sMALL TALK*, October 1973, file.
50. Richard W. Pearce, statement of educational goals, *Bulletin of Methodist College*, November 1973, file.
51. Ibid.
52. Ibid.
53. Gen. John Tolson, secretary, N.C. Dept. of Military and Veterans' Affairs, speaking at a seminar April 6, 1974, *Bulletin of Methodist College*, May 1974, file.
54. Ibid.
55. Ibid.
56. Ibid.
57. Cutline, *The Fayetteville Observer*, March 6, 1974.
58. Ingeberg Dent, interview with Bill Billings, *Methodist College Today*, December 1989, file.
59. Bobby Cobb, interview with Bill Billings, August 19 and September 5, 2005, file.
60. Associated Press and UPI news stories, *The Fayetteville Observer*, March 6-7, 1974.
61. James Lancaster, letter to the editor, *The Fayetteville Observer*, March 13, 1974, file.
62. Carmen Evans, editorial, *sMALL TALK*, April 1974, file.
63. James E. Holshouser, governor of North Carolina, *Bulletin of Methodist College*, May 1974, file.
64. Ibid.
65. Methodist College Board of Trustees, minutes of meeting held April 1-2, 1974, TM, Book 2, file.
66. Richard W. Pearce, comments to Methodist College Board of Trustees, April 1, 1974, TM, Book 2, file.
67. Dr. Mott Blair, and W. Robert Johnson, comments to Methodist College Board of Trustees, April 2, 1974, TM, Book 3, file.
68. Richard W. Pearce, comments to Methodist College Board of Trustees, April 2, 1974, TM, Book 3, file.
69. Bruce Shelley, baseball coach, comments at dedication of Shelley Field, April 20, 1974, *Bulletin of Methodist College*, June 1974, file.
70. Phil Mullen, letter to Coach Bruce Shelley, read by Janet Mullen at dedication of Shelley Field, April 20, 1974, *Bulletin of Methodist College*, June 1974, file.
71. Arnold W. King, commencement address, May 12, 1974, *Bulletin of Methodist College*, June 1974, file.
72. News story, *sMALL TALK*, October 1974, file.

73. Letters to the editor, *sMALL TALK*, December 1974, file.
74. Ibid.
75. Sue Githens, letter of resignation, *sMALL TALK*, December 1974, file.
76. Richard W. Pearce, comments to Executive Committee, Methodist College Board of Trustees, November 3, 1974, TM, Book 3, file.

A Fort Bragg Bicentennial Color Guard conveyed an Ameican Bicentennial flag and the flags of America's 13 original colonies to Methodist College in a colorful ceremony December 3, 1975.

Chapter 5

Survival 101
1975-79

> "Methodist College is not for sale. We do not have an offer for our college and have not had an offer."
> —*The Reverend Vergil Queen, in a resolution unanimously adopted by the Methodist College Board of Trustees, February 27, 1975.*

Methodist College began construction of a home for the college president in February 1975, on a site just north of the Science Building. Totaling 3,300 square feet, the two-story structure was financed with proceeds from the sale of the president's home on Raeford Road and with local donations of cash, labor, and building supplies

Equestrian (horseback riding) classes became part of Methodist's Physical Education Department in the spring semester of 1975. Both beginning and intermediate classes were offered, each carrying two semester hours of credit toward the sophomore P.E. requirement. An outgrowth of the College Lakes Riding Club, the classes were taught by Dona and Dorothy Davis at Cedar Falls Stables just north of the college.

Early in 1975, Robert Christian, chairman of the English Department, announced the establishment of a writing lab/workshop for freshman English students, in which students were expected to write six acceptable 500-word themes, each with an outline in correct form.

The Monarch basketball team compiled a record of 21-5 in 1974-75, winning the Dixie Conference title for the third consecutive year. Elton Stanley of Shallotte and Greg Jones of Durham were named to the All-Conference team, and Coach Joe Gallagher was named Dixie Conference Coach of the Year for the second straight year. The team lost the opening game of the NCAA Division III South Atlantic Regional Tournament, falling to William Paterson, 53-52.

Continuing an effort begun by Methodist's S.G.A. and N.C. Student Legislature delegates, 28 runners from the College participated in a relay race from Methodist College to Raleigh March 14, 1975, in an effort to raise $1,000 for the United Student Appeal.

— CHAPTER 5 —

The Carolina College Alumni Association donated $2,000 in early 1975 to establish a Carolina College Scholarship at Methodist College. Carolina College was a Methodist college for women, which operated in Maxton, N.C. from 1912-26. At the same time, archives and memorabilia from Carolina College were transferred to Davis Memorial Library for safekeeping and preservation.

In the spring of 1975, Lynne Dixon, president of the Methodist College Science Club, presented a $500 check to the N.C. Zoological Park in Asheboro for the purchase of an African Gray parrot. Club members raised the money by selling homemade terrariums, candles, and dried flower arrangements; they also held bake sales, raked leaves, and staged an animal show.

President Recommends Defaulting on Bonds

Speaking to the trustees' Executive Committee January 25, 1975, President Pearce reported that the current number of dormitory students at the College would not produce sufficient funds from room and board to pay the amounts due the federal government on the dormitory bonds and Student Union bonds. He said the college had been forced to borrow funds from its general budget to make principal and interest payments on its bonds. Dr. Pearce said it had also been necessary to borrow funds from local banks over the preceding four years to meet operating expenses ($65,000 in 1970-71, $125,500 in 1971-72, $200,000 in 1972-73, and $135,000 in 1973-74), and to repay these loans each August or September after students had enrolled for the fall semester.

The president presented the following itemized list of the College's $3,184,000 in long-term bonded indebtedness to the federal government: $1,056,000 for the 1962 dormitory bonds (to build Garber and Cumberland halls), $1,134,000 for the 1964 bonds (to build Weaver and Sanford halls), $420,000 for the 1966 Student Union bond (for the addition thereto), and $554,000 for the 1968 Academic Building bonds (auditorium and administration building). In addition, he said the College had long-term bonded indebtedness from private sources (four insurance companies and one individual) totalling $1,104,030: $871,844 for the College's first three buildings, $82,186 for two sets of apartments, and $150,000 for the auditorium. He said the Methodist College Foundation was making payments on the private debt from its annual fund drive receipts. He said the College had $124,177 in sinking funds to meet its federal obligations.

Dr. Pearce said the College would owe $120,000 in total interest for 1974-75 plus $98,000 in principal. He suggested the College apply to the federal government for a waiver of interest in mid-year, when its reserve or sinking funds would be exhausted, and if necessary, default on the auxiliary enterprise bonds (for the dorms, cafeteria, and Student Union addition). The president reported that by increasing College tuition and room and board, the College could meet the principal payments on the auxiliary enterprise bonds, but could not meet interest payments of $60,000 for the coming year.

After some discussion, the trustees' Executive Committee directed the president to implement a policy of not using tuition funds to pay on bonds and auxiliary enterprises.

President Pearce said he was reluctant to borrow money to build the president's home, especially when the College was faced with defaulting on federal bonds. Mr. Wilson Yarborough Sr., chair of the trustees' *ad hoc* committee for construction of the president's home, said $61,000 was available for the project; he projected another $10,000-$20,000 would have to be raised to complete the home. The trustees voted to proceed with construction of the president's home as soon as possible.

Church Committee Studies Plight of Colleges

At the January 25, 1975 meeting of the trustees' Executive Committee, Dr. Pearce reported that the Joint Committee on Higher Education Planning and Strategy of The North Carolina Conference of the United Methodist Church was drafting a final report with eight recommendations for ensuring the future of five United Methodist institutions of higher learning (Louisburg College, Methodist College, N.C. Wesleyan College, High Point College, Greensboro College, and Duke Divinity School) supported by The North Carolina Conference. The resolutions called for more cooperation between institutions of higher learning in the Western and North Carolina conferences and the appointment by the bishop of a special committee to study and monitor the operations of Louisburg, Methodist, and Wesleyan and to make a recommendation regarding future support at the June 1978 Annual Conference meeting. A tentative draft of the report detailed a four-year trend of declining enrollment at the three colleges: a 24.2 percent decline at Methodist, a 15.2 percent decline at Wesleyan, and a 15.5 percent decline at Louisburg.

When the trustees' Executive Committee met February 27, 1975, Dr. Pearce presented a request from Dr. Tom Collins, president of N.C. Wesleyan College, that the boards of trustees of the two institutions meet to discuss forming one board of trustees which would then determine which of the two colleges would be sold. On a motion by Rev. Vergil Queen, the committee declined Dr. Collins' offer. The motion read:

> "We do not join in meeting with the North Carolina Wesleyan Board of Trustees to consider the sale of either of our colleges. Methodist College is not for sale. We do not have an offer for our

— CHAPTER 5 —

College and have not had an offer. We are excited about our future.

We have a grave concern for the current situation of higher education in The North Carolina Conference and have a deep and abiding concern for North Carolina Wesleyan and its faculty, staff, and students. Methodist College will do everything it can do for the students, faculty, and staff of North Carolina Wesleyan." [1]

Speaking to the trustees' Executive Committee February 27, 1975, Dr. Pearce said applications for admission to Methodist College were running ahead of the previous year; he said the budget for 1975-76 would be based on an enrollment of 600, with a $100 increase in tuition and a $100 increase in room and board. He stated further that three faculty positions would be cut, saving $90,000, and that staff raises would be conditional (based on the final enrollment) —either 0 percent, 3 percent, or 5 percent.

Minutes for the April 5, 1975, meeting of the Methodist College Board of Trustees indicate there was a lengthy discussion of Methodist's relationship with North Carolina Wesleyan College. Dr. Pearce reported on a February 28 meeting he had met with Bishop Blackburn and Dr. Tom Collins, Wesleyan's president. On a motion by David Stedman, the trustees authorized Dr. Blair, Dr. Pearce, and the Executive Committee "to negotiate with Dr. Collins and any other appropriate individuals to render whatever aid, within our resources, we can to Wesleyan College in its time of trauma, and to work for the benefit and protection of the students at Wesleyan College." [2]

In another action, the trustees approved a new Bachelor of Applied Science degree program and a new divisional major in science. Dr. Samuel Womack, academic dean, said the B.A.S. program was designed to allow persons with an associate degree in an area of applied science to transfer to Methodist. He said the new B.S. in Science would allow students to do two semesters of work in each of the following science fields: biology, chemistry, physics, and geology.

Trustees Approve 15-Year Plan To Raise $16 Million

At the April 5, 1975 Board of Trustees meeting, Dr. Pearce suggested a 15-year plan for Methodist College that would, by 1990, yield:
1) a student body of 1,000 (600 dorm, 400 day)
2) a faculty of 50, with half holding doctorates,
3) an endowment of $16 million, consisting of :
   a) $4 million for debt retirement
   b) $2 million for physical education facilities,
   c) $4 million for endowed student aid
   d) $3 million for endowed faculty salaries

e) $1 million for endowed administrative costs
f) $2 million for endowed maintenance [3]

The trustee minutes quote Dr. Pearce as saying that he had no plan for raising the $16 million, but "felt strongly that the board must realistically face the needs of the college to properly establish it as a quality, church-involved, liberal arts college." [4]

On a motion by Nelson Gibson, the trustees approved a Development Committee recommendation that the 15-year plan for Methodist College outlined by Dr. Pearce, including the raising of $16 million in endowment funds, "be undertaken with all the zeal and enthusiasm possible, and that the Finance Committee bring to the November board meeting a plan to strive for this goal." [5]

In the June 1975 *Bulletin of Methodist College,* Dr. Pearce said the $16 million endowment was needed "to adequately finance the College and make it the college we all want to have." [6]

sMALL TALK Showcases "Involved" Students

Green and Gold Masque Keys presented *The Lilies of the Field* March 20-21, 1975, in Reeves Auditorium. R. Parker Wilson directed the play, which featured Ervin Smith in the male lead role as the handyman and Ann Thomas as Mother Marie Martha. Kathy Ewing and Jim Nash gave *Lilies* a rave review in the April 17, 1975, *sMALL TALK.*

In the March 20, 1975, Dr. Robert Wayne Preslar, coordinator of a new English 101 writing lab program, explained the program's purpose. Each student would be assigned a diagnostic theme at the beginning of the semester. Students who wrote an exceptional theme would be exempted from the course, while those who did not would have to write six fully acceptable, 500-word themes, each with a formal outline.

Members of the History and Political Science Club visited the State Archives Building in Raleigh April 7, 1975, and also attended a session of the General Assembly at the Legislative Building.

The April 17, 1975 *sMALL TALK* reported that Joe Gallagher had resigned as men's basketball coach to take the same job at nearby Pembroke State University. In his "Sports Spotlight" column, Thomas Pope included the following comment from Gene Clayton, former men's basketball coach, about the outgoing basketball coach: "I think Joe is one of the most knowledgeable young coaches on the East Coast. I don't think Pembroke will be his final resting place." [7]

The same issue reported that the women's tennis team had dropped its debut match with Atlantic Christian College 6-3.

— CHAPTER 5 —

Methodist College staged a highly successful "Media Day '75" April 23, 1975. Consisting of an all-day series of seminars for high school journalism students from eastern North Carolina, the event was sponsored by *The Fayetteville Observer-Times, sMALL TALK,* and *The Forester* (student newspaper) at Pine Forest High School. The day concluded with an evening lecture by CBS TV news correspondent (and North Carolina native) Charles Kuralt, entitled "The America Behind the Headlines."

Guest lecturers during the day included reporters from WRAL-TV (Raleigh) and WTVD-TV (Durham), as well as Roy Parker, editor of *The Fayetteville Times.* Attendees also viewed a film featuring 12 of Charles Kuralt's best "On the Road" segments from CBS TV news broadcasts. Seminar leaders, student newspaper advisors, and student newspaper editors had dinner with Kuralt prior to his lecture in Reeves Auditorium.

Charles Kuralt

The *sMALL TALK* staff and the family of Alan Stowers, College news bureau director and newspaper advisor, enjoyed a night out at Farrell's Restaurant in Fayetteville's new Cross Creek Mall in April. The group consumed Great Onion Burgers with French fries, sasparillas and Cokes, and Farrell's Zoo Sundaes. Farrell's was famous for its late 1800s theme, complete with costumed waiters and waitresses and "loud and exotic" music.

In *sMALL TALK*'s Year-End Review issue for 1974-75, published April 28, 1975, Co-Editor Donna Gemeinhart listed major events from "a year of involvement and leadership" at Methodist College and saluted the students who had involved themselves in a wide range of campus activities—athletic, cultural, social, and academic. [8]

In his "Record Guide" column, Thomas Pope Jr. gave "A" ratings to the LP "Dressed to Kill" by the rock band Kiss and to "Tooth, Fang, and Claw," an LP by Ted Nugent's Amboy Dukes. On the sports page, Pope offered high praise for the baseball team's pitching quintet of Sammy Tolar, Wayne Gooch, Earl Bunn, Mitchell Davis, and Jerry Byrd, saying they were chiefly responsible for the team's 19 wins.

1975–1979

Two Musicals Launch First Circa '75 Season

Summer 1975 saw the inauguration of the Circa '75 Summer Season, subtitled "Come-As-You-Are Outdoor Entertainment." Mrs. Jane Berry served as executive producer, assisted by David Keyte, managing director, and Harlan Deunow, musical director. Two musical productions were staged in O'Hanlon Amphitheater—*Oklahoma!* for four weekends from June 12-July 12, and "The Best of Broadway" July 17-19. Featured on single concert nights were: barbershop quartets, sacred music, country-bluegrass, opera highlights, and "The Salty Dogs" (New Orleans jazz).

The College also offered three terms of summer classes and hosted a basketball camp, the Annual Conference Session of the United Methodist Youth Fellowship, the East Coast Cheerleading Camp, and The North Carolina Conference Leadership School.

Senator Henley Urges Graduates To Get Involved

State Senator John T. Henley of Hope Mills, N.C., was the featured speaker at Methodist College's 12th spring commencement Sunday, May 11, 1975.

Henley urged members of the Class of 1975 to be tolerant of others and to be confident in the future. "Take heart in our government and our community by seeking to right wrongs by becoming involved," said Henley. "'Cop-outs' didn't turn this virgin land of ours into the country it is. An involved individual can make a difference." [9]

Henley said North Carolina should rely on the independent colleges rather than expand existing state institutions to meet enrollment growth. He said the N. C. General Assembly was poised to pass a bill granting $400 tuition grants to needy North Carolina students attending independent colleges.

Of the 82 graduates who graduated in the spring of 1975, 78 received the Bachelor of Arts degree and four received a Bachelor of Science. Sarah Ellen Edge of Fayetteville received the L. Stacy Weaver Award, denoting her selection by the faculty as the outstanding senior.

In a baccalaureate sermon given Sunday morning, The Reverend James H. Bailey, pastor of Jarvis Memorial United Methodist Church in Greenville, told the graduating seniors that to "make it" they must surrender all to God.

Trustees Approve Bare Bones Budget

The Executive Committee of the Methodist College Board of Trustees approved a "bare bones" budget for 1975-76 May 11, 1975. The operating budget totaled $1,868,514 and was based on a full-time equivalent enrollment of 600 students. Another $144,406 was approved for capital expenditures.

CHAPTER 5

Dr. Richard Pearce, college president, reported that the College staff had been reduced by seven persons, which would save approximately $70,000.

When the trustees' Executive Committee met August 27, 1975, Dr. Pearce reported that the College had exhausted all reserve funds for federal mortgages and would shortly default. He said the College had budgeted for payments on the loan principal only and was seeking a waiver of interest from the federal government. He reported that the College had borrowed $300,000 from a local bank to meet summer operating expenses and would repay that loan from September tuition receipts.

MC Begins 16th Academic Year

sMALL TALK's first issue of 1975-76, dated August 31, 1975, reported that Paul Sanderford Jr. '72 had been named Dean of Men and Supervisor of Intramurals, replacing Mason Sykes, who returned to full-time teaching and coaching soccer in the Physical Education Department. The sports page reported that Sanderford and Coach Bruce Shelley had coached the Methodist baseball team to a third place finish (16-15) in the Monarchs maiden season in the N. C. Collegiate Summer Baseball League, behind UNC (20-11) and UNC-W (17-13).

A group photo of S.G.A. officers appeared on Page One of the August 1975 issue, showing: Danny Hood, president; Ken Daniels, vice president; Chris Moore, secretary; and Brian Davis, treasurer. Featured in a separate article were new admissions counselors Paula C. Smith and Jane W. Youngblood. The paper also reported that Dr. B. L. Crisp, assistant professor of education at Methodist, had just received his doctorate in elementary education at the University of South Carolina.

The September 23, 1975 *sMALL TALK* introduced four new faculty members in a front page article and photo: Dr. Janet Cavano, lecturer in English; Martin Stewart, CLU, lecturer in insurance; Mary Hunley, instructor in physical education; and Joe Miller, assistant professor of physical education.

Page One also included an article by Al Phillips reporting that Methodist had received a grant to cover the cost of renting motion pictures to be shown at College convocations every other Wednesday at 10:30 a.m. in Reeves Auditorium. Phillips quoted Dr. Sam Womack, academic dean, as reminding MC students that they were required to attend six of the eight scheduled convocations each semester to meet one of their graduation requirements. The dean said attendance records would be kept by means of slips of paper passed out and collected at the auditorium doors. He said students who failed to attend six convocations in a semester would be charged a fine of $5.00 or required to submit a term paper.

1975–1979

An inside feature in the September 1975 *sMALL TALK* profiled four sound and lighting technicians who worked in Reeves Auditorium: MC students Parker Jones, Richard Williams, and Cooper Canady, and 1975 graduate Bobby Ayers.

Columnist Jim Nash offered a glowing review of the hit movie *Jaws,* based on the Peter Benchley novel and directed by Steven Spielberg. Nash labeled Spielberg "the new master of suspense." [10]

MC Named Bicentennial Campus

To mark Methodist College's designation as a bicentennial campus by the American Revolution Bicentennial Administration, a Fort Bragg Bicentennial Color Guard presented the College with an American Bicentennial flag, certificate, and flags of the 13 original colonies in a colorful ceremony December 3, 1975. The flags and certificate were placed on permanent display in Davis Memorial Library.

With a grant from the North Carolina Humanities Committee, the Methodist College Economics and Business Department launched a series of forums on American society and the American dream December 9, 1975. The guest speakers were Dr. Richard Bardolph, chair of the history department at UNC-Greensboro, and Roy Parker, editor of *The Fayetteville Times.*

Robert Cole Assumes Director of Development Post

sMALL TALK reported October 7, 1975 that Robert G. Cole had joined the College as director of development. Cole came to Methodist from the Brevard Music Center where he had served as general manager since 1973. Prior to 1973, Cole worked as director of development for the University of Tennessee-Martin campus, director of public relations for St. Jude Children's Research Hospital in Memphis, and in community relations with General Electric Company.

The newspaper article indicated that Cole would play the key role in implementing the 15-year development plan and $16 million endowment drive approved by the College trustees in April.

At the October 22, 1975 meeting of the trustees' Executive Committee, President Pearce said Cole would work closely with the Methodist College Foundation to raise $120,000 in unrestricted cash during the 1975-76 school year.

sMALL TALK Reports on Special Events

Homecoming 1975 was celebrated October 9-11 with a talent show, bonfire, and homecoming dance featuring Men of Distinction. Janice Price was crowned Homecoming Queen. The Monarch soccer team lost to Christopher Newport 2-0.

In the November 5 *sMALL TALK,* Entertainment Editor Thomas Pope Jr. described an October 27 concert by Timberline, a four-member rock band, as a "triumph." Pope said the band awed the audience with a wide-ranging program of ragtime music, bluegrass, rock 'n roll, and original material.

In his "Sports Spotlight" column, Thomas Pope lauded the College's decision to enter the Methodist men's basketball team in the Fayetteville Jaycees Tip Off Tournament set for December 5-6, also featuring teams from Fayetteville State University, Campbell College, and Pembroke State University. Pope said he agreed with *Fayetteville Times* reporter Tommy Horton that the Methodist and Fayetteville State basketball teams should play each other at least once a year.

Approximately 200 students attended the Business and Economics Club's annual Halloween Dance featuring Sweet Water October 30, 1975, in the Student Union. Bucky Douthit won first prize in the costume contest for his portrayal of a peasant girl. The Sociology Club staged a Fifties Dance, complete with a cake walk, November 6.

The December 18, 1975 issue of *sMALL TALK* reported that James E. Malloy Jr. had been elected editor of the 1976 *Carillon* (yearbook) and carried feature articles about Steve Quigley, a senior art major from Silver Springs, MD, the rock band Fleetwood Mac, and movie actor David Carradine's portrayal of Woody Guthrie in the upcoming film, *Bound for Glory.*

Enrollment Climbs, Night School Added

The October 1975 *Bulletin of Methodist College* reported that fall enrollment was up 10 percent over the preceding year. Registrar Gordon Dixon said the College enrolled 686 students, 635 in the regular session and 51 in the new night school. The number of residential students increased from 246 to 252.

College Trustees Approve Alumni Representation, Greatest Gift Scholarship, Awarding of Honorary and Associate of Arts Degrees

The Executive Committee of the Methodist College Board of Trustees made several important decisions at its October 22, 1975 meeting. President Pearce opened the meeting by introducing Robert Cole as the College's new director of development and said Cole would be working closely with the Methodist College Foundation to raise $120,000 in unrestricted cash during the 1975-76 year.

First, the committee approved a request from Susan Garrick Motes, director of alumni affairs, that the president of the alumni association be allowed to attend trustee meetings with the privilege of the floor, but without vote. Second, the committee approved a Greatest Gift Scholarship program presented by Mrs. Motes that would allow MC alumni and each College trustee to award a one-fourth tuition scholarship to a deserving person they had recruited to attend Methodist.

The trustees' Executive Committee also approved the recommendations of the Honorary Degree Committee that the College award not more than four honorary degrees a year. It was agreed that the Executive Committee would select recipients from nominations submitted by College trustees and the College president and the resident bishop of The North Carolina Conference of The United Methodist Church. The trustees also decided that one-half of the degree recipients would be members of The North Carolina Conference and one-half would be lay persons who had made significant contributions to the College, society and/or the church.

The Executive Committee also approved an Associate of Arts degree to be awarded to those who had earned 64 semester hours of credit, met all the general education requirements of Methodist College, and completed at least 15 semester hours in residence at the College with a Grade Point Average of at least 2.0.

The full Board of Trustees met November 15, 1975 and approved: the awarding of not more than four honorary degrees per year, an Associate of Arts degree, board privileges for the MCAA president, the Greatest Gift Scholarship Program for MC alumni, and a policy allowing the transfer of up to 64 semester hours of academic credits from technical institutes and community or junior colleges.

President Pearce also informed the trustees that the College was "now in default on the dormitory deeds of trust held by the U.S. Dept. of Housing and Urban Development and had asked for a three-year moratorium on payments of principal and interest and an additional five-year moratorium on interest payments." [11]

Appreciation was expressed to trustee Dillard Teer for the work done by Nello L. Teer Company to expand the tennis courts behind the Student Union from four to six and to resurface the courts.

sMALL TALK Highlights 1975-76

sMALL TALK's December 18, 1975 issue reported that Dr. Sid Gautam, chair of the Economics and Business Department, had staged a symposium December 9 entitled, "What is the American Dream?" The featured speakers were Dr. Richard Bardolph, chair of the History Department at UNC-Greensboro, and Mr. Roy Parker, editor of *The Fayetteville Times*.

In its February 5, 1976 issue, the student newspaper reported that Methodist held its first annual Greek Field Day Sunday, December 14, 1975

— CHAPTER 5 —

and that the men of Lambda Chi Alpha defeated the men of Pi Kappa Phi 14-0 in a game of tackle football (the second annual Frat Bowl).

Methodist began its spring 1976 semester with an enrollment of 672 students, 620 in the day program and 52 in the night school. Speaking at a spring opening convocation Wednesday, January 21, 1976, College President Richard Pearce and S.G.A. President Danny Hood challenged MC students to become involved by saying, "Let's dream, let's plan, and let's change." [12]

Dr. Pearce introduced new staff members James Peterson, director of veterans affairs; Roy Whitmire, comptroller; and James Stanley, admissions counselor. Hood promised S.G.A. support for the Spring Festival, United Student Appeal's Run-a-thon to Washington, D.C., Sunday chapel services, and a peer tutoring program.

In a guest editorial in the February 9, 1976 *sMALL TALK,* Ann Morrow suggested that campus clubs be given the opportunity to make presentations at campus convocations held every other Wednesday. She said this would encourage more student involvement in student clubs and organizations as well as the S.G.A. An inside story by Manuel Maselka recounted the days of *BIG TALK,* a satirical underground newspaper published briefly at Methodist in 1962-63. Maselka said *BT's* first issue ran a cover story entitled, "A Bedtime Story for Students" and described a certain Mollycoddle College, a college which the writer compared to a television show in search of good ratings.

Another article by Maselka, which appeared in the February 16, 1976 issue, chronicled the efforts of Mrs. Norma Womack, assistant librarian (and others) to preserve MC history by collecting college handbooks, newspapers, and articles from periodicals for the college archives located in the basement of Davis Library.

Jim Nash gave *Barry Lyndon,* a Stanley Kubrick film, mixed reviews, while Michael Ellis lauded a February 7 concert by the Fayetteville Symphony, under the direction of Harlan Deunow. In addition to his usual sports stories, Thomas Pope, Jr., offered a glowing review of a New Christy Minstrels concert and gave albums by the rock bands Bad Company and Nazareth an A rating in his record review column.

The March 3, 1976 *sMALL TALK* reported that the girls basketball team, coached by Mason Sykes, compiled a 7-6 record in its second season. Standout players Anita Graves, Jeannie Edwards, and Becky Mundren were dubbed the "Terrific Trio."

The men's basketball team, coached by Joe Miller, finished the season 12-9. Season highs were wins over Fayetteville State and Pembroke; lows were a double overtime loss to Lynchburg, 100-98, and a 65-53 loss to Greensboro in the first round of the Dixie Conference tournament.

A map showing the route of a United Student Appeal Run-a-Thon appeared on the front page of the March 31, 1976 *sMALL TALK*. The 44-hour, 349-mile Run-a-Thon from Fayetteville to Washington, D.C. was scheduled for April 1-3 to raise money for 13 national health-related charities. Fifty-nine MC students pledged to run from one to 41 1/2 miles with various degrees of financial support.

In his March 31, 1976 "Sport Spotlight" column, Thomas Pope said the 1976 baseball team "had much potential," citing powerful hitters Sam Tolar, Robert Bryant, Buddy Gooch, and Mike Hayes.[13]

sMALL TALK Editor Kathy Ewing and her staff were rewarded for their hard work in the spring of 1976, when the newspaper received First Place ratings in contests sponsored by Columbia Scholastic Press Association and Associated Collegiate Press.

The May 6, 1976 *sMALL TALK* reported that a chapter of Pi Gamma Mu, the National Social Science Honor Society, was chartered May 2, 1976, with 20 members. The newspaper also announced the election of Kenneth Daniel Jr., a junior religion major from St. Pauls, as S.G.A. president and the crowning of freshman Chun Hui Song as Miss Methodist College. Editors of student publications elected by the Publications Committee were: Ginny Williams, *Carillon;* and Kathy Ewing, *Tapestry.* Jane Peterson was subsequently elected editor of *sMALL TALK*.

Trustees Comply With Federal Non-Discrimination Laws

At a January 28, 1976 meeting, the Executive Committee of the Methodist College Board of Trustees approved: a federally mandated non-discrimination statement, an Affirmative Action statement, and H.E.W. Title IX statement to comply with new federal laws outlawing race, sex, and other forms of discrimination in admissions, hiring, and administration of athletic programs.

Trustees also approved increases in tuition and fees for 1976-77, setting tuition at $1,380, the general fee at $240, the student activity fee at $100, room rent at $460, and board at $760. The approved increases made the total cost for a resident student $2,940.

Ike O'Hanlon, chair of the Methodist College Foundation's 1976 Fund Drive, reported that a kickoff banquet would be held February 10, with Bishop Kenneth Goodson of The United Methodist Church as guest speaker.

The lead story in the March 2, 1976 *sMALL TALK* reported on the appearance of Dr. Kenneth Goodson, president designate of the Council of Bishops of The United Methodist Church. Dr. Goodson spoke to 200 persons at a kickoff dinner for the MC Foundation's annual Loyalty Fund Drive. He said small private schools like Methodist provide a unique education for youth, and he called on local residents to help Methodist reach its fund-rising goals. He also endorsed state tuition grants to students attending private schools, saying the grants did not violate the doctrine of separation of church and state.

Ike O'Hanlon, chairman of the MC Foundation's 1976 Fund Drive, introduced Dr. Goodson as the "Daddy Rabbit" of The Methodist Church and gave the following history of Fayetteville's religious sects: "The Catholics came to the shores of the Cape Fear, then split up into Methodists and Presbyterians. Somewhere along the line they were excommunicated. I'm an Episcopalian who went to a Baptist school (Wake Forest), so you can see I'm not mad at anybody." [14]

Henry Dixon, chair of the Buildings and Grounds Committee, reported March 13, 1976 that the College's energy conservation program had reduced electricity consumption by 21.5 percent. The program included reducing light bulb sizes and interconnecting air-conditioning units at the men's dorms, women's dorms, and at Reeves Auditorium and Davis Library.

Affirming the April 3, 1976 recommendations of the Executive Committee, the Methodist College Board of Trustees voted April 10, 1976 to reject a Student Government Association resolution to change the room visitation policy at Methodist. The S.G.A. had asked that 1) males be allowed to assist female students by taking luggage to female students' dormitory rooms, and 2) that during dormitory open house periods, room doors could be closed but not locked. The Student Life Committee had recommended that the changes be allowed on a trial basis.

In other action at the April 10 meeting, the trustees approved a schedule of fees already endorsed by the Executive Committee and an operating budget for 1976-77 of $1,924,271. Trustees also re-elected Dr. Mott Blair as chairman, but Dr. Blair said he would have to resign due to personal reasons. He said the board would meet after graduation May 9 to elect a new chairman.

Trustees Elect Richard R. Allen Chairman

In a meeting held May 9, 1976, the Methodist College Board of Trustees elected Richard R. Allen board chairman to replace Dr. Mott Blair and passed a resolution of appreciation to Dr. Blair for his 10 years of service as chairman. The board also approved Affirmative Action and Non-Discrimination Statements mandated by federal law and a $70,566 capital budget for 1976-77. Trustees also approved memorial resolutions to be sent to the surviving spouses of W. Ed Fleishman, John M. Reeves, Graham S. Eubank, Rhoda Holden McMillan, and Chancie D. Barclift.

The Executive Committee of the Methodist College Board of Trustees met July 10, 1976, and approved the employment of a full-time director of the night school. President Pearce predicted an enrollment of 650 students for fall 1976. Chairman Allen said it was imperative for the College to increase its enrollment and suggested that professional help be considered in the preparation of College publications and advertising.

President Pearce said he had asked President Emeritus Stacy Weaver to raise $1 million for the College. Dr. Pearce suggested the college raise $4 million and invest it at 9 percent interest, using interest earnings to pay down its debt.

President Pearce Gives Trustees Five-Year Plan

At a trustees' Executive Committee meeting held August 16, 1976, College President Richard Pearce presented a five-year plan with enrollment goals, calling for: 1) reaffirming the identity goals set in 1973, 2) reaffirming the financial plan adopted in 1973, 3) adopting as goals an enrollment of 1,350 (day and evening) by the fall of 1983, and 4) renewing a request for a waiver of principal and interest payments on HEW and HUD encumbered properties. At the same meeting, Bill Lowdermilk reported that 116 Greatest Gift Scholarships were awarded for 1976-77 and that 81 of the recipients had enrolled at the College.

Enrollment Climbs to 797 / Vann and Joyner Join Staff

Enrollment at Methodist College increased significantly in the fall of 1976, reaching 708 students in the day program and 89 students in the evening. Dr. Sam Womack said the freshman class numbered 332 and was the largest in eight years. The number of dorm students was 330, an increase of 70 over fall 1975.

Another major development, the hiring of Dr. James Vann as Director of the new Division of Continuing Education and professor of education, was announced in the December 1976 issue of the *Bulletin of Methodist College*. Dr. Vann was charged with expanding the Evening College, consisting of two eight-week terms each semester, and implementing several non-credit community service courses. A native of Clinton, N.C. and an active lay leader of the United Methodist Church, Dr. Vann was the founding president of Sampson Technical Institute; he held bachelor's and master's degrees from Duke and a doctorate in adult education and administration from N. C. State University.

Gordon L. Joyner joined the Methodist administration as Dean of Students/Dean of Men in the fall of 1976. A recently retired instructor at the U.S. Air Force Senior Non-Commissioned Officer Academy, Joyner held degrees from Culver-Stockton College and Auburn University; he was also given teaching duties in the Psychology Department.

— CHAPTER 5 —

The women's tennis team, coached by Gene Clayton, was unbeaten during its fall season, compiling a 15-0 record with wins over East Carolina, Campbell, Atlantic Christian College, Pembroke State, and UNC-Wilmington.

Required Convocations Continue

A front page story in the August 29, 1976 *sMALL TALK* profiled Gordon Joyner, the new dean of students; Dr. James Vann, director of continuing education; and Tommy Dent, admissions counselor. Another story noted that Dr. Sam Womack, academic dean, had received approval for the formation of a chapter of Alpha Chi, a national scholarship society.

A short inside article reported that Methodist students were still bound by a requirement to attend six convocations per semester to qualify for a degree. A news article said convocations would be held on specified Wednesdays at 10:30 a.m. in Reeves Auditorium and that the dean of students would be responsible for scheduling the convocation programs. An inside photo showed workers installing a $30,000 Schantz pipe organ in Hensdale Chapel, given by an anonymous donor.

Sports news included a report that Buster Sanderford '72, dean of men and intramurals supervisor, had accepted a position as baseball coach, women's basketball coach, and intramurals director of Louisburg College. Also reported was the selection of pitcher Earl Bunn as first team All-American, following the Monarch baseball team's third place finish in the N. C. Collegiate Summer League (behind UNC and Louisburg).

The Sept. 24, 1976 *sMALL TALK* reported on new academic regulations raising the GPA requirement for Dean's List to 3.2 and the standards for graduation with honors to 3.4 for *cum laude*, 3.7 for *magna cum laude*, and 3.9 for *summa cum laude*. New faculty members profiled in the same issue were: Dr. John Klutz, assistant professor of education and psychology; Dr. Dwight House, professor of mathematics; Regina Daniel, instructor in physical education; Linda Jackson, instructor in English; Dr. W. S. DeLoach, visiting professor of chemistry; and Eleanor Ninestein, visiting instructor in mathematics.

An inside feature article reported that Mrs. Alice Pearce, 79, mother of President Pearce, had enrolled at the College with the intention of earning a degree in English or history. In other student news, MC clubs elected the following presidents: Lambda Chi Alpha, James Malloy; the Methodist College Chorus, Winkie Lee; Alpha Xi Delta (sorority), Debbie Underwood; and Koinonia (ecumenical Christian group), Yvonne Walker.

Sports Editor Thomas Pope Jr. quoted Coach Mason Sykes as saying the soccer team would be much-improved, manned by one senior, four freshmen, four sophomores, and two juniors. Women's Tennis Coach Gene Clayton was also optimistic on the heels of his team's 7-1 record. Kinta Otterman of Roanoke, Va. was the No. 1 seed on the fall team.

Trustees Chairman Meets with Students

The October 4, 1976 *sMALL TALK* reported that Mr. R. R. Allen, chairman of the MC Board of Trustees, met informally with about 125 students in the lobby of Weaver Hall September 15, 1976. Billed as a "reception sponsored by the MC Alumni Association," the event was planned by Susan Motes, alumni director.

Two years of undesignated Loyalty Fund monies were used in the fall of 1976 to purchase two vans and a truck for College use. The funds were also used to purchase draperies for Private Dining Rooms 1 and 2, resulting in these rooms becoming known as the Alumni Dining Room.

Lillian Carter Visits Methodist

Lillian Carter, the mother of Democratic presidential candidate Jimmy Carter, visited the Methodist College campus October 8, 1976, and spoke to an assembly of students in the Student Union. Mrs. Carter was accompanied on her visit by her daughter Ruth Carter Stapleton, a Fayetteville resident and a 1964 graduate of Methodist, and her grandson Dr. Robert Stapleton, a local eye doctor.

Alan Swartz covered the Carter visit for *sMALL TALK*. He reported that Mrs. Carter entered the Student Union about 5:15 P.M. where she was greeted warmly by students and staff. S.G.A. President Ken Daniel and Trustees' Chairman Richard Allen briefly welcomed the lady from Plains, Georgia; then Ruth Carter Stapleton introduced her mother.

Swartz said Mrs. Carter's big smile and sense of humor won over the crowd. Mrs. Carter began her remarks by commenting on the "beautiful decorations" on campus: the toilet paper hanging in the trees (left over from Homecoming). She spoke first about her family, then about her experiences as a housemother at Auburn University and as a Peace Corps worker in India. After she finished talking, Miz Lillian greeted members of the audience and signed autographs.

ETHOS Holds Field Day for Exceptional Children

ETHOS, the Sociology Club of Methodist College, staged a Field Day for Exceptional Children Saturday, October 23. A *sMALL TALK* news article noted that Joe Miller's "Adaptive Physical Education" class helped plan a full morning of outdoor activities for 60 exceptional students from Fayetteville's Hillsboro Street School. Following lunch in the amphitheater, the group toured the Fine Arts Building and viewed a display of "Kiddy Art" by the Art Club.

— CHAPTER 5 —

Pipe Organ Dedicated

Hensdale Chapel's new Schantz pipe organ was dedicated Wednesday, October 27, 1976, at a special worship service/recital. The November 10, 1976 *sMALL TALK* reported that 200 persons attended the service, at which the Methodist College Chorus performed Haydn's "Little Organ Mass" with Betty Neill Guy Parsons '64 as soloist. Other performers included a string ensemble led by Dr. Willis Gates, professor of music and chair of the Music Department, and a brief organ recital (featuring works by six composers) by Mrs. Jean Ishee, assistant professor of piano and organ.

Jean Ishee's dedicatory organ recital included works by six composers.

Two student writers offered some kudos on the editorial page. Editor Jane Peterson praised the College faculty for reversing an earlier vote to end the 10:30 break on Monday, Wednesday, and Friday. She said the S.G.A. Senate had passed a resolution urging restoration of the break.

Al Phillips reviewed an October 22 performance by the Cincinnati Ballet in Reeves Auditorium. He said the troupe danced to six variations from the final act of *Raymonda* (a ballet by Glazunov), to Poulenc's "Concerto for Organ, String Orchestra and Timpani," and to a medley of American folk music designed for the American Bicentennial. Phillips described the group as "fantastic" and said it received three standing ovations from the capacity audience.

Federal Officials Agree to Defer Bond Payments

Trustees Chairman Richard Allen reported to College trustees November 12, 1976 on discussions he and President Pearce had with federal officials in Greensboro regarding a request for a waiver of principal and interest payments. He said U.S. Departments of Health, Education and Welfare (HEW) and Housing and Urban Development officials were willing to grant a moratorium on payments provided the College could demonstrate potential for growth and ultimate payment of the bonds. Dr. Pearce said he had submitted four statements/projections to the federal officials: "Methodist College Identity Goals for 1976-81," "Operations Income Through 1980-81," "Financial Plan 1976-81," "Five year Projections for Operation."

In a 2001 interview, Mr. Allen recalled in great detail the meeting. They traveled from Fayetteville to Greensboro in a jet helicopter owned by D. R. Allen and Sons. Dr. Pearce told Allen he was a little uncomfortable traveling in a jet helicopter to tell federal officials the College could not pay its bills. In deference to Dr. Pearce's feelings, Allen instructed the pilot to land on the tennis courts at Greensboro College instead of the helipad at the HUD building. Allen said he and Dr. Pearce then took a taxi to the HUD building

Allen said Dr. Pearce did an excellent job of presenting his plans for making Methodist College solvent again, but that HUD officials still wanted to know when payments on Methodist's construction bonds would resume. Allen said he told them, "You're not going to get any money, and you have two alternatives. You can go along with this plan or you can repossess those dormitories." [15] Allen said the officials made it clear they did not want to foreclose on the dormitories, and the meeting ended.

Also at the trustees' November 12 meeting, Dean of Students Gordon Joyner reported that residential students had helped paint dormitory hallways, that picture identification cards would be used in the fall of 1977, and that a session for parents and spouses of students would be incorporated into freshman orientation. Mr. Lowdermilk reported that a Methodist College Speakers Bureau had been established, with 27 faculty and staff agreeing to participate.

Student Government Association President Kenneth Daniel presented a report outlining his goals for 1976-77. He said he disagreed with present and former student leaders who felt the S.G.A. should serve as a counter-balance to the power of the College trustees, administration, and faculty. He said he felt the S.G.A. should practice self-governance within the framework of the College and its policies, help communicate College policies and rules to the students, and work with the College president to air and resolve student grievances.

Daniel pledged his best efforts to: 1) further open communication between the College staff and students, 2) promote Methodist College in the local community and the state, 3) promote school spirit and pride in Methodist College, and 4) aid in recruiting students who are potential S.G.A. leaders. [16]

Business Manager Roy Whitmire reported that Methodist College would need to borrow only $100,000 for operational expenses by the end of December, compared to $185,000 the previous year.

In a lengthy report, President Richard Pearce reported that the faculty and Academic Affairs Committee had approved in principle plans to establish a satellite ROTC program at Methodist in cooperation with Campbell College. The trustees voted to approve the ROTC program subject to final negotiations and details being resolved.

The president presented a "needs list" that included a new faculty member in speech/drama, theater, a half-time chaplain, two intramural fields, a 1/4 mile track, scholarships for international students, retiling the showers (16) in the men's dorms, new curtains for Reeves Auditorium, resurfacing three old tennis courts and several streets, and roof repairs. He decried the condition of the inoperable Fleishman Fountain and said the College was looking for ways to rehabilitate it. Dr. Pearce expressed his pride in the College faculty and staff, noting that College salaries were among the lowest in the state, "yet we still retain dedicated, capable persons." [17] At a December 10, 1976 meeting, the Executive Committee of the Methodist College Board of Trustees approved: $25,000 for dormitory repairs, $5,000 for seeding two intramural fields, and the sale of one-eighth interest in land in Alamance and Orange counties willed to the college by John M. McIntyre.

Trustees Approve Faculty Leave Policy

Reporting to the Executive Committee of the Methodist College Board of Trustees February 2, 1977, President Richard Pearce reported that fuel oil consumption at the boiler plant had been reduced from 200 gallons per hour (using four boilers) in 1973 to 48 gallons per hour (using one boiler) in January 1977. He also reported that 600 thermostats on campus had been set at 68 degrees.

In the area of finances, Dr. Pearce said the College was operating within its budget, having borrowed $59,000 December 20, 1976. He projected the College would need to borrow about $150,000 for the next five years. He said an additional appropriation of $7,000 from The North Carolina Conference of The United Methodist Church for debt reduction would be applied to loans on the campus apartments.

A request from the College faculty that the core course requirements be reduced two semester hours by eliminating two hours of required physical education was referred back to the faculty.

At a March 4, 1977, meeting, the trustees' Executive Committee approved the awarding of honorary degrees to John W. Hensdale and the Reverend Charles Mercer; the committee also approved a food service contract with ARA, and fees for 1977-78 totaling $2,990 (tuition-$1,500, general fee-$250, room-$460, and board-$780). Dr. Pearce reported that four faculty members held the M.A.T. degree instead of the M.A. in their teaching field as required by the Southern Association of Colleges and Schools. The committee directed the president to proceed with all due speed to upgrade the faculty.

On April 15, 1977, Dr. Pearce presented a tentative budget for 1977-78 to the trustees' Executive Committee based on 650 full-time equivalent students, with 300 of those being dormitory residents. It was approved and forwarded to the full board of trustees.

The Methodist College Board of Trustees approved a policy for granting leaves of absence to tenured faculty members April 15, 1977. The policy allowed one year leaves to allow faculty to satisfy residence requirements for a terminal degree, leaves of less than one year for personal reasons (with an acceptable substitute paid for by the faculty member), and up to two years of leave (without pay) for a medical reason.

Mr. Robert Cole, director of development, announced that he would be leaving his post in June. In his annual report to the trustees, Dr. Pearce said the College's annual operating deficit had been reduced by $211,000, and the college anticipated borrowing no more than $80,000 in 1977-78. He said 1977-78 would bring a full-time campus minister, a dean of men, a psychology major, a director of financial aid, a speech and drama instructor, and a five percent bonus for faculty. The trustees adopted an operating budget for 1977-78 of $2,351,840 and a capital budget of $70,566. After meeting in executive session, the trustees set the president's annual salary at $30,000 and appointed Bill Lowdermilk vice president.

Trustees Approve Timber Sale, Request for City Annexation

At a May 10, 1977, meeting, the Methodist College Board of Trustees Executive Committee voted to advertise for bids on the harvest and sale of timber from 400 acres on the campus.

When the trustees' Executive Committee met July 7, 1977, Bill Lowdermilk enumerated the five-year goals for the College: 1) enrich the student life program, 2) expand community relations, 3) develop better church relations, 4) operate the College as economically as possible, 5) upgrade the academic program.

At a September 8, 1977, meeting of the Executive Committee, Dr. Pearce said the College was defending itself in a lawsuit brought by a dismissed faculty

— CHAPTER 5 —

member on the basis of the plaintiff's "moral turpitude and inability to meet SACS standards to teach the English courses." [18]

The committee approved a five percent cost of living raise for faculty, a five percent bonus, and the addition of life and disaster insurance to the College's fringe benefits. President Pearce announced a $1,100 gift from trustee Nelson Gibson to establish a Graham Eubank Memorial Conference Room.

Work Begins on Track, Basketball/Volleyball Courts

Construction began early in 1977 on an enlarged soccer field with a quarter-mile track around it and concrete basketball/volleyball courts in the "bonfire area" northeast of the Student Union.

Methodist College's quartermile track was laid in 1977.

The first Mary Jeanne Blackburn Scholarship, established in honor of the wife of Bishop Robert M. Blackburn (resident bishop, Raleigh Area of The United Methodist Church) was awarded to Wanda G. Willett of Sanford, N.C.

Enrollment for the spring 1977 semester reached 803 students, compared to 672 in the spring of 1976. The resident population increased to 306, up from 239 a year earlier, and the Evening College enrollment hit 127 (compared to 52 for the spring of 1976), including 19 in the inaugural Weekend College.

A Reflection of the Arts show February 24, 1977, featured the Methodist College Stage Band, the Methodist College Cloggers, Arnold Pope on the bagpipes, Diane Carlson at the piano, vocalist Allene Aldredge, guitarists Tom Smith and Dave Perry, and dancers Ira Walder, Joan Ann Blyther, and

Betty White. Other spring arts festival events included the 11th Annual Art Exhibition in the Reeves Auditorium lobby (Feb. 25) and a performance of the play *The Lady's Not for Burning* March 3-4.

College Gains ROTC Program, Full-Time Campus Minister
In the spring of 1977, Methodist College reached an agreement with The U.S. Army Reserve Officer Training Corps (ROTC) to begin offering a program at Methodist in the fall. In August, Capt. Glenn Blackburn was appointed to develop the ROTC program, with the rank of assistant professor of military science.

In early April, 1977, after a two-year absence, Methodist sent a delegation to the N.C. Student Legislature and received honorable mention for Best Small School Delegation. In his *sMALL TALK* sports column April 7, Thomas Pope paid tribute to Bruce Shelley, who had announced his resignation as baseball coach. Pope lauded Shelley's coaching skills, character, and knack for telling jokes.

Spring 1977 brought much success for Monarch athletics, as Methodist's men's basketball, baseball, and women's tennis teams were invited to national tournaments. The basketball team finished second in the South Atlantic Regionals, losing to William Paterson 62-60. The baseball team dropped two 2-0 games to William Paterson (NJ) and Lynchburg in the NCAA III Southern Regional. The women's doubles team of Rhonda Moon and Jenny Wright reached the semifinals of the Association of Intercollegiate Athletics for Women national playoffs in Ada, OK.

The April 26, 1977 *sMALL TALK* reported that James Malloy, a junior religion major from Fairmont, N.C., had been elected S.G.A. president, defeating Larry Buffaloe 213-105.

In late April of 1977, President Richard Pearce named William P. Lowdermilk vice president of Methodist College, to be responsible for development as well as public, church, alumni and community relations. Dr. Pearce said Mr. Lowdermilk had been his strong right arm for four years and that the title recognized "the dedication and service of this very hard-working individual." [19]

S.G.A. Pres. James Malloy

In June 1977, Reverend Paul D. Granger was appointed Methodist's first full-time campus minister. A graduate of UNC-Wilmington and Duke Divinity School, Granger came to the college from a pastorate at Longhurst United Methodist Church in Roxboro, N.C.

— CHAPTER 5 —

The North Carolina Conference of The United Methodist Church elected five trustees to the Methodist College board in June 1977: Dr. Lucille W. Hutaff, Fayetteville; James C. Crone, Goldsboro; the Rev. F. Belton Joyner Jr., Mebane; the Rev. Samuel D. McMillan Jr., Henderson; and the Rev. Emerson M. Thompson Jr., Wilmington.

College Begins 18th Year with Many New Faces

Methodist College began its 18th academic year in August 1977 with nine new faculty members and six new staff members.

New faculty included Capt. Glenn Blackburn, ROTC; Mark Bonn, instructor in physical education and baseball coach; Mrs. Deborah Dickerson, instructor in sociology; Dr. Charles Evans, instructor in psychology; Ms. D. Jean Kirkhuff, assistant professor of art; E. Russell Klauk, assistant professor of education; Dr. John C. (Jack) Peyrouse. associate professor of speech and drama; George Calvert Ray; instructor in business administration.

New staff members were: Jim Stanley '75, director of admissions; William G. Morgan Jr., comptroller; Ruth Hoyle, library assistant and director of the Teaching Materials Center; Lynn Moore Barnes '71, assistant in public relations and director of alumni affairs; and Richard E. Coleman, dean of men and Student Union director. MC graduates John Young and Marsha Hudson began work as admission counselors.

Mark Bonn, 26, who succeeded Bruce Shelley as MC baseball coach, told a *sMALL TALK* reporter in August 1977 that he intended to further Methodist's winning tradition. A native of Gillette, N.J. and a graduate of Furman University, Bonn came to MC from Appalachian State University where he served as assistant baseball coach. Bonn was also hired as the Monarch cross country coach.

A front page news story in the September 29, 1977 *sMALL TALK* explained how the courts in a newly organized Student Government Association would work. The five-member S.G.A. High Court was headed by Allan Swartz as chief justice. The S.G.A. public defender was Tom Melvin, and Claudia Harrelston was S.G.A. prosecutor. Jerry Lewis was chief justice of the Community Court, designed to hear infractions involving nonresident students and to serve as an appeals court from the Dormitory Courts. S.G.A. Vice President Randy Blanchard served as president pro tem of the S.G.A.'s Fifteenth Senate.

The four Greek organizations at MC held a Greek Week September 12-18, 1977, followed by Rush Week September 19-23. The president of the Greek organizations were: Tom Holland, Lambda Chi; Bill Parlett, Pi Kappa Phi; Mary Owens, Kappa Delta; and Sarah Jo Young, Alpha Xi Delta.

1975–1979

Students Elect President's Mother Homecoming Queen

Homecoming 1977, held October 3-9, featured a Garber Hall talent show, MC Talent Show, a dance featuring the band Staircase, the staging of two plays by Green and Gold Masque Keys, the annual alumni banquet, and a concert by Bill Deal and the Rondells in Reeves Auditorium. The really big news was the election of Alice Pearce, a 79-year-old student and the mother of College President Richard Pearce, as Homecoming Queen. That event made the national news.

The November 4, 1977 sMALL TALK included a letter to the editor from Susan Putnam and Belinda Chandler criticizing the rude behavior of students at College convocations and the policy of requiring students to attend convocations. In sports news, the women's volleyball team, coached by Mary Jane Hunley, finished its season 14-1 in the conference and 14-5 overall and was invited to the NCAIAW Div. III & IV playoffs at Meredith College. The MC soccer team ended the 1977 season 5-2-1.

A major snack bar renovation was begun in November 1977, using a plan drawn by MC student John Haynes. The project was funded by a $4,000 gift from Home Federal Savings and Loan Co. A part of the plan, College post office boxes were moved to the student story display area to make room for the Graham S. Eubank Conference Room.

Mrs. Alice Pearce is crowned 1977 Homecoming Queen.

A Panhellenic Association was formed October 12, 1977, with officers chosen from the two women's sororities, Alpha Xi Delta and Kappa Delta. Paula Adams was the first president, and Mrs. Janet Cavano was the faculty advisor.

Trustees Approve Request for Annexation, MC Medallion

At an October 20, 1977, Board of Trustees meeting, President Pearce recommended that the College request annexation of the campus by the city of Fayetteville.

— CHAPTER 5 —

The president reported that timber on the campus was now being harvested under the direction of a forester hired by the College. He asked for permission to clear cut the swamp area south and east of the playing fields so the College could build a lake and baseball field in that area. No action was taken on his request.

Trustees approved a recommendation by Dr. Pearce that small scholarship funds be consolidated into a Methodist College Memorial Scholarship Fund, subject to the approval of the person who had created small scholarships.

After considerable discussion of the College's need to borrow funds to complete the fall 1977 semester, the trustees authorized the College president and board secretary to borrow up to $150,000 from local banks at the best rate of interest. Trustees directed that proceeds from the sale of timber be put in the endowment to fund presidential scholarships.

The Pi Kapps in 1978.

In a special meeting October 20, 1977, the trustees' Executive Committee authorized the president to effect loans between the capital, operating and bond accounts and to transfer net amounts resulting therefrom at the end of the fiscal year.

At a special meeting November 17, 1977, the Methodist College Board of Trustees voted to petition the city of Fayetteville for annexation of the campus and approved the awarding of Methodist College Medallions (five per year) to persons who had made significant contributions to the College, The United Methodist Church, or the Fayetteville community.

Bill Lowdermilk reported that 126 Greatest Gift Scholarships had been awarded by MC alumni in Fall 1977, that $111,615 had been raised by the Methodist College Foundation, and that 2,529 persons had attended summer conferences.

Dean Samuel Womack reported a fall 1977 enrollment of 734 in the regular day program and 269 in two terms of Evening College. He said the faculty numbered 42 full-time and four part-time members and that the average salary for all ranks was $11,643.

In a lengthy report on his first four years, President Pearce said the College's financial condition had improved and he anticipated the end of short-term

Soccer Seniors: David Radford, Larry Buffaloe, Dave Perry, Bucky Douthit

borrowing in two years and resumption of payments on bonded indebtedness by 1981. He said the College needed to improve retention, expand continuing education, explore graduate education, raise faculty salaries, improve its facilities, complete a $16 million development program, and launch a capital funds drive.

Louisburg College President Addresses Winter Graduates

Dr. Allen Norris, president of Louisburg College, was the commencement speaker at the 1977 winter graduation Sunday afternoon, December 18. He asked the 31 members of the winter class to look to the future with optimism, yet realize there is always reason for skepticism. "Find a big enough idea to live for and you'll never be unemployed," he said. [20]

Executive Committee Ponders Finances

In a January 27, 1978 meeting, the College trustees' Executive Committee accepted the recommendation of the trustees' Finance Committee and directed that all endowment funds be invested in 90-day certificates of deposit at the best interest rate available from local financial institutions.

President Pearce said 690 students enrolled for the spring 1978 semester and that a Strict Academic Probation (SAP) policy had been

— CHAPTER 5 —

implemented to more rapidly identify students with academic problems (grades of D or F).

When the trustees' Executive Committee met March 20, 1978, President Pearce said the East West Foundation would hold a summer workshop at Methodist and that the $23,000 realized from this event would be applied to the $30,000 estimated cost of air-conditioning the Classroom Building. The committee approved the following annual fees for 1978-79: tuition-$1,650, general fee-$250, activity fee-$100, board-$860, room-$500 for a grand total of $3,360 for a resident student.

sMALL TALK Showcases 1978 Happenings

The Pat Terry Group, an Atlanta-based Christian music trio, presented a concert to over 700 persons February 8, 1978 in Reeves Auditorium. Religious Life Opportunities of Methodist College sponsored the event.

The Preservation Hall Jazz Band of New Orleans appeared in Reeves Auditorium February 23, 1978 under the auspices of the College-Community Civic Music Association.

sMALL TALK reported the results of a student survey regarding summer school in its February 2, 1978 issue. Forty-one percent of the 694 respondents said they did not plan to attend summer school; another 40 percent said they would attend summer school if classes were offered in the morning.

The same issue of the student newspaper also listed 26 spring semester convocations on page three, including the dates, times, sponsors and point values for each event. Students were offered credit for "cultural" performances by the North Carolina Symphony, Goldovsky Theatre Opera ("La Boheme"), the Fayetteville Symphony, the Fayetteville Dance Theatre, as well as concerts by the College chorus and stage band, recitals by music students, and a presentation of *Hedda Gabler* by the MC Theatre Department. [Students were required to earn 16 points a semester by attending convocations to fulfill a graduation requirement.]

A member of the Preservation Hall Jazz Band in concert.

Dr. Joe Bethea, district superintendent of the Rockingham District of The North Carolina Conference of The United Methodist Church, was the guest speaker for Faith-in-Life Week at Methodist March 27-31, 1978. The theme was "That I May Know Him."

"Garden Party" was the theme of the 1978 Spring Festival. The week-long event included a Ms. Monarch contest, a showing of the film *Blazing Saddles*, a Miss Methodist pageant, a coffeehouse featuring John Stanfield, a picnic/concert around the bell tower with New Grass Revival (a bluegrass band), and a semiformal dance with the band Shamrock from Martinsville, Virginia.

Four consecutive *sMALL TALK*s in the spring of 1978 contained full-page ads on the back page promoting MC's ROTC program, specifically snow skiing, whitewater rafting, and scuba diving excursions sponsored by Monarch Company.

In April, 1978, Methodist students elected Ted Hough, a junior from Lumber Bridge, S.G.A. president. The chorus and hand bell choir toured Virginia, West Virginia, and Pennsylvania during spring break. Green and Gold Masque Keys (drama club) took a touring production of *Canterbury Tales* to several local churches and middle schools. Andrea Dunham won the first place purchase prize in the MC Juried Art Exhibit for a sculpture entitled "La Femme." Susan Ipock presented her senior art exhibit in the Student Union. Teresa Culbreth was crowned Miss Methodist College.

Foundation Raises $168,000

A team of 165 Methodist College Loyalty Day volunteers assembled for breakfast February 23, 1978, and then called on local prospects for sustaining gifts to the College. Dr. Charles Speegle, chair of the Development Committee of the Methodist College Board of Trustees, said the volunteer development team operated on two principles: 1) each volunteer must give, and 2) each volunteer must make personal contact with prospects. The campaign surpassed its $120,000 goal by raising a total of $168,000.

"An International Festival of Music, Drama, Dance and Film" came to Methodist in the spring of 1978. Sponsored by the N. C. Southeast Consortium for International Education, the series featured free performances by the Trio A Cordes Milliere of Paris (February 2, 13), "A Night at a German Cabaret" (March 1), the French film *Small Change* (March 1), and the Boston Flamenco Ballet (March 21).

The March 1978 *Bulletin of Methodist College*, profiled Jim Townsend of Fayetteville, who skipped his senior year of high school, took the CLEP exam (earning 30 semester hours of College credit) and entered Methodist as an instant sophomore.

— CHAPTER 5 —

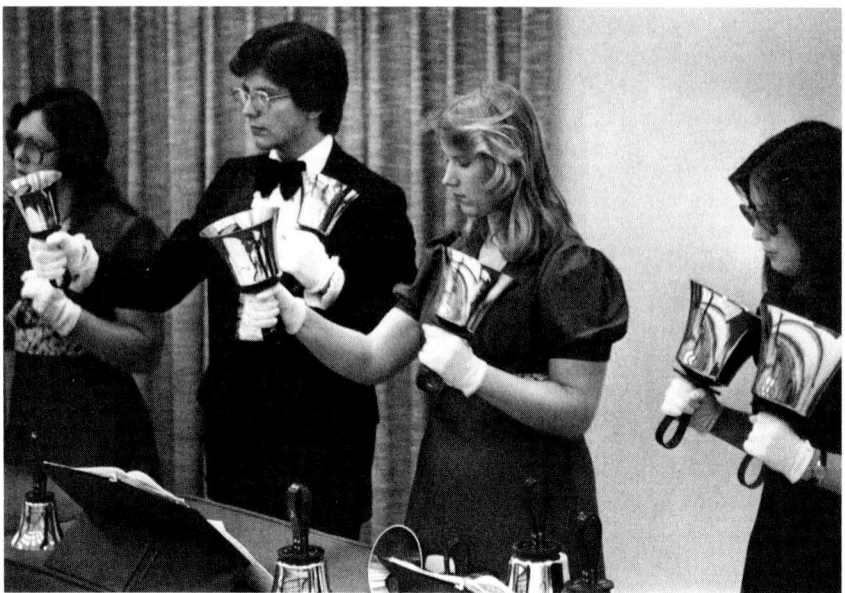

The Methodist College Hand Bell Choir.

Trustees Adopt Retirement, Investment Policies

Meeting April 13, 1978, the Methodist College Board of Trustees approved a retirement policy that conformed to federal legislation, requiring faculty to retire at the end of the academic year in which they attain the age of 70 and administrators to retire at the age of 65. The trustees reserved the right to grant waivers of the retirement policy for one year at a time.

In another major action, the trustees adopted an investment policy requiring that available operating funds be invested in certificates of deposit or U.S. Treasury Bonds and that endowment funds be invested in corporate bonds or stock with Moody rating of "A" or better.

The trustees also approved the design of the Methodist College Medallion (a bronze replica of the college seal attached to a ribbon) and voted to limit the awarding of Greatest Gift Scholarships by MC alumni and trustees to one every other year. Dr. Charles Speegle reported that the Methodist College Foundation's 1978 fund drive had netted $109,500 toward a goal of $120,000. Dr. Samuel Womack, academic dean, reported that 50 percent of the full-time faculty now held doctorates and that enrollment in the ROTC program had reached 72; 12 in the advanced program and 60 in the beginning phase.

Dr. Pearce noted that HEW Title IX's requirement for equal facilities for both sexes would require dormitory modifications in showers, and that ramps would have to be added to make buildings accessible to handicapped persons.

The president concluded his report by saying: "Five years ago the financial picture was a long, dark tunnel with a dim light at the end. Today the tunnel grows shorter and the light brighter. . .The struggle has been long and hard at times, but the college must dare to dream again and again, and to build on the 1956 dream because dreams are what progress is made of. And dreams come true, not overnight, but step by step." [21]

Eubank Conference Room Dedicated

The Graham S. Eubank Conference Room was dedicated April 13, 1978. The late Reverend Eubank was an original member of the Methodist College Board of Trustees and also served as pastor of Hay Street Methodist Church in Fayetteville and superintendent of the Fayetteville District of The North Carolina Conference of The United Methodist Church. Approximately 100 guests attended; speakers included Dr. Richard Pearce, The Reverend Vernon Tyson, Nelson Gibson, S.G.A. President James Malloy, and Koinonia President Dwight Cribb.

Investment Committee Votes to Sell Assets

The trustees' Investment Committee met April 28, 1978, and voted to sell stock in Syntex Corporation, Zoecon Corporation, Katy Industries, Fidelity Trend, Inc., Burlington Industries, and United Guaranty Corporation and to transfer monies in the "Unexpended Plant Fund" to the College's permanent endowment. The committee also voted to sell lots in Sunny Acres, Greenwood, and Edenroc. An investment report showed the college had $88,455 invested with Guaranty Savings and Loan Association (restricted for scholarships). A total of $327,764 was invested in the endowment and other non-expendable funds. This included $216,000 in certificates of deposit at Cross Creek Savings and Loan Association, $12,500 in a CD at North Carolina National Bank, and stocks in seven companies valued at $10,809.

MC Hosts East West Foundation Summer Program

The College's May 1978 *Bulletin* announced that Methodist had been selected as the site of East-West Foundation's Summer Program. Based in Japan, the foundation's seven-week summer program was designed to bridge the cultural gap between Japanese society and the American college campus. It was reported that 160 Japanese students would begin classes at Methodist July 5, studying English as a second language, American culture, composition and speech, and college life.

— CHAPTER 5 —

Horner, Kirby, Weaver Receive Honorary Degrees

William E. Horner, publisher of *The Sanford (NC) Herald,* delivered the commencement address May 7, 1978, telling members of the Class of 1978 that the true road to success involves looking for ways to serve others. Horner also received an honorary Doctor of Letters degree from the college.

The Reverend Wallace Kirby, pastor of Edenton Street United Methodist Church in Raleigh, delivered the baccalaureate sermon, urging the graduating seniors to follow the example of courage set by Jesus Christ. Kirby was awarded an honorary Doctor of Divinity degree at the commencement service.

Dr. L. Stacy Weaver, founding president of Methodist College, was also awarded an honorary Doctor of Divinity degree at the commencement exercise. Claudia Gail Harrison of Cherryville, N.C. received the Stacy Weaver Award for her selection by the faculty as the outstanding senior.

During the summer commencement August 25, 1978, Dr. Charles Speegle, a retired veterinarian, former trustee of the College, and former president of the Methodist College Foundation, received the first Methodist College Medallion for outstanding service to the College and his community.

Trustees Approve New Statement of Purpose

A new Statement of Purpose for Methodist College was approved by the trustees' Executive Committee August 21, 1978. It read as follows:

> The general purpose for the establishment and operation of Methodist College is the development of responsible members of society by providing a liberal arts education for students from the Cumberland County community, from southeastern North Carolina and from United Methodist Church families, as well as for any students whose goals and values can be identified with those of the institution, regardless of their regional, national, racial or ethnic origins. Methodist College is a Christian institution. Since its program is based on the conviction that a liberally educated person can contribute substantially and creatively to the professions and to the business and civic life of his or her community, Methodist College adheres to the following premises:
>
> **1. A liberally educated person should possess an open-minded and a questioning attitude.**
>
> The College was founded in the Methodist educational tradition, which encourages students to inquire actively about the meaning of existence, to maintain a lasting dedication

to truth and to develop consciously their own personal philosophies of life.
2. **A liberally educated person is ethical.**
Responsible citizens conduct themselves in accord with moral principles and accept the consequences of their actions. Methodist College seeks to inculcate high ethical standards in her students, especially by emphasizing the needs and rights of others.
3. **A liberal arts education should promote self-understanding.**
The successful life is based upon sound self-knowledge, and the liberally educated person should have a ready awareness of his or her abilities and shortcomings. Methodist College attempts to foster such self-understanding by encouraging all students to engage in a variety of academic, social, athletic, cultural and civic activities.
4. **A liberal arts education ministers to the whole person.**
The complex human personality has a wide range of potential in diverse aspects of life-experience. Methodist College cherishes for its students the development of capabilities for the appreciation and enjoyment of many areas of knowledge, of the arts, and the attainment of attitudes and skills that may serve to enrich their relationships and experiences throughout life.
5. **A good liberal arts education is acquired through excellence in teaching.**
The College's constant goal is the development of a staff of instructors with the highest professional qualifications, the most effective classroom pedagogy and individual tutorial skills, and the most abiding love for and interest in those persons of all ages who come to them for leadership in the great adventure of learning. [22]

Business Manager Roy Whitmire presented a generally positive report on College finances, saying year-end borrowing had been held to $107,000, that a surplus of $45,180 had been realized in the Evening Division, that a quarter of a million dollars in deferred maintenance had been done in the last three years, and that investment and rental income (from the farm and apartments) had increased.

Bishop Blackburn Speaks At Opening Convocation

Methodist began its 19th academic year September 5, 1978, with a freshman class of 386 and a full-time enrollment of 764, including 50 foreign students. Addressing the student body at the opening convocation, Bishop Robert Blackburn of The North Carolina Conference of The United Methodist Church, said, "If history is defined by key words, then 'liberation' is the word for this generation. Education attempts to liberate people from fear, prejudice and guilt—it is the process of liberation to be the person you are created to be." [23] As the school year began, Dr. Dixon McLeod, a Fayetteville native, assumed the dual posts of dean of students and director of guidance and placement. McLeod had taught at Terry Sanford and Orange high schools before entering graduate school at Duke University.

A fall 1978 orientation issue of *sMALL TALK* profiled seven new faculty members: Dr. Ted Jaeger, psychology; Dr. John Sill, sociology; Dr. Sue Kimball, English; Lloyd Nicks, art; Rose Blakwell, physical education/women's basketball coach and softball coach; Dr. Robert Hersch, head librarians; and Dr. Nadine Landry, Spanish. Feature articles in this issue described things to do in Fayetteville, the MC intramural program, a Christmas break theatre program entitled "Fine Arts in New York,' a pinning ceremony for Deanna Plummer (the first graduate of MC's ROTC program), and exchange student Mamoru Kubota's skill in Kyuda, a Japanese style of archery.

Pastel TP Rains Down on Homecoming

During Homecoming Week, October 9-15, 1978, Jo Anne Jones was crowned Homecoming Queen. Green and Gold Masque Keys presented "Brush Up Your Shakespeare," and hypnotist Larry Garrett entertained students. The Homecoming theme was "Unity within Diversity."

On Thursday night, October 12, 1978, MC students continued a homecoming tradition by "rolling" the campus and the president's home with toilet paper. A *sMALL TALK* news story noted that **pastel** toilet paper (yellow, green, pink) was strewn on trees, fire hydrants, handrails, street signs, and soccer goals. President Pearce and several staff members complimented the students for their creativity. A few students also adorned the president's house with Christmas decorations and serenaded the Pearces with Christmas carols.

The Behavioral Sciences Club (ETHOS) held a Field Day for Exceptional Children from the Fayetteville area October 21, 1978. A two-day Kodaly Music Workshop was held at MC October 6-7, 1978 devoted to teaching children the fundamentals of music. The guest lecturer was Aden Lewis, a music teacher/composer.

Charles Speas won First Place as The Great Pumpkin in the Business and Economics Club's 1978 Halloween Costume Dance.

The November 17, 1978 *sMALL TALK* reported that the 49ers of UNC-Charlotte had dethroned defending champion MC in the NCAIA Div. III

1975–1979

President Pearce: "It must be homecoming!"

state volleyball tournament at Methodist. The MC volleyball team finished the 1978 season with a record of 32-6.

In the same issue, a news story by Jeff Cavano reported that 25 MC students representing many clubs on campus had journeyed to the Falcon Children's Home in northern Cumberland County Sunday, November 2, 1978 and staged a "Love All" picnic and field day.

President Reports On Meeting With Church Officials

At a full Board of Trustees meeting November 9, 1978, Board Chair Richard R. Allen reported on a meeting which he and Dr. Pearce, along with the presidents and board chairs from Louisburg College and N.C. Wesleyan College, had with Bishop Robert M. Blackburn of The North Carolina Conference of The United Methodist Church. He said the bishop had scheduled a program on higher education for Wednesday night at the church's 1979 annual conference. Allen said the conference's Division of Higher Education had decided at a November 8 meeting to create a brochure on the conference's three colleges (Louisburg, Methodist, Wesleyan) giving a comparative cost analysis of the three colleges in relation to North Carolina's public institutions of higher learning.

President Pearce reported that fall 1978 enrollment had increased from 703 to 736 while Evening College enrollment had soared from 271 to 453. He said the college was engaged in two accreditation self-studies, one for the Southern Association of Colleges and Schools and one for the teacher education program.

The president said the Classroom Building had been air-conditioned, but that repaving of roads, repair of roofs, and conversion of one boiler from oil to coal had been deferred until funds became available. Bill Lowdermilk reported on development activities and church relations, and Dean of Students Dixon McLeod reviewed advances in student life.

The Reverend James Bailey expressed concern and frustration over faculty salaries, specifically MC's rank of 36th among 39 private institutions in North Carolina. Trustees' Chair Allen said the low salaries were a primary concern of the Executive Committee.

Dr. Pearce described church support as good, noting the College would receive $183,000 in sustaining funds and $20,000 in capital funds in 1978 from The North Carolina Conference of The United Methodist Church. The president listed the following "current weaknesses" at Methodist College: student retention, S.G.A. reorganization, the Registrar's Office, the cafeteria, and development of corporate and foundation support.

Students Give *sMALL TALK* Plenty To Write About

Methodist College awarded an honorary Doctor of Divinity degree to Dr. Clyde McCarver, superintendent of the Sanford District, North Carolina Conference of The United Methodist Church, at winter commencement exercises December 22, 1978. A College trustee, Dr. McCarver delivered the winter commencement address to 27 students.

The editorial page of the January 26, 1979 *sMALL TALK* reprinted a column by *Washington Post* columnist Jack Anderson in which Anderson criticized the U.S. State Department for allowing California congressman Leo Ryan and four associates to walk into a death trap in Guyana, South America, a trap set by religious cult leader Jim Jones. After Ryan and his associates were gunned down at an air field, Jones and 400 followers committed suicide by drinking poison.

In early February, 1979, a large group of MC students conducted a sit-in demonstration in the Student Union and signed petitions protesting College dormitory regulations [a Sanford Hall demerit system], poor cafeteria service, and the College's required convocation policy. The February 19, 1979 *sMALL TALK* devoted two full pages to news coverage of the sit-in and the three issues which prompted students to hold the demonstration. Arthur H. McDaniel, who became dean of men at Methodist in January 1979, met several times with student protestors and persuaded them to end the sit-in. Meanwhile, letters to the editors of *sMALL TALK* and editorials in the paper welcomed the sit-in as a sign that student apathy was coming to an end.

The February 23, 1979 *sMALL TALK* ran a full-page feature article on religion professor Arnold Pope's participation in the heptathlon games in Scotland, where he tossed the caber (large pole), various other weights and a hay sheaf.

The March 8, 1979 newspaper featured extensive coverage of the Student Government Association's need to reorganize to expedite legislation and increase student participation. A subsequent issue gave considerable space to the 1979 Spring Festival sponsored by the Student Union Board. The festival featured a Ms. Monarch pageant, a showing of the film, *Thank God, It's Friday,* a coffeehouse performance by comedian Tom Parks, the Miss MC pageant, a performance by Loco-Motion Circus (a trio of acrobats), and a semiformal dance with the band Deep South.

In April 1979, *sMALL TALK* reported that Dr. Fred Clark would succeed Dr. Samuel Womack as academic dean September 1, 1979, that Nell Thompson would succeed Dr. James Vann as director of continuing education (Dr. Vann resigned to take a post at the Research Triangle), and that Tommy Dent would become director of admissions, filling the post vacated by Miss Thompson. The April 1979 issue also contained Stella Matthews' glowing review of Dr. Jack Peyrouse's March 1-2 production of *Once in a Lifetime*. Set in the 1920s, the George Kaufman comedy described a group of "actor wannabes" as they tried to make it big in Hollywood. The major players were Lynn Granger as Susan Walker, Dave Perry as George Lewis, and Ann Morrow as Hollywood gossip columnist Hedda Hopper.

The April 30, 1979 newspaper also reported that a chapter of Omicron Delta Kappa, a national leadership honor society, was being organized and that the Publications Committee had announced the selection of Patricia Turner as editor of the 1979-80 *sMALL TALK* and Stella Matthews as editor of the 1980 *Carillon*. A news article on an inside page reported that the following senior athletes had been honored at the 1979 athletic banquet: Jeannie Edwards, tennis; Lois McPherson, volleyball and softball; Elaine Adams, softball and basketball; Clarence Wiggins, basketball; and Bruce Fritz, soccer.

sMALL TALK's August 24, 1979 issue reported that Arthur McDaniel had been promoted from dean of men to dean of students, that Charles K. McAdams (MC's first director of public relations and development and the current treasurer of the N.C. Conference of The United Methodist Church) had received a Methodist College Medallion at the summer commencement, and that the Rev. Milton Earl Sluder-Jordan had been named campus minister.

A fall 1979 orientation issue announced that Greek Week and Formal Fall Rush would be held September 2-8 and 9-11 respectively to acquaint students

— CHAPTER 5 —

with the College's three fraternities: Tau Kappa Epsilon, Lambda Chi Alpha, and Pi Kappa Phi, and two sororities: Kappa Delta and Alpha Xi Delta.

In its September 7, 1979 issue, *sMALL TALK* listed nine new faculty members—in the Science Dept.: Dr. JoAnn Clark, Dr. Linda Sue Donnelly, Dr. Howard D. Tyner, Mrs. Barbara Olcutt; in the Physical Education Dept.: Laura Belton Ferrell, women's volleyball, basketball, and softball coach; Thomas Austin, cross country and baseball coach; Butch English, assistant basketball coach; in the English Dept.: Ms. Beth Cook Mason; in the Music Dept.: Mrs. Rennie Beyer, director of the Preparatory Division.

The September issue also contained a letter to the editor from Jeff Cavano criticizing the College administration for silencing a stereo system previously donated to the Student Union by the S.G.A. and establishing "study desks" in the Union. This issue also announced the appointment of Phil McAllister of Pedricktown N.J. as sports editor. One striking feature of these newspapers was the very professional editorial cartoons drawn by Byron Beall.

In its September 27, 1979 issue, a brief news story gave the results of an S.G.A. questionnaire distributed to students six months earlier. On the question of which convocation plan students favored, 141 opted for an alternate system of raising the graduation requirements by four hours and offering convocations as a optional elective with one hour of credit per year (any course could be substituted to obtain the extra four hours). Another 116 students favored the present fine system of $2 per point, while 34 students answered "neither one."

In the same issue, plans for Homecoming 1979 were unveiled by the S.G.A. and the Student Union Board, which included a 1 p.m. parade on October 13 and a dance on the same date to which 14 previous homecoming queens, 14 previous S.G.A. presidents, and "sweetheart couples" who met at Methodist would be invited.

The October 5, 1979 *sMALL TALK* promoted homecoming with a centerfold spread showing photos of magician Bob Kramer, the band THRESHOLD, and *Little Mary Sunshine*, a parody of 1930s stage musicals slated for O'Hanlon Amphitheater under the direction of Dr. Jack Peyrouse. The paper also announced the appointment of Fred Kistler, an MC junior, as *Tapestry* editor for 1979-80.

A One-on-One Basketball Marathon held on the outdoor courts at Methodist from Thursday, Sept. 27 through noon Saturday, September 29 raised $600 for the College's gymnasium fund. Students signed up to play for 30-minute segments and collected monetary pledges based on the number of continual hours of play.

1975–1979

The front page of the November 8, 1979 issue reported that Polish pianist Misha Dichter would appear in concert with the North Carolina Symphony that evening in Reeves Auditorium. A brief news item indicated the Methodist College Board of Trustees had awarded the faculty a five percent pay increase, which coupled with a spring pay increase would give faculty a 13 percent increase. A double-page photo spread in the center of this issue highlighted a variety of homecoming events. The sports page noted that the women's volleyball team had compiled a 15-2 overall record and went undefeated in Division III play with 10 wins, earning a berth in the NCAIAW Division III Tournament.

The November 16, 1979 *sMALL TALK* reported that the soccer team had finished 4-1-2 in the conference and scored a record 32 goals. Jo Ann Taylor, secretary in the Public Relations Office, was the subject of an inside feature article by Michelle Blackburn. A brief front page news story announced that *sMALL TALK* had received an honors rating first class from the Associated Collegiate Press for its spring 1979 issues. Ann Morrow of New York City and Scott Peterson of Chapel Hill, N.C. served as co-editors of the student newspaper during this period. Mrs. Gwen Sykes, coordinator of college publications, served as newspaper advisor.

A brief news story inside the same issue reported that Byron Beall, a senior art major, had found bits of pottery and projectile points in a clearing near the Methodist College baseball field which could date from between 8000 B.C. and A.D. 400. [Indian arrowheads had been previously collected at many points on the campus, suggesting that Indians once lived in this part of the Cape Fear

— CHAPTER 5 —

River valley.] Beall said he found one perfect arrowhead: "a Morrow Mountain II approximately 2500 years old." [24]

In an early December issue, *sMALL TALK* reported that The Student Union Dinner Theatre Players had presented the Neil Simon play *God's Favorite* November 27 and 28. A modern version of the biblical story of Job, the play featured Dr. John Sill in the lead role of Joe Benjamin, a wealthy New York businessman who suffers many afflictions but refuses the devil's request that he renounce God.

The 1979 Christmas issue of *sMALL TALK* reported that an overflow crowd of 150 persons had attended the Moravian Love Feast in Hensdale Chapel. The Reverend Phil Bauguess '70 led the service, assisted by the Reverend Rick Williams '70; both were residents of Winston-Salem, N.C. The newspaper also reported that over 500 persons attended the College Christmas dinner for students and staff. The sports page noted that the Lady Monarch volleyball team had won the state NCAIAW title at St. Andrews College in Laurinburg, N.C. before falling in the Region II tournament at Radford University to Meredith College.

President Proposes Sale Of Campus Land

Dr. Richard Pearce, College president, informed the trustees' Executive Committee March 26, 1979, that the Methodist College Foundation's 1979 fund drive was proving very successful, having raised $187,645 since January 1: $42,366 in unrestricted gifts, $105,250 in restricted gifts, and pledges of $40,635. He said the increase included $54,996 from the Virginia Rhodes Williams estate and $25,829 from the Samuel Bryan Wilkins estate.

Dr. Pearce said a visitation team from the Southern Association of Colleges and Schools was on campus March 4-7 and that one of its 66 recommendations was the formulation of a long-range plan for debt retirement. He said the team had also recommended that duplicate student records be kept; that an additional person be hired in guidance and placement; that a policy on releasing information on students be printed; and that the funds for a gymnasium not be lost in the priorities.

President Pearce then asked the trustees to consider:
1. selling 400 acres of College land not currently used or needed for college activities,
2. asking The North Carolina Conference to conduct a campaign among member churches to pay the outstanding indebtedness of the College,
3. a campaign to raise endowment funds for student financial aid and faculty salaries,

4. employing a professional firm to assist in the recruitment of dormitory students,
5. seeking a "scaling down" of the HEW and HUD balances.
6. seeking additional uses (rent) of College facilities in the summer,
7. seeking a long-term lease of College land—the 1,000 feet of highway frontage on U.S. 401,
8. seeking a primary health care center for College land south of the campus,
9. supporting construction of a new Cape Fear River bridge and giving land for it,
10. seeking help from the Fayetteville Area Development Commission and Seaboard Coastline Railway to develop industrial and commercial use of college-owned railroad frontage,
11. supporting creation of the Cape Fear Expressway along the west banks of the Cape Fear River from U.S. 301 to Linden. [25]

The board took no action on the president's recommendations.

Trustees Reduce Graduation Requirements

Meeting April 11, 1979, the Board of Trustees reduced College graduation requirements from nine semester hours in religion and philosophy to six semester hours (3 s.h. in religion, 3 s.h. in philosophy) and from four semester hours in physical education to two. The reductions were recommended by the trustees' Academic Affairs Committee chaired by the Reverend Rufus Stark.

Mr. Stark presented a recommendation from the Southern Association visitation team that final approval of graduates be left to the faculty, not the Board of Trustees, which had heretofore approved lists of candidates for graduation. Stark also distributed faculty-approved policies on cheating and plagiarism and suggested that the trustees' Academic Affairs and Student Affairs committees meet jointly to study a "comprehensive code of morality."

Reporting for the trustees' Development Committee, Dr. Charles Speegle said over $250,000 had been raised in Cumberland County since January 1, 1979 and that the base of support for the 1979 Loyalty Fund Campaign had been increased by 50 percent.

The trustees were told that Nell Thompson had replaced Dr. Vann as director of continuing education, that Thomas Dent had replaced Dr. Deloach as director of admissions, that Arthur McDaniel had replaced Richard Coleman as director of the Student Union and dean of students, and that Dr. Fred Clark would succeed Dr. Samuel Womack as academic dean September 1, 1979.

— CHAPTER 5 —

Dr. Pearce listed as his dreams for the College: 65 percent of the faculty holding doctorates, an endowed concert-lecture series, construction of a gymnasium and swimming pool, 1,000-1,200 full-time students, average student SAT scores of 590 (each on math and verbal), a selective freshman class, a graduate program in education and business, endowed faculty salaries, endowed student financial aid, and funds for faculty travel and sabbatical leaves.

Sara Hodgkins Addresses 16th Graduating Class

Sara W. Hodgkins, secretary of Cultural Resources for the state of North Carolina, addressed members of Methodist's 16th graduating class May 6, 1979. The first woman to deliver a commencement address at MC was introduced by her brother, Methodist College history professor R. Parker Wilson.

"The first responsibility of citizenship is to do what you can to better this society through excellence and accessibility," said Ms. Hodgkins. "Maintain the spirit that has brought you so far." [26]

In other commencement activities, the Reverend James H. Bailey of Greenville received an honorary Doctor of Divinity degree and Dr. Samuel J. Womack received a Methodist College Medallion. Graduating senior JoAnne Jones of Ellerbee received the Stacy Weaver Award.

Fred Clark Named Academic Dean

In the spring of 1979, Dr. Samuel J. Womack announced his intention to resign as academic dean (effective in August) to return to teaching in the Religion and Philosophy Department. He was academic dean for a total of 14 years. In May 1979, Dr. Fred Clark of Deland, Florida, was appointed academic dean at Methodist to succeed Dr. Samuel Womack, effective September 1. A graduate of the University of Miami, Dr. Clark came to Methodist from Stetson University where he served as director of special projects. He had previously taught biology at Huntingdon College, the University of Miami, and Stetson University.

In June 1979, Dr. Willis Gates, professor of music, and Mrs. Pauline Longest, assistant professor of biology, retired after 19 years and 17 years of service respectively. Dr. Gates was an original faculty member, accomplished violinist and former conductor of the Fayetteville Symphony Orchestra. Mrs. Longest chaired the Science and Mathematics area for ten years and served as advisor to the Student Education Association.

Also in June, members of The North Carolina Conference of The United Methodist Church elected Dr. Richard Pearce to serve as a lay delegate to the 1980 General Conference of The United Methodist Church at Indianapolis. At the same annual conference, the Reverend Milton Sluder-Jordan was appointed

Dr. Willis Gates (L) and his wife and daughters all played the violin.

campus minister at Methodist to succeed Paul Grainger, who was appointed pastor of Trinity United Methodist Church in Fayetteville. Sluder-Johnson came to Methodist from a pastorate in Nashville, N.C. and held degrees from N.C. State University and Harvard University.

In other news reported in the May 1979 *Bulletin of Methodist College*:

—Michael Servie '71 of Fayetteville was re-elected president of the Methodist College Alumni Association.

—Methodist was named a Servicemen's Opportunity College by a national network of higher education associations.

—*sMALL TALK*, the MC student newspaper, received an honors rating first class in the Associate Collegiate Press's national competition. Editors Scott Peterson and Ann Morrow shared the honors, along with Mrs. Gwen Sykes, advisor and coordinator of college publications at Methodist.

—Mrs. Joyce Elaine Porter, associate professor of French, was named Distinguished Service Professor of French in May 1979. The Cleveland, Ohio native began teaching at Methodist in 1963 and helped establish MC's first sorority, a chapter of Alpha Xi Delta.

College Endowment Reaches One Million Dollars

In a joint meeting of the trustees' Executive and Investment committees June 12, 1979, Dr. Pearce reported that the College endowment would shortly reach one million dollars and that energy-efficient lights had been installed in the library and gymnasium.

In a July 24, 1979 meeting, the trustees' Investment Committee instructed Dr. Pearce to purchase stock in American Telephone and Telegraph, Carolina Power and Light, Kansas City Power and Light and also to invest $100,000 in bonds recommended by trustee Walter Clark.

Member of the trustees' Executive Committee were informed September 24, 1979 that the College endowment had reached $1,067,238 and that the deferred interest owed HEW and HUD on building bonds had reached $361,003.

Trustees Receive SACS Recommendations/College Response

When the Methodist College Board of Trustees met November 8, 1979, Chairman Allen reported that the College had realized fall enrollment growth of seven full-time equivalent students (to 743) and 49 dormitory students (to 348). Enrollment in the Evening Division totaled 181. He said the College borrowed no operating funds in 1979 but needed to spend $100,000 on campus repairs and improvements—to reroof the Classroom Building, convert two boilers to natural gas, and complete modification of the gym, library and outside lighting.

The trustees also reviewed the College's response to 66 recommendations made by the Southern Association of Colleges and Schools visiting team following a March visit to the campus for a reaccreditation review. Among the major SACS recommendations were:

11. improve the development and public relations program and hire an aggressive director of development.
19. bring current the College's long-term debt obligations to the federal government.
20. develop a five-year physical plan and capital expenditure development plan.
37. take steps to meet SACS standards of professional competence in education and business administration.
66. limit regular faculty members to teaching one course per semester in the Continuing Education Division (Evening College). [27]

Dean of Students Arthur McDaniel informed the trustees that a foreign student advisor had been added to the student life staff and that Arnold Pope had been named assistant to the dean of students with responsibility as dean of men and evening supervisor.

President Pearce Shows He Means Business

After six years as president, Dr. Richard Pearce had become known as a tough, hands-on manager. Low enrollment forced him to take drastic measures: terminate personnel, reduce energy costs, and default on federal loans, for example, to keep the College from going bankrupt. "The Southern Association [of Colleges and Schools] finally got on us about our financial problems," he recalls, "and they gave us a year to get things straightened out. That was the year [1979] we finally paid off our revolving debt [bank loans to meet current operating expenses]." [28]

Several incidents recalled by Dr. Pearce in a 2001 interview speak volumes about his priorities. First, he recalled that two of his greatest joys as president was being able to present Methodist College diplomas to his mother, Alice Pearce, and to his wife, Neva. He said he and his wife hosted an annual reception and Christmas dinner for students to teach them social skills, and that Mrs. Pearce held Saturday morning teas in the women's residence halls to teach students how to dress and behave in formal situations.

As he declared when he took office, Dr. Pearce had zero tolerance for drug and alcohol abuse. One of his first tests involved a group of 17 male students found with a keg of beer in Cumberland Hall. "Gene Clayton [dean of students] came to me and said the boys had waived their right to a student trial or a dean's hearing but wanted to meet with me. I said, 'Tell them to come at 2:00 but while they are waiting they might as well pack their clothes.'" [29] When Dr. Pearce met with the students, he told them they would have to leave Methodist, but that the College would help them find transfers to other schools. He said all 17 students were transferred that afternoon.

Dr. Pearce also had a sense of humor. At some point after the College moved to contracted food service, a group of students came to his office with a plate of turkey stroganoff and said it had gone bad. "I looked at it and tasted it," he recalled. "Then I called the cafeteria manager and said, 'Look, this is turkey stroganoff you served them. This is eastern North Carolina. These are meat and taters boys. This is not a stroganoff area.' And I sat there and ate the plate full of food to the kids' shock." [30]

The Pearce Family

Many who served at Methodist College during the administration of Richard Pearce remember his family with great affection. "Neva [Mrs. Richard] Pearce was genuinely caring, welcoming," said Dr. Robert Christian, professor of English. "Theirs was very much a family home. They welcomed students. They welcomed colleagues. Neva was a good cook and housekeeper. She love to work in the yard. She enrolled at Methodist and completed her

— CHAPTER 5 —

Students make a little music in the president's living room.

degree in art. I bought a painting she did of Lake Junaluska which still hangs in my office." [31]

Alice Pearce, the president's mother, also left a lasting impression on the Methodist College community. "She had completed her freshman year of college in Indiana back in 1917," recalled Dr. Christian. "She came to me and said she wanted to complete her degree in English. I encouraged her. She was in her late seventies when she started and 82 when she graduated in 1979. We all loved her. She was a very good student. In 1977, she became an instant celebrity when the students elected her Homecoming Queen at the age of 80. She also played the cello in the Fayetteville Symphony Orchestra. After she received her degree in English, she tutored freshman English students." [32]

1975–1979

END NOTES
Chapter Five

1. Vergil Queen, motion adopted by the Executive Committee, Methodist College Board of Trustees, February 27, 1975, TM, Book 3.
2. David Stedman, motion adopted by the Methodist College Board of Trustees, April 5, 1975, TM, Book 3.
3. Richard Pearce, "15- Year Plan for Methodist College," presented to the Methodist College Board of Trustees April 5, 1975, TM, Book 3.
4. Richard Pearce, remarks to the Methodist College Board of Trustees April 5, 1975, TM, Book 3.
5. Nelson Gibson, motion adopted by the Methodist College Board of Trustees April 5, 1975, TM, Book 3.
6. Richard Pearce, *Bulletin of Methodist College*, June 1975, Vol. 16, No. 4, file.
7. Gene Clayton, quoted by Thomas Pope, *sMALL TALK*, April 17, 1975, file.
8. Donna Gemeinhart, *sMALL TALK*, April 28, 1975, file.
9. John T. Henley, commencement address May 11, 1975, *Bulletin of Methodist College*, May 1975, Vol. 16, No. 3, file.
10. Jim Nash, *sMALL TALK*, September 23, 1975, file.
11. Richard Pearce, remarks to the Methodist College Board of Trustees November 15, 1975, TM, Book 3.
12. Danny Hood, S.G.A. president, remarks at spring 1975 convocation, *sMALL TALK*, February 5, 1976, file.
13. Thomas Pope, *sMALL TALK*, March 31, 1976, file.
14. Ike O'Hanlon, remarks at the Methodist College Foundation Loyalty Fund dinner February 10, 1976, *sMALL TALK*, March 2, 1976, file.
15. Richard R. Allen to Lynn Gruber, interview, August 16, 2001, file.
16. Kenneth Daniel, S.G.A. president, remarks to the Methodist College Board of Trustees, TM, Book 3.
17. Richard Pearce, report to the Methodist College Board of Trustees, November 12, 1976, TM, Book 3.
18. Richard Pearce, remarks to the Executive Committee, Methodist College Board of Trustees, September 8, 1977, TM, Book 3.
19. Richard Pearce, quoted in *sMALL TALK*, April 26, 1977, file.
20. Allen Norris, commencement address December 18, 1977, *sMALL*

— CHAPTER 5 —

TALK, February 2, 1978, file.
21. Richard Pearce, report to the Methodist College Board of Trustees April 13, 1978, TM, Book 3.
22. "Statement of Purpose for Methodist College," Executive Committee, Methodist College Board of Trustees, August 21, 1978, TM, Book 3.
23. Robert Blackburn, speech to fall convocation September 5, 1978, *Bulletin of Methodist College*, November 1978, Vol. 19, No. 8, file.
24. Byron Beall, *sMALL TALK*, November 16, 1979, file.
25. Richard Pearce, remarks to the Executive Committee, Methodist College Board of Trustees March 2, 1979, TM, Book 3.
26. Sarah Hodgkins, commencement address May 6, 1979, *Bulletin of Methodist College*, May 1979, Vol. 20, No. 3, file.
27. "Southern Association of Colleges and Schools Reaffirmation Committee Report," March 4-7, 1979, file.
28. Richard Pearce to Lynn Gruber, interview, June 14, 2001, file.
29. Ibid.
30. Ibid.
31. Robert Christian to Lynn Gruber, interview, June 24, 2003, file.
32. Ibid.

Chapter 6

A New Leader
1980-84

> Dr. Hendricks said he hoped to continue the liberal arts tradition at Methodist 'while moving into the vocational interests of the future.' The president-elect said his top priorities would be to increase: the number of qualified students, the percentage of alumni participating in campus affairs, and the sense of community at Methodist.
> —*from a sMALL TALK news story August 27, 1983, announcing Dr. Hendricks' selection as the third president of Methodist College.*

Methodist College began the spring 1980 semester with an enrollment of 740 day students and 187 evening students. Addressing the trustees' Executive Committee February 4, 1980, Dr. Fred Clark, academic dean, reported that the average faculty salary was $14,000 per annum. The Executive Committee adopted the following fees for 1980-81: tuition—$2,400; activity fee—$100; board—$1,050; and room—$600.

MC Begins Third Decade

A front page story in the February 14, 1980 *sMALL TALK* listed several new courses being offered during the spring 1980 semester: one in 19th century and 20th century art, a theatre course in set design and lighting, a music course in handbells, a N.C. history course, and a sociology course on the aging of older adults.

The Sixteenth Senate of the Student Government Association passed a resolution December 10, 1979 asking the College administration to change the requirement that students earn 16 points per semester by attending convocations. The S.G.A. asked that the administration award one-half semester hour of credit for each 16 points earned by attending convocations each semester and that these credits apply toward the 128 semester hours required for graduation from Methodist College.

Oedipus Rex played to a full Reeves Auditorium Thursday, February 21 and Friday, February 22, 1980. "Overwhelming!" is how Jack Peyrouse, the director, described response to the play, which brought standing ovations for Jeff Cavano, who played Oedipus.

— CHAPTER 6 —

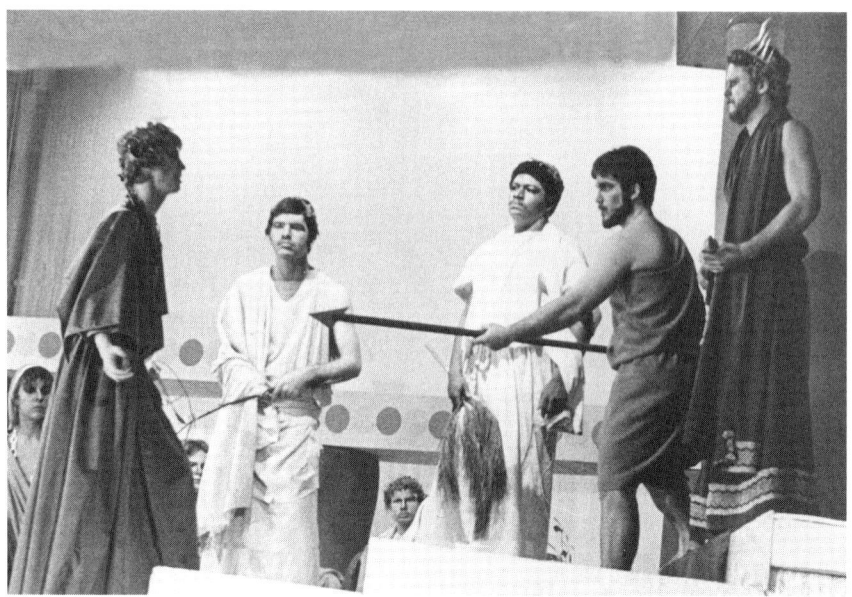

Oedipus Rex *filled Reeves Auditorium and drew standing ovations.*

The Lady Monarch basketball team, coached by Laura Ferrell, won the NCAIAW Division III state title by defeating UNC-G 85-78 on its home court. The Monarchs finished their season 14-7 and advanced to the regional at Maryville, Tennessee March 5-8.

The March 28, 1980 *sMALL TALK* reported that a new food service company, SAGA, had taken over cafeteria operations at Methodist March 10, and that students were very pleased with the food being served. Three candidates filed for election as S.G.A. president: Robin Gottlieb, a junior from Southport, N.C.; Phil Fallin, a junior from Baconton, Ga.; and Lynda Womack, a sophomore from Fayetteville. Lynda Womack won the election, becoming the first female to hold the position of S.G.A. president.

The editorial page of this issue contained a memorial tribute to Huldah Bethune Jones, housemother at Weaver Hall for the preceding 16 years. Mrs. Jones died Saturday evening, March 15, 1980 of a heart attack.

The Golden Knights, the U.S. Army Parachute Team, performed an aerial freefall demonstration Tuesday, April 8 at 11 a.m. over the MC soccer field. The Knights were brought to MC as part of ROTC Recognition Day.

The April 11 issue of *sMALL TALK* reported that John Sam, a junior education major from Fayetteville, was elected president of the Student N.C. Association of Educators at the SNCAE spring convention in Greensboro. The sports page noted that Laura Ferrell, coach of women's volleyball, basketball, and softball, had resigned her post at Methodist to take a coaching job at N.C. Wesleyan College.

Carol Kraus, a junior art major from Salt Lake City, Utah, won the Purchase Award for best-in-show at the Fourteenth Annual MC Juried Art Exhibit. She won with a painting entitled "Carrots and Butter."

The Reverend Bill Presnell '71, pastor of Riverside United Methodist Church in Elizabeth City, N.C., served as minister-in-residence at MC the week of April 21-24, 1980. Teresa Wingenfeld, a sophomore from Fayetteville, was crowned Miss Methodist College at the April 11, 1980 pageant sponsored by the Pi Kappa Phi fraternity.

During the third week in April, 1980, the Monarch baseball team (20-6) was ranked No. 5 in the nation among NCAA Division III schools.

Fayetteville Youth Theatre held its 1980 summer season at MC, presenting *The Skin of Our Teeth* by Thornton Wilder, *King Cole and the Country Witches*, *The Bad Children* by Shirley Jackson, *Fiddler on the Roof* by Joseph Stein, and *Godspell*. All productions were staged in O'Hanlon Amphitheater.

Methodist Accepts UMW Archives

The March 1980 *Bulletin of Methodist College* reported that The United Methodist Women of The North Carolina Conference had established a permanent archive in Davis Memorial Library. A news story said Evelyn Ballance of Raeford, N.C., had contributed her collection of history, files, photographs and journals dating back to 1878.

In other spring news, Athletic Director Gene Clayton announced that Methodist would offer 13 summer day sports camps in June and July 1980, conducted by MC coaching personnel.

At the April 1, 1980 meeting of the Board of Trustees, Dean Clark reported that the social work program had been accredited and that faculty salaries had been increased 6.3 percent. He recommended that Dr. Robert Perkins, Dr. Janet Cavano and Dr. Robert Christian be promoted to full professors and that Dr. Cavano and Mrs. Matthews be granted tenure.

Reporting for the trustees' Building and Grounds Committee, Louis Spilman listed the following needs: replacement of roofs on the Fine Arts

— CHAPTER 6 —

Building ($43,500), Science Building ($10,000-$15,000) and the Student Union ($20,000) and resurfacing of campus roads.

College President Richard Pearce reported that a new roof had been installed on the Classroom Building, that an organ had been purchased for Reeves Auditorium, and that contracts had been signed for new language and piano labs. He said the College endowment was up 25 percent and enrollment was up 32 students. He asked trustees to help fund the "We Need" list for the academic area and "help to make the College the type of college dreamed of at its establishment." [1]

After an executive session, the trustees rehired Dr. Pearce as president for another year, keeping his salary the same but increasing the College's contribution to the TIAA/CREF retirement program from 5 percent to 15 percent of the president's salary.

In a June 10, 1980 meeting, the Board of Trustees approved changes to the retirement program for faculty and administrative staff whereby the college would contribute 5 percent of each eligible employee's annual salary and allow each employee to match the College's 5 percent contribution by having that amount withheld. The mandatory retirement age was set at 70.

Sam Ragan Addresses Class of 1980

Sam Ragan, editor and publisher of *The* (Southern Pines) *Pilot*, called for a reaffirmation of the American system and the American people in a May 4, 1980 commencement address at Methodist. Ragan told the 96 graduates: "Go into the world with wonder, because there is still much to wonder about, and there are still people who believe there are truths which are self-evident, and that life, liberty, and the pursuit of happiness are rights for all to enjoy." [2]

President Pearce awarded an honorary Doctor of Letters degree to Sam Ragan and a Methodist College Medallion to Beth Finch, mayor of Fayetteville. Dr. Pearce also presented the Lucius Stacy Weaver Award to Jeffrey Paul Cavano for excellence in academics, campus activities, character and leadership.

The College's May 1980 *Bulletin* reported that Maj. Glenn Blackburn, coordinator of Methodist's ROTC program and assistant professor of military science, had been selected Distinguished Professor for 1980. The news item said Blackburn had completed his three-year tour of duty at Methodist in July and moved to a new assignment in Anchorage, Alaska.

President Presents Four-Step Fund-Raising Plan

Speaking at the College's fall convocation August 27, 1980, College President Richard Pearce said plans were being made for a gymnasium/physical education complex, including eight new tennis courts, a swimming pool, and relocation of the baseball field. That made front page news in the first issue of *sMALL TALK.* Dr. Pearce said he would ask the Board of Trustees to endorse a capital funds drive for the new gymnasium at the trustees next meeting in November. Referring to MC's metal gymnasium or "tin can," Dr. Pearce said, "It's time we moved out of the biggest two-car garage in Cumberland County." [3]

Richard Pearce called MC's tin can gym "the largest two-car garage in Cumberland County."

The Theatre Department presented Shakespeare's *Twelfth Night* October 9-11 in O'Hanlon Amphitheater. Major players included: Melissa Gentry as Olivia, John Kimball as Malvolio (Olivia's steward), Karl Michael Kroos as Sir Andrew Augecheck and Dr. John Sill as Sir Toby Belch (Olivia's uncle). The musical score was composed by Cliff Wells, a junior at Methodist.

A "coffee house" series sponsored monthly by the Student Union Board opened September 12 featuring student guitarists, pianists, and vocalists. The September 22, 1980 *sMALL TALK* included a feature story on Tom Austin, baseball coach, a story that emphasized his work ethic in high school, at Seminole (Fla.) Junior College, and at Rollins College. The story said Austin began playing in an adult softball league while teaching at Bishop Moore High School in Orlando, Florida. The story said Austin had been named to the All-World Team while playing infield for the Bedsole's Pig and Chicken team of Fayetteville.

A double-page feature in the center of the September 22, 1980 *sMALL TALK* promoted Koinonia (the College's ecumenical religious fellowship), listing upcoming activities and showing photos of some of the 50 students who attended a fall retreat at nearby Camp Rockfish.

In its October 3, 1980 issue, the campus newspaper used a two-page center spread to promote Homecoming Week, October 6-11, the theme of which was "Luau on the South Seas." Major events included a Garber Hall fashion show

— CHAPTER 6 —

Monday, a volleyball game Tuesday, a coffee house with the Covenant Players Wednesday, and a Masque Keys production of *Twelfth Night* in O'Hanlon Amphitheater Thursday. The Saturday schedule included: sidewalk art and games, a homecoming parade and soccer game (MC vs. Francis Marion), and a dance featuring the band Pieces of Eight. Sunday events included a morning worship service and a 3 p.m. recital by Bill Wolfe and Betty Neill Parsons, members of the Class of 1964.

This newspaper also contained a feature article about Cliff Wells, a junior music and English major from St. Louis, Missouri, who wrote the musical score for the College production of *Twelfth Night*.

The front page of the November 14, 1980, *sMALL TALK* announced that Ronald Reagan had defeated Jimmy Carter for president by a landslide. This issue also promoted a November 23 performance of Arthur Honeggar's oratorio *King David* by the Methodist College Chorus. The paper also reported that Neil Simon's *Star-Spangled Girl* would be staged November 24-25 in the Student Union. Directed by Dr. Wayne Preslar, the show starred Jeaneal Whorton, Phil Fallin, and Keith Langford.

In other news:
— William H. Stanley, president of Peoples Bank and Trust Co., was the featured speaker at the Outlook 1981 Symposium Wednesday, December 3, 1980.
— Methodist continued an annual tradition by sponsoring two Moravian Love Feasts (6 p.m. and 8 p.m.) December 7, 1980 in Hensdale Chapel.
— Ben Spitzer, a junior from Fayetteville, organized a November 14 meeting for day students interested in starting their own student organization to get day students more involved in campus life. He told S.G.A. President Lynda Womack it was not fair that day students taking fewer than 15 semester hours were not eligible for inclusion on the Dean's List or President's List.

Trustees Discuss Debt, Fund-Raising Goal

At an October 14, 1980 meeting, the trustees' Executive Committee approved amendments to the college bylaws defining the positions of business manager, dean of academic affairs, and dean of student affairs and the functions of the trustees' Finance, Academic Affairs, Student Affairs, Buildings and Grounds, Development, Investment, and Nominating committees

When the full Board of Trustees met November 14, 1980, the Reverend Samuel McMillan reported that The North Carolina Conference of The United Methodist Church would increase its appropriations to the College $6,000 for sustaining funds (to $192,000) and $5,000 for debt retirement (to $25,000) in 1981. At the 1979 and 1980 annual conference meetings, Reverend McMillan had taken the lead role in persuading conference members to increase their appropriations to Louisburg, Methodist, and N.C. Wesleyan colleges.

President Pearce reported that the College had resumed payments on its bonded indebtedness (federal construction loans) and that fall enrollment had reached 950 students. He predicted that enrollment at Methodist would eventually grow to 1,500 students in the day program and 500 in the evening program.

The president reminded the trustees of the goal set in 1973 to raise $16 million in the next 15 years: $4 million for debt retirement, $2 million for a gymnasium, $4 million to endow student aid, $3 million to endow faculty support, $2 million to endow campus maintenance, and $1 million to endow administrative costs.

To meet the endowment goals, Dr. Pearce suggested that four steps be taken immediately;
1) Each trustee commit to raise $10,000-$15,000 each year for the endowment.
2) A deferred giving program be started.
3) A grant-seeking program be put in full operation.
4) A major challenge gift be secured.

He said a $450,000 gift could be matched readily and lead to a $1 million challenge gift. [4] The trustees took no action on the president's suggestions. In a major action, the trustees accepted with regret the resignation of Mr. R. R. Allen as chairman of the board.

Cultural Offerings Run the Gamut

Arthur Honnegar's oratorio *King David* was presented to a capacity crowd in Reeves Auditorium November 23, 1980. Alan Porter conducted the 34-member Methodist College Chorus and a 15-piece Wind Ensemble. Guest soloists included Michael Best, Leslee Mabee, and Beth Auman.

According to the December 12, 1980 *sMALL TALK*, the S.G.A. and Student Union Board held a "Who Shot J.R.?" party Friday, November 21. The party began with music from Nashville Station, a country-western band, and a J.R. Look-a-like Contest won by Joey Culbreth. The party ended with a viewing of the TV show *Dallas* and the revelation that Kristin had shot J. R. Ewing.

President Pearce's Christmas dinner was held December 5 in the cafeteria, preceded by a reception and followed by a dance featuring Dynaflo, a back-up band for pop singer B. J. Thomas.

— CHAPTER 6 —

s*MALL TALK* Announces Premiere of Anderson Play

The lead story on the front page of the January 31, 1981 *sMALL TALK* announced that Methodist would host the world premiere performance of Maxwell Anderson's *Raft on the River,* a musical version of Mark Twain's *Huckleberry Finn,* April 15-18. The play was to be staged during the College's Fine Arts Festival.

Dr. Sue Kimball, professor of English, said Anderson's widow had given the College permission to stage the musical. Dr. Jack Peyrouse, the show's director, announced tryouts for the 60-member cast February 3-4. Mr. Alan Porter was the musical director, and Mr. Michael Rogers directed the orchestra.

A short article on the editorial page reminded males born in 1962 that they were supposed to register with Selective Service at the nearest post office to become part of a pool of men who could be called to military service in the event of a national emergency. After America's military draft ended in 1972, registration with Selective Service was continued until 1975; in 1979 the system was reorganized.

Among other items reported in late January 1981:

—The Reverend Allen Lee of Red Springs, N.C., delivered the graduation address to 45 seniors at the College's winter commencement December 19, 1980. A retired Methodist minister who had donated a collection of rare Bibles and other books to Davis Library, Mr. Lee received a Methodist College Medallion from President Pearce.

—movies listed for a spring showing at Methodist were: *The Late Show, The Goodbye Girl, Uptown Saturday Night,* and *O, God.*

—Methodist celebrated the release of 52 Americans held hostage in Iran with a service of thanksgiving January 21, 1981 in Hensdale Chapel, the day after the hostages were released. Cheerleaders tied yellow ribbons on the nine cottonwood trees borderng Ramsey Street in front of the College. [The hostages finally reached the U.S. January 25, 1981.]

In other news:

—a 1950s "sock hop" was held in the Student Union January 31, after the Methodist-UNC-G basketball game. A 50s costume contest was held, and students danced to the prerecorded music of Fats Domino and Chuck Berry.

—The sports page carried a news story about MC's new universal weight machine, a system divided into stations that enabled a user to develop arm, leg, shoulder, and stomach muscles and to firm his or her waist.

1980–1984

—A letter to the editor from Robin Pelditz criticized the Student Union Board for spending $633.86 from student activity fees to take 18 students on a three-day ski retreat.

—The men's basketball team coached by Joe Miller had a tough season and stood 4-18 overall and 3-9 in the conference going into the DIAC tournament.

—A sports story by Chris Henn weighed the pros and cons of Methodist shifting from AIAW to NCAA for women's sports. Athletic Director Gene Clayton said there would be a big advantage in switching because the NCAA paid for travel to major tournaments.

College Enrolls 715 In Spring 1981

When the trustees' Executive Committee met February 16, 1981, Dr. Pearce reported a fall enrollment of 795 students and a spring enrollment of 715. He also read a letter from Dr. Allen Norris, president of Louisburg College, announcing a contribution to that school of $1.5 million

Methodist Premiers Maxwell Anderson Play

A story in the March 17, 1981 *sMALL TALK* profiled two cast members from *Raft on the River:* Lynette Blalock of Durham as Mary Jane Wilkes and Mark Mooney of Baltimore as Huck Finn.

The April 10 newspaper reported that Rick Kugelmann, a junior from Fayetteville, had been elected S.G.A. president for 1981-82. Roy Whitmire, MU business manager, issued an invitation to married students to live in one of the College's sixteen 840-square foot apartments on south campus for $225 per month with all utilities paid.

Methodist recorded a major first in April 1981 by staging a world premiere of Maxwell Anderson's *Raft on the River,* a musical version of Mark Twain's novel, *Huckleberry Finn*, during the College's Fine Arts Festival. Dr. Sue Kimball, assistant professor of English, discovered Anderson's handwritten manuscript while reviewing a book on Anderson. She received permission from Mrs. Maxwell Anderson, the playwright's widow, to produce the play at Methodist. The project received a major grant from the North Carolina Arts Council.

Dr. Jack Peyrouse of the Theatre Department directed the musical's cast of seventy persons. Special guests for opening night were Mr. and Mrs. Paul Green, Lee Yopp [director of the Fort Bragg Playhouse], and Dr. Lawrence Avery of UNC at Chapel Hill. In addition to Anderson's play, the festival offered a film series about Anderson's works, three art shows, a lyceum series, a beaux arts ball, and several religious events. The lecture series on Anderson's

CHAPTER 6

A scene from **Raft on the River**

works was the beginning of Methodist's Southern Writers Symposium, which would examine the works of other Southern writers.

In the April 24, 1981 *sMALL TALK,* the Publications Committee announced that Tricia Turner of Fayetteville had been reappointed editor of *sMALL TALK* for another year and that Berry Shelley of Wilmington had been named editor of *Carillon* for 1981-82.

In other April news:
- A news brief reported that Terry Sanford, president of Duke University, would be the featured speaker at the May 1981 commencement.
- In a detailed opinon piece on Page Two, Jeff Coghill gave the College's production of *Raft on the River* a glowing review.
- The baseball team was 20-12 overall and 6-3 in the Dixie Conference, right behind nationally-ranked N.C. Wesleyan.
- The MC chapter of Alpha Xi Delta [sorority] received four awards during the regional conference held in Raleigh.

Trustees Elect Ike O'Hanlon Chair

At a meeting held April 15, 1981, the Board of Trustees elected I. H. "Ike" O'Hanlon board chairman, succeeding R. R. Allen. The trustees also elected Henry B. Dixon vice chairman, R. Dillard Teer secretary, and Wilson F. Yarborough Sr. treasurer.

1980–1984

Reporting for the trustees' Academic Affairs Committee, Rufus Stark recommended approval of a new baccalaureate degree (Bachelor of Music) and changes to the College's core curriculum requirements. After some discussion, the board approved a motion by Dr. James Bailey to require six semester hours of religion (two courses at the 100 level), versus the current requirement of three semester hours.

Dean of Students Calvert Ray recognized Lynda Womack, S.G.A. president, for the purpose of reporting on student opinion regarding Dean of Men Arnold Pope, who had been notified by Dr. Pearce that he would not be rehired. Miss Womack reported strong student support for Pope's retention as evidenced by a petition, and she read a letter from an alumnus supporting Pope. Dr. Paul Carruth moved that the trustees express confidence in and support of Dr. Pearce in his handling of the Pope matter. The motion carried unanimously.

Bill Lowdermilk reported that Miss Nell Thompson would become alumni director in July. The Reverend Sam McMillan reported that The North Carolina Conference of The United Methodist Church had increased its financial support for the College for 1982, but warned, ". . . if the pension fund is budgeted by the conference in the Outreach Ministries budget, this would then compete for College funds." [5] He urged conference members (*i.e.* United Methodists within the conference) to oppose such action.

Dean of Students Calvert Ray reported that the dorms had experienced "conduct and vandalism problems this year," [6] that new furniture had been placed in the lobbies of Garber and Weaver halls and that lobby furniture in Sanford and Cumberland halls had been upgraded.

The trustees went into executive session with Dr. Pearce to discuss Arnold Pope. The trustees' minutes read, "Dr. Pearce explained the eight-year history of the Arnold Pope situation and stated it had necessitated the drafting of the paper, 'First Draft, Philosophy of the Student Life Program.'" [7]

After Dr. Pearce left the executive session, the trustees set the president's salary for 1981-82 at $39,000.

Terry Sanford Addresses Class of 1981

"Truth is the fixed star of liberal education," said Terry Sanford, president of Duke University, at Methodist's 18th spring commencement May 3, 1981. The Methodist College trustee continued, "To seek the truth, to insist on the truth, to recognize the truth is the ultimate aim of liberal education. It isn't enough to cherish books, love music, appreciate fine art. You must also look for the truth in your own life and the lives of those around you. . " [8]

— CHAPTER 6 —

Methodist used this occasion to present Sanford with an honorary Doctor of Laws degree for his "insatiable desire to improve the quality of life for all and his commitment that education is the basis of all that is good." [9]

Methodist College also honored two others at its 18th spring commencement. Dr. Paul Carruth, Fayetteville District Superintendent of The United Methodist Church, was awarded an honorary Doctor of Divinity degree. Dr. Mott Blair, a dentist from Siler City, N.C. and chair of the Methodist College Board of Trustees from 1967-1977, was awarded a Methodist College Medallion.

The Spring 1981 *Bulletin of Methodist College* also reported that Dr. Janet Cavano, professor of English, had been selected Distinguished Professor of 1981 by her peers.

Men's Golf Team Finishes Sixth In NCAA Division III

Methodist's men's golf team finished sixth in the NCAA Division III National Tournament May 19-22, 1981 at Pinehurst, N.C. Coach Gene Clayton described the team average of 310 as "exceptional." This was the first Methodist College team to go to a NCAA national championship tournament. Eddie Dalton, a sophomore form Fayetteville, received All-America honors for his play at Pinehurst.

Playing for the Monarchs were: Ian Joyce, a sophomore from Pittsburgh; Jack Bartanus, a sophomore from Avella, Pa.; Eddie Dalton, a freshmen from Fayetteville; Mickey Sokalski, a freshman from Coopersburg, Pa.; and Mike Baker, a freshman from Bangor, Maine.

Trustees Discuss Energy Conservation, New Gymnasium

Members of the trustees' Executive Committee received an energy report June 30, 1981 from Mr. Irving Ball of Greensboro who said conservation measures already put in effect had cut energy costs in half, to an estimated $254,000, for 1980-81.

Dr. Pearce said the College needed to adopt a Honeywell temperature control program (computerized shutdowns) for the campus heating and cooling systems; put 3M sun shield film on lobby windows in the Administration, Fine Arts, and Student Union buildings; and convert the cafeteria kitchen equipment from electricity to natural gas.

The president offered three major proposals for trustee consideration:
1) installation of Kal-Wall insulated window units in the four dormitories (362 windows at $500 per window).
2) construction of a gymnasium at a cost of $750,000.
3) a fine arts program encompassing a Fine Arts Festival and

Shakespearean Repertory Theatre beginning in August and presenting two plays in September. He said $200,000 was needed to endow this program.

Proposals one and two were docketed for consideration at the trustees' fall meeting, while proposal three was scheduled for discussion at the spring meeting.

College Begins 22nd School Year

sMALL TALK's fall orientation issue August 28, 1981 ran a large front page cartoon of an MC freshman surrounded by alligators.

Fall news stories noted that:
—Guy Braley was the new Dean of Men, and Jane M. Downing was the new Dean of Women.
—Jane Weeks Townsend had joined the faculty as Director of the Community Music Program.
—Ann Clark and Inglelone Holthe had been hired as adjunct instructors of psychology.

The lead story in the September 18, 1981, *sMALL TALK* recounted President Pearce's three-step expansion plans announced at the fall opening convocation marking the College's Silver Anniversary year. Dr. Pearce said the program would involve 1) renovating the exteriors of the four residence halls, 2) building a gymnasium, and 3) founding a Shakespeare Summer Theatre at Methodist.

Dr. Jack Peyrouse announced that Green and Gold Masque Keys would stage four productions in 1981-82: Moliere's *George Dundin*, a Mummer's *Renaissance Christmas Dinner*, Eugene O'Neill's *The Emperor Jones* and James Agee's *All the Way Home*.

An inside news item reported that art professor Lloyd Nick had spent the summer in Europe and exhibited his landscapes at a one-man show in Lovech, Bulgaria.

The October 23, 1981 newspaper reported that Valerie Houston, a senior from Charlotte, was elected 1981 Homecoming Queen.

The November 13, 1981 *sMALL TALK* announced that a Peace Studies Course would be offered in spring 1982, taught by Robert Gosney, director of Quaker House in Fayetteville. Bruce Pulliam, Social Science coordinator, said the upper level course would be a three-semester-hour elective.

In other news:
—The men's soccer team ended its 1981 season 4-10-1.
—Dance Theatre of Fayetteville presented a "Day for Dancing," an interpretation of Christmas carols December 5-6, 1981 at Methodist.

— CHAPTER 6 —

The back page of the December 1, 1980 *sMALL TALK* issue pictured a new painting on the outside wall of the Student Union's east balcony: the words "Home of the Monarchs" and a lion's head, painted in green and gold by the Art Club, under the direction of Silvana Foti.

President Briefs Trustees On Retention, Recruitment

Dr. Pearce reported to the trustees' Executive Committee September 24, 1981 that student retention remained a problem at the College and that the Student Life area was planning more weekend activities. He also announced that a new "highly personalized" student recruitment program was being implemented under the direction of Susan Jaeger. He said the system was patterned after the system used by the Athletic Department and would employ a series of letters and phone calls from College professors.

Mr. Lowdermilk announced that a College speakers bureau had been organized and that all civic clubs in Cumberland County had been sent a list of topics which Methodist faculty or staff could address as guest speakers.

The full Board of Trustees approved a Five Year Financial Plan and Five Year Projections November 20, 1981. After some discussion, the trustees accepted Dr. Pearce's recommendation to keep all four residence halls open; the president said 40 percent of the resident students had private rooms for which they were paying an additional 50 percent over the base room rent.

Dean of Students Calvert Ray praised the students for their volunteer services and S.G.A. President Rick Kugelmann for his positive leadership. Ray said ten students had been suspended from the College during the fall semester.

President Pearce reported that:

—long-term bonded indebtedness stood at $3.9 million.
—fall 1981 enrollment was 759 students, a decrease of 35.
—three faculty chairs should be endowed, two in business and one in religion.
—the College should endow the financial aid program, plant maintenance and faculty salaries; plan for an enrollment of 1,200 students, and "decide how much land we need and consider selling the remainder." [10]
—253 insulated dormitory windows had been pledged for the men's dormitories but, "There is no money for the female dorms." [11]

The board closed its meeting with a moment of silence in memory of Mr. Henry Dixon, a former trustee.

The trustees' Executive Committee met November 20, 1981 and authorized the president and board secretary to sell all Mid-South, Inc. stock at the current market value.

1980–1984

Chorus & Dance Theatre Perform Bach Work

Methodist celebrated the 1981 Christmas season with a joint performance by the Methodist College Chorus and The Dance Theatre of Fayetteville. The chorus performed Bach's *Magnificat in D Major* and a series of nine Christmas carols by contemporary American composer Lloyd Pfautsch. Using the title "A Day for Dancing," the Dance Theatre of Fayetteville, accompanied by the chorus and a small instrumental ensemble, danced interpretively to the nine Christmas carols.

Wells and Wise Make News in Spring 1982

The January 25, 1982 *sMALL TALK* reported that Cliff Wells had been cast in the lead role in *The Emperor Jones,* Eugene O'Neill's tragedy about a black man who becomes a dictator.

A short item on the editorial page invited students and staff to submit original works for the 1982 issue of *Tapestry*, the College literary magazine, in four literary genres: poetry, drama, fiction, and criticism, as well as the visual arts. The editors were Harley Palmer, Jr. and Cary Wilson.

Dr. Jack Peyrouse of the Theatre Department announced a "Weekend Theatre Fling" for March 6-7 in New York City. For $210, MC staff and students could fly to New York (via Piedmont Airlines) and see two Broadway shows: *The Pirates of Penzance* and *Amadeus*.

Cliff Wells

VA Chaplain Corbin Cherry, a decorated Vietnam veteran, was the guest speaker for Faith-in-Life Week January 24-26, 1982, A coffee house performance of contemporary Christian music was held January 25 featuring the God's Way Back band from Raleigh.

Dr. James Cammack, pastor of Snyder Memorial Baptist Church, was the commencement speaker at the College's winter graduation December 18; 32 seniors received degrees.

Kenny Hall, a sophomore from Dublin, N.C., was profiled in a page 5 feature story. Hall skipped his senior year at Tar Heel High School and earned 32 semester hours of college credit by taking CLEP exams. His roommate was Roger Pait from Elizabethtown.

The March 19, 1982 *sMALL TALK* reported that Thomas Pope '78 had received a First Place award in sportswriting from the North Carolina Press Association for his *Fayetteville Observer* story about the Southern 500 at Darlington Raceway won by Terry Labonte.

— CHAPTER 6 —

In other student news from spring 1982:
—the Catalinas band performed for the College's Spring Fest Dance.
—Gil Wise, a junior from Fayetteville, was elected S.G.A. president March 24, 1982.
—Cliff Wells gave his senior voice recital March 30, 1982.
—The baseball team amassed a record of 23-9 "based on superb pitching and clutch hitting." [12]

Gil Wise

Trustees Discuss Possible Land Sale

At a February 16, 1982 meeting, the trustees' Executive Committee approved a Southern Association of Colleges and Schools recommendation that the faculty, not the trustees, approve candidates for graduation. The committee also approved a budget for 1982-83 as presented by Roy Whitmire, College comptroller, a budget based on an F.T.E. of 680 students with 280 dormitory students, and a budget 10 percent larger than the previous year that would increase faculty salaries 4 percent. The yearly cost for a resident student was set at $5,250, which included room, board, tuition and fees.

In an April 16, 1982 meeting, the trustees' Executive Committee voted to ask the full board of trustees to empower the chairman to appoint two committees—one to determine the best use of endowment lands for attracting new students and creating the most efficient income for the College, and one to discuss with the resident bishop of The North Carolina Conference of The United Methodist Church a capital fund raising campaign for the colleges. Dr. Bailey moved that the chairman be so empowered, and the motion carried.

President Predicts Budget Shortfall

At an April 16, 1982 meeting, President Pearce told the Methodist College Board of Trustees:
—he projected a budget shortfall of $30,000-$50,000 for 1981-82 due to an enrollment loss of 20 F.T.E.s, unpaid student accounts, and a 33 percent increase in utility costs.
—the trustees had made little progress on the goal of raising $16 million over 15 years [set in 1973]. "We are halfway through the 15-year period, and the endowment is $1,211,075," he said. [13]
—dormitory governments and the Student Government Association had been reorganized and that every student

1980–1984

Dr. Gautam presents Silver Spoon award to W. L. Smith at the 1982 Stock Market Symposium.

organization had been urged to offer at least one community service per semester *quid pro quo* for operating on campus.

—fall 1982 applications were down 100 from the previous year. "We need to have 225 new freshmen and 145 transfer students next fall," he said. [14]

—again suggested selling 400 acres of College land to build the College's endowment.

—expressed hope that the current economic downturn was bottoming out and that there would be a slow upturn in the American economy.

Following a brief executive session, the trustees employed President Pearce for another year at a salary of $40,500.

MC Honors Watson

At its 19th spring commencement May 2, 1982, Methodist College awarded an honorary Doctor of Divinity degree to the Reverend H. Langill Watson, pastor of First United Methodist Church of Wilson, N.C. Watson delivered the baccalaureate sermon.

— CHAPTER 6 —

A. Dano Davis of Jacksonville, Fla., senior vice president of Winn Dixie Inc., delivered the commencement address. Tricia Ann Turner of Fayetteville received the L. Stacy Weaver Award. President Pearce awarded Methodist College Medallions to Mr. Davis and to Grier Garrick of Jacksonville, N.C., president of Carolina Office Supply and a prominent United Methodist lay leader.

Trustees Receive Bad News

When the Executive Committee met June 28, 1982, Tommy Dent, director of admissions, predicted fall applications would be down 25.3 percent and registration 20 percent. He said an aggressive telemarketing program and new publications aimed at graduating high school students would be employed next year.

Dr. Pearce said a shortfall in student enrollment would require a hiring freeze, an $80,000 reduction in budgeted purchases, and a request to HEW/HUD for deferment of bonded debt payments. A lengthy discussion was held about the best use of Methodist's 575-acre campus, including sale and/or development of the land and possible construction of a golf course and the sale of fairway lots.

MC Stages Shakespearean Summer Festival

The Summer 1982 *Bulletin of Methodist College* reported that Gil Wise, a junior from Fayetteville, was elected S.G.A. president March 24.

The men's golf team finished third in the NCAA Division III National Tournament and placed four players on the All-America team: John Lain, Mickey Sokalski, Mike Hartman, and Brian Hamric.

Methodist College staged its first annual Shakespearean Summer Festival August 19-September 4, 1982, with performances of *West Side Story* and *The Merchant of Venice*.

Trustees Discuss Land Sale, Approve Curriculum Change

When the Executive Committee met October 13, 1982, Dr. Pearce reported a fall semester enrollment of 649 (head count) and an F.T.E. (full-time equivalent) of 607.

Dr. Pearce said three local realtors had been asked to appraise College land. He said Bishop William R. Cannon of The North Carolina Conference of The United Methodist Church had authorized the College to solicit funds within local churches for a capital campaign. The Reverend Sam McMillan was asked to arrange a meeting of the conference's three college presidents with the Division of Higher Education to seek approval for a conference wide capital fund drive for the three colleges.

At a full meeting of The Board of Trustees November 16, 1982, the board approved in principle the sale or other use of College land and authorized the Executive Committee to solicit offers for the purchase or use of College land with the income derived being used for the general endowment of the College. A motion by Dr. James Bailey, which the trustees approved, stated that if a *bonafide* offer for College land was received, a special meeting of the Board of Trustees would be called to evaluate the offer.

Acting on the recommendation of the trustees' Academic Affairs Committee, the trustees approved a major revision in the College's core curriculum, eliminating the requirements for a minor and one course in psychology. The net effect was a reduction in core requirements from 56 semester hours to 49-51 hours and the total hours required for a bachelor's degree from 128 to 124.

The trustees made one change to the committee recommendation, voting to increase the religion requirement from three to six semester hours, pushing the hours required for graduation to 127. The core requirements thus became: Communications—9-11 sem. hrs., Humanities—15 hours, Math and Natural Science—11 hours, Social Science—12 hours, and Physical Education—2 hours.

In other actions, the trustees:

—approved capital and operating budgets. Roy Whitmire, College comptroller, said the school would need to borrow $207,201 to cover a projected deficit in the operating budget. The operating budget totalled $3.2 million; the capital outlay budget $28,050.

—approved a Code of Conduct for the College (See Appendix FF).

—heard Mr. Lowdermilk report that the F.T.E. had dropped from 731 in fall 1981 to 608 in the fall of 1982.

—heard Dean of Students Calvert Ray report that a 34 percent drop in the dorm population had created problems in programming and that day students had organized a "commuter club."

—heard S.G.A. President Gil Wise describe student morale as being at an all-time low. Wise said a student poll taken in the spring of 1982 "revealed a 40 percent vote of 'no confidence' in the College administration." [15] Wise expressed concern over campus security and said a survey taken the night before showed that "70 percent of the dorm students plan to transfer." [16]

—heard Dr. Pearce state that "financial aid for students, recruiting, and quality education" were the three most significant issues facing small, independent colleges and that these areas overlap. [17]

He said Methodist needed to sharpen its recruiting efforts in the face of increased competition for students from public colleges and technical colleges. The president offered three steps as "the solution to Methodist's problems": 1) expanding the evening division, 2) expanding the recruitment of 'our kind' of student, and 3) finding the financial aid to assure applicants they can afford to attend Methodist College. [18]

—heard Steve Harden, president of the Methodist College Alumni Association, report that the association was launching a drive to establish a $50,000 scholarship fund.

—approved a motion by Rufus Stark that the College offer Bachelor of Music and Bachelor of Applied Music degrees.

—were told that a trustee had just made a $10,000 donation to the College.

sMALL TALK Announces Staff Changes

The August 25, 1982 *sMALL TALK* reported that Dr. Lorenzo Plyler had been named Distinguished Professor for 1981-82. The *sMALL TALK* editorial board for 1982-83 was composed of Patty Smith, Shelia Yates, and Kenny Hall.

In other news reported in this issue:

—Tricia Turner was now an admissions counselor and Gerri Williams had become secretary to the president. Susan Yaeger became director of alumni affairs.

—The Methodist College Summer Shakespearean Festival presented *The Merchant of Venice* and *West Side Story*.

—The men's golf team placed third in the NCAA Division III National Golf Tournament and placed four players on the All America team: John Lavin, Mickey Sokalski, Mike Hartman, and Brian Hamric.

Tricia Turner

The September 17, 1982 *sMALL TALK* reported on the fall opening convocation September 3, at which Dr. Pearce estimated Methodist would enroll 800-900 students in the day and evening program and said the new students were "fewer but better." [19] He said 57 of the 107 students placed on Strict Academic Probation the preceding academic year did not return. "Quality is an expensive commodity," he said. [20]

S.G.A. President Gil Wise thanked Dr. Pearce and the faculty for the new once-a-month convocation requirement, and the audience applauded loudly. The S.G.A. announced it had received a $4,000 grant to distribute to clubs and organizations for activities benefiting the entire College community.

The homecoming schedule for October 7-10, 1982 included a new event, a tennis tournament sponsored by the S.G.A. The Theatre Department was slated to present three afternoon performances of *The Birds*, based on a play by Aristophanes. Cast in the lead roles were: Tom Jumalon as Footloose and Sherry Kizzori as Footsore. The Voltage Brothers was the featured band for the homecoming dance.

The soccer team defeated Wingate 2-0 in the homecoming game, and Candy Kearns, a sophomore from Troy, N.C., was crowned the 1982 homecoming queen. This *sMALL TALK* also contained an interview with former N.Y. Jets quarterback Joe Namath, who was in Fayetteville to appear as Sky Masterson in a Fort Bragg Playhouse production of *Guys and Dolls*.

News reported by *sMALL TALK* in November and December 1982 included the following:

—The Reverend Dennis Sheppard, pastor of Lemon Springs United Methodist Church, served as minister-in-residence the week of October 4, 1982. He visited with students, spoke to Dr. Gautam's class about world hunger, and preached at a fellowship breakfast sponsored by Koinonia.

—Jerry Jercle, N.C. Director of the Fellowship of Christian Athletes, spoke at the Methodist College Community Day convocation October 6 in Reeves Auditorium.

—A front page story in the November 12, 1982 issue announced the retirement of Holman Milby, manager of the bookstore for the 16 years. Milby was succeeded by Burl Cunningham.

Students Complain About Lack of Security On Campus

An investigative article on campus security at Methodist appeared on the front page of the December 12, 1982 *sMALL TALK*. Patty Smith and Mark Powell reported that Methodist had only one full-time employee for campus security, supplemented by student workers, compared to 10 security officers at Fayetteville State University and six at Campbell University.

The article noted that a rash of daytime incidents of petty vandalism and thefts and the firing of daytime security guard Fred Miller were cause for concern among students.

Dr. Pearce confirmed Miller's statement that he (the president) had been opposed to daytime security for several years. He said faculty, staff, and students needed to be more responsible.

— CHAPTER 6 —

Guy Braley, dean of men, said students had complained to him and he agreed with them that a 24-hour security force was needed at Methodist.

In other news reported in the closing months of 1982:

—Methodist's new core curriculum was described by Dean Fred Clark as more flexible and giving students a greater choice. The new plan, which was the result of a year-long study by a faculty committee, was approved by the faculty and the College's Board of Trustees.

The major change was the deletion of a requirement that every student have a minor. The English requirement was reduced from six semester hours to three. Students were also allowed to substitute courses in speech and computer language (six hours) for two courses in a foreign language.

"Much work was done to come up with a good solid liberal arts core that had greater options," said Dr. Pearce. [21] He said the new core requirements would take effect in the fall of 1983 but that continuing students could remain in the current core.

Dean Clark said the new core would mean transfer students who had completed a core elsewhere would not lose as many transfer credits at Methodist.

— *sMALL TALK* gave lengthy coverage on two inside pages to a convocation address by Motapula Chabuka, a South African and a professor of divinity at Bennett College in Greensboro, N.C., describing the effects of apartheid on her country. She criticized the Carter and Reagan administrations for defending rulers like Samoza of Nicaragua and Marcos of the Philippines, saying, "This country will pay for its waste and affluence." [22]

Chabuka called on MC students to take up the cause of freedom and human rights and work to bring about changes that would create a more just society.

— In a surprise announcement at the December 8 convocation, Gil Wise resigned as S.G.A. president, citing "academic and miscellaneous reasons." Wise was succeeded by Kenny Hall.

—The back page of the December 13 issue featured a photo of Art Club members on a scaffold inside the Student Union where they had painted several pillars. The page also contained a feature about Mrs. Neva Pearce, the president's wife and an acomplished artist, and a picture of her painting a portrait. A filler photo showed several students playing "Uno" in the Student Union. A short news article indicated the Commuter Club's coffee lounge in the downstairs north stairwell of the Classroom Building was proving popular.

1980–1984

Trustees Receive More Bad News

When the trustees' Executive Committee met January 19, 1983, President Pearce reported that 551 students were enrolled for the spring 1983 semester.

Trustee Sam McMillan said the Board of Higher Education Study Committee of The North Carolina Conference of The United Methodist Church had several recommendatons for Methodist College:

—increase recruitment of resident students.
—reduce the indebtedness,
—create a clear understanding of goals,
—improve the relations between the administration and students,
—develop a strong Development Office,
—conduct a financial drive,
—increase its enrollment. [23]

McMillan said the conference's Board of Higher Education would **not** recommend a capital funds drive [for the three conference colleges] to The North Carolina Conference. He said conference support for Methodist College had increased 8 perecent over the last six years.

In other business, the trustees:
—approved vacation and sick leave policies.
—were told that a January 13, 1983 letter from the U.S. Dept. of Education had granted Methodist deferrals of payments on its federal construction loans, one payment to February 15 1983, and another to December 31, 1983.
—Authorized Dr. Pearce to conduct a feasibility study for a $3 million capital fund drive. [Dr. Pearce suggested $2 million for scholarships and $1 million for a gymnasium.]

In a February 28, 1983 meeting, the trustees' Executive Committee:
—approved sale of Eutaw lots in Fayetteville for $18,750.
—approved the hiring of Johnston & Erwin of Durham, N.C., to do a capital fund drive feasibility study for $1,200.
—was advised that a Spanish instructor would be eliminated and that a tenured English professor who had not been offered a contract for 1983-84 had appealed to the Board of Trustees and that the trustees' Academic Affairs Committee would hear the appeal.
—voted to buy ten computers for a computer lab and six computers for a learning center in the library, at a cost not to exceed $20,000.
—heard Mr. Whitmire report that increased collections and reduced expenditures would eliminate a projected budget deficit and the need to borrow money.
—approved a food services contract with SAGA for 1983-84.

— CHAPTER 6 —

President Expresses Regret Over Loss of Students

In its January 27, 1983 issue, *sMALL TALK* reported on a January 12, 1983 convocation address, in which President Pearce expressed sadness over the loss of a substantial number of students for academic reasons. He said the College had 580 full-time students and 140-160 evening students. He said a grant proposal for a computer study center in the library would probably not be funded until fall 1983.

Ed Kilbourne, a singer, comedian, story-teller, guitarist (and a United Methodist minister) was profiled in a front page story about Faith-in-Life Week. Kilbourne was the resource person for the week, January 31-February 4.

Mark Powell, a freshman from Fayetteville, joined the *sMALL TALK* editorial board in February 1983, replacing Kenny Hall.

***Brigadoon* Highlights Spring Arts Festival**

A front page story in the February 11, 1983 issue announced that Methodist would open its production of the Lerner and Lowe musical *Brigadoon* Thursday, February 17. Directed by Jack Peyrouse, assisted by Alan Porter and Ann Clark, the musical featured Gary Rudd and Ruth Nelson in the lead roles and a cast of fifty.

Methodist's 1983 Fine Arts Festival February 6-19 had a Scottish theme, with slide shows about Scottish gardens and authors Peter Barrie, Robert Burns, and Sir Walter Scott. Also featured were a Ceiligh Party, a Scottish church service, a reading of Scottish love poems, and a Scottish dinner. The staging of the musical *Brigadoon* was the major event of the week.

The 1983 production of **Brigadoon** *played to capacity crowds in Reeves Auditorium.*

1980–1984

In a very complimentary review of *Brigadoon,* Mark Powell said outstanding performances by Richard Bicoy as Charlie Dalyrumple and Roxanne Rodriguez as Jean MacLaren were the highlight of the musical, which played to standing-room-only crowds.

Roger Pait and Jerome Smith, the two candidates for S.G.A. president for 1983-84, were profiled in a front page story by Mark Powell in the March 7 *sMALL TALK.* Both cited a need for better communications with the college administration. Patty Smith wrote a lengthy article on Methodist's "no alcohol policy," debunking the rumor that Methodist might lift alcohol restrictions in the wake of North Carolina legislation raising the drinking age to 21.

First computers on campus

The March 23 issue included a front page story describing Methodist's acquisition of 16 TRS Model Three color computers at a cost of $19,000. Dr. Ted Jaeger said ten units would be housed in the Science Building and six would go to the library.

An inside feature by Mark Powell profiled three MC alumni working as newspaper journalists: Bill Kirby '73, sports editor at *The Fayetteville Times,* Scott Peterson (who had transferred to UNC-Chapel Hill to major in journalism), *Times* sports writer; and Tom Pope '78, *Fayetteville Observer* sports writer.

The men's golf team shot a 600 two-day total score to win the NCAA Division III District 3 Golf Tournament at Quail Ridge Golf Club March 8-9, 1983.

Five writers of contemporary Southern literature were featured at Methodist's Southern Writers Series in March and April 1983: Fred Chappell, Heather Ross Miller, William Price Fox, Joe Ashby Porter, and James Dickey.

Trustees Receive Marketing Study and Internal Audit

A somewhat critical assessment of Methodist College was delivered to the trustees' Executive Committee March 24, 1983 by Jeffrey Johnston of Johnston and Erwin, a Durham, N.C.-based marketing, fund-raising and public relations consulting firm.

After visiting the school and interviewing trustees, current students, alumni and staff, Johnston concluded that Methodist had three immediate needs: 1) to be marketed better, 2) to have its distinctiveness [*i.e.* ability to equip students for leadership] communicated, 3) more affluent trustees who must be able to give or get funds. [24]

More specifically, Johnston said the College needed to sell its surplus land, hire a full-time alumni director and development officer, add admissions personnel, and increase financial aid. "The main problem is moving from a survival mentality," said Johnston. [25] He said good business management during difficult times and the proposal to be presented to the Methodist conference to underwrite the HUD and HEW debt payments were positive factors in launching a fund-raising effort.

Johnston said he found a clear perception at Methodist "that the administration does not listen to students and faculty." [26] He said the top priority for using capital funds should be: 1) financial aid, 2) building of a gymnasium, and 3) more computers, increases in faculty and staff salaries, and "a great deal of deferred maintenance." [27] He reiterated his belief that the College "now must move away from the survival approaches of the last five years so it can compete more effectively for students and for philanthropic support." [28] The consultant urged the trustees to perform Phase II of the study "to see if a capital funds drive could be successful, and if so, at what level." [29]

Following Mr. Johnston's report, Dr. Pearce presented a list of needed repairs to the College plant which totalled $288,000. In other matters, the Executive Committee:

—approved a motion by Mr. McMillan defining the southern half of the campus [south of the stream] as lands the College might be willing to sell.

—approved budgets and fees for 1983-84, increasing tuition and fees $520, making the total cost for a resident student $5,770.

—met with Dr. Pearce after adjourning at the president's request to discuss an unspecified matter.

Dr. Pearce Resigns

Minutes of the trustees' Executive Committee meeting of April 14, 1983 indicate that President Richard Pearce had resigned and that an announcement to that effect would be made to the news media at 3 p.m. by the president and trustees' chairman.

In other matters, the Executive Committee:

—budgeted $10,000 for use by the Presidential Search Committee and $4,000 for the second phase of the Johnston and Erwin study regarding a capital funds drive.

1980–1984

- —authorized Ike O'Hanlon, chairman of the Board of Trustees, to appoint a Presidential Search Committee of five to nine members.
- —agreed to retain Dr. Pearce on a month-to-month basis after June 30, 1983.

Dr. Pearce

Following an executive session April 14, 1983, the Methodist College Board of Trustees accepted the resignation of Dr. Pearce, authorized the board chairman to appoint a Presidential Search Committee, and voted to contract with Johnston and Erwin for the second phase of a capital funds drive feasibility study.

The minutes of this meeting show that Bishop William R. Cannon of The North Carolina Conference of The United Methodist Church praised Dr. Pearce for his service to The United Methodist Church and his leadership in reversing the decline in enrollment at Methodist College.

In other business:

- —The Reverend Sam McMillan reported that the Board of Higher Education and Campus Ministry of The North Carolina Conference of The United Methodist Church had voted to ask the conference to budget $157,742 to underwrite the HUD and HEW payments [on federal construction loans] at Methodist College, increasing church support from $525,000 to $775,000 annually.
- —Dr. Pearce reported that two parties had expressed interest in buying College land but that no offer had been made.
- —heard Ike O'Hanlon, board chairman, report that he had received a letter from Dr. L. Stacy Weaver, Methodist's first president, opposing the sale of any College land.
- —heard Reverend McMillan report that the 1983-84 budget included $25,000 for a development officer and $20,000 for an additional faculty member in English.

sMALL TALK Reports Pearce Retirement On Page 4

The front page of the April 15, 1983 sMALL TALK was filled with a cartoon rendering of "The MC Game," complete with game board caricatures of Gordon Dixon, Dean Braley, Tommy Dent, Maj. Chambers, Bruce Pulliam, and Ted Jaeger. sMALL TALK took a first class honors award in the 1982 Associated Collegiate Press competition with a Mark of Distinction in coverage and content.

— CHAPTER 6 —

A major news story on Page 4 reported that Dr. Richard Pearce had announced his retirement to the Methodist College Board of Trustees April 14. Dr. Pearce said a recommendation of the consulting firm of Johnston and Erwin that the College launch a major capital fund drive would require a five-year commitment from the College president, a commitment he could not make. He said he and Mrs. Pearce would return to Florida.

College Announces Pearce Retirement, Graduates 20th Class

A brief news item in the College's June 1983 *Bulletin* reported that Dr. Richard Pearce had announced his retirement to the Methodist College Board of Trustees April 14, 1983, saying the College's pending capital funds campaign would require a five-year commitment from the president. The story said Trustees Chairman Ike O'Hanlon had named a nine-member presidential Search Committee chaired by R. Dillard Teer of Durham, N.C.

Another story noted that Methodist had awarded Presidential Scholarships worth full-tuition for four years to three high school seniors: Joseph Kidd of Falls Church, Va., Todd S. Krueger of Stafford, Va., and Susan Hyatt of Fayetteville.

The *Bulletin* also reported that U.S. Congressman Charles Rose delivered the commencement address to 67 seniors at Methodist's 20th spring commencement May 1, 1983. The college awarded an honorary Doctor of Letters degree to Wilson F. Yarborough Sr. of Fayetteville, a trustee emeritus, and a Methodist College Medallion to Dr. Lorenzo Plyler, chair of the Religion Department.

In other news, Gene Clayton received the Distinguished Professor of 1982-83 Award at the annual faculty dinner, and Methodist entered the computer age by installing 20 TRS 80 computers in Davis Library.

Trustees Begin Search For College President

When the trustees' Executive Committee met July 7, 1983, Sam McMillan reported that the Presidential Search Committee had placed ads for the president's position in the *North Carolina* and *South Carolina Christian Advocates* [official publications of the North Carolina and South Carolina conferences of The United Methodist Church]. Mr. O'Hanlon commended Mr. McMillan on his successful efforts to persuade The North Carolina Conference to underwrite the College's HEW/HUD payments.

Roy Whitmire advised the committee that no bank borrowing had been necessary for the 1982-83 fiscal year. He presented a proposal to convert the kitchen equipment in the College cafeteria from electricity to natural gas at a cost of $31,000; he was authorized to seek bids.

1980–1984

Dr. Pearce announced that Dr. Robert Perkins would be the new Dean of Students, replacing Calvert Ray who was returning to teaching, and that Charlotte Coheley would be the new Director of Admissions.

The president said the decision of the trustees' Academic Affairs Committee in favor of Dr. Janet Cavano, who had appealed her non-renewal as an English professor, was made on a misinterpretation of SACS standards and that Dr. Cavano was enrolled in two journalism courses at UNC-Chapel Hill.

Trustees Hire Elton Hendricks As College President

The Methodist College Board of Trustees met in special session Thursday morning, August 11, 1983, to receive the report of the Presidential Search Committee. Mr. Dillard Teer, chairman of the Search Committee, said the committee had met frequently and worked diligently "to secure just the right person for Methodist College at this time." [30] He said the committee wished to nominate Dr. M. Elton Hendricks, academic dean at Randolph-Macon College in Ashland, Virginia, to become the third president of Methodist College.

Melvin Elton Hendricks, 47, was born in Savannah, Georgia and reared in Ridgeland, South Carolina. He received a B.A. in history from Wofford College in Spartanburg, S.C. where he was named to Phi Beta Kappa. From 1957-61, he served in the U.S. Navy as a Naval Flight Officer. He earned a Master of Divinity degree from Duke University with honors in 1964 and a Ph.D. in physics from the University of South Carolina in 1971.

Dr. Hendricks taught physics in 1971-72 at Eisenhower College in Pennsylvania. From 1972-77, he taught at Wofford College and served two years as director of admissions. From 1977-83, he was the academic dean at Randolph-Macon College.

Dr. Hendricks

Dr. Hendricks, who was present at the trustees' meeting along with his wife Jerry and children Lynn, Patricia and George, expressed appreciation for the confidence placed in him and his family. He described himself as the product of a small liberal art college [Wofford College] and said he believed in what colleges like Methodist could do.

Trustees Chairman Ike O'Hanlon told Dr. Hendricks he would have the full cooperation of the Methodist College Board of Trustees, which "would work to make Methodist College the finest college in North Carolina." [31]

— CHAPTER 6 —

The trustees then voted unanimously to appoint Dr. M. Elton Hendricks president of Methodist College. Dr. Pearce commended the trustees for choosing a man of Dr. Hendricks' stature. He described his time at Methodist College as "ten wonderful years" [32] and pledged his continued support for the College.

At a trustees' Executive Committee meeting which preceded the full board meeting, Dr. Hendricks' salary as president was set at $47,500 with a $1,000 travel allowance and a $2,500 auto allowance.

A press conference was held after the Board of Trustees meeting to announce Hendricks' selection to the news media. However, *The Fayetteville Times,* the morning newspaper, had already "scooped" the College and run a story with photo *that morning*, saying Dr. Hendricks would be named president "today" at a 10:15 trustees' meeting and that a news conference was scheduled for 10:45 a.m.

Times reporter Ellen Scarborough had learned Dr. Hendricks would be named president from sources at the College and/or members of the Presidential Search Committee. Her news story included a full biography and a photo of the new president and reported that the Search Committee had chosen Dr. Hendricks July 28 after interviewing three finalists.

At the College's press conference, Dr. Hendricks was introduced by Ike O'Hanlon, chair of the Methodist College Board of Trustees, who said the new president would begin work September 15. Accompanied by his wife Jerry, daughters Lynn and Patricia and son George, Dr. Hendricks read a brief acceptance statement in which he stated that Methodist College had a good reputation, that he supported its mission, and promised "creative solutions" and "aggressive" fund-raising to solve the College's problems "because our society needs the service that Methodist was created to offer." [33]

Dr. Hendricks Outlines Goals

At a Board of Trustees meeting October 4, 1983, President Hendricks offered three major goals for 1983-84:

—1) a F.T.E. enrollment of 700, with 50 percent dormitory occupancy.
—2) 30 one-half tuition scholarships for high school seniors in the top 10 percent of their class with an S.A.T. score of 1,000.
—3) a strong annual giving program generating 750 gifts from alumni with an average of $50, a parent program securing 50 contributions totalling $5,000, and 100 percent participation by the College trustees with an average gift of $500. [34]

The trustees accepted the new president's recommendations for allocating $163,775 from the Calvin Little estate and $157,000 in debt retirement funds anticipated incrementally from The North Carolina Conference of The United Methodist Church.

Noting that the College budget included a line item of $25,000 for a director of development, Dr. Hendricks said he felt the College would be better served by funding a full-time alumni director (then a half-time position) and increasing the admissions staff by one person.

MC Today Replaces Trifold *Bulletin*

Methodist abandoned its trifold newsletter, *Bulletin of Methodist College*, for a quarterfold tabloid newspaper in November 1983. Printed on newsprint, the new publication was named *Methodist College Today*. Dr. M. Elton Hendricks was pictured on the cover of the inaugural issue; a "cover story" followed, describing the president's background and summarizing his statement of acceptance.

Another major news story in that issue announced that the College had received $263,795 from the estate of Calvin Little of Mt. Gilead, N.C. The first $100,000 was earmarked for a Little Scholarship.

A double-page spread in the center of this *MCT* provided pictorial highlights of the 1983 homecoming.

Alumni news filled six pages and included a profile of Howard Lupton, president of the Methodist College Alumni Association; a list of MCAA goals; letters to alumni from Pat Clayton, alumni director, Howard Lupton, and Gwen Sykes, director of publications; class notes; and a list of alumni contributors to the MCAA Loyalty Fund in 1983-84. In his letter, Lupton thanked Lynn Gruber '72, Outstanding Alumnus for 1983, for organizing a Methodist College Chorus reunion held in March.

A news brief announced that the MCAA Board of Directors had agreed at its fall meeting that the construction of a physical education building was the greatest need for MC, followed by the raising of scholarship funds. The alumni board challenged alumni to make gifts toward one or both of these needs.

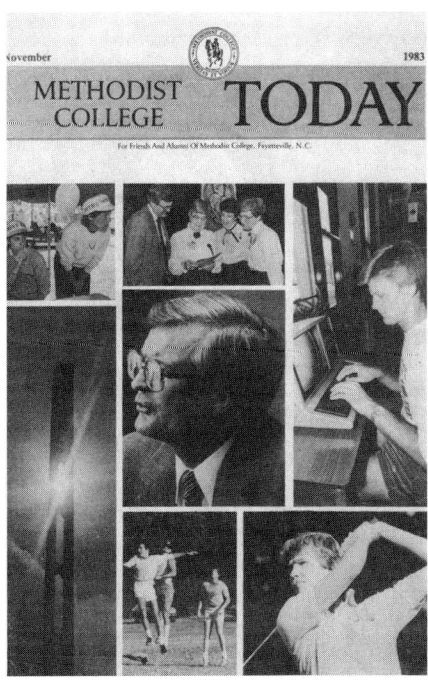

First issue of **Methodist College Today**

— CHAPTER 6 —

Another news story reported that Methodist had awarded honorary doctorates to the Reverend Samuel McMillan Jr., and the Reverend Arthur Winstead and a Methodist College Medallion to Louis Spilman Jr., '64 at the summer graduation. Spilman was then an active member of the Board of Trustees.

sMALL TALK Presents the New President

sMALL TALK began its twenty-first year August 27, 1983 with a front page news story announcing that the Board of Trustees had named Dr. M. Elton Hendricks, academic dean at Randolph-Macon College in Ashland, Va., the third president of Methodist College, effective September 15.

Dr. Hendricks was identified as a native of Savannah, Georgia, with earned degrees from Wofford College, Duke University, and the University of South Carolina. The story said he and his wife Jerry had three children: Joyce Lynn, Leslie Patricia, and George Elton.

The story by Steve Owens and Patty Smith was very upbeat:

> "Dr. Hendricks said he hoped to continue the liberal arts tradition at Methodist 'while moving into the vocational interests of the future.' The president-elect said his top priorities would be to increase: the number of qualified students, the percentage of alumni participating in campus affairs, and the sense of community at Methodist. He said he would also establish close communication with students and aggressively seek new sources of funding for Methodist College." [35]

sMALL TALK editors Patty Smith, Stephen Owens, and Mark Powell meet with President Hendricks.

The campus newspaper also ran a brief farewell interview with Dr. Richard Pearce, in which the outgoing president told Mark Powell that he believed small schools like Methodist "hold the true flame of learning. A small school is the place where everyone has a chance to participate, a chance to become involved, and a chance to excel." [36]

Dr. Pearce said he saw in the choice of Dr. Elton Hendricks as president "good things for Methodist College." [37] He said he had enjoyed his ten years at Methodist and considered the faculty, staff, and students he had known as family. He said he hoped Methodist would have a successful capital funds drive and establish an endowment to fund scholarships.

sMALL TALK Reports Staff Changes

sMALL TALK's first issue of 1983-84, dated August 27, 1983, announced that the newspaper's editorial board would include Patty Smith, Stephen Owens, and Mark Powell.

In a letter printed on the editorial page, S.G.A. President Kenny Hall described the 1982-83 year as "tough," after the S.G.A. president and several senators resigned. "Morale was at an all-time low," he said. [38] Hall said the number of S.G.A. senators had been reduced from twelve to eight and that job descriptions had been written for the S.G.A. officers. Hall and new Dean of Students Robert Perkins were quoted as saying the existence of the Student Union Board was "up in the air." Hall said Gil Wise would serve as Chief Justice and that dorm courts would be continued.

A brief inside story noted that Gordon Dixon had resigned as registrar to teach at The Fayetteville Academy and that Tommy Dent had resigned as director of admissions. Charlotte Coheley '83 was the new director of admissions. Dan Lawrence '81 was named head coach of women's volleyball and softball, replacing Terry Benson Chambers.

The September 16, 1983 *sMALL TALK* featured a graph on the front page projecting a fall enrollment of 643 students. The paper also ran a story about computers on campus, noting that *Time* magazine had named a computer as its "Man of the Year" in 1982.

In this second issue of the 1983-84 school year, Mark Powell proclaimed the MC Shakespearean Summer Festival, which featured *A Midsummer Night's Dream* directed by Jack Peyrouse and *Macbeth* directed by Dr. Edward Hill, a great success. He said Sherry Kizzori as Helena and Elliott Moffitt as Macbeth gave outstanding performances.

The lead story in the October 7 issue reported that Methodist had received $265,000 from the Calvin Little estate. Little, who died in 1982, was described as a bachelor from Mount Gilead, N.C., who owned 2,300 acres of land. He was

— CHAPTER 6 —

reported to have left $6 million to churches, libraries, and colleges. The Reverend Arthur Winstead, a United Methodist minister from Mount Gilead, was credited with persuading Little to provide for Methodist College in his will.

In another of his critical reviews, Mark Powell described the 1983 edition of *Tapestry*, the College literary magazine, as "beautiful and ephemeral." [39] He included brief excerpts from the works chosen for the magazine to prove his point.

When interviewed by Mark Powell, Howard Lupton, president of the Methodist College Alumni Association, said MC needed a full-time alumni director. He also praised the former part-time alumni director, Pat Clayton. Lupton said the MCAA fell short in offering alumni something. He expressed strong support for the Methodist College faculty and staff and for the addition of graduate programs in education and business administration.

Elliot Moffitt as Macbeth

A news brief in the October 7 issue reported that Ruth Carter Stapleton '64 of Fayetteville had died September 26, 1983, after a six-month battle with pancreatic cancer.

The back page featured a photo of The Voltage Brothers, a rock-soul band slated to perform at the homecoming dance October 15. The cutline said a drawing would be held at the dance for an "I Love New York" trip for two. Other events listed under the "New York, New York" homecoming theme were: Friday—a spirit convocation, tennis tournament, and bonfire/pep rally; and Saturday—a street fair, cookout, parade, soccer game, alumni bowl, and homecoming dance.

sMALL TALK's October 31, 1983 issue featured homecoming highlights on a two-page center spread. Those pictured included alumnus Gil Wise dressed as a Lambda Chi hit man, cheerleader Ramona Jackson, soccer goalie Steve Springthorpe, and Sharon Hill, 1983 Homecoming Queen.

A news story in the November 18, 1983 issue promoted a Theatre Department tribute to Tennessee Williams set for November 17-19, 1983. The story said the production would include scenes from 11 of Williams' plays [Williams had died in March 1983].

The sports page noted that the 1983 soccer team finished 4-10-1, while the volleyball team compiled a record of 6-19.

A story in the December 19, 1983 newspaper reported that Hugh McColl, president of North Carolina National Bank, was the keynote speaker at Methodist's Outlook '84 economic symposium. McColl predicted that 1984 would see a strong recovery of the American economy with inflation at 5 percent, prime interest rates just below 10 percent, and a national unemployment rate of 8 percent.

A front page story reported that the College faculty had approved adding a computer science major at Methodist in the fall of 1984. Dr. Ted Jaeger, assistant academic dean, said 15 computer courses would need to be added over a three-year period.

A lengthy inside feature by Calvin McDaniel described an Investigative Reporter and Editors Conference held November 19, 1983 in Washington, D.C. Sponsored by NBC News, the conference was attended by Mark Powell, Bobby Ayers (*sMALL TALK* photographer), James Arvantes, and McDaniel. Jack Anderson, columnist for *The Washington Post*, delivered the keynote address, and James Polk of NBC News lectured on ethics in journalism.

New President Briefs Trustees

In a report to the trustees November 17, 1983, Dr. Hendricks said Methodist needed to:

—develop an area of distinction to give the College the visibility needed to recruit students and to attract financial support. He said plans for adding a computer science major were well under way.

—put a strong admissions program into effect.

—develop a strong development program. He challenged the Board of Trustees to raise $50,000 in 1983-84, with 100 percent support from the trustees. [40]

In other matters, the trustees:

—set April 14, 1984 as the date for the inauguration of President Hendricks.

—granted Dr. Pearce president emeritus status.

—passed resolutions of appreciation in memory of Mr. Joe Tally and Dr. Allen Brantley, former trustees.

At a January 19, 1984 meeting of the trustees' Executive Committee, Dr. Hendricks reported that three developers had been contacted about buying College land, that he had met with Dohn Broadwell and would shortly meet with John Koenig and a representative of North Carolina National Bank.

The committee voted to pay $6,000 for Dr. Hendricks to become a member of Highland Country Club and met over lunch with Mr. Cermette Clardy, the development consultant hired by the College.

— CHAPTER 6 —

When the full Board of Trustees met February 2, 1984, Terry Sanford, president of Duke University, said he opposed the sale of any College land and suggested the College find something from which it could derive income. He offered to have a Duke University real estate person meet with Dr. Hendricks, and the board accepted his offer.

The trustees approved the following fees for 1984-85: tuition--$4,000, activity fee--$200, board--$1,400, room--$800, making the total costs $4,200 for a commuting student and $6,400 for a resident student. The board approved a College budget for 1984-85 of $4,062,734—$3,913,542 for operating expenses and $149,192 for capital expenses.

Reporting on plans for Dr. Hendricks' April 14 inauguration, Mr. Lowdermilk said the day would begin with a panel discussion in the Science Auditorium featuring Dr. Terry Sanford, Dr. Lucile Hutaff, Dr. Samuel Womack, and Mr. John G. Dicks III, followed by a barbecue luncheon on the central mall, followed by the formal inauguration ceremony at 2 p.m. in Reeves Auditorium. He said the inauguration theme would be the same as the title of the president's address: "Truth and Virtue in the Twenty-first Century."

After meeting in executive session, the trustees set President Hendricks' salary for 1984-85 at $49,875 plus $1,500 for travel and a $2,500 auto allowance.

MC Today Profiles Alumni

The February 1984 *Methodist College Today* announced the addition of majors in arts management and computer science and the planned inauguration of Dr. Hendricks April 14. Also included was a photo of Charles McAdams taken at a retirement program and reception held January 15, 1984 at Edenton Street United Methodist Church in Raleigh, N.C. Mr. McAdams was retiring as treasurer of The North Carolina Conference of The United Methodist Church, a post he accepted in 1968, after working nine years at Methodist College as its first director of development and first director of public relations.

An inside feature written by Doug Fellows '83, chronicled the challenges and rewards of being an evening student at Methodist. One inside page was devoted to profiles of 14 MC alumni running for alumni offices.

Loyalty Campaign Nets $127,000

At the March 15, 1984 meeting of the trustees' Executive Committee, Bill Lowdermilk said the Methodist College Foundation's 1984 Community Loyalty Campaign had generated gifts and pledges of $127,000. Dr. Hendricks said master's degree programs in business and education were in the discussion stage and announced that women's golf and soccer would be added to Methodist's intercollegiate athletic program in the fall of 1984. He said applications were up 20 percent and that 225 freshmen were expected in the fall. He also reported that Dr. Fred Clark, academic dean, had been forced to resign for health reasons.

When the Executive Committee met April 12, 1984, Mr. Lowdermilk reported that the Foundation's Loyalty Campaign had reached $140,000. He said 50 United Methodist ministers would be attending Dr. Hendricks' inauguration along with representatives of 53 colleges. The committee accepted an offer of $18,000 for several lots in the Eutaw area of Fayetteville and directed that this money be placed in the College endowment.

Dr. M. Elton Hendricks Inaugurated Third President

Dr. M. Elton Hendricks was inaugurated the third president of Methodist College Saturday, April 14, 1984 at 2 p.m. in Reeves Auditorium. The crowd of 900 included representatives of 47 colleges and universities.

The inauguration ceremony was preceded by a panel discussion Saturday morning in the Science Auditorium and a barbecue lunch on the bell tower mall. The theme for the day, 'Truth and Virtue in the Twenty-first Century,' was also the title of Dr. Hendricks' commencement address.

At the panel discussion moderated by Dr. Sue Kimball, Dr. Terry Sanford spoke of The Liberal Arts, John G. Dicks III of Global Concerns, Dr. Lucile Hutaff of Moral Questions Posed by Technology, and Dr. Samuel J. Womack, Jr., of Religious Concerns.

Panelist Terry Sanford's remarks about the liberal arts were quoted at some length in *The Fayetteville Observer-Times* inauguration story. After all, Sanford had practiced law in Fayetteville, played a major role in founding Methodist College, and served as the first chairman of the College's Board of Trustees before becoming governor and later president of Duke University.

Here is how the local newspaper reported Sanford's remarks:

'When times are bad,' he said, 'people tend to question the usefulness of the liberal arts to say this doesn't do anything. Not so. There is a tremendous practical value in having a trained and disciplined mind. . .

'The great failing of today,' Sanford said, 'might be that graduates don't care about the weaknesses of society. But a liberal arts education teaches deep sensitivity to the values we praise.' [41]

Referring to Alvin Toffler's *Third Wave,* he said those with liberal arts educations must be the ones to talk back to the machines of an increasingly technological world. 'Liberal arts training

— CHAPTER 6 —

Dr. M. Elton Hendricks is inaugurated April 14, 1984.

undergirds the technological genius, reinforces humanitarian instincts,' he said. [42]

In his inaugural address, Dr. Hendricks stressed the College's close ties to The United Methodist Church and to the Fayetteville community which sought the College. "To the community I would say, 'We need each other. Methodist College needs your continuing support and you need the presence of Methodist College.'" [43]

Dr. Hendricks' emphasis on maintaining close ties with the local community and The United Methodist Church dominated the lead paragraph and headline of *The Fayetteville Observer-Times* news story on the inauguration. The story quoted the new president as follows: "It was appealing to me to find at Methodist College an obvious commitment on the part of both parties to be a church-related college and a college-related church." [44]

The May 1984 *Methodist College Today* included Dr. Hendricks' comment that his educational philosophy had been influenced by the Wesleyan tradition and a statement made by Bishop Wightman at the laying of the corner stone at Wofford College in 1854: ". . . education can make men poised and powerful, but only Christian education can make men good." [45]

The College newspaper also reported that Dr. Hendricks had restated the mission of Methodist College as follows:

"As a college we must call men to see the truth. As a college in the Christian and Wesleyan tradition, we must call men to lives of virtue. That is our mission. That you have asked me to participate in this is a call that I view as a high honor but also a sacred trust." [46]

In its August 27, 1983 edition, *sMALL TALK* ran the entire text of Dr. Hendricks' inaugural address and several photos of his inauguration.

Dr. Hendricks began his inaugural address by thanking all at Methodist who had made his first seven months "a joy and delight." He acknowledged the contributions of Dr. L. Stacy Weaver, the College's founding president; Dr. and Mrs. Richard Pearce; the faculty; administrators; trustees; and those in the Fayetteville community and The United Methodist Church who had supported the creation of Methodist College. He specifically thanked Roy Whitmire, business manager; Fred Clark, academic dean; Gene Clayton, athletic director; and Bill Lowdermilk, vice president.

The new president said he embraced the idea that Christian education can make people good. He recalled a conversation he had with a former classmate at Wofford in the fall of 1974. The man asked Dr. Hendricks what he was doing and he answered, "I'm here at Wofford teaching philosophy, trying to determine what the good life is." [47]

At this point, the president posed a rhetorical question to his audience: "What is the good life we want for our students?" He said most parents, like Bishop Wightman, want college to enable their children to be poised and powerful, to live "the good life." He then added, "If all we do is equip our students to live the good life in terms of security and prosperity. . .then we will fail them and our mission in a very fundamental way." [48]

Dr. Hendricks takes the oath of office from Ike O'Hanlon.

Dr. Hendricks said he believed, like John Wesley, in the type of education that seeks to make men good. . .to develop better human beings; to change values, attitudes and behavior. He said he wanted Methodist College to always seek the truth, uphold high academic standards, and promote tolerance for the views of others. [49]

"As a college in the Wesleyan tradition," he said, "we must call men to lives of virtue. That is our mission. That you have asked me to participate in this dual challenge is a call that I view as a high honor but with fear and trembling." [50]

— CHAPTER 6 —

sMALL TALK Finds No Shortage Of News In Spring 1984

In a front page news story in the February 6, 1984, sMALL TALK, Athletic Director Gene Clayton announced that Methodist would add two varsity sports: women's soccer in the fall of 1984 and women's golf in the spring of 1985. Clayton gave two reasons for the move: 1) the NCAA requirement that member schools offer at least four varsity sports for women, and 2) the need for more female students.

The editorial page in this issue focused on two problem areas at Methodist. Patty Smith described the Classroom Building and the Science Building as "dark and deteriorating" and the women's bathroom in the Student Union as "an embarrassment." [51] Mark Powell wrote about student recruitment and how nearby St. Andrews Presbyterian College had increased its enrollment by establishing niche markets for educating and rehabilitating handicapped persons, by entering the computer science field, and by targeting specific high school students. "Methodist needs to modernize its programs in the field which it feels are its best shot at getting a niche in the student marketplace," said Powell, adding, "To establish a strong program in any field, money must be spent." [52]

Guest lecturers at Methodist in January and February 1984 included:; Dr. William McFeely, winner of the 1981 Pulitzer Prize for his biography of Ulysees S. Grant; Malcolm S. Miller, tour guide at Chartres Cathedral in France, and local artist Mellen-Thomas Benedict, who spoke about "Stained Glass From Its Gothic Heritage Through the Modern Age."

Green and Gold Masque Keys presented Anton Chekhov's socio-comedy *The Sea Gull* February 23-15.

Patty Smith devoted most of her column to the formation of FICUS, the North Carolina Federation of Independent College and University Students to represent the interests of independent schools at the state government level. She said Kenny Hall, S.G.A. president, and Mark Powell of the *sMALL TALK* editorial board member, were part of a FICUS delegation that met with North Carolina Governor Jim Hunt and William Friday, president of the UNC system, January 30, 1984 at the Governor's Mansion in Raleigh.

Both Hunt and Friday took questions about the tuition gap between state-supported schools and private schools. Noting that "both public and private schools need more money," Hunt said the problem of equitable state funding would not be solved in the near future or possibly forever. [53]

A Mark Powell news story on the front page of the February 27,1984 *sMALL TALK* dealt with the Raleigh meeting in more detail. Powell quoted Hunt as saying North Carolina did more to aid North Carolina residents attending private schools [through its Legislative Tuition Grants] than any state in the Southeast.

Another front page story reported that Methodist's Greatest Gift Scholarship Program had been changed from a single-year award to a four-year award. The College-funded program paid one-quarter of the current year's tuition to students recruited by MC alumni. Pat Clayton, director of alumni affairs, was quoted as saying the scholarship was renewable if the recipient maintained a 2.0 GPA at the end of each academic year.

Athletes recruited by MC coaches were ineligible to receive a Greatest Gift. Gene Clayton said this exclusion was needed to comply with NCAA rules that athletes in Division III schools could not receive scholarships based on their athletic ability. He said the new Incentive Scholarship program awarding resident students up to $3,000 based on SAT scores and high school rank and guaranteeing work-study jobs for resident students were "more important recruiting tools than the Greatest Gift." [54]

The editorial page reprinted a guest editorial by Gwen Sykes '68, MC's director of publications and cheerleading coach, which had appeared in *The Fayetteville Observer-Times*. In her editorial, Mrs. Sykes quoted the Council of Independent Colleges as saying small private colleges in America were in danger not only from insufficient funds or too few students, but also from a public misunderstanding of "the purpose, place, and the value of small independent colleges in American society." [55]

A news brief on an inside page reported that the Fort Bragg Schools' new middle school had been dedicated November 18, 1982 to the memory of lst Lt. Kenneth H. Albritton, who attended Methodist College from 1964-66. A Fayetteville native who was killed in action in Vietnam, Albritton was awarded the Silver Star posthumously for gallantry against a hostile force.

A sports story reported that Joseph Pereira, 28, former assistant coach of the College's men's soccer team, had been hired as head coach of women's soccer and women's tennis. A native of Fall River Massachusetts, Pereira played soccer at Appalachian State University and Warren Wilson College. He was then teaching at Spring Lake Junior High School. The story said the women's soccer program at Methodist would be the fifth collegiate women's program in North Carolina.

The March 13, 1984 *sMALL TALK* announced that Vickie Smith, a junior from Cape Coral, Florida, was running unopposed for S.G.A. president and profiled the two candidates running for vice president and secretary.

William Faulkner's effect on Southern writers was the subject of Methodist's 1984 Southern Writers Lecture Series March 23-24. Guest lecturers included authors Lucy Daniels Inman, Shelby Stephenson (UNC-P), Madison Jones (Auburn U.) Peter Taylor (U.VA) and Will Campbell.

CHAPTER 6

A feature by Mark Powell profiled Charles Morris, a business major from Newport News, Virginia, and his work as a metal sculptor. A news brief reported that tenor Richard Bicoy, a junior at Methodist, had been named top male vocalist at the annual student auditions at the N.C. Chapter of the National Teachers of Music held March 2-3 at East Carolina University.

The spring sports news was generally good. The Monarch baseball team was ranked second in the South with a record of 15-4, three of the four losses were against Division I schools N.C. State, Wake Forest, and South Carolina.

Methodist's men's golf team won the NCAA Division III District 3 Golf Tournament at Quail Ridge Golf Club with a 618 combined score. Mike Hartman shot 156 to take Medalist honors.

Methodist's cheerleaders won the first annual Dixie Conference Cheerleading Championship at Rocky Mount. Co-captains Ann Johnson and Rennie Stack were understandably elated.

The Methodist College Foundation's 1984 Loyalty Fund Drive netted $102,464 on Loyalty Day February 22 and $126,000 through March 13. Campaign Chairman I. B. Julian led the campaign which had as its theme, "Partners in Progress." Dr. Dennis Jackson predicted the 1984 campaign would exceed the 1983 total of $175,000 and the 1982 total of $141,000.

The Haymount United Methodist Church Youth Choir presented excerpts from an original drama entitled *He Traced Me* Sunday, March 25 in Hensdale Chapel.

A lengthy feature story by James Arvantes in the April 13, 1984 *sMALL TALK* profiled Ike O'Hanlon, 71, chairman of the Methodist College Board of Trustees. A Fayetteville native, O'Hanlon was noted for his booming bass voice and keen sense of humor. He attended Wake Forest College and was accepted to law school there but withdrew because he stammered; he eventually overcame his speech impediment. From 1935-1941, he worked for the National Reconstruction Finance Committee.

When World War II broke out, O'Hanlon was turned down for military service due to age, but worked as an agent for the U.S. government in Texas (monitoring political activity in Mexico). He later worked for Orkin Extermination Co. in New Orleans and Raleigh before founding Antex Exterminating Company in Fayetteville in 1955. He served in the N.C. General Assembly from 1953-55 and 1963-67. He and his wife Emma had three sons; one son, Michael, died in childhood. In 1971, the O'Hanlons donated funds to build O'Hanlon Amphitheater on the Methodist campus in memory of their son Michael.

O'Hanlon predicted Methodist College would have a new gymnasium within five years. He also noted that the Board of Trustees would meet soon

1980–1984

with a Raleigh real estate developer to consider "the amount of land the College should hold on to and how much should be sold." [56]

A news story on the back page reported that Methodist had awarded *full-tuition* Presidential Scholarships to the students from the current sophomore, junior, and senior classes with the highest GPA and to qualified freshmen who had received top marks on the Methodist College Scholarship Exam and personal interviews. Bill Lowdermilk said the scholarships, established to honor Dr. Richard Pearce, the College's second president, were designed to attract academically promising students and to recognize students who had achieved success in academics.

The April 30, 1984 *sMALL TALK* reported that tuition and fees would rise in 1984-85 to $4,200, making the total cost $6,400 for a resident student, (including $800 for room and $1,400 for board) and $4,200 for a commuting student.

The lead editorial by Mark Powell suggested that Methodist might become Eastern Methodist University in the future, but "must remain small to retain its character—truth and virtue." A news brief on the editorial page noted that *sMALL TALK, Carillon,* and *Tapestry* would be governed by a four-man editorial board in 1984-85 made up of Dale Cook, Wendy Smith, Troy Jones, and Richard Briggs. Individual editors of each publication would answer to the editorial board.

A sports story reported that the MC baseball team had won 30 games, was ranked 7th nationally, and stood a good chance of receiving a bid to the NCAA Division III regionals and advancing to the College World Series. Coach Tom Austin said the team had an "awesome" record for offensive production, batting .360 and averaging 10.3 runs per game. He said Dennis Forbes set a new school record with seven home runs, while Mike Currie broke his own record with 56 runs batted in.

An inside story reported that Sgt. Mark T. Ross had received Methodist's first Military Appreciation Scholarship worth $250-$450 per semester. The MAS was designed for full-time military students given a semester to attend college full-time as part of the re-enlistment option and for service members within one semester of attaining an associate or bachelor's degree.

President gives MC's first Military Appreciation Scholarship.

― CHAPTER 6 ―

College Awards Three Honorary Degrees

The May 1984 *Methodist College Today* reported on the inauguration of Dr. M. Elton Hendricks (see previous reference in this chapter), the College's 21st spring commencement, and a successful alumni phonathon.

In a commencement address May 6, 1984, Albert Dunn, president and CEO of Kelly-Springfield Corp., urged the 72 members of the Class of 1984 "to remain positive in attitude and in outlook." [57]

President Hendricks presented honorary doctorates to Bishop William R. Cannon, Fayetteville artist William C. Fields, the Reverend Warren B. Petteway, and the Reverend Ernest R. Porter. Cheryl Lynn Epperson received the Stacy Weaver Award.

In alumni news, *MCT* reported that Fayetteville resident Mark Kendrick '83 had received the Jefferson Award for Community Service at WTVD-TV 11 studios in Durham March 26, 1984. An active Democrat, owner of Kendricks Real Estate and president of the Fayetteville Jaycees, Kendricks estimated he spent 50 percent of his time in volunteer community service.

A center photo spread featured photos and graphic charts of the 1984 alumni phonathon led by Gene and Pat Clayton and a team of staff and student volunteers. Pat Clayton reported that by May 9, 1984, 423 alumni had given $20,000 toward a goal of $38,000.

In sports news, *MCT* announced that Joe Pereira had been hired as the first women's soccer coach at Methodist and would field the first women's team in the fall of 1984.

Trustees Receive Good News

The Board of Trustees received some good news at its May 24, 1984 meeting. Mr. Lowdermilk reported that the Methodist College Foundation's 1984 Loyalty Campaign had generated $155,638 and that the Alumni Loyalty Campaign had garnered over $22,000 (from 436 alumni), a 90 percent increase over the preceding year.

President Hendricks reported that applications were up and that 35 more returning students had registered than last year. He also said 85 percent of the trustees had contributed to the College in 1984, compared to less than 50 percent in 1983.

The Reverend Sam McMillan reported that The Reverend Tom Holtsclaw, pastor of Campground United Methodist Church in Fayetteville, had organized a work team of several ministers and one layman to paint the inside of the dormitories at Methodist. The board directed Ike O'Hanlon, board chair, to send Reverend Holtsclaw a letter of appreciation.

Dr. Hendricks reported that Methodist's men's golf team had placed second in the nation in NCAA Division III, that Golf Coach Gene Clayton had been voted Coach of the Year, and that the Monarch baseball team was runner-up in the Division III regionals.

At a July 19, 1984 meeting of the trustees' Executive Committee, Dr. Hendricks reported that Methodist College had received a Title IV federal grant to fund a three-year program of educational support services for first generation college students. He said Paul Eaglin, a local attorney, had been hired as Director of Special Academic Services. He also noted that Dr. Lynn V. Sadler would begin work August 15 as academic dean.

Gwen Sykes helps with the 1984 phonathon.

Enrollment Climbs

The trustees' Executive and Investment committees held a joint meeting September 18, 1984 and voted to; 1)authorize Dr. Hendricks to invest $500,000 contributed by Mr. Charles Reeves in the Triveset Venture Fund, and 2) recommend to the full Board of Trustees that the firm of Gardner and Preston Moss, Inc. be employed to manage the endowment of Methodist College.

The full Board of Trustees welcomed five new trustees at its October 2, 1984 meeting: Frank Barragan Jr., Admiral Elmo R. Zumwalt, Mrs. Terri Union, the Reverend H. Sidney Huggins, and Mr. Albert W. Dunn.

President Hendricks reported that fall 1984 enrollment had reached 699 full-time students, with an F.T.E. of 727, an evening head count of 195, 281 dormitory students, and a total head count (day and evening) of 959.

Dr. Lynn Sadler, academic dean, reported that new majors in arts management, computer science, and communications had been added, along with a hooding ceremony at graduation. She asked for financial support of two initiatives by the spring 1985 semester: a reduction in faculty teaching loads and the establishment of a Computer Assisted Composition Laboratory that, she promised, would give the College national visibility.

In other matters, the trustees:
- —tabled a contract for management of the College endowment at the urging of Walter Clark.
- —approved a plan for Methodist to teach English and math to 100 Saudi Arabian Army officers per year over a three-year period.

— CHAPTER 6 —

—allocated $364,000 in income from additonal students to fund new positions in the Financial Aid, Development, and Maintenance offices. $15,000 in deferred maintenance, and $151,000 for unbudgeted financial aid.

—Amended the College's TIAA/CREF Retirement Plan, effective January 1, 1985, to cover clerical and maintenance employees, with the College contributing five percent of each employee's salary annually.

College Begins 25th School Year With New Deans

The lead story in *sMALL TALK's* first issue of 1984-85 dated August 26, 1984, described a number of new administrators and faculty: Dr. Mary Lynn Sadler, academic dean; Chuck Lipe, registrar; Dr. Kenneth Collins, campus minister; Ms. Catherine Shuford in religion; Dr. Dwight House in computer science; Ms. Patricia Jones in math; Paul Eaglin, director of special services for the Title IV program; Ms. Nancy Bosher in English (replacing Dr. Janet Cavano, who had taken a one-year leave of absence).

Another front page story listed six new appointees to the Methodist College Board of Trustees: Admiral Elmo Zumwalt Jr. of Arlington, VA, Albert W. Dunn of Cumberland, Md., and Fayetteville residents Frank Barragan Jr., Bobby Allen, Ms. Terri Union, and the Reverend Sid Huggins.

Dr. Lynn Veach Sadler, the new academic dean and successor to the late Fred Clark, came to Methodist from Bennett College in Greensboro where she was head of the English Department and director of the Division of Humanities. A native of Warsaw, N.C., she was a *magna cum laude* graduate of Duke University and held M.A. and Ph.D. degrees from the University of Illinois. She also did post doctoral work at UCLA, Bryn Mawr, and Balliol College of Oxford University.

Dr. Lynn Sadler

An inside news story reported that Dr. Robert Perkins, dean of students, was organizing a Parents' Council and planning MC's first Parents' Weekend for September 28-30, 1984. A story on Page 4 listed the events for Homecoming '84, "A Night in New Orleans," October 12-14, with a large photo of The Fabulous Waller Family Band. This newspaper also contained a half page ad promoting the Methodist College Invitational Soccer Tournament September 14-15.

The sports page reported that the men's golf team had finished as second runner-up in the 1984 National Golf Tournament in May. A large picture of

Coach Gene Clayton and the five members of the golf team appeared on Page 7, with Clayton holding the NCAA trophy. Clayton was also named NCAA Golf Coach of the Year for NCAA District III.

The back page listed 25 cultural events in a Humanities Series, and said students could earn one-half semester hour of credit by attending 12 events. This was described as an alternative to the former system of mandatory convocations. Attendance was to be verified by ticket stubs, and students had to write a brief evaluation of each event on the ticket.

The October 4, 1984 *sMALL TALK* described the Miss Methodist College pageant and the crowning of Tammy Lynn Tolar, a sophomore from Fayetteville, as Miss Methodist College. In a rather unusual news story carried on the editorial page, Troy Jones described a debate between Alex Morrow and Frank Bowden, who were vying for the post of president of the Black Student Movement.

An inside photo showed North Carolina poet laureate Sam Ragan addressing the newly formed Friends of Davis Library September 23. Also pictured inside were 12 members of the Pi Kappa pledge class at the end of Greek Rush '84. A news brief announced that the U.S. Air Force Band and Singing Sergeants would give concerts in Reeves Auditorium the nights of October 15 and 16.

Homecoming 1984 dominated the front page of the October 29, 1984 *sMALL TALK* with a photo of Emma Bet Getachew being crowned homecoming queen and another shot of the MC cheerleaders dumping water on the men's soccer team from the east balcony of the Student Union. A two-page center spread contained other pictorial highlights from homecoming.

A news brief on the back page reported that *sMALL TALK* had received an honors rating of first class for the 13th year in a row following a critical review of the newspaper by the Associated Collegiate Press based at the University of Minnesota.

The October 29 and November 16 issues of the student newspaper promoted the November 18 performance of Cecil Effinger's oratorio *The Invisible Fire* by the Methodist College Chorus and a 35-piece orchestra. Michael Best, a Metropolitan Opera tenor and Durham, N.C. native, was slated to portray John Wesley. The oratorio recounted major events from Wesley's life and was co-sponsored by The North Carolina Conference of The United Methodist Church and Methodist College to celebrate the 200th anniversary of Methodism in America. At its annual meeting in June, The North Carolina Conference had dedicated the concert to the Reverend William P. Lowdermilk "for his immeasurable service to the Conference, the College, and the communities he had served." [58]

— CHAPTER 6 —

The Invisible Fire *oratorio was performed November 18, 1984 in honor of Bill Lowdermilk.*

Methodist College held its first "Iterations" lecture November 30, 1984, at which Dr. John Sill and Dr. Sue Kimball read papers about George Orwell's novel *1984*. In other faculty news, Jean Ishee, assistant professor of music was the subject of a lengthy feature story about her 25 years of teaching organ and piano at Methodist.

The Cape Fear River Research Institute Symposium held at Methodist on Halloween 1984 featured a slide show by Roy Parker, editor of *The Fayetteville Times,* documenting the history of the Cape Fear River and Fayetteville as well as a paper read by Dr. James Clifton of Southeastern Community College.

The 1984 men's soccer team finished its season 5-8-4 overall and 2-2-3 in the Dixie Conference. The women's soccer team finished its inaugural season 6-9 and 2-2 in the conference.

The December 14, 1984 *sMALL TALK* included an announcement by Dr. Lynn Sadler that Dr. Wendy Greene would be joining the College in January as the director of the new Computer Assisted Composition Laboratory. Located in a classroom in the Trustees Classroom Building, the lab was equipped with 12 IBM personal computers for use by the English Department.

In a news story on an inside page, Director of Continuing Education George Bonville reported that 100 active duty soldiers were currently attending Methodist as a result of recruitment efforts by the College's Fort Bragg Office.

On Page 4, *sMALL TALK* ran pictures of three male students the newspaper staff had chosen for submission to the English Leather Musk Man 1985 Competition. The "hunks" so honored were: senior Mike Baker of Bangor, Maine, junior Richard Briggs of Fairfield, Iowa, and sophomore Bill Knowlton of Fayetteville.

Jim Martin Visits Campus

The lead story in the November 1984 *Methodist College Today* described a visit to Methodist by Republican gubernatorial candidate Jim Martin Wednesday, October 31, 1984.

In a convocation address in Reeves Auditorium, Martin said he:
>—supported merit pay for teachers
>—favored using the military (Coast Guard and National Guard) to combat drug trafficking.
>—opposed government funding of elective abortions.
>—opposed the proposed Equal Rights Amendment to the U.S. Constitution.
>—favored a system of burning and burying uranium waste.

Soccer Coach Joe Pereira instructs Lori Silvery.

This *MCT* included two full-page articles by Dr. Lynn V. Sadler, academic dean. One was the full text of a speech she had given to new trustees October 1, 1984 in which she mentioned potential new academic programs at Methodist (*e.g.* a Master of Education program) and the importance of encouraging and supporting scholarly work by faculty. The other Sadler article described the purpose of Methodist's new Computer Assisted Composition Lab in the Classroom Building and how it would change pedagogy in English and related disciplines.

Also included in this newspaper was the full text of remarks by Bill Lowdermilk at the 1984 faculty dinner in which he recalled his first stint hosting the Annual Conference Session (ACS) of United Methodist Youth for The North Carolina Conference in the summer of 1963. He said an adult ACS counselor accused him of "selling his soul" by leaving the ministry to come to Methodist College. He said he had been inspired by the interest taken in students by Charles McAdams, Sam Edwards, and many others. He said he had enjoyed recruiting and ministering to MC students over two decades and was now seeing the fruits of the College's labors in the achievements of its alumni. He urged faculty members to take time to listen to and counsel students "when they knock on your door." [59]

In other news from the fall of 1984, trustee and benefactor John Hensdale was the subject of a feature article and was pictured with four of the eight current recipients of his Hensdale Scholarship. Another news story recounted

— CHAPTER 6 —

Hensdale Scholars meet with their benefactor, John Hensdale.

the organizational meeting of Friends of Davis Memorial Library and the election of Mrs. Sanford Doxey as its first president.

Trustees Change Two Policies

Dr. Hendricks told the trustees' Executive committee November 29, 1984 that a search for a development director would begin in January 1985. At the suggestion of Dr. McMillan, the committee voted to change the criteria for trustee emeritus to reserve that designation for those who had served a minimum of ten years.

Members of the trustees' Investment Committee met December 6, 1984 and approved a Methodist College Investment Policy.

END NOTES
Chapter Six

1. Richard Pearce, remarks to the Methodist College Board of Trustees April 1, 1980, TM, Book 3.
2. Sam Ragan, commencement address May 4, 1980, *Bulletin of Methodist College,* May 1980. file.
3. Richard Pearce, fall convocation address August 27, 1980, *sMALL TALK,* September 5, 1980, file.
4. Richard Pearce, remarks to the Methodist College Board of Trustees November 14, 1980, TM, Book 3.
5. Sam McMillan, report to the Methodist College Board of Trustees, April 15, 1981, TM, Book 3.
6. Calvert Ray, report to the Methodist College Board of Trustees April 15, 1981, TM. Book 3.
7. Minutes of the Methodist College Board of Trustees, April 15, 1981, TM, Book 3.
8. Terry Sanford, commencement address May 3, 1981, *Bulletin of Methodist College,* June 1981, Vol. 22, No. 2, file.
9. Citation presented to Terry Sanford May 3, 1981, *Bulletin of Methodist College,* May 1975, Vol. 16, No. 3, file.
10. Richard Pearce, report to the Methodist College Board of Trustees November 20, 1981, TM, Book 3.
11. Ibid.
12. Sports story, *sMALL TALK,* March 19, 1982, file.
13. Richard Pearce, report to the Methodist College Board of Trustees April 16, 1982, TM, Book 3.
14. Ibid.
15. Gil Wise, S.G.A. president, remarks to the Methodist College Board of Trustees November 16, 1982, TM, Book 4.
16. Ibid.
17. Richard Pearce, remarks to the Methodist College Board of Trustees, November 16, 1982, TM, Book 4.
18. Ibid.
19. Richard Pearce, fall convocation address September 3, 1982, file.
20. Ibid.
21. Richard Pearce, report to the Methodist College Board of Trustees April 13, 1978, TM, Book 3.
22. Motapula Chabuka, speaking at a College convocation December 8, 1982, *sMALL TALK,* December 13, 1982, file.

— CHAPTER 6 —

23. Sam McMilllan, reporting for the Board of Higher Education Study Committee, The North Carolina Conference of The United Methodist Church, to the Methodist College Board of Trustees Executive Committee January 19, 1983, TM, Book 4.
24. Jeffrey Johnston, a report to the Methodist College Board of Trustees Executive Committee March 24, 1983, TM, Book 4.
25. Ibid.
26. Ibid.
27. Ibid.
28. Ibid.
29. Ibid.
30. Dillard Teer, chair of the Presidential Search Committee, reporting to the Methodist College Board of Trustees August 11, 1983, TM, Book 34.
31. Ike O'Hanlon, remarks to Dr. M. Elton Hendricks at the August 11, 1983 meeting of the Methodist College Board of Trustees, TM, Book 4.
32. Richard Pearce, remarks to the Methodist College Board of Trustees August 11, 1983 TM, Book 4.
33. M. Elton Hendricks, remarks at a press conference August 11, 1983, *The Fayetteville Observer*, August 11, 1983.
34. M. Elton Hendricks, remarks to the Methodist College Board of Trustees October 4, 1983, TM, Book 4.
35. M. Elton Hendricks, remarks to *sMALL TALK* editors Steve Owens and Patty Smith, *sMALL TALK*, August 27, 1983, file.
36. Richard Pearce, remarks to *sMALL TALK* editor Mark Powell, *sMALL TALK,* August 27, 1983.
37. Ibid.
38. Kenny Hall, S.G.A. president, letter to the editor, *sMALL TALK*, August 27, 1983, file.
39. Mark Powell, critical review, sMALL TALK, October 7, 1983, file.
40. M. Elton Hendricks, remarks to the Methodist College Board of Trustees November 17, 1983, TM, Book 4.
41. Terry Sanford, remarks at a panel discussion April 14, 1984, *The Fayetteville Observer-Times*, April 15, 1984, file.
42. Ibid.
43. M. Elton Hendricks, inaugural address April 15, 1984, *The Fayetteville Observer-Times*, April 15, 1984, file.
44. Ibid.

45. M. Elton Hendricks, inaugural address April 14, 1984, *sMALL TALK*, May 1984, file.
46. Ibid.
47. Ibid.
48. Ibid.
49. Ibid.
50. Ibid.
51. Mark Powell, editorial in *sMALL TALK*, February 1984, file.
52. Ibid.
53. James B. Hunt, remarks to FICUS delegates January 30, 1984 at the Governor's Mansion in Raleigh, N.C., quoted by Patty Smith in a *sMALL TALK* news story, *sMALL TALK*, February 6, 1984, file.
54. Gene Clayton, athletic director, quoted in a *sMALL TALK* news story, *sMALL TALK*, February 27, 1984, file.
55. Gwen Sykes, *Fayetteville Observer-Times* guest editorial reprinted in *sMALL TALK*, February 27, 1984, file.
56. Ike O'Hanlon, interview with James Arvantes, *sMALL TALK*, April 13, 1984, file.
57. Albert Dunn, commencement address May 6, 1984, *Methodist College Today*, May 1984, file.
58. Front page news story, *sMALL TALK*, November 16, 1984, file.
59. Bill Lowdermilk, feature story, *Methodist College Today*, November 1984, file.

Chapter 7

A 'Miracle' Unfolds
1985-89

"I have been interested in Methodist College since its founding, and I have never seen anything like the progress made since Dr. Hendricks has been president. It's a miracle."

—Ike O'Hanlon, chair of the Board of Trustees, addressing the trustees' Executive Committee September 15, 1988.

At a January 31, 1985, meeting of the Methodist College Board of Trustees, Dr. Hendricks reported that Dr. Ted Jaeger had been appointed interim dean of students and that Dennis Gregory would succeed Jaeger in June. He said the Computer-Assisted Composition Lab in the Classroom Building was open and operating.

Dr. Hendricks announced the receipt of several major gifts: $90,000 from a charitable remainder trust, a $50,000 bequest in memory of an alumnus, 10,000 shares of South Carolina National Bank stock valued at between $580,000 and $590,000, and $25,000 for updating and replacing the lighting and sound systems in Reeves Auditorium. He also announced that trustee emeritus Bill Horner had pledged $20,000 if an additional $20,000 was given to "take advantage of the government's offer to accept 50 percent of outstanding loans." [1]

The board approved the following fees for 1985-86: tuition—$4,700; board—$1,550; room—$800, making the total cost for a resident student $7,100. In addition, the trustees amended the College bylaws to state that any trustee who had served a minimum of ten years could be elected a trustee emeritus.

On the recommendation of Walter Clark, the trustees amended the College investment policy to eliminate percentage restrictions on the investment of funds in stocks and bonds.

Louis Spilman, chair of the trustees' Development Committee, listed short and long term goals, including the hiring of a director of development and the active participation of local trustees in the Methodist College Foundation's annual fund drive.

The trustees' Investment Committee met March 5, 1985, and voted to sell 10,000 shares of SCNB stock and options on 1,000 shares of Exxon Common

— CHAPTER 7 —

Stock and 1,000 shares of GTE Common Stock. The sale of the SCNB stock at $35 a share netted $350,000, with $211,000 going to pay off a loan at Mid-South Bank in Sanford, $20,000 to match Bill Horner's gift, and the balance to support the College's economics and business program.

Members of the trustees' Executive Committee received a positive report on spring 1985 enrollment at the group's March 28, 1985, meeting. Dr. Hendricks said the College had a spring head count of 1,035 (day and evening) with an FTE of 794. He then noted that this increase made $150,000 available for special, unbudgeted items.

The committee discussed the Land Use Study by Rose and Purcell and authorized President Hendricks to talk with developers about implementing Plan B of the study.

Sykes Appointed To Maintenance Post

In its January 31, 1985, issue, *sMALL TALK* reported that Mason Sykes, former soccer coach and tennis coach, had been named superintendent of buildings and grounds. Sykes was succeeded in his coaching position by Mike Parsons, who came to Methodist from Stetson University in Florida. Parsons became head coach of soccer and tennis and director of intramurals.

Elsewhere in that issue:
—The basketball teams struggled in 1984-85. The men's squad lost five players at Christmas for academic reasons. The women were 0-6 in the conference.
—In his record review column, "Tom's Tidbits," Tom Jumalon lauded Lionel Ritchie, who had just won six American Music Awards.

In its March 15, 1985, issue, *sMALL TALK* devoted the entire front page to an interview with College President M. Elton Hendricks; the interviewer was John Marshall Jones. Dr. Hendricks spent a great deal of time explaining a $500 increase in tuition and fees. He said Methodist needed funds to raise faculty salaries and reduce the teaching load from 15 to 12 hours a week. The president said the College also needed to hire a director of development and address some deferred maintenance needs totalling $250,000.

Dr. Hendricks said Methodist has "the possibility of becoming one of the outstanding small liberal arts colleges in the Southeast." [2] He said the College needed to do three things to get to that point: attract people (donors) with financial resources, attract good students, and strengthen the academic programs.

A hot national issue in early 1985 received considerable space in *sMALL TALK*. In a preliminary budget for the U.S. Department of Education, President

1985–1989

Ronald Reagan came under fire from higher education officials for limiting student financial aid to $4,500 a year and disqualifying families with incomes more than $32,500 a year from the Guaranteed Student Loan (GSL) and Pell Grant programs.

In a survey of 200 U.S. college presidents, 43 percent rated Reagan's higher education programs as "disappointing," while 25 persons labeled them as "poor." Reagan had proposed slashing the U.S. Department of Education budget by $3 billion and had appointed William Bennett, former chairman of the National Endowment for the Humanities, secretary of education.

McDaniel Elected S.G.A. President—Twice

Calvin McDaniel, a sophomore from Fayetteville, was elected S.G.A. president March 25, 1985; but Frank Bowden and Jon Ray challenged the results, claiming the S.G.A. constitution called for a primary election when two or more people run for an office. In a second election, McDaniel won a majority of the votes, Bowden came in second, and Ray was eliminated. In a third and final vote April 1, McDaniel defeated Bowden again.

In addition to McDaniel, the student body elected Natalie Barnette vice president, Mark Peary High Court chief justice, four at-large senators, four day senators, and four dorm senators.

The theme of the third annual Southern Writers Lecture Series held April 19-20, 1985, was "Southern Writing in a Feminist Era." Guest lecturers included novelists Daphne Athas of UNC-Chapel Hill, Jill McCorkle, and Sylvia Wilkinson.

Gene Clayton Named Director of Development

The April 16, 1985, sMALL TALK, announced that President Hendricks had appointed Gene Clayton, veteran coach and athletic director, Methodist's director of development July 1. "I think I can sell Methodist College as well as anyone because I believe in it strongly," said Clayton. [3]

"Gene comes into the program with the qualities I was looking for," said Dr. Hendricks. "He is successful in whatever he undertakes, he is hard-working, he is highly organized, and he has phenomenal drive." [4]

Gene Clayton

Although he coached men's basketball, women's tennis, men's tennis, and golf, it was in golf that he brought national recognition to Methodist. Clayton said he had enjoyed watching MC athletes accomplish their goals over the previous 22 years and was especially proud that "we've had eleven All-American golfers in the past five years." [5]

— CHAPTER 7 —

In other news:
— Two of Alan Porter's voice students took first place in auditions of the National Association of Teachers of Singing held March 29-30 at UNC-Charlotte. Richard Bicoy took first place in the college/senior men's division, and Laura Kafka Kernek took first in the junior women's division.
— The women's softball team won the Dixie Conference title in 1985, while the baseball team finished second in the DIAC to N.C. Wesleyan.
— The 1985 men's golf team won the conference title and finished fourth in the national tournament.

Hooding, Flags Become Part of Graduation

Methodist College added a hooding ceremony to its graduation exercise May 5, 1985, in which graduating seniors chose a sponsor (mother/father/husband/wife/friend) to follow them on stage and set their baccalaureate hoods in place as they received their diplomas from the president. Richard Bicoy, a music major from Hawaii, was the first student hooded—by his mother, who also gave her son a lei of fresh flowers.

Al-Azimi presents the flag of Kuwait.

Talal F.M.M. Al-Azimi began another new tradition by presenting the flag of Kuwait, his native country, to the College. Won Hyung Un then presented the flag of Korea. Dr. Hendricks announced that all future international students would be invited to present the flag of his/her country at his/her graduation (if the College did not already have that flag) and that these flags would be carried in future graduation processionals and recessionals.

Eighty-one seniors received degrees at Methodist's 22nd spring commencement. Heather Ross Miller, North Carolina Poet of the Year in 1983, delivered the commencement address. Roger Pait received the Stacy Weaver Award.

President Hendricks awarded three honorary degrees: a Doctor of Letters to Ms. Miller, and Doctor of Divinity degrees to the Reverend Vernon Tyson and the Reverend Al Simonton. Tyson was then serving as pastor of Edenton Street United Methodist Church in Raleigh, while Simonton was the editor of the *North Carolina Christian Advocate*, the newspaper serving The North Carolina Conference of The United Methodist Church.

Clayton and Austin Assume New Jobs

President Hendricks announced two major appointments at the Board of Trustees May 9, 1985, meeting. He said Gene Clayton would become director of development and Tom Austin would become athletic director.

At the same meeting, Dr. Lucille Hutaff reported that the trustees' Academic Affairs Committee had approved granting tenure to Dr. J. Ann Clark, Ms. Silvana Foti, Dr. Sue Kimball, Mr. Walter Swing, and Mrs. Norma Womack. She said the following were approved for promotion: Dr. Sue Kimball and Dr. Wayne Preslar to full professor and Ms. Womack to associate professor. The trustees accepted the recommendations.

President Makes Key Staff Changes

The May 1985 issue of *Methodist College Today,* announced several major staff appointments effective July 1: Gene Clayton, director of development; Dr. Dennis Gregory, dean of students; and Tom Austin, athletic director. In addition, Joy Cogswell was named director of the Community Music Program, and Gwen Sykes was named director of special projects. The publication also noted that Dr. Robert Christian, professor of English, and Dr. Sue Kimball, associate professor of English, had received grants for summer study from the National Endowment for the Humanities; Christian to study English Romanticism at Yale, and Kimball to study Chaucer's Language Games at Columbia.

In an April 26, 1985, address sponsored by the North Carolina Southeastern Consortium for International Education, retired Admiral Elmo Zumwalt praised President Ronald Reagan for taking a hard line in arms negotiations with the Soviet Union.

In alumni news, *MCT* reported that Tommy Yow '66 had been named president of Martin Junior College in Pulaski, Tennessee. Yow was then serving as assistant to the president of Louisburg College. [He was inaugurated president April 19, 1986.] *MCT* reprinted a feature article from *Carolina Magazine* in Columbia, S.C., profiling Roy Philpott '76 and his work as a *guardian ad litem.*

In sports news:
— The 1985 women's softball team, coached by Dan Lawrence, won the Dixie Conference Championship with a record of 11-1.
— The Methodist College cheerleaders won the Dixie Conference Championship February 23, 1985.
— The golf team finished fourth in the NCAA Division III National Championship.
— The baseball team lost to Swarthmore in the NCAA Division III Mid-Atlantic regional, ending its season 32-14.

— CHAPTER 7 —

College Launches Nursing Program

The lead story in the August 16, 1985, *sMALL TALK* reported that Methodist was launching a Bachelor of Science in Nursing degree completion program in the fall. Dr. Hendricks and Dr. Sadler said the new program would add 12 courses and clinical experiences to the College curriculum in the next three years and that four faculty members and an administrator would be added. Dr. Hendricks said 20 full-time and 10 part-time students were expected in the first session, with enrollment growing to between 80 and 100 students.

In other fall 1985 news:

—*sMALL TALK's* editorial board for 1985-86 consisted of Tom Jumalon, Tanya Riley, and Kyle Frost.

—A page one feature story described the development of a nature trail under the direction of Dr. Linda Sue Barnes, with help from Mason Sykes, senior biology major Alan Mintz, and several other students.

New faculty and staff members for 1985-86 included: Alan Robinson, director of public information and public relations; Dennis Gregory, vice president for student affairs and dean of students; Carol Binzer, assistant dean for residence life and Kathie Harrison, assistant dean for student activities; Fiore Bergamasco, assistant professor of physical education and coach of cross country and track for men and women; Marie Blackwell, interim director of the bachelor of science in nursing program; Hal Morrison, assistant professor of physical education and golf coach; Dr. Richard G. Walsh, assistant professor of religion; Samuel Clark, instructor of business; Dr. Kay Huggins, associate professor of history; Jane Weeks Townsend, assistant professor of music.

MCT Notes Alumni Achievements

The August 1985 *Methodist College Today* reported the following alumni news:

—Tom Miriello '70 had been promoted to State Director of Alcohol and Drug Services for the North Carolina Division of Mental Health.

—Jim Darden '69 of Clinton, N.C. had published a second book, *Great American Azaleas*.

—Nancy Ruth Best '65 of Four Oaks, N.C. had published *The Birthing*, a book of poetry.

—A total of 703 alumni had given $34,393 to the Alumni Loyalty Fund.

The College magazine also noted that during the summer of 1985, Methodist had hosted a large number of conferences and events: the North Carolina Quilt Symposium, the North Carolina Annual Conference of The United Methodist Church, The North Carolina Conference Music Workshop, the Eastern Carolina Band Front Camp, the United Pentecostal Family Camp, the Annual Conference Session (ACS) of The North Carolina Conference UMYF, the East Coast Cheerleading Camp, and The North Carolina Conference Summer School.

Safley, Gooch Receive Medallions

Twenty-nine students received degrees at Methodist's summer graduation August 20, 1985. State Senator Tony Rand gave the commencement address. Two 1972 graduates—the Reverend Mike Safley and the Reverend Ray Gooch—received Methodist College Medallions.

The fall 1985 women's soccer team included 12 freshmen and two returnees. *sMALL TALK* announced that 26 students had been named to the Dixie Conference All Academic team for 1984-85.

Power Failure Cancels Classes

Methodist experienced a major power outage at 1:10 a.m. Sunday September 29, 1985, when a break occurred in the main underground electric cable. On Monday, September 30, only two buildings on campus—the Trustees Classroom Building and Horner Administration Building—had electricity. Power was restored to the library and the Student Union Tuesday, October 1, but the residence halls, Science Building, and Reeves Fine Arts Building were still without power. On Tuesday afternoon, College officials decided to cancel classes for the remainder of the week and to close the dorms at 6 p.m. Resident students were moved to local hotel rooms.

The residence halls reopened Sunday, October 6, and day classes resumed Monday, October 7.

A Very Good Year for MC

When the Board of Trustees met October 10, 1985, President Hendricks said 1985 had been a great year for Methodist College, with its largest enrollment, the largest percentage of alumni giving ever, over $1.4 million raised, resurfacing of campus roads, and the paving of the road to the baseball field.

The president reported a fall enrollment of 1,302—942 in the day program and 365 in the evening. He said residence hall occupancy had increased 40 students. He said he had met with the Executive Committee of the North Carolina Independent College Fund and was optimistic Methodist would be accepted as a member.

— CHAPTER 7 —

Dr. Hendricks said the College had been offered the Florence Rogers' home, the oldest home in Cumberland County, by the Florence Rogers Charitable Trust, which would move it to the campus. He said the College had agreed to budget $10,000 for five years to match the trust's $50,000 for renovating the house.

In other matters, the trustees:

—retired the debt on Bond '66 for the addition to the Student Union by paying $170,000.

—were told the developers of Woodcroft in Durham had offered the College $4,500 an acre for 300 acres and to split profits from a proposed housing development 50-50, giving the College $3-5 million. Dr. Hendricks said the offer was not well-received by any land development specialist he had contacted.

—approved budget revisions, applying $800,000 in extra revenue due to increased enrollment.

—voted to pay Ketchum and Ketchum $12,000 to do a feasibility study for a $2 million capital campaign to build a gymnasium.

—heard Dr. John Sill, faculty representative, request that faculty salaries and library funding be increased.

In an executive (closed) session, the board approved the recommendation that fees for 1986-87 be set at $5,200 for tuition and $2,600 for room and board, making the total cost $7,800 for a resident student.

At the same board meeting, the trustees approved a resolution agreeing to indemnify present and future officers and trustees of the College against any costs incurred as a result of any claim or lawsuit in which he or she might be involved as an officer or trustee of Methodist College, Incorporated.

In their final meeting of 1985, Dr. Hendricks briefed the trustees on the summer failure of the College's main underground electric cable. He said Carolina Power and Light Co. had been asked to propose a solution to prevent a recurrence of the extensive power failure and to suggest a means whereby the residence halls would not be without power for over twelve hours.

Alcoholic Beverages Allowed at Homecoming

A homecoming committee headed by Calvert Ray decided to have the October 12, 1985, homecoming dance at the Holiday Inn on Cedar Creek Road. Ray said alumni would be allowed to have alcoholic beverages, but that a uniformed officer would be present to assure that students did not consume alcoholic beverages. The band Mainstream was hired for the dance.

Effective September 1, 1986, North Carolina raised its legal age for drinking beer or liquor to 21. In a *sMALL TALK* editorial, Tom Jumalon said the idea of having alcohol for alumni only at the homecoming dance raised a few questions in his mind: 1) Why do you have to have alcohol at any event? 2) Is it fair to students who are not old enough to drink? 3) If you're old enough to vote, enlist in the military, get married and drive, why not be allowed to drink? [6] His questions notwithstanding, Jumalon urged students planning to attend the homecoming dance to abide by College rules and state law.

Mark Twain's A Medieval Romance *was performed as a cabaret theatre.*

Up, Up and Away With the Arts

Homecoming 1985 celebrated "Twenty Years of American Arts" Saturday, October 12. "North Carolina Arts" was the subject of an afternoon panel discussion. Alvin Reiss gave the keynote address, "Twenty Years of American Arts."

Related arts events included a cabaret theatre production of Mark Twain's *A Medieval Romance*, a one-man show by Ian Frost entitled *Byron in Hell*, a lecture on the arts business by Alvin Reiss followed by a panel discussion on arts management, a tea with Anne Hathaway, and a piano recital by Thomas Turner and Walter Saul.

Mainstream, a North Carolina band, played for the homecoming

Bill Lowdermilk welcomes alumni.

dance at the Green Valley Country Club. Della Raeford, a junior history and biology major from Fayetteville, was crowned homecoming queen.

Pat Clayton '68 received the Methodist College Alumni Association's Alumni Service Award at the group's awards banquet October 12, 1985, at the Holiday Inn after serving three years as Methodist's director of alumni affairs. The MCAA presented its Distinguished Alumnus Award to Dr. Thomas Yow III and the Outstanding Faculty Award to Dr. Samuel J. Womack.

Cultural Arts Make News

The October 25, 1985, *sMALL TALK* ran a front page feature story on Paul Wilson, instructor of communications/mass media. Wilson had served as director of development at WFSS, the radio station at Fayetteville State University. He said he hoped Methodist could establish a 10-watt radio station or develop a partnership with WFSS. Wilson said he reviewed movies for WFNC radio and was a volunteer host at WFSS of Sunday afternoon Broadway music and bluegrass music programs.

The Tommy Dorsey Orchestra, conducted by Buddy Morrow, gave a concert in Reeves Auditorium Tuesday, October 25, 1985.

In other news from fall 1985:

— SABOR, a group of Hispanic musicians and dancers, presented a concert Friday, November 15, 1985, in the Student Union. Dr. David Diaz, professor of Spanish at Fayetteville State University, organized the group, composed of Hispanic soldiers stationed at Fort Bragg.

— The Methodist College Chorus held a Bach-B-Que Benefit November 15 on the lawn of Horner Administration Building to raise funds for a European tour in the spring of 1987. A lunch plate consisting of a barbecue sandwich, baked beans, cole slaw, hush puppies, iced tea and cake cost $3.50. Choral Director Alan Porter said Rainbow's End (five singers) and a barbershop quartet would perform with the 35-member chorus. He said the group would need to raise about $40,000 for a European concert tour.

— An inside news brief announced that Methodist had started a fund drive to buy a concert grand piano for Reeves Auditorium.

— Another news story reported that a Scottish-style bagpipe band was being formed in Fayetteville and invited pipers and drummers to audition. The group was named the Cross Creek Pipes and Drums.

— In their second season, the Lady Monarchs soccer team won the conference championship with a 4-0 record. Standout performers were Lisa Milligan, Jill Starke, Becky Burleigh, and Brenda McKimens. The team's season record of 11-8 included losses to NCAA Division I powers William and Mary and N.C. State.

MC Holds Naturalization Ceremony for Cu Phung

Methodist College was the site of a special naturalization ceremony Friday, November 8, 1985, for Cu G. Phung, 22, a junior chemistry major who was smuggled out of Vietnam on a boat in 1979. Special guests included Brig. Gen. Bernard Leffke, chief of staff of the XVIII Airborne Corps at Fort Bragg and Judge Wallace Dixon, a federal magistrate for the U.S. District Court, who administered the oath of allegiance and presented Cu with a certificate of U.S. citizenship.

After Cu's mother paid someone to smuggle her son to Malaysia, Catholic Social Services found foster parents for Cu in Peoria, Illinois. Army 1sr Sgt. John Moore and his wife Diana accepted Cu as their foster son. When Moore was transferred to Fort Bragg, Cu enrolled at Methodist College.

In alumni news from fall 1985, Lynn Gruber '72 joined the college staff as director of alumni affairs, coming to Methodist from a retail sales position at Marriott Seaview Country Club and Resort in Absecon, N.J.

Cu Phung takes oath.

MC Enrolls 195 Soldiers

A front page story in the December 6, 1985, *sMALL TALK* reported that Methodist had enrolled a record 195 active duty military students in the fall 1985 semester, generating $458,250 in tuition. One hundred fifty-five of the military students were classified as freshmen.

The same issue promoted a December 10 concert by the internationally acclaimed Greg Smith Singers in Reeves Auditorium. The group was organized at UCLA in 1955, when Greg Smith was a graduate teaching assistant there.

Terry Sanford Files for U.S. Senate

The January 24, 1986, *sMALL TALK* reported that Terry Sanford, MC trustee, former governor, and recently retired president of Duke University, had announced he would seek the Democratic nomination for the U.S. Senate.

This issue also reported that State Sen. Lura Tally of Fayetteville spoke to 55 winter graduates December 13, 1985, and that Mrs. Karl Berns had received a Methodist College Medallion during commencement.

— CHAPTER 7 —

As the spring 1986 semester began, Methodist announced a Senior Citizens Scholarship Program, waiving tuition for persons age 65 and older.

A list of 21 movies to be shown in the Student Union during the spring semester included *Romancing the Stone*, *The Flamingo Kid*, *Places In the Heart*, and *Flashdance*.

MC Hosts Educational Computing Conference

The February 1986 *Methodist College Today* reported that Methodist College hosted the North Carolina Assessment of Educational Computing Conference February 6-7, 1986. The brainchild of Dr. Lynn Sadler, academic dean, the conference focused on the use of computers in education, the arts and the humanities.

Attendees were able to attend four sessions Friday, February 6, choosing from 37 scheduled presentations. Dr. C. Stuart Hunter, coordinator of computing at Guelph University in Ontario, Canada, gave the keynote address at dinner Friday. A pre-conference workshop focused on word processing, spread sheeting, and data basing, while a post-conference workshop dealt with "Diagrammatic Writing Using Word Processing."

Methodist hosted three performances of Bertolt Brecht's play *Galileo* February 20-22, 1986. Kevin Sullivan, a professional actor, portrayed the world famous astronomer in a production directed by Paul Wilson.

Kevin Sullivan portrays Galileo.

An inside feature article in this *MCT* profiled Billy Thomas '83, who coached The Fayetteville Academy's 1985 soccer team to a state championship. Another story featured Robin Baxley '84, the first woman to coach a boy's sport in a Cumberland County high school. Baxley coached the Douglas Byrd boys' soccer team in its inaugural season; the team notched a 2-5 league record.

An administrative change was announced in this issue, the appointment of Sam Clark '74 as registrar, effective in mid-December 1985. A business and accounting instructor at Methodist, Clark earned his MBA at Campbell University and a law degree at North Carolina Central University.

The alumni news page memorialized The Reverend David Langston '79 who died January 12, 1986, in Burgess, Virginia, and Steve Little '85, of Mardela, Maryland, a soccer alumnus who died January 4 from injuries sustained in a car crash a week earlier.

Trustees Approve Capital Campaign

In a January 30, 1986, meeting, the Methodist College Board of Trustees approved a capital campaign of $2.5 million to secure funds for building a Student Activities Center. Dr. Hendricks told the trustees the Methodist College Foundation had raised $261,00 for the College in 1985.

Howard Lupton, president of the Methodist College Alumni Association, reported that 19 percent of the alumni gave to the College in 1984-85, compared to only 5 percent three years earlier. He said the current goal of the Alumni Loyalty Fund was to have 900 contributors give $55,000.

Baseball Team Plays in College World Series

The March 7, 1986, *sMALL TALK* reported that the Monarch baseball team had a 39-3-2 season and received a bid to the NCAA Division III Championship, where the team finished fourth.

Elaine Porter, associate professor of French, noted that Methodist would offer two semesters of Latin in the fall if there were sufficient enrollment during pre-registration.

MC Establishes Reeves School of Business

At a press conference Wednesday, March 12, 1986, Methodist College announced the establishment of the Charles M. Reeves School of Business, endowed by a gift from Mr. Reeves, a Sanford, N.C. businessman and trustee of the College.

Reeves had a background in banking, railroad car leasing, and real estate development. He graduated from The University of North Carolina in 1940 with a degree in business administration. During World War II, he was a pilot in the U.S. Navy.

After the war, Reeves operated a bus company and founded Provident Finance Company in 1949. He served as president of Provident until 1977 subsequently selling the company to South Carolina National Bank. He also served three terms on the North Carolina Banking Commission, was a Lee County commissioner, and served on the District Executive Committee of the Boy Scouts of America. He and his wife, Sarah Frances Crosby Reeves, had four children—three sons and a daughter. The Reeves were members of St. Luke's United Methodist Church in Sanford.

— CHAPTER 7 —

The Reeves announcement was followed by a noon luncheon attended by 200 business and community leaders. Michael Novak, author and professor at the American Enterprise Institute in Washington, D.C., gave the keynote address.

Charles Reeves

Dr. Elton Hendricks, college president, introduced Dr. Frank Spreng as the director of the Reeves School of Business. Dr. Spreng came to Methodist from Brescia College in Owensboro Kentucky, where he chaired the Division of Business. He held degrees from Duquesne University and The University of Pittsburgh. He had taught business at Duquesne, Penn State, Hampden Sydney College, and Richmond College in England. He listed his areas of interest as micro managerial and labor economics, managerial accounting, law and economics, and the history of economic thought.

Other news reported in the May 1986 issue of *Methodist College Today* included:

— The study of novelist Carson McCullers and her work at MC's sixth annual Southern Writers Symposium. A Georgia native best known for *The Heart Is a Lonely Hunter*, lived briefly in Fayetteville where she wrote her second novel, *Reflections In a Golden Eye*. The symposium's keynote speaker was Dr. Virginia Carr, author of *The Lonely Hunter*, a McCullers biography. Fifteen papers about McCullers and her writings were read by various literary scholars.

—Murray O. Duggins '66 of Fayetteville was the subject of a feature article by Lynn Gruber. A real estate broker and licensed contractor, Duggins was a principal owner or partner in 19 businesses in North and South Carolina.

College Awards 93 Degrees

Methodist College awarded 93 degrees at its 23rd spring commencement Sunday, May 11, 1986. Lt. Gov. Robert D. Jordan III, the commencement speaker, urged class members to carefully make decisions after graduating and to choose the career path with the greatest opportunity for growth and satisfaction.

The Reverend F. Belton Joyner Jr., executive director of The North Carolina Conference Council on Ministries of The United Methodist Church, delivered the baccalaureate sermon Sunday morning. Jean Lemke received the Stacy Weaver Award.

1985–1989

L to R, Bob Jordan, Joel Fleishman, Reverend Belton Joyner, and President Hendricks.

President Hendricks awarded honorary doctorates to Fayetteville native Joel Fleishman, a vice president at Duke University, and to Reverend Joyner.

In other summer 1986 news:

—Bill Lowdermilk, vice president for church and community relations at Methodist, received an honorary Doctor of Divinity degree from North Carolina Wesleyan College in Rocky Mount in early May.

—Parley and Jean Rasmussen of Hope Mills, N.C. donated their interest in a mill and farm to the College in memory of Parley's grandparents, E.G. Parker and Margaret McCoy Parker.

—Frank Milo McBryde '68 was elected to an at-large seat on the Fayetteville City Council, while Mark Kendrick '83 was elected councilman for District 6.

—The MC baseball team made it to the College World Series and finished fourth, completing its finest season in school history with a 43-6-2 record. Danny Hartline, Mike Brewington, and Doug Garner were named All Americans.

—The men's golf team finished seventh at the national tournament, while John Walsh shot a 75-77-152 to win medalist honors.

—The Tar Heel Quilters Guild created a set of eight ultra suede banners for Hensdale Chapel, presenting them to Bill Lowdermilk (in his honor) April 28, 1986. [The banners still hang in the chapel.]

— CHAPTER 7 —

—The Pauline Longest Nature Trail was completed and opened in the spring to honor the former chair of the Biology Department and director of the Division of Science and Mathematics.

Trustees Approve Plans for Physical Activities Center

When the trustees met May 15, 1986, Dr. Hendricks reported that 300 students were living in the residence halls and projected the number would reach 400 by the fall of 1986. He projected a fall day enrollment of 1,125 students.

Dr. Hendricks said trustee emeritus Bill Horner had pledged $25,000 toward debt retirement if the other trustees would give $75,000. The president said $100,000 for the next two years and $50,000 the third year would retire the debt of Bond 1968; he agreed to write the trustees and invite their participation in matching the Horner gift.

Gene Clayton introduced Mr. Charles Benz, a Ketchum representative, who distributed three documents related to the College's planned capital campaign to build a physical activities center. Benz said he felt Methodist could raise $4 million and recommended: 1) pledges for a three-year period, 2) the use of trained volunteer fund raisers, with each one expected to make five contacts, 3) that solicitations be personal, 4) that the leadership (trustees) set the pace before asking others to give.

The Ketchum handouts proposed a campaign expense budget of $50,000, of which $19,000 would be for promotion, printed materials, and publicity. He said the College should strive for 15 gifts of $50,000-$500,000, 260 gifts of $1,000-$25,000, and $114,625 from 367 alumni donors.

In a special joint meeting May 30, 1986, the trustees' Executive and Buildings and Grounds committees reviewed design proposals from the architectural firms of Mason S. Hicks, MacMillan and MacMillan, The LSV Partnership, and Hayes and Howell Associates (Southern Pines, N.C.) for the College's Physical Activities Center. On a motion by Frank Barragan, the trustees voted unanimously to employ Hayes and Howell Associates to design the new facility.

At a special called meeting July 17, 1986, the full Board of Trustees reviewed plans for the Physical Activities Center and the 'Come of Age" campaign to raise $2.5 million needed to build it.

Dr. Hendricks and Richard Allen reported that three trustees—Mr. Charles Reeves, Dr. Lucille Hutaff, and Mr. Walter Clark—had already pledged over $850,000 toward the campaign. Dr. Hendricks said the new facility would enable the College to attract more summer events that would generate additional revenue. Mr. Ike O'Hanlon, trustees chair, then announced his pledge of $50,000.

College Launches Fund Drive For Womack Endowed Chair

The summer 1986 issue of *Methodist College Today* announced that a 32-member steering committee had met at Methodist June 17, 1986, to lay the groundwork for the Samuel J. Womack Endowed Chair in Religion and Philosophy. Woodrow V. "Woody" Register, a College trustee emeritus, was the catalyst behind the initiative and chaired the steering committee. Pledges made at the initial meeting totaled $25,000 toward a goal of $100,000.

Samuel Womack

College Begins 27th School Year

The August 1986 *sMALL TALK* reported that Methodist would begin its 27th academic year with two new faculty members: Dr. Alex Nakireru, assistant professor of communications, and Dr. Ann Harley, director of the Bachelor of Science in Nursing (B.S.N.) degree completion program. The Reverend William Green assumed the post of campus minister.

In 1986-87, editorial responsibility for *sMALL TALK* shifted from an editorial board to a single editor, Tom Jumalon, and an assistant editor, Linda Krueger.

In an editorial in the September 12, 1986 *sMALL TALK,* Linda Krueger called for a day care center at Methodist, saying Fayetteville State University had one for adult students with children. She asked students to come by the Publications Office in the Student Union to sign a petition requesting such a center.

President Proposes Budget Cutbacks

At a meeting of the trustees' Executive Committee September 11, 1986, Dr. Hendricks said cutbacks in federal funds for military students required the College to increase its financial aid budget by $200,000. He said reductions of $200,000 would be made in other budget areas to compensate.

In other matters, the president reported that:
— Carolina Power & Light was now supplying electricity directly to the residence halls.
— Sod had been laid for the golf driving range.
— The piano fund drive had been completed and a nine-foot Steinway concert grand piano had been ordered for Reeves Auditorium.

— CHAPTER 7 —

Trustees Act on Endowment, Ketchum Contract

The trustees' Investment Committee voted September 24, 1986, to invite representatives of Gordon and Preston Moss of Boston and First Union National Bank of Raleigh to submit proposals for managing the College endowment.

At a meeting of the full Board of Trustees October 9, 1986, Dr. Hendricks said the trustees' Executive Committee had voted in September to terminate the College's capital campaign contract with Ketchum and Ketchum "due to the departure of Mr. Benz."[7] and that Gene Clayton, director of development, would assume responsibility for the campaign with assistance from Mrs. Charlotte Coheley, his new assistant. He said Fiore Bergamasco, cross country coach, would replace Mrs. Coheley as director of admissions.

Gene Clayton reported that 101 alumni had become Distinguished Monarchs by pledging $1,000 to the "Come of Age" campaign to build a Physical Activities Center. He said the trustees had pledged $1,141,880 and that the "Come of Age" campaign would be announced to the public at a press conference Monday, October 13. Clayton also reported that the Methodist College Foundation had received gifts and pledges of $207,900 to its Loyalty Fund Drive for the year to date.

In other matters:
—Dr. Hendricks said a community group had raised $27,500 for a concert grand piano for Reeves Auditorium and that a dedicatory concert would be held Wednesday, October 15.
—The president proposed amending the College bylaws to provide for a trustees committee on Church and Community Relations.
—Mr. Bruce Pulliam, faculty representative, announced plans to retire in 1987 after 25 years with the College. He asked that sabbatical leaves be made available to faculty and that retirees be given an opportunity to continue in the College's health insurance program.
—It was announced that Methodist had been selected as the site of an Elderhostel program.

At the trustees' November 20, 1986, meeting, Dr. Hendricks announced that he had written to the Kresge Foundation in Detroit to inquire about a grant to the capital campaign. He also noted that Cermette Clardy of Clardy and Associates had been hired as a campaign consultant and would visit the College four days a month through February.

Come of Age Campaign Announced

The "Come of Age" campaign to raise $3.5 million needed to build a Physical Activities Center at Methodist College was announced October 13,

1986. The effort was led by Ike O'Hanlon, chair of the Board of Trustees, Louis Spilman, chair of the trustees' Development Committee; and Gene Clayton, vice president for development.

President Hendricks reported that the trustees had already pledged $1.3 million. The initial design included a 1,500 seat gymnasium, olympic-size swimming pool, racquetball and handball courts, a weight room, sauna, classrooms, dressing rooms, and administrative offices. Dr. Hendricks said the campaign would seek $1.5 million from trustees, $800,000 from alumni, $700,000 from the community, and $500,000 from national foundations. He projected construction would start in the fall of 1987, with completion in the fall of 1988. He said the old metal gymnasium would be converted into a warehouse or theater.

A Wet Homecoming

Homecoming 1986, held October 10-12, was hampered by heavy rain Friday and Saturday. "Under the Big Top" was the theme. A pre-game parade led by the Clarkton High School Band and the men's soccer game were held in the rain; the women's soccer game was canceled. Carnival booths and related activities were moved inside the Student Union where the Stage Band, the Men's Quartet, Rainbow's End, and the College Chorus performed. Dedra Tart was crowned homecoming queen.

At the alumni dinner Saturday, Gene Clayton, vice president for development, presented a slide show on the "Come of Age" capital campaign for a physical activities center. Gwen Sykes '68 and Howard Lupton '72 were introduced as co-chairs of the alumni phase of the capital campaign. Howard Lupton received the Outstanding Alumni Award, and Dr. Ted Jaeger was given the Outstanding Faculty Award.

A Saturday night dance held at the Howard Johnson Hotel featured the music of the Kruze band.

On Saturday morning, Dr. Linda Sue Barnes led a tour of the Pauline Longest Nature Trail, and Dr. Sam Womack preached at a worship service in Hensdale Chapel. On Sunday afternoon, Tom Austin's baseball team and baseball alumni played their annual alumni game.

In other news from fall 1986:

—Roya Weyerhauser was the featured performer at the concert premiere of the College's nine-foot grand piano October 15, 1986. The concert was dedicated to Jean Ishee, the recently retired associate professor of piano and organ and chair of the Music Department,

— CHAPTER 7 —

—Dr. J. Allen Norris Jr., president of Louisburg College, addressed 39 summer graduates August 26, 1986, urging them to leave MC "with a 'can do,' caring attitude toward others." [8]

—President Hendricks noted that the fall 1986 day enrollment had reached 1,025, up 60 percent from a figure of 632 three years earlier.

—An academic Honor Code was implemented at Methodist which prohibited "cheating (including plagiarism), theft, and academic misrepresentation." [9] Walter Swing, chair of the Honor Board, said students would be required to write "pledged" on work submitted for academic credit. [10] Violations were to be reported to the Honor Board.

Students sign the Methodist College Honor Code.

—Sam Ragan, North Carolina's poet laureate and publisher of *The (Southern Pines) Pilot,* was honored at a special event Sunday, August 17 sponsored by Davis Memorial Library. The event was used to showcase the release of a new record album, "Poems of Sam Ragan Read by the Poet." Ragan read several poems, and several selections were played from the recording. The album was funded with grants from the North Carolina Arts Council, the National Endowment for the Arts, the Josephus Daniels Foundation, and the John Wesley and Ann Hodgin Hanes Foundation. Invited guests included former N. C. Governor Bob Scott; Dr. William C. Friday, former president of U.N.C.; and Dr. James B. Hemby Jr., president of Atlantic Christian College (Ragan's alma mater).

Sam Ragan reads poems.

—Dr. Lynn Sadler and Dr. Wendy Greene launched a new journal, the *Computer-Assisted Composition Journal,* which contained a dozen articles by college educators on the use of computers and new software to teach composition. The *CACJ* was slated for publication three times a year at an annual subscription cost of $10.

—Jack Langley '70 was profiled in an article reprinted from *The Rocky Mount Telegram*. Left a quadriplegic by a 1982 car accident, Langley had just been named 1985 Salesman of the Year by Ruby Braswell Realty for selling $2.5 million in real estate.

—Both the women's soccer team (13-4-1) and the women's volleyball team (8-4) qualified for their respective NCAA Division III national tournaments and were assigned to the West Regional in San Diego, California.

College Supports N.C. Amendment

In a front page story in the October 24, 1986 *sMALL TALK*, College President Elton Hendricks urged students and staff to vote for an amendment to the North Carolina constitution November 4 that would allow independent colleges to sell tax-exempt revenue bonds through the state bonding authority to fund capital improvements. "Methodist College can save a considerable amount of money over the next several years if this amendment is approved," said Dr. Hendricks. "Without it, we will be unable to move forward with many of our most critical needs." [11] [North Carolina voters approved the amendment, and Methodist went on to issue millions of dollars in revenue bonds on three different occasions from 1990 to 2006 to finance campus improvements.]

In other fall 1986 news:

—Clarinetist Woody Herman and his 15-piece orchestra appeared in concert October 28, 1986, in Reeves Auditorium, as part of Fayetteville's Community Concerts Series.

—"A Touch of Greece," a series of dances and pantomimes, was presented Friday, October 31 and Saturday, November 1, 1986, in the Science Auditorium. Dancers included youth from Saints Constantine and Helen Greek Orthodox Church in Fayetteville. The program was produced by Richard Briggs, a senior majoring in fine arts management.

—Methodist's Center for Entrepreneurship, under the direction of Dr. Sid Gautam, professor of business administration, was formed March 12, 1986.

Convocations Reduced To Four

A news story in the November 14, 1986, *sMALL TALK* reviewed the history of convocations at Methodist. Carol Binzer, chair of the convocation program, said the current system of four convocations per year—two each semester—

— CHAPTER 7 —

would likely continue. Attempts to have "The Great Debates" as a theme for 1986-87 were thwarted when U.S. Senate candidates Terry Sanford and Jim Broyhill and the CEOs of Pepsi Cola and Coca Cola turned down invitations. Binzer said the Student Affairs Office was soliciting "clever" proposals for the spring opening convocation to be held January 23, 1987.

Another story noted that the Cape Fear River Research Institute held its annual meeting and dinner at Methodist October 28, 1986. The guest speaker, Michael Corcoran, spoke about the introduction of catfish into the Cape Fear River. *Fayetteville Times* Editor Roy Parker, Jr. presented the John Pate Award to Mr. and Mrs. Pitt Dickey for their successful efforts to block construction of a nuclear waste disposal plant along the river.

Chicago comedian Tim Cavanaugh, slated to perform in the Center Stage series in the Student Union December 10, was profiled in a feature story.

Safley Appointed V.P. for Student Affairs

The December 5, 1986, *sMALL TALK* reported that Michael Wayne Safley '72 would become vice president for student affairs at Methodist July 1, 1987. Reverend Safley was then working as associate director of youth, young adults, worship, music and the arts for the Council on Ministries of The North Carolina Conference of The United Methodist Church.

Mike Safley

In other news:
—Speaking at the College's Economic Outlook for 1987 Symposium, Glenn Orr, board chairman of Southern National Bank, predicted a 3 percent growth in the nation's GDP in 1987. Richard M. Lewis Jr., president of the Fayetteville Chamber of Commerce, was also bullish about the coming year, saying the local economy would continue to benefit from the $1.3 billion payroll from Fort Bragg and Pope Air Force Base and from booming retail sales.
—the Lady Monarch soccer team lost to St. Mary's College of Minnesota 2-1 in the NCAA Division III National Tournament in San Diego, California. The team finished its season with a 13-4-2 record.

Bishop Minnick Addresses Winter Graduates

Bishop Carlton P. Minnick Jr. of The North Carolina Conference of The United Methodist Church, challenged Methodist's winter graduates December

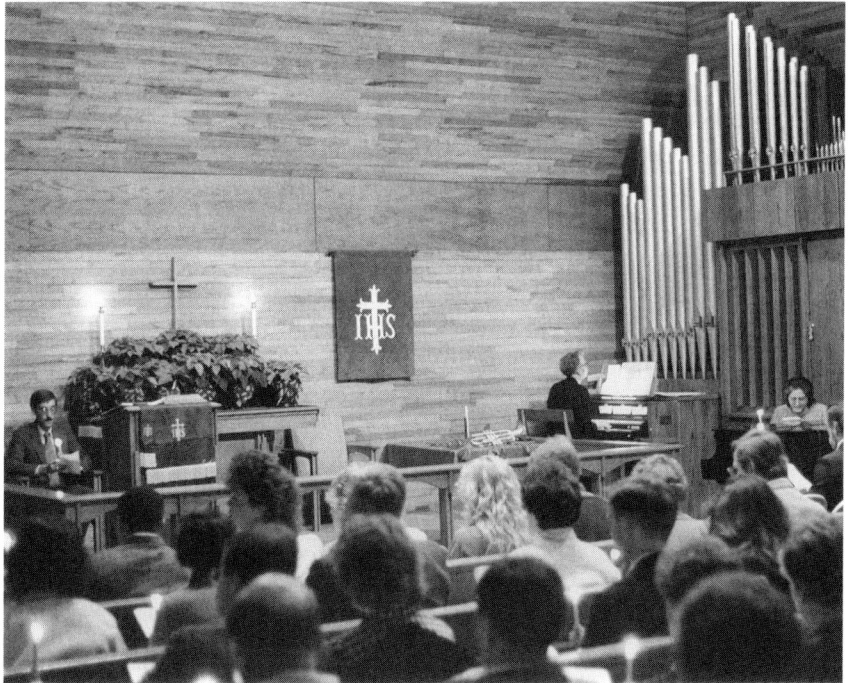

The December 1987 Love Feast featured the Rev. Phil Baugess (liturgist), Paul Tamblyn (organist) and Tammy Hightower Edens (soloist).

17, 1986, to realize they had been born "for such times as these—times that are revolutionary, fearful, seeking, hopeful, and unsettling." [12]

During the commencement, Dr. Hendricks presented Martha Duell of Fayetteville with a Methodist College Medallion for her work to promote closer ties between her native France and Fayetteville. The founder of The Lafayette Society was lauded for her support of Methodist College and other civic organizations.

In other news reported in spring 1987 editions of *sMALL TALK*:

—Ed Kilbourne, a well-known folk singer/humorist and ordained minister, was the resource person for Faith-in-Life Week January 25-30, 1987. The theme for the week was "The Mississippi Squirrel Revival." The week began with a Super Bowl party.

—*Chanticleer*, an eight-member *a cappella* vocal ensemble from San Francisco, performed at Methodist February 3, 1987, as part of the Community Concert Series.

—Jeff DeGraw was named track and cross country coach.

CHAPTER 7

- Women's soccer players Brenda McKimens and Lori Silvasy earned All-American honors for 1986.
- Tom Austin was named the district's Diamond Baseball Coach of the Year.
- The Methodist College Chorus embarked on a spring break tour of Florida and the Bahamas February 28. The group performed at two Florida churches, at Disney World, and at Queens College and Wesley United Methodist Church in Nassau.
- Mary Ellen Anglin wrote a feature story about Charles Bullard '70, director of the 180-member Holland High School Marching Band of Holland, Michigan. The band marched in the Tournament of Roses Parade in Pasadena, California on New Year's Day.

Speaking Across the Curriculum

President Hendricks used the spring 1987 opening convocation to promote the Speaking Across the Curriculum program. The program opened with cast members from *Pygmalion* (a.k.a. *My Fair Lady*) —Professor Henry Higgins (Tom Jumalon) and Eliza Doolittle (Beth Hudson) — performing several scenes from the upcoming musical production. Dr. Hendricks urged faculty, staff, and students to correct speaking errors by responding with a correct variation of what they had heard.

Enrollment Tops 1,400

Reporting to the Board of Trustees January 29, 1987, Dr. Hendricks said that 750 students were enrolled in the regular day program and 725 in the Evening College. He said about 200 military students had moved from the day program to the evening program.

The president said the College had begun work on the reaffirmation of accreditation process with the Southern Association of Colleges and Schools. He said the self study report would be finished by the end of 1988, that a committee would visit in the spring of 1989, and that SACS would vote on reaffirming Methodist's accreditation at the December 1989 meeting.

Trustee Louis Spilman reported that:
- 252 persons had pledged or paid $2,272,039 to the capital campaign.
- 1,203 persons had contributed $237,652.37 to the Methodist College Foundation's Loyalty Fund Drive in 1986, and
- 47 contributors had pledged $33,039 to the fund to establish the Womack Endowed Chair in Religion.

1985–1989

Trustee Dillard Teer introduced Jim Ward, an architect who had worked with Duke University, who had been employed to work with Hayes and Howell Associates, architects for the Physical Activities Center. Mr. Ward said his meetings with Hays & Howell personnel led him to believe the architects did not understand the type of building the College desired. Ward presented a cost estimate for the project of $3.5 million—$2.7 million for the building plus $238,500 in administrative campaign costs, $70,000 for equipment, $110,000 for site development, and $5,000 for preliminary costs. The consultant recommended that the PAC be built on a negotiated (versus bid) basis.

In other business, Dr. Hendricks proposed a 1987-88 budget of $6,768,962 which the trustees approved.

J. P. Riddle Gives $500,000

The lead story in the spring 1987 issue of *Methodist College Today* reported that Fayetteville developer and College trustee J. P. Riddle had made a large gift to Methodist's "Come of Age" campaign to build a Physical Activities Center. Riddle's gift consisted of coastal real estate valued at $500,000.

J. P. Riddle

A related story announced that Fayetteville businessman George Stewart was chairing the Methodist College Foundation's 1987 Loyalty Fund Campaign, with goals of raising $175,000 for operating expenses and $700,000 toward the capital campaign for a physical activities center.

I. H. O'Hanlon, trustees chair and general chair of the "Come of Age" capital campaign, reported that 404 gifts and pledges totaling $2.3 million had been received.

Joe Miller Resigns As Basketball Coach

sMALL TALK reported March 27, 1987, that Joe Miller had resigned as men's basketball coach, after 12 years and a career record of 101 wins and 201 losses. Miller told Gerald Davis that his first four years were good, with winning records, and that his two best memories were of: a win against Campbell in 1983-84 and a trip to the NCAA Division III tourney in 1976-77. Miller said he would remain at Methodist as director of physical education. [13]

In other news:
— "Paul Green's Celebration of Man" was the subject of the Southern Writers Symposium March 27-28, 1987. The event included *Listen to My Song*, an original play about Paul Green, a Harnett County native considered the father of outdoor drama in America.

— CHAPTER 7 —

—"America Alive! The 1920s" was the theme of the 1987 Fine Arts Festival March 27-April 12. A highlight was an outdoor production of Eugene O'Neill's Pulitzer Prize winning play *Lost Horizon*, starring Richard Briggs, Rob Metzger, and Jane Heeckt.
—The baseball team was ranked No. 2 in a postseason *USA Today* poll and had a record of 20-3-1 as of March 21.

Arts Festival Includes Tribute to Paul Green

"America Alive! The 1920s" was the theme of Methodist's seventh annual Fine Arts Festival March 27-April 12. Many of the later events coincided with Fayetteville's Dogwood Festival April 3-12.

The first major event was "Paul Green's Celebration of Man," the fifth annual Southern Writers Symposium. A Pulitzer Prize-winning playwright from Harnett County, Paul Green wrote *The Lost Colony* which premiered in 1937 in Manteo, N.C. It is the most famous and longest-running of his "symphonic" outdoor dramas.

With grants from the Arts Council of Fayetteville/Cumberland County, the National Endowment for the Humanities, the Broyhill Foundation, the Adele M. Thomas Trust, and the Paul Green Foundation, Methodist was able to commission Lee Yopp, director of the Fort Bragg Playhouse, to write a biographical play about Green. Yopp entitled the play *Listen to My Song* and cast Leonard McLeod as a "mature" Paul Green.

Michael Brocki played a young Paul Green, shown here courting his future bride at UNC.

The symposium also included lectures by 12 guest scholars who knew Green or had studied his work, two films, and special music from Green's symphonic dramas performed by the Methodist College Chorus.

Other Fine Arts Festival events included an Art Deco Fashion Show, a program on old time radio by Hope Mills resident John Wallace, a lecture on 1920s architecture by Mason Hicks, a piano recital by Terry Poole Akamatsu '79, and a Theatre Department production of Eugene O'Neill's *Beyond the Horizon*.

A short news item inside this *MCT* announced that Bill Billings '68 had joined the college staff as news bureau director and *sMALL TALK* adviser.

College Awards 100 Degrees

Methodist College awarded 100 degrees—87 bachelor's and 13 associate's—May 10, 1987.

The commencement speaker was Mary Lynn Bryan, historian-in-residence at Methodist. Mrs. Bryan urged the members of the Class of 1987 to keep an open mind, take an active role in solving their generation's problems, and make informed choices based on Christian values.

In an earlier baccalaureate sermon entitled "Life as a Boomerang," Bill Lowdermilk challenged each graduating senior to become a catalyst for good committed to "building up, not tearing down; being caring, not callous; and living a life of sharing, not hoarding." [14]

Cu Phung, a Vietnamese American with a double major in chemistry and mathematics, received the L. Stacy Weaver Award. John Henley, a veteran state legislator from Hope Mills, N.C., received an honorary Doctor of Humanities degree. Lois Lambie, composer of the College alma mater, received a Methodist College Medallion.

Trustees Approve Plans for PAC

At a May 14, 1987, meeting, the Methodist College Board of Trustees accepted trustee emeritus Bill Horner's offer to give $50,000 now and another $50,000 early in 1988 if the College would provide another $250,000 to pay off Bond 1968.

Reporting for the trustees' Building and Grounds Committee, Dillard Teer presented preliminary plans for the proposed Physical Activities Center and recommended that 1) the president be authorized to proceed with the building at an estimated cost of $4.2 million, 2) that the architects be authorized to complete the plans, and 3) that the tennis courts at the site of the new building be moved during the summer. The trustees approved the committee's recommendations by unanimous vote.

— CHAPTER 7 —

The Reverend Ray Gooch, president of the Methodist College Alumni Association, said alumni were delighted that a fountain was being constructed on campus and would support building the PAC as designed. He said alumni had contributed $71,000 in 1987, $52,000 of that for the capital campaign.

Trustees Offer Land For Church Headquarters

The trustees' Executive Committee voted July 9, 1987, to offer property to The North Carolina Conference of The United Methodist Church for new conference headquarters.

When the Executive Committee met again September 10, Dr. Hendricks expressed concern that $1.8 million of the $2.6 million pledged to the capital campaign was non-liquid assets (*e.g.* real estate, stocks, and bonds). A report given to the committee showed the College had only $244,715 in cash for the project.

When Mr. O'Hanlon asked what the plan was for raising the remaining $1.6 million, Gene Clayton responded that "those who have not pledged will be asked again and those who have pledged will be asked to increase their pledges." [15] Clayton said asphalt had been laid for the eight new tennis courts on the lower field and that the courts would cost about $104,000.

Robert Hatfield, chair of the trustees' Ad Hoc Presidential Review Committee, presented a draft of a proposed policy making a Presidential Evaluation Committee a standing committee of the Board of Trustees and stipulating that the committee would evaluate the president and submit a report to the Board every other year.

Regarding the College's offer of land to The North Carolina Conference for a headquarters building, a written proposal was distributed in which the College offered four sites as well as free heating and maintenance of buildings and grounds and access to library services.

***Methodist College Today* Becomes Magazine**

In August 1987, *Methodist College Today* was converted from a quarter fold newspaper to an 8 1/2 X 11-inch magazine printed and assembled in the college print shop. Bill Billings and Lynn Gruber served as co-editors. The lead story in this *MCT* was Gene Clayton's capital campaign report that 563 gifts and pledges had been received toward the physical activities center. He said his office would contact approximately 60 foundations during the next six months with funding requests for Methodist's PAC.

In other news from the spring and summer of 1987:
—In August 1987, Dr. Hendricks had a new fountain constructed on the third level of the campus mall opposite the south (side)

entrance to Reeves Auditorium. The new fountain was built above ground on the site of the original fountain. Built in 1969,

Methodist's "second fountain" was completed in September 1987.

the Fleishman Fountain fell into disrepair in the 1970s and was covered over with concrete.

—A college print shop was established in the basement of the Trustees Classroom Building with a small offset press, folding machine, and stitcher. College printer Debbie Wilson worked under the supervision of Dr. Lynn Sadler, academic dean. Dr. Sadler persuaded Dr. Hendricks to upgrade the print shop, saying new Macintosh computers and desktop software would enable the college to print *Tapestry*, the *CAC Journal*, the college catalog, *Methodist College Today*, the student handbook, and other items that had been formerly outsourced.

—Bruce Pulliam, associate professor of history, retired after 25 years and was the subject of a feature article in the August 1987, *Methodist College Today*. The 63-year-old shared his thoughts about former students and former college presidents—all positive. In May 1987, he and his family established the Pulliam Foundation to fund sabbaticals for MC faculty members. The first recipients, Alan Porter and Parker Wilson, received $1,000 each the following week.

— CHAPTER 7 —

— The women's golf team, coached by Rita Wiggs, won the National Golf Coaches Association Division III National Championship by 36 strokes. Holly Anderson took medalist honors; Anderson and Joy Bonhurst were repeat All-Americans and were invited to participate in the NCAA Women's Golf Championships in Albuquerque.

Women's Golf National Champs 1987

— The men's baseball team finished second to N. C. Wesleyan in the NCAA Division III South Regional. The Monarchs finished their season with a record of 40-12. Danny Hartline, a junior from Laurel Hill, signed a one-year minor league contract with the Baltimore Orioles June 10.

— Assistant Men's Golf Coach Steve Conley was promoted to head coach to succeed Jim Suttie.

— Freezing temperatures (and snow in some areas of the Piedmont) put a damper on Alumni Day April 4, 1987. An alumni golf tournament had to be cancelled, and the picnic was moved indoors. A computer workshop was offered by Dr. Sadler and Sam Clark.

— Following an alumni board meeting, faculty, staff, and graduating seniors attended a banquet in the main dining room. Twenty retired faculty and staff were given certificates for their service to the College. Bruce Pulliam was given the key to the town of Bunnlevel, about 18 miles north of the College. [It seems that Pulliam took a special interest in the crossroads when the U.S. Postal Service threatened to close its post office; for a few years he mailed all his Christmas cards in Bunnlevel. The post office was kept open.]

— *I Love To Cook II*, a 200-page cookbook sponsored by Methodist College Press and authored by Delanie Webb of Macclesfield, N.C., was advertised in *MCT*. The cost was $8. The book contained recipes contributed by MC faculty and staff and other Tar Heels.

1985–1989

A Year Of New Faces

sMALL TALK's September 15, 1987, issue listed the following new faculty: Dr. Suzan Cheek, political science; Mrs. Camille Chigi, nursing; Alan Dawson, physical education and men's soccer coach; Dr. Stephen Emery, chemistry; T. Jerry Hogge, business administration, physical education, and golf management; Dr. Michael Marr, director of the Reeves School of Business; Diane Scherzer, physical education and coach of volleyball and softball; Mrs. Emily Seamon, social work; John Walsh, golf coach; Dr. James X. Ward, director of the CAC Lab and writing program.

New administrative staff included: Chris Grubb, admissions counselor; John Perkinson, director of dining services; Chris Ryan, director of student activities; Michael Safley, vice president for student affairs; Mary Underwood, director of evening and off campus programs; and John Keso, director of financial aid.

Interviewed for the October 6, 1987, *sMALL TALK,* College President Elton Hendricks said he had enjoyed his four years at Methodist where he had found "a committed group of scholars and teachers and hard-working set of administrators." [16]

Enrollment Reaches 1,420

The November 1987 issue of *Methodist College Today* reported that fall enrollment had reached 1,420 students—830 day students and 590 evening students. The day enrollment was down 19 percent from fall 1986 when MC enrolled 200 soldiers as full-time day students. A change in federal regulations ended tuition payments for military enrolled as full-time day students. Fall evening enrollment for 1987 was up 73 percent compared to a year earlier. A total of 349 students were living in the four residence halls, and the College enrolled 407 new freshmen.

The fall 1987 *MCT* also included photo highlights of homecoming events. "A South Seas Weekend" was the theme. Saturday was balmy and included a pre-soccer game parade with floats and a dance at the Holiday Inn Bordeaux.

In other fall 1987 news:
—John Michael Marr became the director of the Reeves School of Business, succeeding Dr. Frank Spreng. Dr. Marr came to Methodist from Elon College, where he taught business administration and directed the M.B.A. program.
—Methodist received a $250,000 Title III Endowment Grant from the U.S. Dept. of Education. Dr. Hendricks said the College would have to hold the money for 20 years and could spend up to one-half the income earned annually (about $25,000). The

— CHAPTER 7 —

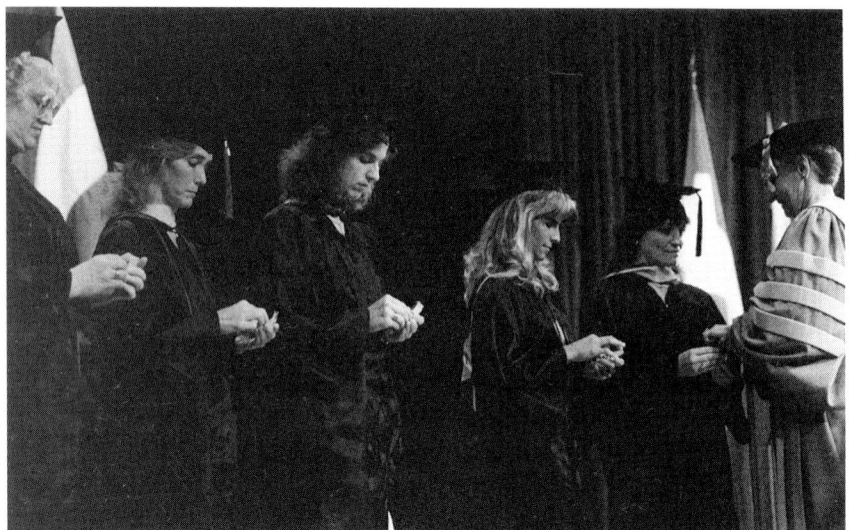

Methodist awarded six nursing degrees August 25, 1987.

president indicated earnings would be used to support the Reeves School of Business.
—The College awarded its first Bachelor of Science in Nursing degrees to six students August 25, 1987. Dr. Ann Harley, chair of the Department of Nursing, presented a special pin to each graduate.
—Cheerleading Coach Gwen Sykes was interviewed by Alison Frankel for an article in *Seventeen* magazine.
— Methodist offered its first Elderhostel, a series of minicourses for senior citizens, September 20-26, 1987. Courses in psychology, sociology, and biology were taught by Dr. Jaeger, Dr. Sill, and Dr. Barnes respectively. Of the 30 Elderhostel students, 24 lived in the residence halls and six commuted to classes. Mrs. Elaine Porter served as Elderhostel coordinator.
—The women's soccer team won the Dixie Conference title with a 4-0 conference record and also won a berth in the NCAA Division III Tournament. Coach Joe Pereira's team finished 16-4 overall, losing only to UNC-Chapel Hill, N.C. State, Cortland, and in NCAA tournament play.
—Dan Lawrence, a MC alumnus, was named head men's basketball coach, succeeding Joe Miller.
—The cross country team, coached by Jeff DeGraw, won its first Dixie Conference title since 1965.

—Eleven "student clowns" from Methodist entertained patients at Cape Fear Valley Hospital and Whispering Pines Rest Home October 28, 1987.

Board Welcome New Members

The Methodist College Board of Trustees welcomed five new trustees October 8, 1987: Charlie Gaddy, Joseph Hatcher, James High, James (Chuck) Noe, and Harrison Williams.

President Hendricks introduced Mike Safley, the new vice president for student affairs. He reported a record fall 1987 enrollment of 1,489 students, but said there were 150 fewer students in the regular day program because of fewer full-time military students.

The president said the College had received a $250,000 endowment grant from a federal program requiring a 50-50 matching agreement. He said part of Charles Reeves' gift for the School of Business would be used as a match, and the endowment would support the Reeves School of Business.

Dr. Hendricks reported that the total cost of the Physical Activities Center was estimated at $4.2 million and that he was optimistic the College would receive a grant from the Kresge Foundation for the project. He also noted that the College's proposal for locating North Carolina Conference headquarters on the campus would be presented to the conference trustees and task force October 23, 1987.

The trustees approved the creation of a Presidential Review Committee as a standing committee of the Board of Trustees, charged with submitting to the Board an evaluation report of the Office of the President every other year.

Homecoming Features Tropical Theme

"A South Seas Weekend" was the theme of the 1987 homecoming October 9-11. Events began Friday with a pep rally, judging of dorm decorations, a tennis tournament, a Popcorn Theatre presentation, a talent show, and a bonfire/pep rally. The Saturday events included a sidewalk carnival, volleyball game, lunch on the central mall with entertainment from the Stage Band and College Chorus, a parade around the soccer field, an alumni reception and luau at the Bordeaux Inn, and a homecoming dance featuring the Fabulous Keys.

A witty *sMALL TALK* reporter wrote a short feature for the October 16 issue, saying that unknown aliens had invaded the campus late Friday, causing resident students to drink large quantities of beverages and drape huge amounts of toilet paper over the trees. A double page photo spread of homecoming highlights showed Fayetteville Mayor J. L. Dawkins and

— CHAPTER 7 —

Alumni President Ray Gooch had a place of honor in the 1987 Homecoming Parade.

President Hendricks riding on a float, a sky diver landing on the soccer field, and the crowning of April Langston as homecoming queen. Both soccer teams won their homecoming games, with the women defeating Erskine College 2-0 and the men winning over USC-Aiken 1-0. Former baseball coach Bruce Shelley and 17 alumni "All Stars" gathered Sunday to play the varsity baseball team.

Newscaster Speaks at U.S. Constitution Program

Methodist held a special convocation Monday, November 9, 1987, celebrating the 200th anniversary of the U.S. Constitution and honoring history professor Bruce Pulliam. Charlie Gaddy, a newscaster with WRAL-TV in Raleigh, was the guest speaker. His topic was "All the News That's Fit to See," Gaddy described the various sources of news—print and broadcast—and how news was gathered.

S.G.A. President Mike D'Arcy told a *sMALL TALK* reporter in the fall of 1987 the S.G.A. should represent student needs and opinions to the College administration. He said the organization was having a successful year, having: repaired trophies and awards for the Athletic Hall of Fame, brought in a caricaturist and a DJ for student orientation, chosen and hired the band "The Fabulous Keys" for the homecoming dance, and brought Star Search comedian Mark Pilla to the Center Stage (snack bar) and getting the residence halls wired for cable TV.

1985–1989

Trustees Discuss PAC, Football

At a November 19, 1987, meeting of the trustees' Executive Committee, Dr. Hendricks said the College's application to the Kresge Foundation for a grant toward the Physical Activities Center had been turned down but that a new proposal would be submitted in May 1988.

The president then presented a proposal and cost analysis for adding football as an intercollegiate sport. The plan called for hiring a coach in the fall of 1988 and giving him one year to recruit players; the College would field its first team in the fall of 1989. After reviewing and discussing the second draft of a football proposal, the trustees approved the addition by unanimous vote.

At a January 28, 1988, meeting, Dr. Hendricks reported that the College held non-liquid assets and pledges of $1,948,000 toward a new gymnasium but only $280,000 in cash. The president proposed: 1) that the scope of the building be reduced to bring the cost down to $3 million, 2) that an additional $1 million be raised, and 3) that any remainder be borrowed, if required. He proposed moving the swimming pool to a second construction phase, adding that the required architectural changes would delay the start of the building by six months. Mr. Wilson Yarborough Sr. asked the president to investigate selling 100 acres of College land and report to the Board at its May meeting.

Fall 1987's Faculty Talent Show was lots of fun.

Dr. Pearce Returns To Give Commencement Address

Dr. Richard Pearce, president of Methodist College from 1973-83, delivered the commencement address at Methodist's 15th winter commencement December 16, 1987. Speaking on the topic, "What Are You Going To Do With Tomorrow?", he listed some of the major achievements of his generation and challenged the degree candidates to adopt a balanced set of values for the future by building on the values of their parents and grandparents and improving society. [17]

A news brief in a January 1988, *sMALL TALK* reported that Dr. Stacy Weaver Jr., son of the first president of Methodist College, had presented the bulk of Dr. Weaver's personal library—654 books and 61 musical scores— to the College. Director of Library Services Norma Womack said she was delighted with the quality and the condition of the collection.

In other news:
— Snow greeted students as they returned to campus for the spring semester.
— Methodist cheerleaders finished fourth among nine college teams in a National Cheerleading Association Championship in Dallas, Texas. The co-captains, Anthony Westbrook and Susie Cox, were pictured holding an NCA trophy.
— "The Big Band Galaxy of Stars" performed in Reeves Auditorium Wednesday, February 3, 1988. Notables on the program included Jimmie Rodgers, Maxine Andrews, The New Ink Spots, and Henry Bobbitt (featured singer with the Kaye Kyser Orchestra).

Cheerleaders finished No. 4 in NCA in 1988.

The addition of football at Methodist made the front page of the February 12, 1988, *sMALL TALK*. A story written by Ernest Pitts, Gregory Blanding, and Rochelle Stokes sampled the views of students and faculty, the Development Office, and the Admissions Office. The article said football was approved to increase enrollment and develop community spirit.

The article noted that a coach would be hired soon and given one year to recruit players, with Methodist fielding its first team in the fall of 1989. Sometime in 1989, a locker room building for 50-75 players would be built behind the old boiler plant. The team would play on the original soccer field and compete against other non-scholarship schools like Guilford and Randolph-Macon in a nine-game season.

This issue of the student newspaper also included feature stories about Earleene Bass, marking her 25th year as faculty secretary, and Mason Sykes, superintendent of buildings and grounds and former coach.

Elizabeth Dole Visits College

The lead story in the January 29, 1988, *sMALL TALK* described a visit to Methodist by Elizabeth Dole, former U.S. Secretary of Transportation, campaigning for her husband, U.S. Senator Robert Dole. Dole was seeking the Republican nomination for president. A Salisbury, N.C. native and Duke University graduate, Mrs. Dole told a crowd of 200 gathered in the Student Union that her husband's twenty years in the Senate and the way he overcame a serious wound in World War II showed he was eminently qualified to be president.

Jonathan Jackson Visits Methodist

Jonathan Jackson, son of the Reverend Jesse Jackson, visited Methodist February 9 to campaign for his father, a candidate for the Democratic presidential nomination. A February 14 story in the student newspaper said Jackson attended a reception hosted by the S.G.A. and the Black Student Movement, then moved to Reeves Auditorium where he spoke of his father's desire to create jobs, raise the minimum wage, and improve the public schools.

An AIDS symposium and panel discussion held February 10, 1988, in Hensdale Chapel made the front page. Col. Gayle Roberts, a physician at Womack Army Hospital, explained how the AIDS virus destroyed the body's immune system, rendering the body vulnerable to infections. Panelists included an Army nurse, a community health nurse, a social worker, and an AIDS patient.

The Reverend William Green, campus minister, wrote an account of the event for *sMALL TALK*. He said an estimated 1.5 million Americans had the AIDS (HIV) virus and that 25-50 percent of those would progress to AIDS in five to ten years. Green said government health officials were estimating there would be at least 54,000 deaths related to AIDS in the year 1991. [18]

In other news:
— The 29-member college chorus was slated to give concerts in Charleston, S.C. February 28 and 29.
— Faculty members Alan and Elaine Porter were subjects of lengthy feature articles
— The Monarch track team performed well in the Lynchburg Invitational where Shanda Mentus finished second in the shot put, Danielle Baker won the 55 meter hurdles, and Brian Cole won the 880 event with a 2:02.9.

College Adds Football

The April 1988 *Methodist College Today* reported on two major decisions reached January 28 by the college trustees. First, the trustees decided to modify the plan for the physical activities center by deleting a swimming pool, putting the pool in Phase II to be built at a later date. Second, the trustees approved the addition of football as a 16th intercollegiate sport, making Methodist the first NCAA Division III school in North Carolina to field a football team.

— CHAPTER 7 —

Dr. Hendricks said a football coach would be hired by September 1 and would be given the 1988-89 year to recruit players. He said the existing soccer field would be converted into the football field, and the large field at the front of the campus would become the soccer field. He said an assistant coach and trainer would be hired in 1989-90.

In other news from spring 1988:

—Dr. Linda Sue Barnes, associate professor of biology at Methodist College, was named Wildlife Educator of the Year by the North Carolina Wildlife Federation. Dr. Lynn Sadler, academic dean, nominated Dr. Barnes, citing her record of teaching excellence, her work in developing the Pauline Longest Nature Trail, and her lectures to garden clubs and school groups about wildflowers, wildlife, and ecology.

—In March 1988, *sMALL TALK* Editor Gerald Davis wrote an editorial addressing the rumor that Methodist would begin to issue condoms on campus in 1988-89. Davis dismissed the idea

Jane Weeks and Terry Poole Akamatsu '79 take a bow following their duo piano recital.

that such a move would foster promiscuity and endorsed the idea for health reasons. [19] [The college administration opted later NOT to distribute condoms.] History professor Parker Wilson and college nurse Sandra Combs were the subject of inside feature stories.

8th Fine Arts Festival Salutes "The Comic Spirit"

The March 1988, sMALL TALK also promoted the 8th annual Fine Arts Festival set for April 8-17. "The Comic Spirit" theme headlined a full page ad. The list of events included: an honors art exhibition, "My Comedy Is Older Than Yours," a duo piano recital by Jane Weeks and Terry Poole Akamatsu '79, the Southern Writers Symposium honoring Reynolds Price, a voice recital by Alice Patterson, and a performance by the Roger Wagner Chorale.

Walter Turner Remembers Teachers

The April 1988, *Methodist College Today* included a memoir by Walter Turner '65 in which he recalled highlights of his years at Methodist. Turner reminisced about teachers like Dr. Marie Fox, Bruce Pulliam and Dr. Sam Womack, listening to the Effigies (a folk music group of George Potts, Allen Hayes, John Avinger, and Larry Green), singing in the college chorus, playing basketball, debating political issues with Henry Grant and becoming the president of North Carolina Young Democrats. [After graduating ,Walter joined the Peace Corps and became a social worker.]

Board Discusses Long Term Debt

President Hendricks informed the Board of Trustees March 17, 1988, that the U.S. Department of Education was willing to accept $1.1 million to settle $2.3 million in outstanding government loans. He said he had asked Bishop Minnick and The North Carolina Conference of The United Methodist Church (Council on Finance and Administration) to continue giving the College $157,000 for debt retirement for 15 years. He said this would enable the College to borrow $1.5 million, pay off its government loans, and have about $800,000 to apply to the Physical Activities Center. He said the church's $157,000 annual appropriation would be applied to the new loan. He said he would know in May if the church would agree to commit the funds.

Trustee Dillard Teer asked the president to see if any developers were interested in purchasing 200 acres of College land.

CFRT Stages Price Play At Writers Symposium

A front page article in the April 13, 1988, sMALL TALK described the April 15-16 Southern Writers Symposium honoring Duke University professor and novelist Reynolds Price. As part of the symposium, the Cape Fear Regional Theatre staged *Private Contentment*, a Reynolds Price play which aired on public television in 1982.

Lee Yopp, veteran director of the Fort Bragg Playhouse, directed three performances featuring local actors Bo Thorp, Leonard McLeod, Michael Brocki, and Margaret Jemison.

— CHAPTER 7 —

Inside this issue were feature articles on Bill Lowdermilk, vice president for church and community relations, and MC sophomore Samantha Fetters, Miss Fayetteville.

Trustees Consider Golf, Debt, Nursing, Alcohol

When the Board of Trustees met May 12, 1988, Dr. Hendricks said the golf management program could grow to 150-200 students and recommended that the College build a nine-hole practice golf course on 50 acres of land at the rate of two holes per year. He said each hole would cost about $50,000.

The president reported that The North Carolina Conference's Council on Finance and Administration had agreed to continue $157,000 debt service payments to the College for 15 years. The trustees then approved a motion authorizing the president to negotiate a payoff on the College's federal debt in the range of $600,000-$700,000 and to borrow $1.3 million to pay off the federal debt, with the balance being used as start-up funds for the Physical Activities Center.

Dr. Hendricks said 20 students were enrolled in the College's nursing program, but "few of them are full-time." [20] He said the program was operating at a deficit of $35,000 annually, which would grow to $100,000 per year if the College hired two additional nurses and a technician (a requirement for accreditation by the State Board of Nursing). He said he would recommend continuation of the program if outside organizations (*e.g.* Cape Fear Valley Hospital or the Cumberland County commissioners) would contribute $75,000 annually.

Trustees approved a motion by Charles Reeves authorizing the Executive Committee to act on continuance or discontinuance of the nursing program at its July meeting, pending an updated report from the president. [The program was discontinued.]

In other matters, Dr. Hendricks reported that The North Carolina Conference Trustees' Advisory Committee had recommended that church conference headquarters remain in Raleigh and that the renovated Mallett-Rogers House would be dedicated Sunday, May 15, 1988.

Trustees approved a proposed student alcohol policy presented by George Johnson, chair of the Student Affairs Committee. Point one of the policy stated that, "Public consumption of any alcoholic beverage is not permitted on campus." [21] Succeeding points stated that possession of an alcoholic beverage container would result in a citation and $25 fine ($50 for a second citation) and that a third citation in any given academic year "may result in suspension from the College." [22]

1985–1989

Trustee Sid Huggins proposed amending point one to read, "Consumption and possession of any alcoholic beverage on campus is not permitted." [23] Ray Gooch, Mike Safley, and Roy Whitmire spoke against the amendment, and it was defeated.

The trustees also approved a revised set of bylaws for the College.

Women Golfers Win Third National Title

The women's golf team won its third NGCA Division III National Golf Championship May 2-5, 1988. Playing in Dubuque, Iowa, the women bested runner-up Mt. Holyoke by 77 strokes. Kristina Kavanaugh was the medalist, and Joy Bonhurst had the second lowest score.

In other sports news from spring 1988:

— The men's golf team finished fifth at the NCAA Division III National Golf Championship May 18-20 in Greensboro. Monarch John McCullough had the best individual score, finishing fourth.

— With three freshmen leading the way, Methodist finished fourth in the NCAA Division III National Indoor Track Championship March 12. John Storms placed second in the 1,500 meter run, Sergio Elmore took third in the 55 meter dash, and Wes Wheeler finished sixth in the 800-meter race.

— Jansen Evans of the baseball team and Lori Silvasy of the women's soccer team were named the Outstanding Male and Female Senior Athletes of 1987-88.

Mallett-Rogers House Opens

The cover story in the August 1988, *Methodist College Today* described ribbon cutting and open house at the restored Mallett-Rogers House Sunday afternoon, May 15, 1988. Nearly 250 persons came out to see the restored structure (in a wooded area near the O'Hanlon Amphitheater), to view an inaugural art exhibit by 14 North Carolina artists, and to hear keynote speaker, Dr. Willam C. Fields.

What had been a coastal plains cottage attached to a larger two-story home, the house was divided when moved to the campus from the Eutaw area of Fayetteville. The older cottage (1778) was placed behind the larger two-story structure (1830); the larger house contained a living room, and two smaller rooms downstairs and two rooms upstairs. When the two houses were oriented side by side, the smaller cottage housed the kitchen and bath; Florence Rogers was the last person to live in the house built by Peter Mallett, an 18th century soldier and merchant who also built the first cotton mill in Fayetteville.

— CHAPTER 7 —

A Mallett-Rogers House Open House was held May 15, 1988.

The house was given to the College by the Florence Rogers Charitable Trust, which had it moved to the campus and paid for half the cost of its restoration. The house was reroofed with cedar shake shingles, rewired, and decorated in period colors. The interior of the large structure was designed as an art gallery with the upper parts of the walls (above the chair rail) carpeted and with track lighting on the ceilings. The upstairs was designed for displaying sculpture. The heart pine floors were retained and refinished.

In other news reported in the August 1988 *MCT*:
—Bill Billings interviewed Mike Safley '72, dean of students, who had just completed his first year at Methodist. Safley said he was especially proud that 85 percent of the resident students had participated in intramurals in 1987-88. He said he felt the two greatest challenges facing the College were: 1) filling the residence halls, and 2) graduating the students who came to Methodist as freshmen. He also expressed the hope that more students would become involved in the religious life program. [24]
—Fayetteville native Rita Wiggs was named assistant athletic director to Tom Austin, while retaining her duties as women's basketball coach and assistant professor of physical education.
—Speaking to summer graduates August 26, 1988, the Reverend Wallace Kirby urged class members to follow the example of Jesus Christ and seek the kind of fame secured through steadfast pursuit of worthy goals. President Hendricks conferred an honorary Doctor of Letters degree on Mary Lynn McCree Bryan

of Fayetteville for her work as editor of the Jane Addams papers and her service to local civic organizations.

—A dance troupe from Marseilles, France, performed at a luncheon on campus August 9.

—In the summer of 1988, Methodist College hosted a Summer Language Institute for training and certifying French and Spanish teachers for the elementary school grades. Thirty teachers from Cumberland County and surrounding school units attended.

Board Approves PAC Plans, AIDS Policy, Long-Range Plan

On the recommendation of the trustees' Building and Grounds Committee, the Methodist College Board of Trustees voted July 14, 1988, to authorize the president to borrow sufficient funds to pay off the College's federal loans and finance construction of the Physical Activities Center until non-liquid campaign assets could be liquidated. Three local banks had offered a line of credit of $3.7 million.

The trustees also approved a draft of a long-range (five year) plan for the College, committing the school to:

—A feasibility study for the addition of a master's degree program.

—Establish a sabbatical program for two faculty members per year.

—Assess outcomes by surveying graduate two, five, and ten years after graduation.

—Design and build a new entrance to the College.

—Replace roofs on the residence halls and windows in the women's residence halls.

—Increase the College's endowment to $7 million.

—Improve retention of resident students so that 65 percent of entering freshmen graduate in four years.

—Employ a psychiatrist to operate a counseling center.

—Complete the Physical Activities Center and initiate a campaign to build a new business and social science building.

—Raise the average SAT scores of entering freshmen 100 points over those entering in the fall of 1987.

—Enroll 500 residential students by 1993.

—Maintain an evening enrollment of 550 students per term.

—Restrict the percentage of the College operating budget going to financial aid to 13 percent. [25]

The trustees also approved an AIDS policy requiring the Office of Student Affairs to conduct an AIDS information program for staff and students and the College nurse to assess infected persons to determine whether there was a medical reason for exclusion from enrollment or employment.

— CHAPTER 7 —

Ground Broken For Physical Activities Center
Methodist College began its 29th school year in August 1988, with 1,502 students—955 in the day program and 547 in the evening program. Residential enrollment grew to 441 students; 35 international students enrolled, representing 15 countries. Site preparation began for the new Physical Activities Center.

A total of 24 new faculty members began work in the fall of 1988, including: Dr. Jo Ann Clark, chemistry; Dr. Carroll Jones, education; Peter

College officials gather for the College's first groundbreaking in more than 20 years.

Kendall, tennis management; Dr. Donald Klein, business; Dr. Jen-Hsiang Lin, business; Dr. Peter Murray, history; Dr. Shivappa Palled, math and computer science. New staff members included Jeff Brock and George Small in admissions; Tricia Turner, director of student affairs programming and counseling; Kathy Woltz, director of career placement and counseling; and Shelia Yates-Tanouye, director of ACES and coordinator of the Evening College.

An official ground breaking for the Physical Activities Center was held Saturday, October 8, 1988. Fifteen persons representing the College's various constituencies wielded green and gold shovels in a brief ceremony to mark the beginning of Methodist's first new building in 19 years. Louis Spilman, Ike O'Hanlon, and Dillard Teer represented the trustees.

Trustees Chair, Executive Committee Laud President Hendricks
Dr. Hendricks informed the Board of Trustees' Executive Committee September 15, 1988, that the College became free of federal debt September 13,

leaving a debt of approximately $1 million, the smallest in the history of the College. He said the federal debt of $1.3 million was retired with a payment of $623,000.

The president also reported that fall 1988 day enrollment was 960 and residential enrollment had grown to 450. He said site preparation had begun for the Physical Activities Center and that a ground breaking ceremony would be held October 8.

Trustees' Chair Ike O'Hanlon ended the meeting by saying he had been interested in Methodist College since its inception but had "never seen anything like the progress made since Dr. Hendricks had been president." [26] He described the progress made during Dr. Hendricks' first five years as a "miracle" and asked the Executive Committee to give the president a standing ovation.

Board Receives More Good News

Dr. Hendricks had more good news for the trustees October 6, 1988. He reported that:

—First Citizens Bank had given the College a $3.7 million line of credit, from which $633,000 had been borrowed to pay off the College's federal loans. He said the payoff of federal debt would not have been possible without the commitment of The North Carolina Conference of The United Methodist Church to pay the College $157,743 for 15 years toward debt retirement.

—550 students were enrolled in the two fall 1988 terms of Evening College.

—The average SAT score for entering freshmen had risen to 907.

A Reeves Auditorium 20th Anniversary Concert was held November 4, 1988.

— CHAPTER 7 —

Concert Marks 20th Year for Reeves Auditorium

Methodist College celebrated the 20th anniversary of Reeves Auditorium November 4, 1988, with a choral concert by the College chorus accompanied by an orchestra and four guest soloists. Two works were featured on the Friday evening program: George Fredric Handel's *Ode to St. Cecilia's Day* and Zolton Kodaly's *Te Deum*. A music enrichment seminar was held the next day.

In other news from fall 1988;
- —Methodist hosted its third Elderhostel, attended by 21 persons.
- —Dr. Scott Peck, noted psychiatrist and author of *The Road Less Traveled,* led a seminar at Methodist October 4.
- —Seven volunteers from Beta Beta Beta (MC's science honorary) picked up 12 bags of trash at Fort Fisher, N.C. September 24 as part of Beach Sweep '88.
- —A classroom (T-243) was converted into a television production studio for the communications program.
- —The College trustees authorized creation of a board of visitors to assist the College in fulfilling its mission.
- —Liz McBride was hired to direct a new business administration major with a concentration in equine management.
- —Methodist's ROTC unit was the largest student group participating in Fayetteville's Crop Walk for Hunger October 9.
- —The alumni association presented a special gift to Mrs. Morie Howard, a long-time friend of the College, at its 1988 homecoming banquet. Ray Gooch received the group's Outstanding Alumnus Award, and Dr. Sue Kimball was named Faculty Member of the Year.
- —In December 1988, Mrs. Susan Pulsipher, a native of England, became director of library services at Methodist. She held an undergraduate degree from King's College, University of London, and a Master of Library Science degree from North Carolina Central University.

Executive Committee Approves Fees

In a November 17, 1988, meeting, the trustees' Executive Committee approved the following fee schedule for 1989-90: tuition—$6,650, board—$1,850, room—$1,000, making the total cost $9,500 for a resident student.

Two Students Killed In Auto Accident

The November 21, 1988, *sMALL TALK* reported that two Methodist College students were killed Friday night November 4, 1988, in a multi-car crash near the college.

A car driven by Craig Thomas Chisum pulled out of Lofton Drive into Ramsey Street and was hit broadside by a northbound vehicle driven by Marvin Morrison of Fayetteville. The impact pushed Chisum's car into the southbound lane where it was struck by a third vehicle. The second impact threw Chisum and a passenger, William Thomas Journey, from the vehicle. Journey died instantly; Chisum died an hour later at Highsmith Rainey Hospital.

Fayetteville police reported that both Chisum and the driver of the second car were intoxicated. Chisum, 19, and Journey, 22, were reportedly on their way back to campus, after attending a party at Weatherstone Apartments. Chisum was from Malone, N.Y.; Journey from Richmond, Va.

A memorial service was held for the students November 8 in the Student Union. The Reverend William Green, college chaplain, and the Reverend Mike Safley, vice president for student affairs and dean of students, presided. Over 300 students and staff attended. [The following April, a small garden and marker were installed around the base of the bell tower in memory of Chisum and Journey.]

In other news from fall 1988:

—The women's soccer team finished 4-0 in the conference, 15-3-1 overall and hosted a NCAA regional where they defeated Kalamazoo 2-1 and advanced to the final four.

—Nancy Phillips was crowned Homecoming Queen Saturday October 8 during halftime of the soccer game. She was sponsored by Sanford Hall.

Chip Dicks Addresses Winter 1988 Graduates

The first *sMALL TALK* of 1989 reported that John G. Dicks III '73 from Chesterfield, Va., had addressed 100 winter graduates December 15, 1988. A lawyer then serving as a member of the Virginia House of Delegates, Dicks urged the graduating seniors to work for "the cause of peace, for the success of commerce, and for the future of democracy." [27]

During the winter commencement, Dr. Hendricks presented Dicks with a Methodist College Medallion.

In other news from January 1989:

—Dr. Hendricks introduced a Five-Year Strategic Plan for the ollege which projected a new main entrance, additions to the Science Building and library and a new building for the Reeves School of Business. In the area of academics, the president set goals for improving the percentage of faculty with Ph.D.s to 75 percent and winning accreditation for the teacher education, social work, and business programs.

—The cafeteria was renovated during the Christmas holidays, receiving new paint, tables and carpet.

—Betty Darden wrote a short news story about the new business administration with a concentration in equine management program.

—Eric Holle reported that John Crea, MC's first football coach, had recruited six transfer students to play for Methodist in the fall.

—Holle also quoted Gene Clayton, director of development, as saying Phase I of the Physical Activiites Center (minus the swimming pool) would be finished by December 31, 1989. He said the College still needed to raise $800,000 for the $3.8 million project.

Trustees Briefed On SACS Visit

Dr. Hendricks briefed the Board of Trustees January 28, 1989, on the April 10-13 visit by a reaffirmation committee of the Southern Association of Colleges and Schools. He said the visiting committee would be looking for financial stability, planning and institutional effectiveness, and faculty qualifications. He shared with the trustees copies of the College's "Self Study," "Strategic Plan," and "Planning, Evaluation, and (More) Planning" documents.

Reporting for the Development Committee, trustee Louis Spilman said contributions to the "Come of Age" campaign for the Physical Activities Center had exceeded $3 million but were not very liquid. He said the campaign had received just over $600,000 in cash.

George Johnson, chair of the Student Life Committee, said an increase in the number of male resident students [generated in large part by the addition of football] would require 1)housing males on one or more floors of one of the female dorms, and 2) renovating 12 of the College apartments to house 72 students.

Trustees approved a revised retirement benefit program to conform to federal law. Under the plan, the College would contribute 5 percent of each employee's salary (after one year's service) to the TIAA Retirement Fund. Disability insurance would be provided to employees after two years' service medical insurance would continue for 18 months after retirement. The ministerial housing allowance was set at $8,000.

Student Dies After Altercation

The February 13, 1989, *sMALL TALK* reported that Joe Cannata Jr., an Air Force veteran and 1987 sociology graduate, had died January 25, 1989, from head injuries sustained in an altercation that took place January 15 in the library parking lot at Methodist. Cannata had confronted a young man who was dating his daughter, a resident student. Cannata, 45, was survived by his wife Dolores and two daughters. [A sociology award is given annually at Methodist in memory of Cannata.]

—Eric Holle reported that the College trustees had approved making one of the female residence halls, Garber Hall, co-ed. Dean Safley said the college expected more male students in the fall than could be housed in Cumberland and Sanford halls. Safley said the co-ed hall would still be run like a female dorm and that second and third floor halls would likely be partitioned, with males on one half and females on the other half.

FSU Chancellor Speaks

Dr. Lloyd Hackley, chancellor of Fayetteville State University, delivered a speech on black history February 19, 1989, in Hensdale Chapel. Recalling his youth in Roanoke, Virginia, Dr. Hackley said older folks cared about black children in those days, giving encouragement or discipline when needed. "Today," he said, "blacks do not have this type of assurance." [28] The March 3, 1989, *sMALL TALK* ran the full text of Dr. Hackley's speech.

In other news from March 1989:

—Ingrid Sauceda, editor of *sMALL TALK*, said lack of funds and a small staff prevented the staff from moving to a weekly publication.

—The men's basketball team, led by sharp shooters Clinton Montford, Quinton Harshaw, and Cedric Brickey, finished its season 14-13

Physical Activity Center construction was in full swing in the spring of 1989.

CHAPTER 7

overall and 7-5 in the conference. Coach Dan Lawrence and the team recorded the first winning season in ten years.
— Track standout Danielle Baker, a junior from Morristown, N.J., won All-Conference honors, finishing second in the 55 meter hurdles, 400 meter dash, and 200 meter dash at the Mason-Dixon Conference Indoor Track and Field Championship February 17 at Virginia Tech. She also finished third in the 55 meter dash.

Applications Soar

In April 1989, Fiore Bergamasco, director of admissions, said 852 students had applied to Methodist for the fall, and the College had accepted 558. He said the average SAT score of those accepted was 900.

In other news from April 1989:
— Pearlette Burton wrote a feature story on the Office of Counseling and Career Placement and the efforts of director Kathy Woltz to upgrade its services to students.
— Two pages of photos showed staff and students at Show You Care Day, laying brick walks and planting trees in the area surrounding the bell tower. This would become the Craig Chisum and Tom Journey Memorial Garden.
— The baseball team set a new school record with 23 consecutive wins. N.C. Wesleyan and Winthrop College broke the win streak by defeating the Monarchs 5-2 and 12-11 respectively. Senior left fielder Mike Brewington ended his career batting .366, with 14 home runs, 57 RBIs, and 34 stolen bases.

Volunteers Build Memorial Garden

Approximately 80 staff and student volunteers spent Show You Care Day April 1, 1989, constructing the Journey-Chisum Memorial Garden at the base of the bell tower. The project included four brick walks radiating outward to four brick circles (for umbrella tables and benches) and the planting of a variety of trees and shrubs.

In other news reported in the summer 1989 issue of *Methodist College Today*:
— The College received a grant from the Sears Roebuck Foundation to establish a Teaching Excellence and Campus Leadership program to reward outstanding faculty performance.
— The Campbell University-Methodist College-Pembroke State U. Army ROTC Battalion (250 cadets) received the General Douglas MacArthur Award at Fort Monroe, Virginia, denoting

1985–1989

Show You Care Day 1989 — a memorial garden takes shape.

its selection as the top small college ROTC battalion in the nation.

SACS Committee Visits Methodist

A Southern Association of Colleges and Schools committee of 12 educators led by Dr. James Jordan, president of Shorter College in Rome, Georgia, visited Methodist College April 10-13, 1989. The committee reviewed a 499-page self-study and met with students, faculty, and staff to assess the College's compliance with new "outcomes assessment" criteria. The committee then drafted a report and recommendation to the full Southern Association regarding reaffirmation of accreditation for Methodist, including suggestions for improvement. Dr. Garland Knott, professor of religion, chaired the Faculty Steering Committee which prepared the self-study.

In other news reported in the Spring 1989 *MCT*:

—Friends of Davis Memorial Library and friends and family of Norma Womack gathered March 12 to dedicate a portrait and plaque in the main reading area in memory of Mrs. Womack.

—A golf driving range was opened on a lower campus field where corn was grown for many years.

—The Methodist College Chorus visited New York City and performed at churches in Mullica Hill, N.J. and Brooklyn, N.Y. on a spring break concert tour.

—Hubert Willis of Fayetteville gave $10,000 to endow the Eutha

— CHAPTER 7 —

L to R, Sam Womack, Lynda Womack. Alan Womack, Jennifer Womack at dedication of Norma Womack Reading Area in Davis Memorial Library.

Neighbors Willis Scholarship in honor of his wife. [Mr. Willis died a few weeks later on February 21. Later that spring, the United Methodist Men of Haymount United Methodist Church established a Hubert M. Willis Scholarship Fund and awarded two $2,500 scholarships to Methodist College students. Willis was a soil and water conservationist and a devoted United Methodist. He led a Kiwanis Club beautification program which resulted in hundreds of dogwood trees being planted across Fayetteville.]

—Reeves Auditorium acquired a new Tectronics lighting system with Producer II control board.
—Lynda Ransdell was hired to recruit a women's field hockey team.
—Pete Kendall was hired as the new men's and women's tennis coach.
—Superintendent of Buildings and Grounds Mason Sykes and the 34 members of his department were saluted in a feature article for their work on the Pauline Longest Nature Trail and efforts to beautify major venues on campus with the planting of trees, shrubs, and flowering plants.
—Brick-faced terraces were constructed in the east bank of the new football (old soccer) field to provide seating for football fans. {Years later, plastic seats would be installed on these terraces.]

Terry Sanford Addresses 26th Class

Addressing the 122 members of Methodist's Class of 1989 May 7, 1989, U.S. Sen. Terry Sanford challenged the graduating seniors to "lift up the weak" by serving others. [29] Sixteen members of the Class of 1964 returned for a 25th class reunion, marching in as a group and sitting together.

Sanford said the late Tar Heel playwright Paul Green once asked a group of college students, "What do you young people care about?" The senator then told the seniors sitting in front of him, "The time has come for you to answer Paul Green's question. Your answer will cost you your life. It might as well be something noble. It would be a pity to have given your life for selfishness, for greed, for nothing." [30]

As part of the commencement, Rebecca Burleigh received the Stacy Weaver Award, and President Hendricks awarded honorary Doctor of Humanities degrees to I. H. O'Hanlon and Lura Tally. Two retiring faculty members—Mrs. Inge Dent (German and French) and Dr. John Tobler (political science) received silver trays.

In an interview with Bill Billings, Terry Sanford:

—praised the N.C. General Assembly for establishing [and increasing the dollar amount of] the N.C. Legislative Tuition Grant [then worth $1,100 a year] for North Carolina residents, a program Sanford first proposed in the1960s.

—declared his opposition to Methodist College becoming a university. "I don't believe great colleges ought to have pretensions about becoming universities. . . . I'd rather see this as a great four-year liberal arts college doing superbly what a four-year liberal arts college can do in the field of education." [31]

—said Methodist should not count on being endowed by a wealthy benefactor (e.g. James B. Duke). "The way to go about raising funds is to reach all the people you can and to draw them into understanding what this College can do." [32]

Athletes Excel at Nationals

Playing at Gates Four Golf and Country Club at Hope Mills, N.C. May 7-10, 1989, the Methodist College women's golf team won its fourth National Golf Coaches Association Division III National Championship by 64 strokes. Joy Bonhurst had the third best individual score, while teammates Holly Andrews and Kristine Kavanaugh tied for fourth. The team was coached by Jerry Hogge.

The men's golf team finished second to Cal State-Stanislaus in the NCAA Division III National Championships in Panora, Iowa. John McCullough was the medalist. Coach Steve Conley was named Golf Coaches of America Division III Coach of the Year.

In other sports news:

— CHAPTER 7 —

—The women's tennis team won its first-ever Dixie Conference Championship, while the men finished second.
—Danielle Baker competed in three events at the NCAA Division III Track and Field Meet and earned All-American honors.
—Mike Brewington '88, a MC baseball alum, was drafted in the 30th round by the Pittsburgh Pirates.
—The 1989 baseball team was denied a third trip to the College World Series by Allegheny College and Ferrum College. They enjoyed a 23-game winning streak and finished 33-3 overall.
—Methodist's first football team (65 players) began practice August 15, 1989.
—Methodist won the Dixie Conference President's Cup (for success in intercollegiate sports) a second year.

Trustees Consider Land Purchase

At a May 11, 1989, meeting of the Board of Trustees, Dr. Hendricks recommended that the College try to purchase seven acres of land bordering the College on its northwest corner, land between the president's home and the Quick Stop. He said the land was zoned multi-family residential. The board authorized the president to offer the owners (Kinlaws) a purchase agreement for the land.

Dr. Hendricks reported that 32 persons had been selected to serve on the Methodist College Board of Visitors, which would hold its first meeting May 18, 1989.

Executive Committee Discusses Cash Flow

The trustees' Executive Committee went into executive (closed) session July 20, 1989, to discuss the College's cash flow situation and the need to build a long-term cash reserve.

Dr. Hendricks informed the committee that the SACS visiting committee had made 41 recommendations to the College, most in the academic area, but some regarding business and accounting procedures.

In a report to the trustees' Development Committee, Gene Clayton said:
—$137,028 had been raised toward the Methodist College Foundation's Annual Fund goal of $175,000 for 1989.
—60 contributions to the Yarborough Endowment Fund had been received in memory of Dr. Wilson Yarborough Sr., bringing the fund to $22,541.
—$216,385 had been received toward the Kresge challenge grant of $541,501. He said the Come of Age campaign had pledges

1985–1989

and gifts totaling $3,484,397, leaving $325,115 to be raised by March 1, 1990, to reach the campaign goal of $3,809,513 and receive the Kresge grant.

Twenty-five Join Faculty

Methodist College began its 30th academic year in August 1989, with 1,461 students—994 in the day program and 467 in the evening. The number of students living on campus increased to 480.

The College welcomed 25 new faculty members, including: Mrs. Gilda Benstead, education; Mr. Robert Bloodworth, communications; Dr. Sue Bowden, education and physical education; Mr. Alton Bridges, business; Mrs. Jane Cherry, advisor to international students; Dr. Michael Colonnese, English and creative writing; Dr. Robert Cooper, accounting; Dr. Anthony DeLapa, education; Ms. Carol Higy, physical education; Dr. George Maguire, chemistry; Mr. Trevor Morris, political science; Dr. JoAnn Parkerson, education; Dr. Janet White, education; Mr. Paul F. Wilson, theatre and speech.

Football came to Methodist in the fall of 1989.

Monarch Athletes Excel

In the fall of 1989, the Lady Monarch soccer team posted a 17-6 record and advanced to the NCAA Division III "final four," losing to Ithaca in the semifinals.

The men's soccer team hosted the Dixie Conference championship, losing to Greensboro College in the finals. The team's overall record was 14-5.

— CHAPTER 7 —

John Storms won the NCAA South-Southeast Regional Cross Country meet hosted by Methodist. He ran the course in 25:12, setting a new course record, was named All-Region, and was invited to compete in the NCAA National Cross Country Meet in Pale Island, Il. November 18.

Methodist' first football team (46 players) finished its inaugural season 0-10, and scored zero points against Washington and Lee, Newport News Apprentice, Ferrum, Bridgewater, Davidson, and Randolph-Macon. Coach John Crea said youth, small player size, injuries, and a tough schedule were the major reasons for the losses.

Trustees Discuss Red Ink

When the trustees' Executive Committee met September 14, 1989, Dr. Hendricks said the college audit for 1988-89 would show an operating deficit between $200,000 and $300,000. He said the deficit was caused by 1) an over-run in budget line items, 2) a greatly overspent financial aid budget, and 3) $580,000 in uncollected student accounts. [33]

The president projected a $330,000 budget surplus for 1989-90, but said that surplus would have to be used to repay $400,000 borrowed from the capital campaign and cash reserve.

Enrollment Grows Five Percent

Dr. Hendricks informed the trustees October 12, 1989, that fall 1989, day enrollment had reached 990, 50 students more than the year before, while residential enrollment had reached 490, up 40 students from fall 1988.

Following an executive session, the trustees authorized the president to borrow an additional $300,000 from First Citizens Bank to complete the construction of the Physical Activities Center.

At the trustees' final meeting of 1989, November 16, Dr. Hendricks said campus security was an increasing concern and that an additional security guard would be added from dark until midnight.

The president also distributed copies of the College's response to the recommendations of the SACS visiting committee.

A Development Office report showed that the Foundation's Annual Fund drive had raised 127 percent of its goal—$221,598 and that $278,936 was still needed to meet the capital campaign goal of $3.8 million.

College Stirs the Caldron

In the fall of 1989, Methodist launched a "Stirring the Caldron" series of luncheon meetings in which College staff and students gathered to discuss important issues. Topics included: whether North Carolina should have a state

1985–1989

lottery, universal public service, and art censorship and public money.

The December 1989, *Methodist College Today* included a two-page feature story on former dean of women Inge Dent and shorter features on faculty members Dr. Michael Colonnese (English) and Robert Bloodworth (communications). Alumnus Tom Bell '69 was profiled for winning a grant from the A. J. Fletcher Foundation to attend a tropical ecology workshop in Belize.

Homecoming Focuses on Roaring Twenties

Homecoming 1989 as held October 27-29 and had as its theme, "The Roaring Twenties." Special activities included a hunt on campus for a facsimile of Al Capone's buried vault, a Charleston dance contest, a casino night, a parade around the football field, a halftime performance by the Cary (N.C.) Marching Band, the crowning of Danielle Baker and Chris Hardy as homecoming queen and king respectively, and a dance at the Holiday Inn of I-95 on Cedar Creek Road.

At the alumni association's homecoming banquet, Susan Yost Jaeger '81 received the outstanding Alumni Service Award, Jack Langley '70 won the Distinguished Alumni Award, and Elaine Porter, associate professor of French, was named Outstanding Faculty Member.

College Commemorates Signing of U.S. Constitution

State and local bicentennial committees combined with Methodist College to commemorate North Carolina's ratification of the U.S. Constitution November 22, 1789, in Fayetteville. *The Patriots*, a play by Sidney Kingsley, was performed at Methodist October 13-15; it focused on the differing viewpoints of Alexander Hamilton and Thomas Jefferson regarding governance of the new democracy.

In other fall 1989 news:

—The Green and Gold Masque Keys presented Samuel Beckett's play *Waiting for Godot* November 10-12. Directed by Robert Bloodworth, the production starred Andy Miller, Dan Covell, Phillip Horne, Pamela Johnson, and Daniel Greene-Colonnese.

—Elaine Porter, associate professor of French, and Mrs. Georgia Grant of the Cumberland County Schools, worked with eleven teams of educators from North Carolina to develop methods courses for training elementary school foreign language teachers.

— CHAPTER 7 —

The Patriots *marked the bicentennial of North Carolina's ratification of the U.S. Constitution.*

—Meeting in Atlanta in December, the Southern Association of Colleges and Schools reaffirmed the accreditation of Methodist College for another ten years.

—Dr. John O. Tobler, founder of the Political Science Department at Methodist, died December 16, 1989, at the age of 79. He taught full-time from 1965 to 1982 and part-time from 1982-89.

—The women's soccer team advanced to the national semifinals in San Diego, losing to unbeaten Ithaca 2-0.

—The men's soccer team finished second in the Dixie Conference Championship to Greensboro College, but finished 14-5 overall with a No. 13 national ranking.

Yow, Reeves Receive Honorary Degrees

Methodist College awarded 107 degrees to 104 persons at its 17th winter commencement December 14, 1989. In his commencement address, Dr. Thomas S. Yow III '66, president of Martin Methodist College in Pulaski, Tennessee, challenged the graduating seniors to maintain a willingness to grow, change, and adapt; a commitment to excellence, and a commitment to Christian values." [34]

Dr. Thomas Yow

President Hendricks awarded Dr. Yow an honorary Doctor of Divinity degree and then presented an honorary Doctor of Humanities degree to Sanford businessman Charles Mercer Reeves, the principal benefactor of Methodist's Reeves School of Business.

Physical Activities Center Named for March Riddle

Methodist College announced December 17, 1989, that its new Physical Activities Center would be named for March Floyd Riddle, wife of College trustee J. P. Riddle.

College athletic officials scheduled the first ten basketball games of the 1989-90 season on the road, to avoid having to play another home game in the old "tin can" gymnasium.

— CHAPTER 7 —

END NOTES
Chapter Seven

1. M. Elton Hendricks, remarks to the Methodist College Board of Trustees, January 31, 1985, TM, Book 4.
2. M. Elton Hendricks, interview with John Jones, *sMALL TALK*, March 15, 1985, file.
3. Gene Clayton, news story, *sMALL TALK*, April 16, 1985, file.
4. M. Elton Hendricks, news story, *sMALL TALK*, April 16, 1985, file.
5. Gene Clayton, news story, *sMALL TALK*, April 16, 1985, file.
6. Tom Jumalon, editorial, *sMALL TALK*, September 13, 1985, file.
7. M. Elton Hendricks, remarks to the Methodist College Board of Trustees, October 9, 1986, TM, Book 4.
8. J. Allen Norris, news story, *Methodist College Today*, Fall 1986, file.
9. Walt Swing, chair of the Honor Board, news story, *Methodist College Today*, Fall 1986, file.
10. Ibid.
11. M. Elton Hendricks, news story, *sMALL TALK*, October 24, 1986, file.
12. Carlton P. Minnick, Jr., news story, *sMALL TALK*, January 23, 1987, file.
13. Joe Miller, interview with Gerald Davis, *sMALL TALK*, March 27, 1987, file.
14. Bill Lowdermilk, news story, *Methodist College Today*, August 1987, file.
15. Gene Clayton, remarks to Ike O'Hanlon, at Methodist College Board of Trustees meeting July 9, 1987, TM, Book 4.
16. M. Elton Hendricks, interview story, *sMALL TALK*, October 6, 1987, file.
17. Richard Pearce, news story, *sMALL TALK*, January 29, 1988, file.
18. William Green, feature article, *sMALL TALK*, February 24, 1988, file.
19. Gerald Davis, editorial, *sMALL TALK*, March 29, 1988, file.
20. M. Elton Hendricks, remarks to the Methodist College Board of Trustees May 12, 1988, TM, Book 4.
21. Excerpt from alcohol policy presented to the Methodist College Board of Trustees May 12, 1988, TM, Book 4.
22. Ibid.
23. Sid Huggins, remarks to the Methodist College Board of Trustees May 12, 1988, TM, Book 4.
24. Michael Safley, interview with Bill Billings, *Methodist College Today*,

August 1988, file.
25. Five Year Plan adopted by the Methodist College Board of Trustees July 14, 1988, TM, Book 4.
26. Ike O'Hanlon, remarks to the Methodist College Board of Trustees' Executive Committee September 15, 1988, TM, Book 4.
27. John G. Dicks III, news story, *sMALL TALK*, January 30, 1989, file.
28. Lloyd V. Hackley, news story, *sMALL TALK*, March 3, 1989, file.
29. Terry Sanford, news story, *Methodist College Today*, August 1989, file.
30. Ibid.
31. Terry Sanford, interview with Bill Billings, *Methodist College Today*, August 1989, file.
32. Ibid.
33. M. Elton Hendricks, remarks to the Executive Committee of the Methodist College Board of Trustees, September 14, 1989, TM, Book 4.
34. Thomas S. Yow III, news story, *sMALL TALK*, February 9, 1990, file.

Dr. Hendricks tosses up the first-tip off in the March Riddle Center

Chapter 8

New Programs Spur Growth
1990-94

> "I challenge you to be a pedaler on the great bicycle of life. Some people pedal, some ride, and some coast."
>
> —*M. Elton Hendricks, president, addressing students at the fall 1993, opening convocation.*

As Methodist College began its fourth decade, the campus was buzzing with excitement over completion of the March F. Riddle Center. The physical education and coaching staff moved into the new physical activities center January 18, 1990. The center opened to the public January 23, when the women's and men's basketball teams played host to Ferrum College.

In a tip-off ceremony held prior to the men's game, Trustees Chairman Ike O'Hanlon took the microphone and, in his famous "basso" voice, exhorted Monarch fans to "stand up and holler." College President Elton Hendricks then tossed up a ceremonial "tip-off" basketball at center court.

The women lost their game 78-60; the men won 91-83. Claudia Lucas scored the first basket for the women, and James Wear scored the first basket for the men.

To commemorate the retirement of the old "tin can" gymnasium, Bill Kirby, assistant sports editor of *The Fayetteville Observer-Times*, wrote a column in which he quoted MC alumni who had played basketball there. Linwood Ferrell, Gene Clayton, and Jerry Huckabee all remembered the stifling heat, the hard, tile-over-concrete floor, and the sound of fans beating on the metal walls behind the bleachers.

Trustees Elect New Officers

In a February 8, 1990, meeting, the Methodist College Board of Trustees approved revisions to the college charter, set the ministerial housing allowance at $8,000, and granted faculty emeritus status to Bruce Pulliam.

Louis Spilman reported that the "Come of Age" capital campaign for the physical activities center had raised $3,713,556 and that $95,956 would have to be raised by March 1 to meet the Kresge Foundation's challenge grant requirement.

— CHAPTER 8 —

Dr. Hendricks reported that Dr. Lynn Sadler, vice president for academic affairs, had been appointed president of Johnson State College in Vermont and that Walt Swing would serve as interim academic dean until a new dean began work in July.

In a February 8, 1990, meeting, the Methodist College Board of Trustees paid tribute to I. H. O'Hanlon May 17, 1990, for his leadership as board chairman since 1981. The board then approved the following slate of officers submitted by the Nominating Committee: Charles Gaddy, chairman; Frank Barragan, vice chairman; Walter Clark, secretary; and Louis Spilman, Jr. treasurer.

The board also approved a tribute to Roy Whitmire, who was retiring July 1 as vice president for business affairs after 15 years service. Dr. Hendricks commended Whitmire for his role in the retirement of $2.2 million in federal debt, energy conservation measures (lighting and windows), and an increase in the College endowment to $2.7 million.

When the trustees' Executive Committee met March 15, 1990, Dr. Hendricks reported that the terms of the Kresge Challenge Grant had been met and the College should receive the $250,000 Kresge grant by March 16. He said the next fund-raising campaign should focus on library expansion and technology, an academic building, and endowment development. A report from the Methodist College Foundation indicated that $44,969 of a goal of $175,000 had been pledged to the Dr. and Mrs. Samuel J. Womack Endowed Chair in Religion and Philosophy.

Dr. Hendricks also introduced Mr. Thomas Williams, the new vice president for development, and Walt Swing, acting vice president for academic affairs. He said two additional holes were being added to the College golf course, making a total of five. After discussing the possibility of buying a parcel of land on the north side of the campus, the committee adjourned and visited the site.

Dr. Hendricks announced the appointment of Methodist's sixth academic dean March 27. He announced that Dr. Erik Bitterbaum, associate provost at Nebraska Wesleyan University in Lincoln, would become vice president for academic affairs at Methodist July 1.

President Taps Gene Clayton, Tom Williams

Dr. Hendricks announced February 20, 1990, that he had appointed Gene Clayton vice president for business affairs effective April 1, to succeed Roy Whitmire. Clayton had served as director of development since 1985. Dr. Hendricks said Clayton's 27 years of experience at Methodist and his knowledge of the Fayetteville community would be valuable assets in the business office.

The president said Thomas W. Williams Jr., would succeed Clayton as director of development, effective March 15. A Fayetteville resident since 1977, Williams had recently retired as senior vice president and Fayetteville area executive for Wachovia Bank and Trust Company. Williams was then serving as president of the Methodist College Foundation. He held degrees from Davidson College and the University of North Carolina

A Student Vents

The following poem by D. K. Doane reflects an experience shared by thousands of Methodist students who have found some of their liberal arts core requirements "challenging." This poem appeared in the February 9, 1990, sMALL TALK:

"Religion 103"

Fire and brimstone, toil and trouble,
Furrowed brows and seeing double,
Doom, despair, eternal woe,
And all the evil man can know.

Wailing, moaning, gnashing teeth,
Howls of anguish, no relief,
The gates of purgatory closed
On these lost, discontented souls.

But what can all this nightmare mean,
This torture cruel, and misery?
Is this inferno Dante's making?
Is it a dream or frightful waking?

There really is no mystery--
It's just Religion 103.

Theodicy, we're here to find
To satisfy inquiring mind,
And learn about hierophany
and maybe eschatology.

To answer questions large and cosmic
Of our beings ontologic,
To show us reason, make us wise,
To open unsuspecting eyes.

Icon, fetish, expiation,
Theophany, Propitiation,
Vishnu, Krishna, Yang, and Yin,
Kali, Siva, grace and sin.

But will I ever learn to tell
The difference between Sheol and Hell?
Or Varna, Moksha--from Sanskrit--
and all the other holy--words?

It's all a blur of something-ism:
Mono-, poly-, pantheism.
and here's the thing that's aggravating--
I need this course for graduating.

I leave to stronger hearts the task
Of seeking immortality--
I'll be happy just to pass
Religion103. [1]

S.G.A. President Receives $1,000 Scholarship

In March 1990, sMALL TALK staff writer Kevin Carlson reported that the S.G.A. Senate had approved changes in candidate eligibility, raising the

— CHAPTER 8 —

required GPA from 2.0 to 2.5. Sophomores with a semester's experience in the Senate could run for vice president. Candidates for S.G.A. president had to be rising juniors or seniors and had to have attended Methodist for two consecutive semesters prior to running for office. The Senate also announced that the S.G.A. president would henceforth receive a $1,000 scholarship from the college, effective in 1990.

In other news:

—At the opening ceremonies for the college golf course February 5, 1990, President Hendricks sliced two golf balls out of bounds and then hit a good third ball off the first tee.

—At the fifth annual Show You Care Day March 24, volunteer faculty, staff, and students planted trees and flowers between the Trustees Building and the Administration Building and remarked and beautified the Paul Longest Nature Trail. Joe Pereira chaired the committee that planned the program.

—The Student Activities Council hosted the second annual Spring Fling April 15-21, 1990. Activities included a live concert by the rock bands "See You" and "The Creek." Other events included team tennis, a volleyball tournament, a scavenger hunt, a baseball bat dash, a pie-eating contest, and an obstacle course.

Student volunteers work on the Pauline Longest Nature Trail at Show You Care Day.

1990–1994

Novelist John Ehle Honored at Symposium

"John Ehle: Born to Be a Writer" was the subject of Methodist College's ninth Southern Writers Symposium March 23-24, 1990. An Asheville, N.C. native and U.N.C. graduate, Ehle was the author of 19 books (11 fiction, six non-fiction), had taught at U.N.C., and had worked as a special assistant to North Carolina Governor Terry Sanford in the early 1960s. While working for Sanford, Ehle developed proposals and secured grants to establish the North Carolina School of the Arts in Winston-Salem, the N.C. Film Office, and the Governor's School (summer classes for talented high school students).

Mr. Ehle and his wife, Rosemary Harris, a British actress, attended the event, along with Terry Sanford and more than a dozen literary scholars who presented papers about Ehle's work. Dr. Sue Kimball, professor of English, directed the symposium.

A three-act play by Lee Yopp, based on Ehle's novel *Time of Drums,* was presented at the Fort Bragg Playhouse. Set in 1862, the play featured actors Robert Bloodworth, Leonard McLeod, Pat Reese, Michael Melcher, Margaret Jemison, and Shannon Bailey.

United Methodist youth sing at a choral workshop in Hensdale Chapel.

Church Officials Praise Church Relations Program

Three representatives of The University Senate of The United Methodist Church visited Methodist College April 19 and 20, 1990. In its report, the committee cited Methodist's church relations program as "one of our best models of effective college-church relations to be found in any of the colleges related to The United Methodist Church." [2] The committee said it was

— CHAPTER 8 —

impressed that 83 church groups had met on the Methodist campus and that college representatives had appeared in 53 churches within The North Carolina Conference of The United Methodist Church during the year.

The group described Methodist's academic programs as "solid, with a competent faculty" [3] and praised Dr. Elton Hendricks, College president, for providing strong "leadership with both vision and enthusiasm." [4]

Schools Superintendent Addresses Class of 1990

Dr. Larry E. Rowedder, superintendent of the Cumberland County Schools, addressed 124 members of the Class of 1990, at Methodist's 27th spring commencement Sunday, May 6, 1990.

Dr. Rowedder urged the graduating seniors to accept the responsibilities of a professional, to: 1) advance the body of knowledge in one's chosen field, 2) maintain personal integrity and a code of ethics in dealing with others, 3) serve one's community, and 4) never stop learning. [5] Connie Kibben, an English major from Pikeville, N.C., received the Stacy Weaver Award. The Reverend Dr. William K. Quick, pastor of Metropolitan United Methodist Church in Detroit and a native of nearby Scotland County, received a Methodist College Medallion for his 37 years of distinguished service to The United Methodist Church. [Quick served nine churches in The North Carolina Conference before accepting the Detroit appointment in 1974.]

Dr. Quick had delivered the baccalaureate sermon earlier, challenging members of the graduating class to seek a new discovery each day and to match their personal efforts to their abilities.

One member of the Class of 1990, was the subject of a feature story in the August 1990, *Methodist College Today*. Celeste DePriest, who had worked as a secretary at Methodist from 1968-73, received a B.A. in English *cum laude*, 22 years after taking her first class at Methodist.

In the summer of 1988, the wife of Todd DePriest '70 and the mother of two, took leave from her job in a pediatrician's office in Maryland and returned to Methodist to take the four courses she needed to earn a Methodist degree. Two years later, after transferring in the last credits she needed, Mrs. DePriest was approved for graduation. Her husband Todd was her sponsor during graduation, and their children Jeff and Jennifer also attended. At the time of her graduation, Mrs. DePriest was teaching mentally and physically handicapped adults at Harford Community College in Bel Air, Maryland.

In other news from spring 1990:

—Roger Pait '85, a chemist at ICI Americas in Fayetteville, was elected president of the Methodist College Alumni Association January 20, 1990.

- Dr. Linda Sue Barnes, professor of biology, received the College's first annual Teaching Excellence and Campus Leadership Award April 10, 1990. The award was funded by a grant of $2,000 from the Sears-Roebuck Foundation.
- College President M. Elton Hendricks was awarded an honorary Doctor of Humanities degree from Wofford College May 20, 1990. [Dr. Hendricks received an undergraduate degree in history from Wofford in 1958.]
- The men's golf team won the NCAA Division III National Championship May 25 at Jekyll Island, Georgia, by 30 strokes. Rob Pilewski took medalist honors with a 289 total score. Coach Steve Conley said, "We were never beaten on any day of the tournament. The guys really stayed focused." [6]
- The women's tennis team won the Dixie Conference tennis title and finished 18-3 overall.
- The softball team won the Dixie Conference Softball Tournament and completed its season 23-11 overall.
- The 1990 baseball team (27-17) advanced to the NCAA Division III Baseball Tournament, but was defeated by N.C. Wesleyan in regional action in New Jersey.

Trustees Elect Charlie Gaddy Chairman

The Methodist College Board of Trustees elected Charlie Gaddy, a newscaster with WRAL-TV 5 in Raleigh, N.C., board chairman May 17, 1990. A graduate of Guilford College, an Army veteran, and a United Methodist, Gaddy succeeded Ike O'Hanlon July 1.

Other officers elected by the board were Fayetteville residents Frank Barragan Jr., vice chairman; Walter Clark, secretary; and Louis Spilman Jr., treasurer. Barragan was the board chairman and former president of North Carolina Natural Gas Corporation. Clark was the chief executive officer and treasurer of Mid-South Insurance Company. Spilman, a 1964, graduate of Methodist, was a retired businessman.

Board Chooses UMF To Manage Endowment Funds

At a joint meeting of the trustees' Executive and Investment committees July 19, 1990, Dr. Hendricks introduced Dr. Erik Bitterbaum, the new vice president for academic affairs.

The president also reported that Carolina Power and Light Co. had assumed responsibility for the College's underground electric cables and would install a loop system over the next two summers. He said CP&L was now serving the Science Building and Reeves Auditorium. Dr. Hendricks said an offer of $175,000 for land bordering the campus on the north had been rejected by the owners, but that negotiations would continue.

After considering three proposals for managing the College endowment—from First Citizens Bank, Branch Banking & Trust Co., and The United Methodist Foundation—the trustees selected The United Methodist Foundation.

Faculty Perform In Scotland and Wales

From July 23 - August 6, 1990, Bob Bloodworth of the Communications Department, and Parker Wilson of the History Department performed in a Cape Fear Regional Theatre production of Thornton Wilder's *Our Town* in Dumfries, Scotland, and Rexham, Wales. Bloodworth played the role of Mr. Webb, and Wilson was cast as Howie. Lee Yopp, director of the Fort Bragg Playhouse, directed the play.

Wilson described the final performance in Dumfries as "very exciting and emotional. There was weeping from the audience when we sang, 'Blest Be the Tie.' I've never experienced anything like it." [7]

Duke Dean Addresses Summer Graduates

The Reverend Dr. Dennis Campbell, dean of the Duke University Divinity School, delivered the address at Methodist's 17th summer commencement August 29, 1990. He challenged the 59 degree candidates to "put down deep roots . . . to: 1) seek that which endures in a world of change, 2) know yourself and sustain your faith 3) never settle for shallow thinking, and 4) look forward to the future; dare to risk and serve. [8]

Troop Deployment Trims Enrollment

Methodist College began its 31st academic year and fourth decade of operation August 22, 1990, with a new chairman of the Board of Trustees, three new vice presidents, and a new soccer field house. The vice presidents were: Dr. Erik Bitterbaum, academic affairs; Gene Clayton, business affairs; and Thomas W. Williams, Jr., development.

Other new personnel included: Charles Plummer, registrar; Samuel Clark, director of institutional computing; and Ann Davidson, women's golf coach.

The College enrolled 1,255 students in the fall of 1990, 969 in the day program and 343 in the evening program. Day enrollment declined 4 percent from a year earlier, while evening enrollment declined 21percent from fall 1989. The deployment of U.S. troops to Saudi Arabia following Iraq's invasion of Kuwait—Operation Desert Shield—had a negative impact on College enrollment.

President Shares Thoughts

In his opening convocation address September 11, 1990, Dr. Hendricks contrasted instruction and education, saying, "Education is not the filling of your mind with data and information. It is the opening of eyes, the stirring of the spirit." [9] The president said four human traits epitomize "education": 1) thinking critically, 2) judging wisely, 3) knowing how to learn, and 4) desiring to learn. [10]

In a September 1990, "extra edition" of *Methodist College Today*, President Hendricks reviewed the major components of "A Strategic Plan for Methodist College: 1989-94." In the area of facilities, Dr. Hendricks said Methodist needed an addition to the library, more classrooms and offices to support business programs, and major improvements to the Science Building.

President Reports On Campus Security

Dr. Hendricks informed the trustees' Executive Committee September 13, 1990, that the College was employing three security guards during evening hours, had hired a new security director, and had installed an eight-foot fence from the back of Weaver Hall to Sanford Hall. He said 18 additional lights would be installed in the residence hall area and undergrowth would be cut.

In a report to the trustees October 11, 1990, Dr. Hendricks said Dr. William Jordan had contributed $50,000 toward the cost of building a soccer field house, and the College was providing an additional $25,000.

The president also reported:

— Fall 1990, enrollment in the day program had dropped to 980 students, compared to 1,013 in fall 1989. He said the Saudi Arabia situation (deployment of U.S. troops) had contributed to a loss of 250 evening students, bringing evening enrollment to 300.

—$1.1 million in endowment funds had been transferred to The United Methodist Foundation.

—CP&L was purchasing one-half acre from the College to expand its electric substation.

College Dedicates Riddle Center

Methodist formally dedicated the March F. Riddle Center Saturday, October 20, 1990, during homecoming weekend. President Hendricks praised the College trustees, the Riddle family, and other major donors to the project. Two plaques were unveiled in the lobby of the physical activities center—one honoring March F. Riddle and another listing more than 300 "Distinguished

— CHAPTER 8 —

Monarchs," alumni who had contributed $1,000 or more to the "Come of Age" capital campaign. Smaller plaques were mounted on interior walls and doors to recognize other gifts that made the building possible.

In other news from fall 1990:

—Cpt. John Bucciarelli and the ROTC cadets built a cannon and brought it to MC football games. The cannon was fired whenever the Monarchs scored.

—MC's Student Council for Exceptional Children staged its first annual Harvest Festival and Kiddie Carnival October 27.

—Jim Darden '69 published a book entitled *Guests of the Emperor—The Story of Dick Darden,* which described the experiences of Jim's father and other U.S. sailors as Japanese prisoners of war. The Americans were captured during the Battle of Wake Island during World War II. Using Navy archives and interviews with his father and other former POWs, Darden told a chilling but inspiring story of how the Americans survived years of physical and psychological abuse.

Dr Hendricks escorts Mrs. March Riddle.

Homecoming 1990 Draws Many Alumni

The cover photo for the November 1990, *Methodist College Today* showed basketball alum Howard Hudson '70 dribbling a basketball for the Gold Team at an alumni reunion game in the Riddle Center. Coached by Gene Clayton, the Gold Team defeated the Green Team, coached by Jim Darden '69, 43-38.

Walter Turner '65, a member of the College's first basketball team, wrote a feature story for *MCT* about the 25th reunion of his graduating class. Turner was photographed with eight other members of his class at the alumni banquet.

Turner said he spotted classmates David Altman, Jerry Marcus, Phil Levine, and Sparky Rapelye at the dedication and tour of the Riddle Center. At the alumni basketball game, Turner saw John Hamilton carrying a large camera. At the football game he met George Potts; the two then moved on to the men's soccer game with Emory University. At the alumni dinner in the

1990–1994

Members of the Class of '65 gather for a reunion photo.

Alumni Dining Room, Turner was reunited with Jerry Keen, Neil Sutton, Paul Brill, Sparky Rapelye, Loche McLean, and Cynthia Walker.

In other homecoming highlights:
— The Cross Creek Pipes and Drums led the homecoming parade.
— Randolph-Macon's football team defeated the Monarchs 20-7, while MC's men's soccer team defeated Emory 2-1, and the women's soccer team shut out Mary Washington 4-0.
— At the alumni dinner, Gene Dillman '73 received the Alumni Service Award and Dr. Robert Christian, professor of English, accepted the Outstanding Faculty Member Award.
— At the homecoming dance, Heather Owen and Jay Kirkpatrick were crowned homecoming queen and king of 1990.

1990 Soccer Teams Excel

In the fall of 1990, the Lady Monarch soccer team advanced to the NCAA Division III semifinals, losing to Ithaca 1-0. Ranked No. 1 in the region and nation, Coach Joe Pereira's 1990 team achieved 14 shut-out victories, allowing their opponents only five goals during the regular season.

— CHAPTER 8 —

The men's soccer team, coached by Alan Dawson, went undefeated in conference play and advanced to the NCAA South Regional, losing to Bethany 1-0. Goalie Lance Watkins posted a school record 11 shut-outs for the season.

Larry Frazier on Positive Thinking

The November 1990, *Methodist College Today* contained a reprint of a *sMALL TALK* feature story about Larry Frazier '70. Linda Welch wrote the story after Frazier, an English teacher at Reid Ross Junior High School, spoke to a special education class at Methodist September 5.

A victim of "arthrogryposis-congenta" which cost him the use of his arms and legs, Frazier had moved to Fayetteville from Phoenix, Arizona when he was two years old. He spent much of his childhood in hospitals and was confined to a wheelchair. His parents divorced when he was 12, and Larry was sent to live with his father in Phoenix, where he was home-schooled until he became a senior at Carl Hayden High School.

Frazier recalled that his student years at Methodist were often difficult because the College had few accommodations for handicapped students. He relied on strong friends to lift his manual wheelchair over barriers large and small.

In his interview with Linda Welch, Frazier described himself as a strict disciplinarian with his junior high English class. Holding a pen or pencil in his teeth, he was able to keep records, correct papers, and turn the pages of books; he had completed 20 years of teaching when he was interviewed. Among his hobbies he listed painting and woodburning; he invented a special holder that allowed him to cast a fishing rod and reel with his mouth. One of his poems, "Alone, Waiting for the Light," which he wrote for his wife, was published.

Frazier and his wife Kay had two children: Aaron, ten, and Lauren, five. Frazier said he had tried to teach his children to be kind to others and to appreciate the value of a good education.

Students Protest Loss of Fall Break

In a front page story carried in the November 19, 1990, *sMALL TALK*, reporter Melissa Rogers decried the fact that the faculty Calendar Committee had met during the summer and eliminated Methodist's fall break. Assistant Dean Walt Swing said some parents had complained that bringing their son or daughter home for fall break, Thanksgiving, and Christmas was a financial hardship. Swing said one and a half days had been added to the Thanksgiving holiday; he also noted that Methodist had operated for many years without a fall break.

Dean of Students Mike Safley said eliminating the fall break was a mistake. "It's too long to go from the start of school to Thanksgiving without a break," he said. [11]

In the same issue, Pauline Blehi reported that Methodist had placed a five-day TV ad campaign on WKFT-TV 40 in Fayetteville, a first for the College. Bill Billings, college PR director, and John Frank of WKFT developed the commercials.

Campus Minister Claire Clyburn announced that the newly formed Christian Life Council (an umbrella organization) had held a fall planning retreat. She said the council planned the fall lineup of religious events: weekly worship Tuesdays at 11 a.m. in Hensdale Chapel, Fellowship of Christian Athletes Wednesdays at 8 p.m., Bible study Thursdays at 7:30 p.m. a Koinonia prayer breakfast Fridays at 7:15 a.m., and vespers every Sunday at 7 p.m.

In other fall news, Pamela Johnson won second prize in a fiction writing contest sponsored by the Sherwood Anderson Foundation. She won for "Garage" and "Ode to Mr. Hughes by Emily Linton." Both stories appeared in *Tapestry*, the College literary magazine.

FSU Chancellor Addresses Winter Graduates

Winter 1990, graduates of Methodist College were urged to reclaim the goodness and promise of America at their commencement December 14.

Dr. Lloyd V. Hackley, chancellor of Fayetteville State University, said material wealth in the last decade and a half had ushered in an era of selfishness, permissiveness, and irresponsibility. He urged the 69 members of the winter class to help make American whole again—"to be human beings in the God-like sense; to be examples of excellence with compassion, decency, equity, and verity; to be the right reflection of what humanity at its best can achieve." [12]

Dr. Hendricks presented an honorary Doctor of Humanities degree to Dr. J. Allen Norris, president of Louisburg College, and an honorary Doctor of Divinity degree to the Reverend Helen Gray Crotwell, Fayetteville District Superintendent of The United Methodist Church. The president also gave a Methodist College Medallion to Mrs. Morie Murray Howard, a retired Cumberland County business and vocational education teacher, and the first annual Sam Edwards Award [for the outstanding Evening College graduate] to Barbara Ratzlaff.

Student Dies in Persian Gulf War

During the last half of 1990, and the first two months of 1991, hundreds of troops from nearby Fort Bragg and Pope Air Force Base were deployed to Saudi Arabia to enforce a United Nations-ordered withdrawal of Iraqi troops

— CHAPTER 8 —

from Kuwait. The operation was called Operation Desert Storm. Thousands of Americans tied yellow ribbons around trees to remember their troops.

The U.S. launched air assaults on Iraq Wednesday evening January 16, 1991, two nights after a small group of College staff and students held a prayer vigil in front of Hensdale Chapel. On Valentine's Day, over 120 staff and students gathered on the central mall to salute American troops. Organized by two military wives enrolled at Methodist, Colleen Witt and Rhonda Hall, the tribute included prayers, speeches, and inspirational singing by Rainbow's End and Stephanie Davisson, an Army wife and student.

A Methodist student, Army Sgt. Major Patrick Robert Hurley, 37, of New Douglas, IL, was killed February 21, 1991, in a helicopter crash in Saudi Arabia. He was scheduled to graduate in May. Weeks later, his degree was presented posthumously to his widow.

When a ground offensive began February 23, the Iraqis began withdrawing from Kuwait. President George Bush suspended hostilities against Iraq February 26. Troops began returning shortly thereafter. Fayetteville staged a homecoming parade and rally Sunday, March 10, which drew about 30,000 persons.

A large group of students assembles for a Valentine's Day Rally for the Troops.

Students Protest Plan To Make Minister Part-time

A front page story in the January 30, 1991, *sMALL TALK* reported that about 20 students had demonstrated in the Student Union January 24 to protest an administration proposal to eliminate the full-time position of campus minister in the 1991-92, College budget. The story also reported that Pam Johnson had led a group of students in a prayer vigil the evening of January 14 in front of Hensdale Chapel, asking that the administration reconsider.

In a report to the trustees February 7, 1991, Dr. Hendricks said the projected average FTE (full-time equivalent enrollment) number had been reduced from 870 to 850 and that the projected amount of the North Carolina Legislative Tuition Grant and the amount of church support had also been lowered. He said these factors would mean a tight resource situation and fewer staff positions in the coming school year.

The president alluded to a plan to make the campus minister position part-time, a plan that had resulted in a student protest. He said the position had been part-time for many years and was still part-time at Louisburg and N. C. Wesleyan colleges. Under the part-time arrangement, he said Bill Lowdermilk would be in charge of campus worship services and a coach would advise the Fellowship of Christian Athletes.

Trustees Chair Charlie Gaddy recognized Pam Johnson, S.G.A. president, who addressed the board concerning student opposition to having the campus minister become part-time. Johnson said 54 students were involved the religious life program, and she felt the campus minister's position should remain full-time

At President Hendricks' suggestion, the trustees went into executive session. During that session, the trustees instructed Dr. Hendricks to study the campus minister issue and report back to them. At a March 21 trustees meeting, Dr. Hendricks reported that the Reverend Helen Crotwell, Fayetteville District Superintendent, N.C. Conference of The United Methodist Church, had presented a strong candidate for the campus minister position whom he expected to be appointed at annual conference in June.

In a letter to the editor, published in the April 26, 1991, *sMALL TALK,* Pam Johnson thanked President Hendricks for deciding to keep a full-time minister at Methodist and for hiring the Reverend Carrie Parrish for the position in 1991-92. "I am grateful that he listened to the opinions of the students when deciding this issue," she wrote. [13]

MC Explores Bill of Rights

Methodist College observed the 200th anniversary of the Bill of Rights February 12, 19, and 26, 1991, with a series of forums entitled "The Bill of Rights in Everyday Life." Dr. Suzan Cheek, associate professor of political science, directed the series, which drew a total of 600 persons, including scores of public school teachers and students.

The series opened February 12 with a panel discussion moderated by Raleigh attorney Chavies L. Becton, former judge on the N.C. Court of Appeals.

— CHAPTER 8 —

In this first forum, "Public Order v. Individual Freedom," Becton explored by question, "Must our personal liberties become casualties in the war on crime?" He then presented a number of scenarios to a panel of 14 local experts; in one, the Cumberland County attorney was asked if the 2 Live Crew rap album "Nasty As You Want to Be" should be allowed in the Cumberland County Public Library. G.B. Johnson said the library purchased the album through a buying service but later removed it when it was judged to be obscene.

A second forum, held February 19, consisted of a mock trial, in which a school teacher was tried for possession of cocaine after his car was searched on a "reasonable suspicion" that he was selling drugs; a vial of cocaine and $5,000 cash were found in his car. Retired Superior Court Judge Maurice Braswell presided. Deborah Koenig was the prosecutor, Gerald Beaver was the defendant, and Jim Parrish was the defense attorney. Members of the audience were empanelled as a jury and found the defendant "not guilty."

Panlists discuss issues related to the Bill of Rights.

The last forum in the series, entitled The Bill of Rights in the 1990s," was held February 26 and featured Robeson County Public Defender Angus Thompson and Wayne Jackson, staff assistant to 7th District Congressman Charlie Rose. Thompson said the Fourth, Fifth and Sixth Amendments might be in danger because of advancing technology and the growing needs of women, children and the aged in American society. Jackson, a former TV journalist, said he was distressed by the decline of newspapers in America and "appalled at the ignorance [among Congressman Rose's constituents] of how our government works." [14]

Copies of *The Courage of Their Convictions,* a paperback book by Peter Irons, were distributed in advance of the forum series, which was supported by a grant from the Commission on the Bicentennial of the United States Constitution. Co-sponsors with Methodist were the Cumberland County Bar Association, the Museum of the Cape Fear, the Cumberland County Public Library, Cumberland County Schools, and the N.C. Department of Public Instruction, Region IV.

In other news from the spring 1991, semester:

—Dr. Erik Bitterbaum, vice president for academic affairs, announced new majors in international studies and criminal justice/legal studies, giving the College a total of 37 baccalaureate degree majors.

—The English Department held its first annual Writers Day for high school students January 21. Organized by Dr. Michael Colonnese, the event drew 70 students from ten area high schools who attended workshops on writing short fiction, writing for visual media, literary essay writing, poetry writing, and business writing. Tar Heel novelist Jill McCorkle read from her works, and Dr. Sue Kimball, director of the Southern Writers Symposium, lectured briefly about Southern writers she had known. Cash awards and certificates were presented to one student from each workshop whose writing was judged outstanding.

—Ben Ruffin, a Winston-Salem business and civil rights leader, spoke at Methodist's spring convocation January 22, 1991. His topic was "The Black Male Identity Crisis." Decrying the scarcity of positive black male role models and the fact that many blacks had gotten away from the church, Ruffin said, "Without faith, we're doomed. Peer pressure will eat our kids alive." [15]

—Betty Neill Guy Parsons '64, directed the Methodist College Chorus during the spring 1991, semester while Alan Porter was on sabbatical studying Mozart. Mrs. Parsons was then teaching choral music at Cape Fear High School in eastern Cumberland County.

President Cites Tight Budget

In a report to the College trustees March 21, 1991, Dr. Hendricks said enrollment for 1990-91, was down about fifty students due to a decline in the number of high school students, the economy, and the deployment of troops to the Middle East.

CHAPTER 8

The president said there had been a $110,000 budget over-run in financial aid and about $80,000 in utility usage. He said the College had eliminated eleven staff positions, postponed reroofing of one residence hall, and moved to 1992, the scheduled replacement of underground electric cable.

Dr. Hendricks reported that telephone jacks would be installed in each residence hall room by July and that students would be charged $75 per semester for telephone service. He said a consultant had estimated Methodist would need $125,000-$150,000 to make the campus handicapped accessible; he said improvements would be made over time.

Acting Workshop, Play Win Kudos

At a "Hail, Dionysus" celebration March 23, 1991, Andrew Reilly, a professional actor from Columbia, S.C., led a four-hour workshop on the subject, "Making a Living as a Movie Actor."

The Dionysus celebration began with drama presentations by high school students from E. E. Smith High School in Fayetteville and Northeastern High in Elizabeth City, N.C. Then Dan Covell performed a scene from *Romeo and Juliet*, and Circuit Players performed *Scruples at the Improv*. In addition, the two winners of Alpha Psi Omega's Student Playwriting Contest were staged. Caroline Kearns presented *Pounding on the Door*, and Brian Smallwood presented *The Vanity* and *Crumbs of Self*. Kearns' play, directed by Bob Bloodworth, received the trophy for "best play."

Local school groups enjoy **Romeo and Juliet** *at O'Hanlon Amphitheater.*

In other theatre news, Monarch Playmakers presented *Romeo and Juliet* April 13-14, 1991, in O'Hanlon Amphitheater, using contemporary costumes and music. Jack Peyrouse directed the show.

Linda Welch gave the 45-member cast and 37-member crew of *Romeo and Juliet* a rave review in the April 26 *sMALL TALK*. The play featured Daniel Covell and Pam Johnson in the lead roles; Bob Bloodworth played Friar Lawrence. Welch quoted an "anonymous groupie" as saying that Dan "Snapper" Covell brought tears to her eyes in the final scene of his final performance at Methodist.

No Smoking Policy, New Grading System Debut

In a front page story April 26, 1991, *sMALL TALK* reported that the faculty had voted at the end of the fall 1990, semester to prohibit smoking in the public areas of all academic buildings at Methodist, beginning in the fall of 1991.

David Leach reported that a new 12-point grading scale (A-F) which provided letter grades with pluses and minuses and decimalized quality points would take effect in 1991-92. A "B-", for example, would now be worth 3.7 quality points per semester hour for computing a student's overall grade point average. He also noted that new majors would be offered in 1991-92, in criminal justice/legal studies and international studies.

In other news from spring 1991:

—Carol Higy, assistant professor of physical education, received the second annual Teaching Excellence and Campus Leadership Award. Funded by the Sears-Roebuck Foundation, the award consisted of $1,000 for Ms. Higy and $1,000 for the Science Department in her name.

—In an election April 7, 1991, students chose Kimberly Ratliff, a junior, S.G.A. president for 1991-92.

—Tasanee Davis reported that the much-maligned English Proficiency Exam had been eliminated by the English Department and that English 100, a developmental course, would replace English 90 and carry course credit. Davis also reported that beginning in the fall of 1991, all students entering Methodist for the first time would have to take an English placement exam and would be placed in English 100, 101, 102, or 207 based on their exam scores.

—Pam Johnson reported that the S.G.A. had passed two constitutional amendments, one allowing only full-time day students to vote in S.G.A. elections and another requiring candidates for S.G.A. president or vice president to have S.G.A. Senate experience.

— CHAPTER 8 —

—Methodist's 1991, baseball team set a new NCAA record by scoring 43 runs against Maryville College Thursday, March 28, 1991, at Monarch Field. Maryville went scoreless. The previous NCAA record of 42 runs in a single game was set by Virginia Tech in 1902.

Congressman Rose Addresses Class of 1991

In a commencement address May 5, 1991, Seventh District Congressman Charlie Rose urged 103 graduating seniors to resist attempts to control the public mind, to safeguard the freedoms guaranteed in the Bill of Rights, and to get involved in government and politics at the grass roots level.

During the commencement, President Hendricks presented a Methodist College Medallion to Mrs. Ruth B. Palmer of Kitty Hawk, N.C., an honorary Doctor of Humanities degree to former Methodist College president Dr. Richard Pearce, and an honorary Doctor of Divinity degree to the Reverend Bill Presnell '71. Kelli Sapp, a biology major from Atlanta, received the Stacy Weaver Award.

Berns Estate Yields $662,592

Following notice that the College would receive at least $662,592 from the Bernice Strassner Berns estate, the trustees voted May 16, 1991, to name the Student Union the Dr. Karl H. and Bernice Berns Student Center. Dr. Karl Berns, who died in 1972, was professor of education and director of development at Methodist in the late 1960s. Mrs. Berns, who died in 1990, endowed a scholarship at Methodist for music students and gave a Schantz pipe organ for Hensdale Chapel in memory of her husband. [A dedication ceremony for the Berns Student Center was held in the fall of 1991.]

At a May 16 meeting of the Board of Trustees, Dr. Hendricks said the College would operate with a deficit for 1990-91, but "one not as large as in the past two years." [16]

Gene Clayton, vice president for business affairs, reported that the College's operating budget had tripled since 1983, moving from $3.2 million to $9.8 million. He said an operating budget deficit began in 1988-89, when financial aid expenditures were $488,000; in 1989-90, the financial aid deficit was $175,000. For 1990-91, he projected an overrun of $125,000. He acknowledged that increased financial aid had attracted more and brighter students.

Clayton said the College would seek to control financial aid costs by 1) reducing incentive and merit scholarship awards, 2) restricting the Greatest Gift Scholarship program, and 3) place a $6,000 award cap on institutional aid per student.

1990–1994

The vice president for business said the president was taking several steps to prevent a budget shortfall in 1991-92, including:
—a more conservative FTE projected enrollment.
—increasing tuition collections from 94 percent to 97 percent.
—requiring that staff stay within budgeted line items.
—a minimum deficit fund transfer service line item of $150,000 each year (to cash reserve) to repay the operating deficit in four years. [17]

Dr. Hendricks reported that the College had received $721,097 from the estate of Bernice Berns and recommended that the funds be allocated as an unrestricted gift to the operating budget, with part being used to eliminate a cash flow imbalance and the remainder being used to establish a Berns account in the cash reserve fund.

Tom Williams reported that gifts to the annual fund (through April 30) totaled $130, 742 and that the Womack Endowed Chair Fund had grown to $73,305.

Trustee Frank Barragan said when foundations and trusts were contacted for contributions, one of the first questions asked was how the College was supported by the trustees on an annual basis. He said the trustees of Methodist College needed to be faithful, with a 100 percent participation record. [Data presented by the Development Office indicated 11 of 35 trustees (31 percent) had given a total of $6,874 to the annual fund. This excluded capital campaign gifts, however. In contrast, 54 percent of the Board of Visitors gave a total of $78,350 and 83 percent of the Methodist College Foundation board gave a total of $13,725.]

Alan Dawson takes roll at a boys soccer camp.

— CHAPTER 8 —

Dr. Hendricks recommended that the Board of Trustees hold a weekend planning retreat in October, led by a trustee from a college similar to Methodist. The plan was approved on a motion by Dr. O'Hanlon.

College Acquires New Phone System

In July 1991, Methodist acquired a new telephone system with direct dial to each office. In addition, the College had telephone jacks installed in all rooms in the four residence halls. The new phone number for general information and the campus operator became 630-7000, while the old number became a toll free number (1-800-488-7110) for the Admissions Office.

President Announces Administrative Changes

College President Elton Hendricks announced several administrative changes in the summer of 1991, appointing Alan Coheley director of admissions, Lynn Clark special assistant for conferences and visiting groups, and Caroline Parsons associate director of development and alumni affairs.

Dr. Hendricks reported to the trustees' Executive Committee July 18 that the College had received an energy management proposal, added two holes to the golf course, and placed $385,688 from the Berns estate in the current budget and $276,872 in the cash reserve. He said the bookstore and snack bar areas had been remodeled, and the Development Office had moved to Horner Administration Building.

In other news from the spring and summer of 1991:

—Kensaku Shimizu, who attended Methodist from 1979-81, returned in March for the premiere peformance of his composition "Suite for Flute and Piano" at Barton College in Wilson, N.C. A Ph.D. student and teaching fellow at Harvard University, Shimizu and his wife visited with College music students and with Mrs. Jean Ishee, Shimizu's former organ teacher at Methodist.

—Dr. James K. Weeks '68 was appointed dean of the Joseph M. Bryan School of Business at the University of North Carolina at Greensboro.

—Frank Eason, who served as College comptroller from 1960-73, died June 17 after a long illness.

Golf Teams Win National Titles

The 1991, men's golf team, coached by Steve Conley, won its second consecutive NCAA Division III Golf Championship in May. The women's golf team, coached by Ann Davidson, won its fifth National Golf Coaches Association Division II championship.

1990–1994

The Monarch baseball team, coached by Tom Austin, made its third trip to the NCAA Division III College World Series in May 1991, and finished in fourth place. Jay Kirkpatrick was named Player of the Year in the Dixie Conference, Most Valuable Player in the NCAA South Regional, and a member of the College World Series All-Tournament Team. Kirkpatrick was drafted in the 30th round by the Los Angeles Dodgers and assigned to a Dodgers farm team in Great Falls, Montana.

Dean Addresses Summer 1991 Class

Members of the summer 1991, graduating class at Methodist were advised to choose their friends and life's work carefully. Dr. Erik Bitterbaum, vice president for academic affairs, cited Abraham Lincoln as one who exemplified true friendship in the face of bitter insults, and the late scientist/teacher J. Henri Fabre as an example of good works because he endured a life of poverty to write science books and incurred the wrath of his peers by admitting females to his science classes.

Enrollment Jumps 9 Percent

Methodist College began its 32nd academic year in fall 1991, with 1,373 students—982 in the day program and 391 in the evening program. A total of 492 students were living on campus.

New faculty members included; Mrs. Terri Moore Brown, social work; Dr. Tryon Lancaster, education; Dr. Donald Lassiter, psychology; M. Kunio Mitsuma, mathematics; Dr. Richard Pratt, chemistry; Ms. Jennifer Jerch, education and English; Dr. Wenda Johnson, physical education.

College Welcomes New Administrators, Faculty

The first *sMALL TALK* of 1991-92, gave front page coverage to the hiring of Alan Coheley as director of enrollment services and the Reverend Carrie Parrish as campus minister.

Coheley was a graduate of Westover High School in Fayetteville. He earned an undergraduate degree at UNC-Chapel Hill and a master's degree from Bowling Green State University.

A resident of Stedman, N.C., Carrie Parrish came to Methodist from the pastorate of Roseboro United Methodist Church. She held degrees from High Point College, Northwestern U./Garrett Seminary, and Southeastern Baptist Theological Seminary.

In an editorial entitled, "What Is College All About?', *sMALL TALK* Editor Caroline Kearns challenged MC students to get involved in extracurricular activities and sports. "There's a lot to do here besides just going to class," she

— CHAPTER 8 —

A November 20, 1991, performance of Mozart's **Requiem in D Minor** *filled Reeves Auditorium*

said. "College can only be what we choose to make it. So let's get involved and have a great year!" [18]

Dr. Sue Kimball, director of Methodist's 10th Southern Writers Symposium, announced that the September 27-28 event would examine the works of novelist and short story writer Lee Smith and would feature a juried art show of works based on Smith's writings.

Alan Porter, professor of music, announced a semester-long Mozart festival, including an October 15 "all-Mozart" faculty recital and a November 20 performance of Mozart's *Requiem in D Minor* by a college and community chorus with orchestra and guest soloists. This chorus would become Cumberland Oratorio Singers.

New faculty members profiled in the October 11, 1991, sMALL TALK were Ms. Terri Brown, assistant professor of social work, and Dr. Don Lassiter, assistant professor of psychology.

Lee Smith Honored At Writers Symposium

Novelist and short story writer Lee Smith was the honoree at Methodist's 10th Southern Writers Symposium September 27-28, 1991. The author of seven novels and two short story collections was living in Chapel Hill and teaching creative writing at N.C. State University. A native of Grundy, Virginia, Smith entertained and amused a dinner audience with an autobiographical account of her experiences as a writer.

Lee Smith spins a yarn.

Those presenting papers about Smith's work included Jill McCorkle, Nancy Parrish, and Dorothy Combs Hill. Dr. Sue Kimball, symposium director, said she was especially pleased with playwright Lee Yopp's stage adaptation of *Family Linen* (a Smith novel) featuring local actors Bo Thorp, Maggie Bunce, Eric Bryant, and others. Fayetteville photographer Rozlyn Masley won First prize in a juried art show for two photos based on Smith's works.

MC Fields College Bowl Team

In early October 1991, Methodist's new College Bowl Team held a tournament to select two five-person travel teams for 1991-92. Dr. Wayne Preslar, College Bowl sponsor, said Methodist would host a Cumberland County high school tournament in October and scrimmage with Elon College and UNC-W in the fall. He said the year's big event would be the College Bowl Regional at Virginia Tech in mid-February.

In other fall news reported in the campus newspaper:

—A Methodist College Veterans Club was organized to represent the interests of veterans and their dependents.

—Sarah Shew and Jeannie Denman gave Lee Yopp's two-act play based on the Lee Smith novel *Family Linen* a "B," saying the play's forward action became bogged down by too many lengthy monologues. The play was staged as part of the Southern Writers Symposium and featured Leonard McLeod, Ed Smith, Bo Thorp, and Eric Bryant.

—At the 1991, homecoming October 13, the football team lost to Bridgewater 34-0, while the men's soccer team tied Maryville 3-3 in overtime. The men's soccer team defeated Greensboro College October 23 at home to win the conference championship and remain unbeaten with a 10-0 conference record.

New Grading System Sparks Protests

A new 12-point grading scale implemented in the fall of 1991, led to protests and a petition from several hundred students. The new grading scale gave pluses and minuses for letter grades with corresponding quality points. For example, a B+ became worth 3.3 quality points for purposes of computing a student's overall grade point average.

Some seniors who had been graded on the old four-point scale petitioned for exemption from the new scale and asked that an A+ be added to the scale. After an S.G.A.-sponsored rally November 4, a forum November 6, and a student-faulty forum November 13, the faculty agreed to add an A+ with a quality point value of 4.3, but refused to abandon what was now a 13-point grading scale or to exempt seniors.

The new grading scale was the subject of a front page story in the October 11 sMALL TALK. Faculty were quoted as saying the new system was fairer to students than the old, seniors as saying they should be exempted from the new policy. Kim Ratliff, S.G.A. president, said she was "appalled" that the faculty had voted down a grandfather clause exempting upperclassmen from the new grading scale.

Dr. Erik Bitterbaum, academic dean, defended the new grading scale, but conceded that only 30 of 53 full-time faculty had voted on the change. Dr. Hendricks also conceded that individual faculty members were still free to use their own grading policy.

In a February 1992, editorial in the campus newspaper, Eric Kimbel criticized a faculty decision to add the grade of "A+," worth 4.3 quality points, to the new grading scale, creating a 13-point scale. He said the "A+"had the effect of making the grades lower than "A+" less substantial than they might seem when viewed on a scale that did not have the 4.3. He said Methodist's "A+" could create problems for transfer students and applicants to graduate school. [19]

Energy Conservation Plan Proposed

At a trustees' Executive Committee meeting November 14, 1991, an energy evaluation report was presented by Stanford Associates. The report said Methodist's heating plant steam distribution system was oversized. The consultants recommended that the boiler plant be abandoned and that natural gas-fired hot water boilers be installed at each building. Also proposed was installation of an energy management (computer-controlled) system to reduce energy consumption, to be operated by EUA/Highland Partners, PA.

At the same November board meeting, Dr. Hendricks said Bishop Minnick had appointed a committee of the North Carolina Annual Conference of The United Methodist Church to study conference liability for related institutions. He said the College could expect less money from the church in the future, having received $260,000 in 1990, for the sustaining fund and $157,000 for debt retirement.

The president said the wife of an evening student had been assaulted and robbed in the fountain area. He said an additional security officer would be added in the evening and that the north gate would be closed at 5 p.m.

In other College news from fall 1991:

—Rita Wiggs was named athletic director after Tom Austin
  resigned from the post. Austin retained the position of head

1990–1994

baseball coach, and Wiggs kept the position of head women's basketball coach.

—Air Force Brigadier General John Handy '66 received the alumni association's Distinguished Alumnus Award at the 1991, homecoming. Cynthia Walker, Handy's classmate, presented the award to Handy. Bill Estes '69 received the MCAA's Outstanding Alumnus Award, and Dr. John Sill, professor of sociology, took the Outstanding Faculty Award.

—The Monarch football team opened its third season with its first win, an 18-8 victory over Charleston Southern. Frankie McLean, a freshman from nearby Laurinburg, N.C., scored a touchdown with a 95-yard kickoff return on the first play of the game. The team later defeated Davidson College 30-28, with Jeff Alton kicking a last-minute field goal.

—The men's soccer team finished its fifth season under Coach Alan Dawson with a 15-0-3 record, undefeated in the conference.

Finbar Clancy closes in for a goal.

—The 1991, women's volleyball team finished second in the Dixie Conference Volleyball Tournament.

—Hampered by injuries, the 1991, women's soccer team won the Dixie Conference Tournament, but did not get a NCAA bid. The team's record was 9-8-1.

Education Department Helps Local School

In January 1992, two members of Methodist's Education Department won grants for a collaborative parent education program designed to improve the reading skills of students at Pauline Jones Elementary School in Fayetteville. Dr. Tony DeLapa and Ms. Jennifer Jerch worked with Pauline Jones Principal Sally Austin to secure a $25,305 grant from the Z. Smith Reynolds Foundation, $17,000 from the United Way of Cumberland County, and additional grants from Methodist College and the Cumberland County Schools.

Named SPIRIT—Students and Parents Involved in Reading Together, the five-month program showed 91 parents things they could do at home

— CHAPTER 8 —

to help their children improve their reading skills. The program also offered free reading materials to all children in grades 4-6 reading below grade level.

Jim Sypult Named Football Coach

James Sypult, an assistant football coach at Davidson College, was named head football coach at Methodist College January 23, 1992.

A native of Fairmont, West Virginia, Sypult played football at West Virginia University and had 18 years of college coaching experience—12 years at Davidson, five at Middle Tennessee State U. and one at Fairmont State College. He also coached the Bologna Towers, a professional football team in Italy, from 1986-89.

Women Netters Win First DIAC Title

The 1991-92, Lady Monarch basketball team won the Dixie Conference Tournament at Greensboro College in February 1992, with wins over Averett, Greensboro, and Ferrum. It was the first time a women's basketball team from Methodist had won the conference tournament.

Coach Rita Wiggs' team won 11 of its last 12 games and finished the regular season 22-6 overall and 6-9 in the conference. Daphne Akridge made

The Lady Monarchs celebrate their Dixie Conference title in 1992.

First Team All-Conference, and Novella McMillan was named Most Valuable Player in the tournament.

President Describes Changes in Church Relationship

Trustees of Methodist College received some good news February 6, 1992. Dr. Hendricks said day enrollment had surpassed 900 and evening enrollment had doubled (reached 440) compared to a year earlier. He said this growth had resulted in a better cash flow position, with $500,000 more available than last year at the same time.

The president said a draft proposal to be considered by The North Carolina Annual Conference of The United Methodist Church in June would create a Board of Institutions which could appoint 40 percent of the College's trustees. He said another change would require the trustees to give College assets and land to a charitable organization if the College went out of business. He said the current charter called for reversion of College assets to The North Carolina Conference in the event of dissolution of Methodist College, Inc.

Dr. Hendricks introduced Mr. Bev Pankey as the new vice president for development. Mr. Pankey came to Methodist from Aquinas College in Michigan.

The trustees approved a resolution presented by Dr. Hendricks stating that Methodist would not sell its Lafayette Collection, and that if at some time in the future it was not able to maintain the collection, it would transfer it to a museum or other appropriate local organization.

In other news from early 1992:

—Methodist dedicated a War Memorial to its fallen alumni May 20. A stone marker was installed at the base of the flagpole facing Horner Administration Building.

—Beverly S. Pankey became director of development January 20. A graduate of the U.S. Naval Academy, Pankey came to Methodist from Aquinas College in Grand Rapids, Michigan where he directed an $8 million capital campaign.

—Richard L. Player Jr. chaired the 1992, Community Loyalty Campaign for the Methodist College Foundation. At a Loyalty Day Breakfast February 18, College cheerleaders led 100 volunteers in a cheer, and the Stage Band serenaded the departing crowd from the east balcony of the Berns Student Center.

—The Education Department announced the formation of the Methodist College Teacher Education Alumni Association.

—The Methodist College Alumni Association sponsored an Alumni Basketball Game February 22. Gene Clayton and Mason Sykes coached separate teams of MC basketball alumni. Sykes' team won 30-20.

— CHAPTER 8 —

—Alumni Association President Roger Pait and board members Janet Mullen and Larry Philpott developed a 1992 Strategic Plan for the association.

President, Senior Staff Address Student Complaints

The Student Government Association sponsored a forum February 24, 1992, to give students a chance to voice their concerns to President Hendricks and the senior administrative staff. Some of the concerns addressed were:

—A non-alcoholic pub and/or extended snack bar hours. The president said extended snack bar hours had been tried but did not lead to greater participation by students.

—New computers for the Computer-Assisted Composition Lab and failure to keep posted hours. Dean Bitterbaum conceded the CAC computers were outdated and that lab staff had failed to report for work a few times. He said new computers would be ordered, and staff would be required to be in the lab when scheduled to be.

—Leaking roofs in the dormitories. The president said roof repairs were planned but deferred because of other important concerns.

College Bowl Team Performs Well in Regional

Methodist's first College Bowl Team performed well in a Region Five Tournament at Virginia Tech February 28-March 1, 1992. Coached by Dr. Wayne Preslar, a team composed of Cathy Griffith, Martin Brack, Ann Morris, Stephen Fann, and Jennifer Seamon (alternate) finished seventh overall and defeated teams from Wake Forest, Duke, Elon, Davidson, and Randolph-Macon.

Theatre Department Stages Musical, Two Farces

The Theatre Department presented the musical, *A Funny Thing Happened On the Way to the Forum,* February 28, 29, and March 1, 1992, in Reeves Auditorium. Dr. Jack Peyrouse directed, Alan Porter served as musical director, and Pam Johnson was the choreographer.

Monarch Playmakers presented two farces by Anton Chekov, *The Bear* and *A Marriage Proposal,* April 3-5, 1992.

In other news from spring 1992:

—An honors art exhibition was held during March in the Mallett-Rogers House. "Keeping An Open Mind," a Rodney Harris sculpture featured in the show, inspired the theme and cover of the *1992 Carillon* (yearbook).

—The faculty approved a campus-wide smoking policy February 25, 1992, which took effect March 16, prohibiting smoking in all classrooms, stairwells, hallways, and offices. The Student Government Association passed a similar "no smoking policy" for the residence halls, prohibiting smoking in all common areas but allowing it in student rooms if all occupants agreed to allow it.

—An editorial in the campus newspaper by Eric Kimbel questioned the validity of a speech competency test, in which students had to give an impromptu speech before a panel of three judges. He said the Registrar's Office reported the test had been given six times since March 13, 1990, and that only13 of 61 test-takers had passed. Those who failed had to take a three-hour speech class to fulfill their core requirement. Kimbel said the Speech and Theatre Department had recently changed the test, allowing students 20 minutes preparation time and one index card from which to speak. [20]

—Monarch golfer Rob Pilewski was chosen to play on the U.S. Golf Team in the United States-Japan Matches June 9-14 in Japan.

Newspaper Probes Issue of Underprepared Students

The March 27, 1992, *sMALL TALK* contained a lengthy investigative article by Ann Morris, headlined, "Why Does Methodist College Have So Many Underprepared Students and What Is It Doing To Help Them?" The author said College administrators admitted to having an "open admissions policy, occasioned by the financial necessity to survive due to our tuition-driven environment and also by our mission to serve first-generation college students from low and moderate income families." [21]

Morris went on to note that Methodist's endowment of $2.9 million ($3,436 per full-time equivalent student) paled in comparison to an average endowment of $26,258 per FTE for all four-year, non-profit colleges. She said MC's retention rate was adversely affected by the fact the college admitted approximately 80 freshmen each year who had an SAT score of 750 or less or a high school grade point average (GPA) of less than 2.5. She said only 18 percent of the freshmen who entered Methodist in 1987, graduated within four years, "while the four-year graduation rate for all private colleges averages 53 percent." [22]

Since 1989, she said, Methodist had added developmental math and English courses, a freshman orientation course on time management, and a "mentor program" that included a study skills class, a tutoring system, and a system to monitor students' academic progress.

Morris said the College had applied for a federal Title III grant to fund a new career development officer position and a Teaching/Learning Center. She ended her article by citing a poem that Dr. Bitterbaum, academic dean, had given her, a poem he said came from one of his college biology professors that summed up his philosophy about the student-teacher relationship in education:

> This bridge will only take you halfway there
> To those mysterious lands you long to see:
> Through gypsy camps and swirling Arab fairs
> And moonlit woods where unicorns run free.
> So come and walk awhile with me and share
> The twisting trails and wondrous worlds I've known.
> But this bridge will only take you halfway there—
> The last few steps you'll have to take alone. [23]

General Handy Addresses Class of 1992

Americans must rediscover moral values if the American dream is to survive. That was John Handy's message to the Class of 1992, Sunday May 17. The Air Force general and 1966, graduate of Methodist asked 144 graduating seniors to reclaim the American dream of democracy peace, and freedom by: 1) defending the idea of liberty, 2) maintaining personal integrity, and 3) claiming a new beginning. [24]

As part of the commencement ceremony, President Hendricks presented three honorary degrees: a Doctor of Humanities to General Handy, and Doctor of Divinity degrees to the Reverend Kermit Braswell and Bishop C. P. Minnick, leaders in The North Carolina Conference of The United Methodist Church. Katherine Grasso, a psychology and social work major from Fayetteville, received the Stacy Weaver Award.

In his baccalaureate sermon, the Reverend Kermit Braswell challenged class members to be faithful to God and themselves by learning from the past, living each day to the fullest, and setting goals for the future. Immediately following the baccalaureate, several members of the Class of 1992, dedicated a time capsule which was buried beneath the bell tower; the capsule was to be unearthed and opened 15 years later, at the 2007, homecoming.

In other news from the spring and summer of 1992:

—Joseph F. Doll Jr. of Washington, D.C. was named director of the Reeves School of Business August 20. A business executive who founded two health care firms in Maryland, Mr. Doll held an M.B.A. from American University and a B.S. degree from the University of Dayton. He succeeded Dr. Michael Marr, who returned to full-time teaching in the Reeves School of Business.

1990–1994

—By November 1, Methodist's professional golf management students were playing golf on the College's nine-hole course spanning 75 acres on the southeastern quadrant of the campus. The nine holes were built by the College maintenance and PGM staffs over a five-year period.

—Dr. Margaret Folsom, professor of biology and director of the Division of Science and Mathematics, received the College's first annual Teaching Excellence and Campus Leadership Award April 22, 1992.

—In March, the College established the Methodist College Endowment Society, enabling friends and alumni to make a planned gift or bequest. By late summer, 36 persons had joined.

—In April, Methodist's teacher education program was reviewed for state and national accreditation.

—In June, representatives of PGA of America visited the campus to evaluate Methodist's PGM program.

—Methodist received $200,000 from the estate of Virginia McKenzie Reeves, widow of John Mercer Reeves, the major benefactor of the Reeves Fine Arts Building.

In sports news:

—Robert McEvoy was named men's basketball coach. A native of Zanesville, Ohio, he played basketball at Kent State and coached the men's basketball team at UNC-Greensboro from 1984-91. He also coached at two Cumberland County high schools, Douglas Byrd and Cape Fear.

—The 1992, men's and women's golf teams won their respective national championships. Rob Pilewski became the first player from Methodist to receive All-American honors four consecutive years. Allyson Greer (medalist), Elizabeth Horton, and Kelly Cap won All-American honors for the women's team.

—The 1992, baseball team advanced to the College World Series and finished third with an overall record of 35-13. Coach Tom Austin reached his 400th win at Methodist, when his team defeated Virginia Wesleyan 5-3.

—The 1992, men's and women's tennis teams won the Dixie Conference Championship. The men finished 17-5. Chip Collins and Chris Collins represented Methodist in the NCAA Division III Championship at Emory University, making their way to the semifinals. The women ended their season undefeated in the conference, with an overall record of 17-9.

— CHAPTER 8 —

Gaddy Resigns As Trustee

Dr. Hendricks began his report to the trustees May 28, 1992, by announcing that Charlie Gaddy, board chairman, had resigned due to increased work responsibilities. Frank Barragan, vice chairman, presided in Gaddy's absence. Later in the meeting, the board elected Frank Barragan Jr. board chairman to succeed Gaddy along with the following: R. Dillard Teer, vice chairman; Walter Clark, secretary; and Louis Spilman, Jr., treasurer.

In a major action, the board approved an Energy Management System and contract with Highland Energy, Inc. for installing boilers and computer controls in each building, installing new energy efficient lamps and ballasts in campus light fixtures, and removing asbestos. The project had been studied and endorsed by the trustees' Building and Grounds Committee.

Gene Clayton explained that the project would require an outlay of $1.5 million (which the College would borrow) but would result in significant savings over ten years: a 20 percent reduction in electricity consumption, a 65 percent reduction in natural gas consumption, and the elimination of three maintenance/boiler workers.

The president also reported that:
—Alan Coheley was the new director of enrollment services.
—The Florence Rogers Charitable Trust had awarded the College grants for a harpsichord, anatomy model, and math calculators.
—The College had the best "cash flow" situation since his arrival, with $850,000 more on hand than the year before.
—Methodist had received a $200,000 bequest from the estate of Mrs. John M. Reeves, which had been placed in the quasi-endowment.

The trustees presented certificates of appreciation to three retiring board members: Dr. Helen Crotwell, Dr. W. Robert Johnson, and Dr. I. H. O'Hanlon.

Parker Wilson Speaks At Final Summer Commencement

History Professor R. Parker Wilson, the senior faculty member at Methodist, spoke at the College's 19th and final summer commencement August 30, 1992. He challenged the 34 seniors to build upon their liberal arts foundation and to live positive lives.

President Shares Good News

In a report to the trustees' Executive Committee July 16, 1992, President M. Elton Hendricks reported that:
—A freshman orientation program was held July 11-12, with over 400 persons in attendance.

—The PGA of America visited the campus on two days in July to review the golf management program and that a PGA endorsement was expected.
—The College ended 1991-92, with $325,000 in cash.
—A contract had been signed with an architect to survey the campus to determine what steps were needed to comply with the Americans with Disabilities Act.
—The College charter and bylaws were being revised to comply with action taken in June by The North Carolina Conference of The United Methodist Church.
—As part of its application for accreditation of the social work program by the American Council of Social Work, Methodist must adopt an Affirmative Action Policy. The Executive Committee approved such a policy with minor changes.

Faculty and Staff Brainstorm

More than 100 members of the Methodist College faculty and staff attended a planning retreat August 13-14, 1992, to generate ideas for improving the College. The retreat was suggested by Gene Clayton, who had participated in a similar activity conducted by the Fayetteville Area Chamber of Commerce. Meeting in groups of seven or eight, the participants generated 14 goals. The top three were: 1) improve intra-campus relationships and communication, and 2) increase incentives to attract more academically talented students, 3) increase funding for academic programs. [25]

Lafayette Collection Reopens

In August 1992, Methodist reopened the Lafayette Collection in Davis Memorial Library and published a new brochure describing its contents. The collection included medals, books, and letters about the Marquis de Lafayette, Fayetteville's namesake.

For nearly a year, Elaine Porter of the French Department and Susan Pulsipher, director of library services, catalogued, rearranged, and preserved the 535 items in the collection. A portrait and bust of Lafayette, a wool rug, and four pieces of antique furniture were moved to the Mallett-Rogers House. Mrs. Porter developed a self-paced user's guide with audio cassette for use by library patrons; in addition, she and Mrs. Pulsipher planned a series of rotating Lafayette displays in the library.

College Opens With 1,437 Students

Methodist College began its 33rd academic year in August 1992, with 1,437 students—1,072 in the day program and 365 in Term I of Evening

CHAPTER 8

Visitors from France inspect the Lafayette Collection.

College. The number of resident students increased to 548. New mattresses were installed in the four residence halls.

President Asks Trustees To Look Ahead

At a September 10, 1992, meeting of the Executive Committee, Dr. Hendricks reviewed proposed changes to the College charter and bylaws and reported a fall 1992, enrollment of 1,079 students (90 more than fall 1991) and residential enrollment of 548 (up 38 over fall 1991). He also reported that the first nine holes of the College golf course were complete.

Gene Clayton reviewed the schedule for the energy management retrofit, including removal of asbestos from four mechanical rooms. He said CP&L would replace the final segment of underground electric cable (to the administration and classroom buildings) in May 1993.

Dr. Hendricks said the board needed to start thinking about the size and kind of institution Methodist would be in the twenty-first century, noting that preliminary work was being done on a new Long Range Plan for the College.

In other news from fall 1992, Dr. Hendricks signed a student exchange agreement with Madero University in Puebla, Mexico, which allowed a foreign student to enroll for one semester in regular classes at the host institution. Dr. Arnal Guzman, associate professor of Spanish, was named program coordinator.

1990–1994

Alumni Gather At Radisson/Prince Charles

Alumni gathered for Homecoming 1992, October 16-18 at the Radisson/Prince Charles in downtown Fayetteville.

The alumni association awarded its Distinguished Alumnus Award to Paul L. "Buster" Sanderford '72, women's basketball coach at Western Kentucky University. Gene Clayton accepted the award for Sanderford. Joanna Cherry Palumbo '69 of Charlotte took the Alumni Service Award, and Dr. Tony DeLapa received the Outstanding Faculty Award.

In sports news from fall 1992:

—The Athletic Department welcomed four new coaches. They were: Bob McEvoy, men's basketball; Jim Sypult, football; Tracy Hubiak, cheerleading; Brian Cole, track and field; and Theresa Worrell, tennis.

—The 1992, men's soccer team won its fourth consecutive Dixie Conference title and its first NCAA Division III South Regional, and made it to the quarterfinals in the national championship.

The College Chorus performs on the mall at the 1992 homecoming.

—The women's soccer team ended the season 9-8-2 and tied N.C. Wesleyan for first place in the Dixie Conference.

—The women's volleyball team recorded its first 20-win season (20-17) since 1988, and finished second in the conference. The coach was Karen Smith.

— CHAPTER 8 —

In other news from fall 1992:
—Methodist was notified October 8 that the National Council for the Accreditation of Teacher Education had continued accreditation of the College's teacher education program, guaranteeing state accreditation as well.
—Cliff Wells '82 wed Constance Felder September 27 in Reeves Auditorium.
—Dr. Mary Frances Boyce and Mrs. Linda Beard built the College's first harpsichord from a kit.
—Davis Library reported that it received a record 83,300 soup labels from United Methodist Women's groups in the North Carolina Conference in 1991-92. Campbell Soup Company's Labels for Education Program enabled the library to exchange the labels for a record player, overhead projector, wall projection screen, book cart, safety stool, and children's books.

College Honors Foundation Leaders

Methodist' honored Dick Player, chair of the 1992, Loyalty Fund Drive; Dr. Stan Griffin, president of the Methodist College Foundation; and other Foundation officers at an appreciation dinner October 26, 1992, at the Radisson/Prince Charles Hotel. Jim Kizer was installed as the foundation's new president.

Gene Clayton Wins Pig-Kissing Contest

In the fall of 1992, Methodist's Students in Free Enterprise chapter sponsored a pig-kissing contest to dramatize the federal deficit, then estimated at $4.1 trillion. A piglet name Pork Barrel was to be kissed at the halftime of a future football game by the person receiving the most "spare change" votes. A large yellow ballot box was placed in the Trustees Classroom Building to receive the votes.

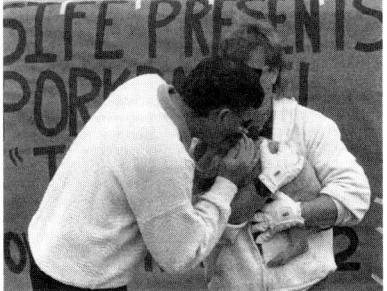

Gene Clayton kisses the piglet by virtue of receiving the most votes for this honor.

Gene Clayton, vice president for business affairs, received the most votes and kissed Pork Barrel during halftime of the Monarchs' final home football game November 7.

Bruce Pulliam Casts Electoral Vote

Bruce Pulliam, Associate Professor Emeritus of Social Science, was the subject of a feature article in the December 17, 1992, *Fayetteville Observer-*

Times. Mr. Pulliam was a member of the Electoral College from North Carolina, which George Bush carried in the 1992, presidential election. He represented the 7th Congressional District.

Mr. Pulliam said Secretary of State Rufus Edmisten invited the state's 14 Electoral College members to a formal ceremony in Raleigh to cast their ballots. Mr. Pulliam said some very good speeches were made, and that he enjoyed voting for Bush and his running mate Dan Quayle, a distant cousin.

RMC President Addresses Winter Graduates

Speaking December 18, 1992, Dr. Ladell Payne, president of Randolph-Macon College, urged Methodist's winter graduates to "always be honorable, even though you may never be recognized or honored for it." [26]

Interim Term Features Travel-Study Courses

Methodist's second annual interim term, January 4-15, 1993, featured three travel-study courses. Dr. Michael Colonnese took a class to Key West, Florida, to study the poetry of Elizabeth Bishop. Mrs. Elaine Porter led a study tour of Montreal and Quebec. Mr. Bob McEvoy taught a course on the volunteer experience in Miami.

College Hires Full-time Director of Career Planning

In January 1993, Ms. Paula Miller became Methodist's first full-time director of career planning and placement. Her office was located in the Berns Student Center.

A new entrance sign at the south entrance to the campus was completed in the spring of 1993. The two-sided structure included small fountains at the base of each side.

In other news from the spring of 1993:

—Football Coach Jim Sypult announced a fight song contest.
—Sarah Shew reported that the Methodist College Honors Program had been changed to 16 honors courses over a four-year period. Dr. Jim Ward, director of the program, said two honors courses would be offered each semester and that Honors Program participants would have to take at least eight honors courses and write a senior thesis in their major to become an Honors Program graduate.

President Appoints Strategic Concepts Committee

In early 1993, President Hendricks appointed a seven-member Strategic Concepts Committee to assist in developing long-range plans for Methodist College. Chaired by the president, the committee also included Dr. Erik Bitterbaum, Gene Clayton, Alan Coheley, and faculty members Joe Doll, Jane

— CHAPTER 8 —

Gardiner, and Emily Seamon. Dr. Hendricks asked the committee to consider the following questions:
1) What should our optimum enrollment be?
2) What kind of academic programs should we have?
3) What priorities should be given to new funds raised by the College?
4) What are the pros and cons of changing the name of Methodist College? [27]

College Wins NCATE Approval

President Hendricks advised the trustees February 4, 1993, that the teacher education program had been approved by the National Council for the Accreditation of Teacher Education.

The board also approved the design and construction of a new sign and fountain at the College's south entrance. The president said the board needed to consider building one or more new residence halls.

Approving the report of the Nominations Committee, the board re-elected six current members and increased board membership from 36 to 40 persons. The board also approved a revised investment policy and the bylaws for the Clergy Friends Association of Methodist College.

At a February 9, 1993, meeting, the trustees' Executive Committee approved an offer to purchase 7.5 acres of Kinlaw property on the northwest side of the campus. The offer was refused.

Local Giving Surges

Early receipts from the Methodist College Foundation's 36th annual Loyalty Fund campaign showed a 70 percent gain over 1992. As of Loyalty Day, February 16, 1993, Fayetteville and Cumberland County residents had pledged $85,795 toward a goal of $200,000. Bob Exum, secretary/treasurer of VanStory-Exum Insurance Agency, chaired the 1993, campaign.

Golden Corral Says Thank You

Officials of Golden Corral Restaurants held a 20th anniversary party January 13, 1993, in Fayetteville and presented a $20,000 check to Methodist College for Davis Library.

In 1973, Golden Corral co-founder Jim Maynard had used Davis Library while developing plans for his first restaurant, which was built on Fayetteville's Bragg Boulevard. Maynard presented a check to President Hendricks in appreciation for the College's hospitality.

1990–1994

Clergy Friends Group Established

A Clergy Friends Association of Methodist College was established in the spring of 1993, consisting of 36 ministers assigned to The North Carolina Conference of the United Methodist Church.

Bill Lowdermilk, Methodist's vice president for church and community relations, said the group would help in identifying and securing support for the College and assist the College in accomplishing its long-range goals.

In other news from spring 1993:

—Enrollment in spring 1993, reached 1,599—987 in the day program and 562 in the evening.

—David G. Wilson, retired president of Fasco Consumer Products in Fayetteville, became Executive-in-Residence in the Reeves School of Business.

—The National Association of Independent Colleges and Universities presented its first annual Award for Advocacy of Independent Higher Education to Dr. Terry Sanford February 4 in Washington, D.C.

—The Theatre Department premiered an original play about Shakespearean actor R. D. MacLean (1887-1945) April 1-4. Written by Dr. Jack Peyrouse and entitled *The Will of R.D.*, the play featured Robert Bloodworth as MacLean, Edwina Lindsay as the actor's first wife Marie, and Susan Paschal as the actor's second wife Odelle.

—The Financial Aid Office acquired a F.E.E.D.S. computer system which performed a student needs analysis and processed FAFSA (federal financial aid) applications in 33 hours.

—Methodist acquired a 29-passenger bus in January.

—The Methodist College Chorus traveled to Florida and the Bahamas for a concert tour.

—Construction began on a new entrance sign with fountains at the College's south entrance.

—The women's basketball team won the regular season title in the Dixie Conference, but came up two points shy of repeating as Dixie Conference Champions, losing to Christopher Newport 85-83.

—The 1992-93 men's basketball team ended the season 6-19 overall and 3-8 in the Dixie Conference.

—Paula Miller filled the newly created position of director of career planning and placement January 15, 1993.

— CHAPTER 8 —

—The College's second annual Writers Day for high school English students drew 181 participants. Guest lecturers included three college instructors: Phil Gerard, a short story writer from UNC-Wilmington, Tim McLaurin, a novelist (and Fayetteville native) from UNC-Chapel Hill, and Robin Greene, a poet from Methodist's English faculty.

Tim McLaurin

Brit Claims Ancestor Wrote Works Attributed To Shakespeare

In a May 9, 1993, lecture at Methodist, Charles Vere, Earl of Buford, claimed that Edward de Vere, the 17th century Earl of Oxford, wrote the works attributed to William Shakespeare. Sponsored by The Fayetteville Publishing Company, the lecture drew 150 persons to Hensdale Chapel.

The Massachusetts resident said Edward de Vere, his ancestor, was a well-educated (at Oxford U.) poet, playwright, musician, dancer, European traveler, and soldier, who paid William Shakespeare, the actor, to be a "front man" in a well-conceived hoax.

Vere said Thomas Looney, a British schoolmaster, analyzed the works of Shakespeare and other literature from the Elizabethan period for content and style. He said Looney found a stylistic match in several anonymous works and some obscure poems by "E. Vere."

Following Mr. Vere's lecture, Raleigh actress Shannon Bailey read several Shakespearean sonnets. A panel of college professors—Jim Ward and Paul Wilson of Methodist and Richard Vela from Pembroke State University—challenged Mr. Vere on several points and questioned his motives for establishing the Shakespeare Oxford Society "to advance knowledge of Edward de Vere and his involvement in the events and literature of his time." [28] Mr. Vere said he was motivated by a love of Shakespeare and a desire to see the rightful author given justice at last.

Clergy Friends Hold First Meeting

The Clergy Friends Association of Methodist College held its first meeting May 16, 1993, and elected the Reverend James Coile chair. Members of the group were briefed on the state of the College by Dr. Hendricks, Dr. Bitterbaum, Ms. Rita Wiggs, and the Reverend Carrie Parrish.

Dr. Bill Lowdermilk, vice president for church/community relations, asked association members to do five things: 1) bring youths to "UMYF Goes to Methodist College Day" October 2, 2) have a Methodist College presence in their churches during the next conference year, 3) identify potential donors, 4) identify potential students, 5) attend the Methodist College luncheon at annual conference in June. [29]

Reverend Stark Speaks At 30th Commencement

Speaking at Methodist's 30th commencement May 11, 1993, the Reverend Rufus Stark II, president of the Methodist Home for Children, challenged 150 graduating seniors to help build a family-friendly environment. He urged them to accept the Christian view that every human being is important and the new "systems theory" that dysfunctional families can be healed.

In his baccalaureate sermon, the Reverend Glen Holt, pastor of First Baptist Church in Fayetteville, asked the seniors to reflect on the most essential things they had learned in college. He then listed five things he had learned "that he really needed to know:

1) To be successful in life, you need a goal or vision.
2) People are more important than things.
3) Dare to dream.
4) Staying power goes further than starting power.
5) Faith and learning go hand in hand." [30]

During the commencement ceremony, Dr. Hendricks presented honorary Doctor of Divinity degrees to the Reverend Rufus Stark II and Reverend Holt and a Methodist College Medallion to Harlan F. Deunow, retiring conductor of The Fayetteville Symphony Orchestra. Chrissy Babb received the Stacy Weaver Award.

Trustees Hold Retreat

At a board retreat held June 5, 1993, at Pine Needles Resort in Pinehurst, the Methodist College Board of Trustees voted to:

—plan for an enrollment of 2,000-2,200 students by 2000.
—build as needed new residential facilities to accommodate 300 students.
—explore the feasibility of a new $10 million capital campaign to build a library addition ($3.5 million), a new academic building ($2.5 million), increase the endowment by $2 million, and renovate the Science Building ($500,000).
—establish a task force to make recommendations by the summer of 1994, regarding the development of unused College land.
—establish a Business Advisory Council.
—Limit the terms of board officers to no more than six consecutive years.

Addressing the trustees' Executive Committee July 5, 1993, Dr. Hendricks reported that:

— CHAPTER 8 —

Gerri Williams '68 hoods her son Jeffrey McDowell.

—The Buildings and Grounds Committee had selected the LSV Partnership to design a new residence hall.
—The College ended 1992-93, with $700,000 in cash.
—A new entrance sign would be completed by July 15.
—The apartment renovations included new paint and funiture and the addition of fire alarms and smoke detectors.
—The gender imbalance was continuing, with estimates the incoming freshman class would be 75 percent male and 25 percent female.

In other news from spring and summer 1993:

—Former U.S. Senator Terry Sanford was honored at an appreciation dinner May 31 in Fayetteville. Sponsored by the Cumberland County Democratic Party, the event drew 1,000 persons to the Charlie Rose Agri-Expo Center. In appreciation for his role in founding Methodist College, Bill Lowdermilk presented Sanford with a framed collage of photos which represented his long association with the College.
—Robert Bloodworth Jr., assistant professor of communications, was named Professor of the Year at Awards Day April 23.
—Methodist College cheerleaders finished fourth in their division at the National College Cheerleading Championship April 19 in San Diego.
—David Zachery "Zach" Hambrick, a rising junior from Midlothian, Va., was elected S.G.A. president for 1993-94, in April.

—The Annual Fund Alumni Phonathon generated gifts totalling $31,000.
—A fund drive was launched for renovations to Hensdale Chapel.
—The women's golf team won a third consecutive National Golf Coaches Association National Championship.
—The men's golf team finished third in the NCAA Division III National Golf Championship in San Diego. Ryan Jenkins became Methodist's third medalist.
—The men's baseball team was ousted in the NCAA South Regional by N. C. Wesleyan and Ferrum.
—The men's and women's tennis teams finished second in the Dixie Conference.
—The Monarch track and field team finished fourth in the Mason-Dixon Conference Championship. Jamelle Ushery competed in the NCAANationals, finishing 8th in his races and winning All-American honors.

Player Family Pledges $100,000 For Building

In August 1993, the son and grandchildren of Richard L. Player, Sr. pledged $100,000 for construction of the Richard L. Player Sr. Golf and Tennis Learning Center at Methodist. Mr. Player founded Fayetteville's Player Realty and Construction Co. in 1938, and co-founded Highland Country Club in 1945.

Richard Player Jr. (Dick), his wife Margaret Ann, and their children Molly and Richard Player III said they wanted to honor the senior Player for his business success and his love of the game of golf.

At the time of the Players' gift, $150,000 had been raised toward the cost of building a facility to house the College's golf management program near the College's golf driving range and golf course.

Trustees Support New Buildings

Dr. Hendricks informed the trustees' Executive Committee September 9, 1993, that the college began its 34th academic year with record enrollment—1,126 students in the day program and 522 in Term II of Evening College.

He said 610 students were living in the residence halls, with some males in triple rooms, forty-eight students in Honors Hall (old apartments) and eight in the "old music building" (small apartment building).

He also reported that a 100 percent loan of up to $1 million had been approved for construction of a new residence hall southeast of Garber Hall. The trustees' Building and Grounds Committee met September 30, 1993, and

— CHAPTER 8 —

selected three construction firms to bid on the new residence hall: Player, Inc., Sigma Construction Co., Inc., and Ellis-Walker Builders.

The president informed the trustees October 7, 1993, that $150,000 had been raised for constructing the Richard L. Player, Sr. Golf and Tennis Learning Center, which was estimated to cost $250,000-$300,000.

He said a proposal for making a new right angle entrance to the College with a stoplight had been presented to the North Carolina Department of Transportation.

Reporting for the trustees' Development Committee, Ms. Terri Union said Cargill Associates of Houston, Texas had been selected to do a feasibility study for a proposed capital campaign.

Meeting in closed session, the trustees approved a revised budget with an increase of $700,000.

College Begins 34th School Year

Methodist began its 34th academic year, 1993-94, with a record enrollment of 1,628 students—1,126 in the day program and 502 in the evening. The College opened with 610 resident students, the largest number in 26 years.

New staff members included: Tom Maze, assistant director of professional tennis management and tennis coach; Dr. Peggy Batten, mathematics; Mr. Darl H. Champion, criminal justice; Summer Brock, director of alumni affairs; John Dixon, printer; Darlene Hopkins, psychologist; and Mike Hogan, sports information director.

New business majors—fashion merchandising/retail management, health care administration, and financial economics—brought the number of undergraduate majors to forty.

Newspaper Staff Seeks Suggestions for New Name

In the fall of 1993, Derek Tang became editor of *sMALL TALK*, and Dr. Sharron Sypult became the faculty advisor.

The newspaper staff announced in its September issue that it was seeking suggestions for a new name, saying some students felt *sMALL TALK* was dated and connoted "chit-chat."

A news brief column on page one noted that MC students were following the latest fashion craze—the baggy, oversized look.

A new column entitled "The Naked Truth" premiered, under the pseudonym Buck Naked. The real author was Tim Benfield, whose first few columns presented little-known facts about college faculty members. For example, Buck Naked reported that English professor Michael Colonnese had contracted a bad case of poison ivy from climbing apple trees. In a subsequent column, Buck summarized the acting credits of communications professor / professional actor Bob Bloodworth: major roles in the 'B movies" *Lady Grey* and *Dogs of Hell* and the role of Dr. Carl Hessler on the TV soap opera Guiding Light.

President Hendricks' fall 1993, convocation remarks were summarized in a photo caption on the back page, in which Dr. Hendricks challenged each MC student to be a "pedaler on the great bicycle of life," noting that "some people pedal, some ride, and some coast." [31]

Among the news items reported in the October *sMALL TALK* were the hiring of Summer Brock as director of alumni affairs and Mike Hogan as sports information director.

Charlotte Wholters reported on the Southern Writers Symposium, featuring mystery writers Margaret Maron and Sharon McCrumb.

After some students objected to having their names and addresses published in the back of the *1993, Carillon*, a long-standing tradition came to an end. Yearbook Advisor Bill Billings said federal law made student addresses "directory information" and that the college was entitled to publish "directory information" unless students filed a nondisclosure request with the college registrar. [32] Because some students regarded publication of their addresses as an invasion of privacy, Dr. Hendricks directed that student addresses not be published in the future.

In December 1993, *sMALL TALK* gave front page coverage to the restoration of the Yarborough Bell Tower and Jones Memorial Carillon. The tower received a new paint job, new lamps in its lighted cross, and a new electronic carillon.

Dan Devlin Jr. became editor of *sMALL TALK* in December 1993, and announced that a name change for the newspaper would be forthcoming.

Mystery Writers Honored

Mystery writers Sharyn McCrumb and Margaret Maron were honored as the "Southern Daughters of Mystery" at Methodist's 11th Southern Writers Symposium October 22-23, 1993.

The event featured two bus tours of local crime sites, in addition to the customary lectures with luncheon and dinner addresses, The Cape Fear Regional Theatre staged Lee Yopp adaptations of Margaret Maron's "Fruitcake, Mercy, and Black-Eyed Peas" and Sharon McCrumb's "MacPherson's Lament."

Dr. Sue Kimball (C) with mystery writers.

— CHAPTER 8 —

"A Midsummer Night's Dream"

The theme for Homecoming 1993, (October 8-9) was built around a Theatre Department presentation of Shakespeare's comedy, *A Midsummer Night's Dream* in O'Hanlon Amphitheater. A pre-play mixer was held Friday evening at the Mallett-Rogers House. The play featured Libby Seymour as Titania and Robert Bloodworth as Oberon.

The first annual William P. Lowdermilk Golf Tournament was held Saturday along with a Harvest Fest staged by the Council for Exceptional Children.

The Methodist College Alumni Association presented the following awards: Outstanding Faculty Award to Dr. Jack Peyrouse, professor of theatre and speech; Distinguished Alumni Award to Lee Warren Jr. '75, vice chairman of the Cumberland County commissioners; Outstanding Alumni Service Award to Roger Pait '85 and Bill Billings '68. Pait had just served as MCAA president for two years and worked for Underwriters Laboratories in Research Triangle Park. Billings, then employed as Methodist's director of public relations, had served on the alumni board for a number of years in the early 1970s and chaired the MCAA Recruitment Committee.

Libby Seymour, Bob Bloodworth

In other news from fall and winter 1993:
— Construction began December 23 on a new $1.2 million residence hall just south of Garber Hall.
— The College's first alumni directory was released for sale by Harris Publishing at a cost of $46.95 plus $5.95 shipping and handling.
— N. C. Natural Gas Corporation presented $100,000 to Methodist September 30 to establish the Frank Barragan, Jr. Scholarship Fund.
— The Board of Visitors toured the golf course and tennis facilities and took the lead role in a fund drive to build the Richard L. Player, Sr. Golf and Tennis Learning Center.
— The Tau Yi chapter of Kappa Delta Pi, an international honor society in education received its charter October 21 and initiated 24 students and 21 faculty members.
— Pauline Longest, Georgia Mullen, and Mrs. Pat Jones presented slide shows of their recent trips to Russia at the October 24 meeting of Friends of Davis Memorial Library.

—The bell tower, carillon, and lighted cross were refurbished in December 1993, at a cost of $13,000. First, the tower was cleaned and repainted. Then new fluorescent tubes were installed in the lighted cross. Finally, new speakers and a new electronic carillon were installed. Starting December 15, the carillon played the Westminster chimes four times each hour and played two hymns daily at 5:01 p.m.

—William E. "Bill" Horner, a charter member of the Methodist College Board of Trustees, died February 7 in Sanford, N.C. at the age of 92. The former editor and publisher of *The Sanford Herald* and former member of the N.C. House of Representatives, was a Durham native. He chaired the trustees' Planning Committee for Methodist College and gave generously to Methodist.

—The Monarch Players staged a children's production of *Snow White* November 19.

Soccer Teams Excel

In the fall of 1993, Becky Morton of the women's soccer team set a new school record by scoring 30 goals in a season.

The 1993, men's soccer team won the Dixie Conference title for the fifth consecutive year and advanced to the NCAA Tournament, losing in the first round to Roanoke College. Michael Scobee was named Player of the year in the Dixie Conference, with 18 goals and two assists. The team finished 14-4.

Football Team Improves

Methodist's 1993, football team won four games and lost a heart-breaker to Maryville College, 18-17. Coach Jim Sypult said the offense set a new school record for points scored (162), and the defense allowed the fewest points in any season to date—244. Sypult praised senior quarterback Ben Pope and senior offensive guard Jeff Baker who won the Iron Man Award and started 40 straight football games.

Sigma Wins Residence Hall Contract

The president informed the trustees' Executive Committee December 3, 1993, that bids for constructing the new residence hall totaled $1.5 million and were rejected. He said new bids were due December 17. The committee voted to raise the cost ceiling for the building from $1 million to $1,150,000.

Dr. Hendricks also reported that Dr. William Jordan of Fayetteville had offered to build a $400,000 soccer complex if the College would make land available and operate the facility. He quoted Dr. Jordan as saying he thought local soccer enthusiasts would provide an additional $400,000. Dr. Hendricks was asked to visit a similar soccer facility in Greensboro and report back to the board at its February meeting.

In the area of academics, Dr. Hendricks said a physician assistant program had been proposed and that Dean Bitterbaum was developing a report on this possibility.

The trustees' Buildings and Grounds Committee met December 17, 1993, and voted to award a conract for a new residence hall with a guaranteed completion date of August 10, 1994. Ellis-Walker Builders was selected, with Sigma Construction as an alternate. When Ellis-Walker declined to accept a contract with a guaranteed completion date, the contract was awarded to Sigma Construction Co. of Fayetteville.

Harrison Addresses Winter 1993 Class

Dr. William Harrison '74, superintendent of the Hoke County Schools, challenged winter 1993, graduates December 17 to plan for the future by adopting a personal mission statement and setting lifelong goals.

President Hendricks presented a Methodist College Medallion to the Reverend Russell Knowles, a United Methodist minister from Bolivia, N.C., who had recruited at least 20 students for Methodist College. The president also presented the Sam Edwards Award to Gary Rhoads, chosen as the outstanding evening student of 1993.

Mr. Edwards (R), Gary Rhoads.

Capital Campaign, Faculty Recognition Win Board Approval

At a February 3, 1994, trustees meeting, Cargill Associates suggested that Methodist could conduct a capital campaign with a base goal of $4.6 million and a challenge goal of $6,550,000. The trustees approved a motion by Ms. Terri Union, chair of the trustees Development Committee, that the board defer a decision on the dollar amount of a new campaign until further work was done by the Executive and Development committees.

Trustees approved a motion by Robert Hatfield, chair of the Academic Affairs Committee, that faculty with 25 years of teaching experience at Methodist and the rank of associate professor be eligible to become a Distinguished Service Professor, upon the recommendation of the Tenure and

Promotion Committee. He also recommended that Dr. Garland Knott, who had retired in December, be granted the status of Faculty Emeritus.

In other matters, Dr. Hendricks reported that renovations to the chapel, bell tower/carillon, and cafeteria had just been completed.

1994 Loyalty Fund Drive Wins Strong Support

The Methodist College Foundation's Community Loyalty Fund Drive for 1994, generated gifts of $173,000 by February 8, Loyalty Day. The 1994, goal was $225,000, with Craig Stewart serving as honorary chair. The 1993, campaign netted $480,725, compared to the Foundation's goal of $200,000.

sMALL TALK Becomes *Pride*

In February 1994, *sMALL TALK*, the MC newspaper, became *Pride*. Valerie Harel, a December 1993, graduate, submitted the winning suggestion in a contest sponsored by the newspaper staff. The staff held a "Pride Jam" in the Student Union, complete with a band and the Energizer bunny, to announced the new name.

In a letter to the editor, Leon Goldstein, instructor of German, argued there was nothing wrong with the name *sMALL TALK*. "Methodist College may be 'small' compared to other institutions, but its students and faculty determine its 'greatness.' If *sMALL TALK* needs a new name, why not add *perri sode magni* to the title? *sMALL TALK*—Great Minds!" [33]

A center spread in the February 1994, *Pride* contained short biographies and photos of famous African Americans in celebration of Black History Month. Some of the persons profiled were: Mary McLeod Bethune, Jimi Hendrix, Ralph Bunche, and Louis Armstrong. Leon Clark, a Methodist College football player, musician and poet, was also featured.

Pride announced that *Fallen Angels,* a comedy by Noel Coward, would be staged March 4-6, directed by Summer Brock. The lead players were: Jeannie Denman, Sam Williams, Camisha Bell, and Michele Burdick.

In his February 1994, column, Buck Naked profiled Dr. Richard Walsh, religion professor, and then bragged, "Buck Naked is among the pantheon of students who will be canonized upon graduation for receiving an 'A' in a Dr. Walsh survey course." [34]

The lead story in *Pride's* March/April 1994, issue reported that Dr. Erik Bitterbaum, academic dean, had resigned to become vice president for academic affairs at Missouri Southern State College in Joplin, Missouri.

A two-page spread in the same issue contained a number of light-hearted tributes to Buck Naked, defending his satirical writing style and rapier wit. Buck's defenders included Dr. Sypult, Nancy Alexander, and Robert Bloodworth. Buck's April column blasted Dr. Jim Ward for trashing "Compu-Chick," a crepe paper bookend which had resided in the CAC Lab for almost two years. The columnist offered a $25 prize to the student who could create the best Compu-Chick II.

The May 1994, *Pride* reported that Peggy McCullen was retiring from the library staff after 31 years and that Dr. Tony DeLapa had been recognized as Professor of the Year at Awards Day in April.

College Magazine Adds Color

The cover of the March 1994, issue of *Methodist College Today* featured a four-color photograph of a waterfall on the Pauline Longest Nature Trail. The back cover used a color photo of students walking in front of Reeves Auditorium as seen through the branches of a pink dogwood tree outside the Trustees Classroom Building.

From this point forward, all College magazines would feature color covers. In 2002, the College began using full color photos throughout the magazine.

Book Honors Paul Green

In early March 1994, Human Technology Interface, Ink published *Paul Green's Celebration of Man, with a Bibliography*. Edited by Dr. Lynn Sadler and Dr. Sue Kimball, the book contained 13 papers about North Carolina's Pulitzer Prize-winning playwright, papers read at Methodist in March 1987, during the Southern Writers Symposium honoring Green.

A 30-page bibliography of works about Paul Green was compiled by Dr. Sadler and Dr. Kimball. The book sold for $20 plus tax, postage, and handling.

Mullen Urges Alumni To Speak Up

Janet Conard Mullen '72, the new president of the Methodist College Alumni Association, was featured in the March 1994, *MC Today*. She urged her fellow alumni to tell her and other alumni board members what they wanted the Association to do.

College Offers Land For Soccer Complex

In the spring of 1994, Methodist College made 30 acres of campus land off Treetop Drive available for construction of an eight-field soccer complex to be used by the Fayetteville Youth Soccer Association. The College leased the land to the group for 30 years at no cost.

At a trustees' Executive Committee meeting March 24, 1994, Dr. Hendricks presented a proposal that the College lease 30 acres of campus land

1990–1994

Dr. Bill Jordan announces challenge gift for soccer complex.

to a non-profit corporation which wanted to build eight soccer fields. Trustees approved a motion by Joe Walker authorizing the College administration to negotiate a "no cost" lease agreement.

Dr. and Mrs. William Jordan of Fayetteville pledged $400,000 June 13 to build the complex, and local residents agreed to raise another $400,000. The College agreed to relocate holes six and seven on the College golf course to make room for the soccer fields.

At the same meeting, Dr. Hendricks reported that Mr. Jay Dowd had been hired to direct the College's next capital campaign, effective June 1. He also reported that Dr. Erik Bitterbaum, vice president for academic affairs, was leaving Methodist to become vice president for academic affairs at Missouri Southern State College in Joplin, Missouri.

Brig. Gen. James Link Addresses Class of 1994

Brig. Gen. James Link '66 told 126 graduating seniors May 22, 1994, their lives would be defined by the choices they made. He urged the seniors to be true to themselves and "be your character. . .the sum of all your parts." [35]

The Army officer offered six lessons he said he had learned in his 27-year career:

1) Money is not a satisfier; material things do not bring happiness.
2) Your family is your most important legacy; take time for your children.

— CHAPTER 8 —

3) There is great joy in being part of something that is bigger than yourself... be it your church, community, nation, or career.
4) People are great; with good leadership they will meet your every expectation.
5) Strive for excellence in all things.
6) Take good care of yourself... physically, spiritually, and mentally." [36]

In his baccalaureate sermon, the Reverend Sid Huggins agreed with journalist Bill Moyers' prediction that the most important news story of the next 50 years will be the search for and interest in spirituality.

He said the word enthusiasm comes from two Greek words meaning "in God." He challenged class members to "Let your spirit come alive in the right relationship with God, and you will be ready to live with enthusiasm." [37]

In other commencement activities, Dr. Hendricks presented an honorary Doctor of Divinity degree to the Reverend H. Sidney Huggins III and honorary Doctor of Humanities degrees to Joseph P. Riddle Jr. of Fayetteville and Brig. Gen. James Link of Kaiserslautern, Germany. The president presented the Stacy Weaver Award to Stephen Fann of Salemburg.

Trustees Elect Barragan, Approve New Mission Statement

When the full Board of Trustees met May 26, 1994, Dr. Hendricks announced the appointment of Dr. Anthony DeLapa as academic dean, effective June 11. He also reported that Dr. William Horner, trustee emeritus, had died and that his home in Sanford, which had been given to the College, had been sold for $80,000.

The trustees elected the following officers for 1994-95: Frank Barragan, Jr., chair; the Reverend Dr. John Bergland, vice chair; Robert Hatfield, secretary; and Vance Neal, treasurer.

The board also approved resolutions of appreciation for Dr. Erik Bitterbaum's four years service as academic dean and for the service of Walter Clark and Louis Spilman as board secretary and board treasurer, respectively.

In another major action, the board approved a new mission statement for the College as presented by Dr. Hendricks. The thesis of the statement read: "The purpose of Methodist College is to develop responsible members of society by providing an education which is firmly grounded in the liberal arts tradition, committed to nurturing moral values and ethical decision-making, and designed to prepare students for a variety of careers." [38]

In other news from spring 1994:

—The North Carolina Conference of The United Methodist Church honored the Reverend Dr. Bill Lowdermilk by presenting him the Francis Asbury Award for Fostering United

Methodist Ministries in Higher Education.
— Dr. Tony DeLapa, professor of education, was named vice president for academic affairs and dean of the College June 11.
— Dr. Ken Collins, an associate professor of religion at Methodist, was appointed to the first Samuel J. and Norma C. Womack Endowed Chair in Religion and Philosophy.
— John Paul "Jay" Dowd joined the Development Office as associate vice president of development for campaigns and major gifts. A graduate of Winthrop University and the University of South Carolina, Dowd came to Methodist from Limestone College in Gaffney, S.C.
— Michael Sullivan joined the Reeves School of Business as director of the new health care administration program.
— The Music Department received three gifts totaling $25,000 to rebuild two grand pianos and buy a new grand piano for Reeves Auditorium. The new piano was made possible by a grant from Mary Fermanides Wright '68 of Fayetteville in memory of her father, Steve John Fermanides.
— The presidents of Louisburg, Methodist, and N. C. Wesleyan colleges pooled funds to hire United Methodist Communications of Nashville, Tenn. to produce a 12-minute video on campus ministries at these colleges. The video was shown to The North Carolina Annual Conference in June when it met in Reeves Auditorium.

In sports news from spring 1994:
— The men's golf team won its fourth NCAA Division III Golf Championship in five years at nearby King's Grant Golf and Country Club.
— The women's golf team won the National Golf Coaches Association Division III title in Des Moines, Iowa. Elizabeth Horton took medalist honors.
— The Monarch baseball team finished the season 25-14-1 and 6-4 in the conference.
— The men's tennis team won the Dixie Conference Championship in April.

Board Approves Bond Application

President Hendricks informed the trustees' Executive Committee July 14, 1994, that consultants had suggested a capital campaign be undertaken to build an addition to the library and a new academic building. He also reported that he had received a proposal from a group of investors willing to build a medical building for family physicians within a proposed office park that might also house the College's physician assistant program. The office park and building were proposed for an area south of the College's main entrance.

In a formal resolution, the trustees' Executive Committee authorized the College administration to proceed with an application to the state treasurer's office for the right to issue $9 million in tax exempt revenue bonds to finance the following:

—a new residence hall
—an energy conservation management system
—Riddle Center/federal debt
—a Science Building addition
—a tennis and golf learning center
—a physician assistant building
—reroofing eight buildings
—a real estate purchase as appropriate. [39]

College Enrolls 1,837

Methodist began 1994-95, with a new residence hall and a fall enrollment of 1,826 students, up 12 percent from fall 1993. There were 1,237 day students and 589 evening students. The day figure marked the first time Methodist had reached its design capacity of 1,200 students. Resident students numbered 568.

Executive Committee Approves Capital Campaign

In a September 9, 1994, meeting, the trustees' Executive Committee approved construction of a new residence hall, establishment of the Lura Tally Leadership Center, and the following goals for a capital campaign:

—a "base goal" of $4.6 million—$1.9 million for a library annex, $1 million for an academic building, and $1.7 million for ongoing support.
—a "challenge goal" of an additional $1,950,000 to build a science annex ($1 million) and to add $950,000 to the College endowment. [40]

Dr. Hendricks reported a fall enrollment of 1,847 students—1,248 in the day program and 589 in the evening. He said the day count was up 108 over fall 1993, while the evening count was up 86.

Trustees Hold Retreat At Wrightsville Beach

At a trustees retreat held October 8, 1994, at Wrightsville Beach, Dr. Hendricks reported that a soccer complex was under construction on College land, financed with $1 million raised by the Fayetteville Area Soccer Association, and that two golf holes had been relocated to make room for the complex.

In separate actions, the trustees approved:

—a budget revision for 1994-95, with total expenditures of $16,316,122.

—a contract with Sigma Construction Co. to build a duplicate of the residence hall completed in 1994, at a cost of $1 million.

—the name, Lura Tally Center for Leadership Development.

In other news from late 1994:

— Enrollment in Methodist's professional golf management (PGM) program reached 204.

—Tenor Richard Bicoy '82 appeared with the U.S. Air Force Band as one of the "Singing Sergeants" in a November 11 concert in Reeves Auditorium.

—Ground was broken for the Fayetteville Area Soccer Complex on 30 acres of College land November 1. Wade Byrd, president of the Fayetteville Area Soccer Association, announced that the original fund drive goal of $800,000 had been raised to $1.4 million. He said 65 persons had pledged $983,750 toward construction of the complex.

—The Miroelectronics Center of North Carolina at Research Triangle Park announced that Methodist and nine other private colleges in the state would soon be connected to the Internet via leased phone lines, thanks to a $284,000 grant from the National Science Foundation. A node was to be installed in the College's Office of Institutional Computing in February 1995.

—Methodist received state approval in August 1994, to have its own campus police department. Director of Security Wilford Saunders said he and five other sworn officers at Methodist would have full arrest powers within a one-mile radius of the campus.

—Dr. Walter Weaver, professor of religion at Florida Southern University, delivered the first Samuel J. and Norma C. Womack Endowed Lecture October 21. In Part I, he reviewed Albert Sweitzer's *The Quest of the Historical Jesus*. In Part II, he presented various scholarly views of Jesus in the 20th century.

—A work team from Methodist spent fall break in Homestead, Florida helping repair homes damaged by Hurricane Andrew in 1992.

—Stained glass windows were added to Hensdale Chapel, a gift from the family of John Hensdale.

CHAPTER 8

—Methodist received the Ray Ehrensberger Institution of the Year Award given by the Commission on Military Education of the American Association of Adult and Continuing Education.
—Julie Kahl and Billie Martin, two members of the Methodist College Debate Team, won the Novice Division title at the James Madison University Debate Tournament November 4-6.
—Becky Burleigh '89 became the first women's soccer coach at the University of Florida in Gainesville. She was given one year to recruit players and staff.

Hard work by the Class of 1969 paid off with a record homecoming attendance.

Class of 1969 Returns In Force

Using their telephones and e-mail, Joanna Cherry Palumbo of Charlotte, Bill Blalock of Dallas, Texas, and Richard Dean of San Francisco, California, persuaded more than 100 of their friends in the Class of 1969, to return to Methodist for a "25th homecoming reunion" October 21-22, 1994. Joanna had "Oldie Goldie Gang" t-shirts made for her classmates, and the gang held a memorable reunion party, with cake, at the Holiday Inn I-95.

At the alumni association dinner, the MCAA board of directors honored the late Howard Lupton '72 by unveiling an MCAA Presidents Plaque given in his memory for permanent display in the Alumni Dining Room. The alumni board also presented the Outstanding Faculty Award to R. Parker Wilson, Distinguished Professor of History, the Distinguished Alumnus Award to Maj. Gen. James Link '66, and the Outstanding Alumni Service Award to George Small '82.

In fall 1994, sports news:
—The football team ended its sixth season with a 5-5 won-loss record.

—Both the men's soccer team (13-4-1) and the women's soccer team (13-5-3) advanced to the NCAA Division III Soccer Championship and were eliminated in the South Regional.

New School Year Brings New Dean, Residence Hall

The October 1994, issue of *Pride* announced the arrival of nine new professors, new majors in health care administration and retail management/fashion merchandising, and the appointment of Dr. Anthony DeLapa as vice president for academic affairs. The newspaper also announced that 56 women had moved into the new residence hall adjacent to Garber Hall.

The new faculty included: Dr. Elizabeth Belford education; Cheryl Kremer, fashion merchandising; Gary Long, history; Dr. Michael Potts, philosophy; Michael Sullivan, health care administration' Dr. Joyce White, social work; Dr. Jeffrey Zimmerman, finance/economics.

Dan Devlin returned as editor of *Pride* for 1994-95, and the newspaper's writing style continued to be colorful and satirical. An Ed Pardue news story was headlined "Hide the Booze and Firearms" and began as follows: "Hide the booze and firearms. Don't even think of speeding. That's right: campus cops are on the prowl. Now, in addition to the security officers, there will be one police officer on campus at all times." [41]

A story by Laura Flanary reviewed the opening of "Emerging and Diverging," an art show at the Arts Center of Fayetteville, featuring the works of Jeff Baker, Yvonne Hair-Pierce, Rodney Harris, and Etsuko Martin.

In the November *Pride*, Dan Devlin wrote a column about "industrial music," as played by the band Nine Inch Nails at the Woodstock 1994, concert. He defined the genre as "music composed of computerized drumbeats called 'loops' repeated over and over . . . raw, unbridled, very heavy sounding, and often violent." [42]

Etsuko Martin's work won kudos.

Presidential Goals Required

At a meeting of the trustees' Presidential Evaluation Committee December 7, 1994, the committee approved five general goals for the president for calendar 1995:

1. The president will operate the College in a fiscally responsible manner.
2. The president will lead the College so as to improve the quality of College programs.

— CHAPTER 8 —

Elton and Jerry Hendricks prepare for a reception at the president's home.

3. The president will lead the College in a way that improves its visibility and reputation.
4. The president will nurture and support a positive relationship between the College and The North Carolina Conference of The United Methodist Church.
5. The president will conduct a program for his own personal, intellectual, and professional growth. [43]

The committee agreed to assess the president's work on each goal as follows:
Goal 1: a review of the audit, enrollment data, and records of contributions
Goal 2: An interview team of trustees will visit the campus every other year to meet with faculty, staff, and students, starting in the fall of 1995.
Goal 3: The president will develop an instrument for surveying members of the Board of Visitors, Methodist College Foundation, and advisory boards for the Reeves School of Business, Social Work, Education, and the Alumni Association.
Goal 4: The president will survey members of the Laity Friends and the Clergy Friends associations of Methodist College.
Goal 5: The president will report to the Evaluation Committee. [44]

Charlie Gaddy Addresses Winter Graduates

In a winter commencement address December 16, 1994, Charlie Gaddy challenged Methodist's graduating seniors to make a difference in the world by voting, serving their communities, and showing concern for others.

The former Methodist College trustee and news anchor/reporter at WRAL-TV in Raleigh also stressed the importance of a free press and the obligation of American citizens to make their views known to their elected officials as well as to local newspapers and TV stations.

The Reverend Tommy Smith, district superintendent of The North Carolina Conference of The United Methodist Church, was the winter baccalaureate speaker. He asked members of the winter class to remember their baptism and hold fast to their faith in the face of worldly temptations.

College President Elton Hendricks presented an honorary doctor of Divinity degree to the Reverend Tommy Smith and an honorary Doctor of Humanities degree to Charlie Gaddy. Dr. Hendricks also presented the Sam Edwards Award (for outstanding evening student) to Ricky John.

— CHAPTER 8 —

END NOTES
Chapter Eight

1. D. K. Doane, poem, *sMALL TALK,* February 9, 1990, file.
2. "Report of the University Senate of The United Methodist Church," quoted in a news story, *Methodist College Today*, November 1990, file.
3. Ibid.
4. Ibid.
5. Larry Rowedder, commencement address, *Methodist College Today*, August 1990, file.
6. Steve Conley, news story, *Methodist College Today*, August 1990, file.
7. Parker Wilson, news story, *Methodist College Today*, November 1990, file.
8. Dennis Campbell, commencement address, *Methodist College Today*, November 1990, file.
9. M. Elton Hendricks, news story, *Methodist College Today*, November 1990, file.
10. Ibid.
11. Mike Safley, news story, *sMALL TALK,* November 19, 1990.
12. Lloyd V. Hackley, commencement address, *Methodist College Today*, April 1991, file.
13. Pam Johnson, letter to the editor, *sMALL TALK,* April 26, 1991.
14. Wayne Jackson, news story, *Methodist College Today*, April 1991, file.
15. Ben Ruffin, news story, *Methodist College Today*, April 1991, file.
16. M. Elton Hendricks, remarks to the Methodist College Board of Trustees, May 16, 1991, TM, Book 4.
17. Gene Clayton, remarks to College trustees, May 16, 1991, TM, Book 4.
18. Caroline Kearns, editorial, *sMALL TALK,* September 6, 1991, file.
19. Eric Kimbel, editorial, *sMALL TALK,* February 26, 1991, file.
20. Eric Kimbel, editorial, *sMALL TALK,* April 30, 1992, file.
21. Ann Morris, news story, *sMALL TALK,* March 27, 1992, file.
22. Ibid.
23. Anonymous poem quoted by Dr. Eric Bitterbaum, news story, *sMALL TALK,* March 27, 1992.
24. John W. Handy, commencement address, *Methodist College Today,* August 1992, file.
25. News story, *Methodist College Today,* September 1992, file.
26. Ladell Payne, commencement address, *Methodist College Today,* April

1993, file.
27. M. Elton Hendricks, news story, *Methodist College Today,* April 1993, file.
28. Edward de Vere, speech, *Methodist College Today,* August 1993, file.
29. Bill Lowdermilk, news story, *Methodist College Today,* August 1993, file.
30. Glen Holt, baccalaureate sermon, *Methodist College Today,* August 1993, file.
31. M. Elton Hendricks, news story, *sMALL TALK,* Septermber 1993, file.
32. Bill Billings, news story, *sMALL TALK,* October 1993, file.
33. Leon Goldstein, letter to the editor, *Pride,* February 1994, file.
34. Tim Benfield, column, *Pride,* February 1994, file.
35. James Link, commencement address, *Methodist College Today,* June 1994, file.
36. Ibid.
37. Sid Huggins, baccalaureate sermon, *Methodist College Today,* June 1994, file.
38. "Methodist College Mission Statement," presented to College trustees by Dr. Elton Hendricks, TM, Book 4.
39. Resolution adopted by Methodist College Board of Trustees' Executive Committee July 14, 1994, TM, Book 4.
40. Campaign goals adopted by College trustees' Executive Committee September 7, 1994, TM, Book 4.
41. Ed Pardue, news story, *Pride,* October 1994, file.
42. Dan Devlin, feature story, *Pride,* November 1994, file.
43. Goals for President (1995) approved by trustees' Presidential Evaluation Committee December 7, 1994, TM, Book 4.
44. Ibid.

Over the Top: Team leaders of the Expanding the Vision campaign celebrate exceeding their campaign goal.

Chapter 9

Campus Grows On Many Fronts
1995-2000

> "Methodist College is reaching a new plateau. We know it will be in the forefront of leadership in the next century."
> —*Terry Sanford, honorary chair of the "Expanding the Vision" campaign, February 29, 1996.*

Methodist College President Elton Hendricks announced January 17, 1995, that Methodist College would establish the Lura Tally Center for Leadership Development and a 21-semester hour interdisciplinary program in leadership development.

He said the College wanted to honor Ms. Tally, a retired public school teacher and counselor, for her strong leadership in serving five terms in the N.C. House of Representatives and six terms in the N.C. Senate. The veteran legislator wrote key legislation to the fields of environmental protection, juvenile detention, day care and public education.

Dr. Suzan Cheek, associate professor of political science, was named program coordinator, charged with recruiting 25 freshmen and sophomores for 1995-96, and 31 more students each year until enrollment reached 120.

In March 1996, Methodist College announced it would launch a physician assistant program in June 1996, and build an allied health building and family medicine clinic on campus. Ron Foster a physician assistant at Methodist was named program director and Dr. Chris Aul, a local family physician, was named medical director.

Dr. Hendricks described the program as "an important undertaking for Methodist College and southeastern North Carolina." [1] The six-semester program was designed for rising juniors with strong science backgrounds and consisted of a didactic year following by a year of clinical rotations. Enrollment was projected to reach 30-40 students.

In March 1995, *MC Today* was chock full of major news, including an architect's rendering of a master development plan for the Methodist campus, news that MC's professional tennis management program had been accredited by the USPTA, and an architectural drawing of the proposed Richard L. Player Sr. Golf and Tennis Learning Center. Construction work on a second new residence hall south of Garber Hall was also pictured.

— CHAPTER 9 —

On the front inside cover of the college's March 1995, magazine, Bill Billings wrote an editorial suggesting that the name "Methodist College" be changed to North Carolina Methodist University or Eastern Methodist University.

The cover of the magazine featured a photo of psychology student Zach Hambrick in front of a PC, doing a flight simulation as part of a federal research study on the performance of general aviation pilots in the Cape Fear Region.

In the back section of the magazine, an annual giving report for 1994, listed 2,481 donors to the college. A cover letter from Dr. Hendricks indicated that the college received gifts totaling $1,349,997 in 1994, a new record. He said the college received 1,006 alumni gifts.

A sports story noted that Monarch basketball legends Greg Jones and Elton Stanley were honored at a reception and dinner December 2, 1994. Jones and Stanley, Nos. 21 and 20, are the only MC basketball players to have their jerseys retired. They were roommates as well as teammates. Jones, a forward, was from Durham, and Stanley, a guard, was from Shallotte. The team of which Jones and Stanley were part won four consecutive Dixie Conference titles (1972-75) and received an NCAA Division III bid in 1975. Jones and Stanley were coached two years by Gene Clayton and two years by Joe Gallagher.

In sports news, Methodist's track team finished third in the Mason-Dixon Conference Track and Field Championships at Virginia Tech. Jamelle Ushery won his third conference title in the 550-meter hurdles and was named All-Conference in the long jump and the high jump.

Hamilton Cuthrell won the 55-meter dash with a time of 6.43. Bjorgvin Fridriksson won the 5,000 meters with a time of 16:02, and Bradley Hicks won the pole vault title with a jump of 14 feet.

Sanford Opposes Name Change

The opinion page in the June 1995, issue of *MCT* contained a letter to the editor from Terry Sanford opposing a name change to Methodist University,

> "As for university versus college, it is my fervent hope that Methodist College never becomes a university. Why be pretentious? The best colleges in America are proud to be colleges. Splendid liberal arts colleges are American treasures. Methodist College should not aspire to have a law school, a medical school, a divinity school, graduate and professional schools being the distinction between colleges and universities. Methodist College should aspire to be the best, at least among the best, of American liberal arts colleges. We're getting there." [2]

Tommy Yow '66 also sent a letter opposing a name change. Robert L. Hostetter '84 endorsed a change to North Carolina Methodist University.

In other news from summer 1995:

—Methodist led all 37 private colleges in North Carolina in enrollment gains.

—J.P. Riddle, a former trustee and benefactor died May 8 at the age of 73. In 1987, Riddle made the lead gift toward construction of the March F. Riddle (physical activities center).

—Also noted was the death of John W. Hensdale at the age of 92. Hensdale was a college trustee from 1962-77, and gave funds to build Hensdale Chapel and to endow a scholarship.

Four Veteran Employees Retire

Mrs. Virginia Godwin retired in February after 20 years service as assistant to the comptroller. Mrs. Jo Ann Taylor retired in March, after 20 years service as administrative assistant to Bill Lowdermilk.

Parker Wilson retired after 32 years and was honored at a retirement dinner April 29. Diane Guthrie sang several show tunes, and at least five college associates offered words of tribute. Wilson said he was grateful for the fellowship and "freedom to teach" he had enjoyed at Methodist. [3] He then sang the Sam Cook tune "Wonderful World", which he dedicated to his former students.

At an April 9 chapel service, Wilson said, "life is meaningful if one remembers three things: place, people, and purpose." [4] He offered a few words of advice under each heading:

"Place- Remember your roots,

People- Associate with creative people,

Purpose- Find out what you can do and go for it." [5]

Bill Lowdermilk addresses friends as his retirement program.

— CHAPTER 9 —

Bill Lowdermilk vice president for church and community relations, was honored at a May 13 retirement dinner attended by more than 400 persons. After dinner, friends gathered in Reeves Auditorium to offer "Uncle Bill" words of thanks and praise.

Dr. Hendricks presented Lowdermilk with a mantel clock engraved with a note of thanks and announced that the main street across the front of the campus would be named Lowdermilk Drive.

"I have had the best possible life here," said Lowdermilk. [6] The program concluded with the audience singing "Hymn of Promise" and the college "Alma Mater."

In other news from spring 1995:

—John Paul "Jay" Dowd was named vice president for development, succeeding Bev Pankey, who accepted a job at Indiana University.

—Pat Jones, associate professor of mathematics, was named Professor of the Year April 21.

—The MC Laity Friends Association held its first meeting April 29.

—Leon Clark, a junior communications major from Savannah, GA, was elected S.G.A. president for 1995-96

—The N.C. Dept. of Transportation agreed to install a stoplight at the main /south/ entrance to the college, on the condition the school move the entrance south and make Lowdermilk Drive intersect with Ramsey Street at a right angle.

—Methodist's first international mission team traveled to Lima, Peru during Spring Break, March 3-11, 1995. The Rev. Carrie Parrish, Paula Miller and eight MC students spent four days painting at the Methodist Seminary and a small Methodist church in Pedregal.

MC students at work on a mission team in Peru

1995–2000

Bruce Pulliam Speaks at 32nd Commencement

Speaking at Methodist's 32nd Spring Commencement May 7, 1995, Professor Emeritus Bruce Pulliam urged members of the Class of 1995, to "merge mind and will" in order to address future challenges. [7]

The four challenges Pulliam enumerated were: "continuing the process of learning, becoming more involved in the political process, finding new ways to excite the tasks of reasoning and of developing moral sensibilities, helping to solve global problems (overpopulation, war, environmental degradation), and distributing wealth in ways that will combat hunger and illiteracy." [8]

Bruce Pulliam

During the Sunday morning baccalaureate service, the Reverend Bill Lowdermilk, Methodist's vice president of church and community relations, compared life to climbing a series of ladders. He advised the graduates to resist the trivial pursuit of material wealth, personal recognition, and social status.

Lowdermilk said those who truly love God will nurture their faith and willingly serve others; moreover, they will be able to climb any ladder and master any of life's transitions. [9]

Among the 136 persons receiving degrees were the first three Bachelor of Social Work graduates.

Dr. Elton Hendricks, college president, presented an honorary Doctor of Humanities degree to Peggy Kirk Bell of Southern Pines, and Methodist College Medallions to Bruce Pulliam and Dr. Mary Emily Miller of Frederica, Delaware.

Tammy Murphy, a December 1994, graduate, received the L. Stacy Weaver Award.

Golf Teams Win National Titles

Methodist's men's golf team won its fifth NCAA Division III championship May 19, 1995, at the Hulman Links Golf Course in Terre Haute, Indiana. Coach Steve Conley's Monarchs shot a 54-hole total of 899, 18 shots ahead of a team from Otterbein College. Ryan Jenkins won the individual title.

The Lady Monarchs of Methodist College won their fifth consecutive National Golf Coaches Association (NGCA) Championship May 10, 1995, at The Links Golf Club in New Palestine, Indiana.

— CHAPTER 9 —

Coach Ann Davidson's team won by 67 strokes over Simpson College of Iowa, Elizabeth Horton won her second individual title.

Baseball Team Finishes Second in World Series

The 1995, Monarch baseball team finished second in the NCAA Division III college World Series, losing to the University of La Verne of California at Salem, Virginia 8-7 and 5-3, Coach Austin's team finished with a record of 36-19-1.

Business School Wins Accreditation

At a June 19, 1995, meeting, the Association of Collegiate Business Schools accredited the undergraduate degree programs offered by Methodist's Charles M. Reeves School of Business. Mr. Reeves, the college trustee who endowed the business school in 1986, died June 30 at the age of 76.

Methodist Begins 36th School Year

Methodist College began its 36th academic year August 22, 1995, with a new 56-student residence hall, West Hall, and 1,779 students (1,265 day, 514 evening).

In August 1995, the college entrance off Ramsey Street was realigned to facilitate a stoplight and ground was broken for the Richard L. Player Golf and Tennis Learning Center near the golf driving range.

Dr. Hendricks said the college would shortly sell $10 million in tax-exempt revenue bonds, using $6.5 million to refinance existing debt, and the remaining $3.5 million to re-roof five buildings and to build a math and computer science building and an enrollment services building.

New faculty included: Dr. Lori Brookman in biology, Dr. Cu Phung in chemistry, and Dr. Lloyd Bailey in religion. Mrs. Darlene Hopkins, a psychologist, was hired as director of a new counseling center.

College Sells Bonds

On Nov. 14, 1995, First Citizens Bank purchased $10 million in Methodist College bonds. Approximately $6.3 million of bond revenue was used to refinance existing loans for the Riddle Center, energy management project, and two residence halls. The balance of $3.6 million was used as follows: $260,000 for roof repairs to Weaver, Sanford, and Cumberland halls, the Berns Student Center, and Reeves Auditorium.

—$210,000 for construction of the Player Golf and Tennis Center
—$95,000 for a new south entrance and sign
—$1 million for a Math and Computer Science Building
—$450,000 for an enrollment services building

Doug Coppeler slides into home on a grand slam, as Methodist defeats N.C. Wesleyan 8-0 at the South Regional at Shelley Field to advance to the College World Series.

—$625,000 to build nine golf holes for the PGM program
—$300,000 for a Science building renovation OR the purchase of land adjacent to the college
—$649,692 for contingencies

In a related matter, the college prepared incorporation papers for the Methodist College Development Corporation, leasing the group 20 acres on south campus to develop an office park.

Chorus Begins Fund Drive

In the fall of 1995, the college chorus held a series of benefit concerts and other activities (barbeque, yard sale, golf tournament, car wash, and walk-a-thon) to raise funds for a spring 1996 concert tour of France.

The chorus needed $30,000 to pay half the cost of taking 40 members to France. Chorus members had to pay the other half, $750 each.

Homecoming 1995

At the 1995 homecoming, the Methodist College Alumni Association presented the Outstanding Faculty Award to Dr. Tryon Lancaster, professor of education; the Outstanding Alumni Service Award to Joanna Cherry Palumbo '69; and the Distinguished Alumni Award to the Reverend Bill Presnell '71.

— CHAPTER 9 —

Johnny Lipscomb '68 shows his college scrapbook to Janet Mullen '72 at 1995 Homecoming.

College Receives $530,000 from Stone Estate

In November 1995, Methodist received $530,000 from the estate of Benjamin Franklin "Doc" Stone of Elizabethtown, N.C. Stone died in January 1995, at the age of 92. A native of Orrum in Robeson County and a graduate of UNC-Chapel Hill, he was a pharmacist, a shrewd investor, and a devoted member of Trinity United Methodist Church in Elizabethtown. President Hendricks announced that the Stone gift would be placed in the college endowment to underwrite the B.F. Stone Endowed Scholarship.

In other news from fall 1995:

—Mrs. Vergil Queen of Raleigh presented the college with a rare pottery bust of John Wesley, the founder of Methodism.

—Delta Mu Delta, a national honor society for undergraduate business students, received its charter November 10, 1995, and inducted 21 members.

—Jesse Smith, director of the college's mentor program, died of cancer Oct. 11.

—The Rev. Bill Lowdermilk began work as assistant in church & community relations at Quail Haven Village in Pinehurst, a facility operated by United Methodist Retirement Homes of NC.

1995–2000

Soccer Teams Finish Second In NCAA

Methodist's men's and women's soccer teams enjoyed remarkable success in the fall of 1995, finishing second in their respective NCAA Division III National Championships.

The 1995 men's soccer team celebrates success.

The men fell one goal short of a perfect winning season November 19, losing to Williams College in Massachusetts 2-1. Coach Alan Dawson's team finished 21-1. Senior goalie Justin Terranova had a record 37 shutouts.

Methodist's women's soccer team advanced to the NCAA Division III title game in Pomona, N.J. November 12, 1995. A 3-0 loss to California-San Diego ended an incredible run by first-year Coach Phil Stephenson's Lady Monarchs, who finished the season 18-4.

PA Program Takes First Applications

Methodist College began taking applications December 1, 1995, for the inaugural class in its physician assistant program, starting in May 1996.

It was also announced that construction of an allied health building on south campus would begin in the spring of 1996. The first floor would house a family medicine clinic and the second floor the PA program.

— CHAPTER 9 —

December 1995 Graduation

Addressing 107 members of Methodist's 1995, winter graduating class December 15, 1995, Dr. John Griffin, superintendent of the Cumberland County Schools, urged them to become true laborers by sharing with and helping those in need.

In the baccalaureate sermon, the Reverend Hope Ward, pastor of Soapstone United Methodist Church in Raleigh, used a text from Matthew 11:2-19 and urged class members "to go forth nobly, humbly, and selflessly . . . to stand and shine." [10]

Mrs. Linda Johnson Hood of Harrells, NC, a May 1995, graduate in business administration, received the Sam Edwards Award, denoting her selection of the outstanding evening college student of 1995.

College Announces Staff Changes

Methodist began 1996 with a new director of admissions, Rick Lowe, and associate director, Eric Brandon. Both reported to Alan Coheley, vice president for enrollment services. Dr. Tryon Lancaster, a former education professor, was named assistant to the president. Dr. Gillie Benstead was named head of the Education Department and director of the Division of Education and Physical Education.

College Launches $6.5 Million Fund Drive

Methodist College launched a $6.5 million "Expanding the Vision" Campaign for Excellence at a press conference February 29, 1996. Trustee Chair Frank Barragen said the three-year campaign would have five goals: $1.9 million for a library annex, $1 million for a new academic building, $1 million for a math and computer science building, $1 million for the college endowment, and $1.7 million for ongoing support. He said $4.2 million or 65 percent of the overall campaign goal had been raised or pledged in the previous 17 months. "This shows great enthusiasm and support for the college," he added. [11]

Honorary Campaign Chair and Trustee Emeritus Terry Sanford thanked all who had supported Methodist College, saying, "Methodist College is reaching a new plateau. We know it will be in the forefront of leadership in the next century." [12]

Frank Barragan announces campaign goals.

College President Elton Hendricks said the math and computer science building would be started in the summer of 1996, using $1 million from the sale of tax-free revenue bonds. He expressed hope that the library annex and academic building could be underway by August 1997.

Jay Dowd, vice president for institutional advancement, said the campaign would have five major divisions, each chaired by a strong supporter of the college. The divisions, goals, and their chairs were: Board of Trustees, $2 million, Walter Clark; Board of Visitors, $200,000, Suzanne Barlow Pennick; Faculty and Staff, $150,000, Dr. Robert Christian; Alumni, $400,000; Friends and Corporations, $1.5 million, Wilson F. Yarborough Jr.

The college also listed a goal of $2.3 million from "The United Methodist Church, foundations, and a bond issue."

Tally Forum Probes Leadership

Methodist's Lura Tally Center for Leadership held its first annual leadership forum February 29, 1996. Terry Sanford gave the keynote address and said,

"Vision is a fundamental part of leadership and self-confidence is an important beginning point. A good leader doesn't mind risking failure. A leader is inspiring and restless. A leader is also a good listener, who has respect for everybody. Leaders aren't made with a cookie cutter . . . but most are trying to make a difference." [13]

Sanford's address was followed by six panel discussions. Dr. Hendricks led a panel which discussed "Spiritual/Ethical Aspects of Leadership," and included the Rev. Cureton Johnson of Fayetteville's First Baptist Church, Sister Jean Rhodes of the CARE Clinic, and Fayetteville native Brad Edwards, a professional football player for the Atlanta Falcons.

Chorus Sings in Paris, Charters, St. Avold, Strasbourg

The Methodist College Chorus, under the direction of Alan Porter, opened its 1996 concert tour of France Sunday morning, March 10 with a concert at the American Church in Paris.

The group also sang March 11 at Chartres Cathedral; March 13 at St. Avold, Fayetteville's sister city; March 14 at Church of St. George in Achenheim (near Strausbourg), and March 15 at Mulhouse.

In a later interview, Alan Porter said the two concerts in St. Avold were a high point. The first was an *a capella* rendition of Randal Thompson's "Alleluia" inside the memorial at the American cemetery. After singing, the chorus members filed outside, walked among 10,000 white crosses, and placed a bouquet of flowers on the grave of William Shaw Jr., a Fayetteville soldier killed in World War II.

— CHAPTER 9 —

The Methodist College Chorus appears in concert with residents of St. Avold, France.

The second high point was a Wednesday evening concert in St. Avold's Municipal Auditorium, attended by over 1,000 local residents. Appearing with the Methodist chorus were two local youth choirs and the city band, Harmonie. In the grand finale, all the groups gathered on stage for a spirited rendition of "O Happy Day!"

Debaters Win ADA Novice Division Title

In a national debate championship held March 11, 1996, at Liberty University in Lynchburg, Virginia, Methodist College debaters David Staiti and Alexis Parmenter finished first in the Novice Division. Staiti and Parmenter debated a team from Liberty by taking the negative side against Liberty's proposal to send nuclear emergency response teams to four Middle East countries.

Debate Coach John Humphreys said Staiti was also rated Best Speaker in the Novice Division. "We worked 45 hours a week for three weeks prior to nationals doing research and preparing our argument briefs," he said. "We incorporated 20,000 individual quotations into the briefs." [14]

The team of Staiti and Parmenter made the final round in all four debates in which they competed in the spring semester, beating teams from Wake Forest and Boston College.

The Methodist debaters' win in the Novice Division marked the second straight national title. In 1995, Julie Kahl and Ha Quach took top honors at Boston College.

College Loses Photographer

Richard Small, Methodist's first-time photographer, died February 6, 1996, of a heart attack just prior to a women's basketball game. He was 53.

Small excelled at his job in the Public Relations Office and was devoted to Methodist athletics. He took over 12,000 photos during his 18 months at the college.

A service of celebration and thanksgiving for Richard Small was held February 9 in Hensdale Chapel and drew an overflow crowd.

Green Remembers With Pride

A guest article submitted by Larry Green '65 for the March 1996 MC TODAY recalled the 30th reunion of members of the Class of 1965 during homecoming in October. A resident of Overland Park, Kansas, Green said he and classmates, Dave Altman, , Gene Coats, Johnny Parker, Steve Holtz, Jerry Marcus, Al Hayes, and Glenn Bell had enjoyed watching their first football game, touring the campus, and visiting the site of the famous "brick-laying stunt" in Cumberland Hall.

Cuthrell Sets Record

Sophomore Hamilton Cuthrell finished second at the NCAA Division III Indoor Championship March 9, 1996, at Smith College in Northampton, Massachusetts. He ran the 55-meter dash in 6.44 seconds.

College Begins Three Buildings

In the summer of 1996, Methodist College began construction of three new buildings— an allied health building/family medicine clinic, the enrollment services building, and the math and computer science building. The Richard L. Player Golf and Tennis Learning Center was completed and occupied in May.

PA Program Wins Provisional Accreditation

In the spring of 1996, Methodist's physician assistant program received provisional accreditation from the Commission on the Accreditation of Allied Health Programs. Ron Foster, program director, said the staff had to write syllabi for 27 courses and submit hundreds of pages of data to win provisional accreditation. "Support from the regional medical community has been outstanding," he said. [15]

The first class of four students—Sayeh Araghi, Melissa Stout, Jason Williams and Robin Lincoln—began the didactic phase (first year) of the two-year program May 13. Ron Foster said the students were "excited and a bit frightened" as they began their course work. [16]

— CHAPTER 9 —

The second of two modern entrance signs had three small fountains.

MC Launches Web Site

Methodist launched a site on the Internet's World Wide Web April 15, 1996. Methodist College's first site was hosted by APCNET, a Fayetteville-based Internet service provider.

The initial site was developed by the Public Relations Office and consisted of a home page and seven additional pages, under the general headings: The Mission, The Place, The Program, Student Life, Athletics, and Admissions/Financial Aid.

Retirees Honored

Four retirees were honored at a special dinner on April 26, 1996: Dr. Jack Peyrouse, theatre professor, with 18 years' service; Dr. Sue Kimbell, English professor, 17 years' service; Mrs. Loretta Swing, college accountant, 15 years' service; Mrs. Earlene Bass, faculty secretary, 33 ½ years' service.

Elaine Porter Named Professor of the Year

Mrs. J. Elaine Porter, Distinguished Service Professor of French, received the college's Professor of the Year Award at the annual awards convocation April 26, 1996.

Mrs. Porter was the head of the department of Foreign Languages; as the senior faculty member (with 33 years of experience), she led all academic processions. A graduate of Mount Union College and Duke University, she

L to R, retirees Jack Peyrouse, Earleene Bass, Sue Kimball, and Loretta Swing.

taught all levels of French, trained foreign language teachers for the public schools, and advised Phi Sigma Iota, (foreign language honorary) and a sorority at Methodist.

College Graduates 168

Don Baer, White House communications director, addressed Methodist College's Class of 1996, Sunday, May 12, urging all present to get involved in their communities and help build a better America. "If we do, we will create an 'Age of Possibility' and a better tomorrow for our children," he said. [17]

In a morning baccalaureate sermon, the Reverend Mike Safley, vice president for student affairs, spoke on the topic, "The Impossible Becomes Possible," describing persons who had overcome seemingly impossible odds: the Apollo astronauts, Abraham Lincoln, Helen Keller, Jackie Robinson, and Christopher Reeve.

President Hendricks presented an honorary Doctor of Humanities degree to Dr. Mott P. Blair of Siler City, N.C. for outstanding service to his community, church, and Methodist College. Dr. Blair was a college trustee from 1965-76, and succeeded Terry Sanford as chairman in 1967.

Laurie Davison, a biology major from Fayetteville, received the L. Stacy Weaver Award.

— CHAPTER 9 —

Golfers Win Again

Methodist's men's and women's golf teams again won their respective national titles in May 1996.

The men's team won its sixth NCAA Division III title May 21-24 in Saratoga Springs N.Y. Mike Adamson won the individual title by five strokes. The Monarchs entered the final round with a nine-shot deficit, but played well and won by two strokes over top-ranked Skidmore College. Coach Steve Conley described the team's comeback as "great, awesome, unbelievable." [18]

The Lady Monarchs golf team defeated a Rollins College team by one stroke May 17, 1996, in Allendale, Michigan, to win the 1996 NCAA Division II/III Championship.

Coach Karen Gray said she was fortunate to have such an outstanding team in her first year of coaching.

In other sports news:

— Methodist's baseball team finished fifth in the NCAA-III College World Series. The Monarchs amassed a run of 35-9, winning the Dixie Conference regular season and tournament titles.

— The men's tennis team, coached by Tom Maze, finished the year with a 14-4 dual match record and a first-ever appearance in the NCAA-III South Regional Tournament in San Antonio. The Monarchs lost in the first round of the South Regional to Washington College (Md.).

— Four members of Coach Brian Cole's men's and women's track and field teams won All-American status at the NCAA-III National Meet in Naperville, Ill. May 24. A 400-meter relay team made up of DeCarlos West, Wilbur Christy, Joe Clark, and Hamilton Cuthrell ran its second-fastest time of the year (41.52 seconds) to take third place in the meet.

— Methodist College won the Dixie Conference Championship in baseball, men's golf, men's soccer, and women's soccer and was runner-up in men's cross country, men's tennis and women's tennis.

College Breaks Ground for New Buildings

A formal groundbreaking for Joe W. Stout Hall, an enrollment services building, was held June 28, 1996. Dr. and Mrs. Frank Stout made a major gift toward the project to honor Frank Stout's late father, Joe W. Stout. Joe W. Stout was a prominent developer who built Eutaw Shopping Center and Bordeaux Motor Inn in Fayetteville.

1995–2000

At the groundbreaking Frank Stout, a college trustee, referred to his father as "a dreamer" and recalled his father's gift of 120 acres to Methodist College 40 years earlier. The wooded tract given by Stout was east of Ramsey Street and bordered the Cape Fear River. It bordered other campus land to the south.

Noting that the Stout home was located on the west side of Ramsey Street, Dr. Stout said he walked on the 120 acres given by his father as a teenager. He said it included a high bluff overlooking the Cape Fear River and some old Civil War ramparts. He said his father used a bulldozer to clear a path into the site and that a committee of Methodist officials which visited the site in early 1956, was overwhelmed by its natural beauty. "Seven days later the bishop's committee recommended that a new Methodist College be built in Fayetteville," he noted. [19]

College Breaks Ground for Office Park

The Methodist College Development Corporation broke ground for a 22-acre professional office park August 14, 1996, near the College's south entrance. Another $1.7 million, 13,000 square foot building was already under construction there. It was to house a family medicine clinic on the first floor and Methodist's physician assistant program on the second floor.

The development corporation, a subsidiary of Methodist College, was given a lease on 22 acres of college land. Governed by a six-member board

College officials break ground for College Centre Office Park.

of directors, the corporation agreed to donate revenues from leases of park properties to the College endowment. Richard R. Allen was named president.

In a site plan, Shuller, Ferris, Johnson and Lindstrom designed the park to house 15 buildings, totaling 100,000 square feet, to be built over a 10-year period.

Player Center Dedicated

The Richard L. Player Golf and Tennis Learning Center was dedicated August 29, 1996. Built adjacent to the College's golf practice green and driving range, the $500,000, 5,400 square foot building contained offices, classrooms, a repair shop, a pro shop, and a conference room for use by the professional golf and tennis management staffs.

The building was named for the founder of Player Realty and Construction Co. in Fayetteville. Mr. Player was an avid golfer and co-founder of Highland Country Club. Mr. Player's son, Richard L. Player, Jr., and other family members, made a $100,000 gift toward the facility in 1993. The senior Player, then 88 years of age, joined other members of the Player family for the dedication. Additional funds were raised by the Methodist College Board of Visitors.

In other news from the summer of 1996:

—A new computerized language lab was installed in Room T-112.

—The Police and Public Safety office moved into a brick house on Ramsey Street.

—Dr. Peter Murray, associate professor of history, took part in a five-week Rotary Group Study Exchange in Japan.

PGM staff members present gifts to Margaret Ann and Dick Player..

1995–2000

The Richard L. Player Golf and Tennis Learning Center.

—Eight teacher educators from the Fayetteville area attended a Teacher Education Scholars Institute at Methodist in August.
—The National Science Foundation awarded Methodist a $75,000 matching grant to furnish a new microbiology lab.
—Brian Scott '95, a 32 year-old *summa cum laude* graduate in political science, landed a summer internship at the White House where he worked as a special assistant in the Office of Public Liaison. His job was to help plan and coordinate visits to the White House by a variety of constituent groups and to manage a youth constituent outreach program targeted to 18-24 year-old Americans. Scott said he was confident President Bill Clinton would be re-elected in November.
—Fourteen rooms in Sanford and Cumberland halls were refurbished with free-standing furniture.

College Opens With Stoplight

Methodist College began its 37th academic year in August 1996, with three new buildings under construction—an Allied Health Building, Math and Computer Science Building, and Enrollment Services Building (Joe Stout Hall). In addition, a long-awaited stoplight was in place at its main entrance. Construction of the "back nine" holes of the College golf course continued. Enrollment reached 1,709 students (1260 day, 457 evening).

— CHAPTER 9 —

Methodist welcomed 13 new full-time faculty—Dr. Mary Wheeling White, and Robin Greene in English; Jacquelyn Hansen in psychology; Lori Stephenson in biology; Mary Kirchner in accounting; Nancy Rivers in mathematics; Edward R. Cohn in theatre; Betty Neill Guy Parsons in music; Paul J. Joseph in communications; Larry Marshall in criminal justice; Patrick D. Fountain in marketing; Dr. Grayson L. Carter in religion; Paul F. Connolly in military science; and Rob Eaton, men's soccer coach.

College Receives Kresge Grant

The Kresge Foundation of Troy Michigan awarded Methodist College a $300,000 challenge grant September 30, 1996, toward construction of an addition to Davis Memorial Library. The grant was contingent on the College raising $1,428,500 by December 1, 1997, to reach a $6.5 million goal for its "Expanding the Vision" campaign.

In other news from Fall 1996:

—Hurricane Fran brought 80 mile per hour winds to the campus, uprooting trees, demolishing a football scoreboard and lifting the roofs from the softball and baseball dugouts.

—Homecoming was observed October 18-19, 1996, with the theme, "Let Us Entertain You!" The Alumni Association presented the following awards at a prime rib dinner: Outstanding Faculty Award to Mrs. Joy Cogswell of Fayetteville, instructor of piano and director of the MC Preparatory School for the Performing Arts; Distinguished Alumni Award to Barry Horne '71 of Raleigh, a broker with Dean Witter Reynolds and a former Air Force pilot; Outstanding Alumni Service Award to Janet Mullen '72 of Fayetteville, principal of Hefner Elementary School and immediate past president of the alumni association.

—U.S. Senator Jesse Helms, accompanied by Sen. Don Nickles (R-OK) made a campaign stop at Methodist November 5, the day before the general election. His appearance was arranged by the Cumberland County Republican Party.

—The Monarch football team achieved its first winning season, finishing 6-4, and defeating Chowan, Bridgewater, Ferrum, Guilford, Maryville, and Davidson. Coach Jim Sypult credited the team's seniors with the turnaround. Receiver DeCarlos West had a 99-yard return against Salisbury State, and kicker Tony Bugeja made 26 of 26 point-after-touchdown kicks.

1995–2000

Hurricane Fran took the roof off the baseball dugout.

College Celebrates 40th Birthday

Methodist College celebrated its 40th birthday October 30, 1996, (two days early), with an hour-long celebration in Reeves Auditorium. Entitled "Celebrate 40!" and produced by the Methodist College Alumni Association, the show mixed a narrated slide-show history with performances of pop tunes from four decades.

Two of the College's original trustees—Terry Sanford from Durham and Robert Johnson from Goldsboro—were present to celebrate the 40th anniversary of Methodist College receiving its charter November 1, 1956. Current College trustees also attended, along with retired faculty and staff, alumni, the Rev. F. Belton Joyner from the N.C. Conference of the United Methodist Church, Fayetteville Mayor J. L. Dawkins, and several hundred students and staff.

The program opened with the Methodist College Chorus singing "Morning Has Broken" and the "Alma Mater" as slides of a campus sunrise were projected on a 13-foot screen on stage. The Rev. Carrie Parrish gave the invocation, and College President Elton Hendricks gave the welcome and introduced guests.

Betty Neill Parsons '64 narrated Part I of the history slide show covering 1956-69. Musical numbers included: Byron Pritchard '90 as Elvis Presley, singing "You Ain't Nothin' But A Hound Dog." Brenda Vandervort, Nanelle Walston, and Ratasha Thompson as The Supremes, singing "Stop In The Name Of Love," and Dr. Paul Wilson as Tevye (from *Fiddler on the Roof*) singing "If I Were a Rich Man."

— CHAPTER 9 —

Rainbow's End *in the finale of Celebrate 40! marking Methodist's 40th anniversary.*

Lynn Carraway '71 narrated Part II of the slide show covering 1970-82. Live musical numbers from that period included: "I Got You Babe," "YMCA," and "Staying Alive."

Leon Clark, S.G.A. president, narrated Part III, covering 1983-96. Featured from this era was: "All I Ask of You," "We Are Family", and "I Heard It Through the Grapevine."

The program ended with Rainbow's End singing and dancing to "Celebration" by Kool and the Gang. The Planning Committee for the celebration consisted of Lynn Carraway, Summer Brock, Lynley Asay, Lynda Beard, Betty Neill Parsons, and Bill Billings.

As part of the celebration, colorful banners were hung on a dozen light poles across campus. The pole brackets and banners were retained for future displays, and the banners were updated for a myriad of other events.

Campus Grows to 584 Acres

Methodist College purchased a 7.5 acre strip of land on the northwestern corner of the campus November 22, 1996. The land was purchased from Mr. and Mrs. Daniel Kinlaw and Mr. and Mrs. George Alred Kinlaw for $375,000. The land was located between the president's home and the Quick Stop. With the additional land, the College campus grew to 584 acres.

In December 1996, Richard R. Allen donated a commercial building and lot on Ramsey Street several hundred feet south of the College's main entrance and opposite Stacy Weaver Drive. The College announced plans to raze the building and construct a new entrance to College Centre Office Park.

Two brick residences that once faced Ramsey Street were moved to new locations on campus. The larger home was placed behind Cumberland Hall to serve as a student lounge/snack bar. The smaller home was moved to a spot opposite the Science Building and adjacent to the president's home to house an Academic Development Center.

Sue Kimball Addresses Winter Graduates

Dr. Sue Kimball, a retired English professor, delivered the commencement address at Methodist's 24th winter commencement December 13, 1996.

Dr. Kimball offered the graduates seven rules for successful living which she said they should have learned at Methodist College: 1) Be curious, 2) Never go anywhere without a ballpoint pen, 3) Never go anywhere without a paperback book or magazine, 4) Don't worry about what others think about you, 5) Love yourself, 6) Find a cause and get behind it, 7) Listen with an open heart and mind to those who love you the most. [20]

In his baccalaureate sermon Sunday morning, the Reverend Bill Braswell, pastor of Haymount United Methodist Church, urged the class members to be "people of joy in all seasons and circumstances." [21]

College President Elton Hendricks presented Methodist College Medallions to two retired faculty members: Mrs. Inge Dent, teacher of German and former dean of women; and Dr. Sue Kimball, English professor and director of the College's Southern Writers Symposium. The president also presented the Sam Edwards Award to Mrs. Mary Frances Williams of Roseboro, N.C.

Mrs. Longest Pens Book

The cover story in the March 1997, *Methodist College Today* previewed Mrs. Pauline Moser Longest's forthcoming book *Going Places*, about her world travels from 1913-1995. Mrs. Longest taught biology and geography at Methodist from 1962-79. She was 83 when she finished the book.

Going Places was divided into two parts: "Early Memories of My Travels" and "Some Serious Travel," which described all her major trips from 1973-95.

Mrs. Longest said her favorite North Carolina destinations were Lewisville (her hometown) northwest of Winston-Salem, Roaring Gap and Chapel Hill. She made a total of 52 trips outside the U.S. between 1971 and 1995. Her favorite travel companions were Georgia Mullen, former MC librarian (32 trips) and Mrs. Phebe Emmons of Raleigh (12 trips), a fellow member of Delta Kappa Gamma, an honor society for women educators.

In her book, the retired professor included her own drawings of things she had seen and vivid descriptions of: glow worms on the rock wall behind Cascade Falls in North Carolina, Lou Gehrig at Yankee Stadium (1934), a morality play at the church of Aimee Semple McPherson (Los Angeles, 1936), a blue-footed booby nesting in the Galapagos Islands (1972), and the World Pillow Fighting Championship in Sonoma, California (1994).

— CHAPTER 9 —

The Methodist College Alumni Association hosted a reception and book-signing for Mrs. Longest May 4 in the Alumni Dining Room, Berns Student Center.

In other news from spring 1997:

Mrs. Pauline Longest works on her book.

— The Cannon Foundation, Inc. of Concord, N.C. awarded Methodist College a $50,000 grant toward construction of the addition to Davis Memorial Library.

— The Council on Social Work Education accredited Methodist's Bachelor of Social Work program. Dr. Joyce White and Ms. Terri Brown conducted an extensive self-study to show compliance with CSWE standards and were visited on four different occasions by CSWE commissioners.

— The Kate B. Reynolds Trust of Winston-Salem, N.C. awarded Methodist College a $59,255 grant to equip an electronic classroom for the new physician assistant program.

— Heritage Family Physicians, a subsidiary of Columbia Highsmith-Rainey Memorial Hospital, opened in April, leasing the first floor of Methodist's new medical arts building in College Centre Office Park.

— Pat Jones, associate professor of mathematics, was profiled in *101 Careers in Mathematics* along with 100 other math teachers. The

The Medical Arts Building housed the PA program and Heritage Family Physicians.

book of autobiographical sketches, published by the Mathematical Association of America to show high school and college students the wide range of careers available to math majors.

Basketball Team Advances To 'Elite Eight'

Methodist's 1996-97 basketball team carried a 20-game winning streak into the NCAA-III Midwest Sectional Game, losing to Illinois Wesleyan 95-63. Coach Bob McEvoy said he was proud of the entire team, but especially proud of the senior tri-captains Taylor Bandy, Tyrone Bennett, and Jason Childers.

Dr. L. Stacy Weaver Dies In Florida

Dr. L. Stacy Weaver, the founding president of Methodist College, died March 25, 1997, in Lakeland, Florida.

A native of Lenoir, North Carolina, Weaver became president of Methodist College in 1957, and served 16 years until 1973. Weaver had a 50-year career in education, including stints as a high school principal, professor of Latin and Greek, coach (football, basketball, and baseball), president of Rutherford College, and superintendent of the Statesville and Durham City schools.

Stacy Weaver held an A.B. degree from Duke University, an M.A. from Columbia University, and honorary doctorates from High Point College, Duke University, and Methodist College.

Methodist College President Elton Hendricks said Weaver gave Methodist "instant credibility because he was one of the most respected educators in North Carolina." [22]

The Fayetteville Observer offered this editorial comment on Weaver's passing, "Before it was fashionable, L. Stacy Weaver was a true Renaissance Man. His contribution to North Carolina, especially to the young people, set high expectations for all." [23]

Stacy Weaver was survived by Elizabeth Hallyburton Weaver, his wife of 70 years; three sons: Dr. Charles H. Weaver of Raleigh, L. Stacy Weaver Jr. of Fayetteville, and Dr. Walter P. Weaver of Lakeland, FL.; seven grandchildren; and five great-grandchildren.

Dr. Weaver's funeral was held March 29 at Hay Street United Methodist Church, with the Reverend Dr. William P. Lowdermilk presiding. Interment followed at Lafayette Memorial Park.

Those offering tributes at the funeral were: Dr. Samuel J. Womack, former MC religion professor and academic dean; Dr. Terry Sanford, College trustee emeritus; and Dr. Weaver's son, Dr. Walter Weaver, a religious professor at Florida Southern College.

CHAPTER 9

Terry Sanford said Weaver was the trustees' unanimous choice to become the first president of Methodist College. "His choice was a guarantee of success," said Sanford. "He came to build and he did so with creativity and vision. He attracted and inspired good people. He wanted quality students. Thanks largely to him, Methodist College is now viewed as one of the two or three best liberal arts colleges in this state." [24] (See Appendix G for a full biography.)

John Templeton Speaks at 20th Stock Market Symposium

More than 1,600 persons gathered April 18, 1997, at the Charlie Rose Agri-Expo Center to hear retired mutual funds manager John Templeton speak. Templeton gave the keynote address at Methodist's 20th annual Stock Market Symposium.

Sir John Templeton

In a speech entitled "Multiplying Multitudes of Blessings: Is Progress Speeding Up?," Templeton cited far-reaching changes that had occurred in economics, medicine, technology, education, and spiritual life during the twentieth century. He drew from 84 years of personal experience, including his boyhood days in rural Tennessee, his college years at Yale and Oxford, his 38 years as manager of the Templeton Growth Fund, and the efforts of the John Templeton Foundation to promote spiritual information through science, free enterprise education, and character development.

In a postscript to his prepared remarks, Templeton predicted America would see bare markets in the future, "carried down to 40 percent below where they are at peak," but counseled investors to hang on. [25] He also advised investors to "search for an expert and mutual fund whose performance has been outstanding." [26] Finally, he recommended that investors "buy long-term U.S. Treasury bonds which are yielding 7.4 percent." [27]

During the program, Methodist College President Elton Hendricks presented Templeton with an honorary Doctor of Business Administration degree.

College Receives Major Gifts

In the spring of 1997, Methodist was notified that Louis D. Thomas of Fayetteville had bequeathed $500,000 to the college to endow the Louis D. and Bernadine Thomas Scholarship. Mr. Thomas, the former owner of Electric Supply Co., died April 18 at the age of 84.

The College received another major gift from David R. Nimocks Jr. to endow the David R. Nimocks Sr. Professorship in the Charles M. Reeves School of Business.

1995–2000

In May, Nolan Clark, trustee of the Florence Rogers Charitable Trust, presented a $10,000 scholarship check for division among the College's four physician assistant students.

Trustees Elect Yarborough Chair

The Methodist College Board of Trustees elected Ramon L. Yarborough chairman May 1997. The president of Fayetteville Publishing Company, Yarborough was vice-chairman and had been a trustee since 1991. He was chosen to succeed Frank Barragan Jr., effective July 1, 1997.

The trustees also elected Richard L. Player, Jr. to succeed Yarborough as vice chairman, and re-elected Walter Clark secretary and Vance Neal treasurer. Fayetteville attorney Wade Byrd was elected to fill a vacancy on the board.

Ramon L. Yarborough

In other news from spring 1997:
- Mrs. Kim Dowd was named vice president for student life and dean of students, effective July 1, to replace the Reverend Mike Safley, who resigned to become president of the Methodist Home for Children.
- Amanda H. Wunder was named director of development effective June 2, to serve as liaison to the Methodist College Foundation and coordinate the Annual Loyalty Fund Drive in Fayetteville.
- The 'Expanding the Vision' campaign reached $6,184,559 as of June 25, 1997, 90 percent of its overall goal of $6,550,000.
- *PRIDE*, the student newspaper at Methodist, won a First Place with Special Merit Award from the American Scholastic Press Association in College Point, N.Y. Mike McDermott served as editor for 1996-97. Jamee Lynch, student media advisor, said the paper received 965 of a possible 1,000 points.

Men's Golf Team Wins National Title

Methodist's 1997, men's golf team captured a fourth straight NCAA-III Men's Golf Championship May 16 at the Medallion Club in Westerville, Ohio. Freshman Brian McLaughlin was the medalist and was named Softspikes Freshman of the Year by the Golf Coaches Association of America; he averaged 76.14 for the season.

The Lady Monarch golfers finished second behind Lynn University at the 1997 NCAA-II III National Championship at Howey-in-the-Hills, Florida.

— CHAPTER 9 —

In other sports news:
—The baseball team finished 31-10, but did not receive a NCAA invitation for post-season play.
—The men's and women's tennis teams won their Dixie Conference championships. Both teams were coached by Tom Maze.
—The softball team, coached by Brenda Hillman, finished 19-17.
—Brian Cole resigned as head men's and women's cross country and track and field coach to take a similar post at Ohio Northern University.

College Holds First Graduation In Riddle Center
Methodist College held its 34th Spring Commencement in a new venue, the March F. Riddle Center, May 11, 1997.

Jerry Richardson, owner of the Carolina Panthers professional football team, was the commencement speaker. A Fayetteville native, Richardson attended Wofford College, played professional football with the Baltimore Colts (1958-59), and made millions as CEO of Flagstar Companies, a major franchise holder of Hardee's restaurants in Spartanburg, S.C.

Richardson shared five lessons he had learned with the 150 members of the graduating class: 1) Teamwork enhances individual effort, 2) Treat people fairly and listen to both sides of every issue, 3) Work hard to achieve worthwhile goals, 4) Build on the strength of diversity to achieve common goals, 5) Be happy in your work and balance work with leisure. [28]

The baccalaureate speaker was the Reverend Dr. Marion Edwards, the new resident bishop of the North Carolina Conference of The United Methodist Church. Edwards shared a story of stagecoach travel in the U.S. penned by the late novelist Louis L'Amour. He said First Class passengers could ride inside no matter what happened, while Second Class passengers had to get out if a

The Class of 1997 was the first to graduate in the March F. Riddle Center.

problem developed, and Third Class passengers were expected to get out and push if the need arose.

Edwards said the Good Samaritan in the Bible was similar to the Third Class ticket holder. "Jesus never issues anything but Third Class tickets," he said. "I challenge you to turn in your First Class and Second Class tickets and purchase a Third Class ticket. Develop a stewardship that follows Jesus." [29]

Dr. Elton Hendricks, College president, presented honorary Doctor of Humanities degrees to Jerry Richardson and to Bill Weisser, diaconal minister of music at Edenton Street United Methodist Church. He also presented the L. Stacy Weaver Award to Cindy Lu del Rosario.

Joe Stout Hall, which houses offices for enrollment services, opened in Spring 1997.

College Dedicates Two New Buildings

Joe Stout Hall, a new home for enrollment services—admissions, financial aid, veteran services—was occupied in the spring of 1997 and dedicated June 17, 1997. The 4,500-square-foot, $600,000 building was designed by Shuller, Ferris, Lindstrom and built on the west front of the campus just south of the flagpole. Player, Inc. was the general contractor.

Stout Hall is named for Joe Wiley Stout, a Fayetteville builder and land developer who built Eutaw Shopping Center and Bordeaux Motor Inn. In 1956, Mr. and Mrs. Joe Stout donated 120 acres to Methodist College. The parcel constitutes the southern leg of the campus and is located across Ramsey Street from where the Stouts lived. In 1996, Dr. Frank Stout and his wife Carol made a large gift toward a new building in memory of Joe Stout, who died in 1988.

— CHAPTER 9 —

The Math and Computer Science Building was later named in honor of Keith Allison.

Methodist College dedicated a $1.2 million, 8,500 square-foot Math and Computer Science Building August 22, 1997, also designed by Shuller, Ferris, Johnson, and Lindstrom and built by Player, Inc.. The building housed four classrooms, two computer labs, seven faculty offices, and a conference room. New furniture and computers were included in the project.

In brief dedicatory remarks, College President Elton Hendricks said, "The Information Age has dawned on us slowly and all at once. This building will help ensure that our students are computer literate." [30]

New Year Brings New Developments

Methodist began its 38th school year and fall 1997, semester with 1,291 day students and 417 evening students for a total enrollment of 1,701.

The College continued work on its third reaffirmation study for the Southern Association of Colleges and Schools. Dr. John Sill, professor of sociology, was self-study director and chair of the Steering Committee. Five committees were charged with gathering data and drafting reports, including plans for improvement. A self-study report was slated for completion in 1998. In the spring of 1999, MC was to host a six-member visiting committee which would then review the self-study and submit a report of its findings to the College and the SACS Commission on Colleges.

In other news from fall 1997:

— Joe Doll, director of the Reeves School of Business, announced the establishment of the Institute of Business and Marketing Research, headed by Dr. Jen-Hsiang Lin. He also announced the promotion of Mrs. Theresa P. Clark to head the Dept. of Business Administration and Economics. The school's third department, the Institute for Golf and Tennis Management, was headed by Mr. Jerry Hogge.

— Walter Clark of Fayetteville, a long-time friend and trustee of Methodist College, died August 8 at the age of 84. The founder and president of Mid-South Insurance Co., Clark served for many years as secretary of the Methodist College Board of Trustees and chairman of its Investment Committee.

— Ruth Palmer of Kitty Hawk, a friend and benefactor of the College, died July 18 at the age of 90. She had made large gifts toward the Samuel J. and Norma L. Womack Endowed Chair in Religion, the renovation of Hensdale Chapel, and the College's current capital campaign.

— Methodist received a $309,000 bequest from the estate of Luther Dean Minges of Fayetteville, who died May 18, 1996, at the age of 86.

— DeeDee Jarman, assistant women's basketball coach, was promoted to head women's coach, succeeding Rita Wiggs. Wiggs remained as director of athletics.

— Jason Childers, the first MC basketball player to gain All-American status, was awarded the 1997 Sykes Cup, denoting his selection as Methodist College Athlete of the Year.

— The second nine holes of the Methodist College Golf Course were sprigged and turfed. The course was to be ready for play in August 1998.

Player Wins Contract To Build Library Annex, Academic Building

In November 1997, Methodist College awarded a general construction contract to Player, Inc. of Fayetteville to build a library annex and academic building.

In December 1997, the College exceeded its $6.5 million goal for the "Expanding the Vision" campaign by 20 percent, raising $7.9 million. In November 1997, Methodist received an anonymous gift of $200,000 toward the academic building in memory of Walter Clark. In recognition of Mr. Clark's support of the campaign, the trustees voted to name the new academic building Walter B. and Margaret T. Clark Hall.

— CHAPTER 9 —

13th Writers Symposium Examines Works of Fred Chappell
"Fred Chappell: Places of Possibility" was the subject of Methodist's 13th Southern Writers Symposium, held September 26-27, 1997.

A well-known novelist, poet, and UNC-G English professor, Chappell was present throughout the weekend to hear what follow teachers, writers, and students had to say about him.

Dr. Mary Wheeling White, assistant professor of English, succeeded Dr. Sue Kimball as the symposium director. It was White who selected Chappell, a native of Canton in western North Carolina, as the symposium honoree. Keynote speakers were Chappell, Dr. Kimball, Dr. Michael McFee of UNC, and Susan Underwood from Carson-Newman College.

Chappell offered the following observations during a question-answer session:
— "Poetry is more like walking through the woods . . . and fiction is like riding a bicycle. [31]
— "The most important aspect of writing is to know how you want the readers to feel when they read the last sentence and close the book." [32]

In other news from winter 1997:
— At Family Weekend, September 27-28, a Methodist College Parents' Association was organized.
— Methodist's Teacher Education program was granted continuing accreditation by the National Council for the Accreditation of

The cast of **Fiddler on the Roof,** *1997.*

Teacher Education (NCATE).
— Monarch Theatre presented *Fiddler on the Roof* November 20-25, 1997, in Reeves Auditorium.
— The Academic Development Center staff moved into a renovated brick residence that had been moved to an area next to the president's home.
— Student volunteers assembled by the Campus Ministry Center spent fall break helping finish two Habitat for Humanity houses in Fayetteville's Habitat Village.
— The theme of the 1997 homecoming November 1, was "Follow The Yellow Brick Road." The Band of Oz performed for the homecoming dance where students and alumni danced the Macarena. The alumni association presented its Distinguished Alumni Award to the Reverend Wesley Brown '73, associate dean for external relations of Duke University Divinity School.

Congressman, Former Dean Address Winter Graduates

Speaking to Methodist's 25th winter graduating class December 12, Seventh District Congressman Mike McIntyre of Lumberton challenged the 98 class members to accept the responsibility that goes with freedom and seize every opportunity to help their fellow man.

During the commencement Dr. Hendricks presented the Sam Edwards Award for outstanding evening student of 1997, to May graduate Jo Ann Bagley.

In a morning baccalaureate sermon, Dr. Samuel J. Womack, Methodist's third academic dean, told the winter class, "We are created for and meant to be lovers of life . . . Find a sovereign good and give yourself to it . . . I hope each of you will be caught up in the great romance and become lovers of life, of our beautiful world and the universe God has given us." [33]

In winter sports:
— The Monarch football team racked up a program-best 9-1 record, including shut-out wins over Bridgewater and Hampden-Sydney. Senior tailback DeCarlos West finished his career as Methodist's all-time leading rusher (2,782 yards on 558 carries), all-time leading scorer (42 touchdowns, 254 points) and all-time leading return specialist (37 kickoffs returns for 1,016 yards). West also collected a school-record 17 touchdowns in his senior season.
— The men's cross country team finished second in the conference.
— The men's soccer team, coached by Adrian Blewitt, finished 8-10 overall and fifth in the conference.

— The Lady Monarch soccer team compiled an 8-10 record and finished third in the conference.
— The volleyball team finished the 1997 season 12-19.

College Breaks Ground For New Buildings

Methodist College trustees and friends wielded shovels February 12, 1998, to break ground for Walter B. and Margaret T. Clark Hall and an annex to Davis Library.

Branch Banking and Trust Co. broke ground for a $1 million branch in College Centre Office Park March 17, 1998. The bank became the second tenant in an office park near the college's main entrance, joining Heritage Family Physicians which completed a family medicine clinic there in 1997.

Tally Forum Focuses on Juvenile Crime

North Carolina Court of Appeals Judge Patricia Timmons-Goodson and Seventh District Congressman Mike McIntyre were the keynote speakers at a Tally Leadership Forum February 23, 1998. The topic was: "The Rocky Years: Pre-empting Juvenile and Young Adult Crime."

Judge Timmons-Goodson said broken homes, poverty and child abuse were major causes of juvenile crime in North Carolina. "Counseling and mentoring can reduce juvenile crime by 80 percent," she said. [34]

McIntyre said crime among juveniles (those under 18) rose 21.5 percent from 1992-96. He said he supported the five goals for addressing the problem put forth by the Commission on the Future of America.

1) Establish opportunities for coaching and mentoring.
2) Ensure adequate health care
3) Establish safe places for those activites
4) Establish new partnerships between public and private groups
5) Give young people opportunities to serve and give back. [35]

During the program, former N.C. Senator Lura Tally presented Judge Timmons-Goodson with the first "100 Percent Award" given by the Lura Tally Center for Leadership Development.

Sanfords Give Set of Audubon Reproductions

In late December 1997, Margaret Rose and Terry Sanford of Durham donated a four-volume set of *The Birds of America* to Methodist's Davis Memorial Library.

The set of books contained 435 color reproductions of Audubon's life-size drawings of birds created between 1826-1838. In 1985, the Sanfords purchased one of the 350 facsimile editions of *The Birds of America* from

Mrs. Pulsipher displays bird print.

the National Audubon Society for $15,000. The prints were reproduced by a Japanese printer. The set of books and a custom-made bookcase and stand were accompanied by a five-volume text entitled *Ornithological Biography*. All were placed in the library's Special Collections Room.

In other news from spring 1998:
- Debaters Daniel Charpentier and Greg Thomas won the ADA Novice National Championship in the Spring of 1998.
- Dr. Michael Potts, assistant professor of philosophy, read a paper entitled "Brain Dead Individuals Are Not Dead" March 5, 1998, at the first annual B.F. Stone Endowed Lyceum.
- Dr. Richard Walsh, professor of religion, took part in a book-signing for *Reading the Bible: An Introduction* a textbook for introductory biblical literature courses.
- Dr. Mary Wheeling White, assistant professor of English, autographed copies of a critical biography entitled, *Fighting the Current: The Life and Work of Evelyn Sutt* (1893-1963).
- An annual giving report published in the Spring 1998 issue of *Methodist College Today* showed the College received gifts totaling $2,627,719 in 1997.
- Eleven representatives of Methodist's newly-formed Residence Hall Association attended a North Carolina Association of Residence Halls Conference February 6-8 at UNC-Wilmington.
- Speaking in Hensdale Chapel January 21, 1998, the Reverend Leonard Fairley, pastor of Soapstone United Methodist Church in Raleigh, compared the late Rev. Martin Luther King, Jr. to the biblical Joseph.
- More that 175 volunteers turned out for "Show You Care Day" March 28 to build an arbor and complete the landscaping of Fannie Farmer Memorial Park located between Cumberland Hall and the Berns Student Center. The late Mrs. Farmer worked at the college for 33 years.
- The Methodist College Alumni Association presented a new mascot (lion) costume to the College cheerleaders.

Women's Team Narrowly Misses NCAA Bench

The Lady Monarchs basketball team fell to Christopher Newport 93-91 in the DIAC championship game February 20, 1998, at Ferrum College. First-year Coach DeeDee Jarman's team finished 16-11, second in the DIAC tournament and second in the league's regular season. Junior forward Amy Todd was elected to the First Team All- DIAC; she led the DIAC in field goal accuracy and ranked seventh in the nation with a .595 clip.

— CHAPTER 9 —

In other spring 1998, sports action:
—Two athletes from Methodist won events at the Mason-Dixon Indoor Track and Field Championship February 22. William Ray won the long jump and triple jump, and Bradley Hicks won the pole vault for a third time in four years by clearing 14.6 feet.
—Men's Golf Coach Steve Conley was selected to coach the United States collegiate golf team against counterparts from Japan in the 23rd Annual USA-Japan matches in Tokyo July 2-4.
—Coach Jim Sypult's 9-1 football squad for 1997, was ranked 20th nationally in both the USA-III Football and Columbus Multimedia final polls.
—Director of Athletics Rita Wiggs announced the formation of a Monarch Booster Club and an Athletic Hall of Fame. Booster Club membership was available for a minimum gift of $25 with five giving levels above that amount. Criteria for election to the Athletic Hall of Fame's inaugural (1998) class were published in the spring 1998, issue of *Methodist College Today*.
—Keljin Adams, a May 1997, graduate and four-year football letterman, was selected for the first annual "Rudy Award" by the *College Football Chronicle* for his unselfish play at the collegiate level.

Terry Sanford Dies At 88

Methodist College Trustee Emeritus Terry Sanford died April 18, 1998, at his home in Durham. He had been fighting cancer for nearly a year.

Sanford's life of public service (former governor, president of Duke University, U.S. Senator) was remembered and praised by many North Carolinians. A native of Laurinburg, it was Sanford (then a Fayetteville attorney) who persuaded Bishop Paul Garber and eastern North Carolina Methodists to build Methodist College in Fayetteville. (See Appendix B for a full biography.)

Eddie Price signs condolence book for Sanford.

Sanford's funeral was held at Duke Chapel, where he was later interred. Students and staff at Methodist signed a book of condolences which was sent to the Sanford family.

1995–2000

College Dedicates Fannie Farmer Park

Methodist College held a dedication ceremony April 1, 1998, for Fannie Farmer Memorial Park. Mrs. Farmer was a cafeteria worker and housekeeper at Methodist from the mid 1960's, until her death in February 1997, at the age of 65. She worked at the College for 33 years.

The park was built in a partially wooded valley between the Berns Student Center and the residence halls. It included a gazebo, brick walks, picnic tables, flowers and shrubs, and a dedicatory plaque. The Reverend Mike Safley, former dean of students, proposed the construction of the park after Mrs. Farmer's death.

Longleaf Press Publishes First Chapbook

Methodist's Longleaf Press published its first poetry chapbook, *Unravelings* by Barbara Presnell, in the spring of 1998. A teacher at Catawba College and a resident of Lexington, N.C., Mrs. Presnell's manuscript (19 poems) won the 1998, Longleaf Press Poetry Chapbook Contest, which drew 46 entries from five southeast states.

Art Faculty Share Award

Art professors Silvana Foti and Peggy Hinson were named Professors of the Year at Methodist's annual awards convocation April 17, 1998.

In other staff and faculty news:

—Jane Cherry, director of international services for ten years, retired in June. She and her husband, retired District Court Judge Sol Cherry, moved to Boone, N.C.

—Cynthia J. Curtis of Hope Mills was named Director of Annual Fund and Parent Programs. She was formerly campaign director for United Way of Cumberland County.

Alan Porter Retires

Nearly 380 persons gathered at Methodist Saturday evening May 2, 1998, to honor Alan M. Porter upon his retirement as professor of music and director of the College chorus. Porter had just completed his 35th year at Methodist.

Organized by Jane Weeks Gardiner, the event was music-filled, with performances by 60 chorus alumni and the College Concert Choir.

Alan Porter takes a final bow after conducting a reunion chorus.

— CHAPTER 9 —

Porter's sons, Greg and David, presented the college with a portrait of their father to be placed in the Music Department.

Several of Porter's former students and fellow staff members offered words of thanks and best wishes. Porter and his wife Elaine (Distinguished Professor of French) were clearly moved by the experience. "It was an evening of great joy," said Porter. [36] He announced that he and Mrs. Porter would be retiring to Kure Beach, N.C.

Texan Addresses Class of 1998

"Look after **all** your lives." [37]

That was Robert H. Dedman's advice to the 35th graduating class of Methodist College May 10, 1998, in an address titled, "Keeping Your Balance."

A lifelong Methodist, Dedman was the founder and chairman of Club Corporation International based in Dallas, Texas. ClubCorp was then operating 260 golf resorts and country clubs around the world; its North Carolina holdings included Pinehurst Resort and Country Club, Capital City Club, and the Carolina Club. A leading philantropist, Dedman was then chairman of the board of trustees of Southern Methodist University.

Using a wooden chair as a prop, Mr. Dedman said the legs could represent four qualities needed for balanced living. He advised the members of the graduating class to: 1)Plan to work and work to plan your lives, 2) Never stop learning, 3) Keep a positive attitude and a sense of humor, and 4) Be nice to others and cultivate long-term, win-win relationships. He also added two bits of philosophical advice: 1)Be decisive, and 2)Look for good role models and learn what works. [38]

In the morning baccalaureate sermon, the Reverend Carl Frazier Jr., pastor of Hay Street United Methodist Church in Fayetteville, urged class members to, "do better than we baby boomers" by turning away from material concerns to what John Wesley described as "social holiness." [39]

He concluded by saying, "Christians should be generous and caring. Overcome evil with good. Go into the world for Christ's sake. Do your best not to fit in." [40]

During the commencement, President Hendricks presented an honorary Dotor of Humanities degree to Robert H. Dedman and a Methodist College Medallion to Alan M. Porter, who had just retired as professor of music. He also presented the Stacy Weaver Award to Jason Anthony Williams.

Kelli Bradshaw Crowned Miss N.C.

Kelli Bradshaw, a May 1998, graduate from Roseboro, N.C. was crowned Miss North Carolina June 23, 1998, in Raleigh. The 22-year old competed as Miss Western Piedmont.

1995–2000

Golfers Win Again

Methodist's men's golf team won its fifth consecutive NCAA-III Championship May 15, 1998, at Jekyll Island, Georgia.

The team surpassed its own national record for the lowest round, firing a third day 277 and final day 279.

Freshman Chad Collins (75-71-68-69-283) was the individual champion and was named NCAA-III National Player of the Year.

The 1998, Lady Monarch golf team regained the national NCAA-II/III title May 15 at Allen, Michigan. Coach Kim Kincer led the Green and Gold to a 1254-1259 victory over Florida Southern.

Junior co-captain Tracey Gage was the lowest scoring Monarch, earning runner-up status in the 63-golfer, 10-team field.

In other spring sports:

—The 1998, baseball team made its 15th NCAA-III Tournament appearance, going 2-2 at the South Regional for runner-up honors. MC fell to top-seeded N.C. Wesleyan, 3-2 in the final. The team ended the year with a 32-13-1 record.

—In track and field, Jody McIntyre took sixth-place in the javelin at the NCAA-III Championship in St. Paul, Minnesota. McIntyre won both the javelin and the hammer at the Mason-Dixon Conference Meet in Newport News, Va., May 2, while finishing second at the shot put.

—The Methodist College cheerleaders took Third Place honors at the National Cheerleaders Association's Collegiate National Championships held at Daytona Beach, Fl., the first weekend in April.

—James Taplie Coile, a *magna cum laude* May graduate and former men's basketball manager and assistant sports information director, won a $5,000 Sears Directors' Cup Postgraduate Scholarship.

Cheerleaders take third place at NCA.

McFaydens Go Sailing

The last of a four-part series by Jim McFayden '78 and his wife Lynn McFayden, in which they recounted their experiences on a 14-month sailboat voyage from North Carolina up the Atlantic Coast and then south to the

— CHAPTER 9 —

Bahamas appeared in the fall 1998, issue of *MC Today*. The McFaydens e-mailed detailed reports and photos of their journey to Summer Brock, alumni director.

Fall '98 Enrollment Reaches New High

Methodist College began the fall 1998, semester with a record 1,972 students, an increase of 7.8 percent over fall 1997. Day enrollment grew 3 percent to 1,332 students, while the evening enrollment grew 19 percent over fall 1997, to 640 students.

Methodist began 1998-99, with a new athletic director—Bob McEvoy. He succeeded Rita Wiggs, who resigned to pursue other interests. David Smith became head men's basketball coach, and Doug Tabbert was named women's volleyball coach.

Methodist's "Expanding the Vision" campaign concluded with total gifts and pledges of $8,590,000.

A newly renovated press box opened at Monarch Field with a second floor and roof observation deck.

The Professional Golfers Association of America sanctioned Methodist's professional golf management program.

The Commission on Accreditation of Allied Health Programs granted full accreditation to Methodist's Physician Assistant Program.

Methodist's first physician assistant graduates with program director Ron Foster

540

Miss North Carolina, Kelli Bradshaw, a 1998, graduate of Methodist College, was First Runner-Up in the Miss America pageant September 19, winning $35,000 in scholarships.

In other fall news:

—The Board of Trustees voted to rename East Hall Pearce Hall, in honor of Dr. Richard Pearce, the college's second president, and his wife, the late Neva Brock Pearce. A naming ceremony was held October 15, attended by Dr. Pearce, family members, and friends.

Kelli Bradshaw

—The 14th Southern Writers Symposium, held September 18-19, 1998, explored "The Idea of Home in Southern Writing;" 48 papers were presented on that subject. Guest speakers included Fayetteville native Tim McLaurin; English professor Shelby Stephenson of UNC-Pembroke; Sylvia Biershank and Vickie Daley, professors at Stephen F. Austin State University; and Donna Kelly, an editor in the N.C. Dept. of Cultural Resources.

Advancement Office Sells Bricks

In the fall of 1998, Methodist's Office of Institutional Advancement launched a campaign to sell engraved brick pavers for a circular plaza at the new entrance to Davis Memorial Library.

Friends and alumni of the College were given the opportunity to purchase a personalized brick for $100. Three lines were available to list a name and class year, a message, or a tribute to someone.

Athletic Hall of Fame Inducts

The Methodist College Athletic Hall of Fame inducted an inaugural class of seven persons October 2, 1998. Those honored were:

—Gene Clayton, former athletic director and coach of basketball, cross country, tennis, and golf,

—Ann Davidson, women's golf coach from 1990-95,

—Karen Grant '87, a four-time national champion in the triple jump and three-time national runner-up in the long jump who also earned top five national finishes in the 55-meter dash and the 100-meter dash.

—Rob Pilewski '92, the 1990, NCAA-III national champion in men's golf,

— CHAPTER 9 —

—Paul Sanderford '72, former baseball standout, who coached highly successful women's basketball teams at Louisburg College, Western Kentucky, and the University of Nebraska,
—Bruce Shelley, who started the baseball program at Methodist and coached nine seasons, was posthumously inducted. Shelley died in 1997.
—Anne Thorpe '91, who set records in women's soccer (for goals and assists from 1987-91) and was an Academic all-American.

Alumni Honor Folsum, Safley

Dr. Margaret Folsom, professor of biology, received the alumni association's Outstanding Faculty Award for 1998. Upon accepting the award, she thanked her former students and said, "This is a great way to celebrate my twenty-fifth year of teaching at Methodist." [41]

At its annual homecoming banquet October 3, 1998, the Methodist College Alumni Association awarded its Distinguished Alumni Award for 1998, to the Reverend Michael Safley, president of the Methodist Home for Children-Child and Family Services and former dean of students at Methodist.

College Loses Three Friends

W. Robert Johnson of Goldsboro, an original trustee of the College died August 7, 1998. Johnson was 92. Methodist awarded him an honorary Doctor of Humanities degree in 1987, and later named a campus street for him.

The Reverend Dr. Charles A. Simonton Jr., editor emeritus of the *North Carolina Christian Advocate*, died October 20 in Charlotte at the age of 74. He was born in Tennessee and served in the Army Air Corps in World War II. He held bachelor's and master's degrees in journalism from Northwestern University. He later earned a Master of Divinity degree at Duke and pastored four churches in the North Carolina Conference from 1959-76. He became editor of the *Advocate* in 1976. Methodist awarded him an honorary Doctor of Divinity degree in 1985.

Verna Brock McAdams, wife of Charles K. Mc Adams, Methodist's first public relations and development director, died November 13 in Raleigh. She was 77. Mr. and Mrs. Mc Adams endowed a scholarship at Methodist.

In other news from fall 1998:
—An 18-member team from Methodist spent fall break, October 17-19, helping residents of Currituck, North Carolina, clean up after Hurricane Bonnie. The team members helped make repairs to eight different homes and slept in the fellowship hall of Moyock United Methodist Church.

—James Link '66 was promoted to three-star general and named head of the U.S. Army Material Command at Alexandria, Va.

—The football team finished its 10th season with a 7-3 record, taking second place in the new Atlantic Central Football Conference. Senior quarterback Brian Turner led the league in passing, total offense, and passing efficiency.

—Four psychology graduates returned to Methodist November 10, 1998, and offered a graduate school colloquium to psychology majors. The presenters were Mike Miller '94, Zach Hambrick '94, Charles E. Brown '91, and Shelli Nobles '93.

Foundation Elects Officers

The Methodist College Foundation installed Sarah O'Hanlon president for 1998-99, at its October 13, 1998, meeting. A Fayetteville civic volunteer, Mrs. O'Hanlon succeeded Mrs. Anne Hodges Smith.

State Schools Superintendent Addresses Winter Graduates

Addressing the winter 1998, graduating class December 18, Dr. Michael Ward, North Carolina's state superintendent of public instruction, urged 112 class members to leave clear footprints "that show evidence of days well-spent" as they began new careers with new responsibilities. [42]

In the morning baccalaureate sermon, the Reverend F. Belton Joyner Jr., assistant to the bishop of the North Carolina Conference, urged 112 class members to walk in faith with the biblical Elijah, saying "You now hold in your hand the mantle of those who went before you." [43]

During the commencement ceremony, College President Elton Hendricks presented a Methodist College Medallion to Fayetteville Mayor J.L. Dawkins for 10 years of work to improve the city. Dr. Hendricks also presented the Sam Edwards Award (for outstanding evening student) to Darrell Lee Finney.

Students Speak At Stone Lyceum

At the first annual B.F. Stone Lyceum December 3, 1998, three MC students made scholarly presentations. Ann Hughes presented a program entitled "The Strategic Analysis of Nordstrum." Glenn Carter spoke on "Restorative Justice's A Return to *Shalom*." Laura Sandler assembled a reader's theatre work "Shades on the Screen," which profiled six famous philosophers.

1998 Annual Report Includes 5-Year Strategic Plan

The spring 1999, issue of *Methodist College Today* included a 1998, annual report entitled "A Banner Year for Methodist."

— CHAPTER 9 —

A letter from President Hendricks cited four major achievements in 1998: construction of Margaret and Walter Clark Hall and the annex to Davis Memorial Library, record summer and fall enrollments, and the conclusion of the "Expanding the Vision" campaign with gifts and pledges of $8.7 million, $2.2 million more than the original goal of 6.5 million.

For the first time, the report included short reports and lists of immediate (1999) goals for each major area of the College: Office of the President, Academic Affairs, Student Life, Business Affairs, and Institutional Advancement. Reports were also included for the Alumni Association, Athletics, Enrollment Services, and Church Relations.

A summary of the College's Strategic Plan for 2000-05, appeared at the end of the annual report. Part I, the Executive Summary, concluded that, "To reach the potential of service, reputation, and effectiveness already present, Methodist College must discover new financial resources and insure that its physical facilities and other resources are appropriate for the mission." [44] The plan included five general recommendations followed by 27 specific recommendations: eight in academics, three in student life, twelve in physical facilities, and four in financial resources.

The general recommendations were:
—Recruit and retain more academically prepared and financially able students through expanded and improved academic programs, including adequate technology, improved recruiting and retention activities and more appropriate physical facilities.
—Increase enrollment by the year 2005, to be distributed as follows: residential, 850 or more; commuting, 700; evening, 600.
—Reverse the decline in new commuting student enrollment.
—Study the advisability of changing the name of Methodist College to Methodist University or some other university.
—Evaluate the advisability and usefulness of developing a residential area for Methodist College faculty immediately south of the Kinwood-by-the River subdivision on the College's land located between the baseball field and the Cape Fear River. [45]

SACS Team Gives Positive Report

Methodist College received a generally positive report from a Reaffirmation Committee of the Southern Association of Colleges and Schools during a visit April 12-16, 1999.

Chaired by Dr. James Taylor, president of Cumberland College, the committee offered three commendations, 16 recommendations, and 16 suggestions. The commendations went to the Student Life staff, the professional golf and tennis management programs, and the College trustees.

In a memo dated April 16, College President Elton Hendricks said, "We did better than I had hoped!" [46] He also thanked the faculty and staff for the hard work they invested in the self-study over a three-year period.

MC Launches ARRIVED Program

In early 1999, Methodist College awarded full academic scholarships to four Russian students to pursue business administration degrees at Methodist.

George Blanc, director of international programs, reviewed the credentials of 15 scholarship applicants and selected Natalia Kyndikova, 23; Alexei Kormschikor, 21; Eugenia Sologub, 21, and Natalva Yakovlena, 21.

Dr. Hendricks announced the ARRIVED program the previous fall at the College's Economic Outlook Symposium. He said the program was designed to assist in the economic development of the Russian Federation by training young entrepreneurs who could return home and promote the development of capitalism, coupled with moral and ethical responsibility.

Stone Lyceum Sparks Hot Debate

The third annual B.F. Stone Lyceum held March 23, 1999, in Yarborough Auditorium, Clark Hall, provoked some lively debate about additional driver's license testing of senior citizens.

Dr. Donald Lassiter, associate professor of psychology, presented a paper entitled "Aging and Driving: The Need for Improved Driver's License Testing." He proposed testing elderly drivers' "useful field of vision." The expert panelists were: Dr. John Sill, MC sociology professor; Mr. Bob White, representing Seniors Call to Action of Fayetteville, Dr. Susan Franzblau, associate professor of psychology of Fayetteville State University; and Mr. James A. DePree, psychologist at Cape Fear Valley Health System.

Dr. Franzblau was highly critical of Dr. Lassiter's findings and proposed solution; Dr. Sill, Mr. White and Mr. DePree also expressed doubts that UFOV testing of elderly drivers was needed.

Students Visit Red Bird Mission

During the 1999, spring break, six Methodist College students and three staff members spent four days performing a variety of tasks at the Red Bird Mission in Beverly, Kentucky. A "missionary conference" of The United Methodist Church, Red Bird serves an eight-county region of 300,000 people, where transportation is difficult and unemployment exceeds 50 percent.

— CHAPTER 9 —

The mission trip was organized by the Reverend Carrie Parrish, who headed the team. Reverend Parrish was joined by Margaret Parrish, Lori Collins, Kristen Butler, Sarah Kerley, Curtis Stephens, Ken Asay, Lindley Asay, and Jessica Asay.

Forum Examines North Carolina Environment

Divergent views of the state of North Carolina's environment emerged at the fourth annual Lura Tally Leadership Forum held February 22, 1999. The keynote speakers were Phil Kirk Jr., president of N.C. Citizens for Business and Industry, and Dan Whittle, senior attorney for the N.C. Office of the Environmental Defense Fund.

Kirk said the state's environment was in "much better shape than several years ago. The water in our 17 water basins is 65 percent cleaner than six years ago," he said. "Chemical emissions in the air are down 14 percent for ozone and 23 percent for sulfur dioxide. There has been a 31 percent drop in carbon dioxide and other pollutants." [47]

Whittle offered a less positive assessment of the state's environment. "Developers have drained 6,500 acres of coastal wetlands since last fall," he said. "Alternative waste technology is needed to replace hog farm lagoons. And last summer was the worst ever in North Caroline for ozone pollution." [48]

Kirk said the 1,880 members of his business organization wanted to protect the environment, supported "sustainable development," and favored regulation based on science. [49]

Whittle said the 300,000 members of his organization had developed an environmental scoreboard to allow citizens to go to the World Wide Web and obtain omissions data for their neighborhoods. He contended that North Carolina's economy was both better and worse than 30 years ago. "We need to celebrate our progress, but continue to look for new solutions to environmental problems," he concluded. [50]

Debaters Win Three Awards

The Methodist College Debate Team won three awards at the 1999, American Debate Association National Championships from March 11-14. Methodist sent four two-member teams to the championship at Mary Washington College in Fredericksburg, VA.

L. Antwan Floyd and Greg Thomas took second place in the junior division. The team of Susan Graves and Khari Floyd won second place in the overall school awards. In the Novice Division, the team of Matthew Whitaker and Ron Berry lost a 2-1 decision to the eventual champions from Liberty University.

In other news from spring 1999:

— Dr. Peggy Batten, professor of mathematics, received the Professor of the Year award. The Reverend Carl King, a Durham native, was appointed chaplain at Methodist. King came to Methodist from Haymount United Methodist Church in Fayetteville, where he had served as associate pastor for three years. King held a B.S. in English from Wake Forest University, a master of divinity from Duke Divinity School, and a master of sacred theology from Yale Divinity School.

— The Student Activities Committee and the Monarch Booster Club staged Methodist's first-ever Sweetheart 5K Road Race February 13, 1999, drawing 160 runners, who competed in nine age categories. A One-Mile Fun Run for Children was also held.

Golf Teams Retain No. 1 Status

Methodist's men's and women's golf teams repeated as NCAA champions in 1999.

The men defeated California-San Diego by 27 strokes May 20 at Williamstown, Ma. Chad Collins became only the second athlete ever to win the individual national title in back-to-back fashion.

The Lady Monarch golfers edged Florida Southern by three strokes May 15 at Howey-in-the-Hills, Fla. Tracey Gage was runner-up for the individual title.

In other sports news:

— The women's basketball team, coached by DeeDee Jarman, finished 19-7, tied for first place in the DIAC, but lost to N.C. Wesleyan in the DIAC Tournament. Senior Amy Todd was named DIAC Player of the Year and an Honorable Mention All-American.

— The men's basketball team finished 16-11 and second in the DIAC. Coach Bob McEvoy announced he was resigning as head men's basketball coach to concentrate on his duties as director of athletics.

— The baseball team finished 29-13, capturing its fourth DIAC title in five years and advancing to its 16th NCAA-III Tournament.

— First-Year Softball Coach Ron Simpson led his team to a 32-12 record, which included a DIAC regular season championship and a first-ever trip to the NCAA-III East Regional.

— Senior triple jumper William Ray earned All-America honors at both the indoor and Outdoor NCAA-III track and field meets and seventh at the outdoor championship.

— CHAPTER 9 —

Duke Dean Speaks at 36th Spring Commencement

"Be faithful, keep hope alive. Be a person of love." [51] That was the advice offered to 170 members of the Class of 1999, May 8. The speaker was Dr. L. Gregory Jones, dean of the Divinity School and professor theology at Duke University.

At the morning baccalaureate service, Dr. Ken Collins, professor of church history at Asbury Theological Seminary in Kentucky, said "the true greatness of God begins with the cross—the humble, sacrificial love of Jesus Christ." [52]

President Hendricks presented the Stacy Weaver Award to Denise Shuey, a math major from Tower City, Pa., and an honorary Doctor of Humanities degree to J. Nelson Gibon Jr., a retired farmer from Gibson, N.C. Gibson was a Methodist College trustee for 32 years, a prominent United Methodist lay leader, and a prominent civic leader in Scotland County.

College Begins 40th Academic Year

Methodist College began its 40th academic year in August 1999, with a record 1,878 students, 1,387 in the day program and 521 in the evening. The number of students living on campus reached 750, an all-time high.

The addition to Davis Library opened in the summer. Other improvements included renovation of 48 rooms in Weaver and Cumberland halls, the installation of four emergency call boxes on campus, and the installation of permanent seats on the home side of Monarch Field.

The annex and entrance plaza at Davis Memorial Library opened in late spring 1999.

New faculty members included Stephen "Pete" Petersen, director of professional tennis management; Hugh Harling, athletic training; Ronnie Martin, director of the social work program; and Dr. Richard Hall, assistant professor of religion and philosophy.

Hurricane Floyd Floods Eastern North Carolina

Hurricane Floyd forced the cancellation of classes at Methodist College from midday September 15, 1999, through Saturday, September 18, as well as the Southern Writers Symposium scheduled for that weekend.

Many resident students went home for a long weekend. Tragically for Methodist, Justin Gambrell, 18, a freshman football player from Jacksonville, Fla., was killed in a traffic accident on the morning of September 15 on his way home. The accident occurred on I-95 near Sumter, S.C.

An only child, Gambrell was remembered in a memorial service at Methodist September 29 as "a fun-loving person who had given his life to Christ." [53]

Hurricane Floyd dumped up to 20 inches of rain in areas of the state east of I-95, causing massive flooding in the Tar and Neuse river basins. East Carolina University in Greenville had to close for a week, and the town of Princeville in Edgecombe County was left uninhabitable.

In Fayetteville, a group of six radio stations held a one-day marathon and raised more than $175,000 for hurricane victims. The funds were given to the American Red Cross and the Salvation Army.

At Methodist, Charles Koonce, assistant director of the Professional Golf Management program, challenged students in that program to start a fund drive. Their drive soon expanded to all of the College community and netted $3,054.

Bob Ziegler, director of the Cumberland County Chapter of the Red Cross, reported October 22, 1999, that local residents had raised $300,000 (about $1 for every resident of Cumberland County) for hurricane victims.

CFE Announces Networking Initiatives

The Center for Entrepreneurship at Methodist College unveiled four new initiatives September 22, 1999, in a "March to the New Millennium Luncheon." The event drew 300 persons to the Holiday Inn Bordeaux.

Linda Lee Allan, chair of the Center's Advisory Board, listed four areas in which the Center would work over the next 25 years: 1) mentoring—building a global network to help budding entrepreneurs, 2) business succession—a network of experts in estate planning, 3) ethnic entrepreneurship, and 4) spirituality and entrepreneurship. [54]

Mrs. Allan asked those present to fill out forms indicating how they would like to help the Center carry out its expanded mission.

— CHAPTER 9 —

College representatives present a hurricane relief check at the WFNC studio.

College President Elton Hendricks announced that Dr. Sid Gautam had rejoined the College staff to serve as full-time director of the Center for Entrepreneurship. He then introduced Mr. and Mrs. Carr Gibson of Lumberton, who presented a $25,000 check to the Center. Dr. Hendricks also presented the first annual Greater Good Award to the Reverend J. Ernest Johnson, pastor of Highland Presbyterian Church in Fayetteville.

The luncheon's keynote speaker was Martin Eakes, founder and CEO of Self-Help, a Durham-based venture fund that has made $325 million in loans to more than 5,800 small businesses, non-profits, and home buyers in North Carolina.

A Greensboro native, Eakes graduated from Davidson College, Princeton University, and Yale Law School. He said he had learned three things during his 19 years of work in community development:
1) to eliminate poverty, you must develop wealth,
2) you cannot understand race or community in America without understanding wealth, and
3) wealth needs to be protected from those who would seek to steal it (unscrupulous mortgage lenders, for example). [55]

Dick Fox '68 Volunteers in Bolivia

Richard "Dick" Fox '68 and his work on behalf of Andean Rural Health Care in Bolivia, was the subject of a two-page feature article in the fall 1999, issue of *Methodist College Today*.

Fox said Dr. Wes Jones, a Fayetteville gastroenterologist, recruited him for an AHRC "Work-Amigos" team in 1993. Jones later invited Fox to AHRC's Lake Junaluska (N.C.) Headquarters and asked him to serve on the ARHC board.

The Methodist alumnus went on to explain how he had just made his fourth trip to Bolivia, where a 15-member team of volunteers spent two weeks helping Bolivians construct a health clinic in Montero. Dr. Elton Hendricks, president of Methodist College, was also a member of the 1999, work team.

College Awards Contract for Apartment-Style Residence Hall

Methodist College awarded a contract for construction of its first apartment-style residence hall October 22, 1999. Sigma Construction Co. of Fayetteville won the $3 million contract. Shuller Ferris Lindstrom and Associates of Fayetteville designed the three-story building to house 68 students in four-bedroom, two-bath apartments which also contained a den and kitchen.

A separate Community Building of 2,500 square feet with a student lounge, meeting room, game room and offices was included in the contract. What would later become known as Cape Fear Commons was to be built in a wooded area behind the Riddle Center.

In other College news:
— Dr. Hendricks delivered a fall convocation address entitled, "Toto, I Don't Think We're in Kansas Anymore." He challenged students to prepare for the "brave new world of the new millennium" by: learning how to learn and to become self-reliant, learning how to speak and write effectively, and exploring moral and ethical questions and answers to the question, "What is the good life?" and "What is worth investing your life in?" [56]
— The Board of Trustees welcomed five new members: W. Lyndo Tippett, Thomas J. Walden, D. Keith Allison, George W. Miller Jr., and Dr. William J. Stewart.
— Lou Tippett was installed as president of the Methodist College Foundation.
— Robin Greene, assistant professor of English, gave a public reading from her new book, *Real Birth: Women Share Their Stories* at the Arts Center in downtown Fayetteville.
— The College's Longleaf Press released three poetry chapbooks: *Lost Languages* by Jonathon Minton, *Mortal* by Judas Riley Martinez, and *The Tar Baby on the Soapbox* by Carole Weatherford.

— CHAPTER 9 —

—Leslie Antoniel, a senior music major from Fayetteville, completed a summer Internship with the New York City Opera's Education Department, based in the New York State Theater at Lincoln Center.
—The Special Collections Room of Davis Library featured an exhibit called "Carolina Echoes," commemorating Carolina College, a Methodist women's college that Operated in Maxton, N.C. from 1912-26.
—Dr. Jen-Hsiang Lin, professor of economics, was selected as the first recipient of the Col. (Ret.) David R. Nimocks, Sr. EndowedProfessorship.
—Janet Conard Mullen '72, immediate past president of the Methodist College Alumni Association, died unexpectedly October 28, three weeks after undergoing heart surgery.
—Michael Molter '94 became the College's first full-time webmaster.
—Summer Brock, MC's alumni director for six years, resigned to take a similar post at Keuka College in western New York. She was succeeded by Tom Maze '93, who returned to his alma mater from a similar position at Fork Union Military Academy.
—Quail Haven Village in Pinehurst, N.C. dedicated a chapel in honor of Bill Lowdermilk June 23. Methodist's former vice president for church and community relations became Quail Haven's chaplain in 1995.
—Dr. Luke Timothy Johnson, a religion professor at the Candler School of Theology, Emory University, spoke at the sixth annual Samuel J. and Norma Womack Endowed Lecture. A former Benedictine monk, Dr. Johnson was highly critical of recent attempts to redefine Jesus Christ.
—The Methodist College Alumni Association Board of Directors adopted a goal of raising the percentage of alumni giving to the College from 15 percent to 20 percent by the end of 2000. From 1964-99, Methodist graduated 7,097 students; meaning the College would need 1,420 alumni donors to meet the 20 percent goal.

Trustees Approve $14 Million Bond Sale

Meeting October 21, 1999, the Methodist College Board of Trustees approved plans for the College to sell $14 million in tax-free revenue bonds to finance four capital improvement projects and to refinance existing debt.

Vice President for Business Affairs Gene Clayton said two banks were interested in underwriting Methodist's bonds. He said the College would use $8.2 million of the bond revenues to refinance existing debt (from a 1995, bond issue) and $5.8 million to pay for capital improvements. He said the bonds would be repaid over a 25-year period.

The bond proceeds were earmarked for the following new projects:
—$3 million for a new residence hall to accommodate 68 students and an area coordinator.
—$1 million for the renovation of science labs.
—$750,000 to buy 33 acres of land adjacent to the campus.
—$600,000 to renovate four residence halls (Cumberland, Garber, Sanford, Weaver).
—$500,000 for contingencies.

Deer Visits Library

Shortly after lunch on Saturday, October 30, 1999, a frightened buck leaped through a side window in Davis Library.

The library staff was able to drive the animal out the back door, but the deer left a trail of blood on the new carpet.

In other activities from homecoming 1999, themed "Still Crazy After All These Years,":
—Members of Coach Bruce Shelley's baseball teams were reunited at King's Grant Golf and Country Club for the Bill Lowdermilk Golf Tournament.
—The football team won a thriller against Greensboro College with a last-minute field goal.
—Friends gathered at the new entrance plaza to Davis Library Sunday, November 1 for a dedication of the new wing.
—The alumni association presented its Outstanding Faculty Award to J. Michael Rogers, Distinguished Professor of Music; its Distinguished Alumni Award to Patric Zimmer '89 of Eden, N.C.; and its Outstanding Alumni Service Award to John B. Lipscomb '68 of Sanford, N.C.
—The Methodist College Athletic Hall of Fame inducted members of its second class Friday, October 29. The inductees were: Becky Burleigh '89, soccer standout and women's soccer coach at the University of Florida; David Holmes '92, three-time All-American soccer player; Jay Kirkpatrick '91, former catcher on the baseball team; and Mason Sykes, who coached the soccer, wrestling, and tennis teams during the period 1966-1983.

— CHAPTER 9 —

College Buys 33-Acre Tract

In November 1999, Methodist College purchased a 33-acre tract of land bordering the southern leg of the campus and the College golf course. Located at the eastern end of Meadowcroft Drive, the property included a brick home, two ponds, and some woodland.

The tract was purchased from the Maurice Taylor family to give the College access to the wooded part of the campus south of the golf course and next to the Cape Fear River. The home was reserved as a parsonage for the college chaplain.

With the Taylor tract, the College campus grew to 617 acres.

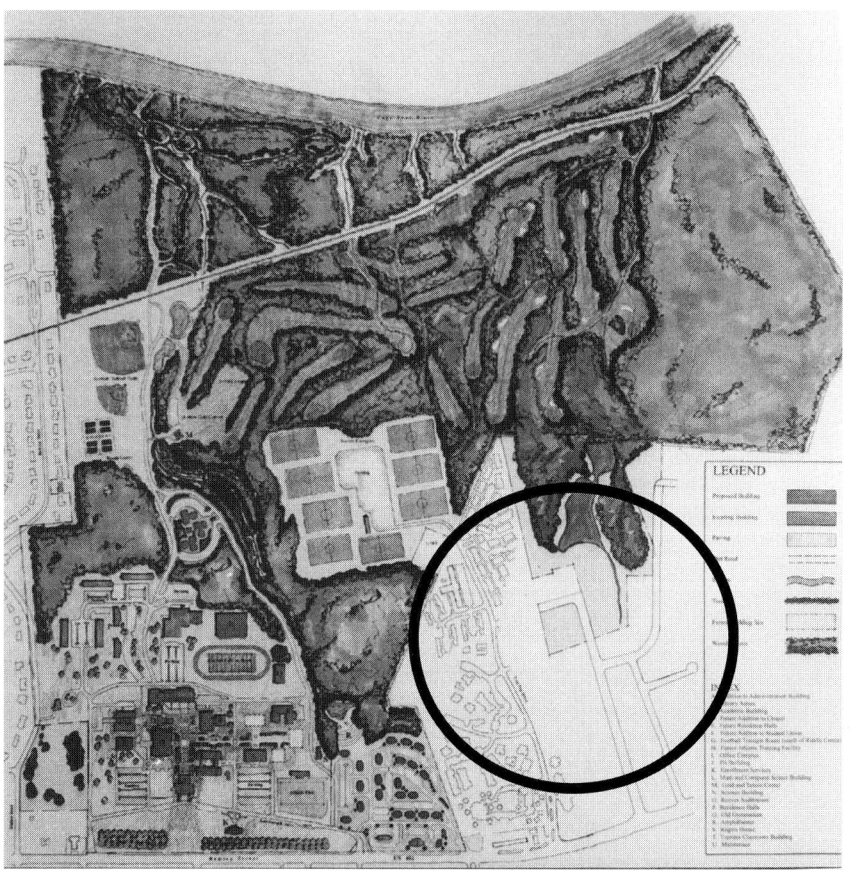

The purchase of Taylor land afforded better access to the golf course and other land.

Dr. Hope Williams Addresses Winter '99 Class

"Celebrate your accomplishments and thank those who helped you. Continue to learn and ask youself at the end of each day, 'Did I make a difference?'" [57]

That was the message given to 120 members of Methodist's winter graduating class December 17, 1999. The speaker was Dr. A. Hope Williams, president of the North Carolina Association of Independent Colleges and Universities.

The baccalaureate speaker, the Reverend Rodney G. Hamm of Burlington, N.C., urged class members to look beyond life's pacifiers or "golden calves"—material goods—to a life based on God's commandments. [58]

President Hendricks presented an honorary Doctor of Divinity degree to Reverend Hamm for 25 years of exemplary service as a minister in The North Carolina Conference of The United Methodist Church. Dr. Hendricks also presented the Sam Edwards Award to Tracy Kessell, voted the most outstanding evening student in the Class of 1999, by the Evening College faculty.

Tally Forum Explores Global Challenges

A Cable News Network (CNN) executive, a congressman, a retired Army general, and a United Methodist missions director shared their views about global challenges and America's proper role in the world at Methodist's fifth annual Tally Leadership Conference February 21-23, 2000.

Gail Evans from CNN and Congressman Robin Hayes were the keynote speakers at a February 21 convocation in Reeves Auditorium. Evans said the news media could never be totally objective, but should be fair and balanced. [59]

A Republican from Concord, N.C., Hayes said America was the world's last superpower and needed to remain strong militarily. He said President Bill Clinton had overcommitted U.S. military forces, with 33 foreign deployments in seven years at a cost of $30 billion. [60]

An afternoon panel discussion of "America's Role in the World," featured Findley Burns Jr., former U.S. ambassador to Jordan and Ecuador; Army General (Ret.) Ted Mataxis; and the Reverend Bruce Stanley, associate director of missions and evangelism of The North Carolina Conference of the United Methodist Church, discussing America's diplomatic, military, and humanitarian responsibilities.

Burns said the United States should not have gone to Somalia, Kosovo or Bosnia; should not promote NATO membership for former Soviet countries; and should lift trade embargos against Iraq and Cuba. [61]

Mataxis said the United States military was overextended and that, "Recruiting is a serious problem." [62]

"Compassion fatigue is a problem today due to disaster everywhere," said Stanley. He expressed regret that churches and United Nations agencies had encountered "corruption" abroad that impeded the flow of aid to those who needed it. [63]

— CHAPTER 9 —

Panelists Bruce Stanley, Ted Mataxis, and Findley Burns.

On the second and third days of the conference, February 22 and 23, groups of 8-12 students met with facilitators for 34 roundtable discussions of specific topics related to the conference theme.

Vatican Astronomer Speaks

Father George Coyne, director of the Vatican Observatory, presented an illustrated history of the universe April 13, 2000, at the first annual Templeton Lecture in Yarborough Auditorium, Clark Hall.

He said he wanted to propose a new way of thinking about God—as a loving parent who nurtures the universe creatively. "Studying the universe helps us know God," he said, "but I don't think science can prove the existence of God." [64]

Financial Analyst Warns Investors

Speaking at Methodist College's 23rd annual Stock Market Symposium April 20, 2000, Michael Culp, director of research of PaineWebber, warned investors to beware of investment information posted on cleverly-named dot com Web Sites.

SIFE Chapter Competes in Kansas City

A six-member team from the MC chapter of Students in Free Enterprise was one of eight college teams invited to participate in the Hallmark Cards SIFE International Exposition and Career Opportunity Fair May 21-23, 2000, in Kansas City.

Methodist's SIFE chapter advanced to Kansas City after making a 24-minute presentation entitled "Economic Education Through Community Involvement" before a panel of 14 business executives. Jeff Zimmerman, associate professor of economics and finance, was named a Sam M. Walton Free Enterprise Fellow to work with Methodist's SIFE team.

Methodist's SIFE team performed well in international competition.

In other College news from spring 2000:

—MC senior Shawn Hartman received the William P. Lowdermilk Student Achievement Award from the Fayetteville Rotary Club March 20.

—Jessica Kupper, a junior from Huntington Valley, PA, was elected president of the Student Government Association for 2000-2001.

—Robin Greene, assistant professor of English, was named Professor of the Year April 24.

—Methodist's teacher education program scored among the top four in the state in a 1998-1999, assessment conducted by the N.C. Department of Public Instruction.

—The Tally Center for Leadership Development at Methodist dedicated a permanent exhibit/display case May 1, 2000, to honor former state senator Lura S. Tally.

—The *Monarch Messenger*, the College's student newspaper, won a First Place award from the American Scholastic Press Association. Co-editors Cindy Bridges and Chuck Heaton headed a newspaper staff of 20 students. Advisor Jami Shepherd, director of student media, said the paper's new name and layout design as well as strong news and feature stories "reflected the time, energy, and talent of the staff members." [65]

—Methodist alumnus John Handy '66 became a full four-star general and vice chief of staff of the United States Air Force April 13, 2000.

— CHAPTER 9 —

—The College dedicated a street May 29, 2000, in honor of the late W. Robert Johnson of Goldsboro, N.C., a charter member of the College's board of trustees.
—Dr. Valery Chukhlomin of Omsk State University in Russia visited MC and agreed to recruit students for MC's ARRIVED program.
—Jay Dowd, vice president for institutional advancement, resigned to take a job as assistant vice chancellor at UNC-Wilmington.
—Methodist launched its first two "MC Online" courses June 26: an advanced course in criminal justice and an introductory course in education.
—The College mourned the passing of two friends; Fayetteville Mayor J. L. Dawkins, who died May 30 at the age of 64; and Richard Lewis Player, who died June 5 at the age of 92.

College Graduates 150

"Run with perseverance the race set before you." [66]
"Use common sense as an everyday strategy." [676]

These were the themes of two speeches delivered to Methodist's 37th spring graduating class Saturday, May 6, 2000.

In the morning baccalaureate sermon, the Reverend Ernest Johnson, pastor of Highland Presbyterian Church in Fayetteville, urged class members to: "1) have a plan for your lives, 2) hold on to your friends, and 3) adopt a morality that puts you ahead of most people." [68]

Earle Leake '73, a business executive from Charlotte, gave the commencement address Saturday afternoon. He advised the Class of 2000, to: "1) use common sense as an everyday strategy for problem solving, 2) understand that continual change is continuous, and 3) keep your internal compass turned to what's right and just." [69]

College President Elton Hendricks presented honorary Doctor of Humanities degrees to two persons closely associated with the College for three decades. Former biology professor Pauline Longest of Fayetteville and trustee emeritus R. Dillard Teer of Durham were honored for their professional achievements, community service, and service to the College.

Dr. Hendricks also presented the Stacy Weaver Award to Eddie Price and recognized Amanda Coffman, a *summa cum laude* graduate in accounting as the first graduate of the Methodist College Honors Program, a 13-semester-hour program with five "great books" seminars and a senior honors project.

Women's Golf Team Wins National Title; Men Finish Second

Methodist's 2000, women's golf team won the NCAA-III National Championship May 16-19, at Prairie Vista Golf Club in Bloomington, Il., finishing 51 strokes ahead of Concordia College of Minnesota. Senior Stacey Smith was the medalist and individual national champion.

The 2000, men's golf team finished in second place in a rain-shortened NCAA-III National Championship at Bedford Valley Golf Club in Battle Creek, MI. Greensboro College's team beat the Monarchs by one shot. The tournament was shortened to 54 holes after heavy rains and lightning struck in the final round making the course unplayable.

In other spring 2000, sports:

—The softball team won the DIAC regular season and tournament championships and took third place in the NCAA-III Atlantic Regional in Roanoke, Va. Coach Ron Simpson's team finished 28-15-1 overall and 10-2 in the Dixie Conference.

—The 2000, baseball team finished 25-15-1. Season highlights included a three-game sweep of Emory University, which won the South Region and advanced to the College World Series. Freshman Dan Gleiss was named Dixie Conference Rookie of the Year.

—Methodist's men's and women's tennis teams finished in fourth place at the 2000, Dixie Conference Tennis Tournament at Christopher Newport University.

—Former baseball players gathered for a spring game against current varsity pitchers and a dinner/roast of Coach Tom Austin. The alumni won 5-1.

—Ninety-one golfers gathered June 16, 2000, for the third annual Hall of Fame Golf Classic at King's Grant Golf & Country Club. Cheer Ltd. was the lead sponsor.

Cynthia Curtis Assumes Development Post

In August, 2000, President Hendricks appointed Cynthia J. Curtis director of development in a reorganized Institutional Advancement Office. Methodist College's director of annual fund and parent programs for two years, Curtis inherited a staff of six persons. Katie Dyke was hired to replace Curtis as director of annual fund and parent programs.

Ike O'Hanlon Dies At 88

I. H. "Ike" O'Hanlon, former trustees chair (1981-90) and president of the Methodist College Foundation, died July 16, 2000, at the age of 88.

— CHAPTER 9 —

A generous supporter of the College, O'Hanlon and his wife Emma O'Hanlon donated a 750-seat amphitheater to the College in 1971, in memory of their son, Michael Terrence. O'Hanlon loved baseball and attended many games at Methodist.

A Fayetteville native, Ike O'Hanlon attended Wake Forest College on a football scholarship. In 1955, he founded Antex Exterminating Co. He served five terms in the N.C. House of Representatives and also served on the Fayetteville City Council.

He was an active churchman of St. John's and Holy Trinity Episcopal churches and held leadership positions with the YMCA, Fayetteville Chamber of Commerce, Kiwanis Club, and Boy Scouts of America.

O'Hanlon was survived by a son, Eddie W. O'Hanlon of Fayetteville, and two grandchildren.

College Begins 41st School Year

Methodist began its 41st academic year in August 2000, with a record fall enrollment of 1,970 students, 11.5 percent more than the previous fall. Day enrollment reached 1,383, and the evening/weekend program enrolled 587.

The College opened its eighth residence hall, Cape Fear Commons, enabling it to house 798 students on campus. Methodist began the fall 2000, semester with 757 students living on campus.

College Hires Resort Manager

In 2000, Methodist College hired John Meeske to direct its new resort management programs and formed a strategic alliance with The Pinehurst Company to provide internships for students at its five resorts.

Meeske had 30 years experience as a resort manager, owner, and consultant. He was president of Club Resorts (forerunner of The Pinehurst Company) from 1985-90, and held degrees from Michigan State and Washington State universities.

Joe Doll, director of the Reeves School of Business, said the new resort management program would have two degree tracks: business administration with a concentration in resort management, and marketing with a concentration in resort management.

College Commemorates 1960 Opening

At a fall convocation September 20, 2000, Methodist commemorated its original opening in September 1960, by inviting back members of the first freshman class and original faculty and staff members. Special guests included Louis Spilman, John Lee Cade, and Amos McLamb (freshmen in 1960); Dr.

1995–2000

Pioneers who were present when the College opened in 1960 return to celebrate.

Elbert Wethington, former assistant to President L. Stacy Weaver; Dr. Samuel Womack, former religion professor; Sam Edwards, the college's first registrar, director of admissions, and P.E. instructor; Charles McAdams, MC's first director of public relations and student recruiter, and Bert Ishee, an early president of the Methodist College Foundation and his wife Jean, who taught piano and organ at Methodist.

College trustees Ramon Yarborough, Bill West, Richard Player Jr., Louis Spilman, and John Wyatt were also present.

S.G.A. President Jessica Kupper, the first to speak, noted that when Methodist opened in 1960, the world was on the brink of nuclear war and young men were subject to the military draft. She recalled that Methodist opened with 86 freshmen, four buildings, 12 faculty members, and a support staff of ten. She praised the hard work of original contributors and students and challenged current students to be active on campus and in the community.

President Hendricks referred to some defining moments of the 1960's- the Woolworth sit-in in Greensboro by four black college students, Arnold Palmer winning the Masters, and MC alumnus Kenneth Albritton losing his life in Vietnam. He recalled that Terry Sanford, the first chairman of the MC Board of Trustees, was a gubernatorial candidate when the College opened. He quoted Bishop Paul Garber's tribute to the 6,000 persons in Fayetteville and

— CHAPTER 9 —

the 30,000 Methodists in eastern North Carolina who contributed funds to build Methodist College. [70]

Dr. Hendricks described the College's founding president, staff, and students as "the patriarchs" who were determined to build a special college. [71]

College Web Site Grows Quickly

In the fall 2000, issue of *Methodist College Today*, College Webmaster Michael Molter described how the Methodist Web site had grown in the first year, to include course schedules, news and information from the college magazine and student newspaper, a virtual tour of the campus, alumni news and archived sports. He said the number of hits (visits) to www.methodist.edu had grown from 244,756 to 382,088 in only one year.

Late Night Express participants enjoy roller skating.

Resident Students Enjoy Late Night Express

Methodist College Late Night Express, a series of Thursday night activities designed to divert students from alcohol and drugs, became a smashing success in 2000, as faculty, staff, and students collaborated to stage talent shows, volleyball tournaments, movies and games, as well as roller skating and bowling excursions. Organized by the Student Development and Services Office, the program attracted several hundred resident students each week.

In a feature article on the "Express", Jami Sheppard quoted Carrie Adcox, editor of *Monarch Messenger* as saying, "Late Night Express offers great opportunities to meet and mingle with students outside of the classroom." [72]

Athletic Facilities Upgraded

During the summer of 2000, 200 chair-back seats were added to Monarch Field's home side, bringing total seating to 800. In addition, a new rubberized surface was installed on the track around Monarch Field.

In other sports news from fall 2000:

— The Monarch football team finished its ninth season under Coach Jim Sypult with a 7-3 record and a second place finish in the Atlantic Central Football Conference. The team also won the Oyster Bowl in Newport News, Va., November 11, defeating Newport News Apprentice School 30-8.

— Heather Hagus, pitcher on the women's softball team, received the Sykes Cup, denoting her selection as athlete of the year 1999-2000.

— Halcyon Blake was named head coach of the men's and women's cross country and track teams.

— Heather Stafford was named Methodist College's first lacrosse coach, with a women's lacrosse team slated to take the field in fall 2001.

— The Monarch Booster Club inducted six persons into the MC Athlete Hall of Fame's third class: Earl Bunn '77, baseball; Greg Jones '75, basketball; Robin Baxley-Long '75, volleyball, soccer, softball, basketball; Joe Pereira, MC's first women's soccer coach (11 seasons); Rita Wiggs, DIAC Commissioner and former athletic director and women's basketball coach at Methodist.

Homecoming Draws Big Crowd

Homecoming 2000, drew a record 2,200 persons to Monarch Field November 4, where the Monarch football game defeated Averett College 51-2. Eleven members of the class of 1965, returned for a 35th reunion.

At its annual dinner November 4, 2000, the Methodist College Alumni Association presented its Outstanding Faculty Award to Jerry Hogge, associate professor of business administration and director of the Institute for Professional Golf and Tennis Management.

Dennis Bruce '68 of Spartanburg, S.C. received the Distinguished Alumni Award, and Lynn Moore Carraway of Fayetteville received the Outstanding Alumni Service Award.

A record crowd competed in the eighth annual William P. Lowdermilk Golf Classic of Kings Grant Golf Club Saturday morning, November 4.

— CHAPTER 9 —

SWS Welcomes Five Tar Heel Writers

Methodist's 15th Southern Writers Symposium, held September 22-25, 2000, addressed the topic "The Limits of Southern Literature." A total of 20 guest lecturers read papers.

Bland Simpson, creative writing teacher at UNC-Chapel Hill and a member of the Red Clay Rambers, read excerpts from three of his novels, and sang three songs from the musical *King Mackerel and the Blues Are Running.*

Judy Goldman of Charlotte described the travails she faced writing her first novel, *The Slow Way Back.*

Robert Morgan, English professor of Cornell University (and a native of western North Carolina) read from his novel, *Gap Creek.*

Poets Keith Cartwright and Joanna Scott read from their chapbooks.

Campus Ministry Leads Mission Trip

During fall break in 2000, 14 students and three staff members, took part in a mission trip to Queens College in Nassau, Bahamas. The team worked on several building projects at Queens, a private prep school for elementary through high school-age students. The group was housed at Ebenezer Methodist Church. Chaplain Carl King and his team raised $8,000 for the trip.

In a novel fund-raiser, the Campus Ministry Office selected favorite daily reflections from College faculty and staff and included them in an inspirational desk calendar for 2001, which it sold for $5.00 a copy.

SACS Gives Green Light to M.S.

In September 2000, officials of the Southern Association of Colleges and Schools in Atlanta authorized Methodist College to award a master's degree to graduates of its physician assistant program. Methodist submitted a revised curriculum to SACS which called for adding three courses worth 18 semester hours to its undergraduate program.

President Hendricks said he looked forward to awarding the College's first master's degrees in physician assistant studies in December, 2003.

Ron Foster, director of the P.A. program, said Methodist's undergraduate program would be phased out over a two-year period.

Winter 2000 Class Totals 117

Joyful living requires service to others. That was the theme of two speeches given at Methodist's 28th winter commencement December 15, 2000.

Dr. Assad Meymandi, a psychiatrist from Raleigh, N.C., discussed 12 characteristics of a joyful person: 1) an appreciation of life, 2) a thirst for knowledge, 3) curiosity and ideas, 4) love, 5) faith, 6) hope, 7) excellence, 8) personal growth, 9) altruism, 10) selflessness, 11) enthusiasm, and 12) service to others. [73]

The baccalaureate speaker was the Reverend Dr. Peter Storey, a retired Methodist bishop from South Africa. Basing his text on three passages from Luke, Dr. Storey challenged the winter class members to "help the poor, help others reach freedom, and bring new light to others." [74]

College President Elton Hendricks presented a citation of appreciation to Louis Spilman Jr. '64, a retired Fayetteville businessman, for his 30 years service on the Methodist College Board of Trustees. He also presented a Methodist College Medallion to Dr. Meymandi and the Sam Edwards Award (for outstanding evening student of 2000) to Sabrina Sabin.

In other news from fall 2000:

—George Blanc, MC's director of international programs, was promoted to vice president of student life and dean of students, effective January 15, 2001, succeeding Kim Dowd, who resigned. A native of Mexico who grew up in San Antonio, Texas, Blanc served 27 ½ years in the U.S. Army, attaining the rank of colonel. He graduated from St. Mary's University.

—Methodist College served as the Fayetteville collection center for Operation Christmas Child, a ministry of Franklin Graham's Samaritan's Purse, November 13-20, 2000. A total of 75 volunteers recruited by the Campus Ministry Office, processed 16,751 shoeboxes filled with Christmas gifts for children in countries devastated by war. The gift boxes were trucked to Charlotte, N.C. and then put on airplanes for shipment abroad.

—Twenty-persons gathered at Methodist November 16, 2000, as granite slabs from Carolina College in Maxton, N.C. (1912-26) and a commemorative plaque were unveiled near the bell tower.

Tally Center Wins CCF Grant

In December 2000, the Cumberland Community Foundation, Inc. awarded Methodist's Lura Tally Center for Leadership Development a $4,500 grant to establish a leadership training facility for the Fayetteville area.

The CCF grant covered one-third the cost of renovating and equipping a classroom on the lower level of the Trustees Classroom Building; the balance was raised by the Tally Center Advisory Board. Dr. Suzan Cheek and Dr. Andrew Ziegler were designated lead instructors for both the "basic" and "advanced" leadership training workshops.

At the time of the grant, Dr. Cheek and Dr. Ziegler had already provided leadership training for the Fayetteville Area Chamber of Commerce and the N.C. Association of Symphony Orchestras.

— CHAPTER 9 —

END NOTES
Chapter Nine

1. Elton Hendricks, news story, January 17, 1995, *Methodist College Today,* March 1995, file.
2. Terry Sanford, letter to the editor, *Methodist College Today*, June 1995, file.
3. Parker Wilson, retirement dinner, April 29, 1995, *Methodist College Today*, June 1995, file.
4. Ibid.
5. Ibid.
6. William Lowdermilk, retirement dinner, May 13, 1995, *Methodist College Today*, June 1995, file.
7. Bruce Pulliam, commencement speaker, May 7, 1995, *Methodist College Today*, June 1995, file.
8. Ibid.
9. William Lowdermilk, baccalaureate sermon, May 7, 1995, *Methodist College Today*, June 1995, file.
10. Hope Ward, baccalaureate sermon, December 15, 1995, *Methodist College Today*, March 1996, file.
11. Frank Barragen, press conference, February 29, 1996, *Methodist College,* March 1996, file.
12. Terry Sanford, press conference, February 29, 1996, *Methodist College Today*, March 1996, file.
13. Terry Sanford, keynote address, February 29, 1996, *Methodist College Today*, March 1996, file.
14. John Humphreys, news story, *Methodist College Today*, March 1996, file.
15. Ron Foster, news story, *Methodist College Today,* June 1996, file.
16. Ibid.
17. Don Baer, commencement address, May 12, 1996, *Methodist College Today*, June 1996, file.
18. Steve Conley, news story, *Methodist College Today*, June 1996, file.
19. Frank Stout, news story, *Methodist College Today*, September 1996, file.
20. Sue Kimball, commencement address, December 13, 1996, *Methodist College Today*, March 1997, file.
21. Bill Braswell, baccalaureate sermon, December 13, 1996, *Methodist College Today*, March 1997, file.

22. Elton Hendricks, news story, *Methodist College Today*, June/July 1997, file
23. *The Fayetteille Observer*, editorial comment, *Methodist College Today*, June/July 1997, file.
24. Terry Sanford, memorial tribute, March 29, 1997, *Methodist College Today*, June/July 1997, file.
25. John Templeton, address to 20th Annual Stock Symposium, April 18, 1997, *Methodist College Today*, June/July 1997, file.
26. Ibid.
27. Ibid.
28. Jerry Richardson, commencement address, May 11, 1997, *Methodist College Today*, June/July 1997, file.
29. Marion Edwards, baccalaureate sermon, May 11, 1997, *Methodist College Today*, June/July 1997, file.
30. Elton Hendricks, dedicatory remarks, August 22, 1997, *Methodist College Today*, Fall 1997, file.
31. Fred Chappell, Southern Writers Symposium, September 26-27, 1997, *Methodist College Today*, Winter 1997, file.
32. Ibid.
33. Samuel J. Womack, baccalaureate sermon, December 12, 1997, *Methodist College Today*, Winter 1997, file.
34. Patricia Timmons-Goodman, keynote speaker, Tally Leadership Forum, February 23, 1998, *Methodist College Today*, Spring 1998, file.
35. Mike McIntyre, keynote speaker, February 23, 1998, *Methodist College Today*, Spring 1998, file.
36. Alan Porter, remarks, *Methodist College Today*, Summer 1998, file.
37. Robert H. Dedman, commencement address, May 10, 998, *Methodist College Today*, Fall 1998, file.
38. Ibid.
39. Carl Frazier, baccalaureate sermon, May 10, 1998, *Methodist College Today*, Fall 1998, file.
40. Ibid.
41. Margaret Folsum, remarks, October 3, 1998, *Methodist College Today*, Fall 1998, file.
42. Michael Ward, commencement address, December 18, 1997, *Methodist College Today*, Fall 1998, file.
43. F. Belton Joyner, Jr., baccalaureate sermon, December 18, 1997 *Methodist College Today*, Fall1998, file.

— CHAPTER 9 —

44. Executive Summary, 1998 Annual Report, *Methodist College Today*, Spring 1999, file.
45. Ibid.
46. Elton Hendricks, memorandum to faculty and staff, April 16, 1999, Summer 1999, file.
47. Phil Kirk, Jr., speech, February 22, 1999, *Methodist College Today*, Summer 1999, file.
48. Dan Whittle, speech, February 22, 1999, *Methodist College Today*, Summer 1999, file.
49. Phil Kirk Jr., speech, February 22-24, 1999, *Methodist College Today*, Summer 1999, file.
50. Dan Whittle, speech, February 22-24, 1999, *Methodist College Today*, Summer 1999, file.
51. L. Gregory Jones, commencement address, May 8, 1999, *Methodist College Today*, Summer 1999, file.
52. Ken Collins, baccalaureate sermon, May 8, 1999, *Methodist College Today*, Summer 1999, file.
53. Family and friends of Justin Gambrell, remarks at a memorial service, September 29, 1999, *Methodist College Today*, Fall 1999, file.
54. Linda Lee Allan, Center for Entrepreneurship luncheon remarks, September 22, 1999, *Methodist College Today*, Fall 1999, file.
55. Martin Eakes, remarks, September 22, 1999, *Methodist College Today*, Fall 1999, file.
56. Elton Hendricks, convocation address, September 13, 1999, *Methodist College Today*, Fall 1999, file.
57. A. Hope Williams, commencement address, December 17, 1999, *Methodist College Today*, Winter 1999, file.
58. Rodney G. Hamm, baccalaureate sermon, December 17, 1999, *Methodist College Today*, Winter 1999, file.
59. Gail Evans, speech, Tally Leadership Conference, February 21, 2000, *Methodist College Today*, Summer 2000, file.
60. Robin Hayes, speech, Tally Leadership Conference, February 21, 2000, *Methodist College Today*, Summer 2000, file.
61. Findley Burns, Jr., remarks in panel discussion, February 21, 2000, *Methodist College Today*, Summer 2000, file.
62. Ted Metaxis, remarks in panel discussion, February 21, 2000, *Methodist College Today*, Summer 2000, file.
63. Bruce Stanley, remarks in panel discussion, February 21, 2000, *Methodist College Today*, Summer 2000, file.

64. George Coyne, Templeton lecture, April 13, 2000, *Methodist College Today*, Summer 2000, file.
65. Jami Shepard, remarks, *Methodist College Today*, Summer 2000, file.
66. Ernest Johnson, baccalaureate sermon, May 6, 2000, *Methodist College Today*, Summer 2000, file.
67. Earle Leake, commencement address, May 6, 2000, *Methodist College Today*, Summer 2000, file. 67. Ibid.
68. Ernest Johnson, baccalaureate sermon, May 6, 2000, *Methodist College Today*, Summer 2000, file.
69. Earle Leake, commencement address, May 6, 2000, *Methodist College Today*, Summer 2000, file.
70. Elton Hendricks, convocation remarks, September 20, 2000, *Methodist College Today*, Fall 2000, file.
71. Ibid.
72. Jami Sheppard, quoting Carrie Adcox, feature article, *Methodist College Today*, Fall 2000, file.
73. Assad Meymandi, commencement address, December 15, 2000, *Methodist College Today*, Winter 2000, file.
74. Peter Storey, baccalaureate sermon, December 15, 2000, *Methodist College Today*, Winter 2000, file.

Chapter 10

College Becomes University
2001-06

> "The name change is something that has been talked about by the Board of Trustees for at least two years. It is coincidental that it is happening at the 50th anniversary, but I think it is appropriate that we are taking this action in our anniversary year."
> —*Alfred E. Cleveland, chair of the Methodist College Board of Trustees, quoted in the Winter 2006 issue of* Methodist University Today.

Mike Sinkovitz, director of intramurals and recreation at Methodist, was profiled in a short feature article in the spring 2001 *Methodist College Today*, which was the Annual Report issue for the year 2000.

In 1991, Sinkovitz started the Outdoor Adventure Club, whose first excursion was a canoeing trip to Camp Rockfish in nearby Hoke County. Later, the club began offering weekend trips and five-day outings during the fall, Thanksgiving and spring breaks. A highlight of 1999-2000 was a trip to Dry Tortugas National Park in Key West, Florida.

Campen Honored At 2001 Loyalty Day

The Methodist College Foundation gathered February 6, 2001 for its annual Loyalty Day kickoff breakfast. Foundation President Steve Blanchard said $103,000 of the Annual Fund's goal of $500,000 had been raised.

College President Elton Hendricks presented a plaque to Henry Campen of Fayetteville, recognizing his work for the College. Campen had been a volunteer fundraiser for Methodist every year since 1956.

Henry Campen

Tally Forum Explores Technology Issues

"Leadership, Ethics and the Technology Revolution" was the topic of the sixth annual Tally Leadership Conference February 19, 2001.

— CHAPTER 10 —

The first keynote speaker was Jane Smith Patterson, director of the N.C. Rural Internet Access Authority. "E-learning and e-help and e-commerce and e-government will change our way of life in North Carolina," said Smith. "Privacy, security, and intellectual property issues will require the enactment of new laws." [1]

The Reverend Bruce Stanley of Duke Divinity School was the second keynote speaker. "No technology is value-neutral," he said. "Everything we shape will afterward shape us." He asked the students and others in the audience to demand: "1) that science and technology admit the presence of ethical values at the time of creation, 2) that technologists create in the image of God and recognize that their creations will shape the users, and 3) monitor outcomes and applications to ensure that we are being reformed not deformed in both our outward and inward selves." [2]

At a luncheon after the convocation, Dr. Suzan Cheek presented the fourth annual 100% Award (for outstanding leadership) to Gary Cooper and Billy Davidson of the Fayetteville Chamber of Commerce. Cooper was the chamber's past chairman (2000), and Davidson was its full-time president.

Pinehurst Makes $25,000 Gift

The Pinehurst Company made its first gift to support Methodist's resort management program February 23, 2001. Pinehurst Company President Patrick Corso presented a $25,000 check to College President Elton Hendricks at the Pinehurst Resort.

The company pledged $50,000 a year for five years to support Methodist's business administration major with a concentration in resort management.

Clayton Reports on Campus Improvements

Speaking to the Methodist College Board of Visitors April 24, 2001, Vice President for Business Affairs Gene Clayton gave a very positive "state of the college" report.

Pat Corso presents the first of five gifts.

Clayton said:
- —The College had an annual budget of $27 million and was in "excellent shape" thanks to record enrollment in 2000-01.
- —Methodist had 325 full-time and 200 part-time employees, with an annual payroll of $15 million.
- —Phase I of an irrigation project at the front of the campus would use city water, while the lower fields and golf course would use water piped from the Cape Fear River.
- —The College had given the city of Fayetteville an easement to allow the Cape Fear River Trail to terminate at the Fayetteville Soccer Complex and the College golf course.
- —Methodist College's 617-acre campus and 40 buildings had an estimated replacement value of $87 million.

Methodist College Students Tour Greece, Italy

A feature story in the Summer 2001 issue of *Methodist College Today* described a spring break tour of Greece and Italy sponsored by the College Honors Program.

Five Methodist College students, accompanied by Jennifer Rohrer-Walsh and her husband Richard, Mrs. Elaine Porter, and five adults from Fayetteville, spent three days in Italy and four days in Greece.

In other College news from spring 2001:
- —Methodist launched a Pastor's Recognition Program, allowing United Methodist ministers in the North Carolina Conference to award certificates worth up to $1,000 per year to youth who enrolled at Methodist.
- —The Florence Rogers Charitable Trust awarded a $4,125 grant to the Methodist College Art Department to support a juried art exhibit for area high school students.
- —Dr. John Sill, professor of sociology, was named Professor of the Year.
- —An octagonal greenhouse was built in front of the Science Building.
- —J. Michael Rogers, distinguished science professor of music, retired in January 2001, after 21 years of teaching instrumental music.
- —Physicist and science writer Margaret Wortheim delivered the second annual John Templeton Endowed Lecture in Science and Religion March 23, 2001. She traced the evolution of physics and said the science was developed, for the most part, by scientists who believed in a divine creator. [3]

CHAPTER 10

—Franklin Douglas Byrd Jr., a trustee emeritus of Methodist College and former superintendent of the Cumberland County Schools, died June 23, 2001 at the age of 93.

College Graduates 187

Methodist College graduated 187 students at its 38th spring commencement May 5, 2001.

New beginnings and happiness were the subjects of the baccalaureate sermon and the commencement address, respectively.

In the baccalaureate sermon, the Reverend Tommy Herndon '70 told class members, "God calls each of us to a new beginning each day." [4]

In a far-reaching commencement address about the pursuit of happiness, Dr. Benjamin Dunlap, president of Wofford College, said Aristotle defined happiness as self-actualization or realizing one's full potential in life.

Dr. Dunlap urged the graduating seniors to: "Get your priorities straight. Keep your creativity alive. Nurture your idealism. Keep the faith." [5]

During the commencement, President Hendricks presented the Stacy Weaver Award to Svetlana Kurs. He also awarded on honorary Doctor of Humanities degree to Dr. Bill Harrison, superintendent of the Cumberland County Schools, and Methodist College Medallions to Dr. Dunlap and the Reverend Tommy Herndon.

Women's Golf Team Claims Another National Title

Methodist's women's golf team, coached by Kim Kincer, won its fourth consecutive NCAA National Championship in May 2001, defeating Concordia College by 50 strokes. MC senior Carol Brogan won the individual title.

In other sports news from spring 2001:

—Methodist College's 2001 men's golf team finished third in the NCAA III National Championship. Chad Collins was the individual national champion.

—Elena Blanina, a member of the women's tennis team, won the NCAA-III Singles National Tennis Championship.

—The Monarch baseball team advanced to regional play in the NCAA and finished the season 29-17-1.

—The men's and women's tennis teams again won the Dixie Conference regular season and tournament titles, the men compiling a 10-1 record and the women finishing 13-2.

2001-2006

Wells Named Campus Minister

The Reverend Benjamin Wells '95, was appointed campus minister in June 2001. He succeeded the Rev. Carl King, who resigned to take a similar post at Columbia College in Columbia, S.C.

Wells received a Master of Divinity degree from Duke Divinity School in 1998 and held pastoral appointments in Morehead City and Goldsboro before coming to Methodist.

Enrollment Grows 3 Percent

Methodist began its 42nd academic year and fall 2001 semester with 2,138 students: 1,425 day students and 821 evening students. Day enrollment increased 3 percent over fall 2000, while evening enrollment decreased 7 percent.

A total of 784 students were living on campus. The freshmen class totaled 376.

New buildings and campus renovations included: a community building and Union Station (student activities center) near Cape Fear Commons. During the summer, Garber and Weaver Halls and four science labs were renovated. In the area of student life, a Greek Council was established to oversee three newly-established sororities and one fraternity.

New faculty for 2001-02 included: Maurice Godwin, criminal justice; Marilyn Vital, sociology; Al Stratta, resort management; Rebecca Wendelken, history; Spencer Davis, business; Lynn Green, social work; Jacqueline Draughan, English education; Evan Bridenstine, theatre; Betty Cline, special education; Sherrie Schmidt, marketing; David Turner, speech; Merirose Moran, advising; Keith Dippre, music; Stephen Clark, Andrea Dickinson, and Kerry Hammond, all in athletic training.

Dr. Jordan Speaks at Mentoring Luncheon

"It all started with blackberries."[6] That's what Dr. William Jordan, a Fayetteville urologist-turned-entrepreneur told an audience of 100 at the fall mentoring luncheon sponsored by Methodist's Center for Entrepreneurship. The event was held September 6, 2001 at the Holiday Inn Bordeaux.

"I'm from Wilson, N.C.," said Jordan "When I was eleven, I wanted an English bicycle. My dad gave me half the money, and my mom said blackberries were in short supply. I picked and sold blackberries to raise my half of the money. I learned if you had the opportunity and the desire, you could be an entrepreneur."[7]

Dr. William Jordan

CHAPTER 10

Dr. Jordan hit the entrepreneurial jackpot in 1985 when he and Joe Jenkins started Carolina Lithotripsy, Inc. to buy and install lithotripsy machines throughout the Southeast. Developed in Germany, the machine uses shock waves to crush kidney stones.

In 1996, Carolina Lithotripsy, Inc. was sold to Lithotripsy, Inc. for $88 million in cash and stock. In 1998, Dr. Jordan and some of his former partners formed a new company called Sonorex to distribute the Sonocur machine developed by Siemens. The Sonocur machine uses electromagnetic shock waves to treat tendonitis.

9/11 Attacks Stun Campus

Tuesday, September 11, 2001, was a day unlike any ever experienced at Methodist College. Between 9 and 11 a.m., Americans learned that two hijacked airliners had crashed into the Twin Towers in New York City, that a third airliner had crashed into the Pentagon in Washington, and that a fourth plane had gone down in Pennsylvania.

New York City firefighters and policemen rushed to the Twin Towers and worked feverishly to clear the buildings and help the injured. Some workers trapped on the upper floors jumped to their deaths.

Students and staff gathered around a television in the Lion's Den and watched in horror as the burning north tower collapsed in a huge cloud of dust; within 30 minutes, the south tower collapsed. Nearly 3,000 persons who had not escaped the towers were killed.

Students watch 9/11 events on Lion's Den television.

2001-2006

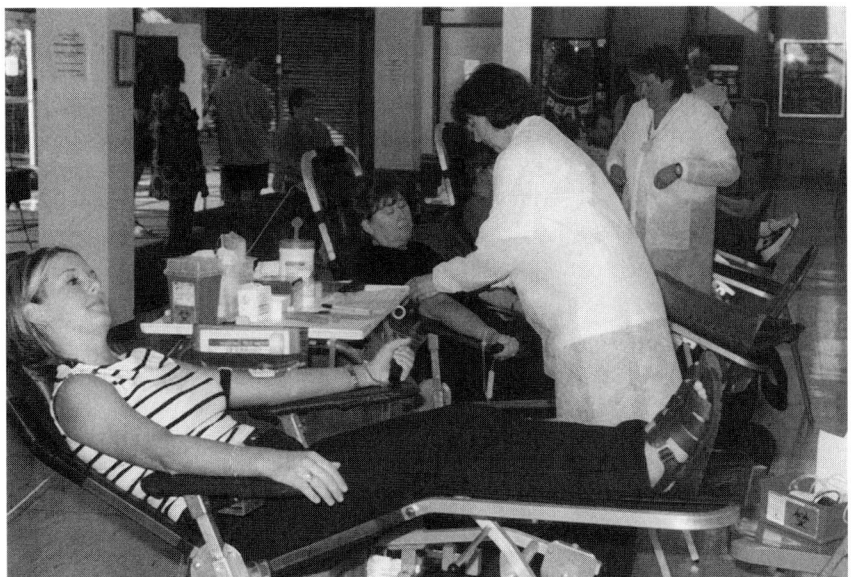

Students donate blood to Red Cross on 9/11.

Immediately following the attacks, air travel in America was halted. Major airports began to shut down. Military bases, including Fort Bragg and Pope Air Force, were placed on alert and began installing concrete barricades and check points. Methodist and other colleges cancelled classes for Tuesday evening.

United States President George Bush was at an elementary school in Sarasota, Florida that morning when he was told that terrorists had flown airplanes into the Twin Towers and the Pentagon. At 1:04 p.m., the President made a brief statement from Barksdale Air Force Base in Shreveport, Louisiana, saying the United States would punish those responsible and that all military forces had been placed on alert.

In a strange twist of fate, the Red Cross Bloodmobile was at Methodist that day. By mid-afternoon, when news of the attacks had been fully disseminated, Red Cross workers had filled all 95 of the bags they brought. Many students rolled up their sleeves. At 5:30 p.m., a dozen persons were waiting to give blood.

The front page of Wednesday's *Fayetteville Observer* displayed a large one-word headline: HORROR, along with a color photo of the second airliner exploding inside the south tower. A crowd of 150 filled Hensdale Chapel Wednesday morning for the College's weekly worship service.

At 11 am, Friday September 14, 2001, more than 400 members of the College community gathered around the bell tower for a moment of silence, hands linked in a show of unity. The brief service that followed included the

Pledge of Allegiance to the American flag, a prayer by William Walker, and the singing of the "Star Spangled Banner" and "Amazing Grace."

At noon Friday, President Bush and his cabinet, four former presidents, members of Congress, and hundreds of federal employees gathered at the National Cathedral in Washington for a prayer service.

In an address to the nation and a joint session of Congress the evening of September 20, President Bush demanded that the ruling Taliban in Afghanistan turn over Osama bin Laden, the Saudi Arabian suspected of planning and financing the terrorist attacks.

By September 17, stock trading had resumed on United States exchanges and airlines had resumed service. The Dow Jones industrials fell a record 1,369 points for the week, and the value of United States stocks plummeted $1.2 trillion.

During the last week of September, the Federal Bureau of Investigation released photos of the 19 terrorists who boarded the four airliners in Boston. Authorities in London and Hamburg, Germany identified and arrested other suspects with ties to Osama bin Laden. The original count of dead and missing, about 4,700, was lowered by more than one thousand. New York Mayor Rudy Giliuani estimated that 25,000 escaped the towers before the buildings collapsed.

Forum Looks at Islam

The History, International Studies and Political Science Club held a public forum on Islam and the Middle East, Monday, October 1, 2001.

A five-member panel sought to answer questions about what provoked the September 11, 2001, terrorist attacks. The panelists were: Dr. Rebecca Wendelken, history professor; Imam Adam Beyah, a Muslim prayer leader from Fayetteville; Dale Comstock, a Special Forces and Delta Force veteran and security consultant; Stephen Williams, geography instructor; and Anne Zahran, a Lebanese American student from Fayetteville.

Beyah said bin Laden had misused the word "jihad" to mean holy war. "It really means struggle, an inner struggle between good and evil. No individual can call for a holy war." [8]

Art Student Remembers 9/11

Following the 9/11 tragedy, senior art major Curtis W. Stephens III created a print named "I Pledge Allegiance." It showed a figure kneeling in prayer before a torn American flag. Where rows of white stars normally appear on a field of blue, he placed rows of white crosses against a gold background.

A pitcher on the Monarch baseball team, Stephens described himself as a Christian artist, and said he would like to work in graphic design or advertising.

2001-2006

Newspaper headlines reflected the far-reaching consequenes of 9/11.

As the theme for his senior art exhibition, he chose "Crossroads," using a text from Jeremiah 6:16.

"Surf's Up" at Homecoming 2001

Homecoming 2001, held October 26-27, included two special athletic events, a luncheon for athletes from the 1960's and the DIAC Cross Country Championship.

Gene Clayton, former Athletic director and coach, served as emcee for the luncheon. All of the sports from that era, including wrestling and bowling, were represented. Former basketball coach Ernie Schwarz also attended. Former basketball players and members of the Class of 1967 turned out in force. Seldon "Sparky" Rapelye '65 of San Antonio, Tx. led the fashion parade in his moth-eaten letter sweater.

Gary Miller '67 of Indianapolis, Ind., had everyone "in stitches" with his recollection of his debut as a soccer goalie.

Gene Clayton recalled an exciting basketball game against UNC-Charlotte played in "the tin can" in 1969. He said the two teams were tied in the final seconds of a third overtime. "I called a time-out and set up a play in which Howard Hudson '69 was to pass the ball to Jim Darden '69 who would take the final shot," said Clayton. [9]

When Darden was double-teamed, Hudson was forced to take the shot himself. He sank it and was given a victory ride on the shoulders of his teammates. Clayton said Methodist won four Dixie Conference championships in the 1960s—in cross country, basketball, volleyball, and bowling. [10]

Mason Sykes, Methodist College's first soccer coach, said he spent a lot of time patching up his battered players. He said Bill Estes '69 sent him a case of adhesive tape after graduating as reimbursement for the hundreds of yards Sykes had used to tape Estes' feet. [11]

In other activities from homecoming 2001:

—Jerry Huckabee, MVP on Methodist's 1965 Dixie Conference Championship team, served as the DIAC cross country meet's honorary starter.

—Jim Darden '69, Holly Anderson '89, and Jansen Evans '88 were inducted into Methodist's Athletic Hall of Fame at a Friday evening banquet.

—The homecoming dance featured beach music. John Haracivet '67 and his wife Brownie came all the way from the island of St. Thomas.

—The alumni association presented awards to two graduates and a retired faculty member at its annual homecoming dinner October 27. Jerry Monday '71 of Raleigh received the Outstanding Alumni Service Award. Wade Byrd '70 of Fayetteville received the Distinguished Alumni Award. Walt Swing, former accounting instructor and assistant academic dean, received the Outstanding Faculty Award.

Wes Brown Addresses Winter Class

"We're not in Kansas anymore." [12] With those words, the Reverend Wesley F. Brown '73, told Methodist's winter 2001 graduating class December 14 that the events of September 11 reminded him of the trials faced by Dorothy and her three companions in *The Wizard of Oz*.

Brown said the events of 9/11 had forced many Americans to face their mortality and had brought a renewal of patriotism, love of family, and faith in God. The associate dean for external relations at Duke University Divinity School, Brown urged the class members to: "Step out in faith and temper it with love. Be faithful. Be thankful. Be generous. Go out and change the world. Be someone's hero. Do something common uncommonly well." [13]

The Reverend Brian Gentle, pastor of Haymount United Methodist Church, gave the winter 2001 baccalaureate sermon, which he entitled, "Welcome to Fast Company."

Citing rapid change in the world, Gentle said those who build their lives on a strong spiritual foundation will be able to weather the storms of life. "I hope you never lose your passion and purpose and persistence for living," said Gentle. "We need a sense of justice and mercy." [14]

In other commencement activities:

—College President Elton Hendricks presented an honorary Doctor of Divinity degree to the Reverend Wes Brown for 20 years of exemplary service to The United Methodist Church and to ministerial education.

—Included in the winter class of 108 were two "second generation" students: Chris Barber, son of the Reverend Eddie Barber '68, and Mark Benton, son of Mickey Benton '67.

College Awards Contracts for Cape Fear Commons II

In a meeting held October 15, 2001, the Methodist College Board of Trustees awarded a $2.7 million contract for construction of a second apartment-style residence hall to Player, Inc. of Fayetteville.

Cape Fear Commons II was financed with a $3 million commercial loan from Wachovia Bank, which included $300,000 for furnishings and architectural engineering fees.

Women's Soccer Team Excels

The 2001 women's soccer team, coached by Bobby Graham, finished 12-5-2 overall, losing to Greensboro 1-0 in the DIAC Tournament semi-finals.

The men's soccer team, coached by Adrian Blewitt, ended the 2001 season with an 8-8 record.

The Monarch football team ended its 2001 campaign 5-5 overall and 3-3 in the Dixie Conference. Defensive tackle Quincy Malloy was named Defensive Player of the Year in the conference.

The 2001 volleyball team reached the Dixie Conference Tournament finals, losing to top-seeded Christopher Newport. The Lady Monarchs finished the season 9-26 in Head Coach Eddie Matthews' first year at the helm.

"The Lucky Seven"

The spring 2002 issue of *Methodist College Today*, the annual report for 2001, contained a feature story on Methodist's first master's degree candidates; seven students who entered the physician assistant program in August 2001.

— CHAPTER 10 —

The group was introduced at a white coat and oath ceremony January 31, 2002. Four of the College's first master's students already held bachelor's degrees from Methodist. The members of the first master's class were: Kelli Bradshaw '98; William Cotton '00; Sean Wilson '01; Rebecca Howard '01; Genevieve C. Hanson, a 1993 graduate of Saint Louis University; Jason Perrow, a 1997 graduate of N.C. State University; and Jennifer Whiteley, a 1994 graduate of the State University of New York at Plattsburgh.

The master's students described their first semester of course work (21 semester hours) as "very demanding." [15] Each was enrolled in nine classes.

Destined to Teach

Jane Stroud Cade '73, a third grade teacher from nearby Long Hill Elementary School, was profiled in a feature story in the spring 2002 *Methodist College Today*. Mrs. Cade was completing her 29th year of teaching when Bill Billings visited her class.

A former Teacher of the Year in her school and school district (Pine Forest), Jane Cade began her day with 24 third graders by reading aloud and discussing a short story entitled "Two Bad Ants" and other stories about a magic pig and a scirroco (desert wind).

Mrs. Cade said she was inspired to become a teacher by her mother, who was a high school home economics teacher for 30 years. She estimated she had taught about 750 students over three decades.

Mayor Speaks of Diversity

Fayetteville Mayor Marshall Pitts Jr. was the guest speaker at Methodist's spring convocation February 4, which marked the beginning of African-American History Month.

Pitts said he was four years old when his parents showed him a Negro almanac listing the contributions of African-Americans, "beyond the history book icons." [16]

The mayor said he learned that four Negro regiments distinguished themselves in the War of 1812. "I discovered C. J. Walker, a man who established a cosmetics business in 1910 and became a millionaire," he added. [17]

"As we move into the new millennium," said Pitts, "Americans need to learn more about other cultures and how to appreciate them. Our diversity is our greatest strength. We need to walk a mile in each other's shoes. We are each responsible for who we become." [18]

Voluntary Simplicity

Americans should consume less and work fewer hours. That was the thesis of a paper read March 7, 2002 at the College's sixth annual B. F. Stone Endowed Lyceum.

Dr. Spencer Davis, assistant professor of financial economics, said he joined the "voluntary simplicity" movement about four years prior, noting it is tied closely to environmental and conservation groups. "When I moved here from Utah, I brought all my possessions in my car," he said. "Voluntary simplicity frees up time and energy for family, children, leisure and relationships—the beautiful intangibles of life." [19]

Reverend Gentle Rethinks Leadership

How to be a spiritual leader in a world of virtual reality was the theme of the seventh annual Pastors' Day Lectures held March 4, 2002 at Methodist College.

The Reverend Dr. Brian Gentle, pastor of Haymount United Methodist Church in Fayetteville, was the guest speaker. "Leadership is a gift," he said, "but we can all learn to be leaders. Just remember that a good leader knows where he is going and make sure the one you follow really knows where he is going." [20]

Dr. Gentle continued, "Just as Jesus taught his disciples to dance with God, we pastors must seek to empower others." [21]

College Launches Campaign for $11 Million

At a May 2, 2002, press conference, the Methodist College Board of Trustees announced a comprehensive campaign to raise $11 million. Named *Seeds on Good Soil, A New Season*, the three-year campaign was designed to secure:

—$4.5 million for an addition to the Science Building
—$3.5 million to build a fitness center and intramural field house
—$1.5 million for current operating expenses
—$1 million for the College's endowment.

The Board of Trustees selected Richard R. Allen, Sr. and Ramon Yarborough to serve as campaign co-chairs. The board also selected Shuller, Ferris, Lindstrom, and Associates to design the new buildings.

During the press conference, Yarborough said the new facilities were greatly needed "to keep up with the caliber of students we are now attracting and our advancing curricula." [22]

Two students—Lindsay Spitzer, S.G.A. president, and Kenyetta "Rey" Little, a senior chemistry major, addressed the need for the fitness center and Science Building addition, respectively.

The *Seeds on Good Soil* campaign actually began with a "silent phase" 18 months earlier, during which the College trustees were solicited. The trustees pledged $4.5 million; others pledged $500,000.

— CHAPTER 10 —

Ramon Yarborough speaks at the Seeds on Good Soil Campaign kickoff.

"Methodist College has enjoyed incredible support from the community and our growing number of alumni," said College President Elton Hendricks. "In return, we have worked hard to build a college and programs worthy of this community and that support." [23]

College Holds 39th Spring Commencement

Addressing the Class of 2002 at Methodist College's 39th spring commencement, a business leader and a religious leader extolled the traditional "family values" of character and compassion for others.

Phillip J. Kirk Jr., chairman of the State Board of Education and president of N.C. Citizens for Business and Industry, urged 183 class members to, "Live so that when your family and friends think of fairness, caring and integrity, they think of you." [24]

A former state legislator and cabinet official, Kirk concluded his speech by urging class members to have a positive but realistic outlook on life, pick their battles, establish flexible goals, reach out to those in need, stand up for their beliefs, and take part in community affairs. [25]

In his morning baccalaureate sermon, Bishop Marion M. Edwards resident bishop of The North Carolina Conference of The United Methodist Church, told the graduating seniors the most important thing they would take from Methodist College would be their character, which he defined as a development of the human soul. "Crisis and hard times will reveal your true character, which consists of the capacity to give, to create, to be proactive," said Edwards. [26]

During the 39th commencement, College President Elton Hendricks presented:

2001-2006

—An honorary Doctor of Divinity degree to Bishop Marion Edwards for 42 years of exemplary service to The United Methodist Church.
—A Methodist College Medallion to Thomas F. Miriello '70 for 31 years of outstanding service as a mental health program manager in North Carolina, and
—The Stacy Weaver Award to Carole Blanc of Fayetteville, who received a Bachelor of Social Work, graduating magna cum laude.

Trustees Tap Dick Player As Chair

The Methodist College Board of Trustees elected Richard L. Player Jr. chairman May 18, 2002, to succeed Ramon L. Yarborough. A trustee since 1991, Yarborough had reached the five-year term limit as chairman, but he was reappointed a trustee.

Richard L. Player

A Fayetteville resident and Duke university graduate, Player was the CEO of Player, Inc. and previously served as vice chairman. Other officers elected by the trustees were: Alfred E. Cleveland, vice chairman; James E. Bledsoe, treasurer; and A. Howard Bullard, treasurer.

Trustees also elected four new members—Charles B. C. Holt, O. Ray Manning, the Reverend Hope Vickers, Dr. Mark Miller—and re-elected the following to four-year terms: Wade Byrd, Alfred Cleveland, Dr. Loleta Wood Foster, Mrs. Jane Hook Johnson, Edwin A. Hubbard, J. Wesley Jones, the Rev. Dr. William P. Lowdermilk, and Ramon L. Yarborough.

College Hires New RSB Director

During the summer of 2002, Methodist College named Michael R. Truesdell, a California business executive, director of the Reeves School of Business, effective September 1. Truesdell succeeded Joe Doll, who returned to full time teaching.

Methodist College Mourns Passing of Seven Friends

The summer 2002 issue of *Methodist College Today* included obituaries for:
—Dr. Samuel MacMillan Jr., of Raleigh, a former trustee who died May 28.
—The Rev. Emerson M. Thompson Jr., a former trustee.
—Marie Murray Howard, a former Cumberland County teacher and lifelong friend of Methodist College, who died March 4.

— CHAPTER 10 —

—Frank H. Jeter Jr., former executive director of the Methodist College Foundation, who died June 10.
—Elizabeth H. Weaver, widow of the College's founding president, L. Stacy Weaver. She died July 8 in Lakeland, Florida. She was 95.
—Leona Martin, administrative assistant to the cafeteria manager at Methodist.

In other news from the spring 2002 semester:
—The Theatre and Music departments presented the musical *Godspell* in February.
—Common Grounds Coffee House opened in Union Station (the old Safley House).
—Construction of the Cape Fear Commons II apartments continued.
—Silvana Foti, professor of art and head of the Art Department, received the Professor of the Year Award at Awards Day April 1.
—The Foreign Language Department announced it would offer a certificate program in "Teaching English as a Second Language" in the fall.
—Mike Brown, a rising senior from Chapel Hill, N.C., was elected S.G.A. president for 2002-03.
—Newspaper editor Ashleigh Radford and her staff reclaimed the paper's original name, *sMall Talk*, after using *Monarch Messenger* for three years.

Women Golfers Win Again

Methodist's women's golf team won a fifth consecutive NCAA-III crown in May 2002, winning by 31 strokes at The Orchards Golf Club in South Hadley, Ma.

The men's golf team finished third at the NCAA-III National Championship in Lincoln, Ne.

In other spring sports news:
—Elena Blanina won her second consecutive NCAA-III Women's Tennis Singles Championship,
—Methodist College baseball players Dan Glies and Mike Oldham were selected as NCAA-III All Americans. Glies was named to the second team, while Oldham garnered third team honors,
—In its inaugural season, the women's lacrosse team finished third in the Dixie Conference with a 5-8 overall record,
—The third annual Methodist College Hall of Fame Golf Classic drew 88 golfers to King's Grant Golf Club June 29, raising $8,000 for Monarch athletics.

Cafeteria Renovated

During the summer of 2002, Sodexho, the College's food service provider, began major renovations to the cafeteria, spending $375,000 on new tables and chairs, convertible hot and cold storage units, an expanded deli area, new countertops and displays, modern track lighting, and a mechanized tray and dish return conveyor system. The new facility was dubbed the Green and Gold Café.

College Begins 43rd School Year

Methodist began its fall 2002 semester with 2,180 students—1439 day students and 741 evening students. Residential enrollment reached 833 students, as Cape Fear Commons II, Methodist College's second apartment complex, opened.

New faculty for 2002-03 included: Dr. Emily Powers Wright, English; Dr. Robert Ritzema, psychology; Dr. Storen Walker, marketing; Dr. Colleen Griffiths Walker, education; Dr. Don Saxon, medical science; Ms. Regina Varas, athletic training; and Vici Pate, women's golf coach.

Dr. Hendricks Presents Vision Statement

In the fall of 2002, College President Elton Hendricks shared his thoughts about Methodist College and its future in a vision statement. As a graduate of a liberal arts college (Wofford), he said he supported a liberal arts core curriculum.

The president said he was convinced upon his arrival at Methodist in 1983, that "it would be hard to increase Methodist College's enrollment if we focused only on the traditional liberal arts majors, such as English, history, or

Sodexho and the College spent $475,000 renovating the cafeteria in summer 2002.

philosophy. I was convinced that goal of increasing our enrollment would be served by strong career-oriented programs." [27]

Dr. Hendricks said new programs like business administration with a concentration in golf management were responsible for Methodist doubling its enrollment in less than two decades. "Small colleges or universities need to develop special and specialized niches," he noted. "I believe Methodist offers the best of both worlds—contemporary, career-oriented majors with a traditional liberal arts core." [28]

CFE Launches Thank-You Series

Methodist's Center for Entrepreneurship held its first "thank-you" day for an existing local industry September 26, 2002. The first honoree was Kelly-Springfield Tire Company, Cumberland County's largest private employer and Methodist's closest industrial neighbor.

The day began with a welcome ceremony at the Kelly plant on Ramsey Street. More than 100 plant associates gave visitors a tour of the two million-square-foot facility. At that time, the plant had a workforce of 3,000 and produced 57,000 tires a day.

At an appreciation luncheon held in Methodist's Alumni Dining Room, John Palhemus, president of Goodyear Tire & Rubber Co./North America, Kelly's parent, praised the plant's work force. After the luncheon, he answered questions from business students in Yarborough Auditorium, Clark Hall.

Kelly-Springfield Appreciation Day ended with a banquet at the Holiday Inn Bordeaux. A souvenir booklet, "The Untold Story of Kelly-Springfield," was distributed. "We are proud to have hosted Kelly-Springfield Day," said Dr. Sid Gautam, director of Methodist's Center for Entrepreneurship. [29]

The Soup Label Lady

Mrs. Louise Peterson, a member of Wesley Heights United Methodist Church in north Fayetteville, was the subject a feature story in the fall 2002 issue of *Methodist College Today*.

During 26 years, Mrs. Peterson forwarded more than one million labels from Campbell's soups and other products to the College library. The library staff was then able to redeem the labels for materials and equipment through Campbell's "Labels for Education" program.

The labels collected by Mrs. Peterson were donated by United Methodist Women's groups in churches throughout The North Carolina Conference. In 2002, the staff of Davis Library used 161,799 labels from Campbell's products to order a Dell computer and a Panasonic digital camera for the library's Teaching Materials Collection.

College Makes Staff Changes

Methodist College announced several staff changes in the summer of 2002. Cynthia Curtis moved from director of development to director of public relations. Robin Davenport was appointed director of development. Bill Billings moved from public relations to the position of university historian, charged with writing a history of Methodist College's first 50 years.

In the Athletic Department, Justin Terranova '95 was named men's soccer coach and Goncalo Marques '02 was named head coach of women's tennis.

Alumni Board Sets Scholarship Goal

At a fall 2002 meeting, the Methodist College Alumni Association's Board of Directors approved a goal to increase the Alumni Scholarship Fund to $100,000 (from the current $20,000) by 2005. The Fund was then awarding one $1,000 scholarship to a deserving student.

Alumna To Lead Teaching Center

Mary Dix McDuffie '75 was profiled in the fall 2002 issue of *Methodist College Today*. Dr. McDuffie was named director of the North Carolina Center for the Advancement of Teaching July 12, 2002. She had been superintendent of the Northampton County Schools since 1999. Before that, she served as principal of Seventy-First High School and taught U.S. history and government at Terry Sanford High School in Fayetteville.

Homecoming '02 Has Patriotic Theme

"Let Freedom Ring!" was the theme of Methodist's 2002 homecoming, October 25-26, 2002. True to form, Johnny Lipscomb '68 brought his scrapbook from his College years, along with business cards promoting his woodcrafting skills.

Three former athletes were inducted into the Methodist College Athletic Hall of Fame at a banquet Friday, October 25. They were: Elaine Adams Anderson '80, who lettered in basketball, volleyball, and softball; John McCullough Jr. '89, three time NCAA-III All-American golfer; Alan Dawson, men's soccer coach from 1987-95.

The homecoming banquet concluded with Parker Wilson, professor emeritus of history, giving a history trivia quiz. The alumni association presented the following awards: Distinguished Alumni Award to F. Milo McBryde '68; Outstanding Alumni Service Award to Larry S. Philpott '73; Outstanding Faculty/Staff Award to Wilford Saunders, the College's chief of public safety.

— CHAPTER 10 —

Jerry Hogge Wins PGA Award

Jerry Hogge, director of the College's Institute for Golf and Tennis Management, received the PGA of America's Bill Strausburgh Club Relations Award at its 86th annual meeting in Philadelphia in late October.

The award was created in 1979 to honor a PGA professional who, through his or her daily efforts, creates dramatic improvement in employment conditions in the local PGA sections or at the national level. Hogge had been a PGA member since 1977.

In other news from fall 2002:
— Seven political science students helped stage a candidates forum at the Cumberland County Courthouse. Thirty-five candidates for local and state offices participated.
— The Theatre Department performed a modified version of the Dickens' classic, *A Christmas Carol*.
— Fayetteville attorney L. Stacy Weaver, Jr., presented the College with $100,000 from the estate of his mother, Elizabeth H. Weaver, for the Stacy and Elizabeth Weaver Endowed Scholarship Fund.
— Claudia Dudley '67 established a scholarship at Methodist to assist older women.

Hazing Incident Proves Costly

A November 11, 2002 hazing incident in the football locker room at Methodist resulted in a lawsuit, 16 months of bad publicity for the College, and the dissolution of the campus police department.

Football players has returned to the locker room after a Monday evening practice when seven players allegedly held down a freshman player, stripped him of his underwear, smacked him on the buttocks and wrote on his buttocks with a Sharpie marking pen. One player was alleged to have sexually assaulted the victim with the Sharpie.

The victim was taken to Cape Fear Valley Hospital, treated and released. A student reported the incident to campus police. Six players were suspended from the football team, and campus police launched an investigation.

Two days after the incident, campus police charged seven players with hazing, a violation of state law. One player was additionally charged with second degree sexual assault.

When contacted by local news media, Head Football Coach Jim Sypult, Athletic Director Bob McEvoy, and College President Elton Hendricks all refused comment. Cynthia Curtis, public relations director, said the College was still investigating and that, "This appears to be a case of horseplay gone awry." [30]

On November 19, two of the suspended football players met with Dean of Students George Blanc. The student charged with sexual assault was suspended from the College for the rest of the school year, while a second student was required to pay a fine and undergo counseling. Blanc also ordered the students to write written apologies to the victim.

A new story in the next day's *Fayetteville Observer*, written by sports editor Brett Friedlander, alleged that Methodist College football players had been engaging in locker room horseplay for a long time, and that College officials had done nothing to stop it. Friedlander also reported that some of the players who had been punished "taunted members of the media" as they left the press conference. [31]

In a December 15, 2002 story, Friedlander identified the victim as Kent Murphy, 18, of Southern Pines, N.C. and wrote that Murphy had issued a statement December 13, saying, "They might think I am a crybaby, but I am not. Being sodomized in a locker room full of teammates stripped me of my dignity and my self-respect." [32]

The Fayetteville Observer also reported that Murphy had withdrawn from Methodist.

In mid-May 2003, Dr. Hendricks reported to the College trustees that a new College policy on hazing had been presented to student athletes after the Christmas break and that Kent Murphy had filed a lawsuit against the College. He said the local district attorney had declined to prosecute the students charged with hazing, citing a State Court of Appeals ruling involving the Pfeiffer University police that campus police at church-related colleges lacked jurisdiction because of the "separation of church and state" clause in the U.S. Constitution. He said the local D.A. had also refused to prosecute students arrested by campus police for selling drugs. [33]

The president said the state attorney general notified independent colleges in North Carolina that their police forces should continue to function. Dr. Hendricks said the local D.A. had turned the hazing cases over to the Cumberland County Sheriff's Department which had investigated and presented findings to a grand jury, which ruled there was insufficient evidence to charge the students.

President Hendricks said the College had $15 million in liability insurance and that the insurance company would like to settle the case. He said Murphy's attorney had made inaccurate statements to the news media about the College's handling of the incident.

Finally, Dr. Hendricks told the trustees that because of the D.A.'s interpretation of the court ruling, the College would dissolve its police department June 30, and contract with the Cumberland County Sheriff's Department to provide coverage 24/7 for the campus, effective July 1, 2003.

— CHAPTER 10 —

On March 17, 2004, Murphy's lawsuit against the College was dismissed in Cumberland County Superior Court, based on a settlement reached in mediation March 5. According to an April 2, 2004, news story in *The Fayetteville Observer*, Murphy said he was "somewhat" happy with the amount of the settlement, which he could not disclose. [34]

Safley Addresses Winter Graduates

Addressing Methodist's 2002 winter graduates December 13, the Reverend Michael Safley '72 challenged them to formulate a vision of the kind of person they wanted to be "and then live toward becoming that person." [35]

The president of the Methodist Home for Children also asked the class members to live a life of service to others. [31]

In a morning baccalaureate sermon, the Rev. Camille Yorkey, compared the graduates' work at Methodist to building an ark, "You have made sea-worthy vessels," she said. "You are the captain of your ship, and you will face floods." [36]

Yorkey recalled her work as a chaplain at Ground Zero in New York City after the 9/11 attacks. "Out of the rubble of two towers, one great, loving giant has risen," she said. "God has not abandoned us." [37]

In other commencement activities, President Hendricks awarded an honorary Doctor of Humanities degree to Lexington, N.C. artist Bob Timberlake and an honorary Doctor of Divinity degree to the Reverend Michael Safley, president of the Methodist Home for Children.

Dr. Hendricks also presented the Sam Edwards Award to Tammy Maxwell, a *summa cum laude* graduate in criminal justice, denoting her selection as the outstanding evening student of 2002.

Alumni Recruit Students

The spring 2003 issue of *Methodist College Today*, which contained the annual giving report for 2002, reported that 129 Methodist College alumni helped recruit new students in 2001-02 by awarding Greatest Gift Scholarships to prospective full-time undergraduates. Each year the College allows each alumnus to award one scholarship to a full-time day student whom he or she actively recruits for undergraduate admission.

Budget Shortfall Leads to Staff Cuts

President Hendricks reported to the Methodist College Board of Trustees May 15, 2003, that he learned in late March that the College had used inaccurate income projection figures to formulate the 2003-04 budget. He then shared a handout on the budget problem he had presented to Methodist College faculty and staff the preceding week.

The handout explained why the president had asked the trustees' Executive Committee April 8 to approve his recommendation that the College cut its retirement contribution from 10 percent of each employee's salary to 6 percent for 2003-04. It also noted that 15-20 staff reductions would be necessary to avert a budget deficit. Dr. Hendricks also stated that he had informed the chairman of the board of trustees that he would not accept a salary increase for 2003-04. [38]

The president's handout said Gene Clayton, vice president for business affairs, and Dawn Ausborn, College accountant, had given him an analysis March 28, showing that faulty income projections would result in a budget deficit at the end of the current fiscal year and an even larger deficit in 2003-04, unless budget cuts were made.

Dr. Hendricks said a spring semester drop in full-time military students to 15, normally 40-50, and projected declines for fall 2003 of 30 continuing students and 30 new students could result in a $1 million budget shortfall. He said the College's contingency fund needed to be increased as well. Finally, the president's handout said he had asked Dawn Ausborn to create an Income Projection Committee, charged with projecting by September 15 income for the current year and by November 15 a projection for the forthcoming year.

The president announced that the College was deferring capital projects and banning overtime and the hiring of temporary workers to forestall a deficit in the current budget year.

On April 10, 2003, Dr. Hendricks sent a letter to 27 contract employees age 60 or older asking if any planned to retire in the next year or so.

On June 30, the College laid off 15 persons. College Registrar Harvey Adams, 72, told *The Fayetteville Observer* that Dean DeLapa gave him a letter from President Hendricks the afternoon of June 30 saying his position was being eliminated, effective that day. [39]

The same *Observer* news article quoted Cynthia Curtis, PR director, as saying Dawn Parker, assistant registrar, would replace Adams, and that those whose jobs were cut included a mixture of hourly support staff (secretaries and maintenance workers) and other contract employees. She was quoted as saying some of the duties of former employees were being assigned to other persons, meaning some employees would take on the duties of laid-off persons, working a half-day in one position and a half-day in another position. [40]

In addition to the 15 persons laid off, said Curtis, several employees retired or announced plans to retire. Dr. DeLapa retired June 30, as did Elaine Porter, chair of the foreign language department, and Robert Perkins, assistant dean. Tryon Lancaster, assistant to the president for church and community relations, said he would retire at the end of August.

CHAPTER 10

Wilson Donates College Mace

Early in 2003, R. Parker Wilson, distinguished service professor emeritus of history, commissioned the design and construction of a Methodist College mace. He gave the mace in memory of his father, Martin Morehead Wilson.

Derived from medieval times, the mace is a ceremonial staff borne or displayed as a symbol of authority. Methodist's mace was topped by the "cross and flame" symbol of The United Methodist Church and a globe fashioned out of pewter. The College seal was affixed to one side of the globe. The walnut staff had eight ribs to represent eight groups that support the College.

A cotton blossom carved into the base of the shaft is a reminder of the 1964 inaugural address given by Methodist's founding president, Stacy Weaver, which he entitled, "From Cotton Field to College." Two dark green streamers with gold letters are attached at the base of the globe; these feature words from Methodist's "Alma Mater."

The Methodist College mace was carried at the front of the processional and recessional of graduates May 10, 2003.

College Graduates 138

Methodist College graduated 138 students at its 40th spring commencement May 10, 2003.

Dr. Mary McDuffie '75 was the commencement speaker. A former high school principal and history teacher, she was then serving as executive director of the North Carolina Center for the Advancement of Teaching. Dr. McDuffie urged class members to concentrate on God, family, and friends, not success. She them listed five steps to lifelong fulfillment:

—Love your family; nurture your friends and faith.
—Do the right thing
—Remember that attitude is everything
—Give everything you do, everything you've got.
—Cherish laughter and joy. [41]

During the commencement, President Hendricks awarded Dr. McDuffie a Methodist College Medallion and presented the Stacy Weaver Award to Irina Jorgenson, a December 2002 graduate.

The Reverend Dr. Willliam Simpson, district superintendent of the Rocky Mount District of the North Carolina Conference at the United Methodist Church, was the baccalaureate speaker.

He challenged the graduating seniors to boldly state to employers, their parents, the College, the world that "I am here." He said it was time for them to show others they were ready to move forward with vision and purpose. He

Elaine Porter and Chris Raines, the mace bearer, lead the processional.

said they could rely on the presence of God to see them through all of life's celebrations and trials. [42]

Four Faculty Members Retire

At the end of the spring 2003 semester, Elaine Porter, Dr. Robert Perkins, Dr. Anthony DeLapa, and Dr. Tryon Lancaster retired from the College.

Mrs. Porter, distinguished service professor of French and head of the Foreign Languages Department, retired with 40 years' service, Dr. Robert Perkins, associate dean and former history professor, served 29 years. Dr. Anthony DeLapa, vice president for academic affairs and former professor of education, served 14 years. Dr. Tryon Lancaster, assistant to the president for church and community relations and former education professor, had worked at Methodist for 12 years.

Staff Changes Announced

Methodist College welcomed Dr. Phillip Williams as its new academic dean and vice president for academic affairs July 1, 2003. Dr. Williams succeeded Dr. Anthony DeLapa.

— CHAPTER 10 —

Dr. Williams came to Methodist from Gardner-Webb University where he was assistant vice president for academic affairs and assistant professor of business administration. He held a J.D. degree from Columbia University School of Law, and the Ph.D.. M.P.H., and B.A. degrees from the University of North Carolina at Chapel Hill. At UNC, he was a Morehead Scholar and a member of Phi Beta Kappa.

Michelle Heinen was named director of Methodist's Medical Science Division and Physician Assistant Program in the summer of 2003. She replaced Ron Foster, who resigned. She came to Methodist from East Carolina University.

Dawn Congleton Parker '99 was appointed registrar and academic records manager after serving as assistant registrar for two years.

In the Athletic Department, Jill Penrose replaced Brian Kruger as lacrosse coach, and Kelly Brown replaced Goncalo Marques as women's tennis coach.

DIAC Becomes USA South

Effective July 1, 2003, the Dixie Intercollegiate Athletic Conference became the USA South Athletic Conference.

In spring sports for 2003:
—The women's golf team claimed another national championship.
—The men's basketball team shared the DIAC championship.
—The women's basketball team (19-10) and the softball team (38-10) appeared in the NCAA Division III Tournament.
—The men's tennis team finished 12-2 and the women's tennis team finished 10-5.

College Launches New Programs

Methodist launched a program in Occupational Environmental Management in 2003 to prepare graduates for industry, government mining, agriculture, public health, educational and research organizations. Carla Raineri, assistant professor of biology for 11 years, was named program director.

Several majors began offering new concentrations. Biology added a conservation biology concentration and a health occupations concentration. Business majors were offered a management information systems concentration. Computer science majors were offered a computer art, multimedia and programming concentration.

In other news from spring and summer 2003:
—College President Elton Hendricks received the 2003 Chairman's Award from the Fayetteville Chamber of Commerce for his leadership in and contributions to the community.

—Methodist launched its third generation Web site featuring a new look and menu system. Biz Tools One, a Fayetteville web design firm, worked on the project with the College's webmaster and the offices of Admissions and Public Relations.
—Dr. Suzan Cheek, professor of political science and director of the Tally Leadership Center, retired in summer 2003, after 16 years of service.

Methodist Begins 44th School Year

The fall 2003 semester was marked by continued enrollment growth at Methodist College. Day students numbered 1,441, while evening/weekend enrollment reached 908.

Forty-seven states and 27 foreign countries were represented in the student body. A total of 807 students were living on campus, compared to 833 in fall 2002.

Three members of the Class of 2003 joined the College staff as student recruiters: Nick Rose in resort business, Brandy Helm in day admissions, and Justin Rimbey in professional golf management.

The Methodist College Board of Trustees welcomed three new members: Mrs. Dorothy Bell Hubbard of Sanford, N.C.; Earl Leake '73 of Charlotte, N.C.; and the Reverend Jerry Lowry of Sanford, N.C.

Members of the Administrative Committee as well as faculty and staff began discussing issues raised by Jim Collins in his national best selling book, *Good to Great*.

Methodist College's Center for Entrepreneurship sponsored Dupont Appreciation Day September 23, 2003.

SWS Explores 'Region'

Methodist's 17th Southern Writers Symposium September 19-20, 2003, explored the influence of "region" on southern writers. The passage of Hurricane Isabel along the Carolina coast cut into attendance; about 60 persons were present to hear nine featured speakers and 30 scholarly presenters.

The featured speakers included Carmen Deedy, a story teller from Cuba; Gary Hawkins, an independent filmmaker from Thomasville, N.C.; Lucinda MacKethan, English professor at N.C. State University; Jon Smith, editor of *Mississippi Quarterly: the Journal of Southern Culture*; and John Shelton Reed, William Kenan Rand Jr., professor emeritus of sociology at UNC-Chapel Hill.

— CHAPTER 10 —

Staff Member Dies in Tragic Accident

Chris Ryan, a dedicated and very popular staff member, died suddenly Wednesday, September 24, 2003. Ryan was director of student activities at the time.

While attending a soccer game, Ryan was stung by an insect. After he left the game and went to his parked car, he suffered a fatal allergic reaction. He was survived by his wife Susan Ryan (Class of 1990) and three sons, Christopher, Joshua, and Caleb Ryan.

During his 16 years at the College, Ryan worked in the area of student life, student employment and residence life.

A memorial service for Ryan was held Sunday afternoon, September 28, 2003, in Reeves Auditorium. The College subsequently honored Ryan by naming the student activities center (former Safley house) near Cumberland Hall Chris's House.

Chris Ryan

MCT Features Students of the Environment

The cover story in the fall 2003 issue of *Methodist College Today* featured four students who were majoring in environment-related disciplines.

Doug Austin had worked as a U.S. Forest Service firefighter in the western U.S. the previous summer. He was majoring in biology with a concentration in conservation biology.

Philip Crawford, a member of the U.S. Army with a specialty in power generation, was enrolled in the College's new occupational environmental management program.

Cynthia Webb, an Air Force veteran, interested in helping government agencies solve environmental problems, was also enrolled in the OEM program.

The third OEM major profiled in the article was Rashe Malcolm, a former employee of Marriott Food Services. The mother of two said she wanted to be a health inspector.

College Recruits Softball Star

Caryn Moreland, a freshman from Waldorf, Md., was also featured in the Fall 2003 *Methodist College Today*. The previous summer, her Maryland All-Star summer softball travel team defeated Latin America 3-1 in the finals of the Big League Softball World Series in Kalamazoo, Mi.

An outfielder for the Monarchs, Moreland graduated early in criminal justice. Softball coach Ron Simpson said Moreland now works in the Washington, D.C. area.

2001-2006

Board Hosts Student Am Tournament

In the fall of 2003, the College's Board of Visitors hosted its first Student Am Golf Tournament at Baywood Country Club. More than 50 players participated, raising $2,900 for the golf management program and student activities.

Keith Dippre Premiers Composition

Keith Dippre, assistant professor of music at Methodist College, premiered his composition *Pilgrim's Blues* at Northampton, Ma. in the fall of 2003. Scored for piano, violin, and cowbell, the work was commissioned for the Jonathon Edwards Tercentenary.

Richard Hall, former philosophy and religion professor, chaired the conference which honored the life and work of Jonathon Edwards, an 18th century Puritan preacher, writer, and theologian, who wrote "Sinners in the Hands of an Angry God." Dippre was able to research the life of Edwards while serving as artist-in-residence at the Artist's Enclave in East Haddam, Ct. during the summer.

Women's Soccer Team Wins Conference Title

The 2003 women's soccer team finished 12-6-1 with a 7-1 mark in the USA South Athletic Conference. Senior goalkeeper Ken La Salla was selected as a third team NCAA Division III All-American. Women's Coach Bobby Graham was named conference coach of the year.

In other fall 2003 sports:

—The football team finished 4-5 overall and 3-3 in the USA South Athletic Conference.

—The men's soccer team posted a 10-7-1 season, 4-3 in the USA South Atlantic Conference.

—The volleyball team finished 10-24 and 6-10 in the conference.

—The women's cross country team finished third in the conference and the men's cross country team finished fourth.

MCAA Honors Three

During the 2003 homecoming, which had a safari theme, the college alumni association presented the following awards: Distinguished Alumni Award to Dr. Jim Weeks '68, dean of the Bryan School of Business of UNC-Greensboro; Alumni Service Award to Nona Fisher '88, a Fayetteville accountant; and the Outstanding Faculty Staff Award to Theresa Clark, professor of business administration and Fayetteville attorney.

— CHAPTER 10 —

During a luncheon for 1960s alumni October 31, Walter Turner '65 presented Dr. Hendricks with a copy of *Paving Tobacco Road,* a history of road-building in North Carolina, published by the N.C. Department of Transportation.

Athletic Hall of Fame Inducts Three

The Methodist College Athletic Hall of Fame inducted three new members at the Athletic Booster Club banquet October 31, 2003.

Alumni inducted were:
— Clinton Montford '90, basketball player who set College and NCAA-III records for rebounding.
— Daphne Akridge '93, the first women's basketball player to garner 1st team Dixie Conference honors and who set school records for points scored, field goals, and free throws.
— Elizabeth Horton '95, four-time All-American golfer.

Alumni-Owned Business Wins State Award

In December 2003, *Business North Carolina* magazine gave Cheer Ltd., a Fayetteville cheerleading company co-owned and operated by Gwen and Tim Holtsclaw, '68, '92, and Dick Fox '68 its Small Business of the Year award.

College Receives Major Gifts

In December 2003, David R. Nimocks Jr., his wife Elisabeth and their family businesses, of which David R. Nimocks III was president, pledged $1 million toward construction of the College's new fitness and intramural center.

In addition, the College was notified that the late Robert Dedman Sr., board chairman of Club Corp., had bequeathed $1 million in Club Corp stock to fund scholarships for Methodist College students enrolled in the resort management, golf management, and tennis management programs.

Dr. L. Elbert Wethington and wife, Lois, of Durham, N.C., established a "Wesley Heritage Fund" in the fall of 2003 to support lectures, dramas, and other approved projects.

College Awards First Master's Degrees

Methodist College awarded its first master's degrees December 12, 2003, to seven graduates of the physician assistant program. The Master of Medical Science recipients shared the stage with 137 undergraduates.

Dr. Loleta Wood Foster, a Fayetteville psychologist and College trustee, gave the commencement address.

2001-2006

L to R, David R. Nimocks, Jr., his wife Elisabeth, Dr. Hendricks, David R. Nimocks III.

The speaker took the audience and graduates on a visual and figurative journey across the commencement stage, which she likened to a bridge. She measured the stage to be approximately 22 steps, broken into five sections, each with its own message contained in a poem she wrote entitled, "The Bridges We Cross."

Dr. Foster concluded by encouraging class members to repeat the following statements as often as needed in their life journeys:

"1) I only have the power to work on changing me,

2) I owe it to myself to believe in me,

3) I deserve to be more intentional as I manage my life's journey." [43]

Dr. Hendricks presented a Methodist College Medallion to Dr. Foster and to Nolan Clark, of Fayetteville, trustee of the Florence Rogers Charitable Trust. He also presented the Sam Edwards Award to Francesea Rolando Heller.

The Rev. Raymond Gooch '72, was the winter baccalaureate speaker. He said living a successful life is about finding the right rhythm and believing that God will hold you steady. [44]

Celebrate All Cultures

At the College's spring opening convocation February 2, 2004, Dr. Terri Moore Brown '65, spoke of the significance of Black History Month but encouraged the audience to celebrate all cultures equally. A former professor at Methodist, Dr. Brown was then chair of the Department of Social Work at Fayetteville State University.

— CHAPTER 10 —

McIntyre Chairs 2004 Loyalty Day Drive

Seventh District Congressman Mike McIntyre chaired the Methodist College Foundation's 2004 Loyalty Day fund drive February 10, 2004.

McIntyre shared his many connections to the College and praised Methodist for its growth and ethical education of students. He also encouraged 160 volunteer fund-raisers to think of three *L's* as they went out on behalf of the College: loyalty, learning, and leadership. [45]

President Hendricks presented the "Loyalty Day Supporter of the Year" award to D. P. Russ, a member of the original Fayetteville College Steering Committee and a consistent donor to the College for nearly 50 years.

College Loses Trustee

The College mourned the passing of John Wyatt Jr. of Fayetteville January 30, 2004, at the age of 73. A College trustee and founder of Valley Motors, Wyatt was active in church and civic affairs.

In June 2004, friends and family of John Wyatt gathered for a luncheon at Methodist College, and the Board of Trustees presented Wyatt's wife, Dot, with a resolution of appreciation for John Wyatt's service to the College and to the Fayetteville community.

Lady Monarchs Capture 7th Straight National Title

In the spring of 2004, the women's golf team captured its seventh straight NCAA Division III National Championship in Great Lakes, Wi., winning by two strokes over Mary Hardin-Baylor. Charlotte Williams, Hope Thomas, and Heather Martin garnered All-American honors, and Williams was selected NCAA Division III Freshman of the Year.

In other sports action from spring 2004, the men's golf team, men's basketball team, and women's tennis team won their USA South Conference tournaments. The baseball, men's basketball, men's golf, and men's track and field teams appeared in their respective NCAA-III tournaments.

College Upgrades Golf Practice Facility

During the summer of 2004, the College maintenance staff installed irrigation lines for the central mall, upgraded the golf practice facility, laid fiber optic cable to the Pines Apartments, and replaced the lamps in the Yarborough Bell Tower.

The cover story in the summer 2004 *Methodist College Today* described the College's internship program for professional golf management students. Methodist College's Jerry Hogge, director of Institute for Golf and Tennis Management, said Methodist's internships surpass the P.G.A.'s requirements.

The seven-month internships, which take students to some of the world's most famous golf courses, are the last hurdle students have to clear before graduating. Students are placed and supervised by Charles Koonce, internship director, who traveled more than 7,200 miles in the summer of 2004, visiting more than 100 students in 18 states.

Students begin applying for internships each fall, sending their résumés to golf professionals and undergoing interviews. In addition to world-class courses like Pebble Beach, Congressional, Oakmont, TPC Sawgrass and Kiawah Island Turtle Point, PGM students also work for Titleist and in PGA section offices. Upon completion of an internship, each student must submit a written report and be evaluated by an on-site golf professional and a faculty member.

General Shelton Stresses the Three *F's*

Speaking at the College's 41st spring commencement May 8, 2004, retired Army General Hugh Shelton urged each graduating senior to "become a person of value and remain true to yourself and your family." [46]

He said the importance of faith, family, and friends—the three *F's*— were reinforced to him when he suffered a spinal cord injury and paralysis in 2002. [47]

The former chairman of the Joint Chiefs of Staff also said he discounted much of the negative opinion he hears about today's youth, saying he had had the honor of watching thousands of young men and women in uniform perform superbly in difficult missions around the world. [48]

In a morning baccalaureate sermon entitled "Not Yet," the Rev. Woodrow W. Wells Jr. '69 extolled the virtues of delayed gratification, saying heaven is the ultimate example of that credo, "Jesus wants us to say 'No' to what is cheap and easy and 'Yes' to what is precious, worthwhile, and everlasting," he said. [49]

In other commencement activities:
— President Hendricks presented honorary Doctor of Humanities degrees to General Hugh Shelton and to College trustee Louis Spilman Jr. '64, a retired Fayetteville businessman.
— Sarika Bellis-Rodriguez received the Lucius Stacy Weaver Award.

College Restructures

In anticipation of more graduate programs, Methodist College reorganized its academic program into six "schools" in the summer of 2004. A dean was appointed for each school, and all degree programs were grouped under the appropriate "school."

The schools and their deans were: School of Graduate Studies, Dr. Donald Lassiter; Reeves School of Business, Dr. Jeff Zimmerman (interim); School of Arts and Humanities, Dr. John Sill; School of Science and Human

Development, Dr. Wenda Johnson; School of Public Affairs, Dr. Trevor Morris; School of Information & Technology, Dr. Willis Watt.

Methodist College Hires Symphony Conductor

During the fall of 2004, Methodist provided office space for Fouad Fakhouri, the new conductor of the Fayetteville Symphony, and hired him to teach an orchestra class. The initial class contained 22 musicians; membership was opened to faculty and staff and other interested members of the Fayetteville community.

A native of Jordan, Fakhouri previously conducted the Bulgarian Symphony. He earned a bachelor's degree at West Texas A & M University, two master's degrees from Penn State, and a Doctor of Musical Arts in composition at the University of North Texas.

Fall 2004 Day Enrollment Tops 1,500

Methodist opened its 45th school year in August 2004 with a day enrollment of 1544, an increase of more than 100 students from fall 2003. Evening and weekend enrollment reached 818. A total of 860 students were living on campus.

A dozen freshmen were recruited with the help of The Davis Foundation of New York through $10,000 grants per student, per year, for four years. The foundation established the scholarship program at Methodist to recruit students from member institutions of United World Colleges, an international, multi-cultural school system which offers the international baccalaureate degree.

The fall 2004 class of Davis Scholars represented Ethiopia, Mongolia, Kazhakstan, India, Poland, Swaziland and Gambia. The total enrollment of international students in fall 2004 was 54.

Trustees Reject River Easement

In April of 2004, the Sandhills Area Land Trust (SALT) offered to pay Methodist College $715,000 for a conservation easement on 60 acres of college-owned land bordering the Cape Fear River.

President Hendricks reported to the board May 13, 2004, that an *ad hoc* committee which included five trustees, Gene Clayton, and himself had met with SALT officials for many hours, but had been unable to reach a consensus on how to respond to the offer.

In a written analysis, Dr. Hendricks said most of the 60 acres under discussion consisted of deep ravines and could not be developed. He said the College had no plans to develop the land in question.

The president said the trustees needed to consider reducing the size of the easement to 30 acres or whether the current board of trustees should grant any kind of easement in perpetuity (forever). He said the *ad hoc* committee could not reach a consensus.

Dick Player presented a written opinion to the board, stating his opposition to "giving up our full rights to use the acreage purchased by the founders of the College." [50] The trustees instructed their Executive Committee to gather more information on the matter and report back to the full board.

The trustees settled the river easement issue at an October 21, 2004, meeting, accepting an Executive Committee suggestion that in lieu of granting as easement for river land to SHALT, the board adopt a resolution stating its intent to protect the river, but noting it was not prepared to give an easement. After a lengthy discussion, the trustees adopted a resolution committing the college to protect its riverside property and the water quality of the Cape Fear River by a vote of 24-2.

At the same board meeting, the trustees were advised that the College ended the fiscal year June 30 with a budget surplus of $1,136,777, "due to an increase in enrollment, coupled with expense reductions in hospitality and travel budgets and a 10 percent reduction in staff and benefits." [51]

BB&T Boosts Campaign

In October 2004, the BB&T (Branch Banking & Trust Company) Charitable Foundation pledged $750,000 toward the College's *Seeds on Good Soil, A New Season Campaign*.

This gift brought to $10.9 million the amount pledged in the $12.85 million campaign to build a fitness center and an addition to the Science Building, add to the College endowment, and provide operating funds.

Tea With John Wesley

Methodist's first annual Wesley Heritage celebration began with a lecture by David Lowes Watson, director of the Office of Pastoral Formation, Nashville Area of The United Methodist Church. The lecture was entitled "A Matter of Heart and Life: John Wesley's Protestant Course-Correction."

In the afternoon, Denny Wise, pastor of Oxford (N.C.) Methodist Church, portrayed Wesley in a historical monologue entitled "Afternoon Tea with John Wesley." Both events were funded by Dr. Elbert Wethington and his wife, Lois.

Methodist College Today Features MC at Night

The cover story in the fall 2004 issue of *Methodist College Today* featured non-traditional students like Susie Biddle, a divorced mother of eight who

— CHAPTER 10 —

earned a degree in education and became a teacher of children with learning disabilities.

Mrs. Linda Gravitt, assistant dean for MC at Night and Summer School, said the average age of evening students was 35 and that approximately 100 "non-traditional" students graduated from Methodist each year. [52]

Jarman Promoted

Athletic Director Bob McEvoy announced that DeeDee Jarman, head women's basketball coach and senior woman administrator had been promoted to associate athletic director. "Coach Jarman is a key reason for the overall success of our athletic program," said McEvoy. [53]

In other sports news:
—Eddie Luck became the men's tennis coach, coming to Methodist from Ferris State in Michigan.
—Adam Horton, a member of the men's golf team, was voted the best overall athlete of 2003-04 and received the Sykes Cup.
—It was announced that Methodist would host the 2005 NCAA Division III Women's Golf National Championship at the Mid Pines Inn and Golf Club in Southern Pines, N.C.

"Methodist Always Salutes Heroes"

Thanks largely to Laurie Cherry, Methodist College's alumni director, homecoming 2004 carried out its patriotic theme in great style. Members of the Green Beret Parachute Team dropped in during a homecoming pre-game show. Mrs. Cherry also presented a slide show at the alumni banquet, showing what life was like for American soldiers (like her husband) in Iraq.

Homecoming 2004 festivities began October 22, with a sports banquet and induction of four athletes into the Methodist College Athletic Hall of Fame. The banquet was staged in the Riddle Center by the Methodist College Booster Club.

The former Monarch athletes inducted were: Mike Currie '84, who pitched for the baseball team and was a two-time All-American; Mickey Sokalski '84, a member of the men's golf team and Methodist College's first three-time Division III All-American in that sport; Kelly Cap '95, an LPGA pro golfer who helped lead the women's golf team to four consecutive national championships; and DeCarlos West '97, a former tailback on the football team who set three scoring records at Methodist.

Three Fall Teams Have Winning Seasons

The Monarch football team ended its fall 2004 season 7-3 overall and 4-2 in the USA South Athletic Conference. It was the first winning season for the team since 2000.

Tailback Demarcus Wilson finished his career ranked second at Methodist in rushing yardage and rushing attempts. Chris Roncketti became the first Methodist College quarterback to eclipse 2,000 career passing yards and 1,000 career rushing yards.

The 2004 men's soccer team finished 11-6-2 overall and second in the conference. Season highlights included 3-1 victory over UNC-Pembroke and a 2-1 overtime victory at home over Christopher Newport.

The women's soccer team compiled a 12-7-2 record and also finished second in the USA South Conference.

Methodist College Athletes Win Cans Competition

In a winter 2004 Cans Across the Conference food drive, members of the Methodist Student-Athlete Advisory Committee collected 2,325 items and won a first place trophy from the USA South Athletic Conference. The food items were donated to the Salvation Army's Fayetteville office.

College Awards 154 Degrees

Methodist College awarded 148 undergraduate degrees and nine master's degrees at its 38th winter commencement December 10, 2004.

North Carolina Secretary of State Elaine Marshall encouraged graduates to invest in their interpersonal relationships and stressed the importance of morality and serving others. [54]

In the winter baccalaureate sermon, Dr. Reggie Ponder, president of Louisburg College, encouraged graduating seniors to live lives of integrity to demonstrate the ability to think critically and clearly, to be committed, and to become servant leaders. [55]

Dr. Hendricks presented an honorary Doctor of Science degree to Dr. Linda McPhail '70 a biochemical researcher and faculty member of the Wake Forest University School of Medicine.

— CHAPTER 10 —

Darden Named Horticulturalist

In December 2004, Jim Darden '69 became Methodist's first full-time horticulturalist, charged with beautifying the campus through landscape, irrigation, and drainage design. He was given two staff assistants.

Darden retired from Sampson Community College in Clinton, N.C. in 2004, having served 25 years as chair of the Horticulture Department. He was also the owner and operator of Darden's Nursery and Landscaping in Clinton.

Kresge Offers Challenge Grant

In December 2004, the Kresge Foundation of Troy, Michigan, offered Methodist College a $550,000 challenge grant toward construction of an addition to the Science Building. The grant was contingent on the College raising $2.6 million by October 1, 2005. The $2.6 million was the amount needed for the College to complete its $12.85 million *Seeds on Good Soil, A New Season* campaign.

The Kresge Foundation had given Methodist two previous challenge grants—$250,000 in 1989 for the physical activities center and $300,000 in 1996 for an addition to Davis Memorial Library.

Citing new concentrations in biology and the master's program in physician assistant studies, President Hendricks said, "The demand for sciences has grown rapidly. Our friends and alumni have responded well to past challenges from the Kresge Foundation, and I am confident we will raise the money needed to meet or exceed the conditions of this newest challenge grant." [56]

CFE Honors Business Owners

In January 2005, Methodist's Center for Entrepreneurship honored Ron and Sharon Matthews of Fayetteville, proprietors of Family Foods, Inc. at its first-ever "Legacy Lunch" at the Holiday Inn Bordeaux. The two were honored for their community involvement as well as their business success as Taco Bell Corp. franchise holders, with 20 restaurants in eastern and southeastern North Carolina.

The Matthews were cited for their generous support of their church (Hay Street United Methodist Church) as well as area non-profits and civic organizations such as Boys and Girls Clubs of Cumberland County, the 4-H Foundation, YMCA, the Dogwood Festival Rodeo, Fayetteville Force hockey and activities at Fort Bragg.

Foster Returns

In January 2005, Ron Foster returned to Methodist as director of Methodist College's physician assistant program. Foster founded the program in 1996 and directed it until 2003, when he left to pursue clinical work.

Berns Center Renovated

During the semester break in December 2004, the Berns Student Center underwent a $30,000 "makeover," that included renovations to the Lion's Den (snack bar), new flooring inside and out, and the addition of informal lounge areas on the east side of the great hall.

Alumnus Jim Link Visits Methodist

Retired Army Lt. General James M. Link '66 visited his alma mater in December 2004 and was interviewed by Laurie Cherry, director of alumni affairs.

A resident of Huntsville, Alabama, Link was then serving as president of Teledyne Brown Engineering, Inc., which provided systems engineering and technology and manufacturing solutions for space, defense, environmental and homeland security requirements. The Fayetteville native majored in history at Methodist, joined the Army and served in Vietnam, and went on to earn an M.B.A. at the University of Tennessee.

When asked to give his thoughts about Methodist and its future, Link said,
"I am impressed that Methodist has embraced change and is remaining relevant to today's students. Tradition is a touchstone for an institution, but tradition unburdened by progress is a recipe for irrelevance. The College must not be satisfied with the status quo. As we say in Huntsville, 'The sky is NOT the limit.'" [57]

Tony DeLapa Passes

Dr. Tony DeLapa, former vice president for academic affairs and professor of education, died January 6, 2005 at the age of 68. He had been suffering from cancer. He retired in 2003, after 14 years at the College, and then served as pastor of Parkton United Methodist Church.

In 2004, the Anthony J. De Lapa Art Award was established in his honor, to recognize a junior or senior art or art education major for academic and artistic excellence.

France Honors General John Handy

General John Handy '66, commander of the U.S. Transportation Command and Air Mobility Command, was inducted into the French Legion d'Honneur October 25, 2004 in Washington, D.C.

The highest award given by the French Republic for service to France was presented at the residence of the French ambassador to the U.S., Jean-David Lavitte. Fewer than 60 Americans have received this honor since the Legion was introduced by Napoleon Bonaparte in the early 1800s. Handy visited Methodist in June 2005 and met with a group of faculty and staff.

CHAPTER 10

Pinehurst Partners With Methodist

Early in 2005, Pinehurst Resort and Methodist's Reeves School of Business collaborated to establish a Professional M.B.A. at Pinehurst program, starting in the fall of 2005.

The 24-month program was designed for professionals already working in golf, tennis, or resort management, with classes meeting at Pinehurst one weekend a month, and with supplemental coursework completed online between residency sessions. In addition to core business courses, students were to be offered courses in agronomy and food and beverage management. Other components of the program were the Executive Speaker Series and a Capstone Experience (final project).

College Thanks Donors

Methodist College held its annual Donor Appreciation Dinner April 7, 2005, at the Highland Country Club to honor donors who made a gift of $1,000 or more to the college in 2004.

The highlight of the evening was the presentation of a Methodist College Medallion to Mrs. Mary Butler Yarborough, widow of Wilson F. Yarborough, Sr., one of the College's original trustees. Mrs. Yarborough was honored for her generous support of the College and the Fayetteville community.

Alumni Survey Results Published

The summer 2005 issue of *Methodist College Today* shared the results of an alumni survey conducted in 2004 and 2005 and commissioned by the Alumni Association Board of Directors. Approximately 400 alumni responded to the survey, the results of which were presented to the College's Administrative Committee April 23, 2005.

Alumni said their favorite part of the College magazine was alumni news. Twenty-five percent of the respondents said Methodist should improve academics (and add more graduate programs). Many wanted more alumni events. The survey showed that only 30 percent of the respondents had ever awarded a Greatest Gift Scholarship to an incoming freshman. [58]

As part of the survey story, the Alumni Office unveiled its monthly e-newsletter and invited alumni to subscribe. The office also announced plans to publish a new alumni directory in 2006.

Methodist College Today Touts Lady Monarchs' Dynasty

The summer 2005 *Methodist College Today* featured the women's golf team in its cover story. The story said 18 national championships in 20 years constituted a dynasty for the Lady Monarchs. Attention was also given to the outstanding play of Katie Dick and Charlotte Williams at the 2005 NCAA-III National Championship at Mid Pines Golf Club in Southern Pines.

Women's Golf Coach Vici Pate said her team was young but very talented. She said the players needed to "stay loose and have fun to play well" in the tournament. [59] Obviously the team followed that recipe, winning the title by 12 strokes over Mary Hardin-Baylor. In addition, sophomore Charlotte Williams won the individual national title by three strokes.

Congressman Speaks at 42nd Commencement

Methodist conferred 157 degrees at its 42nd spring commencement Saturday, May 7, 2005.

Second District Congressman Bob Etheridge of Lillington delivered the commencement address. He congratulated the graduating seniors on reaching this milestone and said, "The road is not at its end. If you think it is, you're in for a rude awakening. Never, ever, ever forget: Education is not a destination. Education is a journey." [60]

The Rev. Dr. Charles Smith delivered the baccalaureate sermon, entitled "Let This Mind Be In You."

President Hendricks presented a Methodist College Medallion to Rep. Etheridge and an honorary Doctor of Humanities degree to Charles K. McAdams, the College's first director of development and public relations. Dr. Hendricks also presented the Stacy Weaver Award to Enausa Davis-Robinson.

College Celebrates the Life of Bill Lowdermilk

The Rev. Dr. William P. Lowdermilk died July 18, 2005, after a 10-month battle with brain cancer. He was 72.

To hundreds of students and alumni, Bill Lowdermilk was known affectionately as "Uncle Bill." He joined Methodist's public relations staff in 1963, after serving five years as pastor of Culbreth Memorial United Methodist Church in Fayetteville. He became director of public relations in 1968, assistant to the president in 1974, vice president in 1977 and vice president for church and community relations in 1985. He retired in 1995.

Lowdermilk was revered by students and staff alike for his skill at recruiting quality students, his work to enhance religious life at Methodist, and his ability to make visitors, especially Methodists, feel welcome on the campus. He officiated at scores of weddings, baptisms, and funerals of Methodist alumni and staff.

"Uncle Bill" helped launch the Methodist College Alumni Association and the Greatest Gift Scholarship, an award alumni may give to new students. He coordinated 25 annual sessions of the N.C. Conference of The United

— CHAPTER 10 —

Methodist Church and countless Annual Conference Sessions of the N.C. Conference United Methodist Youth Fellowship (UMYF) held at the College each summer.

A past president of the Fayetteville Rotary Club, he endowed the club's William P. Lowdermilk Student Achievement Award and an annual program on values and ethics in the workplace. In 1986, he received an honorary Doctor of Divinity degree from N.C. Wesleyan College. In 1994, he received the Francis Asbury Award for Fostering United Methodist Ministries, first from the N.C. Conference, and then from the Southeastern Jurisdiction of The United Methodist Church. In May 2005, the College awarded him a Methodist College Medallion.

Rev. Dr. William Lowdermilk

Bill Lowdermilk was born and reared in Norman, N.C., a small community in northern Richmond County. After graduating from Ellerbee High School, he earned a B.A. in English at Emory University and a Bachelor of Divinity degree at Duke University. He was survived by two brothers.

The College held memorial services for Lowdermilk July 21 and again August 31. The Reverend Ray Gooch '72, presided at the July service. Dr. Lowdermilk was interred at a rural cemetery in Norman where his mother and father were buried. Dr. Lowdermilk's family asked that memorial gifts be made to the Lowdermilk Scholarship Fund at Methodist College.

A member of the College's Board of Trustees at the time of his death, Dr. Lowdermilk left the College an estate gift of $1,010,627, designated for endowment.

Methodist College Begins 47th School Year

Methodist College began the 2005-06 academic year with six new trustees: Mrs. Kathy Wright, General John W. Handy, the Reverend Dr. Carl Frazier Jr., Dr. John W. Shrader, Dr. Eric L. Mansfield, and Mr. Ron B. Matthews.

New faculty members included: Mike Roberts, English; Dr. Andrew Jameson, physical education; Dr. John Dembosky, geology; Dr. Chris Slivva, Spanish; Dr. Gregory Combs, sports management; Dr. Cynthia Sawchuk, computer science; Mr. Anthony Holderied, library services; Mrs. Mary

Deyampert McCall, social work; Dr. James McCandless, biology; Mrs. Jan Turner, ESL/TESL; Ms. Rosario Lara, Spanish; Dr. Jennifer Purvis, political science; Mr. David Page, English; Ms. Jennifer Cuchna, athletic training; Ms. Whitney Larrimore, English; Dr. Berry Avner, pharmacology; Ms. Karen Kletter, history; Ms. Kristine Thomas, justice studies.

New staff members in fall 2005 included:

—Fred Gilbert, manager of dining services

—Duane Grooms, director of student activities

—Garland J. "Guy" Stewart, director of career services

—Lauren Cook Wike, director of annual fund and alumni affairs

—Lindsay Hanson, director of student media/College photographer

—Michael Molter, assistant dean for distance education

—Michelle Petty, director of College events.

The enrollment for the fall 2005 semester reached 2,147 students, 1,530 in the day program and 706 in the evening/weekend program. Residential enrollment reached 825.

Mike Safley Rejoins College Staff

The Reverend Michael Safley '72 returned to Methodist College in May 2005 as vice president for church and community relations and College chaplain. Safley came to the post after serving as president and CEO of the Methodist Home for Children from 1997-2004. In that capacity, he led a $7 million campaign which resulted in construction of the Jordan Child and Family Enrichment Center in Raleigh.

From 1988-97, he served as vice president for student life and dean of students at Methodist. Prior to 1988, he served as director of youth and young adult ministries, led a prison ministry, pastored a local church, and worked at the Methodist Home for Children.

Methodist awarded Safley an honorary Doctor of Divinity degree in 2002. In 2005, he received the Order of the Long Leaf Pine from North Carolina's Governor Mike Easley. In 1998, the College alumni association awarded him the Distinguished Alumni Award.

Former Governor Pays Tribute to Lura Tally

Former North Carolina Governor James B. Hunt was the featured speaker at an October 18, 2005 luncheon honoring former state senator Lura Tally and celebrating the tenth anniversary of the Tally Center for Leadership Development at Methodist College.

— CHAPTER 10 —

Trustees Approve $24.5 Million Bond Issue

In October 2005, Methodist College issued $24.5 million in tax-exempt revenue bonds through the North Carolina Educational Finance Agency. Wachovia Bank, National backed the bonds with a letter of credit.

The Board of Trustees approved bond resolutions in September and October to secure funds needed to start construction on three new buildings. This was the third such bond issue for the College.

Proceeds from the 2005 bond issue were used as follows:
1) $14.2 million to pay off the Series 2000 bond.
2) $2.5 million to refinance a loan with Wachovia Bank used to build Cape Fear Commons II.
3) $4 million for construction of a new science building and a fitness center.
4) $504,537 to refinance a loan with First-Citizens Bank & Trust Co. used to construct the Walter and Margaret Clark Hall (School of Business building) and a library annex in 1998-99.
5) $4.4 million to build a 95-room, apartment-style residence hall on campus. [74]

Under terms of the bond issue, the College agreed to pay off the bonds over a 20-year period at a blended interest rate (half fixed and half variable) which has thus far averaged 4.04 percent per year. In 2007, MU's bond payments totaled just under $2 million.

Friends Break Ground for New Buildings

College friends and staff gathered October 31, 2005 to break ground for the science building addition and the fitness and wellness center to be built as part of the *Seeds on Good Soil* campaign. Special guests included Second District Congressman Bob Etheridge, members of the David Nimocks family, campaign co-chairs Richard R. Allen Sr. and Ramon Yarborough, Richard L. Player Jr., Robert Shuller, Alfred E. Cleveland, the Rev. Dr. Brian Gentle, and Shauna Bunn (S.G.A. president).

In an October 20, 2005 meeting, the Methodist College Board of Trustees awarded Player, Inc. the contracts to build the science building and the fitness center. The trustees also awarded Construction Systems, Inc. a separate contract to build a three-story, two-wing, 95-room apartment-style residence hall, to be financed by a bond issue.

In related matters:
—First Citizens Bank pledged $100,000 toward the fitness center, and
—North Carolina Natural Gas made a gift of $15,000 toward the addition to the Science Building.

Homecoming '05 Breaks New Ground

In keeping with the theme, "Breaking New Ground," alumni returning for homecoming October 22, 2005, received yellow plastic hard hats. Members of the Class of 1965, including former "Yama-yama" men (Cumberland Hall intramural team members), took on Ron Simpson's softball team.

For the first time ever, the alumni association held a "Lunch on the Green" in a tent behind Clark Hall in lieu of a banquet. Mark Moses '97, proprietor of Carrabbas' Italian Grill and his staff catered the lunch. Lynn Carraway, homecoming chair, emceed a short program in which Dr. Bill Lowdermilk was remembered for his faithful service to the college.

During the luncheon, the Alumni Association presented the following awards:
—Distinguished Alumni Award to Dr. William Harrison '74, superintendent of the Cumberland County schools
—Outstanding Alumni Service Award to Jim Darden '69, College horticulturalist
—Outstanding Faculty/Staff Award, given posthumously to Dr. Bill Lowdermilk.

Former athletes inducted into the Methodist College Athletic Hall of Fame October 21, 2005 included:
—Joy Bonhurst, women's golf, 1986-89
—Mike Brewington, baseball, 1986-89
—Jeannie Edwards, tennis and basketball, 1975-79
—Kenneth Hoey, men's soccer, 1992-95.

College Recruits for MJA Program

In the fall and winter of 2005, Methodist College began accepting applications for its first Master of Justice Administration class. The two-year weekend and online program was slated to begin in January 16, 2006, at the North Carolina Justice Academy in Salemburg, N.C.

Football Team Claims Conference Title

The Monarch football team finished the 2005 season 8-2 overall and 6-1 in the USA South Athletic Conference, winning the USA South championship. Senior quarterback Chris Roncketti was named USA South Offensive Player of the Year.

A Good Year for Giving

Methodist College's *Seeds on Good Soil, A New Season* campaign exceeded its $12.8 million goal in 2005, reaching $14,295,216 in gifts and pledges by the end of 2005.

— CHAPTER 10 —

The *Seeds on Good Soil* campaign generated four $1 million gifts. In addition, more than 2,400 individuals, corporations and foundations (including 1,281 alumni) contributed.

By meeting its campaign goal before October 1, 2005, the college secured a $550,000 challenge grant from the Kresge Foundation. The campaign added $3.4 million to the College endowment. Challenged by Campaign Co-chair Ramon Yarborough, the College trustees raised an additional $625,000 during the year.

Total giving to Methodist reached a record $3,145,107 in 2005, and the College endowment grew to $10.6 million. Annual Fund gifts toward current operations totaled $276,282. The alumni gave $236,377, and the North Carolina Conference of The United Methodist Church contributed $137,084.

Surgeon Defines Success for Winter Graduates

"There is a world of difference between success and significance," said Dr. Bruce Steffes at Methodist's 33rd winter commencement December 17, 2005. [61]

The surgeon-in-residence in Methodist College's Department of Medical Sciences continued, "Success is when you invest in yourself; significance is investing in others." [62]

President Hendricks conferred 174 degrees and presented Danny Marchant with the Sam Edwards Award.

The Reverend Hope Vickers delivered the baccalaureate sermon, entitled, "One of the Wise Guys."

College Remembers 'Pioneers'

Methodist College lost some of its oldest and dearest friends in 2005. The College marked the passing of:

—Dr. J. Nelson Gibson Jr., an original trustee, April 18.
—Mr. Samuel Reese Edwards Sr., former registrar, director of admissions, and physical education instructor, April 21.
—Mrs. Jane Peyrouse, wife of retired theatre professor, Dr. Jack Peyrouse, April 16.
—The Rev. Dr. Bill Lowdermilk, July 18.
—Mr. Charles H. Von Rosenberg, an organizer and board member of the Methodist College Foundation, October 29.
—Mrs. Pauline Longest, assistant professor emeritus of biology, November 1.
—Mrs. C. Wallace Jackson, a founding member of the Fayetteville College Foundation, September 28.
—Dr. Lorenzo P. "Joe" Plyler, professor emeritus of religion, November 9.

—Dr. Bert Ishee, a former president of the Methodist College Foundation, November 16.
—Mrs. Margaret T. Clark, widow of former trustee Walter Clark, November 26.
—Mr. Henry L. Campen Jr., a longtime friend of and fundraiser for the college, August 16.

Five Join College Staff

Methodist began 2006 with several new staff members:
—H. Ray Baker Jr. '71, director of grants and research and scholarship coordinator in the Development office.
—Kimberly Genova, director of career services.
—Melissa Jameson, director of college events in the Office of College Relations.
—Tiffany Nabors, director of student media and campus photographer in the office of Student Development.
—Maria Sikoryak-Robins, assistant director of college relations.
—Ryan Pretlow and Ed Salisbury, programmers; and Jason Joseph, network engineer in Institutional Computing.

College Receives $50,000 from Longest Estate

In March 2006, Methodist received news of a $50,000 gift from the estate of Mrs. Pauline Longest, who died the previous November. Mrs. Longest established a dual endowment to maintain the Pauline Longest Nature Trail and to support the Science Department.

Women Win 9th Straight National Title

Methodist's women's golf team won its ninth straight NCAA-Division III national title in May and Charlotte Williams was again named Player of the Year.

The men's golf team won its fourth straight conference title and finished third in the national tournament.

The women's tennis team, coached by Francie Barragan, won a sixth straight conference title.

The men's tennis team finished second in the conference and Keith Criscoe was named conference "Player of the Year."

The women's lacrosse team finished 11-4 and senior Lindsey West was named conference "Player of the Year."

Chad Collins '01, former three-time individual national medalist golfer, tied for 40th in his first U.S. Open, shooting 76-71-72-77.

— CHAPTER 10 —

College Plans 50th Anniversary Celebration

During the fall 2005 and spring 2006 semesters, a 50th Anniversary Committee met and planned a celebration of the 50th anniversary of the Methodist College receiving its charter from the state of North Carolina.

During the spring of 2006, a ribbon-type logo that read, "Celebrating 50 Years" was added to the college logo for use on commemorative objects and the MC postage meter stamp. In late fall, a gold ball Christmas ornament commemorating the College's 50th anniversary went on sale in Methodist's bookstore.

In the summer 2006 issue of *Methodist College Today*, Methodist unveiled plans for a week-long celebration, scheduled to coincide with homecoming, November 1-4.

Exhibits consisting of old College photos and artifacts would appear in the fall in the library and in Horner Administration Building.

The first "official" event would be a Fourth Friday (October 27) appearance at the Rainbow Room and the Market House in downtown Fayetteville by the cheerleaders and *One Spirit*, the honors vocal ensemble. Historic exhibits featuring photos from the College's first five decades, were set up at both locations.

On Wednesday, November 1, the College's 50th birthday, an open house, live art demonstration, and convocation were scheduled. *One Spirit* and the Jazz Ensemble would perform, and an afternoon alumni art exhibit would follow in the Mallett-Rogers House.

An appearance by the Vienna Choir Boys was slated for Thursday evening, November 2 in Reeves Auditorium.

A concert by the Fayetteville Symphony Orchestra was scheduled for Friday evening November 3, featuring a commissioned work by Dr. Keith Dippre, associate professor of music. The annual Athletic Hall of Fame Dinner and Induction in the Riddle Center gymnasium would precede the concert

The alumni scholarship luncheon, the newest homecoming tradition, was set for Saturday, November 4 at noon, along with the presentation of the annual alumni awards.

A 50th anniversary dinner and dance were planned for Saturday evening, in the Riddle Center gymnasium. The Breeze Band, a Charlotte-based "beach music" band, would play for the dance. A silent auction would follow the dinner to benefit the Methodist University Alumni Association Scholarship Fund.

The 50th Anniversary celebration would conclude with a special church service Sunday, November 5 at Hay Street United Methodist Church.

2001-2006

Rep. McIntyre Speaks at 43rd Spring Commencement

Addressing 138 graduating seniors May 6, 2006, 7th District Congressman Mike McIntyre stressed three words: reject, inject and project. [63]

McIntyre urged the class members to:

"1) Reject false notions that pull freedom down.

2) Inject freedom in a positive way and a true sense of responsibility in all they did.

3) Project themselves forward in time to make a better world." [64]

The morning baccalaureate speaker was Bishop Alfred Gwinn, resident bishop of The North Carolina Annual Conference of The United Methodist Church. He reminded the graduates they did not reach this milestone by themselves and that they were indebted to family, friends and God for bringing them to this point.

"Determine today to never lose the vision of your importance," said Gwinn. "I challenge you also to remember that you have promises to keep and miles to go before you sleep." [65]

During the commencement, President Hendricks presented an honorary Doctor of Humanities degree to College trustee Richard R. Allen Sr. and the Stacy Weaver Award to Lori Ann Knutson.

Trustees Approve Budget & Fees for 2006-07

At an executive session May 18, 2006, the Methodist College Board of Trustees approved a budget of $40,195,197 for 2006-07. The budget assumed the College would have a full-time equivalent day enrollment (FTE) of 1,349 with 785 resident students and collect 99 percent of its accounts receivable.

Tuition was set at $18,780, board at $3,570, and room at $3,600, making the total cost for a resident student $25,950. Evening and weekend tuition was set at $190 per semester hour. Tuition for day part-time students was set at $605 per semester hour.

Among North Carolina's 35 independent four-year colleges and universities, Methodist ranked 14th in total cost for 2006-07. The most expensive school was Duke University at $43,115.

Soccer Team Trains in Brazil

The men's soccer team spent part of the summer of 2006 at Santo Filomena, a soccer training facility located on the outskirts of São Paulo, Brazil. This was the first Methodist College athletic team to travel abroad.

College Begins 48th Year

As Methodist opened for its 48th school year, 91 resident students moved into the new Creekside Apartments, two three-story buildings overlooking the golf course and a creek. [In 2008. these apartments were renamed the McLean Residential Complex: Thomas R. McLean Hall and Elizabeth E. McLean Hall.]

The complex included 22 apartments with four students in each, one apartment with three students, and an apartment for the area coordinator. All apartments contained a private bedroom and bath for each occupant.

Designed by Shuller, Ferris, Lindstrom and Associates, the new complex cost $4.7 million. The College's tenth residence hall brought the total residential capacity to 980 students.

The College enrolled 2,116 students in the fall of 2006—1,588 day students and 528 in the evening program. A total of 887 students were living on campus. The student body included 72 international students, representing 37 countries.

Fifteen Join Faculty

Methodist opened the 2006-07 school year with 15 new faculty members: Dave Pauly, forensic science; Anne Galloway, English; Sarah Drake, mass communication; Valeria Russ, academic services; Dr. Rene Turcato, Spanish; Rocio Ochiltree, Spanish; Stephany Newberry-Davis, English; William Greg Thomas, mass communication and debate; Larry Wells, instrumental music; John Herring, physical education; James Marcin, Marketing; Karen Reid, financial economics; Dr. Warren McDonald, health care administration; George Hendricks, social work.

Nine Join Athletic Staff

The Methodist College Athletic Department welcomed nine newcomers in 2006-07: Rachel Bowman, assistant athletic trainer; Kirbie Britt, sports information director; Eric Brown, assistant football coach; Wylie Crisanti, women's lacrosse coach; Rachel Quesada, assistant women's soccer coach; Tim Ryerson, head men's and women's cross country coach and assistant men's basketball coach; Tony Tommasi, head women's soccer coach; Crystal Williams, head men's and women's track and field coach and assistant cross country coach; Nicole Yard, assistant athletic director.

Congressman Presents $600,000 Check

U.S. Rep. Bob Etheridge presented Methodist University with $600,000 in federal funds October 20, 2006, to support the occupational environmental management and forensic science programs. A total of $500,000 was earmarked for a virtual reality environmental laboratory, and $100,000 was allotted for forensic equipment.

The McLean Residential Complex honors Thomas R. and Elizabeth McLean.

Etheridge secured the funding in the Energy and Water Development Appropriations Act 2006 and the Science, State, Justice, Commerce and Related Agencies Appropriations Act 2006.

Trustees Approve Name Change

The Methodist College Board of Trustees voted October 28, 2006, to change the name of the institution to Methodist University, effective November 1, 2006. The effective date coincided with the 50th anniversary of the College receiving its charter from the state of North Carolina. The vote was unanimous.

"The truth of the matter is that the name change is something that has been talked about by the Board of Trustees for at least two years," said Alfred Cleveland, chair of the Board of Trustees. "It is coincidental that it is happening at the 50th anniversary, but I think it is appropriate that we are taking this action in our anniversary year." [66]

President Hendricks announced the name change at a 50th Anniversary Founders Day Convocation held Wednesday, November 1, 2006, in Reeves Auditorium. Faculty and staff learned early that week that the Board of Trustees had considered two "new names"—Methodist University and Eastern Methodist University. A graphic designer had already created new logos using both names.

— CHAPTER 10 —

"Words in higher education are used differently today," said Dr. Hendricks. "A word that signaled something in 1956 does not necessarily send the same signal today. The label that was appropriate in 1956 is not necessarily appropriate today." [67]

A trumpet fanfare preceded the actual announcement, after which a new "Methodist University" banner was lowered over the main curtain. Audience members responded by rising to their feet and applauding loudly.

Methodist became the tenth "independent" College in North Carolina to make the transition from college to university, and the fourth such school to do so in the 21st century. The school charter and bylaws were then amended, so that Methodist's legal name became "The Methodist University, Inc."

The president appointed the Reverend Dr. Michael Safley, vice president for church and community relations and university chaplain to chair a Marketing Committee charged with facilitating the name change with new signage and logos and developing a "usage standards manual" for faculty and staff. A graphic designer was retained to create new logos for the University and for the athletic programs.

Almost immediately, Monarch Press, the campus print shop, began applying the new logos to forms, letterhead, business cards, and brochures. The front entrance sign was changed within 60 days, following by new building signs over the next four months. A large marble sign with "Methodist College" on it, a sign that had stood on the center lawn for 46 years, was removed. The student store began ordering new school supplies, decals, and sportswear with the MU logos.

Trumpeters and **One Spirit** *perform the Alma Mater.*

Dr. Hendricks announces the trustees' decision to adopt the name Methodist University.

Reverend Joyner Looks to the Future

The Reverend Dr. F. Belton Joyner delivered the keynote address at Methodist's 50th Founders Day Convocation. The former trustee entitled his speech, "Let's Meet Back Here in Fifty Years."

"What questions should we (this school) ask at the age of 50?" he began. The seven questions he raised were:

- **Why bother with church-related higher education?** He then referred to the Charles Wesley hymn, "Come, Father, Son, and Holy Ghost," which speaks of combining heart and mind, knowledge and piety, truth and virtue.
- **Who's hurting?** How is Methodist helping, in Christlike fashion, those who are educationally undernourished, lost, and lonely?
- **What's happening?** How does a church-related college measure its results? Be patient. Effectiveness may best be measured over time by what people *know* about themselves, the world, others, God, and how all these things interact.
- **What are the values? What's important?** A good leader is not the one with the right answers, but the right questions. It must be clear that this school is here for the student, not the administration, faculty or trustees.
- **What's next?** Birthdays put matters in perspective. What should the kingdom of God look like at 5400 Ramsey Street? Ideally,

— CHAPTER 10 —

Alumni, former staff and trustees applaud the name change announcement.

Methodist University should show the world how to live with differences in opinion, experience, and background.

—**How do we balance academic freedom and denominational intentionality?** As one of 123 schools tied directly to The United Methodist Church, Methodist University is in charge of Methodist University. I am glad the school has chosen to keep its family name.

—**Who's responding to our Church and school's mission to be a presence of Jesus Christ?** Are students here being channeled and led to be more human and godlike? [68]

In his conclusion, Dr. Joyner said his first and last questions had come full circle and become, "How does a church-related commuity of higher education invite persons into a relationship with Jesus Christ? I did say it was a question, didn't I? Why don't we agree to meet back here in 50 years to see how the answer is coming along." [69]

Methodist's 50th Founders Day convocation ended with the congregation singing, "Be Thou My Vision."

Vienna Choir Boys Perform

One of the highlights of Methodist's 50th anniversary celebration was a concert by the Vienna Choir Boys Thursday evening, November 2, 2006, in Reeves Auditorium.

This group consisted of 24 boys ages 10-14 from all parts of the world (including America and Africa). The choirmaster was a virtuoso conductor and pianist named Andy Icochea Icochea. [yes, the name is repeated]. A native of Lima, Peru, Icochea studied music at the Conservatorio Nacional de Musica del peru, Westminster Choir College in Princeton N.J., and the Vienna Konservatorium.

On this occasion, the Vienna Choir Boys performed a program of 26 works divided into four parts: Sacred Music From Europe, Sacred Music From Around the World, International Folk Songs, and Austrian Folk Songs. The

The Rev. Dr. Mike Safley and The Rev. Dr. Belton Joyner visit after the convocation.

boys sang from memory in at least four different languages, for the most part, accompanied by Icochea on the piano. Speaking from the stage, the choirmaster provided interesting background information about the Boys Choir selection and schooling, individual members, and some of the works the Choir was performing.

Among the featured works were: *O Fortuna* from *Carmina Burana* by Carl Orff, *Ave Verum Corpus* by Mozart, *Jerusalem* by Charles Parry, *Psalm 61* by Andy Iccochea, *O, Shenandoah* (arr. by Gerald Wirth), and several folk songs by Johann Strauss, Jr.

At the end of the program, the audience gave the Vienna Choir Boys and Choirmaster Andy Icochea a standing ovation.

A "University" Homecoming

Methodist University's first homecoming under its new name began Friday evening, November 3, 2006, with the ninth annual Athletic Hall of Fame Banquet.

— CHAPTER 10 —

The Vienna Choir Boys impressed the audience with their mastery of music and language.

Four former athletes and one former coach were inducted into the ninth class:
—Catherine Byrne '91, women's soccer, a former All-American then serving as head women's soccer coach at The University of Akron.
—Heather Hugus Purgason '00, softball, holder of six school pitching records.
—Ernie Schwarz, first director of athletics, men's basketball and golf coach, inducted posthumously.
—Amy Todd '99, women's basketball, school record holder for rebounding.
—Jamelle Ushery '95, track, NCAA All-American and school record holder in three events.

MUAA Presents Awards

At the 2006 homecoming luncheon November 4, under a big white tent behind Clark Hall, the Methodist University Alumni Association Board of Directors presented the following awards:
—Distinguished Alumnus Award to Dr. M. Elton Hendricks, university president.
—Outstanding Alumni Service Award to the Rev. Dr. Dennis R. Sheppard '71.
—Outstanding Faculty Award to Jane Weeks Gardiner, dean of the School of Arts and Sciences.

King Makes Debut

"King," Methodist's new Monarch (lion) mascot, entered Monarch Field during the football pre-game show Saturday, November 4, riding on the back of a Harley Davidson motorcycle and carrying the game ball.

The new mascot uniform was purchased through the collaborative efforts of the University, the Athletic Boosters Club, and the Alumni Affairs, University Relations, and Admissions offices.

"The old mascot (lion) was in need of a face-lift," noted Cheerleading Coach Melissa Hay. [70]

Women's Soccer Team Excels

In the fall of 2006, Methodist's women's soccer team, led by first year Head Coach Tony Tommasi, won the regular season USA South conference

Milo McBryde '68 presents Dr. Hendricks with the Alumni Association's Outstanding Faculty and Staff Award.

championship, lost a 3-2 shootout for the conference tournament championship game to Christopher Newport, and received an at-large bid to the NCAA-III National Soccer Tournament. The program swept the conference post-season awards, winning Coach, Player, and Rookie of the Year.

On November 11, the Lady Monarchs lost in the first round of the NCAA national tournament to Maryville 2-0, playing in Maryville, Tn. in rain and 35-degree weather.

— CHAPTER 10 —

In other fall sports news:

—Bob McEvoy, director of athletics, completed a two-year term as president of the USA South Athletic Conference, and a four-year term as South Region chair of the National NCAA III Men's Basketball Committee.

MUT Publishes Commemorative Edition

In December 2006, *Methodist University Today* published a commemorative edition with pictorial highlights of Methodist's 50th anniversary celebration and homecoming held October 27-November 5, 2006.

Winter 2006 Class Numbers 186

Methodist graduated 186 students December 16, 2006, the largest number in the school's history. Although Methodist was now a university, winter class members received "Methodist College" diplomas, and the baccalaureate and commencement programs for the 35th winter commencement retained the words "Methodist College."

Because the diplomas were already in production when the trustees voted October 28, 2006, to make Methodist a university, "Methodist College" was used one more time. Winter graduates were, however, given the opportunity to have their diplomas reprinted with "Methodist University" and the new MU seal on them.

Brian Whitcomb, president of the Professional Golfers Association of America, was the commencement speaker. In 2004, Whitcomb donated his time and services to help Methodist renovate its golf practice facility.

The PGA president dared the graduating seniors to dream and to follow their hearts. "The opportunities laid out in front of you are vast and wonderful," he said. "You've already given yourself the best chance to succeed." [71] Dr. Elton Hendricks, University president, awarded Whitcomb with a Methodist College Medallion. He also presented the Sam Edwards Award (for outstanding evening student of 2006) to Michael Carrion.

The Rev. Dr. John Tyson Jr., pastor of Fayetteville's Hay Street United Methodist Church, delivered the morning baccalaureate sermon, entitled "Wrestling God."

Gifts to MU Exceed $3.8 Million

Calendar 2006 was a record-breaking year for gifts to Methodist, as noted in the Spring 2007 *Methodist College Today*, which contained the annual giving report for 2006.

Total giving to Methodist hit $3,852,996 in 2006, bolstered by a $1 million gift from the Davis United World College Scholars Program (providing

2001-2006

Bob and Betty Jones '69 look at old yearbooks on Founders Day.

Dr. Colonnese welcomes class visitors at Founders Day Open House.

Dr. Michael Potts (L) admires art at the Alumni Art Exhibit.

scholarships to 27 international students at MU) and a $1 million gift from the Thomas R. and Elizabeth E. McLean Foundation for the Science Building addition.

In addition, Methodist received large gifts from:

—trustee Ramon Yarborough, who offered a challenge gift of $200,000 toward the *Seeds on Good Soil* campaign, if his fellow trustees would pledge an additional $800,000. The other trustees met his challenge.

—Howard and Marta Bullard of Fayetteville to endow a science and religion lecture series.

—$100,000 from the Thomas R. and Elizabeth E. McLean Foundation to establish the Elizabeth E. McLean Endowed Professorship in the area of English and writing. The late Mrs. McLean was a graduate of Vassar College who greatly valued education. (Dr. Emily Wright, professor of English, was later named the first McLean Professor of English.)

—Dr. Louis Spilman Jr. '64, who made a gift of appreciated stock to complete funding for the Dr. Louis Spilman, Jr. Endowed Scholarship in Religion.

—George Armstrong '68 and his wife Carolyn gave $69,000 to provide stadium lights for the baseball field. The College provided another $50,000 to fund the project. [In 2007, what had been known as Shelley Field became Armstrong-Shelley Field.]

Campaign Yields $14.7 Million

As the *Seeds on Good Soil, A New Season* campaign concluded in late 2006, Methodist University President Elton Hendricks noted with pride that the campaign had raised the largest amount in the school's history—$14,739,839.

"It would not have been possible to raise this amount of money without the leadership of Bob Allen and Ramon Yarborough, as well as a strong Board of Trustees who gave a significant amount of the total raised," said Dr. Hendricks.[72]

A final report for the campaign, which appeared in the 2006 Annual Giving Report (Spring 2007) issue of *Methodist University Today*, noted that 2,857 individuals, corporations, and foundations contributed to the campaign, including 1,385 Methodist alumni and former students. For the first time in the school's history, Methodist received four $1 million gifts, including two from philanthropist Shelby M.C. Davis and his foundation to fund scholarships for international students.

2001-2006

A Fayetteville Symphony concert November 3 premiered a work by Dr. Keith Dippre.

Diners at the 50th Anniversary Banquet watch a video about the school's founding.

Gene Clayton gives a MC trivia quiz.

The elegant banquet included ice sculptures and a 50th birthday cake.

The $14.7 million was allocated as follows: $7,638,726 to build and equip the Nimocks Fitness Center and the Science Building, $4,638,726 to the endowment, $1,564,578 to annual support, and $1,591,585 to "other restricted (annual scholarships, *etc.*)." [73]

Where did the $14.7 million come from? A total of $6,601,018 came from the Board of Trustees. Other principal sources were:
—friends, $3,079,150
—corporations, $2,641,000
—foundations $1,063,834.
—The United Methodist Church, $450,245.
—Alumni and former students, $385,618.
—Current and former faculty and staff, $361,637.
—North Carolina Independent Colleges and Universities, $100,361.
—Current and former parents, $56,973. [74]

Trustees Grant Tenure to New Academic Dean

In November 2006, the Methodist University Board of Trustees voted to grant tenure to Dr. Delmas S. Crisp Jr. as a professor of English. On November 21, 2006, President Hendricks appointed Dr. Crisp the new vice president for academic affairs, effective June 1, 2007. The new dean succeeded Dr. Phillip C. Williams, who resigned from Methodist in the summer of 2006 to become president of the University of Montevallo, Ala.

Dr. Crisp was the academic dean at Wesleyan College in Macon, Georgia, where he had previously served as chair of the Division of Humanities and Fuller E. Calloway Professor of English. He received his B.A., M.A. and Ph.D. from the University of Southern Mississippi, where he specialized in linguistics and British Medievel and Renaissance literature.

At the time of Dr. Crisp's appointment, Dr. Wenda Johnson was serving as interim academic dean; she agreed to become associate vice president for academic affairs upon the new dean's arrival. [After Dr. Johnson died suddenly in March 2007, Jane Weeks Gardiner was named associate vice president for academic affairs.]

Trustees Approve Golf Course Purchase

After considerable discussion December 19, 2006, the Methodist University Board of Trustees approved the purchase of a 51 percent interest in the nearby King's Grant golf course for $1.4 million. The 153-acre course was seen as a second learning laboratory for the school's 300 golf management students, in addition to the University golf course.

The sale closed in January 2007, with members of King's Grant using membership fees to buy a 49 percent interest in the course. Wachovia Bank provided financing for MU in the form of a 15-year loan. King's Grant Golf Management, LLC, a subsidiary of Methodist University created to manage the course, hired a manager, golf professional, and several others to operate and maintain the course.

President Hendricks said MU was fortunate that the golf course at King's Grant became available at a time when Methodist had won PGA approval to increase its PGM enrollment from 300 to 400 students. [75]

King's Grant Golf and Country Club

— CHAPTER 10 —

END NOTES
Chapter Ten

1. Jane Smith Patterson, speech, February 19, 2001, *Methodist College Today*, Summer 2001, file.
2. Bruce Stanley, speech, February 19, 2001, *Methodist College Today*, Summer 2001, file.
3. Margaret Wortheim, lecture, March 23, 2001, *Methodist College Today*, Summer 2001, file.
4. Tommy Herndon, baccalaureate sermon, May 5, 2001, *Methodist College Today*. Summer 2001, file.
5. Benjamin Dunlap, commencement address, May 5, 2001, *Methodist College Today*, Summer 2001, file.
6. William Jordan, speech at mentoring luncheon, September 6, 2001, *Methodist College Today*, Fall 2001, file.
7. Ibid.
8. Imam Adam Beyah, forum, October 1, 2001, *Methodist College Today*, Fall 2001, file.
9. Gene Clayton, remarks at homecoming luncheon, October 26, 2001, *Methodist College Today*, Winter 2001, file.
10. Ibid.
11. Mason Sykes, remarks at homecoming luncheon, October 26, 2001, *Methodist College Today*, Winter 2001, file.
12. Wesley F. Brown, commencement address, December 14, 2001, *Methodist College Today*, Winter 2001, file.
13. Ibid.
14. Brian Gentle, baccalaureate sermon, December 14, 2001, *Methodist College Today*, Winter 2001, file.
15. Master's degree candidates in the physician assistant program, interviewed for a news story, January 31, 2002, *Methodist College Today*, Spring 2002, file.
16. Marshall Pitts, Jr., convocation speaker, February 4, 2002, *Methodist College Today*, Summer 2002, file.
17. Ibid.
18. Ibid.
19. Spencer Davis, lecture, March 7, 2002, *Methodist College Today*, Summer 2002, file.
20. Brian Gentle, Pastors' Day lecture, March 4, 2002, *Methodist College Today*, Summer 2002, file.
21. Ibid.

22. Ramon Yarborough, press conference, May 2, 2002, *Methodist College Today*, Summer 2002, file.
23. M. Elton Hendricks, press conference, May 2, 2002, *Methodist College Today*, Summer 2002, file.
24. Phillip J. Kirk, Jr., commencement address, May 11, 2002, *Methodist College Today*, Summer 2002, file.
25. Ibid.
26. Marion M. Edwards, baccalaureate sermon, May 11, 2002, *Methodist College Today*, Summer 2002, file.
27. M. Elton Hendricks, Vision Statement, October 18, 2002, *Methodist College Today*, Fall 2002, file.
28. Ibid.
29. Sid Gautam, remarks at industry appreciation luncheon, September 26, 2002, *Methodist College Today*, Fall 2002, file.
30. Cynthia Curtis, public relations director, quoted in a news story *The Fayetteville Observer*, November 15, 2002, file.
31. Brett Friedlander, news story, *The Fayetteville Observer*, November 22, 2002, file.
32. Kent Murphy, quoted in news story, *The Fayetteville Observer*, December 15, 2002, file.
33. M. Elton Hendricks, report to Methodist College trustees, May 15, 2003, TM, Book 6.
34. Kent Murphy, quoted in news story, *The Fayetteville Observer*, April 2, 2004, file.
35. Michael W. Safley, commencement address, December 13, 2002, *Methodist College Today*, Winter 2002, file.
36. Camille Yorkey, baccalaureate sermon, December 13, 2002, *Methodist College Today*, Winter 2002, file.
37. Ibid.
38. M. Elton Hendricks, report to Board of Trustees, May 15, 2003, TM. Book 6.
39. Harvey Adams, quoted in news story, *The Fayetteville Observer*, June 30, 2003, file.
40. Cynthia Curtis, public relations director, quoted in news story, *The Fayetteville Observer*, June 30, 2003, file.
41. Mary McDuffie, commencement address, May 10, 2003, *Methodist College Today*, Summer 2003, file.
42. William Simpson, baccalaureate speaker, May 10, 2003, *Methodist College Today*, Summer 2003, file.

— CHAPTER 10 —

43. Loleta Wood Foster, commencement address, December 12, 2003, *Methodist College Today*, Winter/Spring 2004, file.
44. Raymond Gooch, baccalaureate sermon, December 12, 2003, *Methodist College Today*, Winter/Spring 2004, file.
45. Congressman Mike Mc Intyre, commencement address, February 10, 2004, *Methodist College Today*, Winter/Spring 2004, file.
46. Hugh Shelton, commencement address, May 8, 2004, *Methodist College Today*, Winter/Spring 2004, file.
47. Ibid.
48. Ibid.
49. Woodrow W. Wells, baccalaureate sermon, May 8, 2004, *Methodist College Today*, Winter/Spring 2004, file.
50. Dick Player, trustees chair, written statement to Board of Trustees, October 21, 2004, TM, Book 6.
51. Resolution, Methodist College Board of Trustees, October 21, 2004, TM, Book 6.
52. Linda Gravitt, assistant dean, quoted in news story, *Methodist College Today*, Fall 2004, file.
53. Bob Mc Evoy, quoted in news story, *Methodist College Today*, Fall 2004, file.
54. Elaine Marshall, commencement address, December 10, 2004, *Methodist College Today*, Fall 2004, file.
55. Reginald Ponder, baccalaureate sermon, December 10, 2004, *Methodist College Today*, Fall 2004, file.
56. M. Elton Hendricks, news story, *Methodist College Today*, Winter 2005, file.
57. James M. Link, news story, *Methodist College Today*, Winter 2005, file.
58. Alumni survey, *Methodist College Today*, Summer 2005, file.
59. Vici Pate, quoted in news story, *Methodist College Today*, Summer 2005, file.
60. Congressman Bob Etheridge, commencement address, May 7, 2005, *Methodist College Today*, Summer 2005, file.
61. Bruce Steffes, commencement address, December 17, 2005, *Methodist College Today*, Spring 2006, file.
62. Ibid.
63. Mike McIntyre, commencement speaker, May 6, 2006, *Methodist College Today*, Summer 2006, file.
64. Ibid.

65. Alfred Gwinn, baccalaureate sermon, May 6, 2006, *Methodist College Today*, Summer 2006, file.
66. Alfred Cleveland, trustees chair, news story, October 28, 2006, *Methodist College Today*, Winter 2006, file.
67. M. Elton Hendricks, news story, *Methodist College Today*, Winter 2006, file.
68. F. Belton Joyner, convocation address on the 50th anniversary of Methodist College receiving its charter, Novembr 1, 2006, text, file.
69. Ibid.
70. Melissa Hay, cheerleading coach, quoted in news story, *Methodist College Today*, Fall 2006, file.
71. Brian Whitcomb, commencement address, October 28, 2006, quoted in a news story, *The Fayetteville Observer*, December 17, 2006, file.
72. M. Elton Hendricks, *Methodist College Today*, Spring 2007, file.
73. News story, *Methodist College Today*, Spring 2007, file.
74. Ibid.
75. M. Elton Hendricks, remarks to the Methodist University Board of Trustees, December 19, 2006, TM, Book 6.

"Elevated Visions," a sculpture which now stands in front of Reeves Auditorium, was presented to Methodist in September 2007 by Dr. Gerald Ellison and Mrs. Naomi Ellison. The Ellisons commissioned Michael Baker of Salisbury, N.C., to create the work.

Epilogue: MU's Future

> "I am impressed that Methodist has embraced change and is remaining relevant to today's students. Tradition is a touchstone for an institution, but tradition unburdened by progress is a recipe for irrelevance. The college must not be satisfied with the status quo. As we say in Alabama, the sky is NOT the limit."
>
> —retired Army Lt. Gen. James M. Link '66, during a visit to Methodist College in December 2004.

About twenty years ago, I prepared a newspaper ad for the Methodist College Foundation's Annual Loyalty Fund Drive. The ad was headlined with a quote attributed to Robert F. Kennedy: "Some men see things as they are and ask 'Why?' I dream things that never were and ask 'Why not?'"

A few days after the ad appeared, an Irish student named Mike D'Arcy told the academic dean, "Kennedy didn't say that. That was George Bernard Shaw!" After the dean relayed D'Arcy's comment to me, I set out to see who said what.

Yes, Shaw was the original author. Kennedy changed Shaw's second person, originally "You see things. . .," to the third person, "Some men see things . . . ," and the phrase became Robert's trademark. Ted Kennedy cited the phrase in the eulogy he gave at Robert's funeral. The words are now attributed more to Robert Kennedy than to George Bernard Shaw.

For those of us who came of age in the 1960s, these words about dreams were a fitting mantra. They embodied our sense of idealism and the belief that "baby boomers" could change the world. We were looking for heroes, and even after JFK, MLK, and RFK were assassinated, we continued to look. Like the founders of Methodist College (University), we wanted to be led in the right direction.

In the 50 years since Methodist College was established, some remarkable things have happened. Americans put a man on the moon and broke down the walls of racial injustice. A global village, linked by television, satellites, and the Internet emerged. The Iron Curtain was lifted and the Berlin Wall torn down. Dreams came true!

So what do the leaders of Methodist University dream for the future? The Methodist College Strategic Plan for 2005-10, adopted by the Board of Trustees at a planning retreat in May 2005, offers a few hints. This plan has five priorities:

First priority—Analyze and develop new academic programs. Examples cited include nursing programs, a program in Christian youth leadership, certificate programs for physician assistants (including one in tropical medicine), and a master's degree in education. Also to be studied is the possible expansion of MU at Night to off-campus sites.

Second priority—Identify new sources of revenue, including a program of planned and deferred giving, additional income from leasing and other non-academic business activities, and campaigns targeting endowment growth.

Third priority—Upgrade and, where necessary, expand existing infrastructure according to a five-year schedule of capital projects to be developed by the Buildings and Grounds Committee of the Board of Trustees.

Fourth priority—Establish an objective assessment system for the purpose of evaluating and improving the effectiveness of all academic, athletic, student life and administrative programs and the performance of all personnel. Special attention shall be focused upon the identification of factors that could lead to a more satisfying campus life experience for students, thereby aiding in retention.

Fifth priority—Commission a marketing study to determine the advantages and disadvantages of the "Methodist College" name and whether university status should be reflected in the name.

The strategic plan includes a series of benchmark dates, by which some studies will be completed and some actions taken. Progress on the plan was recently assessed as part of the self-study process for reaffirmation of accreditation by the Southern Association of Colleges and Schools.

In a recent interview, University President Elton Hendricks said Methodist needs to build its endowment to $100,000 per student or about $200 million. At five percent annual interest, he said a $200 million endowment would generate $5,000 annually toward the cost of educating each student.

In the year 2025, Dr. Hendricks envisions a Methodist University of 2,500-3,000 students, "with more undergraduate innovation and a few more graduate programs."

Of four major building projects now in the final planning stages, the president said, "I only have the money for the art building (William F. Bethune Center for the Visual Arts)." That center will cost $2.2 million.

Other buildings now planned include a football field house (2009), lab and lecture hall buildings for the physician assistant program (price tag: $2.5 million), and a world ministry center (to replace Hensdale Chapel). About five years ago, the school's Institute for Golf, Tennis, and Resort Management was authorized to raise funds for a two-wing expansion of the Richard L. Player Golf and Tennis Learning Center.

A long range master plan for the campus (see Appendix J J) developed in 1994, envisions construction of a conference center, an addition to the Berns Student Center, an addition to Horner Administration Building, and a small cultural arts center or theatre. All these projects will require millions of dollars, funds raised through gifts or borrowing or a combination of both.

If the past 25 years are a harbinger of things to come, Methodist University has a bright future ahead of it. I believe the history of our school's first 50 years shows first and foremost that God is with us and always has been. Those of us who studied here owe much to the administrators, faculty, and friends who have made our school what it is today, overcoming many obstacles and hardships. Our world is a better place because of their efforts.

As I reflect upon the rich history of Methodist University, I rejoice that so many of its staff, students, and faculty have made the quest for excellence a lifelong credo. To the extent that this school has inspired and challenged people to "be the best they can be," it has succeeded beyond the wildest dreams of its founders.

As Ralph Waldo Emerson once wrote, "Nothing great was ever achieved without enthusiasm."

—WHB

On the Horizon

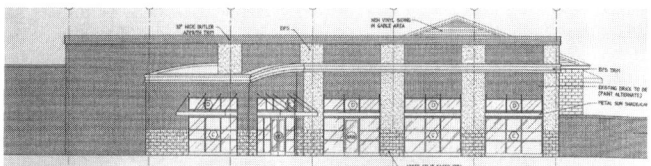
Football Field House / Conversion of Old Boiler Plant Building

William F. Bethune Center for the Visual Arts

PA Lab Building   *Medical Lecture Hall*

World Ministry Center

Expansion of Richard L. Player Golf and Tennis Learning Center

About the Author

William Harmond "Bill" Billings, a native of Durham, N.C., has worked at Methodist University since 1987—15 years as director of public relations and the last five years as college/university historian and director of Monarch Press, the college/university print shop. He has also taught freshman English in Methodist's evening and weekend program.

He graduated from Methodist College in 1968 with a B.A. in English and taught junior and senior high school English in Chesterfield County, Virginia and Cumberland, Durham, and Person counties in North Carolina. He earned a M.A. in journalism from The University of North Carolina at Chapel Hill in 1974. After that, he worked eight years as a newspaper editor, reporter, and feature writer, first in Louisburg, N.C. and later in Roxboro, N.C.

He lives in Fayetteville with his wife, Cynthia. His principal avocations are music (listening, singing, playing keyboards), attending cultural events, photography, traveling to new places, and vacationing with his wife, stepchildren and stepgrandchildren. He is an active member of Hay Street United Methodist Church, where he sings in the chancel choir.

Never at a loss for words, Bill enjoys people and frankly admits he can "talk the horns off a billy goat." He describes working at Methodist University as "both a joy and a blessing."

Appendices

A	Charter Members of the Fayetteville College Foundation
B	Terry Sanford Biography
C	Bishop Paul Garber Biography
D	Certificate of Incorporation
E	Topographic Map, Methodist College Campus
F	Plan for Ultimate Enrollment by William Davis
G	L. Stacy Weaver Biography
H	Cost Estimates for Methodist College Buildings
I	Architect's Site Plan for Methodist College
J	Methodist College Milestones
K	Eulogy for John F. Kennedy by Dr. Samuel J. Womack/
L	Inaugural Address of Dr. L. Stacy Weaver
M	Honorary Degree Recipients
N	Methodist College Medallion Recipients
O	Stacy Weaver Award Winners
P	Sam Edwards Award Winners
Q	Alumni Association Distinguished Alumni Awards
R	Alumni Association Outstanding Alumni Service Awards
S	Alumni Association Outstanding Faculty/Staff Awards
T	Student Government Association Presidents
U	Athletic Hall of Fame Members
V	Sykes Cup Winners
W	Business Award Winners
X	Alumni Association Presidents
Y	Foundation Presidents
Z	*Tapestry* Editors
AA	Student Newspaper Editors
BB	*Carillon* Editors
CC	Lowdermilk Student Achievement Award Winners
DD	2006 Annual Report
EE	2006 Freshman Profile
FF	Alcohol Policy (1973)
GG	Computing Milestones at Methodist College
HH	Methodist College Board of Trustees, 2006-07
II	Board of Trustees Members, 1956-2000
JJ	1994 Master Plan for Campus J
KK	Growth of Methodist University / Hendricks Era

— APPENDICES —

APPENDIX A

Charter Members of the Fayetteville College Foundation
(June 22, 1956)

Officers
Franklin S. Clark, President
Wilbur Clark, 1st Vice President
D. P. Russ, 2nd Vice President
Norman Suttles, Secretary
Mel Thompson, Treasurer

Mrs. Harry Stein	Richard E. Taylor
Thomas Hood	Mrs. V. F. Tally, Jr.
Alton Murchison	Dr. C. F. Siewers
J. W. Pate, Jr.	Dr. W. E. Howie
John Ormsby	Dr. Walker B. Healy
Bernard Stein	The Rev. Henry F. Speight, Jr.
Mrs. J. O. Tally, Jr.	The Rev. Lloyd O. Barker
Mrs. George Tinning	Jack McArthur
Roscoe Blue	Vick Dawson
Charles Warren	Ralph Hess
Nathan Fleishman	Ed Edgerton
John Hensdale	W. C. Holland
Tom McLean	R. D. Buie
Ed Brower	W. F. Griffin
Billy Godwin	George Herndon
R. M. Lilly	F. D. Byrd
Arthur Moore	C. Reid Ross
Hector McKethan	Mrs. B. T. Williams
F. M. Averitt	I. B. Julian
Tildon Walker	Billy Huske
Mrs. C. Wallace Jackson	William Smith
Mrs. Dan Currie, Jr.	Bill Bailey
Mrs. Floyd Souders	E. S. Bosher
Charlie Rose	Mrs. W. T. Rainey
Bert Ishee	Mrs. Elizabeth Ellis
Joe Stout	L. P. Crispell
J. D. Kinlaw	J. T. Pharr

APPENDIX B
Terry Sanford
1917-1998

Terry Sanford, the first chairman of the Methodist College Board of Trustees, was born in Laurinburg, N.C., the son of Cecil L. Sanford and Elizabeth Martin Sanford. He earned his A.B. degree in 1939 and his law degree in 1946 from the University of North Carolina at Chapel Hill.

Sanford was a special agent in the F.B.I. from 1941-1942 when he enlisted in the U.S. Army. He served in the 501st Parachute Infantry Regiment and the 517th Parachute Combat Team from 1943-45. He saw action in five European campaigns and was awarded the Bronze Star and the Purple Heart.

From 1946-48, Sanford was assistant director of the Institute of Government at the University of North Carolina at Chapel Hill. While engaged in the practice of law, he was a partner in the law firms of Rose and Sanford from 1949-57; Sanford, Phillips, McCoy and Weaver from 1958-60; Sanford, Adams, McCullough and Beard from 1965-86; and Sanford and Holshouser from 1993-98.

In 1956, when Sanford was a young lawyer in Fayetteville, N.C., he was enlisted by the Presbyterian College Steering Committee to help secure a new Presbyterian college for Fayetteville. When Fayetteville lost its bid for the new Presbyterian college (now St. Andrews Presbyterian) to Laurinburg in March 1956, Sanford and other civic leaders reorganized as the Fayetteville College Steering Committee and asked people who had pledged to the Presbyterian College campaign to lend their support to the campaign for a Methodist college. Pledges of $1.7 million and 577 acres of land just north of Fayetteville were then offered to the North Carolina Conference of The Methodist Church. The Conference accepted Fayetteville's bid at a special session in Goldsboro May 14, 1956.

An active Methodist layman and a member of Fayetteville's Hay Street Methodist Church, Sanford was present Nov. 1, 1956, at the State Capitol in Raleigh when Secretary of State Thad Eure signed the charter creating Methodist College, Inc. He served as chairman of the Methodist College Board of Trustees from 1956-67 and remained a trustee until 1993.

A lifelong Democrat, Sanford was president of the North Carolina Young Democrats in 1949 and managed Kerr Scott's campaign for the U.S. Senate in 1954. He served North Carolina in the state Senate (1952-54), as governor (1960-64), and as United State senator (1986-92). He was a delegate to the Democratic National Convention in 1956 and sought the Democratic nomination for president of the United States in 1972.

In 1962, while he was governor of North Carolina, Sanford secured passage by the N.C. General Assembly of a state sales tax which gave impetus to the state's community college system and allowed him to make good on his promise to North Carolina youngsters: "If you have the will and the skill, we (the state) will help you find a way to attend college." Because the sales tax was collected on food and medicine, Sanford was branded by some Tar Heels as "Termite Terry." Continuing his educational entrepreneurship, Governor Sanford established the North Carolina School of the Arts in Winston-Salem, the Governor's School (a summer enrichment program for talented high school juniors sited in Winston-Salem and Laurinburg), and the Learning Institute of North Carolina.

It was at a Methodist College Founder's Day convocation in November 1966 that Sanford first proposed state grants to assist North Carolina residents who wanted to attend one of the state's independent colleges or universitites. The first such grants were awarded in 1972-73. Today, North Carolina residents attending Methodist or one of the state's 35 other independent colleges or universities on a fulltime basis receive a North Carolina Legislative Tuition Grant worth nearly $2,000 per year; many also receive state-funded contractual scholarships.

Terry Sanford was president of Duke University from 1970-85. During his tenure at Duke, the Medical Center doubled its capacity, the Fuqua School of Business was constructed, and the university endowment increased from $70 million to $200 million.

Sanford published several books, including *But What About the People?*, *Storm Over the States*, and *Outlive Your Enemies*. He was an active member of the Veterans of Foreign Wars, Shriners, Masons, Fayetteville Chamber of Commerce, and the Children's Home Society of North Carolina.

Some of Sanford's political stands were not popular. In the late 1960s, he encouraged college students across the state as they sought repeal of North Carolina's "Speaker Ban Law," a bill the state legislature had enacted to prevent Communists from speaking on UNC campuses. In 1991, the former U. S. Army paratrooper spoke out in the U.S. Senate against American involvement in the Persian Gulf War.

Sanford maintained his interest in and support of Methodist College throughout his lifetime. In the late 1980s and the mid-1990s, he was honorary chair of the College's "Come of Age" and "Expanding the Vision" fund drives. In May 1989, Sanford, then a U.S. Senator, delivered the spring commencement address at Methodist and visited with members of the College's first class, the Class of 1964, at their 25th reunion.

When the Methodist College Alumni Association staged a 40th birthday convocation for the College Oct. 30, 1996, Sanford was the guest of honor and seemed to thoroughly enjoy the retrospective review of the College's first 40 years. In March 1997, Sanford was one of three persons who eulogized Stacy Weaver, Methodist's founding president, during Weaver's funeral at Hay Street United Methodist Church in Fayetteville. In 1997 and 1998, Terry and Margaret Rose Sanford made two major gifts to Methodist College.

Several months after undergoing a heart valve replacement and losing his bid for re-election to the U.S. Senate, Sanford was honored by his Fayetteville friends at an appreciation dinner/tribute sponsored by the Cumberland County Democratic Party. Held March 30, 1993, at the Charlie Rose Agri-Expo Center, the event drew more than 1,000 persons. On that occasion, the Rev. Bill Lowdermilk, vice president for church and community relations at Methodist, presented Sanford with a Methodist College windbreaker and a large framed collage of photos of Methodist College milestones in which Sanford had been involved. Entitled "Portrait of a Visionary," an exact replica of the collage now hangs outside the Special Collections Room of the College's Davis Memorial Library.

Terry Sanford died of cancer April 18, 1998, at his home in Durham, N.C. He was 80 years old. He was survived by his wife, Margaret Rose Knight; his children, Terry Sanford, Jr. and Betsee Sanford; two grandchildren; and his sisters, Mary Glenn Rose of Wyndover, Pennsylvania, and Helen Wilhelm of Berne, Switzerland.

Sanford's funeral at Duke University Chapel was "the Methodist funeral" he wanted, with several of his favorite hymns and eulogies by some of his oldest friends. It was also a celebration of a life well-lived, a life of public service and devotion to education that was extraordinary in the annals of this state.

—*WHB*

NOTE: In 1965, the Methodist College Board of Trustees honored Terry Sanford by naming its second residence hall for men Sanford Hall. A commemorative plaque in the lobby of Sanford Hall reads: "This building is dedicated in honor of Terry Sanford, first chairman of the Board of Trustees, Governor of North Carolina 1960-64, educational stateman."

APPENDIX C

Bishop Paul Neff Garber
1899-1972

Paul Neff Garber was elected bishop of the Richmond Area of The Methodist Church in 1951. At that time, the North Carolina Conference was part of the Richmond Area. In 1964, Garber was assigned to the newly-created Raleigh Area; he thus presided over the North Carolina Conference for 17 years, from 1951-1968. After his retirement in 1968, he and his wife Nina returned to Geneva, under the assignment of the Council of Bishops of what had just become The United Methodist Church, to write the history of European Methodism. He died there Dec. 19, 1972 at the age of 73.

A native of New Market, Virginia, Garber received the A.B. degree from Bridgewater College, the M.A. and Ph.D. degrees from the University of Pennsylvania, and did post graduate work at Crozer Theological Seminary. He held honorary degrees from several institutions of higher learning. He was ordained to the ministry in the Western North Carolina Conference of The Methodist Episcopal Church South in 1926.

From 1926 until 1944, Garber held several different positions. He was assistant professor of history, registrar, and dean at Duke University's School of Religion, now known as Duke University Divinity School. Before coming to Duke, he was an instructor of history at the University of Pennsylvania and Brown University. From 1944-1951, he served as bishop of the Geneva Area of The Methodist Church, made up of ten countries in Europe and North Africa.

In the 1973 Journal of the North Carolina Conference of The United Methodist Church, the Rev. Chancie Barclift wrote a memorial tribute to Paul Garber. Excerpts from that tribute follow:

> "The phrases 'the Garber era' and 'the miracle conference of American Methodism' are not misnomers but are quite appropriate for his tenure of leadership and service. Many statistics justify these epithets. The following data give full credence to same. The number of pastoral charges increased 88 percent; the church membership 23 percent; and total money raised 152 percent. The Retirement Home in Durham and the Headquarters Building in Raleigh were built; several camps across the conference were developed; and other advances, too numerous to detail, were made. In fact, he fully

supported every area of the work of the Church, but the two outstanding emphases of his leadership were Christian Higher Education and Church Extension. He gave encouragement and guidance to the establishment of two new colleges, Methodist College in Fayetteville and North Carolina Wesleyan College in Rocky Mount, and to the expansion of Louisburg College in Louisburg.

Approximately eighty new churches were organized during his administration. Not all of these churches have grown as expectation projected, but most of them are on a solid growth basis and many of them are now strong churches. Doubtless, it would be well within the bounds of truth to say that no bishop in modern Methodism officiated at more ceremonies for groundbreaking, cornerstone laying, consecration and dedication of church buildings than did Bishop Garber while presiding over the Richmond and Raleigh Areas.

[. . .] He was an eminent church historian, who not only studied and taugh the history of the church in all of its details and drama, but, what is more important, through his love of the church and his labors in it, he made church history by adding to her long line of spendor many chapters rich in achievements and abounding in kingdom fruits.

He had a positive outlook on life and preached and practiced contagious optimism and hopefulness. He often quoted the late Dr. William Preston Few, a lontime president of Trinity College and Duke University, as saying, 'If one has a good cause, somebody will help him.' History validates the truth of this dictum.

He had a strong body and his energy seemed unlimited. He scarcely ever had a physical ailment. Great was his stamina for work and, like John Wesley, he and leisure parted company early in life. He had a spartan discipline for mental and physical toil.

[. . .] Of a humble spirit, he was readily accessible and approachable. All felt at ease in his presence. When preachers and laymen talked to him about appointments, they left the meeting feeling that their desires and requests would be granted, if he could possibly do so [. . .] He was unusually patient and had a large measure of kindness [. . .] He was uncommonly generous in giving of his finances to needy individuals and good causes, even to the extent of denying himself.

He loved people and found much pleasure in being and working with them. In fact, most of the illustrations in his sermons had to do with persons he had known and with whom he had worked in many parts of the world. He was beloved by minsters and laymen alike for his brotherly spirit and his unfailing graciousness [. . .] His usual salutation to a congregation was 'my dear brothersand sisters.'

[. . .] His love for his Saviour was genuinely expressed in words and deeds.He lived in the contemplation of the immensities of the greatness of God.

[. . .] If we would see his monument in the North Carolina Conference, weneed only to look around us and across the conference at the accomplishments ofhis dedicated labors among us."

NOTE: In 1964, the Methodist College Board of Trustees honored Bishop Paul Garber by naming its first residence hall for women Garber Hall. A commemorative plaque in the lobby of Garber Hall reads: "This building is dedicated in honor of Paul Neff Garber, bishop of The Methodist Church, whose vision, courageous leadership, and devotion to the cause of Christian higher education led to the establishment of this institution." Garber United Methodist Church in New Bern, N.C. is also named for Paul Garber.

— APPENDICES —

APPENDIX D

Certificate Of Incoporation Of Mehodist College, Incorporated

This is to certify that we, the undersigned, hereby associate ourselves into a corporation under and by virtue of the laws of the State of North Carolina for such purpose made and provided, and do severally agree to become members thereof; and to that end do hereby execute this certificate of incorporation in manner and form as follows:

ARTICLE I

The name of this corporation is Methodist College, Incorporated.

ARTICLE II

The principal office of this corporation is at the City of Fayetteville, in the County of Cumberland, in the State of North Carolina.

ARTICLE III

The objects for which this corporation is formed are to establish, maintain and operate at Fayetteville, Cumberland County, North Carolina, a co-educational institution of collegiate grade to be known as Methodist College, under the control and direction of the North Carolina Conference, Southeastern Jurisdiction, subject to the appropriate provisions of the Discipline of the Methodist Church.

ARTICLE IV

In order properly to prosecute said objects, this corporation shall have full power and authority to purchase, lease, and otherwise acquire, hold mortgage, sell, convey and otherwise dispose of, all kinds of property, both real and personal; to borrow money; to construct, equip and maintain buildings, works and plants; to install, maintain and operate all kinds of machinery and appliances; and generally to perform all acts which may be deemed necessary or expedient for the proper and successful prosecution of the objects for which this corporation is formed.

ARTICLE V

This corporation shall have no capital stock. Through its Board of Trustees, hereinafter provided, this corporation shall be conducted and operated as a non-profit corporation, for the purpose of Christian higher education and to extend the influence of science, art, and Christian culture.

The members of this corporation shall be The Board of Trustees of this corporation as constituted from time to time as hereinafter provided.

The original Board of Trustees shall be and they are the Incorporators of this corporation; and their names and addresses and the expiration dates of their terms of office as Trustees are as follows:

ARTICLE VI

Subject to the control and direction of the North Carolina Conference, Southeastern Jurisdiction, the Methodist Church, as hereinafter more fully set forth, the business and affairs of this corporation shall be vested in, administered and managed by the Trustees of Methodist College, Incorporated.

There shall be twenty-four trustees. At least one-fourth of these shall be ministerial members of the North Carolina Conference, Southeastern Jurisdiction, the Methodist Church; at least one-fourth shall be residents of Cumberland County; and at least three-fourths shall be members of the Methodist Church. Trustees may succeed themselves. All trustees shall serve until their successors are elected.

The trustees shall be divided into four classes of six members each, whose term of office shall expire respectively, July 1, 1957, July 1, 1958, July 1, 1959, July 1, 1960.

ARTICLE VII

Upon the expiration of the term of office of each class, the Board of Education of the North Carolina Conference, Southeastern Jurisdiction, and Methodist Church, after consultation with the nominating committee of the Board of Trustees, shall nominate their successors to serve for a period of four years or until their successors are elected, and submit the names of persons nominated to the North Carolina Conference, Southeastern Jurisdiction, of said church for election or rejection.

— APPENDICES —

The North Carolina Conference, Southeastern Jurisdiction, the Methodist Church, shall have power at any time, by a majority vote of its members to remove from office any trustee.

Should there exist a vacancy by death, resignation, or otherwise, of any trustee, the same shall be filled for the unexpired term in the same manner described above for the election of trustees, provided persons so nominated by the Board of Education of the North Carolina Conference, Southeastern Jurisdiction, shall exercise all powers conferred under these articles of incorporation until they have been either elected of rejected by the said Conference of the Methodist Church.

All members of this Board of Trustees shall be at least twenty-one years of age.

ARTICLE VIII

The said Board of Trustees shall administer the affairs of this corporation and conduct its business in trust for the Methodist Church and subject to the will, control and direction of the North Carolina Conference, Southeastern Jurisdiction of the said church, or any committee or agency to which the said conference delegates this authority; provided however, said Board of Trustees shall have full power to see, convey, mortgage or otherwise dispose of any of the real estate owned by this corporation upon consent and permission of the executive committee of the Board of Education of the said church.

ARTICLE IX

This corporation is authorized to solicit, acquire and receive real and personal property by purchase, gift, devise or otherwise, and to hold and to administer such property for the benefit of Methodist College, Incorporated, and in accordance with the uses and trusts, if any, declared in any and all conveyances or other instruments under which such property is acquired. Specifically, this corporation is authorized to succeed to and own all property, real, personal, and mixed, tangible and intangible, and hold the title thereto, and to succeed to and own all rights, privileges and powers, including all powers necessary to administer all trust funds upon the uses and trusts declared in any will, deed or other instrument, and this corporation shall assume and be liable for the payment of all debts and liabilities of Methodist College, Incorporated, to the full extent authorized and provided and conferred upon this corporation by Chapter 55 of the General Statutes of North Carolina as amended, provided, however, that the Board of Trustees shall not in any way or manner be personally liable for any debts, obligations, or liabilities of Methodist College, Incorporated.

ARTICLE X

The said Board of Trustees shall have power to make rules, regulations and by-laws, not inconsistent with law and not inconsistent with the provisions hereof. The said Board of Trustees shall fix the time and place of holding their annual and other meetings and shall elect the following officers of this corporation, namely, a chairman of its Board of Trustees, a Secretary, a Treasurer, and such other officers as it may determine. Also the said Board of Trustees shall elect the faculty, including the President of Methodist College, Incorporated and such other employees as it may deem necessary. The said Board of Trustees shall annually elect, from members of said Board of Trustees, an executive Committee consisting of at least five and not more that nine members, which Executive Committee shall have the powers and shall perform the duties to be fixed by the by-laws not inconsistent with the charter. The President of Methodist College, Incorporated, shall be ex-officio a member of said Executive Committee.

ARTICLE XI

Twelve (12) trustees shall constitute a quorum for the transaction of business at any regular or called meetings of said Board of Trustees; and it shall be the duty of said Board of Trustees, or of its said Executive Committee, as shall be determined, to fix the salaries of the faculty and other employees, and to make all contracts and agreements necessary to the business and management of the corporation.

ARTICLE XII

The faculty of Methodist College, Incorporated, and the Board of Trustees of Methodist College, Incorporated, when licensed or authorized to do so under the laws of the State of North Carolina, shall have power to confer degrees and marks of honor such as are conferred by colleges and universities generally.

ARTICLE XIII

The said Board of Trustees shall have power to make, and from time to time, alter, such by-laws as it may deem necessary.

—APPENDICES—

ARTICLE XIV

The Division of Educational Institutions of the Board of Education of The Methodist Church shall have full visitorial privileges and powers as provided by the Discipline of the Methodist Church in respect to the corporation herein formed and in relation to the college operated under said corporation's management.

ARTICLE XV

The period of existence of this corporation is unlimited.

ARTICLE XVI

Amendments may be made to this charter which are not inconsistent with the principles as set forth in the preceding articles by a two-thirds vote of the
Board of Trustees and confirmation by the said North Carolina Conference. Such amendments must be executed in accordance with the procedure as set forth in the laws of North Carolina.

In Testimony Whereof, we, the said incorporators have hereunto set our hands and seals, this 27th day of September, 1956.

Mrs. E. L. Hillman	(SEAL)
Mrs. Earl W. Brian	(SEAL)
Vergil A. Queen	(SEAL)
W. A. Crow	(SEAL)
O. L. Hathaw	(SEAL)
Graham S. Eubank	(SEAL)
Lenox G. Cooper	(SEAL)
Frank McBryde	(SEAL)
W. Ed Fleishman	(SEAL)
W. Robert Johnson	(SEAL)
Wilson F. Yarborough	(SEAL)
Joe Talley, Jr.	(SEAL)
John R. Hodge	(SEAL)
J. M. Wilson	(SEAL)
W. L. Clegg	(SEAL)
Allen P. Brantley	(SEAL)
W. E. Horner	(SEAL)
Terry Sanford	(SEAL)
R. L. Pittman	(SEAL)

— APPENDICES—

L. Stacy Weaver	(SEAL)
J. W. Page	(SEAL)
J. Nelson Gibson, Jr.	(SEAL)
Dr. William M. Spence	(SEAL)
E. L. Sanders	(SEAL)

NORTH CAROLINA
CUMBERLAND COUNTY

I, Jean D. Nunalee, a Notary Public of said County and State do hereby certify that Mrs. E. L. Hillman, Mrs. Earl W. Brian, Vergil E. Queen, W. A. Crow, O. L. Hathaway, Graham S. Eubank, Lenox G. Cooper, Frank McBryde, W. Ed Fleishman, W. Robert Johnson, Wilson, F. Yarborough, Joe Tally, Jr., John R. Hodge, J. M. Wilson, W. L. Clegg, Allen P. Brantley, W. E. Horner, Terry Sanford, R. L. Pittman, L. Stacy Weaver, J. W. Page, J. Nelson Gibson, Jr., Dr. William M. Spence, E. L. Sanders personally appeared before me this day and acknowledged the due execution of the foregoing instrument.

Witness my hand and Notarial Seal, this the 26th day of October, 1956

Jean D. Nunalee

— APPENDICES —

TRUSTEES	ADDRESSES	EXPIRATION DATES OF TERMS OF OFFICE
J. M. Wilson	Fayetteville, N. C.	1 July 1957
Allen P. Brantley	503 Tarleton St. Burlington, N. C.	1 July 1957
W. Ed Fleishman	Fayetteville, N. C.	1 July 1957
William Spence	Elizabeth City, N. C.	1 July 1957
O. L. Hathaway	P. O. Box 2346 Fayetteville, N. C.	1 July 1957
Mrs. Earl W. Brian	2111 White Oak Road Raleigh, N. C.	1 July 1957
Wilson Yarborough	Fayetteville, N. C.	1 July 1958
W. A. Crow	Warrenton, N. C.	1 July 1958
John R. Hodge	Fayetteville, N. C.	1 July 1958
J. Nelson Gibson	Gibson, N. C.	1 July 1958
L. Stacy Weaver	1724 Vista St. Durham, N. C.	1 July 1958
W. Robert Johnson	1512 Evergreen Ave. Goldsboro, N. C.	1 July 1958
Vergil E. Queen	1516 Market St. Wilmington, N. C.	1 July 1959
Joe Tally, Jr.	Fayetteville, N. C.	1 July 1959
Jack W. Page	117 Brooks Ave. Raleigh, N. C.	1 July 1959
Frank McBryde	Fayetteville, N. C.	1 July 1959
W. E. Horner	Sanford, N. C.	1 July 1959
Lenox G. Cooper	Wilmington, N. C.	1 July 1959
W. L. Clegg	1002 W. Knox St. Durham, N. C.	1 July 1960
R. L. Pittman	Fayetteville, N. C.	1 July 1960
Mrs. E. L. Hillman	Siler City, N. C.	1 July 1960
Terry Sanford	Fayetteville, N. C.	1 July 1960
Ernest L. Sanders	Tabor City, N. C.	1 July 1960
Graham S. Eubank	Box 1225 Fayetteville, N. C.	1 July 1960

— APPENDICES —

APPENDIX E

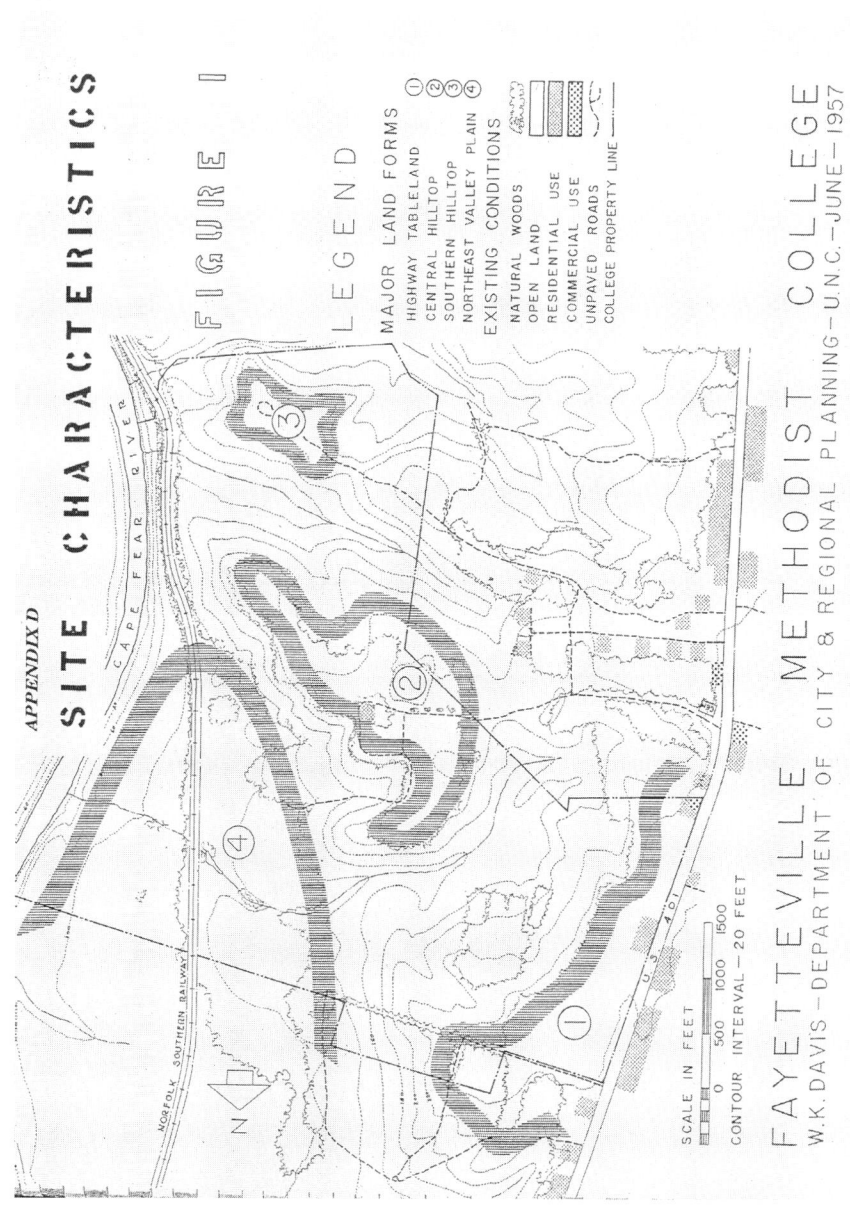

—APPENDICES—

APPENDIX F

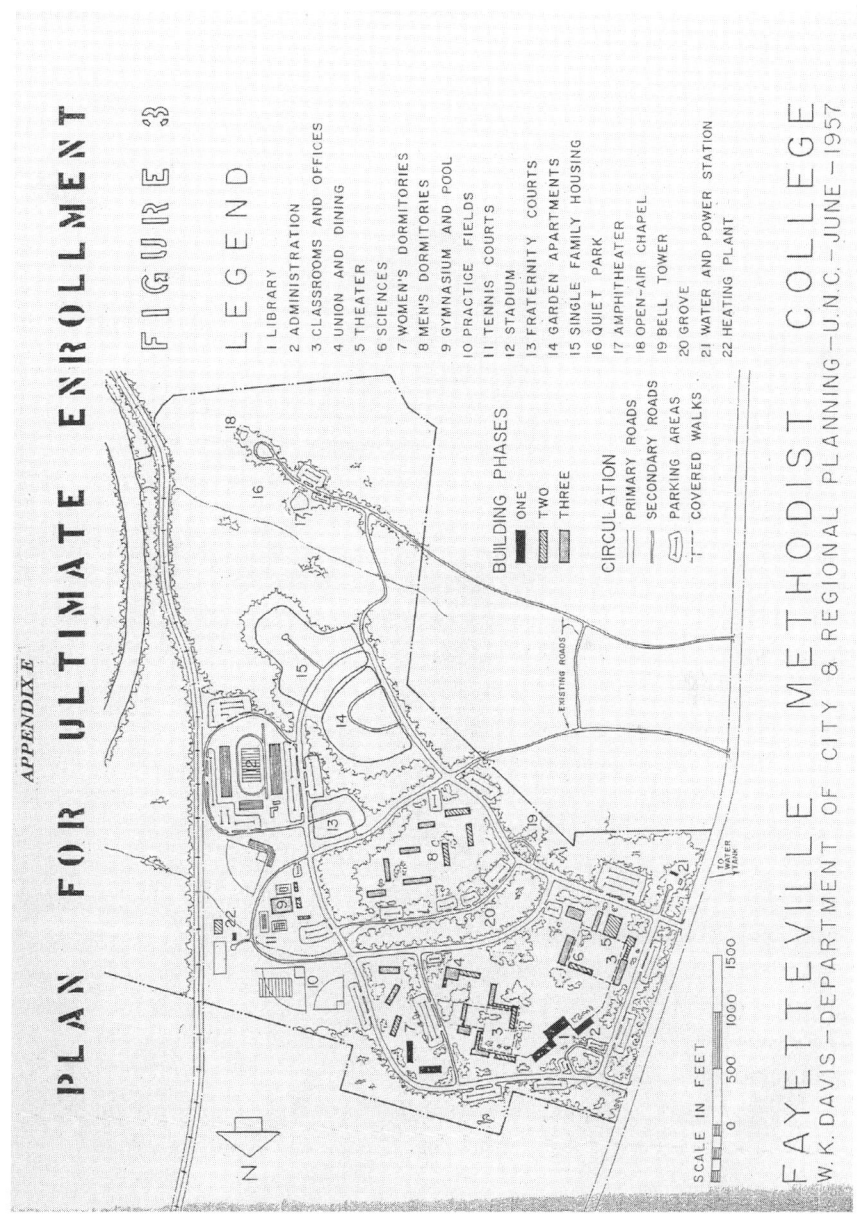

— APPENDICES—

APPENDIX G

Lucius Stacy Weaver
1904-1997

Lucius Stacy Weaver, the first president of Methodist College, was a native of Lenoir, North Carolina. Dr. Weaver served as president of Methodist College from 1957 to 1973, capping a distinguished, 50-year career in education. Before coming to Methodist, Weaver was a school principal in Union County and Jonesville; a professor of Latin and Greek, a coach, and president of Rutherford College; president of Mountain Park Junior College; and superintendent of the Statesville and Durham city schools.

Stacy Weaver was one of five children of Dr. Charles C. and Florence Stacy Weaver. His father was a Methodist minister and served as president of Davenport College (a precursor of Brevard) and Emory and Henry College.

His siblings were noted for outstanding educational leadership. His brother Philip was superintendent of the Greensboro City Schools. Jim was commissioner of the Atlantic Coast Conference and athletic director at Wake Forest. His sister Janie was a teacher and counselor at Reynolds High School in Winston-Salem. His brother C. C. Weaver, Jr. once served as principal of the Methodist Orphanage in Raleigh.

Almost everyone familiar with the history of Methodist College agrees that Stacy Weaver was the primary reason for its early success. As Methodist College President Elton Hendricks told *The Fayetteville Observer-Times* in 1997, "Having Dr. Weaver as president gave Methodist College instant credibility. He was one of the most respected educators in North Carolina. Even after all these years, we still benefit from that reputation."

In an editorial comment on Weaver's passing, *The Fayetteville Observer-Times* said, "Before it was a fashionable phrase, L. Stacy Weaver was a true Renaissance Man. His contribution to North Carolina, especially to its young people, set high expectations for all."

Stacy Weaver received an A.B. degree from Duke University, an M.A. from Columbia University, and honorary doctorates from High Point College, Duke University, and Methodist College. He met and married Elizabeth Hallyburton while teaching at Rutherford College; in August 1996 they celebrated their 70th wedding anniversary at their home in Lakeland, Florida.

Dr. Weaver had been superintendent of the Durham City Schools for ten years when the Methodist College Board of Trustees elected him president in June 1957. He was then 52. Methodist College was still an infant, having received its charter from the state of North Carolina only eight months earlier.

Because he had held many leadership positions in public education and was a very prominent Methodist lay leader, Dr. Weaver's appointment was hailed by Trustees Chairman Terry Sanford, Rev. Vergil Queen (Chairman of the Selection Committee), Bishop Paul Garber of the N. C. Conference of The Methodist Church, and Dr. Hollis Edens, president of Duke University.

Three different governors appointed Dr. Weaver to state commissions, dealing with Public School Law, Public School Finance, and Public Television.

He was a member of *Who's Who in American Education*, *Who's Who in the South*, and *Who's Who in Methodism*. He was president of the North Carolina Education Association and the Horace Mann League, Lieutenant Governor of Kiwanis International and District Deputy Grand Master of the Masonic Order.

He wrote articles for religious and educational journals, broadcast a weekly Sunday school lesson on a Durham radio station, and was a representative from the North Carolina Conference to six General Conferences of The Methodist Church.

Upon accepting the presidency of Methodist College, Stacy Weaver pledged that the fledgling liberal arts college would be "Christian in concept and dedicated to academic excellence." As Dr. Weaver went about raising funds for Methodist College, overseeing its construction, and recruiting its faculty, staff, and students, he never lost sight of that original pledge. During his 16-year tenure he would see the college grow from a 1960 opening enrollment of 80 students to a high of 1,100 students in 1967.

When he delivered the commencement address to the Class of '73 just prior to his retirement, Dr. Weaver used the title "This I Believe" and discussed three beliefs which he said had guided him over the years: "1) I believe in the divinity of human personality. 2) I believe in the improvability of human personality. and 3) I believe that Christian education is the best means yet devised for the development of human personality."

Even after he and Mrs. Weaver retired to Lake Junaluska and later Lakeland, Florida, the Weavers maintained an interest in Methodist College.

On his last visit to the campus, Dr. Weaver walked through the newly completed March F. Riddle Physical Activities Center. The Elizabeth Weaver Award is still given annually to an outstanding student, while the Stacy Weaver Award honors an outstanding graduating senior each May.

Dr. L. Stacy Weaver died March 25, 1997, in Lakeland, Florida. He was 92. He was survived by his wife, Elizabeth Hallyburton Weaver; three sons, Dr. Charles H. Weaver of Raleigh, N.C., L. Stacy Weaver, Jr. of Fayetteville, N.C., and Dr. Walter P. Weaver of Lakeland, Fla.; seven grandchildren; and five great-grandchildren.

Weaver's funeral was held March 29, 1997, at Hay Street United Methodist Church in Fayetteville, with the Rev. William P. Lowdermilk presiding. Interment followed at Lafayette Memorial Park in north Fayetteville.

Those offering tributes and remembrances at the funeral were: Dr. Samuel J. Womack, former Methodist College religion professor and academic dean; Dr. Terry Sanford, Methodist College trustee emeritus; and Stacy's son, Dr. Walter Weaver, a professor of religion at Florida Southern College.

Sam Womack: "He stood tall. He was the recipient of a goodly sum of talents. He had the qualities of a great teacher, an educational statesman, and a builder—integrity, honor, loyalty, vision, and humility. He was my mentor, leader, and friend. It was a blessing to work with him."

Terry Sanford: "He was the unanimous choice of the trustees to become president of Methodist College. His choice was a guarantee of success. He had a vision of what a college should be and the church's responsibility in higher education. He came to build and he did so with creativity and vision. He attracted and inspired good people. He wanted quality students. Thanks largely to him, Methodist College is now viewed as one of the two or three best liberal arts colleges in this state."

Walter Weaver: "My father was something of an endangered species—the last and best of his kind. He lived by his word. He was precise and highly organized. He had a well-defined set of values. He was an old Roosevelt Democrat. Duty to him was a constant. He loved old-style country music as well as Shakespeare. He loved baseball, which he played in college. He had a headfull of wonderful anecdotes. He was devoted to his family."

The legacies that Dr. Weaver most wanted to leave to his children were, in his words, "A good name, a good education and a good example." In all three he succeeded.

— APPENDICES—

NOTE: In 1965, the Methodist College Board of Trustees honored L. Stacy Weaver by naming its second residence hall for women Weaver Hall. A commemorative plaque in the lobby of Weaver Hall reads: "This building is dedicated in honor of Lucius Stacy Weaver, builder and first president of the college. 'If you would see his monument look around you.'"

APPENDIX H

Methodist College Building Estimates

Unit	Sq. Ft.	Cost Per Sq. Ft.	Total Coat
1. Classroom Building	35,362	12	$ 424,344
2. Library	19,833	14	277,662
3. Science Building	28,130	12	337,560
4. Cafeteria - Student Union	28,040	12	336,480
5. Administration Building	8,809	14	123,480
6. Bell Tower	----------	----------	15,000
7. Auditorium and Fine Arts Bldg.	35,030	14	490,420
8. Chapel	1,600	20	32,000
9. Gymnasium	35,159	14	492,226
10. Two Dormitories - 350 Boys	55,874	13	762,362
11. Two Dormitories - 250 Girls	39,910	14	558,740
12. Heating Plant and Utilities	----------	----------	250,000
13. Architects' fee - 4 $^{1}/_{2}$%	----------	----------	182,885
14. Equipment - 10%	----------	----------	406,412
			$4,653,417

These estimates take no account of landscaping and paving for which we have no schedule of cost as yet. In addition approxmiately $150,000 of Capital Funds will be required to purchase library books. These can be supplied over a 4 - year period beginning with the opening of the College.

Total of first 6 Items, plus Items 12 -------------	1,764,372
Architects' fee - 4 $^{1}/_{2}$%-------------------	79,396
Equipment - 10%------------------------	176,437
	$2,020,205

Presented to Board of Trustees 1/30/58

—APPENDICES—

APPENDIX I

Architect's Site Plan for Methodist College

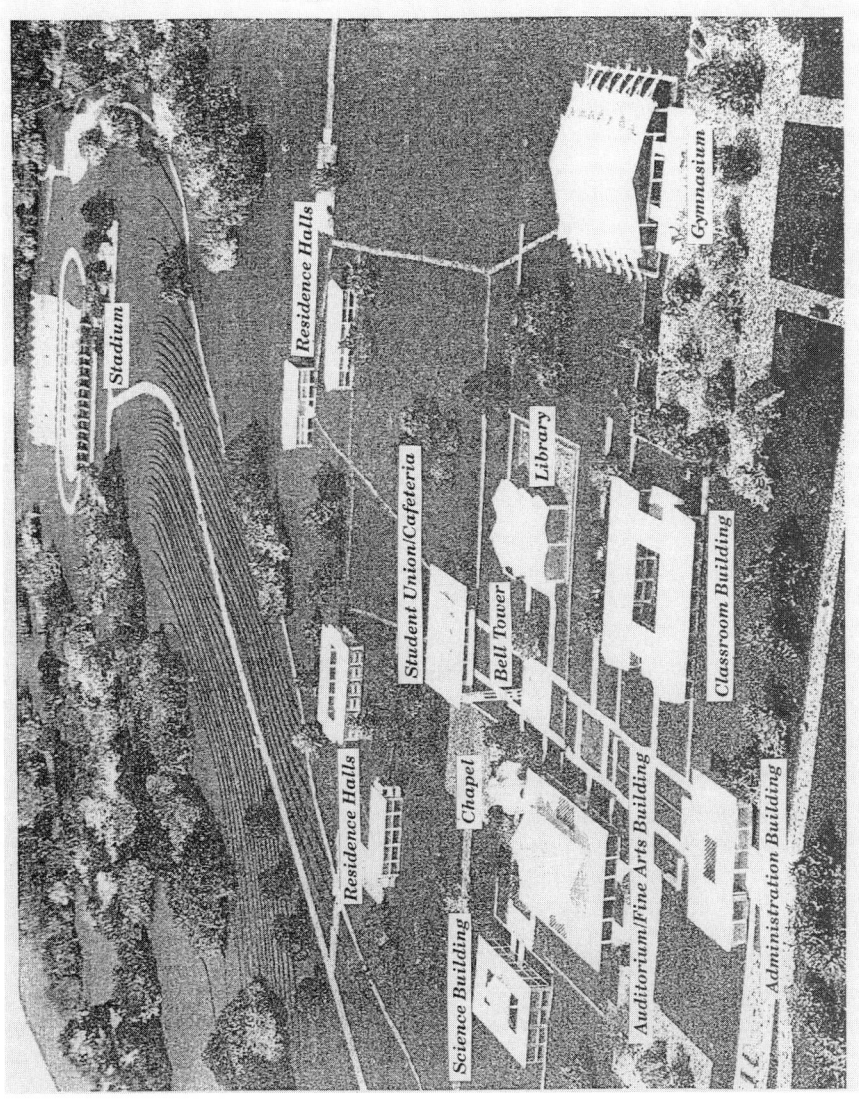

— APPENDICES—

APPENDIX J

Methodist College Milestones

• 1956

• On March 13, Terry Sanford and seven other Fayetteville residents appear before Bishop Paul Garber's Cabinet at Trinity Methodist Church in Durham, N.C., to invite the North Carolina Conference of the Methodist Church to consider Fayetteville as the site for a new Methodist college. The Fayetteville group offers $2 million for construction, a 600-acre site, and at least $50,000 in annual support.

• A site committee from the North Carolina Conference of the Methodist Church, chaired by the Rev. W. L. Clegg, tours Fayetteville March 15 and reviews a proposal from the Fayetteville College Steering Committee for securing a Methodist college for the city.

• On March 27, Reverend Clegg's Site Committee recommends that the North Carolina Conference of the Methodist Church: 1) build a new four-year college in Fayetteville, and 2) move Louisburg College, a junior college, to Rocky Mount and expand it into a four-year college.

• At a special called session held May 14, in Goldsboro, N.C., the North Carolina Conference of the Methodist Church votes to build new four-year colleges in Fayetteville and Rocky Mount, N.C. and to retain Louisburg College in Louisburg as a two-year, junior college.

• Meeting in Fayetteville June 19, the Board of Education of the North Carolina Conference of the Methodist Church approves a proposed charter for Methodist College and nominees for the Methodist College Board of Trustees.

• The Fayetteville College Foundation is formed June 23 to aid, foster, and promote the growth, progress, and general welfare of the new Methodist college in Fayetteville.

• Meeting in annual session June 25, in Greenville, N.C., the North Carolina Conference of the Methodist Church approves the charter for Methodist College and nominees for the Methodist College Board of Trustees.

• The Methodist College Board of Trustees holds its first meeting July 18 and elects Terry Sanford chairman. • Methodist College, Inc. is formally

• Methodist College, Inc. is formally chartered Nov. 1, 1956, by the state of North Carolina after filing a Certificate of Incorporation with Secretary of State Thad Eure.

— APPENDICES —

• 1957
- In a brief ceremony held Feb. 21, at the site of the Methodist College campus, Fayetteville College Foundation President Franklin Clark conveys 577 acres of land to Bishop Paul Garber of the North Carolina Conference of the Methodist Church.
- In a meeting held June 22, the Methodist College Board of Trustees elects L. Stacy Weaver, superintendent of the Durham (N.C.) City Schools, president of Methodist College. The board hires architects Stevens and Wilkinson of Atlanta, Ga., to design and supervise construction of the Methodist college campus.
- Meeting in special session Feb. 21, in Fayetteville, N.C., the North Carolina Conference of the Methodist Church approves a $5 million Capital Funds Campaign designed to provide $2 million to construct Methodist College in Fayetteville and $2 million to build N.C. Wesleyan College in Rocky Mount.

• 1958
- Methodist College trustees approve an architectural site plan for the College January 30 and authorize Stevens and Wilkinson to draw final plans and specifications for the Classroom Building.
- Trustees award a $441,100 construction contract for the Classroom Building August 7 to McDevitt and Street Co. of Charlotte, N.C.
- At its August 11 meeting, The Fayetteville College Foundation board hires Robert B. Isner as executive secretary.
- Trustees and supporters of the College attend a groundbreaking ceremony August 26 at the site of the College.

• 1959
- The Fayetteville College Foundation meets January 13 and elects Alton G. Murchison president to succeed Franklin C. Clark.
- Trustees meet April 3 and award a $402,600 construction contract for the Science Building to Anderson Construction Co. of Dunn, N.C.
- At a meeting held April 20, the Fayetteville College Foundation board hires Frank H. Jeter, Jr. as executive secretary.
- Trustees meet May 5 and award a $416,630 construction contract for the Student Union-Cafeteria to McDevitt and Street Co. of Charlotte.
- At a May 8 meeting, The Board of Education, N.C. Conference of the Methodist Church, approves the Methodist College Board of Trustees'

request for authority to borrow $1 million from First Citizens Bank and Trust Co. to finance construction needed for the college to open in the fall of 1960.
• In June and July, college trustees award contracts for grading, water/sewer lines, Boiler Plant, underground electrical system.
• The Trustees' Academic Affairs Committee meets October 8 and approves a proposed curriculum for Methodist College.
• Trustees meet November 3 and approve a fee schedule for the college and authorize President Weaver to obtain bids for constructing sidewalks, parking lots, dressing and bath facilities at the Boiler Plant, and campus lighting.
• At a December 17 meeting, the Fayetteville College Foundation board elects Bert Ishee president for 1960.

• 1960
• In January, Methodist College publishes its first catalogue; announces the hiring of key administrators and faculty; sets Sept. 19, 1960, as the opening date for the College.
• In February, the college accepts its first students, seven freshmen from the Cape Fear Region.
• The Fayetteville College Foundation reports April 1 that it has collected $720,488 locally on five-year pledges totaling $1,725,880.
• In May and June 1960, the college completes construction of the Science Building, Classroom Building, Student Union, Boiler Plant, streets, sidewalks, and parking lots.
• Methodist College holds a formal opening ceremony September 19 in the Student Union. Speakers include College President L. Stacy Weaver, Fayetteville Mayor George Herndon, Trustees Chairman Terry Sanford, Methodist Bishop Paul Garber, Fayetteville College Foundation President Bert Ishee, and North Carolina College Conference President Dr. W. H. Plemmons.
• Methodist College begins classes September 20, with 128 day students, 41 evening students, and 12 faculty members.
• In October, college trustees authorize President Weaver to seek $120,000 in financing to build two 16-room apartment buildings to serve as temporary dormitories.

1961

- At a January 12 meeting, the Fayetteville College Foundation sets a college fund-raising goal of $300,000 per year for the next four years: $250,000 per year for the building fund and $50,000 per year for operating expenses.
- Methodist College Board of Trustees meets May 2 and re-elects N.C. Governor Terry Sanford board chairman. Dr. Weaver reports that the College has spent $2.7 million on buildings and equipment, using $1,729,559 in cash and $1 million in loan funds from First Citizens Bank.
- First student music recital is given May 14, featuring Paul Ostborg, violinist; Patricia Jackson, pianist; Anne Bradford, soprano.
- On July 19, President Weaver announces a $50,000 gift from R. J. Reynolds Tobacco Co. to the college's Building Fund. Trustees authorize construction of a third apartment building to house 88 students; D. R. Allen and Sons, Inc. of Fayetteville agrees to build it for $97,942.
- In November, the first issue of *sMALL TALK*, the campus newspaper, is published.

1962

- In March, The University Senate of the Methodist Church accredits Methodist College for the undergraduate training of ministers.
- At a May 1 meeting, the Board of Trustees awards construction contract for two three-story residence halls (one to house 160 men, one to house 150 women) to T.A. Loving & Co. of Goldsboro, N.C. totaling $1,137,800. Construction funds are secured through a 40-year loan by the Community Facilities Administration, U.S. Housing and Home Finance Agency.
- In June and July, the Fayetteville College Foundation votes to move its offices from the Grace Pittman Building in downtown Fayetteville to the college campus.
- On July 10, college trustees authorize construction of a temporary metal gymnasium at a cost of $90,000. D. R. Allen & Sons of Fayetteville wins contract, assists college with financing.
- Trustees Chairman / N. C. Governor Terry Sanford delivers a major policy address on higher education in the state at Methodist College's third Founders' Day program November 15. Sanford endorses the establishment of a community college system in North Carolina and new public four-year colleges at Asheville, Charlotte, and Wilmington.

— APPENDICES—

- **1963**
  - At a February 12 meeting, trustees approve a program of intercollegiate athletics at Methodist College, starting in the fall of 1963, limited to basketball and minor sports.
  - In March and April, faculty and students ratify a proposed constitution for a Student Government Association. Students elect four S.G.A. officers and three senators from each class.
  - In April, *sMALL TALK* reports that Methodist has joined five other colleges-N.C. Wesleyan, St. Andrews, Charlotte College, College of Charleston, and Lynchburg College-to form the Dixie Intercollegiate Athletic Association and will field teams in 1963-64 in basketball, tennis, and golf.
  - At a May 7 meeting, trustees accept low bids for construction of the library ($434,543) and the bell tower($90,000) as submitted by D. R. Allen & Sons of Fayetteville.
  - On November 15, Board of Trustees votes to apply for a federal loan to build two additional residence halls (one for men, one for women).

- **1964**
  - The first senior music recital is given February 9 by Betty Neill Guy (soprano) and William Wolfe (pianist).
  - On April 10, Dr. L. Stacy Weaver is inaugurated as first president of Methodist College, seven years after taking the job.
  - In May, Reese Edwards '64 presents a copy of the first college yearbook, the Carillon, to Trustees Chairman Terry Sanford, to whom the book is dedicated. Edwards was the yearbook editor.
  - On June 1, Methodist College graduates its first class of 43 students. Methodist Bishop Paul Garber gives the commencement address. On the same date, trustees award a $1,165,634 contract for construction of two additional residence halls (Weaver and Sanford Halls) to D. R. Allen & Sons of Fayetteville.
  - Students help move books and equipment November 23 from old library in Classroom Building to the newly completed Davis Memorial Library.
  - On December 16, the Southern Association of Colleges and Schools accepts Methodist College as a candidate for membership.

- **1965**
  - On February 8, M.C. students approve four revisions to the S.G.A. Constitution which clarify Judicial Council authority in disciplinary matters and establish a Student-Faculty Judicial Committee.

- In a May 4 meeting, the Board of Trustees amends the college charter, expanding the board to 36 members and specifying that six members would be members of the N.C Conference of the Methodist Church, six would be Cumberland County residents, and three-fourths would be members of the Methodist Church. President Weaver announces that John M. Reeves of Pinehurst, N.C. has pledged $200,000 toward construction of an auditorium/fine arts building at the college.
- The Methodist College Alumni Association holds its first alumni banquet May 29 and announces the election of Julian Jessup as its first president.
- At its second spring commencement May 31, the college dedicates Yarborough Bell Tower and Jones Memorial Carillon.
- Fall 1965 enrollment increases 33 percent over the previous year to 818 students; college enrolls 407 freshmen and first black student, Mary Monroe. Faculty grows by 17 members. Freshmen are required to wear Monarch caps(beanies) and follow other provisions of the S.G.A. Freshman Orientation Code during the first month of school.
- In September, trustees name five newest buildings: Horner Administration Building, Sanford Hall, Weaver Hall, Davis Memorial Library, Reeves Auditorium/Fine Arts Building and vote to seek federal grants and loans to finance construction of a Student Union addition, Horner Administration Building, and Reeves Auditorium/Fine Arts Building.
- In December, Monarch cross country and volleyball teams win their respective Dixie Conference championships, the first for Methodist College. In a special referendum, M.C. student body rejects a proposed Honor Code by a nine to one margin.

• 1966

- In January, The Executive Committee of the Methodist College Board of Trustees votes to apply for a federal loan of $1,276,480 toward construction of the administration building and the fine arts building/auditorium and a federal grant of $425,493 for construction of a Student Union addition. Trustees meet October 11 and reject construction bids for the Student Union addition, administration building, and chapel because they exceed available funds.
- In May, the first issue of *Tapestry*, the college literary magazine, is published by Pastiche, the literary club.
- On May 28, the Methodist College Alumni Association board adopts a constitution and by-laws; defines an active member as anyone who attended Methodist College at least one year and is in good standing with the college.

— APPENDICES—

- Speaking at Methodist College's Founders' Day (and 10th anniversary) November 2, Trustees Chairman Terry Sanford proposes that the state of North Carolina institute a scholarship program that would award any state resident attending a private college at least $200 toward tuition.
- On November 16, *The Fayetteville Observer* publishes a 12-page special section to commemorate the tenth anniversary of the founding of Methodist College.
- Trustees meet November 22 and award construction contracts for administration building, fine arts building, and Student Union addition to Player, Inc. of Fayetteville at a total cost of $1,764,300.
- Meeting in Miami Beach November 30, the Southern Association of Colleges and Schools awards full accreditation to Methodist College.
- In November, Methodist College Press publishes *Leaves Before the Wind*, a collection of 98 poems written by Dr. Walter Blackstock, professor of English at the college.

• 1967

- On March 13, the Methodist College student body selects a college song-alma mater-after an assembly at which four proposed songs are performed. Students vote for a song written by Lois Lambie, choral director at Seventy-First High School in Cumberland County.
- In April, the college buys a collection of letters and memorabilia relating to the Marquis de Lafayette, the French general who helped the United States win its war for independence from Britain and for whom Fayetteville is named.
- The M. C. student body approves revisions to the S.G.A. Constitution May 31 which continue "equal representation" in the S.G.A. Senate: four senators and an alternate from each of the four classes.
- College begins eighth academic year September 14 with an enrollment of 1,069 students (626 living on campus) and 15 new faculty members.

• 1968

- The first wedding ceremony at Methodist College is held March 9 in the "classroom chapel" on the ground level of the Classroom Building, uniting underclassmen Robert Flynn and Jeannine Faulkner.
- On April 2, the trustees Executive Committee votes to name the chapel for John William Hensdale, the Fayetteville trustee who had endowed a chapel fund.
- From June 4-7, The North Carolina Annual Conference of the

Methodist Church meets at Methodist College; 540 of those attending are housed in college residence halls.
- In July, the Fayetteville College Foundation, Inc. changes its name to the Methodist College Foundation, Inc., submitting an amended charter and by-laws to the Secretary of State's Office, State of North Carolina.

• 1969
- The Monarch basketball team, coached by Gene Clayton, wins its first Dixie Conference Championship by defeating the N.C. Wesleyan College Bishops 86-65.
- Denomination-based religious clubs vote to combine forces and form a new religious fellowship called Koinonia.
- Hensdale Chapel completed and dedicated.
- New assembly attendance policy takes effect requiring students to attend 13 assemblies each semester. One assembly per week, held each Wednesday at 11:30 a.m., replaces the two required assemblies formerly held each Monday and Wednesday.

• 1971
- O'Hanlon Amphitheater built and dedicated.

• 1973
- Dr. Richard Pearce named president, following Dr. Weaver's retirement.
- Lafayette Room in Davis Library dedicated.
- Dr. Sid Gautam, professor of economics, establishes the Center for Entrepreneurship at Methodist College to "assist entrepreneurs in converting dreams into realities, exploring new frontiers of opportunity while promoting, creating, and preserving wealth."

• 1974
- Shelley Baseball Field dedicated.
- Fraternities and sororities established.
- Center for Entrepreneurship stages first annual Economic Outlook Symposium in the fall.

• 1975
- College launches evening program.
- President's home completed on campus.

— APPENDICES —

- Phil Bauguess, a Moravian student from Winston-Salem, N.C., introduces the Moravian Love Feast to Methodist College; the feast becomes an annual tradition.
- Trustees approve Greatest Gift Scholarship program allowing each MC graduate to give a scholarship worth one-fourth tuition to a prospective MC student.

• 1976
- Schantz pipe organ, a gift from Mrs. Karl Berns, is installed in Hensdale Chapel.
- Methodist College named an American Bicentennial campus.

• 1977
- College awards its first honorary degree, a Doctor of Divinity, to the Rev. Vergil E. Queen.
- Army ROTC program established.
- Student body elects Mrs. Alice Pearce, the college president's 79-year-old mother, Homecoming Queen

• 1978
- College begins offering associate or two-year degrees.
- Center for Entrepreneurship stages first annual Stock Market Symposium in the spring.
- Methodist hosts 170 Japanese students at the East-West Foundation's summer orientation.
- College awards first Methodist College Medallion to Dr. Charles Speegle August 25, 1978.

• 1979
- Dr. Fred Clark succeeds Dr. Sam Womack as academic dean following Dr. Womack's retirement.
- Methodist designated a "Serviceman's Opportunity College.
- College enrollment increases to 990, with 360 living on campus.
- *sMALL TALK* receives honors rating first class in Associated Collegiate Press national competition.

• 1980
- Lady Monarch basketball team wins NCAIAW Division III state championship and advances to regionals.
- Theatre Department presents Sophocles' *Oedipus Rex* to packed houses in Reeves Auditorium.
- Dr. Richard Pearce, college president, receives first Methodist College Medallion.
- The president of Peoples Bank and Trust Co. gives keynote address at the Economic Outlook for 1981 Symposium.

• 1981
- Dr. Sue Kimball, English professor, edits and produces the world premiere of Maxwell Anderson's *Raft on the River*, a musical version of *Huckleberry Finn*. Dr. Jack Peyrouse, professor of theatre, directs.

• 1982
- College stages first annual Shakespearean Summer Festival, featuring *West Side Story* and *The Merchant of Venice*.
- Men's golf team, coached by Gene Clayton, finishes third in NCAA Division III Nationals.
- Methodist launches Southern Writers Symposium with a festival honoring James Agee. Dr. Sue Kimball, English professor, plans and directs the symposium.

• 1983
- Dr. M. Elton Hendricks succeeds Dr. Pearce as president in mid-September.
- *Methodist College Today*, a quarterfold newspaper, replaces the *Methodist College Bulletin*, a quarterly newsletter.

• 1984
- Dr. M. Elton Hendricks inaugurated as third president of Methodist College.
- Women's soccer added to intercollegiate athletic program.
- Fall enrollment increases 15 percent to 760.

• 1985
- Work begins on Pauline Longest Nature Trail.
- Flag presentations by international students incorporated into graduation ceremonies
- Major in special education added
- Computer-Assisted Composition Lab established.

• 1986
- Charles M. Reeves School of Business established to honor a Sanford businessman, college trustee, and benefactor.
- Honor Code adopted
- Tuition waived for senior citizens
- College launches $3.5 million "Come of Age" capital campaign to build a physical activities center
- Fund drive launched to establish Samuel J. Womack Endowed Chair in Religion and Philosophy.

• 1987
- *Methodist College Today* upgraded to magazine format
- Major in Business Administration with a Concentration in Professional Golf Management added
- College hosts first Elderhostel.

• 1988
- College dedicates restored Mallett-Rogers House to serve as art gallery.
- Golf driving range, eight tennis courts, nine golf holes built.

• 1989
- Soccer field house built.
- MC fields first football team.

• 1990
- March F. Riddle (physical activities) Center opens; men's golf team wins first NCAA Division III National Championship by 30 strokes.

— APPENDICES—

- **1991**
- New majors added in criminal justice and international studies; college celebrates bicentennial of U.S. constitution with series of three forums; 12-point grading scale adopted; mentor/tutoring program started.

- **1992**
- The College contracts with EUA/Highland Partners for installation of new energy-saving, computer-controlled heating and lighting systems.

- **1993**
- The Board of Trustees approves a five-year Strategic Plan which calls for building additional residence halls and raising funds to build a library addition, a new academic building, and a science building.
- Construction begins on a new residence hall adjacent to Garber Hall.

- **1994**
- The Board of Trustees agrees to lease 30 acres of land to a local nonprofit group for construction of a youth soccer complex.

- **1995**
- The Lura Tally Center for Leadership Development is established.
- West Hall, a coed residence hall similar to one built the previous year, opens next to Garber Hall.
- The main (south) entrance to the campus is realigned to meet a new stoplight; a new entrance sign with three small fountains is added.
- The men's and women's soccer teams finish second in the NCAA Division III National Championships.
- The College sells $10 million in tax-free revenue bonds to refinance a $6.3 million debt and to pay for capital improvements totaling $3.6 million (roof repairs, Golf & Tennis Learning Center, new south entrance, math and computer science building, nine golf holes, land purchase).
- The Methodist College Development Corporation is chartered and granted a 50-year lease of 22 acres of College land for development of College Centre Office Park.
- The Charles M. Reeves School of Business is accredited by the Association of Collegiate Business Schools and Programs.

— APPENDICES —

• 1996
- The College announces a $6.5 million "Expanding the Vision" campaign to build the endowment, a library annex, a math and computer science building, and a new academic building.
- MC launches a physician assistant program.
- Methodist goes online with a site on the World Wide Web.
- The Methodist College Chorus completes a spring concert tour of France.
- The Richard L. Player Golf and Tennis Learning Center, located next to the golf driving range, is completed and dedicated.
- Construction begins on Joe Stout Hall (for Admissions and Financial Aid), a math and computer science building, and an Allied Health Building (for the physician assistant program) in College Centre Office Park.
- Methodist celebrates the 40th anniversary of receiving its charter with an hour-long retrospective/stage show in Reeves Auditorium.
- Clearing and grading work begins for the second nine holes of the College golf course.
- The College buys seven acres of land adjacent to Kinwood and the north boundary of the campus.
- Two brick residences that fronted Ramsey Street are relocated to make way for a new tenant in College Centre Office Park.

• 1997
- Joe Stout Hall and the Math and Computer Science Building are completed and opened.
- The social work program receives national accreditation.
- Sir John Templeton is the featured speaker at the College's 20th annual Stock Market Symposium.
- Work begins on the College's self-study for reaffirmation of accreditation by the Commission on Colleges of the Southern Association of Colleges and Schools.
- A brick residence is renovated to house the Academic Development Center.
- The Methodist College Parents Association holds its first meeting and Family Weekend.

• 1998
- Two Methodist College debaters win an ADA national debate tournament in the Novice Division.

— APPENDICES—

- The College's Longleaf Press publishes its first poetry chapbook.
- MC's professional golf management program is endorsed by the PGA of America.
- Construction begins on a library annex and a new academic building for the Reeves School of Business.
- The Expanding the Vision campaign concludes with a total of $8.5 million, $2 million over its original goal.
- College dedicates Fanny Farmer Memorial Park.
- BB&T completes and opens a new branch in College Centre Office Park.

• 1999

- A new entrance to College Centre Office Park (with stoplight) is completed at the intersection of Ramsey Street and Stacy Weaver Drive.
- Methodist launches the ARRIVED scholarship program, awarding full scholarships to four outstanding Russian students who will major in business and return home to help Russia make the transition to a free market economy.
- The College sells $14 million in tax-free revenue bonds to refinance $8.2 million in debt and to fund capital improvements worth $5.8 million (a new residence hall, renovation of science labs, land purchase, renovation of four residence halls).
- The Methodist College Board of Trustees approves a Strategic Plan for 2000-2005 which includes five general recommendations and 27 specific recommendations for improving College programs and facilities.
- A visiting team from the Southern Association of Colleges and Schools gives a very positive report after evaluating the College's self-study for reaffirmation of accreditation.
- The College opens its new annex to Davis Memorial Library, as well as Margaret and Walter Clark Hall, the new home for the Reeves School of Business.
- Work begins on Cape Fear Commons, an apartment-style residence hall, in a wooded area east of the March F. Riddle Center.
- The College buys a 33-acre tract of land off Meadowcroft Drive for improved access to the south campus.
- The Southern Association of Colleges and Schools reaffirms the accreditation of Methodist College.

— APPENDICES —

• 2000
- MC publishes its first Annual Report Issue *of Methodist College Today* (for the year 1999).
- The Tally Leadership Conference probes global challenges for the 21st century.
- A Vatican astronomer delivers the first annual Templeton Lecture at Methodist.
- "MC Online" debuts by offering a criminal justice course and an education course online.
- The College launches a resort management program.

• 2001
- The Tally Leadership Forum explores the ethics of new technology.
- Fall enrollment exceeds 2,000 for the first time.
- The physician assistant program admits its first class of master's degree candidates.
- A brick residence is renovated and opened as Union Station to provide space for the S.G.A., Student Activities, Student Employment, and a coffee house.
- MC alumni who participated in intercollegiate athletics during the 1960s relive their glory days at a luncheon reunion held during Homecoming.
- The College grants easements to the City of Fayetteville for a hiking and biking trail along the Cape Fear River that will terminate at the Fayetteville Soccer Complex and the Methodist College golf course.

• 2002
- The College fields its first women's lacrosse team.
- The Methodist College Board of Trustees announces a *Seeds on Good Soil, a New Season* comprehensive campaign to raise $11 million: $5 million for an addition to the Science Building, $3.5 million for a fitness center/intramural field house, $1.5 million for operating expenses, and $1 million for the College endowment.
- President Hendricks releases a vision statement in which he suggests that Methodist will need to become a "small university" to ensure continued growth.
- Cape Fear Commons, the College's second apartment-style residence hall, opens to students.

• 2003
• College awards first master's degrees to seven graduates of the physician assistant program.
• Methodist adds major in Occupational Environmental Management.

• 2004
• Methodist College restructures curriculum, creating six schools, each with its own dean.
• Fall enrollment reaches an all-time high of 2,277 students, 1,544 in the day program and 818 in the evening/weekend program.
• Jim Darden '69 joins college staff as horticulturalist.

• 2005
• College launches Professional MBA at Pinehurst program at Pinehurst Resort.
• Construction begins on the Science Building addition, the fitness and wellness center, and Creekside Apartments.
• Master of Justice Administration program established at the N.C. Criminal Justice Training Academy at Salemburg, N.C.
• Methodist's *Seeds on Good Soil, A New Season* campaign surpasses its revised goal of $12.8 million, reaching a total of $14.3 million in gifts and pledges, helped by four $1 million gifts received since 2003.

• 2006
• Creekside Apartments completed and occupied in August.
• In October, Methodist receives two federal grants totaling $600,000-$500,000 to fund an Environmental Simulation Center for the Occupational Environmental Management program and $100,000 for its Forensic Science Education and Training Program.
•Trustees vote to change the name of Methodist College to Methodist University.
• Methodist College celebrates the 50th anniversary of receiving its charter with special activities November 1-5, 2006, coinciding with Homecoming Weekend. At a 50th anniversary convocation November 1, 2006, President Hendricks announces that Methodist College will henceforth be known as Methodist University.

—compiled by Bill Billings, October, 2006

— APPENDICES—

APPENDIX K

John F. Kennedy
In Memoriam

A eulogy delivered at Methodist College November 25, 1963 by Dr. Samuel J. Womack, College Chaplain

One terrible weekend of hate and violence, spawned by the poisons within the soul of America has changed this beautiful autumnal season of 1963 from a period of national thanksgiving into one of national-and international?mourning. Even as we pause on our own campus here today to express our grief and pay our homage, a caisson bearing the body of our fallen leader is on its way to the Washington cathedral where it will be committed to the care of the God in whom we as a nation profess to trust, a God in whom John Fitzgerald Kennedy expressed his trust in almost every public utterance.

In such a time as this we mortals discover that there is within our souls some infinite sadness that bespeaks our acquaintance with tragedy; some infinite tenderness and compassion, some silent outreach of spirit to others more bereaved; some fragment of an infinite Trust and a sharing which we have not yet found the means to communicate or express. And so, amidst the unending torrent of words that have poured forth during the past several days, there is no tribute more eloquent nor more fraught with meaning than that which we have paid to the memory of our late President in the moments of silence and of silent prayer which we observed a short time age.

The tragedy of this fateful November weekend has wrought its own miracle, however. It has brought America to her knees, and it is upon her knees that America finds her true strength; it has forced us to search our very souls; it has awakened in us through our common grief a new and deeper realization of the very real brotherhood of man; it has brought forth from the depths of our beings a capacity for sorrow and love we had begun to think we had lost. Somehow, we seem to have felt in our own bodies, sympathetically, the impact of those fateful bullets from the assassin's gun, and we have felt an agony of after math that he who died was mercifully spared. We have been drawn closer together for the moment in our common grief, and through our deep sympathy with and tremendous admiration for that beautiful, courageous, noble woman who played so large

— APPENDICES—

a part in his life until its very end; who comforted him as she could even as his life ebbed away, and who has remained at his side through the long dark hours of mourning.

Yes, we have had a tremendous share in the so-nearly universal grief of this hour. But it if a share in the grief, we have, perhaps a share also in the universal guilt-and perhaps it is the deep suspicion of this guilt that adds to our sorrow. For if, in a sense we were with John Kennedy in his martyrdom, we were also with the assassin as his finger pulled the fateful trigger. The act of violence that has so horrified us all is one of which any one of us is potentially capable, as yesterday's sequel of violence so readily demonstrated. The fate that befell our young President, furthermore, was not a new phenomenon in human history; indeed, he joins a distinguished company who have paid with their lives for the sickness, the evil within the soul of mankind. His was a martyrdom shared by such men as Abraham Lincoln, James A. Garfield and others, including in our own day the late Dag Hammarskjold, who died in the cause of peace.

In his famous BALLARD OF READING GAOL Oscar Wilde has these lines:

"…..And each man kills the thing he loves…"
by each let this be heard; some do it with a bitter look,
Some with a flattering word…"

Perhaps it might be well to rephrase Wilde's statement; turn it around a bit so as to read:

"And we as men kill those who give us leadership and love."

It was not too many human natures ago, for instance, that angry men, outraged men, screamed for the blood of One whose only "crime" was that of an infinite, forgiving compassionate love for those who lusted for His death. It is Golgotha, or Calvary, which shows us the kind of beings we can allow ourselves to be; and it is Calvary which shows us the one force alone which offers this world any hope, whatever. It is such a love working in the hearts of men that alone will put an effective stop to deeds such as that which has taken from us our young President; it is such a love alone that can cleanse and free us from the hatreds, the rages, the poisons that per and it is Calvary which shows us the one force alone which offers this world any hope, whatever. It is such a love working in the hearts of men that alone will put an effective stop to deeds such as that which has taken from us our young President; it is such a love alone that can cleanse and free us from the hatreds, the rages, the poisons that perpetuate man's inhumanity to man.

Nothing else is powerful enough to tame the beast that flexes its muscles within each of us; the beast that causes us to broadcast hatred and exhorts us to acts of violence and uses our tongues to spray abroad the poisons of calumny of disrespect and lawlessness which cannot but influence the minds of such as those who become the actual pullers of triggers. "And some men kill with the inflammatory word." Wherein is our guilt? It is in the degree of our failure to dedicate ourselves in the last ounce of our strength and devotion to the development of a world, a society, an atmosphere, a brotherhood in which the poisons that warp and destroy God's image within us are wiped out. It is in the degree to which we fail to shoulder the responsibilities to which our religious faith calls us, as well as the responsibilities of enlightened citizenship to which leaders like John F. Kennedy have called us.

Let us in these grim hours see ourselves for what we really are or may become. Let us not forget that those whom we are so ready to condemn for their terrible deeds are our brother's keepers. Let us not become ourselves victims of the very poison of hate which has so horrified us in the deeds of these past few days.

Nor let us in these hours despair of man and his world. Despite the violence that has dominated our agonized attention, this is not a world gone mad; it is a world in which human dignity, human decency, the nobility of human character is being manifest all about us, as it was manifested so splendidly by the leader we mourn. He was the leader who, addressing the nation at the height of the Berlin Crisis in July, 1961, ended with this plea:

"In meeting my responsibilities in these coming months as President, I need your good will and your support, and, above all, your prayers." He was a leader who, in September of that same year, in an address which was in part a eulogy for the fallen Dag Hammarskjold, told the United Nations General Assembly:

"His (Dag Hammarskjold's) tragedy is deep in our hearts, but the tasks for which he died are at the top of our agenda. A noble servant of peace is gone. But the quest for peace lies before us."

He was a leader who was a special friend to higher education, too. In a review of foreign policy, delivered in March, 1962 he said:

"As we press forward on every front to realize the flexible world order, the role of the university becomes ever more important both as a reservoir of ideas and as a repository of the long view.... Today a world of knowledge--a world of cooperation-- just and lasting peace-may well be years away. But we have no time to lose. Let us plant our trees this very afternoon."

He, the author of PROFILES IN COURAGE, just before his

inauguration in January, 1961, set forth for the legislature of his home state, Massachusetts, the qualities he would desire in America?s leaders. To meet the challenge of this age, said Mr. Kennedy, we need:

". . . men of courage, with the courage to stand up to one's enemies, and the courage to stand up, when necessary, to one's own associates."

. . . men of judgment, with perceptive judgment of the future as well as the past.

. . . men of integrity, who never run out on the principles in which they believe or on the people who believe in them

. . . men of dedication."

Could anyone have written a more fitting epitaph for John F. Kennedy himself?

Of utmost significance in this hour, however, is the strong religious faith manifested by the late President. Few of his public statements are more eloquent testimonials to the character of this man than He went on to speak of the sweeping changes that are taking place in this crisis age, and concluded his address with the following statement:

"Today we still welcome those winds of change?and we have every reason to believe that our tide is running strong. With thanks to Almighty God for seeing us through the perilous passage, we ask His help anew in guiding the Good Ship Union."

— APPENDICES—

APPENDIX L

The Inaugural Address Of Dr. Lucius Stacy Weaver

April 10, 1964

"FROM COTTON FIELD TO COLLEGE"
Governor Sanford, our distinguished guests, ladies and gentlemen:

It would be a poor soul who would not be grateful for your presence here today. And so please allow me to begin by expressing my deep appreciation for your coming. So many of my professional colleagues and my personal friends are present that I could not attempt to enumerate them. To mention some would be to omit others. But perhaps I may be pardoned if I express the gratitude of my heart that my mother and other members of my family are able to be here; and if I say a special word of appreciation for the presence of the speaker of the morning. He has come a great distance, taking time from a busy schedule, to honor us by his presence and to share his wisdom with us. I count it a blessing that I am able to number him among my friends. He is a great Christian educator of world-wide repute.

New institutions are not bound by tradition. And so, we are probably establishing a "first" here today by holding these exercises almost seven years after the incumbent took office. And the mathematics of the calendar would suggest, if nothing else, that we are probably holding them as near the end as the beginning of my term of office. But for the first three years after I undertook the commission of turning a cotton field into a college there was no insititution here, and thus no opportunity to celebrate an inauguration. When the college opened its doors four years ago and admitted a freshman class, we decided that it might be appropriate to further defer these exercises until we became a full-fledged college, having four classes on the campus. And so I welcome today the presence of the first senior class of the college, who are participating in the academic procession.

Many questions must be answered by one who undertakes to build an institution from the ground up. Questions of size, design, and construction must be determined. These answers require much time and study before anything tangible begins to appear and take shape. But I shall not dwell on these. Suffice it to say that answers were provided and action taken on the basis of these decisions. I wish rather this morning to make a few suggestions about the direction an institution such as we envision here ought to take in today's world.

I am not interested in the exercise in semantics which attempts to draw fine lines of distinction between the terms 'church college', 'church-connected college', and 'church-related' college. I prefer rather to speak of the 'church-supported' college. Educational history amply demonstrates that those institutions which are supported with reasonable adequacy by their constituent body remain church institution church institutions; those that are not, do not.

The church was the fountain head of education in the early days. The first nine colleges founded in America were church-related. But the church is no longer the mass educator. The demands of our industrial society have created an educational need so great, so varied, and so complex that all elements of our society have been called upon to help meet the need. It is literally true that the hewers of wood and drawers of water of this generation have to know more than did the professional people of a few generations ago.

So the church college has come to play a more selective role in the scheme of higher education. This role is likely to proportionately diminish, rather than increase, in the future, in my judgment. Assuming that the role of the church college in the future will be more qualitative than quantitative, what direction should the emphasis of such an institution take?

The church college should prepare and train the future leadership of the church both lay and clerical. Indeed the church must be in the business of education for its own self-preservation. If all segments of our society demand a higher and higher level of education, can the church do less? Can the vital and eternal truths of the Christian faith be entrusted to the ignorant and the ill-informed in a world which needs to hear the message of the Christian church as never before? To ask the question is to answer it. If the church is to continue to contribute the leaven to our society which only the church can contribute, the church college must continue to send into the bloodstream of our culture men and women who will take their place as leaders of our society, in the professions, as teachers, and in all walks of life, who are dedicated to the Christian ethic and whose pursuit of truth gives deserved consideration to the truths of religion. The corollary duty of the church college to train the clerical leaders of the future goes without saying. Even if we dared entrust this duty to the State, constitutional prohibitions would stand in the way.

The church college should also contribute its part of the answer to two unanswered questions in higher education today. (1) Who shall be taught and (2) What shall they be taught? Educators constantly change the answers to these questions, as perforce they must. Our answers today are little better than expedients. We are still selecting college students on the basis of the economic competence of their parents. The Creator in His divine wisdom did not distribute intelligence on that basis. Then, as a further expedient, we have adopted so-called objective tests to make onerous decisions for us. Now please do not misunderstand me. Testing has value when properly used. We could hardly do without it in any modern system of education. But test results should be evaluated and considered along with other criteria. I do not accept the theses that a prospective student who makes a specific score on a given test should be admitted to educational opportunity. While one who makes one point less should be cast into outer darkness. I fear we shall look back in wonderment a generation hence at some of the uses we are making of testing now. The great percentage of failures and drop-outs, between the freshman and senior years, indicates that our present methods of selecting candidates for higher education leave much to be desired. The results of a recent four-year experiment at Harvard University, which has caused a change in admission requirements at that institution, give evidence of a return to sanity in this area.

The difficulty is that we have never yet been able to devise a test which will tell us whether a young man or woman has, in addition to intelligence, the fundamental strength of character to meet and overcome hard tasks; to refuse to be discouraged in the face of disappointment and adversity; whether he is genuinely interested in getting an education or is more concerned to participate in the country-club activities of the weekend; whether he is motivated to prepare himself to make his maximum contribution to his day and generation or whether he would prefer to join the great horde of beer-bloated sex-seekers who swarm over the Florida beaches during spring vacation masquerading as college men and women. But perhaps the colleges should not be asked to bear too much responsibility for this latter group. They are the product of the culture which has produced them; too much money, too little work, too irresponsible parents. They are the froth and foam and effervescence of a too-affluent society.

The second question relates to the curriculum of the church college. If it is to meet its objectives this must be in the liberal arts. It is evident that the concept of liberal education has undergone considerable change since its introduction by the Greek philosophers. They conceived of it as education for a leisure class. We have no such purpose today. We have

APPENDIX M

Honorary Degree Recipients

May 1977	Rev. Virgil E. Queen, Doctor of Divinity Mr. John W. Hensdale, Doctor of Humanities Rev. Charles H. Mercer, Doctor of Divinity
May, 1978	Mr. William Horner, Doctor of Letters Rev. Wallace Kirby, Doctor of Divinity Dr. L. S. Weaver, Doctor of Humanities
Dec. 1978	Rev. Clyde McCarver, Doctor of Divinity
May 1979	Rev. James H. Bailey, Doctor of Divinity
May, 1980	Mr. Samuel T. Ragan, Doctor of Letters
May, 1981	The Honorable Terry Sanford, Doctor of Law Rev. Paul Carruth, Doctor of Divinity
May 1982	Rev. Langill Watson, Doctor of Divinity
Dec. 1982	Dr. Offie L. Hathaway, Doctor of Divinity
May, 1983	Mr. Wilson F. Yarborough, Doctor of Letters
Aug. 1983	Rev. Samuel D. McMillian, Jr., Doctor of Divinity Mr. Arthur W. Winstead, Doctor of Divinity
May, 1984	Mr. Ernest R. Porter, Doctor of Humanities Bishop William Ragsdale Cannon, Doctor of Humanities Mr. William C. Fields, Doctor of Humanities Rev. Warren Petteway, Doctor of Divinity
May, 1985	Mrs. Heather Ross Miller, Doctor of Letters Rev. Vernon Tyson, Doctor of Divinity Rev. Charles A. Simonton, Jr., Doctor of Divinity

— APPENDICES —

May 1986	Mr. Robert B. Jordon III, Doctor of Humanities Mr. Joel L. Fleishman, Doctor of Letters Dr. F. Belton Joyner, Jr., Doctor of Divinity
May 1987	Mr. John T. Henley, Doctor of Humanities
Dec. 1987	Mr. William Robert Johnson, Doctor of Humanities
May, 1988	Mr. J. Roy Parker, Jr., Doctor of Letters
Aug. 1988	Ms. Mary Lynn McCree Bryan, Doctor of Letters
May 1989	Mr. Isaac Hawley O'Hanlon, Doctor of Humanities Senator Lura S. Talley, Doctor of Humanities Rev. Charles M. Smith, Doctor of Divinity
Dec. 1989	Dr. Thomas S. Yow III '66, Doctor of Divinity Mr. Charles Mercer Reeves, Doctor of Humanities
Dec. 1990	Dr. J. Allen Norris, Jr., Doctor of Humanities Rev. Helen Grey Crotwell, Doctor of Divinity
May 1991	Rev. William Presnell, Doctor of Divinity Dr. Richard Pearce, Doctor of Humanities
May 1992	Brig. General John W. Handy, USAF '66, Doctor of Humanities Rev. Kermit L. Braswell, Doctor of Divinity Bishop Carlton P. Minnick, Jr., Doctor of Divinity
May 1993	Rev. Rufus H. Stark II, Doctor of Divinity Rev. E. Glen Holt, Doctor of Divinity
May 1994	Mr. Joseph P. Riddle, Jr. (posthumously), Doctor of Humanities Brig. Gen. James M. Link '66, Doctor of Humanities Rev. H. Sidney Huggins III, Doctor of Divinity
Dec. 1994	Rev. John Thomas Smith, Doctor of Divinity Mr. Charlie Gaddy, Doctor of Humanities

— APPENDICES —

May 1995	Ms. Peggy Kirk Bell, Doctor of Humanities
May 1996	Dr. Mott P. Blair, Doctor of Humanities
April 1997	Mr. John Marks Templeton, Doctor of Business Administation
May 1997	Mr. Jerome "Jerry" Richardson, Doctor of Humanities Mr. William James Weisser, Doctor of Humanities
May 1998	Mr. Robert Henry Dedman, Doctor of Humanities
May 1999	Mr. J. Nelson Gibson, Jr., Doctor of Humanities
Dec. 1999	Rev. Rodney Gene Hamm, Doctor of Divinity
May 2000	Mr. R. Dillard Teer, Doctor of Humanities Mrs. Pauline Longest, Doctor of Humanities
May 2001	Dr. William C. Harrison '74, Doctor of Humanities
Dec. 2001	Rev. Wesley F. Brown, Doctor of Divinity
May 2002	Bishop Marion M. Edwards, Doctor of Divinity
Dec. 2002	Mr. Bob Timberlake, Doctor of Humanities Rev. Michael W. Safley '72, Doctor of Divinity
May 2004	Gen. H. Hugh Shelton, Doctor of Humanities Mr. Louis Spilman, Jr. '64, Doctor of Humanities
Dec. 2004	Dr. Linda C. McPhail '70, Doctor of Science
May 2005	Mr. Charles K. McAdams, Doctor of Humanities
May 2006	Mr. Richard R. Allen, Sr., Doctor of Humanities

— APPENDICES —

APPENDIX N

Methodist College Medallion Recipients

August 25, 1978	Dr. Charles Speegle
May 6, 1979	Dr. Samuel Womack
August 12, 1979	Charles K. McAdams
May 4, 1980	Beth Finch Dr. Richard R. Pearce
August 15, 1980	Estelle Hillman
December 19, 1980	Reverend Allen Lee
May 3, 1981	Dr. Mott P. Blair
August 1981	Walter Davis Henry Dixon (posthumously; one additional Medallion to Mrs. Dixon)
December 18, 1981	Bobby O. McCoy, Jr.
May 2, 1982	Dano Davis Grier Garrick
August 20, 1982	Musette Kitchen Dunn Londa Shamburger Johnson Margie Grace Mann Ruth L. Cade Mildred Powell Fry Catherine Allen Vick
May 1, 1983	Lorenzo Pierce Plyler
August 19, 1983	Louis Spilman, Jr. '64

— APPENDICES—

December 22, 1983	Virginia M. Thompson
December 20, 1984	Charlotte T. Yarborough John W. Hurley
August 20, 1985	Michael W. Safley '72 Ray Thomas Gooch '72
December 13, 1985	Mrs. Karl H. Berns
December 17, 1986	Martha A. Duell
May 10, 1987	Lois Janet Lambie
October 2, 1987	Margaret R. Saunders
December 15, 1988	John G. Dicks III '73
August 30, 1989	Roger W. Ireson
May 6, 1990	William Kellon Quick
December 14, 1990	Morie Murray Howard
May 5, 1991	Ruth H. Palmer
October 4, 1991	Jane Hook Johnson
December 13, 1991	The Rev. Wesley Freeland Brown '73
May 16, 1993	Harlan Duenow
November 10, 1993	Erskine B. Bowles Sid Gautam
December 17, 1993	Russell R. Knowles
May 7, 1995	Mary Emily Miller Bruce R. Pulliam

— APPENDICES—

December 13, 1996	Ingeborg Dent Sue Laslie Kimball
December 12, 1997	Samuel J. Womack
May 10, 1998	Alan Porter
October 10, 1998	Tibbie Roberts
October 9, 1999	Jeanne Rouse
December 15, 2000	Dr. Assad Meymandi Dr. Louis Spilman, Jr. '64 (Special Presentation)
May 5, 2001	Dr. Benjamin B. Dunlap Rev. Ernest Thompson Herndon, Jr. '70
May 11, 2002	Mr. Thomas F. Miriello '70
May 10, 2003	Dr. Mary Dix McDuffie '75
December 12, 2003	Dr. Loleta Wood Foster Mr. Nolan Clark
April 7, 2005	Mary Butler Yarborough
May 7, 2005	Congressman Bob Etheridge
May 6, 2006	Congressman Mike McIntyre
December 16, 2006	Mr. Brian Whitcomb

APPENDIX O

The Lucius Stacy Weaver Award Winners
(Outstanding Seniors)

1964	Ralph Finton Hoggard
1965	Barbara Allen Holmes
1966	Roberta Dawn West
1967	Ima Jean Hutchinson
1968	Donna Merre Davis
1969	Jamar Francis Loschiavo
1970	Diane Qualliotine
1971	John Wayne Brown
1972	Larry Edward Lugar
1973	Kenneth Lee Williams
1974	Nancy Coleen Shaw Loucette
1975	Sara Ellen Edge
1976	No recipient
1977	Frank Guy Braley
1978	Claudia Harrelson
1979	Jo Anne Jones
1980	Jeffrey Paul Cavano
1981	Ruby Annette Wilson
1982	Patricia Anne Turner
1983	Allen Lee Borgardis
1984	Cheryl Lynn Epperson
1985	Roger Durham Pait
1986	Jean Lemke
1987	Cu Gia Phung
1988	Richard Albert Butler, Jr.
1989	Rebecca Lund Burleigh
1990	Connie Kibben
1991	Kelli Kathleen Sapp
1992	Katherine H. Grasso
1993	Christine Lynn Babb
1994	Stephen Austin Fann
1995	Tammy Jean Murphy
1996	Laurie Ann Davison
1997	Lindy Lu Del Rosario
1998	Jason Anthony Williams
1999	Denise Roni Shuey
2000	Edward G. Price
2001	Svetlana Kurs
2002	M. Carole Blanc
2003	Irina Jorsenson
2004	Sarika D. Bellis
2005	Enausa Davis-Robinson
2006	Lori Ann Knutson

APPENDIX P

The Sam Edwards Award
(Outstanding Evening College Graduates)

1990	Barbara Ratzlaff
1991	Frank Steven Taylor
1992	Judith W. Blake
1993	Gary Doran Rhodes
1994	Ricky Darwin John
1995	Linda Johnson Hood
1996	Mary Francis Williams
1997	Jo Ann Bagley
1998	Darrell Lee Finney
1999	Tracey Kassel
2000	Sabrina J. Sabin
2001	Charles P. Brigman
2002	Tammy R. Maxwell
2003	Frances Rolando Heller
2004	Kevin C. Bradley
2005	Danny R. Marchant
2006	Michael Carrion

APPENDIX Q

Methodist College Alumni Association Distinguished Alumni Award

1973	L. Stacy Weaver & Karl Berns
1975	William P. Lowdermilk
1978	Louis Spilman, Jr.
1980	Terry Sanford
1982	Richard Pearce & Ralph Hoggard
1984	Howard J. Lupton
1985	Thomas S. Yow, III
1989	Jackson L. Langley, Jr.
1991	John W. Handy
1992	Paul "Buster" Sanderford
1993	Jamison Lee Warren, Jr.
1994	James M. Link
1995	William M. Persnell
1996	Barry Horne
1997	Wesley F. Brown
1998	Michael W. Safley
2000	Patric S. Zimmer
2001	Wade E. Byrd
2002	F. Milo McBryde
2003	James K. Weeks
2004	Scott Ellender
2005	William Harrison
2006	M. Elton Hendricks

APPENDIX R

Methodist College Alumni Association Outstanding Alumni Service Award

1970	Charlotte Carmine
1971	Larry M. Barnes
1972	William P. Lowdermilk
1973	Thomas S. Yow, III
1974	Cynthia A. Walker
1975	Mike J. Alloway
1976	Louis Spilman, Jr.
1977	Gwen Pheagin Holtsclaw
1978	D. Michael Servie
1980	Betty Neill Guy Parsons
1981	Steven Hardin
1982	Nell B. Thompson
1983	Lynn Gruber Clark
1984	Jerry & Faye Huckabee
1985	Pat Bracewell Clayton
1986	Howard J. Lupton
1987	Faith Finch Tannenbaum
1988	Ray T. Gooch
1989	Susan Yost Jaeger
1990	Eugene B. Dillman
1991	William P. Estes
1992	JoAnna Cherry Palumbo
1993	Roger D. Pait & William H. Billings
1994	George A. Small
1995	JoAnna Cherry Palumbo
1996	Janet Conrad Mullen
1999	John B. Lipscomb, Jr.
2000	Lynn M. Carraway
2001	Jerry R. Monday
2002	Larry S. Philpott
2003	Nona D. Fisher
2004	Tom Maze
2005	James Darden
2006	Dennis R. Sheppard

APPENDIX S

Methodist College Alumni Association Outstanding Faculty/Staff Award

1980	Garland Knott
1981	Alan Porter
1982	Gene Clayton
1984	Bruce Pulliam
1985	Sam Womack
1986	Ted Jaeger
1988	Sue Jaeger
1989	Elaine Porter
1990	Bob Christian
1991	John Sill
1992	Tony DeLapa
1993	Jack Peyrouse
1994	Parker Wilson
1995	Tryon Lancaster
1996	Joy Cogswell
1998	Dr. Margaret Folsom
1999	J. Michael Roger
2000	T. Jerry Hogge
2001	Walt Swing
2002	Wilford Saunders
2003	Theresa P. Clark
2004	Michael Sinkovitz
2005	William Lowdermilk
2006	Jane Weeks Gardiner

— APPENDICES —

APPENDIX T

Student Government Association Presidents

1963-64	Julian Jessup
1964-65	David Altman
1965-66	Thomas Yow
1967-68	Edward Barber
1968-69	Bob Swink
1969-70	Jim Russell
1970-71	John W. Brown
1971-72	Donald F. Leatherman
1972-73	John G. Dicks III
1973-74	Robert A. Peele
1974-75	Frederick A. Paddock
1975-76	Daniel L. Hood
1976-77	Kenneth K. Daniel
1977-78	James E. Malloy III
1978-79	Ted W. Hough
1979-80	G. Thomas Holland
1980-81	Lynda K. Womack
1981-82	Richard R. Kuglemann
1982-83	William K. Hall Jr.
1983-84	William K. Hall Jr.
1984-85	Victoria J. Smith
1985-86	Calvin McDaniels
1986-87	Chris Grubb
1987-88	Mike D'Arcy
1988-89	Patric S. Zimmer
1989-90	Kevin Carlson
1990-91	Dawn Thompson
1991-92	Kimberly Ratliff

— APPENDICES —

APPENDIX T

Student Government Association Presidents

1992-93	Abigail Findlay
1993-94	Zach Hambrick
1994-95	Shawn Cucciardi
1995-96	Leon Clark
1996-97	Leon Clark
Fall 97	Brett Davis
Spring 98	Felix Sarfo-Kantanka
1998-99	Eddie Price
1999-2000	Eddie Price
2000-01	Jessica Kupper
2001-02	Lindsay Spitzer
2002-03	Michael Brown
2003-04	Danielle Smith
2004-05	TJ Johnson
2005-06	Shauna Bunn
2006-07	Kevin Page

APPENDIX U

Methodist College Athletic Hall of Fame

Class of 1998
Gene Clayton
Ann Davidson
Karen Grant
Rob Pilewski
Paul Sanderford
Bruce Shelley
Ann Thorpe

Class of 1999
Becky Burleigh
David Holmes
Jay Kirkpatrick
Mason Sykes

Class of 2000
Robin Baxley-Long
Earl Bunn
Greg Jones
Joe Pereira
Elton Stanley
Rita Wiggs

Class of 2001
Holly Anderson
Jim Darden
Jansen Evans

Class of 2002
Elaine Adams
Alan Dawson
John McCollough, Jr.

Class of 2003
Daphne Akridge
Eizabeth Horton
Clinton Montford

Class of 2004
Kelly Cap
Mike Currie
Mickey Sokalski
DeCarlos West

Class of 2005
Joy Bonhurst
Mike Brewington
Jeanne Edwards
Kenneth Hoey

Class of 2006
Catherine Byrne
Heather Hugus Pergerson
Dr. Ernie Schwarz
Amy Todd
Jamelle Ushery

APPENDIX V

Sykes Cup Winners

1986 -	Doug Garner (Baseball)
1987	Karen Grant (Track/Field)
1988	Jansen Evan (Baseball)
1989	Mike Brewington (Baseball)
1990	John McCullough (Men's Golf)
1991	Anne Thorpe (Women's Soccer)
	Jay Kirkpatrick (Baseball)
1992	Mike Rohr (Baseball)
1993	Ryan Jenkins (Men's Golf)
1994	Anne Uleman (Women's Basketball)
1995	Kelly Cap (Women's Golf)
1996	Mike Adamson (Men's Golf)
1997	Jason Childers (Men's Basketball)
1998	Tracey Gage (Women's Golf)
1999	Tracey Gage (Women's Golf)
2000	Heather Hugus (Softball)
2001	Elena Blanina (Women's Tennis)
2002	Elena Blanina (Women's Tennis)
2003	Michelle Meadows (Women's Golf)
2004	Adam Horton (Men's Golf)
2005	Charlotte Williams
2006	Katie Dick

— APPENDICES—

APPENDIX W

BUSINESS AWARD WINNERS
Methodist University Center for Entrepreneurship

Given at the Annual Stock Market Symposium

Small Business Excellence Award

2007	Wade Hardin
2006	Thomas Bradford
2005	Richard Guy
2004	Ralph and Linda Huff
2003	Garry & Tyler Nelson
2002	Ernest Stanley Owen
2001	G. Michael Pleasant
2000	Ron and Sharon Matthews
1999	Larry and Brenda Tinney
1998	Judy Cashwell
1997	Bobby and Barbara Hawley
1996	Luke Wheeler
1995	Woodrow Bass
1994	James Peaden and Family
1993	John Lampros
1992	Howard Bullard
1991	Ronald Stone
1990	Keith Allison
1989	R. Leonard Ellis and Joe Walker
1988	Michael Franklin Currin
1998	David Martin
1997	M. Carr Gibson
1996	William Daniel Ratley
1995	James Patrick Godwin
1994	Robert and Barbara Briggs
1993	Larry Godwin
1992	Daniel Dudley P.M. Williams (Melrose)
1991	James Soffe
1990	Al and Mary Grace Cain
1989	Ray Manning, Sr.
1988	Jerry McDonald
1987	Timothy Smith
1986	Dorothy Noe
1984	James Maynard
1983	Hugh Robert Haire, Sr.
1982	W. L. Smith
1981	David Stedman

Silver Spoon Award

2007	Irvin Warren
2006	Felton Capel
2005	Paul Lawing, Jr.
2004	Wendell Murphy
2003	John Wyatt, Jr.
2002	Marvin Johnson
2001	Edward Melvin
2000	Larry Allman
1999	Jim and Sylvia Faircloth

Outstanding Woman Entrepreneur of the Year Award

2008 Carolyn Armstrong and Sharlene Williams
2007 Doris McPhail Williams and Carolyn Naylor
2006 Carolyn Fincher
2005 Grace Henderson
2004 Olga 'Bo' Thorp
2003 Pauline Harger
2002 Jane Smith
2001 Celia McGuire
2000 Sandy Berger
1999 Debra Williams
1998 Jan Johnson and Pat Wright
1997 Linda Lee Allan
1996 Peggy Kirk Bell
1995 Iris Thornton
1994 Sharon Valentine
1993 Jo Ann Kirkman
1992 Terri Union
1991 Jan Britt and Anne Ashe
1990 Mildred Starling
1989 Suzanne Barlow Pennink
1988 Jean Hodges

American Business Ethics Award

2008 Joseph 'Joey' Boles
2007 David Lane
2006 Charles Warren
2005 Robert Schuller
2004 John and Kay Poulos
2003 Robert and Fay Jones
2002 Nathan Page
2001 R. David Ruth
2000 Gene and Pat Howell

— APPENDICES—

Given at the Annual Economic Outlook Symposium

Economics and Business Alumnus of the Year Award

2007 Jonathan Mark Moses
2006 David Herring
2005 Jason Williams
      Jimmy Wood
2004 Phyllis Owens
2003 B. Davis Horne, Jr.
2002 Robert Dunn
2001 Lawrence Walsh
2000 Bradley Minshew
1999 Patric Zimmer
1998 Jurgen Stanley
1997 George Copeland
1996 John Butler
1995 Terry Sasser
1994 James Townsend
1993 Ray Manning, Jr.
1992 David Foster
1991 James Weeks
1990 James Bledsoe
1989 David Altman
1988 Jo Ann Palumbo
1987 Mark Kendrick
1986 Harvey Wright
1985 Douglas Fellows
1984 Regina McLaurin
1983 Howard Lupton
1982 Murray Duggins
1981 Ralph Hoggard
1980 Eugene Cote
1979 David Yount
1978 Joe Shepard
1977 James Peterson
1976 Jerry Keen

Entrepreneur of the Year Award

2007 Thomas Wood
2006 Carlie McLamb
2005 Houston Brisson, Jr.
2004 David Clark
2003 Robert 'Bob' Bleecker
2002 D.M. "Mac" Campbell
2001 Bonner Hubbard
2000 Carlton Martin
1999 Clarence Briggs III
1998 Gregory Stadermann
1997 Stephen Smith
1996 William Rand Jordan
1995 James Robert 'Bob' Smith
1994 Lewis Jourden
1993 Franklin Clark and John Henley
1993 Ray Manning, Jr.
1992 Rajan Shamdasani
1991 David McCune, Sr.
1990 Don Clayton
1989 Charlie Holt
1988 Vance Neal
1987 Dohn Broadwell
1986 Albert McCauley
1985 Ramon Yarborough
1984 W. Don Brewer
1983 M. J. Weeks
1982 William Wellons, Sr.
1981 Von Autry, Jr.
1980 Norman Suttles

— APPENDICES —

Business Person of the Year Award

2007 Dr. Frank Stout
2006 Gary Smith
2005 Sylvia Ray
2004 Don Price
2003 William 'Bill' Bowman
2002 Norwood Bryan
2001 Wyatt Upchurch
2000 Graham Moore
1999 John Carlisle
1998 Wilson Yarborough, Jr.
1997 Michael Lallier
1996 W. A. Bissette
1995 Calvin Wells
1994 Fritz Healy, Sr.
1993 Richard Player, Jr.
1992 A. B. Bryant
1991 Walter Clark
1990 Frank Barragan, Jr.
1989 Joe Wiley Stout, Jr.
1988 David Wilson
1987 Michael Girone

Greater Good Award

2007 Linda 'Jo' Lucas
2006 Dr. Linda McAllister
2005 Dr. Mark Miller IV
2004 Roy Parker, Jr.
2003 Martha Duell
2002 Moses Mathis
2001 Dr. John Wesley Jones
2000 J. L. Dawkins
1999 J. Ernest Johnson

— APPENDICES —

APPENDIX X

Alumni Association Presidents

1965-66	Julian Jessup
1966-67	Roger Williams
1967-68	Jerry Wood
1968-70	Larry M. Barnes
1970-72	Tommy S. Yow
1972-73	Cynthia Walker
1973-74	Tommy S. Yow
1974-76	Gwen Pheagin Sykes
1976-78	Michael J. Alloway
1978-80	Mike Servie
1980-81	Betty Neill Guy Parsons
1981-83	Steve Harden
1983-86	Howard J. Lupton
1986-89	Ray Gooch
1989-94	Roger Pait
1994-96	Janet Conard Mullen
1996-2000	Lynn Moore Carraway
2000-04	Bryan W. May
2004-08	Nona D. Fisher

APPENDIX Y

Foundation Presidents
Fayetteville College Foundation (1956-1967)
Methodist College Foundation (1968-2006)
Methodist University Foundation (2007-Forward)

1957-58	Franklin S. Clark	1991	James Cherry
1959	Alton G. Murchison	1992	Dr. Stan Griffin
1960	Bert Ishee	1993	Jim Kizer
1961	Bert Ishee	1994	Jean Hodges
1962	Newton Robertson, Jr.	1995	Dr. C.T. Daniel
1963	Dr. C. F. Siewers	1996	Craig Stewart
1964	Richard L. Player, Jr.	1997	John Holmes
1965-66	George W. Vossler	1998	Anna H. Smith
1967	Jerome B. Clark, Jr.	1999	Sarah O'Hanlon
1968	John C. Pate	2000	Lou Tippett
1969	I. H. O'Hanlon	2001	Steve Blanchard
1970	William O. Cordes	2002	Danny Highsmith
1971	Norman J. Suttles	2003	Ellis Felton
1972	C. C. Ingram	2004	Dave Foster
1973-74	J. Scott McFadyen, Jr.	2005	Kevin Bunn
1975	Dr. Charles M. Speegle	2006	Louis Feraca
1976	Wilson F. Yarborough, Jr.		
1977	Ray A. Muench, Jr.		
1978	Joseph L. Vogel		
1979	John Corbett		
1980	Marie Stewart		
1981	Walter Moorman		
1982	L. Stacy Weaver, Jr.		
1983	D. P. Russ		
1984	Dr. Dennis Jackson		
1985	Hal Broadfoot		
1986	Rus Crowell		
1987	Robert G. Cogswell, Jr.		
1988	C. C. (Larry) Ingram		
1989	John H. Wheeler		
1990	Tom Williams		

APPENDIX Z

Tapestry (Literary Magazine) Editors

1966	Theodore F. Boushy	1993-95	Ms. Pamela Thibodeau-Dick
1967	Theodore F. Boushy	Fall 1995	Lynn Flanary
Fall 1967	Dennis L. Bruce	1996	Lisa Rogers
1969	William Parker	1996-97	Caroline F. Kearns
1970		1997-98	Tricia Riordan
1971		1999-00	Mary Dewey
1972	Cletus E. Cronrath	2001-02	Rachel Beaulieu
	Hal Stephan White	2003-04	Melissa M. Taylor
1973		2005-06	Shannon Williams
1974	David Atwood		
	Donna Kiki Parrous		
	Glen Carter		
1975	Patricia Meeks		
1976	Luz M. Baumann		
1977	Not Listed		
1978	Anne Fisk Wilce		
1979	Jo Anne Jones		
	Anne Fish Wilce		
1980	Fred Kistler		
1981	Jaci Zwan		
1982	Harley Palmer		
1983	Carol Reichle		
1984	Kathryn Locey		
1985	Karen M. Parker		
	Tanya L. Riley		
1986-87	Tanya L. Riley		
	Connie Kibben		
	Jane Heecht		
1987-88	Connie L. Kibben		
1988-91	Mr. John Hawkins		
1991-93	Ms. Cathy Griffith		

— APPENDICES—

APPENDIX AA

(Student Newspaper) Editors
Small Talk, Pride, Monarch Messenger, Small Talk

Nov. 1961-May '62	Elaine Barbee
Oct. '62-April '63	Kermit Norris
Oct. 1963-64	Lois Stephenson
1965- 66	Larry M. Barnes
1966- 67	William H. Billings
Spring 1968	Susan Sharp
Fall 1969	Kenneth R. Murray
1969	Sonja F. Kendrick
1970	William A. Flowers
1971-72	Sarah Brady
1973	Gene Dillman
Spring 1974	Carmen Evans
Fall 1974	Sue Githens
Spring 1975	Donna Geneinhart & Bill Krumpter
March 1975	Bill Krumpter
April 1975	Kathy Ewing & Donna Gemeinhart
Fall '75- Spring '76	Kathy Ewing
Fall 1976	Jane Peterson
Spring 1977	Jane Peterson, Kathy Ewing
Fall 1977	Ann Morrow & Jim Outlaw
Spring 1978	Ann Morrow & Jim Outlaw
Fall 1978	Ann Morrow & Scott Peterson
Spring 1979	Ann Morrow & Scott Peterson
Fall 1979 - Spring '82	Patricia Turner
1982-83	Patty Smith, Shelia Yates, & Kenny Hall
1983-84	Patty Smith, Mark Powell
Spring 1985	Dale Cook, Richard Briggs, & Smith Simmons

— APPENDICES—

APPENDIX AA

Newspaper Editors

Aug. - Oct. 1985	Tom Jumalon, Tanya L. & Kyle Frost
Spring 1986	Tom Jumalon & Stephanie Williams
Fall 1986	Tom Jumalon
Spring 1987	Mary Ellen Anglin
Sept. - Oct. 1987	Mary Ellen Anglin
Dec. 1987	Joseph W. Vernon
Spring 1988-Fall '88	Gerald Davis
Spring 1989	Ingrid Sauceda
Fall 1989- Spring '90	Betty Darden
Fall '90- Spring '92	Caroline F. Kearns
Fall '92- Spring '93	Martine Lowry & Kim Shackleford
Sept.- Oct. 1993	Derek Tang
Dec. '93-Feb. '96	Dan Devlin, Jr.
Fall 1996- Spring '97	Mike McDermott
Fall '97- Spring '98	Amanda Fellers
Sept. '98- April '99	Cindy Hawkins
Sept.-Oct 1999	Cindy S. Bridges & Mary S. Kinney
Nov.- Dec. 1999	Cindy S. Bridges
Spring & Fall 2000	Cindy S. Bridges
Spring 2000	Cindy S. Bridges & Chuck Heaton
Fall 2000	Cindy S. Bridges
Spring & Fall 2001	Carrie Adcox
Spring 2002	Kelley McGonnell
Sept. '02	Amanda Ritz
Nov. '02	Ashleigh Radford
Spring 2003	Ashleigh Radford
Fall 2003-Spring '04	John W. Arnold III
Fall 2004	Malia Kalua
Spring '05-Spring '06	Will Montoya
Fall 2006	Ashley Genova

APPENDIX BB

Carillon (Yearbook) Editors

1964	Reese Edwards
	Ralph Hoggard
1965	Wayne Autry
1966	Bobbie West
	Wade Mapp
1967	Bill Church
	Wesley Guthrie
1968	William H. Billings
1969	Diane Qualliotine & Linda McPhail
1970	Camellia Sizemore
1971	Ray Gooch
	Valera Snider
1972	William Costin
1973	Coleen Shaw
	Steve Hall
1974	Mike Voss & Pam Walker
1975	Leon Graves
Fall '76	Leon Graves
Spring '76	James Malloy
1977	Kathy Ewing
1978	A.C. Brenda Ellyson
1979	Stella Matthews
1980	John Braden
1981	Carla McLamb
1982	Barry Shelley
1983	Patty Smith, Shelia Yates, & Mark Powell
1984	Mark Powell
1985	Dale Cook, Wendy Smith Simmons
1986	Marie Dexter
1987	Marie Dexter
1988	Susan Osborne

APPENDIX BB

Yearbook Editors

Year	Editor
1989	Susan Osborne
1990	Sherry L. Overton
1991	Sherry L. Overton
1992	Rachel Juren & Amanda Cook
1993	Rachel Juren & Jeannie Denman
1994	Kellie S. Fernandez & Barbie Ward
1995	Kellie S. Fernandez
1996	Kellie S. Fernandez
1997	Lauren Caulder
1998	James Lynch
1999	Jeremy Plumley
2000	
2001	
2002	Andrea Allen
2003	Andrea Allen
2004	Laura Phillips
2005	
2006	

— APPENDICES—

APPENDIX CC

William P. Lowdermilk Student Avchievement Award
*given by the Fayetteville Rotary Club
and endowed by Dr. Lowdermilk*

1995	Jason Williams
1996	Samuel Hudson
1997	Leon Clark
1998	J. Taplie Coile
1999	Lalique Metz
2000	Shawn Hartman
2001	John Morris
2002	Leigh Stevens
2003	Justin Rimbey
2004	Ryan Steele
2005	Nicholas Kimps
2006	Katrina Campbell, Ben Hansen, William Kamffer, Julia Parker, Krystal Richardson, Latoya Robertson, Veronica Romero, Ryan Taylor, Anastasiya Zavyallova

— APPENDICES —

APPENDIX DD

2006 Annual Report

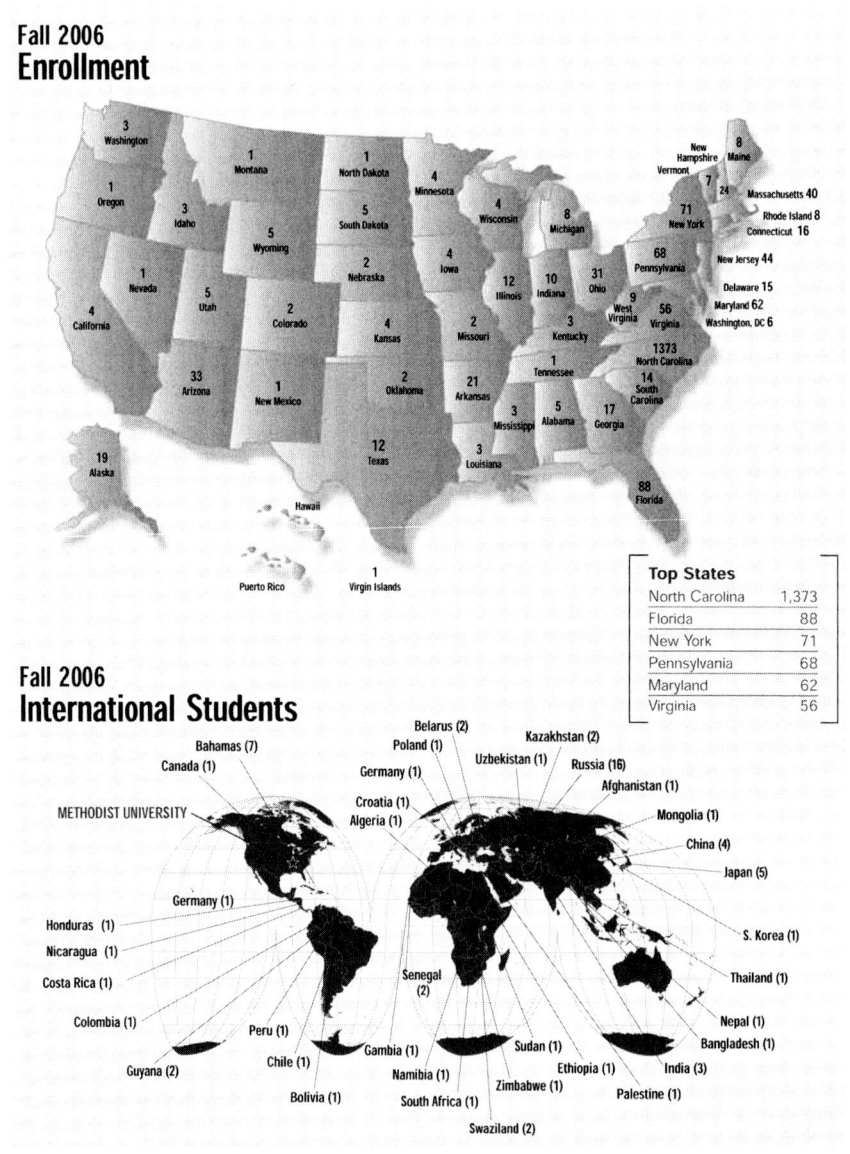

— APPENDICES —

APPENDIX DD

2006 Annual Report

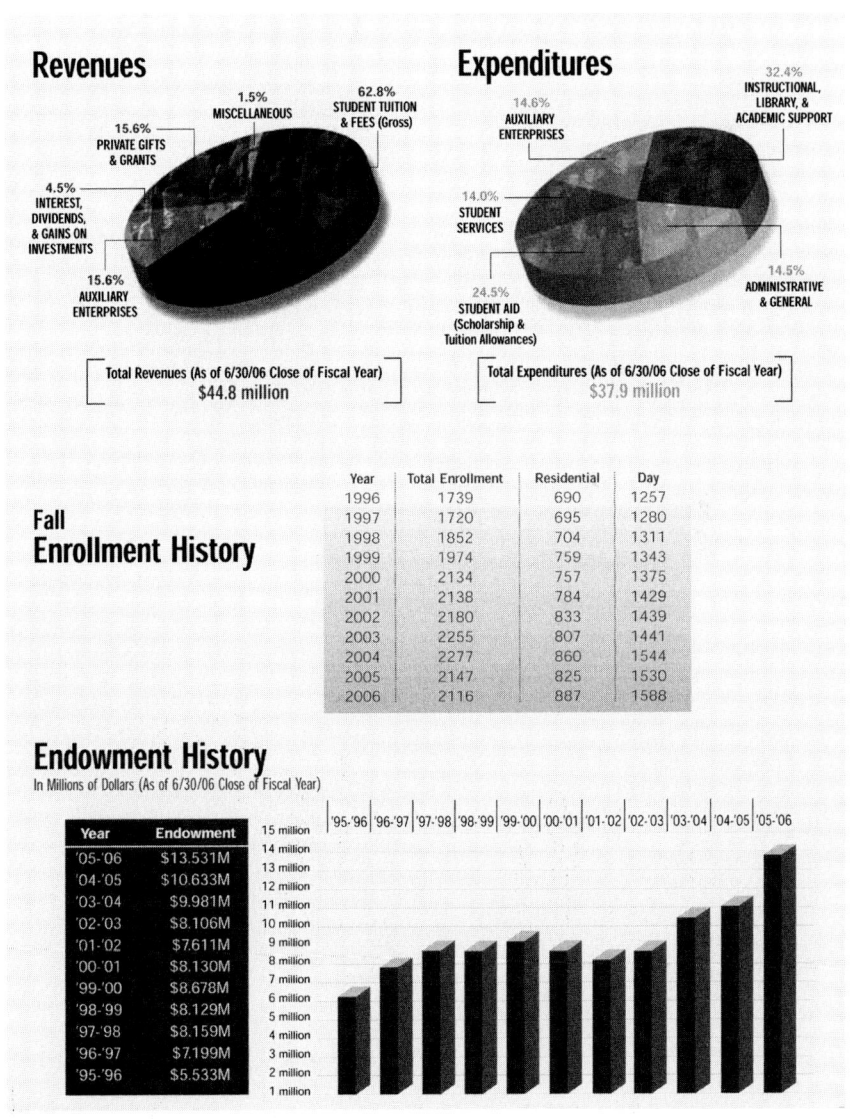

Revenues

- 62.8% STUDENT TUITION & FEES (Gross)
- 1.5% MISCELLANEOUS
- 15.6% PRIVATE GIFTS & GRANTS
- 4.5% INTEREST, DIVIDENDS, & GAINS ON INVESTMENTS
- 15.6% AUXILIARY ENTERPRISES

Total Revenues (As of 6/30/06 Close of Fiscal Year) $44.8 million

Expenditures

- 32.4% INSTRUCTIONAL, LIBRARY, & ACADEMIC SUPPORT
- 14.6% AUXILIARY ENTERPRISES
- 14.0% STUDENT SERVICES
- 24.5% STUDENT AID (Scholarship & Tuition Allowances)
- 14.5% ADMINISTRATIVE & GENERAL

Total Expenditures (As of 6/30/06 Close of Fiscal Year) $37.9 million

Fall Enrollment History

Year	Total Enrollment	Residential	Day
1996	1739	690	1257
1997	1720	695	1280
1998	1852	704	1311
1999	1974	759	1343
2000	2134	757	1375
2001	2138	784	1429
2002	2180	833	1439
2003	2255	807	1441
2004	2277	860	1544
2005	2147	825	1530
2006	2116	887	1588

Endowment History
In Millions of Dollars (As of 6/30/06 Close of Fiscal Year)

Year	Endowment
'05-'06	$13.531M
'04-'05	$10.633M
'03-'04	$9.981M
'02-'03	$8.106M
'01-'02	$7.611M
'00-'01	$8.130M
'99-'00	$8.678M
'98-'99	$8.129M
'97-'98	$8.159M
'96-'97	$7.199M
'95-'96	$5.533M

— APPENDICES —

APPENDIX EE

Methodist University

2006 FRESHMAN CLASS PROFILE

The Admissions Funnel

Total Freshman Applications	1826
Total Freshman Acceptances	1302 (71%)
Enrolled Freshman	425 (33%)

Academic Profile For First-Time Freshman

Average GPA = 3.24
Average SAT = 998

The middle 50% of deposit paid freshman scored between 900 and 1090 on the SAT I
The middle 50% of deposit paid freshman had a GPA between 2.81 and 3.63

Class Rank dispersal
Top 10% = 10%
Top 20% = 24%
Top 25% = 34%
Top 33% = 45%
Top 50% = 71%

171 deposit paid freshman (40% of the class) were Presidential Scholars
Average GPA for Presidential Scholars = 3.73
Average SAT for Presidential Scholars = 1113
Average Presidential Scholarship amount = $7,716

Geographic Profile

- 45% (192) of enrolled freshman are North Carolina residents.
- 27% (51) of North Carolina residents are from Cumberland County.

Largest states represented:		Largest counties represented:	
Florida	42	Wake, NC	11
Maryland	21	Mecklenburg, NC	8
New York	20	New Hanover, NC	8
New Jersey	19	Harnett, NC	8
PA/VA	18	Robeson, NC	8
Ohio	13	Guilford, NC	6
Massachusetts	12	Cabarrus, NC	6
Georgia	7	Baltimore, MD	6
CT/NH	6	Burlington, NJ	6
DE/SC/TX	4	Brevard, FL	5

States represented - 31   International freshman - 17   Countries represented – 14

— APPENDICES—

APPENDIX EE

Additional Enrolled Class Analysis

RESIDENT = 387 (91%)
COMMUTER = 39 (9%)

Top 10 anticipated majors or concentrations
Professional Golf Management concentration
Business Administration/Marketing/Accounting
Biology/Pre-Med/Pre-Physician Asst
Education/Physical Education/Teacher Certification
Athletic Training
Sports Management concentration
Justice Studies
Political Science
Psychology
Resort Management concentration

Religious Affiliation
Baptist = 66
Roman Catholic = 64
Methodist = 63
Presbyterian = 15
Lutheran = 13
Other = 76
Unknown = 129

Course Requirements

16 College Preparatory courses required:
4 years of English
3 years of Mathematics (Math beyond Algebra II is **strongly recommended**)
3 years of Social Sciences
3 years of Science (At least 1 lab science)
2 years of the same Foreign Language are **strongly recommended**

Financial Aid Information

2006-2007 costs:
Tuition & Fees $18,968 per year
Room & Board $7,170 per year
Total $26,138 per year

Methodist College requires only the FAFSA from students and their families. Financial aid is awarded with consideration given to the level of need a student demonstrates (as determined by the FAFSA) and the cumulative grade point average the student carries (higher need and/or higher GPA will net more scholarship money). Over 85% of our students receive more than 15 million dollars of financial aid each year. For the 2006-2007 academic year the college awarded over $8 million in Presidential scholarships, need-based scholarships, performance scholarships (music, drama, debate, and ROTC), and institutionally funded on-campus employment. The average financial aid award for 2006-2007 was over $14,500.

Important Dates and Deadlines

Methodist College operates on a rolling basis for both admissions and financial aid. Early application for both is **strongly** encouraged. It is ***strongly recommended*** that students apply for admissions no later than March 1 of each year, and that financial aid information is completed prior to May 1 of each year. Notification for both admissions and financial aid is also rolling. Students are typically notified of their admissions status within 2 weeks of receiving all admissions materials, and financial aid is typically awarded within 2 to 4 weeks of receiving all necessary information. Students interested in the more popular majors are encouraged to apply well before the dates listed above because of space limitations.

— APPENDICES—

APPENDIX FF

Alcohol Policy (1973)

Methodist College prohibits the use or possession of alcohol by its students, on as well as off campus. This rule stresses the historic concept of Methodism—that of total abstinence. It was not entered into lightly, but after much deliberation.

The trustees of the college call upon the entire college community to observe and dedicate themselves to total abstinence at all times.

Methodist College calls upon its students to abstain from the use of alcohol as a matter of conscience. However, the college realizes there are students who violate the rule and is concerned with realistically supporting the rule in a manner which respects the students as trustworthy individuals. The college does not intend to set itself up as a policeman or spy, and it does not operate on the principle that all students are suspect until proven otherwise.

Methodist College considers its students to be responsible persons who have accepted college regulations by choosing to enroll.

It will act with utmost regret and with deep disappointment when a student flagrantly abuses the trust placed in him or her. In these cases, the student will force an action which cannot be avoided or escaped, unless the college is to betray its own principles.

— APPENDICES—

APPENDIX GG\

Computing Milestones at Methodist College

• Summer, 1982— 8 Radio Shack TRS-80 computer terminals in Davis Library become the first computers on campus.

• Summer, 1983—10 Radio Shack Color Computers installed in the Computer Science Laboratory.

• November, 1984—12 new IBM PCs installed in the Classroom Building to create the Computer Assisted Composition Laboratory.

• January, 1985—Computer Assisted Composition Laboratory opened (CAC is a term coined by the Dean of the College, Lynn V. Sadler, to describe the new concept of creative writing using the latest computer technology).

• Summer, 1985—CAC lab size increased to 20 computers.

• Summer, 1985—First summer computer classes offered to the general public.

• December, 1985—2 IBM PC ATs acquired to begin automation of the Registrar's Office and Business Office.

• November, 1986—Apple Macintosh acquired for the Academic Dean's Office to begin in-house publishing.

• December, 1986—First computerized transcript printed in the Registrar's Office.

• April, 1987—First computerized account statement printed in the Business Office.

• Summer, 1988—Development/Alumni Office records computerized.

• Summer, 1991—Business/Education Laboratory outfitted with 15 386 PCs and 6 Apple IIs.

— APPENDICES—

Computing Milestones

• Summer, 1991—Computer Science Laboratory network put on line.

• Summer, 1992—CAC Laboratory gains 20 new 80386 PCs.

• March, 1993—Development Office network put on line.

• Summer, 1993—Library network put on line.

• June, 1993— Financial Aid Office network put on line.

• July, 1993—Business Office network put on line.

• April, 1994—Payroll network put on line.

• July, 1994—Registrar's Office and Admissions network put on line.

• Spring, 1995—56,000 BPS link completed with Internet supplier to give Methodist College Internet access. Faculty and staff are able to dial up the service from office or home.

• March, 1996—Microsoft presented Methodist College with 500 free licenses for Microsoft products.

• August, 1996—First fiber optic link established between Library and Teaching Materials Center.

• August, 1996—Business/Education Laboratory re-opens with 17 new Pentium based Windows 95 PCs.

• March, 1997—Admissions and Financial Aid networks merged and installed in the first fully network wired building on campus, Stout Hall. Stout Hall is linked by fiber optics to the Trustees' Building.

• Summer, 1997—21 new Pentium class computers and associated hardware were acquired to outfit the CAC lab.

— APPENDICES —

Computing Milestones

• Summer, 1997—21 new Pentium class computers and associated hardware were acquired to outfit the Mathematics Building.

• Summer, 1997—Medical Science Building put on line.

• August, 1997—CAC Laboratory gains 20 new Pentium based Windows 95 PCs connected to MCNET and complete laser printing.

• August, 1997—Methodist College Network (MCNET) put on line. MCNET allows direct connection of computers for 10 megabit access to the resources of the main academic server located in the Trustees' Building, as well as T-1 (non-dial-up) access to the Internet.

• August, 1997—New Mathematics Building opens with three new computer laboratories.

• August, 1997—New Mathematics Building, Berns Center, and Reeves Auditorium linked by fiber optics to the Trustees' Building.

• December, 1997—All rooms in Trustees' Building internally wired for connection to MCNET.

• January, 1998—Business/ Education Lab networked and each workstation given direct Internet access and ability to print to a laser printer.

• January, 1998—Direct internal wiring finished in Administration Building for each office to be connected to MCNET.

• April, 1998—All rooms in Science Building wired for MCNET.

• June, 1998—Fiber optic connection to President's House, Academic Resources Center, Riddle Center, and East, West, Garber, Weaver, Sanford, and Cumberland Halls.

• Summer, 1998—5 new Pentium class computers were networked in an English Writing Lab in Trustees' Building.

—APPENDICES—

Computing Milestones

• Summer, 1998—Business/Educational Technology Lab put on line in Trustees' Building.

• Summer, 1998—Sanford, Weaver, Cumberland, Garber, East, and West Halls category 5 wired for MCNET accessibility with one jack per pillow.

• November, 1998—All rooms in Player Center linked by fiber optic and internally wired for MCNET connection.

• October, 1998—All rooms in Riddle Center internally wired for MCNET connection.

• January, 1999—Clark Hall Business Laboratory comes on line.

• January, 1999—All rooms in the Fine Arts Building internally wired for MCNET connection.

• January, 1999—Nearly 300 Pentium class computers acquired by Methodist College over the last two and a half years in order to enable everyone to share in the Microsoft software gift of 1996.

• March, 1999—All rooms in Berns Student Center internally wired for MCNET connection.

• Summer, 1999—New Davis Library addition comes on line.

• Summer, 2005—Clark Hall, Davis Library, Medical Science building went wireless.

• Summer, 2006—Berns Student Center went wireless.

• Summer, 2008—All Residence Hall lobbies went wireless.

— APPENDICES—

APPENDIX HH

METHODIST COLLEGE BOARD OF TRUSTEES 2006-07

Officers

Mr. Alfred E. Cleveland, Chair
Mr. Harvey T. Wright II, Vice-Chair
Mr. O. Ray Manning, Secretary
Mr. A. Howard Bullard, Treasurer

Trustees Emeriti

Dr. Mott P. Blair, Siler City
Dr. R. Dillard Teer, Durham
Mr. W.V. Register, Dunedin, Florida
The Reverend Dr. Clyde McCarver, Hartsville, South Carolina

Honorary Trustee

Bishop Alfred W. Gwinn, Jr.
The United Methodist Conference

Terms Expiring July 1, 2007

Mr. D. Keith Allison, Fayetteville
Mr. A. Howard Bullard, Jr., Fayetteville
Dr. Eric LeMoine Mansfield, Fayetteville
Mr. Vance B. Neal, Fayetteville
Dr. Louis Spilman, Jr., Fayetteville
Ms. Terri Union, Fayetteville
The Reverend Hope A. Vickers, Wilson
Mr. Thomas J. Walden, Youngsville
Mr. Harvey T. Wright II, Fayetteville

Terms Expiring July 1, 2008

Dr. Richard R. Allen, Sr., Fayetteville
Mrs. Mary Lynn Bryan, Fayetteville
General (ret.) John W. Handy, Charlotte
Mr. Jerry A. Keen, Goldsboro
Mr. Earl D. Leake, Charlotte
Mr. George W. Miller, Jr., Durham
Dr. Frank P. Stout, Fayetteville
Mr. David K. Taylor, Jr., Fayetteville
Mrs. Ann H. Thornton, Clinton

Terms Expiring July 1, 2009

Mr. Frank Barragan, Jr., Fayetteville
Mrs. Betty Upchurch Hasty, Maxton
The Rev. Dr. Brian G. Gentle, Fayetteville
The Rev. David O. Malloy, Laurinburg
Mr. O. Ray Manning, Jr., Fayetteville
Mr. Ron B. Matthews, Linden
Mr. Charles E. Warren, Fayetteville
Mr. Richard L. Player, Jr., Fayetteville
Mr. William R. West, Fayetteville
Mrs. Kathy Wright, Fayetteville

— APPENDICES—

APPENDIX II

METHODIST COLLEGE TRUSTEES 1956-2006

NAME		TERM
Mr. Richard R. Allen	Chairman 1976-1981	1975-
Mr. D. Keith Allison		1999-
Rev. James H. Bailey		1976-1982
Mr. Frank I. Ballard		1992-1997
Dr. C.D. Barclift		1968-1971
Mr. Frank Barragan, Jr.	Chair 1992-1997	1984-2000
Rev. John K. Bergland		1991-1995
Dr. Mott P. Blair	Chairman-1967-1976	1965-1982
Mr. James A. Bledsoe		1996-2006
Rev. Clyde S. Boggs		1969-1977
Mr. Hargrove Bowles, Jr.		1965-1967
Dr. Allen P. Brantley		1961-1969
Mrs. Earl W. (Blanche) Brian		1961-1984
Mr. Dohn Broadwell		1998-2005
Mr. J. Allen Brown		1983-1985
Mrs. Mary Lynn Bryan		1997-
Mr. A. Howard Bullard		1996-
Mr. Wade E. Byrd		1997-2006
Mr. F. D. Byrd, Jr.		1958-1977
Mr. Norman J. Campbell		1967-1983
Mrs. Nancy C. Capel		1988-1990
Rev. Paul Carruth		1979-1982
Mr. Walter B. Clark		1981-1997
Dr. W. L. Clegg		1960-1962
Mr. Alfred E. Cleveland	Chair 2005-	2000-
Mrs. Buena Vista Coggin		1991-1994
Rev. Stephen C. Compton		1995-1998
Mr. Lenox G. Cooper		1959-1982
Mr. M. C. Cottingham		1964-1968
Mr. S. M. Cozart		1969-1974
Mr. J. C. Crone		1977-1979
Rev. Helen Crotwell		1989-1992
Rev. W. A. Crow		1958-1962
Rev. B. L. Davidson		1964-1967

— APPENDICES—

TRUSTEES 1956-2006

Mrs. Walter R. Davis	1963-1966
Mr. William Davis	1975-1986
Rev. Grady Dawson	1962-1970
Mr. Henry B. Dixon	1964-1981
Mr. Sanford Doxey, Jr.	1982-1989
Mr. Murray O. Duggins	1988-1993
Mr. Al Dunn	1984-1986
Rev Camille Yorkey Edwards	1992-1996
Rev. Graham S. Eubank	1960-1975
Rev. Edgar B. Fisher	1969-1976
Rev, F. Owen Fitzgerald	1983-1986
Mr. W. Ed Fleishman	1961-1975
Dr. Loleta Wood Foster	1993-
Rev. R.Carl Frazier, Jr.	2005-
Mr. Charles Gaddy Chairman 1990-92	1988-1992
Rev. William H. Gattis	1988-1998
Rev. Brian G, Gentle	2000-
Mr. J. Nelson Gibson, Jr.	1958-1987
Mr. John Bond Gillam III	1985-2000
Rev. Carol W. Goehring	2006-
Mr. Dan W. Gore	1994-1999
Rev. N. W. Grant	1965-1968
Mr. M. F. Grantham	1975-1981
Gen. John W. Handy	2005-
Mrs. Betty Upchurch Hasty	1989-
Mr. Joseph M. Hatcher, Sr.	1988-1996
Mr. Robert Hatfield	1985-1996
Rev. O. L. Hathaway	1961-1974
Mr. J. W. Hensdale	1963-1978
Mr. James C. High	1988-1991
Mrs. E. L. Hillman	1960-1964
Gen. John R. Hodge	1958-1962
Mr. E. V. Hogan	1981-1982
Mr. Ralph Hoggard	1981-1992
Mr. Charles B. C. Holt	2002-2005
Mr. W. E. Horner	1959-1971
Mr. Edwin A. Hubbard	1999-2003

TRUSTEES 1956-2006

Mrs. Dorothy B. Hubbard	2003-
Rev. H. Sidney Huggins III	1985-1989
Dr. Lucille W. Hutaff	1978-1987
Mr. L. D. Isenhour	1962-1966
Rev. George W. Johnson	1987-1993
Mrs. Jane Hook Johnson	1990-2008
Mr. W. Robert Johnson	1958-1990
Dr. J. Wesley Jones	1998-
Mr. Robert B. Jordan IV	1995-1998
Mr. F. Belton Joyner, Jr.	1977-1985
Mr. Jerry A. Keen	1993-
Rev. Wallace H. Kirby	1973-1975
Mr. Michael G. Lallier	1995-2000
Mr. Earl D. Leake	2003-
Mr. Jack R. Lindley	1999-2002
Rev. William P. Lowdermilk	1998-2005
Mr. Robby Lowry	1993-1998
Rev. David O. Malloy	2000-
Mr. O. Ray Manning, R.	1994-
Dr. Eric L. Mansfield	2005-
Dr. Allen Greene Mask, Jr.	2006-
Mr. Ron B. Matthews	2005-
Mr. Frank McBryde	1959-1963
Mr. James H. McCallum	1975-1983
Rev. C. G. McCarver	1966-1982
Mr. Albert O. McCauley	1993-1996
Mrs. Rhoda H. McMillan	1972-1976
Rev. Samuel D. McMillan, Jr.	1977-1991
Mr. James H. Miller	1975-1983
Dr. H. W. Mark Miller IV	2002-
Mr. George W. Miller, Jr.	1999-2006
Mrs. Maria Minges	1984-1991
Mr. Vance B. Neal	1991-2006
Mr. James B. Noe	1988-2004
Mr. James H. O'Hanlon Chairman 1981-1990	1975-1992
Rev. Jack W. Page	1959-1966
Mrs. JoAnna Cherry Palumbo	1992-1999

— APPENDICES —

TRUSTEES 1956-2006

Mr. W. Daniel Pate	1984-1994
Mr. J. M. Peden, Jr.	1967-1975
Dr. R. L. Pittman	1960-1964
Mr. Richard L. Player, Jr. Chair 2002-2005	1994-
Rev. William M. Presnell	1994-1998
Rev. Vergil E. Queen	1959-1977
Rev. William K. Quick	1970-1978
Mrs. Dorothy Raymond	1979-1987
Mr. J. M. Reeves	1962-1975
Mrs. Sarah Frances Crosby Reeves	1995-2005
Rev. W. V. Register	1966-1984
Mr. J. P. Riddle	1979-1995
Mrs. March F. Riddle	1997-2001
Mr. Fred S. Royster	1969-1972
Mr. J. Paul Russell	1983-1985
Mr. Ernest C. Sanders	1959-1960
Mr. Terry Sanford Chairman-1960-1967	1960-1984
Dr. John W. Schrader	2006-
Rev. William W. Sherman	1988-1994
Dr. Grant S. Shockley	1988-1990
Mr. Timothy R. Smith	1988-1991
Mr. W. L. Smith	1975-1986
Mr. Wilbur R. Smith	1965-1976
Mr. T. Lynwood Smith	1966-1982
Rev. J. Thomas Smith	1994-1998
Mr. Charles Speegle	1976-1980
Dr. William Spence	1961-1981
Mr. Louis Spilman	1968-
Mr. Rufus H. Stark	1977-1984
Mr. W. D. Stedman	1968-1975
Mr. J. Bernard Stein	1977-1984
Dr. William L. Stewart	1999-2003
Dr. Frank P. Stout	1992-
Mr. Joe O. Talley, Jr.	1959-1966
Mr. David K. (Bud) Taylor, Jr.	1993-2005
Mr. R. Dillard Teer	1966-1999
Mr. Emerson M. Thompson, Jr.	1979-1985

733

— APPENDICES —

TRUSTEES 1956-2006

Mrs. Ann H. Thornton		2004-
Mr. W. Lyndo Tippett		1999-2003
Rev. Vernon Tyson		1975-1983
Mrs. Terri S. Union		1984-
Mrs. Anne Upchurch		1982-1986
Mr. T. B. Upchurch		1969-1973
Rev. Hope A. Vickers		2002-2006
Rev. Theodore VonCarter, Sr.		1990-1998
Mr. Thomas L. Walden		1999-
Mr. Joe W. Walker		1990-2002
Mr. Charles E. Warren		2003-
Dr. H. Langill Watson		1982-1986
Mr. Ernest J. Wendell		1988-1990
Mr. William R. West		1993-
Mr. William H. White		1965-1973
Mrs. Sherrill Williams		1985-1990
Mr. Harrison H. Williamson		1988-1997
Mr. J. M. Wilson, Sr.		1956-1967
Rev. Herman S. Winberry		1983-1986
Mrs. Kathy Wright		2005-
Mr. Harvey T. Wright II		1994-
Mr. John W. Wyatt, Jr.		1988-2004
Mr. Wilson F. Yarborough		1958-1982
Mr. Ramon L. Yarborough	Chair 1997-2002	1991-
Adm. Elmo Zumwalt		1984-1986

— APPENDICES —

APPENDIX JJ

1994 Master Plan for Campus
by Shuller, Ferris, Lindstrom and Associates

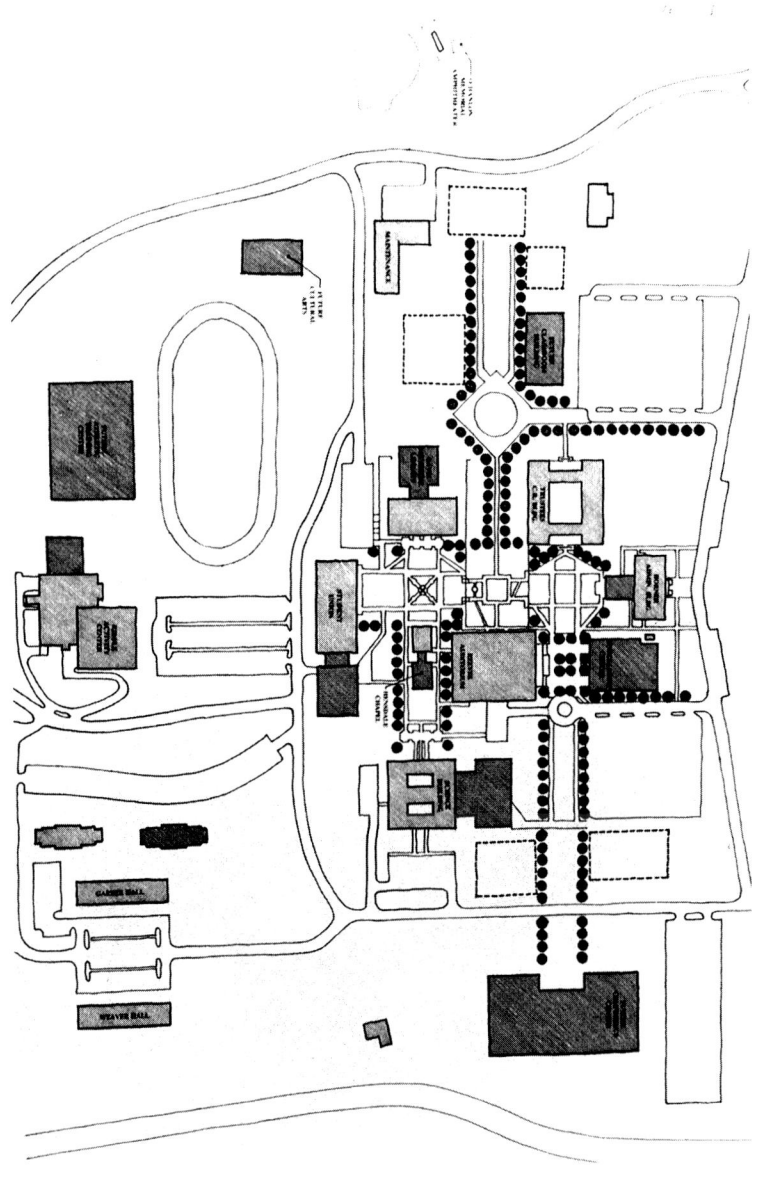

APPENDIX KK

Growth of Methodist University / Hendricks Era

	1983	2008
Est. Replacement Value of Campus Buildings	$29,536,000	$172,346,250
Endowment	$1,262,818	$15,325,129
Enrollment (Fall)	771	2,069
Residential Enrollment	248	908
Employment	110	519 (377 full-time / 153 part-time)
Operating Budget	$3,200,000	$45,835,561
External Debt	$3,645,884	$24,009,622
Salaries/Benefits	$1,500,000	$20,796,918
Utilities	$350,571	$1,527,905
No. of Buildings / Facilities	21	51
Academics	19 majors	43 undergraduate majors; three master's degree programs
Athletics	11 intercollegiate sports	19 intercollegiate sports

— INDEX —

A

Abel, Fran 103, 136
Academic Affairs Committee 56, 57, 331, 339, 343, 349
Academic Development Center 523, 533
Adams, Arthur 17, 62
Adams, Elaine 307
Adams, Harvey 593, 635
Adams, Keljin 536
Adamson, Mike 516
Adams, Paul D. 24
Adcox, Carrie 562, 569
Ad Hoc Presidential Review Committee 402
Adler, Richard 131
Administrative Committee 206
Advisory Committee 19, 20, 22, 414, 607
Affirmative Action Policy 283, 284, 471
Agnew, Donald C. 22, 23, 63
AIAW 329
A. J. Fletcher Foundation 431
Akamatsu, Terry Poole 401, 412
Akridge, Daphne 600
Alan and Elaine Porter x, 411
Al-Azimi, Talal F.M.M. 378
Albritton, Kenneth H. 361, 561
Alexander Graham Junior High School 6
Alexander, Mary 188
Alexander, Nancy 488
Allan, Linda Lee 549, 568
Allen, Bob 630
Allen, Bobby 366
Allen, George V. 217, 266
Allen, Richard R. 284, 305, 317, 518, 522
Allen, R. R. 287
Allen Sr., Richard R. 614, 619

Allied Health Building/Family Medicine Clinic 513, 519
Allison, D. Keith 551
Allvord, Linda 249
Alma Mater 149, 173, 174, 175, 178, 187
Alpha Chi 286
Alpha Xi Delta 251, 257
Alston, Patricia 215
Alston, Richard 154, 208
Altman, Dave 513
Altman Jr., David 117
Alumni Loyalty Fund 380, 387
Alvarez, Christina x
American Association of Universities 28
Americans with Disabilities Act 471
A Midsummer Night's Dream 484
Anderholdt, C. H. 161
Anderson Construction Co. 53
Anderson, Elaine Adams 589
Anderson, Holly 404
Anderson, Jack 306
Anglin, Mary Ellen 398
Antoniel, Leslie 552
Araghi, Sayeh 513
Archie, William C. 124
Arden, Howard 166, 200, 207, 214, 215
Arden, Howie 196
Armstrong, E. E. 52
Armstrong, George 630
Arnold, Frederick 219
Asay, Lynley 522
Asbury, Francis 44, 53, 490, 612
Associated Collegiate Press 238, 347, 367
Association of Collegiate Business Schools 506
Association of Methodist Colleges of The North Carolina

— INDEX —

Conference of the Methodist Church 142
A Strategic Plan for Methodist College: 1989-94 445
Athletic Hall of Fame 536, 541, 553
Atlanta, Ga. 23, 31, 167, 231
Atlantic Christian College ix, 105, 275, 286, 394
Atlantic Coast Conference 30
Atlantic Coast Railroad 49
Atwater, Mary Monroe 147, 208
Auman, James 142, 163, 177, 203
Ausborn, Dawn 593
Austin, Thomas 308, 325, 363, 379, 393, 398, 416
Avinger, John 413
Avner, Berry 613
Aydlett, Virginia 217
Ayers, Bobby x, 243, 279, 355

B

Babb, Chrissy 479
Bachelor of Science in Nursing (B.S.N.) 380, 391, 406
Baer, Don 515, 566
Baggett, Dr. and Mrs. J. W. 27
Bagley, Jo Ann 533
Bailey, James H. 277, 306, 312, 331, 339
Bailey, Lloyd 506
Bailey, Shannon 441, 478
Bailey, Sue 253
Baker, Danielle 411, 424, 428, 431
Baker, Jeff 485, 495
Baker Jr., H. Ray 617
Balaez, Ofelia M. 146
Baldwin, Richard 242
Ball, Walter C. 5
Bandy, Ray 9
Baptist College 156, 157
Barbee, Emma 69

Barber, Eddie 175, 184, 186, 209
Barbour, R. H. 38
Barclift, C. D. 5, 8
Barclift, Chancie D. 284
Bardolph, Richard 279, 281
Barefoot, Irving 69, 72
Barefoot, Vicki 220
Barger, James 247, 248
Barker Jr., Addison R. 111
Barnes, Larry 130, 131, 148, 156, 181, 193, 208
Barnes, Linda Sue 380, 393, 412
Barnes, Lynn Moore 294
Barnhardt, Marlen 113
Barragan, Francie 617
Barragan Jr., Frank 365, 366
Barton College ix, 458
Bass, Earleene x, 410, 515
Batten, Peggy 482
Bauguess, Phil 230, 310
Baxley-Long, Robin 386, 563
B & B Bowling Lanes 81
BB&T (Branch Banking & Trust Company) Charitable Foundation 605
Beall, Byron 308, 309, 318
Beard, Mrs. Linda 474
Beattie, Bud 106, 117
Beattie, Guy 125, 127
Beaver, Gerald 452
Belford, Elizabeth 495
Belk Foundation 190
Belk-Hensdale Company 94
Belk-Hensdale Stores 190
Bell, Glenn 513
Bellis-Rodriguez, Sarika 603
Bell, Peggy Kirk 505
Benedict, Mellen-Thomas 360
Benfield, Tim 482, 499
Benstead, Mrs. Gilda 429
Benton, Mark 581
Benz, Charles 390

— INDEX —

Bergamasco, Fiore 380, 392, 424
Bergland, John 490
Berns, Bernice Strassner 147, 170, 385, 456
Berns, Karl H. 147, 170
Berns Student Center 456, 465, 475
Berry, Jane 277
Best, Nancy Ruth 125, 380
Bethune, Alex 82
Beyah, Adam 578, 634
Beyer, Mrs. Rennie 308
B.F. Stone Endowed Lyceum 535, 543, 545
Bicoy, Richard 345, 362, 378
BIG TALK 282
Billings, Bill 152, 162, 175, 208, 209, 401, 402, 416, 427, 434, 435, 643
Billings, Colleen x
Billings, Cynthia x
Binzer, Carol 380, 395
Bishop's Cabinet 3, 4
Bishop's Long Range Planning Committee xiii
Bitterbaum, Erik 438, 443, 444, 453, 459, 462, 475, 487, 489, 490
Blackburn, Glenn 293, 294
Blackburn, Lois 147
Blackburn, Robert M. 246, 304, 318
Black, Loraine 129
Blackmer, Sidney 132
Blackstock, Walter 161, 167, 168, 209
Blackwell, Marie 380
Blair, Mott P. 141, 158, 176
Blake, Halcyon 563
Blake, Wayne 203
Blakwell, Rose 304
Blalock, Bill 184, 189, 201, 494
Blalock, Lynette 329

Blanc, Carole 585
Blanc, George 545, 565
Blanchard, Steve 571
Bland, Peggy 231
Blanina, Elena 574, 586
Bledsoe, James E. 585
Blewitt, Adrian 533
Bloodworth Jr., Robert 429, 431, 441, 444, 447, 454, 455, 480, 483, 484, 488
Blount, Dick 254
Board of Education 4, 5, 8, 13, 14, 15, 17, 20, 46, 50, 52, 53, 58, 122, 124, 178, 204, 226, 228, 231, 236, 584
Board of Visitors 457, 484, 496
Boggs, Clyde S. 3
Bonhurst, Joy 404, 415, 427, 615
Bonn, Mark 294
Bonville, George 368
Booker, Ivan 183
Bosher, E. S. 104
Bosher Jr., Ernest Sheridan 91, 113, 136
Bosher, Nancy 366
Bott, Ronnie 200
Boushy, Edith C. 147
Boushy, Ted 160, 170
Bowden, Sue 429
Bowles Jr., Hargrove 131, 132
Bowman, Rachel 620
Boyce, Mary Frances 474
Boyd, Bernard 100
Bradford, Anne 87
Bradley, Davis 157
Bradshaw, Kelli 538, 541, 582, 596
Brady, Sarah 223, 231, 233, 267
Braley, Guy 333, 342
Branch Banking & Trust Co. 6, 38, 133, 444
Brandon, Eric 510
Brantley, Allen P. 15, 16, 77, 81,

— INDEX —

84, 96, 128, 135, 137, 141, 163
Braswell, Bill 523, 566
Braswell, Kermit 468
Braswell, Maurice 452
Brewer, Coy 3
Brewer, Don 71, 134
Brewington, Mike 389, 424, 428, 615
Brian, Mrs. Earl W. 15, 16, 53, 70, 264
Brickey, Cedric 423
Bridenstine, Evan 575
Bridges, Alton 429
Bridges, Cindy 557
Bridgewater College 6
Brigadoon 344, 345
Briggs, John 175, 183
Briggs, Richard 363, 368
Brill, Paul 447
Britt, Herman 117
Britt, Kirbie 620
Broach, Larry 254
Broadwell, Charles xi
Broadwell, Dohn 355
Brocki, Michael 400, 413
Brock, Jeff 418
Brock, Summer 482, 483, 487
Brogan, Carol 574
Brookman, Lori 506
Brower Sr., E. N. 81
Brown, Charles E. 543
Brown, David 175
Brown, Eric 620
Brown, John 217, 222, 227, 266
Brown, Kelly 596
Brown, Mike 586
Brown, Terri Moore 459, 601
Brown vs. Board of Education 58
Brown, Wesley F. 533, 580, 634
Bruce, Dennis 162, 173, 175, 209, 563
Bryan Jr., Norwood 155

Bryan, Mary Lynn 401
Bryant, Eric 461
Bryant, Robert D. 194, 283
Bucciarelli, John 446
Buck Naked 482, 487
Bugeja, Tony 520
Building and Grounds Committee 56
Building Committee of the Methodist College Board of Trustees 69
Bullard, A. Howard 585
Bullard, Charles 398
Bullard, Howard and Marta 630
Bunce, Betty Graham 92, 120, 127, 143, 160
Bunce, Maggie 461
Bundy, Mrs. James. B. 218
Bunn, Earl 276, 286, 563
Bunn, Shauna 614
Burleigh, Becky 494, 553
Burleigh, Rebecca 427
Burns Jr., Findley 555
Burt, Millard B. 105
Burton, Hugh 37, 64, 172
Butler, Anne 161
Butler, W. G. 90
Byrd, Bernon E. 183
Byrd Jr., F. D. 20, 114
Byrd Jr., Franklin Douglas 574
Byrd, Wade 493, 580, 585
Byrne, Catherine 626

C

Cable News Network (CNN) 555
Cade, Jane Stroud 582
Cade, John Lee 560
Cade, W. A. 10
Cain, Bill R. 147
Cammack, James 335
Campbell College 79, 117
Campbell, Dennis 444, 498

— INDEX —

Campbell, Norman J. 203, 231
Campbell's "Labels for Education" Program 588
Campen Jr., Henry L. 571, 617
Cannata Jr., Joe 422
Cannon Foundation, Inc. 524
Cannon, William R. 202, 210, 338, 347, 364
Cape Fear Commons 551, 560
Cape Fear Commons II 581, 586, 587, 614
Cape Fear Regional Theatre 413
Cape Fear River 2, 4, 27, 28, 198, 309, 311, 368, 396, 517, 544, 554, 573, 604, 605
Cape Fear River Research Institute 368, 396
Capital Funds Campaign 33, 177
Cap, Kelly 607
CARE Clinic 511
Cargill Associates 482, 486
Carillon x, 113, 124, 125, 144, 145, 175, 249, 257, 280, 283, 307, 330, 363, 466, 483
Carlyle, Irving E. 101
Carmine, Charlotte 158
Carolina College Alumni Association 238
Carolina Panthers 528
Carolina Power & Light Co. 57, 433
Carolina Telephone 77
Carolina Transformer Co. 79
Carrabbas' Italian Grill 615
Carraway, Lynn Moore 522, 563
Carr, George Watts 25
Carrion, Michael 628
Carroll, Charles F. 124, 161
Carruth, Paul 33, 36, 53, 57, 64, 331, 332
Carter, Grayson L. 520
Carter, Lillian 287

Casey, Mike 242, 257
Cavano, Janet 278, 295, 323, 332, 349, 366
Cavano, Jeffrey Paul 305, 308, 324
Cawman, Diane 161
Cedar Falls Equestrian Center and Riding Stables 234
"Celebrate 40!" 521
Center for Entrepreneurship 395
Central Carolina Bank xiv
Champion, Darl H. 482
Chandler, George P. 111
Chandler, Suey 10
Chanticleer 397
Charles M. Reeves School of Business 387
Charlotte College 109, 117
Charlotte, N.C. 41, 54, 188, 228, 565, 597
Charpentier, Daniel 535
Chaves, Jose Maria 147, 157
Cheek, Suzan 405, 451
Cheer Ltd. 600
Cherry, Jane 537
Cherry, Joanna 175, 183, 184, 189
Cherry, Laurie 606, 609
Cherry, Mrs. Jane 429
Chigi, Camille 405
Chisum, Craig Thomas 421
CHOICE 68 196
Christian, Kathy and Robert x
Christian Life Council 449
Christian, Robert S. 194, 271, 315, 318, 379
Clardy, Cermette 355
Clark, Fred 307, 311, 312, 321, 342, 357, 359, 366
Clark, J. Ann 379
Clark, Jerome 180, 190
Clark, JoAnn 308
Clark Jr., Franklin S. 14, 19, 22, 27, 28, 36, 40, 42, 47, 48, 49, 63, 65,

— INDEX —

72, 134, 167
Clark Jr., Jerome B. 179
Clark, Leon 504, 522
Clark, Lynn ix, x, 458
Clark, Mrs. Margaret T. 617
Clark, Nolan 527
Clark, Samuel 380, 386, 404
Clark, Stephen 575
Clark, Theresa P. 531, 599
Clark, Walter 365
Clark, Wilbur 3, 14, 24, 124
Clay, Charles 12
Clayton, Gene T. x, 111, 141, 151, 154, 183, 199, 208, 232, 242, 248, 251, 257, 262, 275, 286, 315, 317, 323, 329, 332, 348, 359, 360, 361, 365, 367, 373, 377, 379, 390, 392, 393, 402, 422, 428, 434, 437, 438, 444, 446, 456, 465, 470, 471, 472, 473, 474, 475, 498, 502, 541, 553, 572, 579, 593, 604, 631, 634
Clayton, Georgena 200, 202
Clayton, Pat 351, 354, 361, 364
Clegg's Site Committee 4
Clegg, W. L. 4, 5, 9, 15, 16, 20, 21, 53, 70
Clergy Friends Association of Methodist College 476, 477, 478
Cleveland, Alfred E. 571, 585, 521, 614, 621, 637
Cline, Betty 161, 575
Clyburn, Claire 449
Cobb, Bobby 255, 268
Code of Conduct 339
Coffman, Amanda 558
Cogswell, Joy 379
Coheley, Alan 458, 459, 470, 475
Coheley, Mrs. Charlotte 349, 353, 392
Cohn, Edward R. 520
Coile, James 478
Coile, James Taplie 539
Coker College 23
Cokesbury College 44
Cole, Brian 473
Coleman, Richard E. 294
Cole, Robert G. 279
College Bowl Team 461, 466
College Centre Office Park 517, 522, 524, 534
College Chorus 147, 164, 172, 173, 174, 189
College Lakes 37, 38, 271
College Level Examination Program (CLEP) 237
College of Charleston 109
College Parents' Association 532
College Wind Ensemble 164, 173
Collins, Chad 539, 547, 574, 617
Collins, Chip 469
Collins, Chris 469
Collins, Kenneth 366, 491, 548, 568
Collins, Tom 273, 274
Colonnese, Michael 429, 431
Columbia College 25, 237, 575
Columbia University 30, 228, 525, 596
Combs, Gregory 612
"Come of Age" campaign 392, 399, 422
Commercial & Industrial Bank 6
Commission on Christian Higher Education of The North Carolina Conference of The Methodist Church 33, 96
Commission on Colleges and Universities 23
Commission on Educational Emphasis of the Quadrennial Program 6

— INDEX —

Commission on Education Beyond the High School 101
Commission on the Accreditation of Allied Health Programs 513
Commission on World Service and Finance 5, 8
Community Council 88, 89, 91, 109
Community Loyalty Campaign 213, 218, 264
Computer-Assisted Composition Journal 394
Computer Assisted Composition Laboratory 365, 368
Comstock, Dale 578
Concert-Lecture Series 140, 147
Conference Advisory Committee to the College 19
Conference College Sustaining Fund 9
Conley, Raymond 201
Conley, Steve 404, 427, 443, 458, 498, 505, 516, 536, 566
Connolly, Paul F. 520
Consolidated Presbyterian College Board of Trustees 2
Construction Systems, Inc. 614
Contardi, Edna 183
Cook, Dale 363
Cooke, Dennis H. 20
Cook, Kitty 217, 224
Cooper, Dave 151
Cooper, Gary 572
Cooper, Lenox G. 15, 16, 110
Cooper, Robert 429
Cooper, William C. 161
Coppeler, Doug 507
Cordes, William O. 218
Corn, Patrick 201
Corso, Patrick 572
Costello, Bob 201
Cotton, William 582

Council, Louise Freeman 127
Council on Social Work Education 524
Council, Susan 158
Cowley, Yolana 161
Cox, Susie 410
Coyne, George 556, 569
CP&L 443, 445, 472
Crea, John 422, 430
Creekside Apartments 619
Cribb, Dwight 181, 301
Crisanti, Wylie 620
Crisp, Bobby L. 147
Crisp Jr., Delmas S. 632
Croce, Jim 239
Crone, James C. 294
Croom, Lela 107
Cross Creek Building & Loan Association 6
Cross Creek Pipes and Drums 447
Crotwell, Helen Gray 449
Crowell Construction Co. 70
Crowell, Russell 155, 262
Crow, W. A. 15
Crozer Theological Seminary 6
Crutchfield, Philip 223
Cuchna, Jennifer 613
Culbreth, Don 170
Culbreth, Oliver C. 246
Cumberland Community Foundation, Inc. 565
Cumberland County ix, xi, xiii, 4, 6, 7, 11, 15, 20, 21, 26, 29, 40, 42, 45, 50, 55, 59, 78, 84, 94, 98, 104, 108, 114, 125, 132, 141, 146, 165, 174, 176, 184, 204, 243, 245, 302, 305, 311, 325, 334, 382, 386, 400, 414, 417, 431, 442, 449, 452, 453, 461, 463, 469, 476, 480, 484, 510, 520, 537, 549, 574, 585, 588, 590, 591, 592, 608, 615

— INDEX —

Cumberland County Council of Civil Defense 104
Cumberland County Democratic Party 480
Cumberland County Public Library ix, xi, 452, 453
Cumberland County Republican Party 520
Cumberland County Schools 510
Cumberland Hall xv, 66, 96, 105, 107, 111, 114, 125, 156, 181, 197, 198, 250, 259, 315, 513, 522, 535, 598, 615
Cumberland Oratorio Singers 460
Cunningham, Burl 341
Currie, Mike 606
Curtis, Cynthia J. 537, 559
Cuthrell, Hamilton 502, 513, 516

D

Dailey, Gloria 215
Dale, Thomas L. 27
Daniel, Joseph M. 96
Daniel Jr., Kenneth 283
Daniel, Regina 286
Daniels, Ken 278
D'Arcy, Mike 408
Darden, Jim 157, 173, 198, 199, 380, 446, 580, 608, 615
Davenport, Robin 589
David R. Nimocks Sr. Professorship 526
Davidson, Ann 506, 541
Davidson, Billy 572
Davies, Jim 125
Davis, A. Dano 338
Davis, Donna 183, 191, 194
Davis, Gerald 399, 412, 434
Davis, Geraldine Tyson 150, 176, 185
Davis Memorial Library x, 129, 150, 185, 220, 238, 272, 279, 323, 370, 394, 425, 426, 471, 484, 520, 534, 541, 544, 548, 608
Davis, Mitchell 276
Davis, Mrs. Geraldine Tyson 98, 150
Davison, Laurie 515
Davis-Robinson, Enausa 611
Davis, Shelby M.C. 630
Davisson, Stephanie 450
Davis, Spencer 575, 583, 634
Davis United World College Scholars Program 628
Davis, Walter R. 176
Davis, William 20
Davis, Willliam K. 25
Dawkins, J. L. 521, 558
Dawson, A. C. 124
Dawson, Alan 405, 589
Dawson, R. Grady 97, 114
Dean Clark 323, 342
Dean, Richard 175, 187, 188, 189
Dedman, Robert H. 538, 567
DeGraw, Jeff 397, 406
DeLapa, Anthony J. 429, 463, 473, 488, 490, 491, 495, 593, 609
DeLapa, Anthony J. Art Award 609
DeLoach, W. S. 286
Delta Mu Delta 508
Dembosky, John 612
Dent, Inge 523
Dent, Ingeborg 93, 194
Dent, Tommy 253, 338, 347, 353
Department of City and Regional Planning at UNC 20
Depp, Mark 125, 127
DePriest, Celeste 442
Dept. of Business Administration and Economics 531
Deunow, Harlan F. 277, 282, 479
Development Committee 80
Devlin Jr., Dan 483, 495, 499

— INDEX —

Dickens, John 44
Dickerson, Deborah 294
Dickinson, Andrea 575
Dicks III, John G. 224, 235, 238, 240, 241, 267, 421
Dickson vs. Sitterson 117
Dillman, Gene 238, 447
Dippre, Keith 575, 599, 618, 631
Distinguished Alumni Award 507, 520, 533, 542, 553, 563
Division of Continuing Education 285
Division of Educational Institutions 14, 17, 46
Dixie Intercollegiate Athletic Conference 109, 141, 151, 152, 173, 187, 199, 201, 207, 378, 379, 381, 406, 428, 429, 432
Dixon, Gordon 262
Dixon, Henry B. 176, 284
Dixon, John 482
Dixon, Lynne 272
Doane, D. K. 439, 498
Dogwood Festival 400
Dole, Elizabeth 410
Doll Jr., Joseph F. 468, 531, 560
Donaldson Academy and Manual Labor School 148
Donnelly, Linda Sue 308
Donor Appreciation Dinner 610
Doucette, Leonard 259
Doucette, Mrs. Nancy Coleen Shaw 261
Doug Clark and the Hot Nuts 197
Douglas, Anne 161
Douglas, Frances 146, 151
Douthit, Bucky 280, 297
Dowd, John Paul "Jay" 489, 491, 511, 558
Dowd, Mrs. Kim 527
Dowd, O. E. 102, 131
Dowd, Orren E. 96

Downing, Jane M. 333
Doxey, Mrs. Sanford 370
Drake, Sarah 620
D. R. Allen and Sons 83, 110, 120, 289
Draughan, Jacqueline 575
Dudley, Claudia 590
Duell, Martha 397
Duggins, Murray O. 388
Duke University 6, 20, 22, 30, 31, 33, 41, 43, 45, 68, 73, 92, 96, 99, 109, 111, 112, 165, 192, 217, 222, 228, 245, 304, 330, 331, 349, 352, 356, 357, 366, 385, 389, 399, 411, 413, 444, 514, 525, 533, 536, 548, 580, 612, 619
Duke University Divinity School ix, 6, 444, 533, 580
Duncum, Greta 89, 90, 99
Dunham, Andrea 299
Dunlap, Benjamin 574, 634
Dunlap, George 156
Dunn, Albert W. 364, 365, 366, 373
Dunn, Millard C. 78, 134
Durham xiv, 3, 4, 5, 10, 15, 20, 23, 25, 30, 64, 80, 120, 156, 158, 164, 175, 187, 217, 257, 271, 276, 329, 343, 345, 348, 364, 367, 382, 485, 502, 521, 525, 534, 536, 547, 550, 558, 600, 643
Durham City Schools xiv, 30
Durham High School xiv
Duvon, Jay 17
Dyke, Katie 559

E

Eaglin, Paul 365, 366
Eakes, Martin 550, 568
Earnhardt, D. E. 10
"Earth Day" 215

745

— INDEX —

Eason, F. H. 57
East Carolina College 5, 9, 20, 73, 167
East Coast Cheerleading Camp 277
Eastern Methodist University 363
East Hall Pearce Hall 541
East West Foundation 298, 301
Eaton, Rob 520
Edens, Hollis 31, 41, 43, 64
Edenton Street Methodist 86, 180
Edenton Street Methodist Church 53
Edgecombe County 45, 549
Edge, E. J. 245
Edge, Sarah Ellen 277
Edmisten, Rufus 475
Edwards, Brad 511
Edwards, Jeannie 282, 307, 615
Edwards, Marion M. 528, 567, 584, 635
Edwards Military Institute 79
Edwards, Reese 113, 117, 120, 124, 125
Edwards, Samuel R. xiv, 68, 72, 73, 85, 86, 90, 105, 111, 114, 135, 194, 200, 245, 260, 369, 449, 486, 497, 510, 523, 533, 543, 555, 561, 565, 592, 601, 616, 628
Edwards, Steve 243
Effigies 413
Ehle, John 441
Elderhostel 392, 406, 420
Elfmon, Mrs. S. L. 52
Elkin, John x
Ellis, Bob 151
Ellis, Mrs. Elizabeth 52
Emerson, Ralph Waldo 641
Emery, Stephen 405
Emory and Henry College 30, 164
English, Butch 308
Epperson, Cheryl Lynn 364

Ervin, Sam 58
Escudero, Esperanza 99
Estes, Bill 463
Etheridge, Bob 611, 614, 620, 636
ETHOS 287, 304
EUA/Highland Partners, PA 462
Eubank Conference Room 295, 301
Eubank, Graham S. 3, 4, 14, 15, 16, 70, 184, 209, 284, 292, 295, 301
Eure, Thad 20, 21
Evans, Carmen 243, 248, 256, 268
Evans, Charles 294
Evans, Gail 555, 568
Evans, Gayle 243
Evans, Jansen 415
Evening College 285, 292, 296, 305, 314
Everette, Mrs. B. B. 10
Ewing, Kathy 263, 275, 283
Executive Committee 14, 31, 32, 34, 38, 40, 41, 47, 48, 49, 50, 51, 52, 53, 55, 57, 65, 139, 149, 150, 155, 166, 176, 178, 190, 191, 204, 205
"Expanding the Vision" Campaign for Excellence 510
Exum, Bob 476

F

50th Anniversary Celebration 618
50th Anniversary Founders Day Convocation 621
Fairley, Leonard 535
Fakhouri, Fouad 604
Falcon Children's Home 305
Fallin, Phil 322, 326
Family Weekend 532
Fannie Farmer Memorial Park 535, 537
Fann, Stephen 466, 490
Faulkner, Jeannine 189
Fayetteville Chamber of Commerce

— INDEX —

2, 24, 251, 396, 560, 572, 596
Fayetteville College Foundation
xiii, 2, 5, 13, 15, 18, 19, 22, 24,
25, 26, 27, 28, 31, 32, 35, 36, 40,
42, 47, 48, 49, 51, 52, 53, 54,
56, 57, 58, 59, 63, 65, 70, 71, 75,
76, 80, 84, 92, 94, 104, 110, 113,
119, 121, 124, 132, 134, 135,
142, 154, 158, 160, 163, 167,
177, 179, 190, 193, 209, 616
Fayetteville College Steering
Committee xvi, 2, 4, 5, 7, 10,
11, 13, 14, 57, 602
Fayetteville Dance Theatre 298
Fayetteville District 3, 45, 46, 78,
105, 184, 301, 332, 449, 451
Fayetteville High School 27, 48
Fayetteville Soccer Complex 573
Fayetteville State College xiii, 24,
204
Fayetteville State University 147
Fayetteville Symphony Orchestra
107, 122, 125, 282, 298, 312,
316, 604, 618, 631
Fayetteville Technical Institute 204
Fayetteville Youth Soccer
Association 488
Ferrell, Laura Belton 308
Ferrell, Linwood 437
Ferris 518, 620
Fetters, Samantha 414
Ficken, Clarence E. 68, 72, 73, 81,
93, 94, 95, 135
Fiddler on the Roof 521, 532, 533
Fields, Arleen x
Fields, William C. 89, 364
Finch, Beth 324
Finch, George 219
Fine Arts Festival 157, 400, 401,
413
Finlater, W. W. 170
Finney, Darrell Lee 543

First Citizens Bank & Trust Co.
xiii, 6, 38, 53, 58, 70, 79, 84,
121, 155, 158, 177, 180, 419,
430, 444, 506, 614
First Methodist Church in Wilson 4
First Presbyterian Church 1, 4, 120,
202
Fisher, E. B. 5, 8
Fisher, Nona 599
Five-Year Strategic Plan 421
Fleishman, W. Ed xiv, 14, 15, 30,
31, 62, 104, 141, 167, 284, 290,
389
Flipping, Harry "Flip" 242
Florence Rogers Charitable Trust
382, 416, 573, 601
Flowers, Bill 207
Flynn, Jonathan 190
Flynn, Robert 189, 190, 210
Folsom, Margaret D. 247, 469
Ford Foundation 204
Fort Bragg 2, 3, 4, 9, 11, 41, 50, 51,
69, 83, 86, 112, 126, 141, 142,
150, 204, 238, 270, 279, 329,
341, 361, 368, 384, 385, 396,
400, 413, 441, 444, 449, 577,
608
Fort Bragg Bicentennial Color
Guard 270, 279
Foster Jr., Ivan L. 248
Foster, Loleta Wood 585, 600, 636
Foster, Ron 501, 513, 540, 564, 566
Foti, Silvana 379, 537
Founders Day 77, 100, 102, 115,
128, 135, 136, 137, 231, 232,
240
Fountain, Patrick D. 520
Fowler, Danny 243
Fox, Larry 100
Fox, Marie C. 74, 100
Fox, Richard "Dick" 550
Francis Asbury Award 490

— INDEX —

Franklin County 13
Frazier Jr., Carl 538, 612
Frazier, Larry 448
"Fred Chappell: Places of Possibility" 532
Freshman Orientation Code 148, 149
Friday, William 41, 360
Fridriksson, Bjorgvin 502
Friedlander, Brett 591, 635
Friends of Davis Library 367
Fritz, Bruce 307
Future Shock 242

G

Gaddy, Charlie 407, 408, 443, 451, 470, 497
Gage, Tracey 539, 547
Galileo 386
Gallagher, Joe 247, 253, 271, 275
Galloway, Anne 620
Gambrell, Justin 549, 568
Garber Hall 96, 111, 114, 125, 127
Garber, Paul Neff xi, xiv, 1, 3, 4, 6, 7, 8, 10, 26, 27, 28, 31, 33, 41, 42, 43, 44, 45, 46, 58, 59, 60, 61, 76, 77, 79, 114, 122, 123, 125, 127, 134, 177, 189, 191, 192, 536, 561
Gardiner, Jane Weeks 475, 537, 626, 632
Gardner, John 130, 131
Garner, Doug 389
Garrett, Frances C. 194
Garrick, Grier 338
Garthly, Elizabeth F. 111
Gates, Willis 74, 77, 90, 91, 102, 107, 114, 122, 125
Gautam, Sudhaker "Sid" 194, 248, 251, 252, 550
Gavin, Bob 80
Gemeinhart, Donna 276, 317

General Conference of The Methodist Church 1, 4, 6, 7, 61
General Conference of The Methodist Church's Board of Education 4
Geneva Area of The Methodist Church 6
Genova, Kimberly 617
Gentle, Brian 581, 583, 614, 634
Georgia Tech 36
Getachew, Emma Bet 367
Gettysburg College 69, 74
Gibon Jr., J. Nelson 14, 15, 16, 62, 240, 244, 275, 292, 301, 317 548, 616
Gibson, Mr. and Mrs. Carr 550
Gilbert, Fred 613
Githens, Susan 254
Giving It the Good Old College Try 169
Gladys' 219
God's Favorite 310
Godwin and Bell 38
Godwin, Gayle 260
Godwin, Maurice 575
Godwin, Virginia 503
Golden Belt Peach Orchard, Inc. 38
Golden Corral Restaurants 476
Golden Knights 323
Goldsboro xvi, 6, 8, 10, 12, 15, 33, 61, 96, 172, 207, 214, 294, 521, 542, 558, 575
Goldwater, Barry 129
Gooch, Buddy 283
Gooch, Ray 181, 192, 381, 402, 408, 415, 420, 601, 612, 636
Gooch, Wayne 276
Goodson, Kenneth 283
Gosier, Jim 107
Gottlieb, Robin 322
Grace Pittman Building 15, 32, 104
Graham, Bobby 581, 599

— INDEX —

Graham, Frank Porter 17, 20
Graham, Gary 513
Granger, Paul D. 293
Grant, Henry 152
Grant, Karen 541
Grasso, Katherine 468
Graves, Anita 282
Gravitt, Linda 606, 636
Gray, Karen 516
Greatest Gift Scholarship Program 361, 280, 281
Green and Gold Café 587
Green and Gold Masque Keys 120
Green, Donald 161, 195
Greene, Robin 520, 551, 557
Greene, Wendy 368
Green, Larry 413, 513
Green, Lynn 575
Greensboro City Schools 30
Greensboro College 20, 33, 173, 214, 242, 273, 289, 429, 432, 461, 464, 553, 559
Greenville 5, 9, 13, 14, 15, 96, 215, 277, 312, 549
Green, William 391, 411, 421, 434
Greer, Allyson 469
Gregory, Dennis 375, 379, 380
Griffin, Stan 474
Grooms, Duane 613
Gross, John O. 17
Grubb, Chris 405
Gruber, Lynn 385, 388, 402
Guilford College 69, 73, 117, 206
Gum, Walter C. 192
Guy, Betty Neill 86, 107, 109, 113, 120, 135, 136

H

Habitat for Humanity 533
Hackley, Lloyd V. 423, 449, 498
Hagus, Heather 563
Hair-Pierce, Yvonne 495
Halcyon Blake 563
Hale, Michael 156
Hall, Frances 69
Hall, Johnny 107
Hall, Kenny 335, 340, 342, 344, 353, 360, 372
Hall of Fame Golf Classic 559
Hall, Rhonda 450
Hall, Richard 549, 599
Hambrick, David Zachery "Zach" 480, 502, 543
Hamby, Dawn 95, 109
Hamilton, Johnny 106
Hammond, Kerry 575
Hamm, Rodney G. 555, 568
Hamric, Brian 338, 340
Handy, John W. 160, 463, 468, 557, 609, 612
Hansen, Jacquelyn 520
Hanson, Genevieve C. 582
Hanson, Lindsay 613
Haracivet, John 580
Harden, Steve 340
Hardin Jr., Paul 144
Harel, Valerie 487
Harley, Ann 391, 406
Harling, Hugh 549
Harmon, Carson 117, 126
Harnett County xiv, 399, 400
Harris, Larry 117
Harrison, Bill 574
Harrison, Kathie 380
Harrison, Mike x
Harrison, William 486, 615
Harris, Pierce 179
Harris, Rodney 466, 495
Harris, Shearon 252
Harshaw, Quinton 423
Hartline, Danny 389, 404
Hartman, Mike 338, 340, 362
Hartmann, Charles C. 25
Hartman, Richard O. 146, 169

— INDEX —

Hartman, Shawn 557
Hartsville, S.C. 23
Hatchell, David 189
Hatcher, Joseph 407
Hatfield, Robert 402, 486, 490
Hathaway, O. L. 3, 15, 46, 48, 64, 141, 163, 216
Hauser, Barbara 126, 127, 132, 137
Hayes, Allen 413, 513
Hayes and Howell Associates 390, 399
Hayes, Mike 283
Hayes, Robin 555, 568
Hay, Melissa 627, 637
Haymount United Methodist Church 5, 523, 547
Hay Street 2, 3, 4, 13, 15, 32, 33, 41, 43, 45, 50, 73, 77, 89, 91, 125, 127, 184, 301, 525, 538, 608, 618, 628, 643
Hay Street United Methodist Church 3, 4, 13, 33, 41, 43, 73, 77, 89, 125, 127, 184, 301, 525, 538
Healy, Walker B. 3, 4, 202
Heath, Brenda 157
Heaton, Chuck 557
Heffern, James R. 87
Heinen, Michelle 596
Heller, Francesea Rolando 601
Helms, Jesse 520
Henderson, Roy 199, 215
Hendricks, George 620
Hendricks, Jerry 496
Hendricks, M. Elton ix, x, xv, 321, 349, 350, 351, 352, 353, 355, 356, 357, 358, 359, 364, 365, 370, 372, 373, 375, 376, 377, 378, 380, 382, 387, 388, 390, 391, 392, 393, 395, 397, 398, 399, 402, 403, 405, 407, 409, 412, 414, 418, 419, 421, 422, 428, 430, 434, 435, 436, 437, 438, 442, 443, 444, 445, 449, 451, 453, 454, 456, 457, 458, 462, 465, 470, 472, 476, 478, 479, 481, 483, 485, 486, 487, 488, 489, 490, 492, 497, 498, 499, 501, 502, 504, 505, 506, 511, 521, 523, 525, 526, 529, 530, 533, 543, 545, 550, 551, 555, 558, 562, 565, 566, 567, 568, 569, 571, 572, 581, 584, 587, 588, 590, 591, 592, 593, 596, 600, 601, 604, 607, 611, 622, 623, 626, 627, 628, 630, 635, 636, 637, 640
Henley, John T. 277, 317, 401
Hensdale Chapel 215, 250, 251
Hensdale, John W. 3, 52, 98, 110, 142, 159, 216
Henwood, Janelle 161
Herald-Sun Papers xiv
Herbert, Gordon 187, 210
Heritage Family Physicians 524, 534
Herndon, George B. 1, 3, 11, 27, 61, 75, 134, 213
Herndon, Tommy 574, 634
Herring, David 106, 109, 118, 136, 160
Herring, John 620
Hersch, Robert 304
Hester, Brenda 253
H.E.W. Title IX 283
Hiatt, Bruce 196
Hicks, Bradley 502, 536
Higher Education Act 150
High, James 407
Highland Country Club 355
High Point College 20, 30, 33, 111, 228, 273, 459, 525
Higy, Carol 429, 455
Hill, George Watts xiv

— INDEX —

Hillman, James E. 5, 10
Hillman, Mrs. E. L. 15, 16, 70
Hill, Rodney 161, 164, 173
Hinson, Peggy 537
History 578
History, International Studies and Political Science Club 578
Hixson, Ivy May 122
Hobgood, Hamilton 9, 10, 61
Hodge, John R. 3, 4, 15, 16
Hodges, Bobby 215
Hodges, Luther H. 42, 45
Hodgkins, Sara W. 312
Hoey, Kenneth 615
Hogan, Mike 482, 483
Hoggard, Ralph 91, 126, 127
Hogge, Jerry 405, 427, 531, 563, 590, 602
Holderied, Anthony 612
Holland, Connor 95, 109, 116, 135, 136
Holland, Tom 294
Hollis, Patrick D. 230
Holmes, Barbara Allen 144
Holmes, David 553
Holmes, Mrs. James D. 146
Holshouser, Jim 256
Holt, Charles B. C. 585
Holt, D. D. 48, 65
Holt, Glen 479, 499
Holtsclaw, Gwen Pheagin Sykes 154, 208
Holtsclaw, Tom 364
Holtz, Steve 513
Honeycutt, Bill 157
Honorary Degree Committee 281
Honor Code 151, 152, 394
Honors Hall 481
Honor System 151, 153
Hood, Danny 253
Hood, Gurney P. 8
Hood, Mrs. Linda Johnson 510

Hood, Thomas A. 49
Hopkins, Darlene 482, 506
Hopkins, Steve 158, 162, 171, 173
Horne, Barry 520
Horner Administration Building 261
Horner, W. E. 18, 15, 16, 17, 23, 39, 52, 62, 63, 64, 65, 110, 114, 149, 227, 375, 376, 390, 401
Horner, William W. 230
Horton, Adam 606
Horton, Elizabeth 469, 491, 600
Hostetter, Robert L. 502
Hough, Ted 299
Houghton Jr., Amory 132
House, Dwight 286, 366
Houston, Valerie 333
Howard, Mrs. Morie 420
Howard, Mrs. Morie Murray 449
Howard, Rebecca 582
Howell Construction Co. 55
Howell, Eleanor 205
Howell, James 194
Howze, Hamilton H. 41
Hoyle, Ruth 294
Hsin, Ying 182
Hubbard, Edwin A. 585
Hubbard, Elmer 243
Hubbard, Mrs. Dorothy Bell 597
Hubiak, Tracy 473
Huckabee, Jerry 117, 151, 437
Hudson, Howard 202, 446
Hudson, Marsha 294
Huggins III, H. Sidney 365, 490, 499
Huggins, Kay 380
Hugo, Victor 1, 61
Hulley, Clarence C. 182, 220
Hummer, Keith 201
Humphreys, John 512, 566
Hunley, Mary 278
Hunt, James B. 613

— INDEX —

Hunt Jr., Earl 224
Hurley, Patrick Robert 450
Hurricane Daisy 41
Hurricane Floyd 549
Hurricane Fran 520, 521
Hurricane Isabel 597
Hutaff, Dorothy 52
Hutaff, Lucille W. 294
Hutchinson, Jean xi, 156, 158, 160, 178, 209, 219
Hutson, Harold W. 20
Hutto Jr., David N. 194

I

Icochea, Andy Icochea 625
Igor 161, 162, 163
I Love To Cook II 404
Institute for Golf and Tennis Management 531
International Studies and Political Science Club 578
Investment Committee 301, 314, 375, 392
Isenhour, Lewis D. 97
Ishee, Bert 47, 52, 65, 75, 76, 80, 84, 92, 134, 561, 617
Ishee, Jean B. 74, 288
Isner, Robert B. 48, 49
"Iterations" 368

J

Jaber, Trudi 189
Jackson, Jonathan 411
Jackson, Joy A. 146
Jackson, Linda 286
Jackson, Mrs. C. Wallace "Pinky" 5, 61, 616
Jackson, Patricia 69, 87
Jackson, Ramona 354
Jaeger, Susan 334
Jaeger, Ted 304, 375, 393
James, Connie 126

Jameson, Andrew 612
Jameson, Melissa 617
Jarman, DeeDee 531, 535, 547
Jenkins Jr., Arthur C. 25
Jenkins, Ryan 505
Jerch, Jennifer 459, 463
Jernigan, Glenn R. 213, 245
Jessup, Julian 109, 122
Jeter Jr., Frank H. 51
J. J. Barnes Inc. 55
J. L. Stokes 20
Joe W. Stout Hall 516
John, Ricky 497
Johnson, Cureton 511
Johnson, Deryl F. 205
Johnson, D. S. 9
Johnson, George 414, 422
Johnson, George M. 108
Johnson, Jane Hook 585
Johnson, J. Ernest 550
Johnson, Jimmy 126
Johnson Jr., Henry 89
Johnson, Luke Timothy 552
Johnson, Lyndon 129, 132
Johnson, Mrs. Guler 161
Johnson, Pamela 449
Johnson, Sandra E. 202
Johnson, Stacey H. 205
Johnson, Wenda 459, 604, 632
Johnson, W. Robert 15, 16, 110, 142, 159, 216, 259, 268, 470, 542, 558
Johnston & Erwin 343
Johnston, Jeffrey 345, 372
John Templeton Endowed Lecture in Science and Religion 573
Joint Committee to Study the Future of United Methodist Higher Education 264
Jones, Carroll 418
Jones, D. Trigg 124
Jones, Greg 253, 271, 502, 563

— INDEX —

Jones, Helen Elizabeth 111
Jones, Huldah Bethune 181, 322
Jones, James Archibald and Mary McNair 145
Jones, JoAnne 312
Jones, J. Wesley 551, 585
Jones, L. Gregory 548, 568
Jones Memorial Carillon 483
Jones, Patricia 366
Jones, Pauline 181
Jones, Troy 363, 367
Jordan, Charles E. 20, 22, 63
Jordan III, Robert D. 388
Jordan, William 445, 485, 489, 575, 634
Jorgenson, Irina 594
Josten's 113
Journey-Chisum Memorial Garden 424
Journey, William Thomas 421
Joyner, Jr., F. Belton 37, 60, 64, 65, 131, 294, 388, 521, 543, 567, 623, 624, 637
Joyner, Gordon L. 285
Julian, I. B. 180
Jumalon, Tom 341, 376, 380, 382, 391, 398, 434

K

Kalina, Anthony 161
Kangaroo Court 184
Kate B. Reynolds Trust 524
Kearns, Candy 341
Kearns, Caroline 454, 459, 498
Kearn, Virginia 95, 135
Keen, Jerry x, 447
Keller, Theresa 215
Kelly, Billy 100
Kelly, Joseph 69
Kelly-Springfield Appreciation Day 588
Kemp, Rita "Baez" 106

Kendall, Pete 426
Kendall, Peter 418, 426
Kendrick, Sonja 199, 207
Kennedy, John F. 74, 117
Kennedy, Robert F. 639
Keppel, Francis 132
Kernek, Laura Kafka 378
Kershaw, Theodore 3, 4
Kervin, Fred 260
Keso, John 405
Kessell, Tracy 555
Ketchum and Ketchum 382, 392
Ketchum, Inc. 51, 56
Kibben, Connie 442
Kilbourne, Ed 344
Kimball, Sue ix, 304, 328, 329, 357, 368, 379, 420, 488, 523, 532
Kimbel, Eric 462, 467, 498
Kincer, Kim 539, 574
Kinder, Ray J. 146, 248
King (Mascot) 627, 633
King, Arnold K. 20, 261
King, Carl 547, 564
King David 326, 327
King's Grant Golf and Country Club 553, 633
King's Grant golf course 632
King's Grant Golf Management, LLC 633
King, Willis J. 192
Kinlaw, Daniel 522
Kinlaw, George Alred 522
Kinlaw, Mr. and Mrs. John C. 27
Kinston 3, 4
Kirby, Bill 345, 437
Kirby, Wallace 259
Kirchner, Mary 520
Kirkhuff, D. Jean 294
Kirk Jr., Phillip J. 546, 584
Kirkpatrick, Jay 447, 459, 553
Kistler, Mrs. Charles 52

— INDEX —

Kizer, Jim 474
Kizzori, Sherry 341, 353
Klauk, E. Russell 294
Klein, Donald 418
Kletter, Karen 613
Klutz, John 286
Knight, Craig 242
Knott, Garland T. 156
Knowles, Russell 486
Knutson, Lori Ann 619
Koinonia 225, 286, 325, 341
Koonce, Charles 549
Kremer, Cheryl 495
Kresge Challenge Grant 438
Kresge Foundation 392, 407, 409, 520, 608, 616
Krueger, Linda 391
Kruschev, Nikita 103
Kubisty, Ed 252
Kugelmann, Rick 329, 334
Kupper, Jessica 557, 561
Kuralt, Charles 276
Kurs, Svetlana 574

L

Lafayette Collection (Papers) 176, 465, 471, 472
Lain, John 338
Lake, I. Beverly 74
Lambda Chi Alpha 257
Lambert Jr., Otis P. 74
Lambie, Lois 174, 175, 187, 209, 401
Lancaster, James 256, 268
Lancaster, Tryon 459, 507, 510
Landry, Nadine 304
Landsberger, Robert 158
Langston, April 408
Lapke, Robert 120
Lara, Rosario 613
Largent, William "Chip" 205
Larkins, John 74

Larrimore, Whitney 613
Laslett, Basil G. 25
Lassiter, Donald 459, 545, 603
Laurinburg 1, 2, 145, 148, 151, 256, 310, 463, 536
Lawrence, Dan 353
Leake, Earle 558, 569, 597
Leatherman, Donald 217, 223, 224
Leathers, Dale 200
Leaves Before the Wind 167, 168, 209
Ledford, Jim 235
Lee, Allen 328
Lee, Jackson 245, 251, 264
Lee, Winkie 263
Lehman, Faye 194
Lehman, Jerry D. 194
Lennon, Alton 94
Lenoir, N.C. 30
Leslie, Alvin 257
Levine Jr., Phil 117, 446
Lewis, Jerry 294
Lewis, John 217, 266
Lilly, Richard M. 52
Lincoln, Robin 513
Lin, Jen-Hsiang 418, 531, 552
Link, James M. 489, 490, 494, 499, 609, 636
Lipe, Chuck 366
Lipscomb, Betty 179
Lipscomb, John B. 508, 553
Listen to My Song 399, 400
Little Anthony and the Imperials 184
Little, Calvin 350, 351, 353
Llanos, Juan xi
Lloyd Advertising Inc. 22
Lloyd, Tim 263
Longest, Mrs. Pauline Moser 96, 174, 205, 523, 524, 616, 617
Long, Gabriel 44
Long, Gary 495

— INDEX —

Longleaf Press 537, 551
Long Range Planning Committee xiii, 3, 4, 5, 8, 10
Loschiavo, James 202
Louisburg xiii, 3, 4, 5, 8, 9, 10, 12, 13, 20, 22, 24, 33, 44, 45, 53, 57, 203, 273, 286, 297, 305, 327, 329, 379, 394, 449, 451, 491, 542, 607, 643
Louisburg College xiii, 3, 4, 5, 8, 9, 10, 12, 13, 20, 22, 24, 33, 45, 273, 286, 297, 305, 329, 379, 394, 449, 542, 607
Louisburg College Board of Trustees 9, 10
Love, Margaret 219
Lowdermilk, William P. x, xv, 111, 180, 192, 193, 194, 209, 210, 264, 285, 291, 296, 306, 331, 356, 359, 363, 368, 369, 373, 383, 389, 401, 414, 434, 451, 477, 478, 480, 490, 499, 503, 504, 505, 508, 552, 553, 585, 611, 612, 615
Lowenstein, Allard 125
Lowe, Rick 510
Lowry, Jerry 597
Loyalty Fund Drive 283
Loyer, Milton W. 194
LSV Partnership 480
Lucas, Claudia 437
Lucius Stacy Weaver Award 127
Luck, Eddie 606
Lugar, Larry Edward 195, 237
Lumberton 3, 4, 533, 550
Lupton, Howard 351, 354
Lura Tally Center for Leadership Development 492, 493, 546
Lynchburg College 109
Lynch, Jamee 527

M

Mabson, Robert 131
Macarena 533
Macdonald, Dune 71, 134
MacMillan, Dan 2, 25, 61, 252
MacPhail, Arthur and Portia 82
Magnificat in D Major 335
Maguire, George 429
Mallett, Peter 415
Mallett-Rogers House 414, 415, 416
Malloy Jr., James E. 280, 286, 293, 301
Manning, O. Ray 585
Manning, Thomas 219
Manning, Tommy 103, 136
Mansfield, Eric L. 612
Marchant, Danny 616
March F. Riddle Center 437, 445
Marcin, James 620
Marcus, Jerry 446, 513
Margaret and Walter Clark Hall 37, 544
Market House 9, 15, 50, 618
Maron, Margaret 483
Marques, Goncalo 589
Marquis de Lafayette 176
Marr, John Michael 405
Marshall, Dale 151
Marshall, Elaine 607, 636
Martin, Earl D. 194
Martin, Etsuko 495
Martin, Heather 602
Martin, Jim 368
Martin, Ronnie 549
Mary Babcock Reynolds Foundation 121
Mary Jeanne Blackburn Scholarship 292
Masley, Rozlyn 461
Mason, Beth Cook 308

— INDEX —

Mason, Lester 107
Mason, Rom 140, 141, 152, 208
Massengill, Nancy C. 183
Master of Justice Administration 615
Mataxis, Ted 555, 556
Math and Computer Science Building 506, 519, 530
Matteson, Rowland 161, 222, 223
Matthews, Charles E. 147
Matthews, Eddie 581
Matthews, Ron and Sharon 608
Matthews, Ron B. 612
Matthews, Sandra 219
Matthews, Stella 307
Maxwell, Dudley 261
Maxwell, Harold 102
Maxwell, Tammy 592
May Dance 140, 157, 189
Maynard, Jim 476
Maze, Tom 189, 482
McAdams, Charles K. x, xiv, 10, 55, 57, 66, 68, 79, 91, 92, 106, 111, 114, 138, 156, 180, 189, 193, 194, 356, 369, 561, 611
McAdams, Verna Brock 542
McAlexander, John A. 146
McAllister, Phil 308
McBride, Liz 420
McBryde, Frank 1, 3, 15, 16, 17, 20, 25, 31, 40, 53, 63, 70, 84, 110
McBryde, Frank Milo 175, 389, 589
McBryde, Leon 155
McBryde, Vearl G. 96, 121
McBryde, Winnie 235
McCall, Mary Deyampert 612
McCandless, James 613
McCarver, Clyde 306
McChesney, Janet 108
McClelland, Roy F. 194

McClellan, Winston 80, 83, 84, 120
McColl, Hugh 355
McCorkle, Jill 453, 461
McCrumb, Sharyn 483
McCullen, Peggy 488
McCullers, Carson 388
McCullers, Charles 194
McCullough Jr., John 589
McDaniel, Arthur H. 306
McDaniel, Calvin 355, 377
McDavid, Fred 219
McDermott, Mike 527
McDevitt & Street Company 41, 54, 55
McDonald, Warren 620
McDuffie, Mary Dix 589, 594, 635
McEvoy, Robert T. 469, 473, 475, 590, 606, 628
McFadyen, Bruce 3
McFadyen Jr., J. Scott 264
McFayden, Jim 539
McFayden Jr., Mrs. O. L. 92
McFayden, Lynn 539
McFeely, William 360
McIntyre, Mike 533, 534, 567, 602, 619, 636
McKee Jr., Paul A. 170
McKimens, Brenda 385, 398
McLamb, Amos 89, 560
McLaughlin, Brian 527
McLaurin, Tim 478
McLawhorn Jr., H. R. 25
McLean, Loche 129
McLean Residential Complex 620, 621
McLean Residential Complex: Thomas R. McLean Hall and Elizabeth E. McLean Hall 620
McLean, Tom 3, 37
McLeod, Dixon 304, 306
McLeod, Leonard 400, 413
McMillan Jr., Samuel D. 294, 326,

— INDEX —

331, 338, 343, 347, 348, 352, 364, 371
McMillan, Rhoda Holden 284
McPhail, Linda 215, 607
McPherson, Lois 307
MC Preparatory School for the Performing Arts 520
MC Stage Band 239
MC Wind Ensemble xiv
Meacham, Cheryl 156
Medical Arts Building 524
Meeske, John 560
Meissner, Dick 125
Melvin, Patsy 126
Memorial Auditorium 44
Mercer, Charles 291
Merchant, Francis 160, 170
Messick, J. D. 5, 9, 20
Methodist College Alumni Association 143, 160, 178, 181, 193, 340, 351, 354
Methodist College Athletic Hall of Fame 541, 553
Methodist College Board of Visitors 572
Methodist College Chorus 384, 398, 401, 425
Methodist College Cloggers 292
Methodist College Concert Lecture Series 82
Methodist College Debate Team 546
Methodist College Development Corporation 507, 517
Methodist College Foundation 2, 193, 213, 218, 226, 229, 232, 237, 240, 241, 247, 248, 264, 265, 266, 267, 272, 279, 280, 283, 296, 300, 302, 310, 317, 356, 362, 364, 375, 387, 392, 398, 399, 428, 438, 439, 457, 465, 474, 476, 487, 496, 527, 543, 551, 559, 561, 571, 586, 602, 616, 617, 639
Methodist College Honors Program 475
Methodist College, Inc. 14, 16, 20, 21, 63, 465
Methodist College Late Night Express 562
Methodist College Medallion 296, 300, 302, 307, 312
Methodist College Memorial Scholarship Fund 296
Methodist College Scholars 215, 246
Methodist College Strategic Plan for 2005-10 639
Methodist College Teacher Education Alumni Association 465
Methodist College Today x, 163, 254, 268, 351, 356, 358, 364, 368, 373, 379, 380, 386, 388, 391, 399, 402, 403, 405, 411, 413, 415, 424, 431, 434, 435, 442, 445, 446, 448, 488, 498, 499, 523, 535, 536, 543, 550, 562, 566, 567, 568, 569, 571, 573, 581, 582, 585, 588, 589, 592, 598, 602, 605, 610, 618, 628, 634, 635, 636, 637
Methodist College Veterans Club 461
Methodist College Wind Ensemble 164, 173
Methodist Conference 10
Methodist Home for Children 592, 613
Methodist University 3, iv, v, x, xi, xiii, xv, 363, 502, 538, 544, 571, 618, 620, 621, 622, 623, 624, 625, 626, 628, 630, 632, 633, 637, 639, 640, 641, 643

— INDEX —

Methodist University Today 571, 628, 630
Meymandi, Assad 564, 569
Mid-South, Inc. 334
Milby, Holman 341
Miller, Gary 151, 166, 579
Miller, Heather Ross 378
Miller, Joe 278, 282, 287, 399, 406, 434
Miller Jr., George W. 551
Miller, Malcolm S. 360
Miller, Mark 585
Miller, Mary Emily 96, 107, 505
Miller, Mike 543
Miller, Paula 475, 477
Milner, Robert 177
Minges, Luther Dean 531
Minneapolis 1, 6, 7, 61
Minnick Jr., Carlton P. 396, 468
Miriello, Thomas F. 380, 585
Miss Boiler Plant 188, 207
Mitsuma, M. Kunio 459
Molter, Michael 552, 562, 613
Monarch Booster Club 536, 547, 563
Monarch Messenger 557, 562
Monarch Players 485
Monarch Press 622
Monday, Jerry 580
Monroe, Mary Ann 147, 148, 202, 208
Montford, Clinton 423, 600
Mooney, Mark 329
Moore, Dan K. 129
Moran, Merirose 575
Moravian Love Feast 310
Morgan Jr., William G. 294
Morgan, Marilyn 205
Morris, Ann 466, 467, 498
Morris, C. P. 9, 10, 124
Morrison, Hal 380
Morris, Trevor 429, 604

Morrow, Ann 282, 307, 309, 313
Morton, Becky 485
Moses, Mark 615
Motes, Susan Garrick 262, 280
Motes, William Harold 230
Mount Park Junior College 30
Mullen, Georgia C. 205
Mullen, Janet Conard 260, 268, 488, 508, 520
Mullen, Phil 260, 268
Mundren, Becky 282
Murchison, Alton G. 5, 49, 53, 57, 65, 179
Murchison and Bailey, Inc. 179
Murphy, Kent 591, 635
Murphy, Tammy 505
Murray, David 43, 64
Murray, Johnson 262
Murray, Ken 153, 187, 195
Murray, Peter 418
Murry Jr., Melvin M. 262

N

9/11 576, 577, 578, 579, 580, 592
Nabors, Tiffany 617
Nakireru, Alex 391
Nardone, Bob 152, 156, 208
Nash County 45
Nash, Jim 263
National Cheerleading Association 410
National Council for the Accreditation of Teacher Education (NCATE) 532
National Science Foundation 493
Nature Trail, Pauline Longest 380, 390, 393, 412, 426, 440, 448
Nau, Danny 103, 109, 136, 153, 208
NCAA 323, 329, 332, 338, 340, 345, 360, 361, 362, 363, 365, 367

— INDEX —

N.C. Dept. of Transportation 49, 504
N.C. General Assembly 29, 126, 362, 427
N.C. House of Representatives 24, 485, 501, 560
N. C. Natural Gas Corporation 484
N.C. Student Legislature 271, 293
N.C. Wesleyan College xiii, 33, 57, 58, 91, 92, 187, 199, 273, 305, 323, 612
Neal, Vance 490
Nelson, Ruth 344
Newberry-Davis, Stephany 620
New Market, Virginia 6
Nguyen, Leven 215
Nichol, Doug 260
Nicks, Lloyd 304
Nimocks Fitness Center 632
Nimocks Jr., David R. 526
Ninestein, Eleanor 286
Nisbet, Andrew 150
Nobles, Shelli 543
Nobles, Sondra M. 205, 222
Noe, James (Chuck) 407
Noell, John W. ix
Norman, Caroline 202
Norris Jr., J. Allen 297, 317, 394, 449
Norris, Kermit 95, 103, 135, 136
North Carolina Association of Independent Colleges and Universities 555
North Carolina Christian Advocate 9, 12, 34, 61, 62, 64, 378, 542
North Carolina Collection at UNC ix
North Carolina College Conference 75, 112, 122, 130
North Carolina Department of Public Instruction 106, 130
North Carolina Educational Finance Agency 614
North Carolina Legislative Tuition Grant 451
North Carolina Methodist University 502
North Carolina Natural Gas 614
North Carolina Student Legislature 223, 257
North Carolina Symphony 298, 309
North Carolina Wesleyan College 14, 45, 109, 117, 159, 274, 389
Northwestern Life Insurance Co. 155

O

Occupational Environmental Management 596
Ochiltree, Rocio 620
Oedipus Rex 321, 322
Office of Education 155, 159
O'Hanlon Amphitheater 232, 233, 267
O'Hanlon, I. H. "Ike" 155, 188, 193, 283, 284, 317, 559
O'Hanlon, Mrs. I. H. 188
O'Hanlon, Sarah 543
Ohio Wesleyan University 68, 73
Oklahoma! 277
Olcutt, Barbara 308
Omicron Delta Kappa 307
One Spirit 618, 622
Operation Desert Shield 444
Ormond, John 113, 221
Ormsby, John 155
Ostborg, Marie C. 74
Ott, Charles 69, 73, 89, 94, 108, 114, 122
Otterman, Kinta 287
Outdoor Adventure Club 571
Outlaw, Wilbur 185, 209
Outstanding Alumni Service Award 507, 520, 553, 563

— INDEX —

Outstanding Faculty Award 507, 520, 542, 553, 563
Owen, Guy 183, 209
Owens, Mary 294

P

Paddock, Fred 253, 257
Page, David 613
Page, Jack W. 15, 16
Pait, Roger 378, 442, 466, 484
Palled, Shivappa 418
Palmer, Mrs. Ruth B. 456, 531
Palumbo, Joanna Cherry 473, 494, 507
Pan American Life Insurance Co. 155
Pankey, Beverly S. 465
Pardue, Ed 495, 499
Parker, Dawn Congleton 596
Parker, John "Knocky" 106, 513
Parker, John R. 111
Parker, Roy 276, 279, 281
Parkerson, JoAnn 429
Parker, Tommie 96
Parks, Beverly 158
Parlett, Bill 294
Parmenter, Alexis 512
Parmley, Ingram C. 146
Parrish, Carrie 451, 459, 478
Parsons, Betty Neill Guy 86, 107, 135, 136, 520
Parsons, Don 87, 89, 109, 117
Pastiche 160
Pastors' Day Lectures 583
Pastor's Recognition Program 573
Pate, John C. 193
Pate, Vici 587, 611, 636
Patrick, David 222
Patterson, Jane Smith 572, 634
Patterson, Paul 182
"Paul Green's Celebration of Man" 399

Paul Green's Celebration of Man, with a Bibliography 488
Pauly, Dave 620
Payne, Ladell 475, 498
Pearce, Alice 286, 295, 315, 316
Pearce, George 151
Pearce, Neva Brock 315, 342, 541
Pearce, Richard W. 213, 244, 245, 246, 247, 248, 249, 250, 251, 252, 254, 255, 257, 258, 259, 260, 261, 263, 264, 265, 267, 268, 269, 272, 273, 279, 280, 281, 285, 286, 289, 292, 295, 299, 297, 298, 304, 305, 310, 315, 541
Peck, Scott 420
Peele, Bob 243, 260
Pemberton, Robert 254
Pembroke State College 206
Pennick, Suzanne Barlow 511
Penrose, Jill 596
Pereira, Joseph 361, 563
Perkinson, John 405
Perkins, Robert C. x, 247, 323, 349, 353, 366
Permian Corporation 106
Perrow, Jason 582
Perry, Hank 119
Perry, W. E. 33
Person County ix, 46
Persons, Babette 125, 126
Petersen, Stephen "Pete" 549
Peterson, James 282
Peterson, Jane 283, 288
Peterson, Louise 588
Peterson, Scott 309, 313, 345
Petteway, Warren B. 364
Petty, Michelle 613
Peyrouse, John C. (Jack) 294, 514, 515
Peyrouse, Mrs. Jane 616
Pfeiffer College 20

— INDEX —

PGA of America 469, 471
Pharr, Jim xvi, 11
Pheagin, Gwen 154, 158, 208
Phillips, Al 278, 288
Phillips, Charles 20
Philpott, Larry S. 466, 589
Phi Sigma Iota 515
Phung, Cu 385, 401, 506
Physical Activities Center 390, 392, 399, 401, 407, 409, 413, 414, 417, 418, 419, 422, 430, 433
Physician Assistant Program 501, 509, 513, 517, 524, 564
Piercy, Fred G. 146
Pierson, W. W. 20
Pi Gamma Mu 283
Pi Kappa Phi 251, 257, 260
Pilewski, Rob 443, 467, 469
Pinehurst Resort 572, 610
Pines Apartments 602
Pittman, R. L. 1, 2, 3, 4, 5, 7, 11, 15, 16, 32, 37, 42, 57, 61, 64, 70, 79
Pitts Jr., Marshall 582
Planning Committee 16
Player Construction Co. 172
Player, Inc. 166
Player Jr., Richard L. 92, 124, 585, 614
Plemmons, W. H. 75, 134
Plummer, Charles 444
Plummer, Deanna 304
Plyler, Lorenzo P. "Joe" 161, 189, 200, 340, 348, 616
Ponder, Reggie 607
Pope Air Force Base 2, 3, 4, 11, 41, 396, 449
Pope, Arnold 170, 181, 183, 197, 209, 210
Pope, Ben 485
Pope, Carol x
Pope, Dean 197

Pope Jr., Thomas 276, 280, 286
Pope, Samuel Marsden 69
Pope, Thomas Arnold 183, 275, 276, 280, 282, 283, 286, 293, 317, 335
Pope, William P. 120, 154
Porter, Alan M. 111, 147, 157, 173, 174, 189, 205, 537, 538
Porter, Ernest R. 364
Porter, Joyce Elaine 111, 313, 514
Potter, W. Stanley 15
Potts, George 117, 413
Potts, Michael 495, 535
Powell, Glenn 155
Powell, Howard P. 86
Powell, Mark 341, 344, 345, 352, 353, 354, 355, 360, 362, 363, 372, 373
Prather, Gibson 42, 87
Pratt, Richard 459
Presbyterian College Steering Committee 1, 2, 5
Presbyterian Synod of North Carolina 1
Presidential Review Committee 402, 407
Presidential Scholarships 348, 363
Presidential Search Committee 240, 241, 244, 245, 267, 346, 347, 348, 349, 350, 372
Preslar, Robert Wayne 247, 275, 379, 461, 466
Presnell, Barbara 537
Presnell, Bill 323, 507
Preyer, Richardson 125
Price, Janice 279
Price Jr., James H. 194
Price, Reynolds 413
Pride 487, 488, 495, 499
Prince Charles Hotel 15, 25, 474
Pritchard, Byron 521
Professional M.B.A. at Pinehurst

761

— INDEX —

program 610
Public Works Commission 46, 51, 57, 84
Pulliam, Bruce R. x, 96, 107, 136, 150, 170, 208, 333, 347, 392, 403, 404, 408, 413, 437, 474, 505, 566
Pulsipher, Mrs. Susan 420
Purcell, E. C. 10
Purgason, Heather Hugus 626
Purvis, Jennifer 613
Pygmalian 230

Q

Qualliotine, Diane 202, 215, 217
Queen, Vergil E. 15, 16, 21, 110, 271, 273, 317, 508
Quesada, Rachel 620
Quick, William K. 216, 442
Quigley, Steve 280
Quillin, Mr. and Mrs. G. S. 27

R

Radford, Ashleigh 586
Raeford, Della 384
Raft on the River 328, 329, 330
Ragan, Sam 324, 367, 371, 394
Raineri, Carla 596
Raines, Chris 595
Raleigh Road 2, 9, 47
Ramsey Street iv, xi, 4, 15, 37, 49, 54, 84, 104, 222, 328, 421, 504, 506, 517, 518, 522, 529, 588, 623
Randolph-Macon College ix, 28, 349, 352, 475
Rand, Tony 381
Rankin, Charles 82
Rapelye, Peter 151
Rapelye, Seldon "Sparky" 95, 117, 143, 446, 447, 579
Rasmussen, Eugene M. 248

Ratliff, Kimberly 455, 462
Ray, George Calvert 294, 331, 334, 339, 349, 371
Ray, William 536, 547
R. B. House 20
Reardon, Fred 182
Reavis, Ken 253
Red Bird Mission 545
Reeves Auditorium/Fine Arts Building xiii, 150, 191, 193, 199
Reeves, Charles Mercer 365, 388, 390, 407, 414, 432
Reeves, John M. 97, 138
Reeves, Virginia McKenzie 469
Register, Woodrow V. "Woody" 391
Reid, Frank 239
Reid, Karen 620
Reinke, Arthur 161
Reisinger Jr., Howard W. 205, 222, 223
Reynolds, Bob 90, 91, 92, 95, 135
Reynolds High School 30, 181
Rhine, J. B. 92
Rhoads, Gary 486
Rhodes, Jean 511
Richard L. Player 482
Richard L. Player Golf and Tennis Learning Center 506, 513, 518, 519
Richard L. Player, Sr. Golf and Tennis Learning Center 482, 484
Richardson Foundation, Inc. 92
Richardson, Jerry 528, 529, 567
Richmond Area of The Methodist Church 6, 76, 122, 192
Richter, Eugene P. 41
Riddle Jr., Joseph P. 399, 433, 490
Riddle, March Floyd 433
Rider, John 205
Rine, Barbara 90, 96

— INDEX —

Ritzema, Robert 587
Rivers, Nancy 520
R. J. Reynolds Tobacco Co. 87, 88, 110
Robb, Felix 178, 209
Robbins, Cecil 20, 22
Robbins, Stella 146, 169
Roberts, Brenda Gail 253
Roberts, John 106, 252
Roberts, Mike 612
Robertson Jr., Newton 80, 92
Roberts, Ronald 215
Robinson, Alan 380
Rocky Mount xiii, 3, 4, 5, 8, 9, 10, 12, 14, 18, 23, 45, 46, 58, 81, 91, 92, 151, 173, 187, 199, 362, 389, 395, 594
Rodriguez, Roxanne 345
Rogers, Florence 382, 415, 416
Rogers, J. Michael 553
Rollins, Steed xiv
Romeo and Juliet 454, 455
Roncketti, Chris 607, 615
Rosa, Yvette 243
Rose, Charles G. 2, 348
Rose, Charlie 252, 452, 456, 480
Rosehill Road 38
Rose, Margaret 534
Rose, Sol C. 38, 79
Ross, C. Reid 260
Ross, Mark T. 363
ROTC 290, 293, 294, 299, 300, 304
Rowe, Charles Gilbert 82, 183
Rowedder, Larry E. 442
R. Parker Wilson x, 157, 275, 312, 470, 494, 594
Rudd, Gary 344
Ruffin, Ben 453, 498
Rummans, Al 218
Run-a-Thon 283
Ruskin, John 204, 210

Russ, D. P. 14, 602
Russell, Jim 202
Russell, Leon 9
Russell, Ronnie 196, 199, 206
Russ, Valeria 620
Rutherford College 30, 165, 525
Ryan, Chris 405, 598
Ryan, Dr. Christopher 170
Ryerson, Tim 620

S

SACS 139, 159, 166
Sadler, Mary Lynn 365, 366, 368, 369
Safley, Michael Wayne 181, 192, 396, 405, 434, 592, 613, 622
SAGA 322, 343
Salas-Calero, Maria 182
Sam Edwards Award 449, 486, 497
Samuel J. Womack Endowed Chair in Religion and Philosophy 391, 491
Samuel J. and Norma C. Womack Endowed Lecture Series in Religion 493
Sanderford, Buster 286
Sanderford Jr., Paul 278
Sanderford Jr., Paul L. "Buster" 242
Sanderford, Paul L. "Buster" 473
Sanders, Ernest L. 15
Sandhills Area Land Trust (SALT) 604
Sanford Hall 128
Sanford, Terry xi, xiv, xvi, 1, 2, 3, 4, 7, 9, 11, 13, 14, 15, 16, 19, 20, 21, 24, 26, 31, 32, 35, 36, 39, 40, 42, 48, 49, 52, 53, 58, 59, 61, 62, 63, 64, 65, 69, 70, 74, 75, 76, 80, 83, 84, 88, 97, 98, 100, 102, 110, 111, 122, 123, 124, 125, 131, 132, 134, 135, 138, 142, 149, 159, 163, 165, 176, 209, 222,

— INDEX —

228, 235, 245, 304, 330, 331,
356, 357, 371, 372, 385, 396,
426, 427, 435, 441, 477, 480,
501, 502, 510, 511, 515, 521,
525, 526, 534, 536, 561, 566,
567, 589
Sapp, Kelli 456
Sarenac, Vessalin 161
Satterfield, Byrd I. 46, 64
Saunders, Earlyne 194
Saunders, Wilford 493, 589
Sawchuk, Cynthia 612
Saxon, Don 587
Scarborough, Ellen 350
Scherzer, Diane 405
Schmidt, Sherrie 575
Schutz, Barbara 200
Schwarz, Earnest W. 96, 579, 626
Schwoyer, Natalie 199, 214, 223
Scotland County 14, 442, 548
Scott, Brian 519
Scott, Kerr 3, 58
Seamon, Emily 405
Seawell, Malcolm 74
Seeds on Good Soil, A New Season Campaign 583, 605, 608, 614, 615, 616, 630
Seitz, Richard J. 251
Selective Service 328
Self, Terry 202
Sellers, Sharon Ruth 183
Senior Citizens Scholarship Program 386
Servie, Michael 313
Seymour, Libby 484
Shaffer, Denny 251
Shakespearean Summer Festival 338, 353
Sharpe, Bill 50, 65
Sharp, Paul F. 144
Sharp, Susan 156, 164, 175, 185, 187, 209
Shaw, George Bernard 639
Shaw Jr., William 511
Shelley Baseball Field 259
Shelley, Bruce 161, 187, 278, 293, 294
Shelton, Hugh 603, 636
Sheppard, Dennis R. 341, 626
Sheppard, Jami 562, 569
Shimizu, Kensaku 458
Show You Care Day 424, 425
Shrader, John W. 612
Shuey, Denise 548
Shuford, Catherine 366
Shuller, Ferris, Johnson and Lindstrom 518
Shuller, Ferris, Lindstrom and Associates 620
Shuller, Robert 614
Shumelda, Jacob 156
Sigma Construction Co. 482, 486, 493
Sikes Brothers, Inc. 53, 55
Sikoryak-Robins, Maria x, 617
Sill, John 304, 310, 573, 603
Silvasy, Lori 398, 415
Simonton Jr., Charles A. 378, 542
Simpson, Bland 564
Simpson, Myron L. 69, 74
Simpson, Ron 547, 559
Simpson, Willliam 594
Sinkovitz, Mike 571
Site Committee 4, 5, 27
Sizemore, Camellia 202
Slivva, Chris 612
Sluder-Jordan, Milton Earl 307
Small, George 418, 494
Small, Richard x, 513
sMALL TALK x, 88, 90, 91, 92, 93, 94, 95, 99, 100, 103, 105, 106, 107, 109, 112, 113, 116, 117, 118, 120, 125, 129, 135, 136, 137, 140, 148, 150, 151, 152,

— INDEX —

153, 154, 155, 156, 162, 164, 165, 167, 171, 172, 173, 175, 176, 183, 184, 185, 186, 187, 188, 189, 194, 195, 196, 199, 200, 201, 206, 207, 208, 209, 210, 213, 214, 217, 219, 220, 221, 222, 223, 229, 230, 231, 233, 234, 235, 238, 239, 240, 241, 242, 243, 248, 249, 252, 254, 256, 262, 263, 266, 267, 268, 269, 275, 276, 278, 279, 280, 281, 282, 283, 286, 287, 288, 293, 294, 295, 298, 304, 306, 307, 308, 309, 310, 313, 317, 318, 321, 322, 323, 325, 326, 327, 328, 329, 330, 333, 334, 335, 340, 341, 342, 344, 345, 347, 352, 353, 354, 355, 358, 360, 361, 362, 363, 366, 367, 368, 371, 372, 373, 376, 377, 380, 381, 382, 384, 385, 387, 391, 395, 396, 397, 399, 401, 405, 407, 408, 409, 410, 411, 412, 413, 421, 422, 423, 434, 435, 439, 448, 450, 451, 455, 459, 460, 462, 467, 482, 483, 487, 498, 499
Smith, Charles 611
Smith, David 540
Smith, Ella Rose (Hall) 178
Smith, Ervin 275
Smith, Eugene 248
Smith, Jesse 508
Smith, John Owen 161
Smith Jr., Phillip C. 183
Smith Jr., Raymond H. 202
Smith, Karen 473
Smith, Lee 460, 461
Smith, Leta Anne 215
Smith, Mike 243
Smith, Patty 340, 341, 345, 352, 353, 360, 372, 373
Smith, Paula C. 278
Smith, Stacey 559
Smith, T. Lynwood 216
Smith, Tommy 200, 214, 223, 235, 497
Smith, Vickie 361
Smith, Wendy 363
Snyder, Grady K. 74, 86, 112, 114
Snyder, Mrs. Grady 112
Sodexho 587
Sokalski, Mickey 332, 338, 340, 606
Souders, Mrs. Floyd B. 49, 80
South Carolina National Bank 375, 387
Southerland, Warren 200
Southern Association of Colleges and Schools 17, 23, 112, 130, 133, 139, 149, 159, 166, 178, 214, 226, 291, 306, 310, 314, 318, 336, 398, 422, 425, 432, 530, 544, 564, 640
Southern Writers Symposium 330
Sparkman, John 58
Sparrow, Dorothy T. 248
"speaker ban law" 115, 116
Speaking Across the Curriculum 398
Spears, Marshall T. 10
Spears, R. Wright 25, 237
Speas, Charles 304
Special Committee to Recommend a President for Methodist College 30
Speed, James 147
Speegle, Charles 264, 265
Spence, William 15, 141
Spilman Jr., Louis 120, 216, 248, 259, 260, 264, 352, 603, 630
Spilman, Mary 243
SPIRIT—Students and Parents Involved in Reading Together

— INDEX —

463
Spreng, Frank 388, 405
Spring Fling 440
Spring Lake Times 113
Springthorpe, Steve 354
Sprouse, Beverly 156
Spruill, Cecil 20
Stacy and Elizabeth Weaver Endowed Scholarship Fund 590
Stacy Weaver Award 324, 338, 364
Stafford, Heather 563
Staiti, David 512
St. Andrews Presbyterian College 2, 109, 117, 148, 151, 196, 214, 220, 234, 256, 360
Stanley, Bruce 555, 556, 568, 572, 634
Stanley, Elton 234, 242, 253, 271
Stanley, Jim 294
Stanton, Mildred 181, 198
Stapleton, Ruth Carter 287
Stark II, Rufus 311, 479
Statement of Purpose for Methodist College 302, 318
State Student Legislature 117, 188, 196, 199
Statesville City Schools 30
Staton Jr., Jesse 187
Stedman, W. David 216, 274, 317
Steering Committee xvi, 1, 2, 3, 4, 5, 7, 10, 11, 13, 14, 57, 425, 530, 602
Steffes, Bruce 616, 636
Stein, J. Bernard 3, 89
Stephens III, Curtis W. 578
Stephenson, Lois 112
Stephenson, Lori 520
Stevens and Wilkinson 30, 31, 34, 36, 37, 38, 39, 46, 50
Stewart, Alva W. 68, 73, 114
Stewart, Charles 126
Stewart, Craig 487

Stewart, Francis 120
Stewart, Garland J. "Guy" 613
Stewart, Martin 278
Stewart, William J. 551
Stilwell, Joe 150
Stinson, Gorrell R. 25
"Stirring the Caldron" 430
Stock Market Symposium 526, 556
Stone, Benjamin Franklin "Doc" 508
Storey, Peter 565, 569
Storms, John 415, 430
Stout, Frank x, 4, 61, 516, 517, 529, 566
Stout, Joe 4, 59, 519, 529
Stout, Melissa 513
Stout, Mr. & Mrs. Joe W. 27, 35
Stowers, Alan 262
St. Paul Methodist Church 8, 33, 61
Strategic Concepts Committee 475
Strategic Plan for 2000-05 544
Stratta, Al 575
Strict Academic Probation (SAP) 297
Student Activities Council 440
Student Christian Association 90
Student Council for Exceptional Children 446
Student Government Association 91, 100, 109, 117
Student Life Committee 161, 162, 206
Students in Free Enterprise 474, 556
Student Union xiii, 34, 35, 36, 38, 41, 46, 50, 54, 55, 66, 69, 72, 75, 87, 91, 93, 96, 102, 108, 109, 111, 117, 121, 127, 128, 139, 149, 155, 159, 162, 163, 164, 165, 166, 167, 173, 177, 178, 182, 185, 191, 193, 217, 222, 235, 245, 251, 257, 259, 260,

INDEX

261, 272, 280, 281, 287, 292, 294, 299, 306, 307, 308, 310, 311, 324, 325, 326, 327, 328, 329, 332, 334, 342, 353, 360, 367, 381, 382, 384, 386, 391, 393, 396, 411, 421, 450, 456, 487
Student Union Board 251, 257
Sullivan, Michael 491, 495
Suttie, Jim 404
Suttles, Norman 3, 14, 17, 47, 48, 218, 237
Sutton, Neil 447
Swartz, Allan 294
Swing, Loretta 514, 515
Swing, Walter 379, 394, 580
Swink, Bob 175, 188, 189, 199
Swink, Richard 200, 202
Sykes, Gwen Pheagin 216, 379, 393, 406
Sykes, Samuel Mason 156, 165, 166, 207, 209, 553
Sypult, James 464
Sypult, Sharron 482

T

Tabbert, Doug 540
Tally Jr., Joe 3, 4, 11, 15, 16, 52, 114, 115, 124
Tally, Lura 385, 427
Tang, Derek 482
Tapestry x, 160, 283, 308, 335, 354, 363, 403, 449
Tar Heel Quilters Guild 389
Tarr, Bill 130, 131
Tau Kappa Epsilon 308
Taylor, James 544
Taylor, JoAnn 181, 309
Taylor Jr., D. K. 151
Taylor, Key W. 9
Taylor, M. T. and Lillian Mae 27
Taylor, Richard E. and Linda H. 27

Teague, Harold J. 67, 72, 214
Teer, R. Dillard 330, 348
Teer Sr., Nello 70
Temple, Shirley ix
Templeton, John 526, 567
Templeton Lecture 556
Terranova, Justin 509, 589
The Birds 341
The Breeze Band 618
The Bulletin of Methodist College x, 131, 166, 202
The Courage of Their Convictions 453
The Courier-Times ix
The Davis Foundation 604
The Durham Morning Herald xiv
The Effigies 157
The Embers 119
The Emperor Jones 333, 335
The Fayetteville Observer xi, xvi, 6, 11, 31, 36, 42, 45, 47, 48, 52, 61, 62, 64, 65, 67, 68, 69, 79, 87, 94, 123, 126, 132, 134, 137, 147, 165, 242, 254, 256, 268, 276, 357, 358, 361, 372, 437, 525, 591, 592, 593, 635, 637
The Fayetteville Observer-Times 357, 358, 361, 372
The Fayetteville Times 276, 279, 281, 345, 350, 368
The Flim-Flam Man 184
The General Conference of The Methodist Church 6
The Invisible Fire 367, 368
The Kelly Springfield Tire Company 214
The Lafayette Society 397
The Lilies of the Field 275
The Methodist Church xiii, 1, 3, 4, 6, 7, 8, 12, 13, 15, 17, 20, 21, 23, 25, 26, 27, 28, 31, 33, 34, 35, 36, 43, 45, 46, 49, 50, 53, 54, 56, 57,

— INDEX —

59, 60, 61, 62, 73, 75, 76, 77, 78, 81, 84, 94, 96, 97, 109, 122, 123, 124, 128, 130, 141, 144, 163, 203, 216, 284
The Methodist University, Inc. 622
The Miracle Worker 253
The News and Observer of Raleigh 12
The North Carolina Conference xiii, xvi, 1, 3, 5, 6, 7, 8, 9, 12, 13, 15, 19, 20, 21, 25, 26, 27, 33, 34, 35, 43, 45, 50, 51, 52, 53, 54, 56, 57, 58, 59, 60, 61, 62, 75, 76, 81, 84, 91, 96, 97, 99, 123, 141, 142, 177, 180, 189, 203, 216, 225, 226, 232, 236, 246, 264, 273, 274, 277, 281, 290, 294, 299, 301, 304, 305, 306, 310, 312, 323, 326, 331, 336, 338, 343, 347, 348, 351, 356, 367, 369, 372, 378, 381, 388, 396, 402, 413, 414, 419, 442, 465, 468, 471, 477, 490, 496, 497, 555, 584, 588
The North Carolina Conference of The Methodist Church xiii, 1, 3, 8, 12, 13, 15, 20, 25, 26, 27, 33, 34, 35, 43, 50, 53, 54, 56, 57, 59, 62, 75, 81, 84, 96, 97, 123, 216
The North Carolina Conference's College Site Committee 5
The Patriots 431, 432
The Person County Times ix
The Pinehurst Company 572
The Roxboro Courier ix
The Sanford Daily Herald 23
The Southern Fellowships Fund in Chapel Hill, N.C. 18
The Special Collections Room 552
The State 50, 65
The United Methodist Foundation 444, 445

Thomas, Billy 386
Thomas, Greg 535
Thomas, Hope 602
Thomas, Jack 153
Thomas, Kristine 613
Thomas, Louis D. 526
Thomason, Mrs. Raymond 180
Thomas R. and Elizabeth E. McLean Foundation 630
Thomas R. McLean Hall and Elizabeth E. McLean Hall 620
Thomas, William Greg 620
Thompson, Ann Scott 182
Thompson, J. Mel 2, 3, 14, 31, 49, 61
Thompson Jr., Emerson M. 294
Thompson, Kathy S. 229
Thompson, Neil H. 194
Thompson, Ratasha 521
Thorp, Bo 461
Thorpe, Anne 542
TIAA/CREF Retirement Plan 366
Timberlake, Bob 461, 592
Timmons-Goodson, Patricia 534
Tippett, Lou 551
Tippett, W. Lyndo 551
Title III Endowment Grant 405
Tobler, John O. 146, 164, 169, 173, 174, 432
Todd, Amy 626
Toffler, Alvin 242
Tolar, Sammy 276, 283
Tolar, Tammy Lynn 367
Tolson, John 252, 268
Tommasi, Tony 620, 627
Tommy Dorsey Orchestra 384
Town and County Commission 9
Townsend, Jane Weeks 333, 380
Tribble, Harold 20
Trinity Methodist Church 3, 19
Trousdale, Wayne 188, 193
Truesdell, Michael R. 585

— INDEX —

Trustees' Executive Committee 69, 70, 80, 88, 92, 98, 110, 111, 114, 128
Turcato, Rene 620
Turner, Bob 262
Turner, Brian 543
Turner, Cora Ann 181
Turner, David 575
Turner, Jan 613
Turner, Tricia Ann 307, 330, 338, 340, 418
Turner, Walter 92, 129, 600
Twelfth Night 325, 326
Tyner, Howard D. 308
Tyson, Henry Page 222
Tyson Jr., John 628
Tyson, Mrs. Ruth 222
Tyson, Vernon 301

U

Uncle Bill's Recipes and Related Reflections 181
Underwood, Debbie 286
Underwood, Mary 405
Union, Terri 365, 366, 482, 486
United Methodist Women to the Annual Conference Session (A.C.S.) of the United Methodist Youth Fellowship 192
United Student Appeal 256, 257
University of Georgia ix, 36, 111, 147, 167, 256
University of North Carolina 17, 19, 23, 41, 42, 43, 74, 93, 96, 100, 101, 105, 111, 115, 131, 144, 156, 244, 261, 264, 387, 439, 458, 596, 643
University of Pennsylvania 6, 111, 169
University Senate of The Methodist Church 94, 130
University Senate of The United Methodist Church 441, 498
U.S. 401 2, 15, 28, 29, 49, 54, 108, 263, 311
U.S. Army Reserve Officer Training Corps (ROTC) 293
USA South Athletic Conference 596, 599, 607, 615, 628
U.S. Dept. of Housing and Urban Development 281
Ushery, Jamelle 481, 626
U.S. Housing and Home Finance Agency 17, 69, 88, 96, 149
Usrey, Miriam L. 120
Ussery, Ray 173

V

Valentine's Day Rally for the Troops 450
Vandervort, Brenda 521
Vann, James 285, 286, 307
Varas, Regina 587
Vere, Charles 478
"Veritas et Virtus" 53
Verney, Mrs. Gilbert 128
Vickers, Hope 585, 616
Vienna Choir Boys 618, 624, 625, 626
Vietnam Day 150, 151
Vincellette, Barney 197
Virginia Wesleyan College 173
Vital, Marilyn 575
Von Rosenberg, Charles H. 49, 616
Voorhees, Ed 151
Vossler, George 80
Vurnakes, Angie 221

W

Wachovia Bank, National 614
Wadsworth Jr., Allen P. 111
Waiting for Godot 201, 431
Wake Forest College 20, 30, 73, 111, 362, 560

— INDEX —

Walden, Thomas J. 551
Walker, Colleen Griffiths 587
Walker, Cynthia 99, 100, 109, 245, 447, 463
Walker, Henry 92
Walker, Storen 587
Walker, Yvonne 286
Walsh, John 389, 405
Walsh, Richard G. 380
Walston, Nanelle 521
Walter B. and Margaret T. Clark Hall 531, 534
Wang, King 161
Wansley, Fred C. 146
Ward, Dresham and Reinhardt, Inc. 33
Ward, Hope 510, 566
Ward, James X. 399, 405
Ward, Michael 543, 567
Warren Jr., Lee 484
Warren, Larry 89
Warrenton, N.C. 33
Warren, Wayne 170
Washington, D.C. 17, 58, 62
Watkins, Lance 448
Watson, H. Langill 337
Watt, Katherine x
Watt, Willis 604
Wear, James 437
Weaver, Charles C. 30, 228
Weaver, Charles H. 525
Weaver, Elizabeth H. 586, 590
Weaver Hall 128
Weaver, Janie 30, 181
Weaver, Jim 30
Weaver Jr., L. Stacy 525
Weaver, L. Stacy xi, xiv, 1, 10, 15, 20, 30, 32, 36, 38, 39, 41, 42, 43, 46, 48, 49, 50, 52, 53, 54, 57, 58, 59, 63, 64, 65, 66, 68, 69, 72, 75, 77, 79, 80, 81, 84, 114, 121, 122, 124, 127, 132, 134, 135, 136, 137, 138, 139, 140, 143, 144, 145, 150, 155, 159, 160, 161, 162, 163, 164, 165, 170, 174, 175, 176, 177, 178, 180, 181, 185, 186, 191, 195, 202, 203, 204, 206, 208, 210, 216, 217, 218, 225, 228, 231, 237, 240, 244, 245, 246, 261, 266, 267, 277, 285, 302, 312, 324, 338, 347, 359, 364, 378, 388, 401, 409, 427, 442, 456, 468, 479, 490, 505, 515, 522, 525, 529, 538, 548, 558, 561, 574, 585, 586, 590, 594, 603, 611, 619
Weaver, Philip 30, 82
Weaver, Philip J. 81
Weaver, Walter P. 493, 525
Webb, Jimmy 230
Weeks, Ben 41
Weeks, James K. 458, 599
Weeks, Jane 380, 412, 413
Weeks, Kermit 92
Weeks, M. J. 48, 49, 52
Weisser, Bill 529
Welch, Linda 448, 455
Weldon, William O. 237, 267
Wells, Benjamin 575
Wells, Cliff 325, 326, 335, 336, 474
Wells Jr., Woodrow W. 202, 603
Wells, Larry 620
Wendelken, Rebecca 575, 578
Werner, Hazen G. 192
Wesley Foundation 33, 44
Wesley Heritage Fund 600
Wesley, John 115
West, Bill 561
Westbrook, Anthony 410
West, DeCarlos 516, 520, 533, 607
West, Edwin A. 194
West Hall 506, 507
Westlake, James R. 252
Westmoreland, William C. 151

— INDEX —

Weston, Margaret Ann 69
West, Paul 194
West, Roberta Dawn 161
Wethington, L. Elbert 10, 55, 56, 57, 61, 67, 561, 600
Weyerhauser, Roya 393
Weyrauch, Paul R. 3, 4
WFSS 384
Whitcomb, Brian 628, 637
White, Janet 429
White, Joyce 495
Whiteley, Jennifer 582
White, Mary Wheeling 520, 532, 535
Whitmire, Roy 282, 290, 303
Whittle, Dan 546, 568
Wicke, Myron F. 224, 228, 266
Wicker, Terry 170
Wiggins, Clarence 307
Wiggs, Rita 404, 416, 531, 536, 540, 563
Wike, Lauren Cook 613
Willard, Barry 260
William F. Bethune Center for the Visual Arts 640, 642
William P. Lowdermilk Golf Classic 563
William P. Lowdermilk Student Achievement Award 557
Williams, A. Hope 555, 568
Williams, Charlotte 602, 611, 617
Williams, Crystal 620
Williams, Dennis 80
Williams, Gerri 340
Williams, Harrison 407
Williams, Jason Anthony 513, 538
Williams, John 201
Williams Jr., Thomas W. 439
Williams, Kenneth Lee 246
Williams, Mrs. Dennis 52
Williams, Mrs. Mary Frances 523
Williams, Phillip 595

Williams, Roger 160
Williams, Sammy 173, 174, 175
Williams, Stephen 578
Williams, Thomas 438
Willis, Hubert 425
Wilmington, N.C. 3, 4, 15, 41, 60, 94, 101, 117, 126, 198, 206, 286, 293, 294, 330, 478, 535, 558
Wilson, David G. 477
Wilson, Debbie 403
Wilson, Demarcus 607
Wilson, Elizabeth 161
Wilson, Elizabeth W. 205
Wilson, J. Allan 161
Wilson, J. M. 15, 16, 141
Wilson, Paul F. 384, 386, 429, 521
Wilson, R. Parker x, 444, 470, 494, 498
Wilson, Sean 582
Winstead, Arthur 352, 354
Winston-Salem 25, 30, 125, 127, 181, 310, 441, 453, 523, 524
Wise, Denny 605
Wise, Gil 336, 338, 339, 340, 342, 353, 354, 371
Withers, Loren 99
Witt, Colleen 450
Woelfel, Karl 207, 215
Wofford College ix, 183, 349, 352, 358, 443, 528, 574
Wolfe, Bill 119
Wolfe, William 120
Woltz, Cindy 235
Woltz, Kathy 418, 424
Womack Jr., Samuel J. 68, 73, 78, 82, 95, 108, 114, 117, 135, 136
Womack, Lynda 322, 326, 331
Womack, Norma x, 282, 379, 409, 425, 426, 552
Woman's College, UNC 20
Woodall Jr., William E. 182
Woodbury, Dusty 259, 262

— INDEX —

Woodcock, Eldon 161
Wood, Jerry 93, 94, 113, 126, 143
Worrell, Theresa 473
Wortheim, Margaret 573, 634
Worth Printing, Inc. xi
Wright, Bill 123, 137
Wright, Emily Powers 587
Wright, Frank Lloyd 37
Wright, Fred D. 182
Wright, Mary Fermanides 491
Wright, Mrs. Kathy 612
Writers Day 453, 478
WTIP 107
Wunder, Amanda H. 527
Wu, Tsung-Hsun 182
Wyatt Jr., John 561, 602

Y

Yaeger, Susan 340
Yarborough Bell Tower 144, 145, 197
Yarborough Endowment Fund 428
Yarborough Jr., Wilson F. 511
Yarborough, Mrs. Mary Butler 27, 610
Yarborough, Ramon L. 181, 527, 561, 583, 584, 585, 614, 616, 630, 635
Yarborough Sr., Wilson F. 3, 5, 15, 20, 27, 142, 159, 330, 348, 409, 428
Yard, Nicole 620
Yates-Tanouye, Shelia 418
Yopp, Lee 400, 413
Yorkey, Camille 592, 635
Youngblood, Jane W. 278
Young, John 294
Young, Sarah Jo 294
Yow III, Thomas S. 108, 240, 379, 432

Z

Zahran, Anne 578
Ziegler, Andrew 565
Zimmerman, Jeffrey 495, 603
Zimmer, Patric 553
Zollars, Pam 158
Zumwalt, Elmo R. 365, 379